PHOBIAS

PHOBIAS

The Psychology of Irrational Fear

Irena Milosevic and Randi E. McCabe, Editors

GREENWOOD

AN IMPRINT OF ABC-CLIO, LLC
Santa Barbara, California • Denver, Colorado • Oxford, England

Library of Congress Cataloging-in-Publication Data

Phobias : the psychology of irrational fear / Irena Milosevic and Randi E. McCabe, Editors.

   pages cm

Includes bibliographical references and index.

   ISBN 978-1-61069-575-6 (alk. paper) — ISBN 978-1-61069-576-3 (ebook)

   1. Phobias—Encyclopedias.   2. Anxiety disorders—Encyclopedias.   I. Milosevic, Irena (Clinical psychologist), editor.   II. McCabe, Randi E., editor.

   RC535.P52 2015

   616.85'22003—dc23   2014039583

ISBN: 978-1-61069-575-6
EISBN: 978-1-61069-576-3

19   18   17   16   15   1   2   3   4   5

This book is also available on the World Wide Web as an eBook.
Visit www.abc-clio.com for details.

Greenwood
An Imprint of ABC-CLIO, LLC

ABC-CLIO, LLC
130 Cremona Drive, P.O. Box 1911
Santa Barbara, California 93116-1911

This book is printed on acid-free paper ∞

Manufactured in the United States of America

CONTENTS

ACKNOWLEDGMENTS

We would like to thank the many individuals who have given their time and expertise to this book. We greatly value their contributions.

INTRODUCTION

For as children tremble and fear everything in the blind darkness, so we in the light sometimes fear what is no more to be feared than the things children in the dark hold in terror and imagine will come true.

Lucretius (Titus Lucretius Carus), *De Rerum Natura*, 99–55 BC

Fear is a fundamental and universal emotion that has been adaptive in ensuring our survival as a species—it serves as an alarm system that enables us to perceive and react to danger in an instant, without conscious thought. If you have ever been confronted by an angry dog, experienced butterflies when peering down the ledge of a cliff, or rushed to the aid of a loved one who has been injured, it is likely that your fear response facilitated a quick reaction to ensure your or others' safety. However, when the fear alarm system goes awry—by misfiring in response to nonthreatening stimuli, for example—the consequences may be significant. Maladaptive fear can lead to severe psychological distress and interference in one's ability to engage in daily activities and function normally. With this presentation, fear becomes what we call a phobia—an excessive and persistent fear that is disproportionate to the degree of danger in a situation.

The topic of phobias is a fascinating one for a number of reasons. They are highly prevalent and one of the most common types of anxiety disorders. Everyone either has a phobia or knows someone who has a phobia. In fact, in a given year, approximately 19.2 million American adults, an estimated 8.7% of the population in this age group, experience a phobia. The types of situations and stimuli that people become phobic of are wide-ranging, including everyday situations such as riding in an elevator or traveling on a bridge; encountering animals like snakes, insects, or dogs; seeing blood or getting a needle or a medical procedure; encountering phenomena in the natural environment such as heights or storms; and other types of situations such as those that may lead to choking or vomiting. Phobias are a highly popular topic in the media both for the degree of interest they generate in the public and for all of the interesting original names, many of ancient Greek origin, which each phobia has. For example, most recently the term *nomophobia* was used to describe the fear of being out of mobile phone contact.

Phobias also capture our curiosity because they can take rationally minded people and leave them cowering in terror despite the knowledge that the fear is not based in actual threat. Consider the following example. Justin was a university professor who had always been high achieving. He was married and had a two-year-old child. Although Justin has had a phobia of fish for as long as he can remember, he was not overly distressed by it as he was always able to accommodate the fear in the choices that he made. For instance, he avoided swimming in lakes or streams where he might encounter a fish. This was not too disruptive until he realized on a family vacation at a beach house that he needed to go into the lake with his small child who could not be unattended for risk of drowning. The terror that he felt forcing himself in the lake that day was almost unbearable. Furthermore, he desperately tried to hide his fear because he was greatly concerned about transmitting the fear to his daughter. The rest of the trip he dreaded going down by the water and attempted to fill the family time with excursions so he could avoid being in the situation of having to encounter fish. It was at this point that he realized he had to better address his phobia of fish if he was going to be able to truly enjoy his family vacations.

Humans have had phobias like Justin's for thousands of years. This long history can be traced in clinical accounts that date back to the Greek physician Hippocrates who described a man with a severe fear of flute music. Five hundred years later, Roman physician Celsus (25 BC–AD 50) used the word *phobia* for the first time to characterize an individual's extreme fear of water due to rabies, which he termed *hydrophobia*. The word *phobia* itself originates from the Greek word *phobos*. Phobos was the son of Ares, the Greek god of war. Throughout modern history, our scientific understanding of phobias has advanced significantly, from the writings of Freud in the late 19th and early 20th centuries to the work of modern-day researchers who study fear and phobias in their laboratories. The first classification of phobias as a diagnostic category in the *International Classification of Diseases* (1947) and the *Diagnostic and Statistical Manual of Mental Disorders* (1952) set the stage for the scientific community to study this anxiety disorder by providing a common understanding of the definition of a phobia. Developments in behavioral science, cognitive science, and neuroscience in the last century and the first part of this century have led to great progress in our understanding of the etiology and phenomenology of phobias as well as effective treatments.

In *Phobias: The Psychology of Irrational Fear* we provide a comprehensive, evidence-based review of the topic of phobias in one volume. Readers are provided a user-friendly book, organized so that they can easily read the specific entries of interest that are written by scientific leaders in the field. Themes covered in this book include the historical and cultural context of phobias; phenomenology, classification, and diagnosis; etiological models; and treatment approaches. The book also highlights the major figures and organizations that have advanced our understanding of phobias, including contemporary researchers who are contributing to the ever-advancing scientific literature. The reader will be taken from the research laboratory to the clinician's office, from the depths of the brain to the social context, and from the pages of history to the cutting edge of contemporary knowledge.

Entries in this volume are organized alphabetically and include cross-references to other relevant content in the book. In addition to the standard entries, numerous sidebars are presented, which highlight interesting facts, research methods, and clinical cases. Although phobias are the principal focus of this volume, we also present content on related anxiety disorders in an effort to provide a comprehensive context for the understanding of phobias. By bringing together the key concepts and addressing the current state of our scientific understanding of phobias, we hope to provide a volume that provides broad appeal, from the curious layperson to those developing their clinical and research expertise in anxiety disorders who will find this volume a useful resource for their library.

Irena Milosevic and Randi E. McCabe

A

Acarophobia (Imagined Infestation)

Acarophobia (from the Greek *akari*, meaning mite, and *phobos*, meaning fear), also known as delusional parasitosis, delusional infestation, or Ekbom's syndrome, is a psychiatric disorder in which individuals erroneously believe that their skin and body are infested with parasites. The term *acarophobia* was coined by Thibierge, a French dermatologist, in 1894, and it is now considered to be a misnomer since the disorder is not characterized by phobic fear but rather by delusional beliefs. The term *entomophobia* (fear of insects) has also been inaccurately used to describe the disorder and similarly pertains to fear rather than false beliefs. Contemporary clinicians and researchers prefer to use the terms *delusional parasitosis* or *delusional infestation*. In cases where fear or anxiety is present, it is thought to be a consequence of the delusions.

Delusional parasitosis is not uniform in its presentation and can occur either in *primary form*, as a stand-alone psychiatric disorder, or in *secondary form*, as a consequence of a medical condition, mental disorder, or intoxication. In its primary form, delusional parasitosis is classified in the *Diagnostic and Statistical Manual of Mental Disorders*, fifth edition as a type of psychotic disorder called delusional disorder, somatic type. Causes of the secondary form of delusional parasitosis vary widely and can include cerebrovascular disease, cancer, dementia, schizophrenia, major depression, and chronic use of substances (e.g., methamphetamine, cocaine, alcohol), among others. The prevalence of delusional parasitosis is not known, but researchers believe that it is more common than was once thought. The primary form of delusional parasitosis is more common in women than in men, with the average age of onset ranging from 50 to 69 years. The cause of the disorder is not well understood. Hypotheses about its origins have focused on the possible misperception of actual physical sensations that subsequently become associated with paranoid ideas, and on the role of neurotransmitters such as dopamine and serotonin.

The hallmark feature of delusional parasitosis is the fixed belief that one is infested by parasites or very small "bugs" or insects. In some cases, individuals with delusional parasitosis also believe that their family members, friends, pets, home, and belongings are infested. They commonly report that they feel itching and other physical sensations, such as crawling and biting, on their skin and bodies. Their beliefs about being infested persist despite a lack of evidence upon medical examination and microbiological analysis. Behaviors commonly associated with delusional parasitosis include time-consuming examination of the skin and body, use of instruments (e.g., tweezers, magnifying glasses) to facilitate examination or to extract the parasites, maintenance of notes or drawings of the infestation, attempts to photograph or catch the parasites as proof of the infestation, and frequent visits to dermatologists, general practitioners, and other health-care providers, as well as to pest control specialists and entomologists. Visits to mental health providers are much rarer, as individuals with delusional parasitosis do not believe that the source of their problem is psychiatric in nature. Notably, individuals diagnosed with the primary form of the disorder typically present with a pattern of logical thinking and appropriate behavior in all other aspects of their life.

Individuals with delusional parasitosis often reject their diagnosis. When left untreated, the course of the disorder in the primary form tends to be chronic. Atypical antipsychotic medication is the first-line treatment for the primary form, whereas in cases where delusional parasitosis is secondary to another condition, treatment is geared toward the underlying condition.

Irena Milosevic

See also: DSM-5; Entomophobia (Fear of Insects)

Further Reading

Freudenmann, Roland W., & Lepping, Peter. (2009). Delusional infestation. *Clinical Microbiology Reviews, 22*, 690–732.

Acrophobia (Fear of Heights)

Originating from the Greek words *akron* (peak or summit) and *phobos* (fear), acrophobia is an unrealistic or excessive fear of heights that may be triggered by a wide range of situations that involve being high off the ground, such as being on a high floor of a building; standing on a bridge, balcony, ladder, or chair; taking an elevator to a high floor; and climbing stairs. In the *Diagnostic and Statistical Manual of Mental Disorders*, fifth edition, acrophobia is classified as a specific phobia, situational type, and is among the most prevalent of the phobias, affecting up to 5% of individuals in their lifetime (Depla, ten Have, van Balkom, & de Graaf, 2008). Individuals with acrophobia fear that they might fall or lose their balance when they are a certain distance off the ground; consequently, they experience anxiety symptoms that may escalate into a full-blown panic attack when in feared situations. Often feared situations are avoided altogether. Given the breadth of situations that can trigger the fear, individuals with acrophobia experience significant impairment in their life (Depla et al., 2008). For example, they may avoid taking certain jobs (e.g., a construction worker who is asked to work on a high floor) or be unable to do certain things (e.g., change a light bulb that requires standing on a ladder), and their mobility may be greatly affected (e.g., driving over a bridge, traveling in an airplane). In some cases the phobia has a detrimental effect on their health and well-being. For example, they may avoid attending their doctor's office if it is on a high floor of an office building.

Evidence points to a non-associative model of fear acquisition in height phobia (i.e., the fear does not develop due to a traumatic experience related to heights). The origins of height phobia have been linked to abnormalities in balance control and visual perception of movement, as well as sensitivity to bodily symptoms and space and motion discomfort (Coelho & Wallis, 2010). It has been proposed that acrophobia may represent an extreme response to the body's normal warning signal termed *heights vertigo* (Coelho & Wallis, 2010). Heights vertigo is a loss of postural control that occurs when the distance between an individual and visible stationary objects becomes too large. The lack of depth cues leads to a conflict between signal detection of the vestibular and somatosensory receptors resulting in a shift in posture (postural sway or loss of balance) to reactivate visual control. In support of this hypothesis, research has found that individuals with height phobia do more poorly on tasks involving posture control and cognitive activity compared to nonphobic individuals (Boffino et al., 2009).

Treatment for acrophobia consists of exposure to feared situations. In addition, given the impairments of visual perception and posture control associated with acrophobia, vestibular physical therapy may hold some promise; however, further research is needed (Whitney et al., 2005).

Randi E. McCabe

See also: Exposure Treatment; Phobia, Situational Type; Phobia, Specific

Further Reading

Boffino, Catarina C., Cardoso de Sá, Cristina S., Gorenstein, Clarice, Brown, Richard G., Basile, Luis F. H., & Ramos, Renato T. (2009). Fear of heights: Cognitive performance and postural control. *European Archives of Psychiatry and Clinical Neuroscience, 259*, 114–119.

Coelho, Carlos M., & Wallis, Guy. (2010). Deconstructing acrophobia: Physiological and psychological precursors to developing a fear of heights. *Depression and Anxiety, 27*, 864–870.

Depla, Marja F., ten Have, Margreet L., van Balkom, Anton J., & de Graaf, Ron. (2008). Specific fears and phobias in the general population: Results from the Netherlands Mental Health Survey and Incidence Study (NEMESIS). *Social Psychiatry and Psychiatric Epidemiology, 43*, 200–208.

Whitney, Susan L., Jacob, Rolf G., Sparto, Patrick J., Olshansky, Ellen G., Detweiler-Shostak, Gail, Brown, Emily L., & Furman, Joseph M. (2005). Acrophobia and pathological height vertigo: Indications for vestibular physical therapy? *Physical Therapy, 85*, 443–458.

Age of Onset

Frequent and varied fears are a normal part of childhood. As children have increased exposure to the world, and develop cognitively, they tend to "age out" of their fears as they learn that particular stimuli are not dangerous. For some children, this kind of learning fails to occur. This can be due to family avoidance of the stimuli, learning to fear the stimuli from other family members, or (albeit less likely) a negative experience with the stimuli. In these cases, a phobia can develop. The hallmark of a phobia (in contrast to a normal, transient fear) is the expression of extreme distress when exposed to the feared stimuli and/or impairment in functioning.

A recent literature review suggests that the age of onset for animal phobias, natural environment phobias (fear of heights, storms, and water), and blood-injection-injury (BII) phobias are remarkably similar (LeBeau et al., 2010). These subtypes of phobias tend to emerge between 5 and 13 years of age. In contrast, situational phobias (fear of flying, driving, enclosed places) tend to emerge later, between the ages of 13 and 21. It is important to note that most studies on age of onset of phobias are based on retrospective data (i.e., adults looking back on their childhoods), suggesting that these data should be viewed with some caution.

In a clinical setting, the youngest patients with phobias tend to fear specific animals and insects. Very young children (ages 3–5) also present for treatment fearing imaginary creatures (e.g., ghosts, witches) and the dark. Later in childhood (ages 6–9), we continue to see children with the aforementioned fears and we also begin to see children with fears pertaining to their physical health. At this age, children retain memories of going to the doctor for yearly immunizations or blood tests. They might remember a negative experience of being ill or of seeing a friend or family member being ill, or they might learn about illnesses from school or the media. For some children, these experiences lead to the onset of a full-blown phobia of BII and other bodily concerns (including vomit).

In the later elementary school years and through middle school (ages 9–13), phobias shift more into the realm of general worries (doing well at school) and social concerns. This makes sense because at this time, life revolves around school and peers. Even at this young age, there can already be a great deal of pressure to perform well in school and extracurricular activities. For youth who are predisposed to anxiety, messages communicated by schools and parents can be strongly internalized and translated into overwork, expectations that are impossible to meet, and negative thoughts about the self when performance is anything less than perfect. Other anxious children who receive these messages sometimes underperform. The standards that they set for themselves (and which they perceive are set for them by others) can seem so difficult to attain that they end up procrastinating and not being able to complete work in a timely manner, resulting in poor grades. Socially, this is the age where peer relations become more complex, leading some anxious youth to avoid talking to peers, going to parties, or joining new activities for fear of looking foolish. Youth who experience performance anxiety also tend to start suffering distress and impairment at this time. While they might have been able to avoid speaking up in class, making class presentations, or doing other activities in front of others in the younger grades, these kinds of behaviors become increasingly important as the school years continue.

Later still (late teens and early 20s), we see the emergence of phobias of driving and stimuli associated with travel like tunnels and bridges. This of course correlates with the age at which most youth begin driving and traveling independently. This is also the age where panic attacks onset. It is very typical for people to start avoiding situations that might bring on their panic attacks in the years following their first attacks. Over time, panic attacks begin to be associated with the situations in which people experienced them. For example, people who experience a panic attack at the mall might begin to fear and avoid the mall. Similarly, if a person has a panic attack on the subway, he or she might begin to avoid the subway and even other situations that elicit the same cognitions (e.g., "I can't get off if needed to") such as trains, airplanes, or being the passenger in someone else's car. Accordingly, it makes sense that the onset for agoraphobia (avoidance of situations that may provoke panic, for fear that escape will be difficult or impossible) is in the late 20s.

Deborah Roth Ledley

See also: Childhood, Phobias in; Phobias, Causes of; Phobias, Family Influences on the Development and Maintenance of

Further Reading

Antony, Martin M., & Swinson, Richard P. (2000). *Phobic disorders and panic in adults: A guide to assessment and treatment*. Washington, DC: American Psychological Association.

Chansky, Tamar. (2004). *Freeing your child from anxiety: Powerful practical solutions to overcome your child's fears, worries, and phobias*. New York, NY: Broadway Books.

LeBeau, Richard T., Glenn, Daniel, Liao, Betty, Wittchen, Hans-Ulrich, Beesdo-Baum, Katja, Ollendick, Thomas, & Craske, Michelle G. (2010). Specific phobia: A review of DSM-IV specific phobia and preliminary recommendations for DSM-V. *Depression and Anxiety, 27*, 148–167.

Agliophobia (Fear of Pain)

The Greek word *algos* and suffix *-algia* refer to pain or a pain condition, such as neuralgia (nerve pain), arthralgia (joint pain), and cephalgia (headache). Depending on the source, *agliophobia* (sometimes spelled algiophobia or algophobia) refers to the fear of pain or fear of suffering.

The International Association for the Study of Pain defines pain as "an unpleasant sensory and emotional experience associated with actual or potential tissue damage, or described in terms of such damage." Pain is universal and essential for our survival because it motivates us to withdraw from harmful situations (e.g., hot stoves), to protect the injured body part while it heals (e.g., run hand under warm water, apply a bandage), and to avoid similar experiences in the future. For most individuals, the initiation of short-term adaptive processes in response to acute pain facilitates recovery, and pain diminishes quickly as healing occurs. For at least 10% of adults, however, pain persists long after any identifiable organic pathology has healed (Waddell, 1987). Persistent pain can lead to catastrophic thinking about what the pain means. Pain catastrophizing invariably leads to pain-related fears that can amplify the pain experience. It is not clear whether the primary object of pain-related fears is the painful sensations per se, the activities associated with those sensations ("kinesiophobia"), or painful reinjury. In any event, pain-related fears can trigger a cascade of hypervigilance (excessive attention to pain), guarding or "safety" behaviors (restricting range of joint motion), and escape/avoidance behaviors (limiting or not participating in physical, occupational, or social activities). Although intended to reduce pain, in the long term these actions can perpetuate and/or exacerbate the pain.

According to fear-avoidance models of pain, pain-related fears lead to withdrawal from important domains of functioning, such as work, leisure, social, and sexual activities. This reduced functioning can result in mood disturbances (e.g., irritability, frustration, anger, and depression). In explaining the development and maintenance of chronic pain, fear-avoidance models highlight three anxiety-related constructs associated with pain-related disability: pain catastrophizing, pain anxiety, and anxiety sensitivity (fear of arousal-related somatic sensations associated with anxiety). Pain-related fear differs from pain anxiety in that the former tends to motivate defensive behaviors (escape), whereas the latter tends to motivate preventative behaviors (avoidance). Avoidance behaviors can be difficult to correct because they arise from the anticipation of pain rather than in response to pain itself. Studies show that pain catastrophizing predicts current pain, pain anxiety predicts task-related pain, and anxiety sensitivity predicts functional disability and negative pain-related affect. Studies also show that anxiety sensitivity exacerbates fear of pain and, in turn, pain-specific avoidance behaviors in individuals with chronic pain. Evidence indicates that fear of pain plays a role in both dental phobia and blood-injection-injury phobia.

Clinicians commonly employ self-report measures to assess overall pain severity, beliefs about pain, fear of work-related activities, fear of movement and/or reinjury, degree of pain focus, and perceived disability across important domains of functioning (e.g., self-care, occupational recreational). Not surprisingly, individuals with pain-related fear are more apt to seek biomedical (vs. psychological) explanations and solutions for their pain problems. Accordingly, they are more likely to seek pain relief versus restoration of activities. Unfortunately, this can lead to dissatisfactory health-care encounters, increased stress, and even more pain. Moreover, individuals with pain-related fear often have comorbid mood and anxiety disorders, which can make assessment and treatment even more difficult.

To reduce pain-related fear, psychological approaches tend to include psychoeducation (information about the fear-avoidance behavior and "managing" versus controlling or avoiding pain); cognitive restructuring (intended to target errors in thinking, such as pain catastrophizing); and exercise (e.g., lifting weights) to increase muscle strength and physical activity. Treatment also may involve graded *in vivo* exposure, whereby individuals are encouraged to engage in activities that activate their fears, without relying on safety behaviors. This is intended to target dysfunctional beliefs such as "If I lift my child, I will tear all the muscles in my neck." In this way, individuals can test their assumptions that pain signals injury (i.e., hurt = harm) and that activities are dangerous. In the absence of catastrophic consequences, exposure enables individuals to correct their fear expectancies and discover that hurt does not equal harm.

Margo C. Watt and Christianne Macaulay

See also: Anxiety Sensitivity; Cognitive Restructuring; Exposure, *In Vivo*; Phobia, Blood-Injection-Injury Type; Psychoeducation

Further Reading

Vlaeyen, Johan W. S., & Crombez, Geert. (2007). Fear and pain. *Pain: Clinical Updates*, XV, 1–4.

Waddell, Gordon. (1987). Volvo award in clinical sciences. A new clinical model for the treatment of low-back pain. *Spine, 12*, 632–644.

Agoraphobia (Fear of Panic-Like Symptoms)

Agoraphobia, which translates from Greek to *fear of the marketplace*, is far more complex than a fear of shopping venues. Although the term *agoraphobia* implies that this is a specific phobia, the *Diagnostic and Statistical Manual of Mental Disorders* (DSM) does not classify it as such. According to the fifth edition of the DSM (DSM-5; American Psychiatric Association [APA], 2013), *agoraphobia* refers to fear of being in situations where one might have panic-like or other embarrassing symptoms and in which escape is perceived as difficult or help unavailable. Although it is commonly believed that being agoraphobic means that a person is fearful of leaving his or her home, the range of situations that are feared by individuals with agoraphobia is considerably more expansive and includes enclosed spaces (e.g., a movie theatre or a crowded restaurant), wide open spaces (e.g., parking lots or parks), standing in a line, being in a crowd, being home alone or away from home, bridges, driving, or using public transportation. These situations are frequently avoided or tolerated with significant levels of fear or distress. In some cases, individuals are able tolerate the feared situation with the aid of behaviors designed to ensure their safety. Examples of such safety behaviors include always carrying a cell phone, locating the nearest exit, always sitting on the edge of the aisle, driving only within a certain radius around the home (often referred to as a *safety zone*), or leaving the house only with certain "safe" individuals. In very severe cases, the individual with agoraphobia may be housebound.

Many experts consider agoraphobia to occur as a consequence of experiencing panic attacks; thus, until recently, the diagnosis of agoraphobia was linked to panic disorder in the DSM. Individuals could be diagnosed with either panic disorder with agoraphobia or agoraphobia without a history of panic disorder, whereas agoraphobia itself was not considered to be a stand-alone disorder. It was believed that agoraphobia without a history of panic disorder developed as a result of so-called limited symptom panic attacks, where the number of panic symptoms experienced, such as pounding heart or sweating, was not enough to warrant a diagnosis of panic disorder (Kessler, Ruscio, Shear, & Wittchen, 2009). However, alternative diagnostic systems, such as the World Health Organization's *International Classification of Diseases*, do not specify that the source of fear must be related to an ability

Passengers boarding a bus during rush hour. People with agoraphobia commonly avoid taking public transportation, particularly when it is crowded, for fear of being unable to escape in the case of experiencing a panic attack or panic-like symptoms. (Troppobella/Dreamstime.com)

to escape or obtain help, calling into question the causal link between panic disorder and agoraphobia. Furthermore, recent studies have shown that a diagnosis of agoraphobia increases the probability of developing panic disorder (Kessler et al., 2006), suggesting that the implied one-way relationship of panic disorder leading to the development of agoraphobia may not be accurate. As a result of this body research, agoraphobia is now listed as a distinct anxiety disorder in the DSM-5, which describes the focus of agoraphobic fear to be of not only panic-like symptoms but also of other embarrassing symptoms such as vomiting, falling in the case of older adults, or getting lost in the case of children.

Epidemiological research suggests that approximately 1.1% of the population is diagnosed with panic disorder with agoraphobia during their lifetime and 0.8% of the population is diagnosed with agoraphobia without a history of panic disorder during their lifetime (Kessler et al., 2006). On average, individuals develop agoraphobia in late adolescence or early adulthood, with more women than men being diagnosed with the disorder (APA, 2013). Without treatment, symptoms are unlikely to improve (APA, 2013). Furthermore, research suggests that the presence of agoraphobia in the context of panic disorder is associated with poorer outcomes than panic disorder alone (Kessler et al., 2006). Individuals with agoraphobia are also frequently diagnosed with many other mental disorders such as all other anxiety disorders, including social anxiety disorder (social phobia) and specific phobias.

Given the theoretical link between agoraphobia and panic disorder and the large proportion of individuals with agoraphobia who are also diagnosed with panic disorder, nearly all psychological treatments for agoraphobia also focus on the treatment of panic disorder. One of the first-line treatments for agoraphobia and panic disorder is cognitive behavioral therapy (CBT). The cognitive model (see Woody & Nosen, 2009) suggests that individuals develop panic disorder when they interpret their bodily sensations as being dangerous. Research suggests that heightened expectation of having a panic attack and focus on the negative personal (e.g., that physical danger is likely) and social (e.g., humiliation) consequences of such an attack may result in the development of agoraphobia (Woody & Nosen, 2009). CBT involves educating individuals about the cognitive behavioral model of panic disorder and agoraphobia, examining and reevaluating negative beliefs about panic symptoms and the costs and likelihood of the occurrence of catastrophic events as a result of a panic attack, exposure to feared sensations (e.g., elevated heart rate), and exposure to places and situations that are avoided due to one's fear of being unable to cope or escape. Numerous studies have found CBT to be effective for the treatment of panic disorder and agoraphobia both immediately and in the long term (McCabe & Gifford, 2009).

Andrea R. Ashbaugh

See also: Anxiety and Related Disorders; Anxiety Sensitivity; Barlow, David H. (1942–); Carbon Dioxide Challenge Test; Craske, Michelle G.; Exposure, Interoceptive; Exposure, *In Vivo*; Panic Attacks; Panic Disorder; Safety Behavior

Further Reading

American Psychiatric Association. (2013). *Diagnostic and statistical manual of mental disorders* (5th ed.). Arlington, VA: American Psychiatric Publishing.

Kessler, Ronald C., Chiu, Wai T., Jin, Robert, Ruscio, Ayelet M., Shear, Katherine, & Walters, Ellen E. (2006). The epidemiology of panic attacks, panic disorder, and agoraphobia in the National Comorbidity Survey Replication. *Archives of General Psychiatry, 63,* 415–424.

Kessler, Ronald C., Ruscio, Ayelet M., Shear, Katherine, & Wittchen, Hans-Ulrich. (2009). Epidemiology of anxiety disorders. In Martin M. Antony & Murray B. Stein (Eds.), *Oxford handbook of anxiety and related disorders* (pp. 19–31). Oxford, UK: Oxford University Press.

McCabe, Randi E., & Gifford, Shannon. (2009). Psychological treatment of panic disorder and agoraphobia. In Martin M. Antony & Murray B. Stein (Eds.), *Oxford handbook of anxiety and related disorders* (pp. 308–320). Oxford, UK: Oxford University Press.

Woody, S. R., & Nosen, E. (2009). Psychological models of phobic disorders and panic. In Martin M. Antony & Murray B. Stein (Eds.), *Oxford handbook of anxiety and related disorders* (pp. 209–224). Oxford, UK: Oxford University Press.

CASE STUDY: PANIC DISORDER WITH AGORAPHOBIA

The case of Brandon illustrates how agoraphobia develops in the context of panic disorder. Take note of the focus of Brandon's fear and his change in behavior, which exemplify common symptoms of agoraphobia.

Brandon is a 28-year-old married father of a young son. He has been on a leave from his job as a physiotherapist for the past six months. Brandon first experienced an unexpected panic attack when he was 26 years old, shortly after the birth of his son. While he was driving to work, his heart began to pound rapidly, he had difficulty breathing, and he felt very dizzy. Brandon felt as though he was losing control of himself, and he thought that he would "pass out." He pulled his car over at the side of the road for fear of causing an accident. After his symptoms subsided, Brandon called in sick to work and carefully drove home, worrying that there might be something terribly wrong with him.

After his initial panic attack in the car, Brandon began to experience recurring attacks. They happened several times per month and always unexpectedly. Brandon became very vigilant to any changes in physical sensations in his body, monitoring for signs of another attack. He also considerably changed his daily behavior to reduce the likelihood of having panic symptoms in the "wrong" place.

In particular, Brandon began to avoid situations where he thought it would be dangerous or embarrassing to experience a panic attack. He was especially concerned that he might faint in public, although this had never happened. He avoided driving on the freeway to get to work, instead taking side roads that lengthened his commute by 30 minutes each way. He also began to avoid crowded settings where rapid escape might be difficult, such as shopping centers, grocery stores, and movie theaters. When his wife pressed him to pick up items at the store, Brandon would anxiously acquiesce and follow a routine to ensure he could leave the store as quickly as possible. He risked parking in the handicapped spot that was closest to the exit, wanting to get to his car quickly should he experience panic. He additionally avoided lining up at the checkout, choosing instead to proceed through the self-checkout. Indeed, even though Brandon's family was dealing with financial constraints, he would go to the more expensive grocery store because it had a self-checkout. Eventually, Brandon got a parking ticket for parking in the handicapped spot. He felt a great deal of shame about this.

Brandon continued to struggle with driving to work. He would lay awake at night, anxiously anticipating his long commute and worrying that he might experience a panic attack while driving. He began to ask his wife to drive him, but she was unable to do so on a daily basis. On the days that he did not have a ride, Brandon started to increasingly call in sick to work. When his employer expressed concern about his absences, Brandon decided to take a sick leave.

Irena Milosevic

Ailurophobia (Fear of Cats)

Ailurophobia (from the Greek *ailuros* meaning cat and *phobos* meaning fear) is an excessive and persistent fear of cats. This phobia is also recognized by other names, including elurophobia, gatophobia, and felinophobia. In the DSM-5, ailurophobia is classified as an animal type specific phobia, one of the most prevalent phobia types. Compared to other animal phobias (e.g., fear of snakes and spiders), ailurophobia is less common, although its exact prevalence has not been reported.

Ailurophobia can develop through several pathways. A person might become fearful of cats after having a negative experience with a cat, such as getting severely scratched after trying to pet a seemingly docile cat. The fear might also develop as a result of seeing another individual express significant fear of cats or as a result of hearing negative information about cats (e.g., a parent telling a child to stay away from cats because they are unpredictable and dangerous). It is also possible that humans have a predisposition to acquire fear of cats, as our early ancestors lived in environments in which predators such as big cats posed a threat to their survival. It was therefore adaptive for early humans to readily acquire fear of such animals.

Individuals with ailurophobia are typically fearful of being bitten or scratched by a cat. They might hold unrealistic beliefs about the dangerousness of domestic cats and view them as predatory or evil creatures. When exposed to a cat, they exhibit intense distress and may even experience a panic attack. Hearing a cat's meow or purr might also provoke fear. Accordingly, individuals with this phobia avoid being in the presence of cats, touching them, or even, in some cases, seeing photographs or videos of them. Ailurophobia may hinder a person's ability to visit friends or family with pet cats and to be in or near other settings where cats might be present (e.g., near neighbor's yard). This phobia further may considerably interfere with travel to many areas of the world with high populations of stray cats.

Like other phobias, ailurophobia can be successfully treated with exposure therapy, which involves graduated and repeated exposure to cat-related stimuli. For example, an individual might begin by looking at photographs and videos of cats and then move on to touching or petting a plush cat before ultimately completing exposures that involve being in the presence of a real cat and handling it.

Irena Milosevic

See also: DSM-5; Exposure Treatment; Phobia, Animal Type; Phobia, Specific

Further Reading

Antony, Martin M., & McCabe, Randi E. (2005). *Overcoming animal and insect phobias*. Oakland, CA: New Harbinger Publications.

American Psychiatric Association

The American Psychiatric Association (APA) is the leading professional organization for psychiatrists in the United States. Its membership is comprised of 36,000 American and international psychiatrists and psychiatry trainees, making it the largest psychiatric organization in the world. The APA publishes a number of scholarly journals focused on psychiatry and mental health, and it is also the publisher of a widely used classification system for mental disorders, the *Diagnostic and Statistical Manual of Mental Disorders* (DSM). In addition to its professional resources for mental health providers, the association offers educational resources for the general public.

The APA was founded in 1844 with the formation of the Association of Medical Superintendents of American Institutions for the Insane. Its membership at the time was limited to superintendents of mental hospitals and asylums. In 1892, the association was renamed to the American Medico-Psychological Association, and its membership was expanded to include physicians employed in mental hospitals and private offices. Its current name, the APA, was adopted in 1921.

The stated mission of the APA is to promote the highest quality care for persons with mental disorders, as well as to promote education, research, and advancements in the profession of psychiatry. One of its most influential contributions is its development of the DSM (currently in its fifth edition; American Psychiatric Association, 2013), which is the standard in North America for the diagnosis of mental disorders. The APA also publishes several scientific journals and many books on a broad range of topics relating to mental health. Additionally, since 1991, it has been developing and disseminating practice guidelines for evidence-based assessment and treatment of psychiatric disorders. The association hosts two annual educational conferences that highlight advancements in the field of psychiatric research and treatment, and it further offers educational and professional programs to its members.

The APA has been active in advocating for increased awareness of mental health problems and improvements in accessibility to mental health care. Members of the general public can access a variety of mental health–focused educational resources, including brochures, videos, and blogs on the APA website. Anxiety disorders, including phobias, are included among the many topics covered.

Irena Milosevic

See also: DSM-5; Psychiatry; Treatment, Evidence-Based

Further Reading

American Psychiatric Association. (2013). *Diagnostic and statistical manual of mental disorders* (5th ed.). Arlington, VA: American Psychiatric Publishing.

Website

www.psych.org

American Psychological Association

The American Psychological Association (APA) is a scientific and professional organization representing psychologists. With a membership of more than 137,000 researchers, practitioners, educators, consultants, and students, it is the largest psychological association in the world. The APA's stated mission is to "advance the creation, communication and application of psychological knowledge to benefit society and improve people's lives" (www.apa.org).

The APA was founded in 1892 at Clark University. Its first president was G. Stanley Hall, a pioneer in American psychology and the first individual in the United States to receive a doctorate in psychology. At the time of its formation, the APA had only 31 members, but its membership increased rapidly after World War II. Today, the organization boasts a vast membership and is comprised of 54 divisions or special interest groups organized by its members. The divisions represent broad areas of psychology, including various subdisciplines of the profession (e.g., experimental, clinical, developmental), as well as particular topics such as addictions, aging, measurement, and psychotherapy. Perhaps most relevant to the understanding and treatment of phobias is Division 12, the Society of Clinical Psychology, which has been responsible for identifying empirically supported treatments for mental health problems based on the current research literature.

The APA provides a broad range of services and resources to its members and affiliates, to the field of psychology at large, and to the general public. Its goals across all of these domains are to promote the recognition of psychology as a science and to advance health through psychological knowledge and principles. The association is responsible for accrediting psychology doctoral programs in North America, and it has also established a code of ethics to which professional psychologists in America are expected to adhere. Furthermore, the APA holds an annual research and professional convention that is well attended by psychologists and psychology trainees, and it publishes or maintains a vast array of psychologically focused academic journals, books, databases, manuals, videos, magazines, brochures, and web pages, some geared toward professionals and students and others toward the general public. For individuals seeking information about psychology topics that affect their well-being (e.g., phobias, depression, sexuality, trauma), the APA hosts an online consumer resource, the Psychology Help Center.

Irena Milosevic

See also: Treatment, Evidence-Based

Websites

www.apa.org
www.psychologicaltreatments.org

Amygdala

The amygdala is a collection of anatomically and functionally distinct nuclei located deep within the temporal lobes of the brain and critically involved in fear, threat-related processing, and fear/aversive associations. Pathological fear, which is a defining characteristic of anxiety disorders, is suggested to manifest in part from amygdala dysfunction.

In 1888, Sanger Brown, an American physician, and E. A. Schäfer, a professor of physiology, began a series of experiments examining the behavioral consequences of temporal lobe damage in monkeys. They removed the entire temporal lobe on both sides of the brain in a group of monkeys and discovered a profound change in one monkey's emotional disposition. Specifically, they noticed that prior to the surgery the monkey was aggressive and wild; however, upon removal of the temporal lobes, it became very docile and failed to show any evidence of fear even when attacked by a wild monkey. The importance of these findings was overlooked until the 1930s, when work by Heinrich Klüver, an experimental psychologist, and Paul Bucy, a neurosurgeon, also revealed similar changes in the emotional responses of monkeys following temporal lobe damage that included damage to the amygdala. These changes in emotion were later reproduced in monkeys by removal of only the amygdala while keeping the surrounding brain structures. Furthermore, other studies found that monkeys with neonatal amygdala damage had enhanced social fear and that human patients with amygdala damage were impaired in making accurate judgments regarding trustworthiness and approachability based on photographs of faces.

Since then, convergent evidence from animal and human studies has highlighted the role of the amygdala in the mediation of fear, threat-related processing, and anxiety. The amygdala has been particularly implicated in fear and aversive conditioning, processes intimately related to phobias and other anxiety disorders. During fear acquisition, sensory information about the conditioned stimulus, such as a tone, and the unconditioned stimulus, such as a shock, converge at the amygdala and become associated (i.e., producing the fear memory) and translated into conditioned fear responses. Neuroimaging studies have shown increased amygdala activation in healthy individuals during fear conditioning, which has also be correlated with fear responses. Of particular relevance to social anxiety disorder (social phobia), the amygdala is thought to play a critical role in the social processing of emotionally significant information and in heightening watchfulness and interpreting ambiguity. For instance, brain imaging has consistently identified amygdala activation to facial expressions of threat/danger (e.g., fear) and to socially threatening/negative faces (e.g., anger, disgust), but also more generally to emotionally expressive faces regardless of the type of emotion. Furthermore, the amygdala is activated during evaluative judgments of trust, and the intensity of amygdala activation is related to the level of trustworthiness.

Compared to healthy individuals, individuals with fear-based disorders, such as social anxiety disorder, specific phobia (e.g., animal), panic disorder, and post-traumatic stress disorder, consistently exhibit exaggerated amygdala reactivity to harsh (e.g., angry, fearful, contemptuous) versus accepting (e.g., happy) faces, and to angry versus neutral faces. Enhanced amygdala activity has also been observed in individuals with social anxiety disorder when exposed to an anxiety-provoking public speaking task, and during aversive conditioning. Further, adults who were characterized in infancy as "behaviorally inhibited," a temperament that predisposes the development of social anxiety disorder, showed an elevated response in the amygdala to novel (vs. familiar) neutral faces relative to those previously characterized as uninhibited. Studies have also shown that exaggerated amygdala reactivity is positively associated with social anxiety symptom severity and negative social-evaluative beliefs. Consistent with these findings, increased amygdala activation has also been observed in individuals with specific phobias when engaged in tasks or when viewing pictures related to their specific fear (e.g., spiders). Recent studies have reported changes in the volume of the amygdala associated with phobia; however, the direction of change is inconsistent. For instance, one study reported that spider phobia was associated with decreases in amygdala volume, whereas another study reported increased amygdala volume. Despite these conflicting findings, alterations in amygdala volume may be a brain marker for vulnerability to develop phobic disorders or may emerge as a consequence of the disorder.

There is emerging evidence to suggest that treatment for phobia, either by cognitive behavioral therapy or by medications, normalizes abnormal amygdala function and that pretreatment amygdala activity predicts treatment outcome in individuals with anxiety disorders. For instance, in a public speaking task, individuals with social anxiety who responded to treatment showed reduced amygdala reactivity to the speaking challenge, regardless of the type of treatment (behavioral or medication). In another study, individuals with spider phobia exhibited exaggerated amygdala reactivity to disorder-related cues prior to cognitive behavioral therapy; the reactivity decreased following treatment and was associated with self-reported symptom improvement. These findings are particularly exciting because they demonstrate that specific brain regions, which are observed to be altered before treatment, are the same ones that change/adapt following successful treatment. Moreover, they suggest that pretreatment activation in the amygdala may predict treatment response. Thus, given that hyper-responsivity is observed specifically in the amygdala in fear-based disorders at baseline, amygdala activation may serve as a potential brain marker for treatment response.

Shoko Mori and Christine A. Rabinak

See also: Fear; Fear, Neural Pathways of; Limbic System; Neuroimaging; Treatment Outcome, Predictors of

Further Reading

Whalen, Paul J., & Phelps, Elizabeth A. (Eds.). (2009). *The human amygdala*. New York, NY: Guilford Press.

Antony, Martin M. (1964–)

Martin M. Antony is a clinical psychologist and leading contemporary figure in the field of anxiety disorders. He is known as an engaging speaker, prolific writer, program builder, and influential mentor, having shaped the career paths of a multitude of students who have now become leaders in the field themselves. One of his early research interests was in the area of phobias. His workbook *Mastering Your Fears and Phobias*, coauthored with David Barlow and Michelle Craske, is now in its second edition and is one of the most popular workbooks for therapists and clients striving to overcome a specific phobia.

Born and raised in Toronto and the surrounding area, Antony attended the University of Toronto. He took a range of science courses but found he was naturally drawn to psychology, in which he decided to major. He received his bachelor's degree in 1987 and then took a year to work as a research assistant in the Anxiety Disorders Clinic at the Toronto General Hospital, under the direction of Richard Swinson. There, Antony coordinated a large study investigating the relative and combined effects of alprazolam and exposure therapy for the treatment of panic disorder and agoraphobia. It was during this period that Antony realized he wanted to become a psychologist. In 1994, he received a PhD in psychology from the University at Albany, State University of New York, where he was supervised by a number of prominent anxiety disorders researchers, including David Barlow, Timothy Brown, Michelle Craske, and Ron Rapee.

Since completing his PhD, Antony has held a number of professional positions. He was a psychologist in the Anxiety Disorders Clinic at the Clarke Institute of Psychiatry (now the Centre for Addiction and Mental Health, Toronto) from 1994 to 1998, was chief psychologist and founding director of the Anxiety Treatment and Research Centre at St. Joseph's Healthcare Hamilton from 1998 to 2006, and has been a professor in the Department of Psychology at Ryerson University in Toronto from 2006 to the present. He was also the founding director of several training programs, including the Clinical Psychology Residency Program at St. Joseph's Healthcare Hamilton and the MA and PhD programs in psychology at Ryerson University. In 2009–2010, Antony served as president of the Canadian Psychological Association. Currently, he is professor and chair in the Department of Psychology at Ryerson University and director of Research at the Anxiety Treatment and Research Clinic, St. Joseph's Healthcare Hamilton.

Antony has published 29 books and over 200 scientific articles and book chapters, mostly on the nature, assessment, and treatment of anxiety-based problems such as phobias, obsessive-compulsive disorder, panic disorder, social anxiety disorder (social phobia), generalized anxiety disorder, and perfectionism. His books have sold over 180,000 copies and have been translated into 14 different languages. Antony is best known for research that examines practical ways to assess and treat anxiety-based problems, and for disseminating evidence-based treatments to therapists and individuals who struggle with anxiety, through his books and treatment manuals. Antony also trains and supervises numerous students in psychology, psychiatry, social work, and other disciplines in the area of cognitive behavioral therapy for anxiety-based problems, and he has received a number of career awards for his contributions to research, training, and education. He is a fellow of the Royal Society of Canada, as well as the American and Canadian Psychological Associations, and the Association for Psychological Science. Antony has given more than 300 workshops and presentations to health-care professionals from across North America, Europe, and Australia. He has also been interviewed, featured, or quoted more than 300 times in various print, radio, and television media outlets, including the *CBC, Chatelaine Magazine, CTV, Discovery Channel*, the *Globe and Mail, National Post, O*, the *Oprah Magazine, Reader's Digest, Scientific American Mind, Washington Post*, and many others.

Antony's research interests are wide-ranging within the field of anxiety disorders and reflect his keen ability to see the broad perspective. The popularity and global accessibility of his treatment manuals and clinical guides reflect Antony's talent at translating empirical research findings into straightforward, effective clinical strategies and applications. On the personal side, Antony is known for his down-to-earth nature, approachability, and engaging sense of humor. These personal qualities, combined with his extraordinary work ethic and visionary ability, make Antony a greatly admired and highly respected member of the field of anxiety disorders.

Randi E. McCabe

See also: Anxiety and Related Disorders; Barlow, David H. (1942–); Craske, Michelle G.; Phobia, Specific; Phobias, Assessment of; Phobias, Diagnosis of; Phobias, Prevalence of

Further Reading

Antony, Martin M., & Norton, Peter J. (2009). *The anti-anxiety workbook: Proven strategies to overcome worry, panic, phobias, and obsessions*. New York, NY: Guilford Press.

Antony, Martin M., Craske, Michelle G., & Barlow, David H. (2006). *Mastering your fears and phobias (client workbook)*, 2nd ed. New York, NY: Oxford University Press.

Anxiety and Depression Association of America

The Anxiety and Depression Association of America (ADAA) is a nonprofit organization focused on increasing awareness and improving diagnosis and treatment of anxiety and related disorders in adults and children. The organization is also highly involved in supporting and disseminating scientific research related to these disorders. Its stated mission is "to promote the prevention, treatment, and cure of anxiety, depression, and stress-related disorders through education, practice, and research" (www.adaa.org).

Originally called the Phobia Society of America, the ADAA was founded in 1980 by a group of practitioners and patients who sought to promote awareness of treatments for phobias. Its name was reflective of the early state of knowledge about anxiety disorders, most of which were called phobias at the time. With the advancement of research in the field, the association was renamed the Anxiety Disorders Association of America in 1990. It placed greater emphasis on the application of scientific methods to the understanding of anxiety disorders, which included increased membership of researchers and the addition of a research program to its annual conference. The ADAA was renamed to its current name in 2012 with the intention of recognizing the high degree of co-occurrence between anxiety and depression.

The ADAA boasts a diverse membership of clinicians, researchers, students, and consumer advocates. It offers many resources for professionals working in the area of anxiety and related disorders, including educational resources, teaching tools, and research funding, the latter which has totaled to $1.5 million. It also hosts a well-attended annual conference that targets both professionals and consumers and emphasizes the integration of biological and psychological approaches. The association additionally publishes a prestigious academic journal in psychology, *Depression and Anxiety.*

The ADAA has led several nationwide educational campaigns to raise awareness about anxiety disorders and their treatment. It offers extensive informational resources on its website to individuals affected by anxiety, depression, and related problems. Consumers can access information about symptoms, treatment, and research. Available tools include factsheets, self-administered screening questionnaires, self-help books, informational videos, a list of support groups, and a therapist database.

Irena Milosevic

See also: Anxiety and Related Disorders

Website

www.adaa.org

Anxiety and Related Disorders

The broad category of anxiety disorders encompasses psychological disorders that are defined by excessive fear and anxiety and associated behavioral disturbances, such as avoidance. Although all individuals experience some degree of anxiety or fear in various situations, the anxiety and fear that defines anxiety disorders is excessive given the actual threat posed by the object or situation, developmentally inappropriate, chronic, and is associated with functional impairment in one or more domains (e.g., school, work, or social relationships). As a group, anxiety disorders are the most prevalent mental disorders, with a 12-month prevalence rate of 18%.

Anxiety has been discussed by philosophers and poets since antiquity. Early Greek philosophers attributed anxiety and panic reactions to encounters with mythological gods and to imbalances between bodily humors. The first medical models of anxiety were developed early in the 18th century and viewed anxiety symptoms as having a biological origin and playing a causal role in other medical and psychiatric conditions, such as "insanity." Sigmund Freud (1856–1939) was the first to propose a psychological underpinning for anxiety disorders. Freud viewed anxiety disorders as a unitary construct that he termed *anxiety neuroses*. Although Freud's conceptualization of anxiety as resulting from repressed sexual impulses and unconscious conflicts fell out of favor in the 1960s, with the shift to behaviorism (i.e., and its focus on observable symptoms and characteristics), his work had an important impact on the development of the modern classification system for psychiatric disorders.

The *Diagnostic and Statistical Manual of Mental Disorders* (DSM) describes the criteria used by clinicians in the United States (and in many places throughout the world) to diagnose psychological disorders, including anxiety disorders. The first edition of the DSM, published in 1952, conceptualized anxiety as neuroses and focused on the role of unconscious conflicts in anxiety. The third edition of the DSM, published in 1980, revolutionized the conceptualization of anxiety disorders by introducing the term *anxiety disorders* and dividing the category into specific disorders with clear diagnostic criteria. The manual is currently in its fifth edition (DSM-5) and includes 11 distinct anxiety disorders: separation anxiety disorder, selective mutism, specific phobia, social anxiety disorder (social phobia), panic disorder, agoraphobia, generalized anxiety disorder, substance/medication-induced anxiety disorder, anxiety disorder due to another medical condition, other specified anxiety disorder, and unspecified anxiety disorder. These anxiety disorders differ from one another based on the specific objects and situations that induce feelings of fear and anxiety, as well as the specific thoughts and beliefs that individuals have about the feared object or situation. In addition, the DSM includes a number of anxiety-related disorders (e.g., obsessive-compulsive disorder, posttraumatic stress disorder, illness anxiety disorder) that are listed in other categories.

Separation anxiety disorder is characterized by fear and anxiety about being separated from one's attachment figures; in children this is most commonly one's parents and in adults this is most commonly one's children. Individuals with separation anxiety disorder are afraid that harm may come to the attachment figure and that they may permanently lose the attachment figure. Separation anxiety disorder results in a reluctance to leave the attachment figure and is associated with nightmares and physical symptoms of distress, including headaches, stomachaches, nausea, and vomiting. Separation anxiety disorder is the most common anxiety disorder in children under the age of 12 years with a 12-month prevalence rate of 4%.

Selective mutism is defined by a consistent failure to speak in specific situations (e.g., at school) despite speaking in other situations (e.g., at home). There is a lack of clear evidence as to the specific thoughts and beliefs that underlie the lack of speech, although the problem may be related to social anxiety. The prevalence rate of selective mutism in children is currently estimated to be between 0.03% and 1%.

Specific phobia is characterized by excessive fear or avoidance of a specific object or situation. Specific phobias are classified into the following categories based on the focus of the fear: animal (e.g., dogs, spiders), natural environment (e.g., thunderstorms, water), blood-injection-injury (e.g., getting a needle, seeing blood), situational (e.g., heights, elevators), and other (e.g., vomiting). The 12-month prevalence rate for specific phobias in the general population is 7% to 9%.

Social anxiety disorder (social phobia) is characterized by excessive anxiety and/or avoidance of social (e.g., attending parties, meeting unfamiliar individuals) or performance (e.g., public speaking) situations in which an individual may be judged or scrutinized. Individuals with social anxiety disorder fear being negatively evaluated, embarrassed, or rejected by others. The 12-month prevalence rate of social anxiety disorder in the general population is about 7%.

Panic disorder is defined by recurrent, unexpected panic attacks that are followed by persistent concerns about having another panic attack and/or a change in behavior as a result of the panic attack (e.g., not exercising due to a fear of physical symptoms, avoiding locations or activities during which one has previously had a panic attack). A panic attack is characterized by a sudden onset of intense fearfulness and/or terror that is accompanied by four or more of the following physical and cognitive symptoms: hyperventilation, increased heart rate, sweating, trembling or shaking, chest pain, nausea, dizziness, derealization (feelings of unreality) or depersonalization (feeling detached from oneself), fear of losing control or going crazy, and fear of dying. The panic attack symptoms develop abruptly and reach a peak within minutes. The 12-month prevalence rate of panic disorder in the general population is 2% to 3%.

Agoraphobia is characterized by fear and anxiety about panic-like symptoms or other embarrassing physical symptoms occurring in two or more of the following situations: using public transportation, being in open spaces, being in enclosed places, standing in line or being in a crowd, or being alone in situations outside one's home. Individuals with agoraphobia fear that escape might be difficult or that help might not be available in the event of experiencing distressing physical symptoms. The 12-month prevalence rate of agoraphobia in the general population is 1.7%.

Generalized anxiety disorder is defined by excessive, uncontrollable worry about a number of domains (e.g., work, school, one's health and safety, the health and safety of loved ones). The worry is accompanied by at least three out of six physical and cognitive symptoms, including: restlessness or feeling on edge, fatigue, difficulties concentrating, irritability, muscle tension, and disturbed sleep (i.e., difficulties falling asleep or staying asleep). The 12-month prevalence rate of generalized anxiety disorder in the general population is 2.9%.

Although the DSM-5 did not include major changes to the diagnostic criteria for most anxiety disorders, three anxiety disorders from the fourth edition (obsessive-compulsive disorder, posttraumatic stress disorder, acute stress disorder) were reclassified in the DSM-5 under new sections. Obsessive-compulsive disorder is defined by the presence of obsessions (repetitive thoughts, images, or urges, such as intrusive thoughts about contamination or of harming others) or compulsions (repetitive behaviors aimed at decreasing feelings of anxiety caused by the obsessions, such as repeatedly checking the stove or the lock on the door). Obsessive-compulsive disorder is classified as an Obsessive-Compulsive and Related Disorder in the DSM-5, a category that groups together disorders defined by the presence of obsessive preoccupation and repetitive behaviors. Posttraumatic stress disorder is characterized by persistent reexperiencing of a trauma (e.g., intrusive memories), avoidance, cognitive and mood symptoms, and arousal symptoms that occur for a period of more than one month after exposure to a traumatic event. Acute stress disorder includes similar symptoms as posttraumatic stress disorder, although the duration is shorter (between three days and one month). The DSM-5 lists posttraumatic stress disorder and acute stress disorder under the category, Trauma and Stressor-Related Disorders, which groups together disorders that include exposure to a traumatic or stressful event.

Illness anxiety disorder, which is included in the Somatic Symptom and Related Disorders section of the DSM-5, is characterized by a preoccupation about having or developing a serious illness. Individuals with illness anxiety disorder are vigilant for physical symptoms and misinterpret normal physical symptoms as indicating the presence of a serious medical condition (e.g., interpreting a headache as a symptom of a brain tumor). The anxiety is maintained despite medical tests that fail to find an underlying medical condition. If a medical condition is present, the anxiety is excessive given the severity of the medical condition. While some individuals with illness anxiety disorder engage in various health-related excessive behaviors, including seeking excessive reassurance from others (e.g., family members and medical doctors) about their physical health, spending a significant amount of time researching medical conditions, and repeatedly checking their bodies for signs of serious physical illness, other individuals engage in maladaptive avoidance behaviors, such as completely avoiding doctor's visits and medical procedures. Specifiers are used to indicate whether the individual frequently seeks out (i.e., care-seeking type) or avoids (i.e., care-avoidant type) medical care, including physician visits and medical tests. The one- to two-year prevalence of illness anxiety disorder in the general population is between 1.3% and 10%.

Although there are differences among specific disorders, anxiety disorders are more commonly diagnosed in females than males, with an average age of onset during childhood or adolescence. Without treatment (psychological or medication), anxiety disorders tend to have a chronic course and can cause significant functional impairment in a person's life.

The most extensively studied treatments for anxiety disorders include psychological approaches (especially cognitive and behavioral strategies) and medication. Cognitive strategies focus on identifying, evaluating, and changing anxiety-provoking thoughts and predictions. Behavioral strategies include engaging in therapeutic exposures (i.e., repeatedly facing anxiety-provoking situations), using progressive muscle relaxation to reduce generalized anxiety, skills training (e.g., improving communication skills in social anxiety), and mindfulness-based approaches, to name a few.

Matilda E. Nowakowski and Martin M. Antony

See also: Agoraphobia; Classification; DSM-5; Obsessive-Compulsive Disorder; Panic Disorder; Phobia, Specific; Posttraumatic Stress Disorder; Social Anxiety Disorder (Social Phobia)

Further Reading

American Psychiatric Association (2013). *Diagnostic and statistical manual of mental disorders, fifth edition (DSM-5).* Arlington, VA: American Psychiatric Publishing.

Antony, Martin M., & Stein, Murray B. (Eds.) (2009). *Oxford handbook of anxiety and related disorders.* New York, NY: Oxford University Press.

Anxiety and Related Disorders Interview Schedule

The Anxiety and Related Disorders Interview Schedule (ADIS-5; Brown & Barlow, 2014) is a semistructured clinical interview assessing a range of anxiety and related disorders, including specific phobias, based on criteria set forth in the *Diagnostic and Statistical Manual of Mental Disorders*, fifth edition (American Psychiatric Association [APA], 2013). The interview allows researchers and clinicians to determine not only if diagnostic criteria for a given disorder are met but also the severity of the symptoms. The ADIS-5 also includes modules to assess a number of disorders which have symptoms that overlap with anxiety and which frequently co-occur with anxiety disorders, such as depression and substance use disorders. Two adult versions of the ADIS-5 are available, one assessing current symptoms and a lifetime version that assesses both current and past symptoms. A version, based upon DSM-IV criteria (APA, 1994), assessing anxiety symptoms in children using interviews of both the child and the child's parents is also available (Silverman, Saavedra, & Pina, 2001).

Andrea R. Ashbaugh

See also: Barlow, David H. (1942–); Differential Diagnosis; DSM-5; Phobias, Assessment of; Structured Clinical Interview for DSM Disorders

Further Reading

American Psychiatric Association. (2013). *Diagnostic and statistical manual of mental disorders* (5th ed.). Arlington, VA: American Psychiatric Publishing.

American Psychiatric Association (1994). *Diagnostic and statistical manual of mental disorders* (4th ed.). Washington, DC: Author.

Brown, Timothy A., & Barlow, David H. (2014). *Anxiety and related disorders interview schedule for DSM-5 adult and lifetime version: Clinician manual.* New York, NY: Oxford University Press.

Silverman, Wendy K., Saavedra, Lissette M., & Pina, Armando A. (2001). Test–retest reliability of anxiety symptoms and diagnoses using the Anxiety Disorders Interview Schedule for DSM-IV: Child and parent versions (ADIS for DSM IV: C/P). *Journal of the American Academy of Child & Adolescent Psychiatry, 40,* 937–944.

Anxiety Sensitivity

Anxiety sensitivity (AS) is the fear of arousal-related bodily sensations, such as a racing heart, dizziness, rapid breathing, and sweating. This "fear of fear" is caused by the belief that the sensations signal impending physical, psychological, or social harm. AS consists of three components (physical, cognitive, and social concerns), each reflecting a different feared harmful consequence of arousal-related sensations. A person with high physical concerns fears that arousal sensations signal future physical harm or illness (e.g., fearing that racing heartbeat signals a heart attack). A person with high cognitive concerns fears that arousal signals impending cognitive dyscontrol (e.g., fearing that dizziness and racing thoughts mean one is "going crazy"). Finally, social concerns reflect the fear that other people will notice one's anxious arousal (e.g., sweating and trembling) and that this will lead to embarrassment or rejection. A person with low AS perceives the same sensations as unpleasant but nonthreatening.

According to Reiss's (1991) expectancy theory, there are three "fundamental fears" that underlie and can explain many other, more specific fears. AS is one of the three, along with fear of illness or injury, and fear of social evaluation. Many other, more specific fears can be explained by the underlying fundamental fear. For example, a person might be afraid of flying or giving a presentation, because he or she has an underlying fear of becoming anxious in flight or becoming anxious on stage. In both cases, the person is afraid of the experience of anxiety. Specifically, the individual is afraid of experiencing anxiety because of a belief that anxiety signals impending harm. This individual is high in AS.

Fear of arousal sensations once was believed to be a conditioned fear, learned from previous panic experiences. Subsequent research, however, has demonstrated that AS tends to precede and predict the onset of panic and many other anxiety disorders. In the 1980s, "fear of fear" was identified as a dispositional (trait-like) factor caused by cognitive beliefs (i.e., anxiety is harmful), rather than by associative learning. Whereas most people find anxiety aversive, we differ in our beliefs about how much we need to fear and avoid experiencing it.

AS has a strong heritable component; research suggests that genetic factors explain nearly half of the individual variability in AS levels. Other studies indicate that childhood learning experiences and interpersonal factors are also heavily implicated in the development of AS. Children being rewarded by parents for displaying sick role behavior in response to anxiety symptoms, parents modeling fear reactions to anxiety symptoms or expressing their beliefs about the harmfulness of such symptoms, and attachment styles have all been linked to the development of elevated AS.

When we are anxious or afraid, the sympathetic nervous system's natural, adaptive, and automatic response prepares the body to deal with threat by freezing, fighting, or fleeing. Physiological changes include increased heart rate, blood pressure, and breathing rate; sweating; blushing; inhibited digestion and bladder relaxation; increased muscle tension; shaking; and tunnel vision. People high in AS tend to look for and notice these physical changes and associated sensations, and tend to misinterpret them as harmful. This serves to intensify the physiological fear response and the experience of anxiety-related physical sensations. AS is like an amplifier of anxiety; people high in AS experience anxiety more often and more intensely, and therefore may develop maladaptive behavioral strategies to avoid unpleasant, feared arousal sensations.

AS predicts the development and maintenance of a variety of psychological problems (reviewed in Olatunji & Wolitzky-Taylor, 2009). These include panic attacks and panic disorder; agoraphobia; posttraumatic stress disorder and symptom severity; social anxiety disorder (social phobia); depression; health anxiety and hypochondriasis (intense fear of having a serious disease); alcohol abuse, notably the use of alcohol to relieve stress and social anxiety; smoking; and decreased general function and heightened pain-related distress in chronic pain sufferers. Many individuals high in AS avoid activities that arouse similar bodily sensations, such as aerobic exercise and sex. Exercise avoidance and high AS are particularly common in individuals with a high body mass index, suggesting that AS may have a role in the development and maintenance of obesity. Research has found that each of the three dimensions of AS is uniquely associated with different anxiety-related disorders: physical concerns with panic; cognitive concerns with depressive symptoms; and social concerns with social anxiety (Olthuis, Stewart, & Watt, 2013).

Because AS predicts and helps to maintain a wide variety of psychological disorders and other health concerns, it is an excellent target for preventive and therapeutic interventions. Brief cognitive behavioral therapy (Watt & Stewart, 2008) is the intervention of choice and includes psychoeducation, cognitive restructuring, and interoceptive exposure. Psychoeducation involves learning about the body's natural, adaptive arousal response, and about AS and its links to psychopathology. Cognitive restructuring entails identifying, examining, and modifying the maladaptive thoughts and beliefs involved in misinterpreting arousal sensations as harmful. Interoceptive exposure includes safe, controlled exposure to feared arousal sensations, so that the individual learns that arousal sensations do not lead to harm. For example, breathing through a straw simulates feeling short of breath, running simulates elevated heart rate and sweating, and spinning in a chair can simulate dizziness and feeling nauseated.

Christianne Macaulay and Margo C. Watt

See also: Cognitive Behavioral Therapy; Exposure, Interoceptive; Fear, Physiology of; Hypochondriasis; Panic Attacks; Panic Disorder; Posttraumatic Stress Disorder; Social Anxiety Disorder (Social Phobia)

Further Reading

Olatunji, Bunmi O., & Wolitzky-Taylor, Kate B. (2009). Anxiety sensitivity and anxiety disorders: A meta-analytic review and synthesis. *Psychological Bulletin, 135*, 974–999.

Olthuis, Janine V., Watt, Margo C., & Stewart, Sherry H. (2014). Anxiety Sensitivity Index (ASI-3) subscales predict unique variance in anxiety and depressive symptoms. *Journal of Anxiety Disorders, 28*, 115–124.

Reiss, Steven. (1991). Expectancy theory of fear, anxiety, and panic. *Clinical Psychology Review, 11*, 141–153.

Watt, Margo C., & Stewart, Sherry. (2008). *Overcoming your fear of fear: How to reduce your anxiety sensitivity*. Oakland, CA: New Harbinger Publications, Inc.

Apiphobia (Fear of Bees)

Derived from the Latin *apis* (bee) and Greek *phobos* (fear), apiphobia (also called apiophobia or melissophobia) is an excessive or unrealistic fear of bees. Individuals with this phobia are also commonly fearful of wasps and hornets. Apiphobia is closely related to entomophobia (fear of insects) and is classified as a specific phobia, animal type, in the *Diagnostic and Statistical Manual of Mental Disorders*, fifth edition.

As an animal type phobia, apiphobia belongs to the most common category of specific phobias and is typically acquired in childhood. Some individuals develop the phobia after being stung by a bee and experiencing a painful reaction, whereas others might develop it by observing someone close to them responding fearfully to bees or by hearing about the dangers of bee stings or bees' volatile temperament. Considerable misinformation about bees among the general public might play a role in the development or maintenance of apiphobia. Indeed, research shows that knowledge about bees is inversely related to perceptions of danger, anxiety, and disgust (Münstedt & Mühlhans, 2013). Many people who are fearful of bees falsely believe that bees have a tendency to attack when around humans and that humans are therefore highly vulnerable to being stung when they encounter a bee. However,

Bumblebees are drawn to the nectar of the *Echium candicans* flower. Although bumblebees are not known to be aggressive toward humans, individuals with apiphobia nevertheless avoid them for fear of being stung. (Courtesy of Irena Milosevic)

this is generally the case only when bees are defending their hive or when they are stepped on or otherwise squashed. An exception to this is the markedly more aggressive Africanized honey bee (also known as the "killer bee"). The threat of this particular type of bee, which in reality is relatively minimal, has been sensationalized in popular culture, thus reinforcing the unrealistic beliefs held by individuals with apiphobia. Further confusion regarding bees relates to the perceived dangerousness of their sting, which can be painful but is not dangerous unless a person happens to be allergic to them. Importantly, individuals who avoid bees because they have this allergy are not considered to be phobic; a phobia is diagnosed only if a person's fear is *disproportionate* to the danger associated with the feared object.

Individuals with apiphobia typically avoid places (e.g., gardens, parks) and activities (e.g., eating on a patio, being outdoors during the day) that might involve the presence of bees. They might also be highly vigilant to bees in their environment, frequently scanning for them and possibly mistaking other insects for bees. When they encounter a bee, they become highly distraught and might experience a panic attack. Rapid escape from the situation is a common response, although this is not always possible (e.g., while driving). Some individuals might attempt to kill a bee to reduce the risk of being stung, which paradoxically increases this risk.

Exposure treatment is the first-line treatment for specific phobias, including apiphobia. This time-limited and highly effective intervention involves graduated exposure to bee-related stimuli and situations (Antony & McCabe, 2005).

Irena Milosevic

See also: DSM-5; Entomophobia (Fear of Insects); Exposure Treatment; Phobia, Animal Type; Phobia, Specific

Further Reading

Antony, Martin M., & McCabe, Randi E. (2005). *Overcoming animal and insect phobias*. Oakland, CA: New Harbinger Publications.

Münstedt, K., & Mühlhans, A. K. (2013). Fears, phobias and disgust related to bees and other arthropods. *Advanced Studies in Medical Sciences, 1*, 125–142.

Applied Relaxation

Relaxation is a physiological state that includes a decrease in one's heart rate, respiration rate, blood pressure, muscle tension, metabolic rate, oxygen consumption, and analytical thinking. *Applied relaxation* refers to the practice of relaxation techniques rather than activities like simply unwinding in front of the TV. Relaxation training alone is typically not sufficient for the treatment of phobias and other anxiety disorders, and it is not a standard treatment approach for these problems. However, it may be used as an adjunct in cases where individuals have heightened distress and difficulty engaging in cognitive behavioral therapy intervention.

The ability to bring on a state of relaxation is a skill that can be developed with training. Daily relaxation practice of 20–30 minutes can improve symptoms of anxiety (Smith, Hancock, Blake-Mortimer, & Eckart, 2007) and can generalize to feeling more relaxed in one's daily life (Bourne, 2010). There are several forms of applied relaxation techniques, which can be used in the treatment of phobias, including abdominal breathing, guided visualization, progressive muscle relaxation, and passive muscle relaxation.

Abdominal breathing is a relaxation technique that can be helpful for people who have phobias. People with phobias usually have one of two problems with their breathing: (1) shallow breathing or (2) hyperventilation, where they breathe out too much carbon dioxide relative to the amount of oxygen in their blood stream. When people are tense, their breathing typically becomes quick and shallow and occurs high in the chest, whereas when they are relaxed they breathe more fully and deeply from the abdomen (this occurs by contracting the diaphragm, a large horizontal muscle located between the chest and stomach cavities). It is difficult to remain tense and to breathe from the abdomen at the same time. Therefore, using abdominal breathing when anxious can help a person to turn off the physiological stress response and become more relaxed. Abdominal breathing involves first noticing how one is breathing, placing a hand on the abdomen, inhaling slowly through the nose and feeling the abdomen rise, pausing for a moment, then exhaling slowly through the mouth or nose and feeling the abdomen fall.

Guided visualization is a relaxation technique that can help clear the mind from anxious thoughts. This relaxation technique involves the use of an audio recording or live voice that guides the person through creating a peaceful scene in his or her mind. This form of relaxation requires minimal training as all that is necessary is for the person to lie down, close his or her eyes, and listen to the instructions. Examples of peaceful scenes that people often visualize include a quiet beach, a stream, a calm lake, their bedroom, and a cozy fireside, although whatever peaceful scene the individual can imagine will suffice. The scene should be visualized in enough detail in order to grab and sustain the person's full attention. It is recommended that all five senses be engaged in the visualization, such that the person imagines what he or she sees, hears, smells, tastes, and touches when immersed in the peaceful scene.

Progressive muscle relaxation (PMR) is a relaxation technique that involves purposely tensing and releasing muscles throughout the body. PMR is especially helpful for people who experience muscle tension as a result of their phobia, as it helps individuals recognize when their muscles are tight, and purposely release this tension. To practice PMR, the person should tense each muscle group for 10 seconds and then release for 15–20 seconds, with the aim of observing how the muscles feel when relaxed compared to when they are tense. Although instructions regarding how to tense the muscles and the number of muscle groups included can vary, generally most of the major groups (e.g., biceps, triceps, shoulders, chest, back, abdomen, buttocks, thighs, calves) are tensed and released in turn. Once all of the muscle groups have been tightened and released, the person should scan his or her body to see if there is any remaining tension and reapply this technique to target the tense muscle group. Throughout the relaxation, the person should keep attention focused on the muscles and bring his or her attention back to the muscles if it wanders.

Passive muscle relaxation is a relaxation technique similar to PMR, except that the person simply focuses on a particular muscle group and then relaxes this area rather than actively tensing each muscle group. If tensing muscles results in pain or discomfort, passive muscle relaxation can be practiced in the place of PMR.

Another variant of PMR, called applied tension, is commonly used in the treatment of individuals with blood-injection-injury (BII) phobias (Hood & Antony, 2012). As many individuals with BII phobias faint when exposed to a feared situation (e.g., blood test), applied tension can be used to prevent the fainting response. Fainting results from a sudden drop in blood pressure, which can lead to decreased blood flow to the brain. Muscle contractions (which are intentionally induced during PMR and applied tension) can be used to elevate blood pressure to counteract the fainting response. Once the person has practiced applied tension, he or she can be exposed to feared situations without fainting.

Although applied relaxation techniques vary widely, there are common recommendations for how to get the most benefits from relaxation practice. It is recommended that applied relaxation be practiced in a quiet location, at regular times, in a comfortable position, and with a detached attitude (trying too hard to relax can result in increased tension). Starting with brief periods of relaxation practice and working up to longer practices can help to ease any frustration. It is also important to recognize that relaxation is a skill that needs repeated practice before it can be used successfully in anxiety-provoking situations. The more that the applied relaxation is practiced the more it will become a habit or come naturally.

Brenda L. Key and Caitlin Davey

See also: Applied Tension; Cognitive Behavioral Therapy; Fainting Response; Phobia, Blood-Injection-Injury Type

Further Reading

Antony, Martin M., Craske, Michelle G., Barlow, David H. (2006). *Mastering your fears and phobias*. New York, NY: Oxford University Press.

Bourne, Edmund J. (2010). *The anxiety & phobia workbook*. Oakland, CA: New Harbinger Publications, Inc.

Hood, Heather K., & Antony, Martin M. (2012). Evidence-based assessment and treatment of specific phobias in adults. In T. E. Davis III, T. H. Ollendick, & L.-G. Ost (Eds.), *Intensive one-session treatment of specific phobias* (pp. 19–42). New York, NY: Springer Science and Business Media. doi: 10.1007/978-1-4614-3253-1_2

Smith, Caroline, Hancock, Heather, Blake-Mortimer, Jane, & Eckart, Kerena. (2007). A randomized comparative trial of yoga and relaxation to reduce stress and anxiety. *Complementary Therapies in Medicine, 15*, 77–83.

Applied Tension

Applied tension is a behavioral intervention used primarily to treat blood-injection-injury (BII) phobia. Developed by Kozak and Montgomery (1981) and investigated extensively by Öst and colleagues (e.g., Öst, Fellenius, & Sterner, 1991), this approach targets the fainting response experienced by many individuals with BII phobia. Research has supported the effectiveness of applied tension in reducing physiological responding and fear in the presence of BII stimuli, making it the psychological treatment of choice for this phobia.

Compared to other phobias, BII phobia is linked to a unique physiological reaction that often results in fainting. That is, many individuals with this phobia experience a rapid initial increase in blood pressure followed by a sharp decrease when they are exposed to BII-related situations like seeing blood or receiving injections. A key element of effective treatment for BII phobia therefore involves helping individuals learn to circumvent this fainting response.

Applied tension is a time-limited and structured treatment, with a typical duration of five weekly one-hour sessions. The treatment consists of two key components. During the first component, the individual is taught to recognize early signs of a drop in blood pressure and then to apply a tension technique to reverse this drop. The tension technique involves briefly tensing one's arm, chest, and leg muscles and releasing the tension when one's face starts to become warm. This tension-release sequence is repeated several times, with brief pauses between each repetition. Individuals are instructed to practice applied tension on a daily basis between treatment sessions.

Once a person has achieved mastery of detecting a blood pressure drop and applying tension to counteract it, the second component of applied tension is implemented. This involves *in vivo* exposure to a broad range of BII-related stimuli or situations (e.g., blood tests, blood donations, photographs or videos of surgeries), which provides further opportunity to practice early detection of lowered blood pressure and subsequent application of tension.

Applied tension has been used extensively in various clinical settings, such as medical laboratories and blood donation clinics, to help individuals (both phobic and nonphobic) combat the fainting response during BII-related procedures. This method has been shown to be effective in treating BII phobia in several studies, with 60–100% of treatment recipients benefiting from significant improvements in symptoms such as the fainting response and self-reported fear (Ayala, Meuret, & Ritz, 2009). A five-session treatment protocol of applied tension is typical, but there is evidence to suggest that a one-session format is also effective when paired with an exposure-based maintenance program following treatment (Hellström, Fellenius, & Öst, 1996).

Although applied tension is aimed specifically at preventing fainting in BII phobia, it is notable that this method appears to be similarly effective in modifying physiological and subjective fear symptoms for individuals with or without a history of fainting. Therefore, applied tension is considered to be a broadly effective treatment for BII phobia, irrespective of an individual's propensity toward fainting.

There is currently no consensus among researchers regarding the relative effectiveness of the two components of applied tension, with earlier studies suggesting that tension is the critical ingredient of this intervention (Öst et al., 1991), whereas more recent studies have suggested that *in vivo* exposure may in fact be the most important component (Ayala et al., 2009). Further research is thus required to better understand the respective roles of tension and exposure techniques in BII phobia treatment.

Irena Milosevic

See also: Fainting Response; Exposure, *In Vivo*; Exposure Treatment; One-Session Treatment; Öst, Lars-Göran; Phobia, Blood-Injection-Injury Type

Further Reading

Ayala, Erica S., Meuret, Alicia E., & Ritz, Thomas. (2009). Treatments for blood-injection-injury phobia: A critical review of current evidence. *Journal of Psychiatric Research, 43,* 1235–1242.

Hellström, Kerstin, Fellenius, Jan, & Öst, Lars-Göran. (1996). One versus five sessions of applied tension in the treatment of blood phobia. *Behaviour Research and Therapy, 34,* 101–112.

Kozak, Michael J., & Montgomery, George K. (1981). Multimodal behavioral treatment of recurrent injury scene, elicited fainting (vasodepressor syncope). *Behavioural Psychotherapy, 9,* 316–321.

Öst, Lars-Göran, Fellenius, Jan, & Sterner, Ulf. (1991). Applied tension, exposure in vivo, and tension-only in the treatment of blood phobia. *Behaviour Research and Therapy, 29,* 561–574.

Aquaphobia (Fear of Water)

Aquaphobia (from the Latin, *aqua*, meaning water, and *phobos*, meaning fear) is an excessive and persistent fear of water. It is classified in the *Diagnostic and Statistical Manual of Mental Disorders*, fifth edition as a natural environment type of specific phobia. The prevalence rate of aquaphobia in the general population is 2.4% (Stinson et al., 2007), and it is more common among children than adults. Its onset is typically in childhood, and both non-associative (e.g., biological preparedness) and associative (e.g., learning experiences) factors have been proposed to play a role in its development (Poulton, Menzies, Craske, Langley, & Silva, 1999).

Generally, the core focus of aquaphobic fear is danger of harm, which commonly manifests as a fear of drowning, even among individuals who have adequate swimming skills. In cases in which the fear is circumscribed to deep water, some individuals report being fearful of what might be lurking in the depths below the surface. A broad range of situations might elicit aquaphobic fear, such as being in or near a body of water (e.g., ocean, creek, swimming pool), swimming in water that is dark or opaque so one cannot see what is in the water, submerging one's head below water, being near fountains, and traveling on a boat. In more rare cases, even bathing in a bathtub might provoke a fear response. Accordingly, aquaphobia can disrupt a number of activities and is associated with considerable distress or embarrassment. Individuals might avoid poolside gatherings, attractions with ponds or

A woman with aquaphobia learns aquatic skills in a SOAP and Water class. SOAP, which stands for Strategies for Overcoming Aquatic Phobias, is a program that facilitates cognitive awareness, emotional support, and aquatic skills building to individuals who are fearful of water. (AP Photo/Diane Bondareff)

fountains, cottage or beachside vacations, fishing, and boating trips. When near water, if playfully splashed or pushed by a companion, individuals with aquaphobia might respond with intense fear or even experience a panic attack. Some individuals never learn to swim due to their complete avoidance of water, whereas others might have difficulty learning when they try because they cannot sufficiently relax their body to facilitate floating or swimming.

Aquaphobia can be treated effectively with exposure treatment, whereby individuals gradually and repeatedly face feared situations. Treatment begins with exposure to less fear-provoking situations, such as walking close to shore or dipping one's feet in water, and progresses to confrontation of situations that elicit greater fear, such as row boating across a lake or jumping into the deep end of a pool.

Irena Milosevic

See also: DSM-5; Exposure Treatment; Learning Theory; Non-Associative Model; Phobia, Natural Environment Type; Phobia, Specific; Preparedness Theory

Further Reading

Poulton, Richie, Menzies, Ross G., Craske, Michelle G., Langley, John D., & Silva, Phil A. (1999). Water trauma and swimming experiences up to age 9 and fear of water at age 18: A longitudinal study. *Behaviour Research and Therapy, 37,* 39–48.

Stinson, Frederick S., Dawson, Deborah A., Chou, S. Patricia, Smith, Sharon, Goldstein, Rise B., Ruan, W. June, & Grant, Bridget F. (2007). The epidemiology of DSM-IV specific phobia in the USA: Result from the National Epidemiologic Survey on Alcohol and Related Conditions. *Psychological Medicine, 37*, 1047–1059.

Arachnophobia (Fear of Spiders)

Arachnophobia (from the Greek words *arachne*, meaning spider, and *phobos*, meaning phobia) is a specific phobia characterized by an excessive and persistent fear of spiders or other arachnids (e.g., tics, mites, scorpions) that results in marked distress and impairment in functioning. This fear is often excessive and may be evident not only in the presence of a spider but also in anticipation of seeing, or even imagining, a spider. It is not unusual for people with spider phobia to refuse to go to parks or camping and to avoid many places where they fear a spider may live. Some individuals with arachnophobia may even experience a panic attack when faced with a spider or spider-related stimuli.

Spider phobia is one of the more common phobias, with approximately 3.5% of the population meeting diagnostic criteria at any given time (Fredrikson, Annas, Fischer, & Wik, 1996) and with many more individuals reporting extreme fear that does not meet diagnostic criteria. Cultural factors and related exposure to spiders

A woman responds with fear upon seeing a tarantula in its terrarium in a laboratory. Tarantulas are a commonly used fear stimulus in studies of arachnophobia and other fear-related phenomena. (Courtesy of Irena Milosevic)

may influence the prevalence of spider phobia. For instance, some cultures are geographically bound to areas where spiders are more common, thus reducing fear due to regular exposure. This is likely the reason that spider phobia is more common in the United States than in warmer climates, such as South America or Asia, where large spiders are more frequently seen.

Spider phobia most commonly develops during early to middle childhood and is more common in women than men. There are multiple pathways that may lead to the development of the phobia, including a biological propensity toward anxiety, direct or indirect learning (e.g., seeing someone get bitten by a spider or personally experiencing a spider bite), and/or behavior modeling (e.g., observing others' fear of spiders). Further, the preparedness hypothesis suggests that humans have evolved to have a fear of spiders (Merckelbach, de Jong, Muris, & van den Hout, 1996). While mostly maladaptive now, during prehistoric periods, a fear of spiders may have been adaptive in protecting humans against infection and disease caused by arachnid bites. In addition to fear, disgust is commonly associated with spider phobia, with many people avoiding spiders because they find them "gross" (Connolly, Olatunji, & Lohr, 2008).

Exposure therapy is the first-line treatment for spider phobia and usually involves graded exposure to spiders. Although this treatment commonly incorporates live spiders, it may also be conducted with the aid of virtual reality. There is evidence that spider phobia can be eliminated in as little as one extended exposure therapy session.

· *Jessica R. Beadel and Bethany A. Teachman*

See also: Disgust Sensitivity; Exposure Treatment; One-Session Treatment; Phobia, Specific; Preparedness Theory; Virtual Reality Treatment

Further Reading

Connolly, Kevin M., Olatunji, Bunmi O., & Lohr, Jeffrey M. (2008). Evidence for disgust sensitivity mediating the sex differences found in blood-injection-injury phobia and spider phobia. *Personality and Individual Differences, 44*, 898–908.

Fredrikson, Mats, Annas, Peter, Fischer, Hakan, & Wik, Gustav. (1996). Gender and age differences in the prevalence of specific fears and phobias. *Behaviour Research and Therapy, 34*, 33–39.

Merckelbach, Herald, de Jong, Peter J., Muris, Peter, & van den Hout, Marcel A. (1996). The etiology of specific phobias: A review. *Clinical Psychology Review, 16*, 337–361.

Association for Behavioral and Cognitive Therapies

The Association for Behavioral and Cognitive Therapies (ABCT) is an organization for researchers and practitioners specializing in cognitive behaviorally based research and therapy. The organization was founded in 1966 by 10 behaviorists with the goal of promoting the "advancement of scientific approaches to the understanding and improvement of human functioning through the investigation and application of behavioral, cognitive, and other evidence-based principles" (abct.org).

ABCT was originally known as the Association for the Advancement of Behavioral Therapies. The name was first changed to the Association for the Advancement of Behavior Therapy following the publication of an article in *Behavior Therapy*, an academic journal published by ABCT, suggesting that all behavioral therapies are based on the same learning theory. The name was revised again in 2005 to the Association for Behavioral and Cognitive Therapies to reflect current evidence-based treatments.

ABCT holds an annual conference for cognitive behavioral researchers and practitioners. It also publishes two academic journals that focus on cognitive behavioral research and therapy, *Behavior Therapy* and *Cognitive Behavioral Practice*, as well as the newsletter, *Behavior Therapist*. ABCT additionally has a number of resources available to educate the public on psychological problems and cognitive behavioral treatments, including factsheets that describe various psychological disorders and the scientific research on their causes and treatment. ABCT further offers an international "Find-a-Therapist" directory of cognitive behavioral practitioners that is accessible to the public. The resources that are available for both members of the association and the general public include, among many others, topics relating to the development, maintenance, and treatment of phobias.

Andrea R. Ashbaugh

See also: Cognitive Behavioral Therapy; Treatment, Evidence-Based

Website

www.abct.org

Astraphobia (Fear of Thunder and Lightning)

The term *astraphobia* is derived from the Greek *astrape*, meaning lightning, and *phobos*, meaning fear. More specifically, astraphobia is an excessive and irrational fear of thunder and lightning, or of thunderstorms. Astraphobia falls within the category of natural environment phobias (i.e., phobias related to heights, water, and thunderstorms), one of five specific phobia types in the *Diagnostic and Statistical Manual of Mental Disorders*, fifth edition. Natural environment phobias are second only to the animal phobias as they are most frequently reported in adult clinical samples, although they are the least commonly reported in community samples. Most individuals with natural environment phobias are female (55–90%). Ollendick, Raishevich, Davis III, Sirbu, and Öst (2010) found that youth with natural environment phobias reported significantly more physical symptoms of anxiety and depression, as well as more comorbid anxiety diagnoses (e.g., panic disorder) and less satisfaction with their quality of life, than youth with other phobias (e.g., animal). Among youth with natural environment phobias, the most commonly reported fear is thunderstorms.

In 1996, psychologist John Westefeld coined the term *severe weather phobia* to describe individuals who reported an intense, debilitating, and unreasonable fear of severe weather, particularly of severe thunderstorms or tornadoes. Individuals with this phobia report symptoms characteristic of anxiety (e.g., increased respiration and perspiration, trembling and dizziness) plus a need for reassurance. They also engage in behaviors specific to the phobia, such as unusual anticipation of weather events and constant monitoring of weather via television weather networks, radio, and other media, as well as seeking refuge from storms in ways that go beyond normal precautionary measures (e.g., hiding under beds or in closets).

The main risk factors for astraphobia include temperament (e.g., high anxiety sensitivity) and environmental influences (e.g., parental overprotectiveness, parental loss and separation, physical and sexual abuse). A negative or traumatic experience with thunder and lightning may precede the phobia. Westefeld (1996) found that most (65–80%) of the participants in his studies had direct experience with a severe storm. Other conditioning experiences can include observational learning (e.g., parental modeling of fears, watching television coverage of storms like Hurricane Katrina in 2005) and vicarious transmission (e.g., parents warning about the potential harmful consequences of storms; Watt & DiFrancescantonio, 2012).

In the short term, distraction techniques (e.g., playing a video game during a storm) could reduce one's astraphobic fears. In the long term, cognitive behavioral therapy is advised, whereby individuals are taught strategies for self-soothing during storms, challenging cognitive distortions (e.g., overestimating the probability of being struck by lightning), and exposing oneself to the feared stimuli (via reading or watching documentaries about thunder and lightning) to desensitize to the sights and sounds. One study successfully used a virtual reality system to simulate thunder and lightning and reduce storm phobia in a 70-year-old woman.

Margo C. Watt

See also: Anxiety Sensitivity; Exposure Treatment; Panic Disorder; Phobia, Natural Environment Type

Further Reading

Ollendick, Thomas, Raishevich, Natoshia, Davis III, Thompson, Sirbu, Cristian, & Öst, Lars-Göran. (2010). Specific phobia in youth: Phenomenology and psychological characteristics. *Behaviour Therapy, 41*, 133–141.

Watt, Margo C., & DiFrancescantonio, Samantha L. (2012). Who's afraid of the big bad wind? Origins of severe weather phobia. *Journal of Psychopathology and Behavioral Assessment, 34*, 440–450.

Westefeld, John. (1996). Severe weather phobia: An exploratory study. *Journal of Clinical Psychology, 52*, 509–515.

Attention

Attention is a broadly defined term referring to the cognitive processes involved in selectively attending to environmental stimuli by filtering out irrelevant information. There are different types of attention depending on the task or situation, such as sustained attention (focusing on a stimulus over a period of time) and divided attention (engaging in multiple activities simultaneously). Every second of the day we are bombarded with an overload of information from the environment, yet our capacity for processing this information is limited; therefore, we have to make choices to attend to what we perceive as most important. It is thought that biases in attention and information processing may play a role in the development and maintenance of anxiety disorders, including phobias.

Although there are many factors that influence attention, such as characteristics of stimuli (e.g., size, motion, novelty), perception of danger, and personal factors (e.g., interests, goals), the process can be controlled. Shifting attention from one stimulus to another, or directing our attention toward something in the environment, allows us to exert some control over the information in our awareness. Try shifting your attention to your breathing for a few seconds. Although we are always breathing, we are not aware of this process unless it is a target of attention.

Perception of feared stimuli is related to the information attended to while processing an event. From an evolutionary perspective, humans are primed to attend to threats in their environment. Noticing and attending to a dangerous animal, for example, is beneficial for our survival. However, in clinical phobias focusing on the *perceived* threat of a stimulus, and the strong irrational response to this threat, is related to subsequent anxiety. Cognitive theories have suggested that attentional biases related to threatening stimuli are important in anxiety disorders (Beck & Clark, 1997). For example, individuals who are afraid of spiders may constantly scan their environment for spiders, focusing on the perceived threat. Individuals with phobias also tend to ignore information that disproves their beliefs, or they avoid anxiety-provoking stimuli, which limits access to information to disprove beliefs. This bias to attend to information that is consistent with anxious beliefs, while *not attending* to information inconsistent with beliefs, results in the maintenance of fear and phobias.

Clark and Wells's (1995) model suggests that biases in attention and information processing in individuals with social anxiety disorder (social phobia) result in a negative perception of themselves and social situations. A bias in favor of the detection of threatening social cues, such as critical facial expressions, may lead individuals with social anxiety disorder to focus on these negative cues or to interpret neutral interactions negatively. Self-focused attention has also been demonstrated in social anxiety disorder, whereby socially anxious individuals attend more to internal information in social situations than nonsocially anxious individuals. Focusing on internal cues (e.g., sweating, shaking, or thoughts such as "I will look stupid") can lead to the assumption that others also perceive them as anxious or incompetent, and it shifts focus away from external cues (e.g., others smiling or nodding in interest). Humans are only capable of attending to limited information at one time; therefore, self-focused attention competes with the resources available to attend to external information. Focusing on symptoms of anxiety, or planning and rehearsing what to say next, can inadvertently lead to *not attending* to the information being presented in a conversation. These behaviors can also mistakenly give the impression that the socially anxious person is uninterested in the conversation. After the social situation, individuals with social anxiety disorder may also selectively focus on the negative aspects of the interaction, rather than the experience as a whole. These maladaptive attentional processes result in negative evaluations of social performance and maladaptive predictions of future interactions.

Cognitive therapy for phobias and other anxiety disorders involves recognizing biases in thought patterns by teaching individuals to examine the evidence for their threat-focused beliefs, and to consider alternative beliefs. Treatment attempts to remove the biased attentional filter, allowing for greater cognitive flexibility. Exposure treatment is another effective intervention for phobias, and it typically involves attending to fear-provoking stimuli. Some studies have compared the effects of exposure treatment when individuals either focused on feared stimuli or engaged in distraction techniques during an exposure. Results appear to be mixed on whether or not attending to stimuli is necessary for exposure treatment to be effective. A more novel paradigm, attention training, is aimed at reducing attentional biases toward perception of threat, and is currently being studied as a possible treatment method for phobias and other anxiety disorders. Preliminary evidence suggests small therapeutic effects, and further research is needed to establish whether attention training is an effective intervention. Nevertheless, current theory and research support the importance of understanding attentional processes in the development and treatment of phobias.

Jeanine E. M. Lane

See also: Cognitive Bias Modification; Cognitive Therapy; Distraction; Exposure Treatment; Information Processing Biases

Further Reading

Beck, Aaron T., & Clark, David A.(1997). An information processing model of anxiety: Automatic and strategies processes. *Behaviour Research and Therapy, 35*, 49–58.

Clark, David M., & Wells, Adrian. (1995). A cognitive model of social phobia. In Richard G. Heimberg, Michael R. Liebowitz, Debra A. Hope, & Franklin R. Schneier (Eds.), *Social Phobia: Diagnosis, Assessment and Treatment* (pp. 69–93). New York, NY: Guilford Press.

Atychiphobia (Fear of Failure)

Atychiphobia (from the Greek *atyches* meaning unfortunate, and *phobos* meaning fear) is an irrational and persistent fear of failing at something. This fear may paralyze individuals; they may stop trying things for fear that they will fail at them, leading to significant problems in their daily lives and numerous missed opportunities.

The fear of failing at something exists on a continuum of severity. Most people have experienced at least mild fears at some point in their lives that they will not be able to succeed at something that is new or challenging. When this fear is mild, people can often persevere and continue to work toward their goals. However, for some people this fear becomes so severe that they will not even try something. At a severe level, this fear can be out of proportion to reality. For example, some individuals may be afraid of doing poorly on an exam, even though they have studied for the exam and have passed similar exams previously. In some cases, a fear of failure can even cause a person to sabotage his or her efforts; this phenomenon has been called *self-handicapping*. Many people engage in self-handicapping in an attempt to preserve their self-esteem—it's easier on one's self-esteem to fail because of not trying versus failing after putting in strong effort. The fear of failing an exam that one has studied for may cause the individual to not even take the exam, thus ensuring the very outcome the person was dreading! This outcome only strengthens the original fear, setting up a vicious cycle that is difficult to break.

Fear of failure is not classified as a phobia itself but can instead be seen across many different mental disorders, such as anxiety disorders, mood disorders, and eating disorders. Fear of failure can exist even when someone does not have a diagnosis of a mental disorder. It is likely closely linked to perfectionism, which is common across the aforementioned disorders.

Karen Rowa

See also: Phobias, Impairment Related to; Safety Behavior; Test Anxiety

Aversions

Aversion is a repugnance or dislike toward something that leads one to want to avoid it. For example, some people have an aversion to seafood that leads them to avoid eating it because they do not like the texture. Alternatively, some people may have an aversion to wool and avoid wearing sweaters containing wool because they find it extremely uncomfortable. Although from the outside it may look like an aversion is a form of phobia because they both involve avoidance of a specific stimulus, they are in fact two separate phenomena that can be differentiated by examining the motive for avoidance. In phobia, the avoidance is fear-based whereas, in aversion, the avoidance is preference-based. There are other differences as well. Aversions are typically accommodated by people by the choices they make (e.g., avoiding ordering seafood or buying wool sweaters), whereas phobias are associated with significant distress and avoidance in functioning.

In addition to being a preference, aversions can be learned, through a process of classical conditioning, when something is paired with a noxious stimulus such as nausea or vomiting. For example, if a person ate butternut squash soup (unconditioned stimulus) and then a short time later vomited (unconditioned response), there would be a high likelihood that he or she would not want to eat butternut squash soup (conditioned stimulus) anytime in the future so as to avoid any chance of a recurrence of nausea (conditioned response). Even the smell or thought of butternut squash soup might trigger a nauseous reaction given the negative experience with it. This type of aversion is termed a *conditioned taste aversion* and is not limited to humans.

A lot of the research conducted to facilitate our understanding of the biological and behavioral mechanisms underlying conditioned taste aversion has been done using mice and rats. The brain region that has been identified to play a key role in the formation of memories for conditioned taste aversion is the amygdala. Avoidance resulting from conditioned taste aversion is considered to be adaptive since learning to avoid a substance if its taste is followed by temporary illness helps organisms to learn which foods are potentially unsafe to eat, thereby improving their chance of survival. This is considered to be an example of the evolution of biological preparedness. Conditioned taste aversions can be short term or long lasting.

Another type of aversion, which has been a focus of research integrating psychology and economics, is risk aversion in decision making. Risk averse individuals tend to choose certain gains over uncertain gains. Risk aversion is affected by many different factors such as age, gender, and the cost or stakes associated with a decision outcome. A recent study comparing risk aversion in children, adolescents, and young adults found that risk aversion increases with age, paralleling maturation of decision-making brain regions including the insula, hippocampus, amygdala, and prefrontal cortex (Paulsen, Carter, Platt, Huettel, & Brannon, 2012).

Randi E. McCabe

See also: Amygdala; Classical Conditioning; Phobia, Specific; Preparedness Theory

Further Reading

Paulsen, David J., Carter, R. McKell, Platt, Michael L., Huettel, Scott A., & Brannon, Elizabeth M. (2012). Neurocognitive development of risk aversion from early childhood to adulthood. *Frontiers in Human Neuroscience, 178*, 1–17.

Reilly, Steve, & Schachtman, Todd R. (2008). *Conditioned taste aversion.* New York, NY: Oxford University Press.

Aviophobia (Fear of Flying)

Thought to originate from the Latin *avi* (bird) and the Greek *phobos* (fear), aviophobia (also known as aerophobia or aviatophobia) is the fear of flying on an airplane or other aircraft such as a helicopter. The focus of fear in aviophobia is rather heterogeneous and may include fear of crashing, being out of control, heights, or being trapped. Diagnostically, aviophobia is considered a situational type specific phobia when the fear is circumscribed to flying. If flying is just one feared situation among many, it may be conceptualized as claustrophobia, panic disorder, or agoraphobia depending on the focus of fear. The prevalence rate of fear of flying is estimated as high as 40% and ranges from moderate to severe levels.

In aviophobia, flying is associated with significant anxiety and distress that may escalate into a full-blown panic attack. The thought of going on a flight leads to substantial anticipatory anxiety. In response to their anxiety, individuals with aviophobia may use substances such as alcohol or motion sickness medication with sedating properties to help manage their anxiety symptoms. These types of coping strategies are not recommended as they may actually increase fear or have other unintended negative consequences. There is some research to suggest that individuals with aviophobia might have enhanced interoceptive sensitivity to respiratory sensations

A woman anxiously waits for her flight at an airport. Individuals with aviophobia experience a great deal of anticipatory anxiety prior to flying. For some, this anxious anticipation begins weeks or even months in advance of the flight. (tirc83/iStockphoto.com)

(a condition called hypoxia) triggered by pressure and temperature changes when flying at a high altitude (Vanden Bogaerde, Derom, & De Raedt, 2011). Thus individuals with aviophobia tend to experience more physical sensations such as feelings of breathlessness, palpitations, and dizziness, which in turn increase levels of fear and anxiety associated with flying.

Individuals with aviophobia typically accommodate their fear by arranging their lives so that they do not have to take an airplane. The associated avoidance can cause significant impairment as it limits travel for leisure or work purposes. For example, someone with aviophobia might turn down a promotion that would require travel, thus hindering his or her ability to reach work-related performance goals, as well as to obtain the financial benefits that come with promotion. Aviophobia can also significantly impact family relationships in a negative way when one family member wants to travel and the individual with aviophobia cannot. For example, consider the case where one spouse loves to travel the world and wants to share the adventure with her partner but due to the partner's fear has resigned herself to solo travel. When the partner tries to go along in an effort to overcome the fear, it ultimately results in a cancelled trip that puts great strain on the relationship due to the consequent stress and disappointment. Entertainers with aviophobia have been known to travel thousands of miles by train or bus to get to a performance, losing days of travel time in what could have taken mere hours.

The onset of aviophobia might occur following a harrowing experience in a plane (e.g., experiencing extreme turbulence, a dramatic storm, having a panic attack, or becoming ill) in what is a conditioned fear process. However, many people who have this fear report that they have never had a negative experience on a plane. Media reports of plane crashes and terrorism plots might also trigger aviophobia for some people.

Aviophobia is a highly treatable fear. The treatment of choice is cognitive behavioral therapy emphasizing exposure, including situational exposure, imaginal exposure, and virtual reality exposure. Given the cost of air travel, therapy often involves the application of imaginal exposure (having the individual vividly imagine that he or she is on a plane) and/or virtual reality exposure (simulation of being on a plane through virtual reality equipment), which are geared toward working up to situational exposure to the airport and airplane-related triggers, and then an actual flight. Cognitive therapy may be used in conjunction with exposure to challenge feared beliefs and expectations regarding flying. In addition, some airlines offer fear of flying programs that include an educational component delivered by a pilot or member of the flight crew in conjunction with a psychological component delivered by a psychologist or trained mental health clinician. These programs are typically four to six sessions and often wrap up with the option of taking an actual flight. In addition, there are online programs that offer treatment through videos or DVDs along with telephone counseling sessions. The SOAR Fear of Flying Program is one example of such a program.

Randi E. McCabe

See also: Agoraphobia; Claustrophobia (Fear of Enclosed Spaces); Cognitive Behavioral Therapy; Cognitive Therapy; Exposure Treatment; Panic Disorder; Phobia, Specific

Further Reading

Oakes, Margaret, & Bor, Robert. (2010a). The psychology of fear of flying (part I): A critical evaluation of current perspectives on the nature, prevalence and etiology of fear of flying. *Travel Medicine and Infectious Disease, 8*, 327–338.

Oakes, Margaret, & Bor, Robert. (2010b). The psychology of fear of flying (part II): A critical evaluation of current perspectives on approaches to treatment. *Travel Medicine and Infectious Disease, 8*, 339–363.

Vanden Bogaerde, Anouk, Derom, Eric, & De Raedt, Rudi. (2011). Increased interoceptive awareness in fear of flying: Sensitivity to suffocation signals. *Behaviour Research and Therapy, 49*, 427–432.

B

Bandura, Albert (1925–)

Albert Bandura (1925–) is a renowned Canadian-born psychologist and Stanford University professor. He is widely recognized as one of the most eminent psychologists of all time and as one of the greatest living psychologists. Bandura is credited with developing social learning theory, later expanded to social cognitive theory. He is also known for related work on human agency and self-efficacy. Bandura's work critically introduced observational learning to learning theory and provided a bridge between behaviorism and cognitive psychology. It has influenced models of psychopathology and psychotherapy, including phobias and their treatment.

The youngest of six children of Eastern European immigrants, Bandura was born on December 4, 1925, in Mundare, a small village in Alberta, Canada. Bandura's father laid tracks for the trans-Canada railroad and his mother worked in the town's general store. After saving enough money, they purchased wild land and began the arduous task of converting it to farmland. Although the family experienced struggles in this pioneering work, Bandura's parents had a celebratory attitude toward life and raised their children in a festive household where a strong work ethic and education were valued.

Bandura attended elementary and high school in Mundare's only school, where limited access to teachers and educational resources led him to conclude that "the students had to take charge of their own education" (Stokes, 1986, p. 2). Accordingly, Bandura learned to value self-directedness. In the summer of his senior year in high school, he took on a job in the northern tundra region of the Yukon to earn money for university tuition. As a member of a road crew making repairs to the Alaskan highway, Bandura experienced numerous adventures that left an impression on his understanding of the human condition.

Escaping the severe Alberta weather, Bandura enrolled in undergraduate studies at the University of British Columbia in Vancouver. He did not initially set out to study psychology but after registering for a psychology course to fill a time slot in his schedule, he became captivated by the topic and pursued it as a major. Bandura excelled in his studies and earned a bachelor's degree in 1949 as the top student in psychology.

Bandura subsequently enrolled in graduate studies in psychology at the University of Iowa, a hotbed of renowned psychology faculty. At Iowa, Bandura was exposed to social learning theory, which established the roots for his future work in this area. He earned a Master's degree in 1951 and a doctoral degree in clinical psychology in 1952. While in graduate school, Bandura met Virginia Varns, whom he married in 1952. The couple went on to have two daughters.

After Bandura's graduation from Iowa, Bandura and Varns moved to Wichita, Kansas, where Bandura completed a postdoctoral internship at the Wichita Guidance Center. In 1953, the couple moved to Stanford, California, where Bandura joined the Department of Psychology at Stanford University and where he remains on faculty to this day. In 1964, he was appointed full professor and in 1974, he became the David Starr Jordan Professor of Social Science in Psychology. He is currently appointed as the David Starr Jordan Professor Emeritus of Social Science in Psychology.

Over the years, Bandura pursued numerous lines of research, often concurrently. His interests have focused on adolescent aggression, children's self-regulation and self-reflection, social modeling, human agency, self-efficacy, and psychotherapy. Among Bandura's best-known work are his now classic *Bobo doll experiments*, conducted in the 1960s. In this series of experiments, children observed social models of violent or nonviolent behavior toward an inflatable Bobo doll, a popular children's toy. Bandura discovered that children who observed a model behaving aggressively toward the doll and then being rewarded or experiencing no consequence for this behavior were themselves likely to behave aggressively toward the doll. By contrast, children who observed aggressive behavior that was subsequently punished were reluctant to behave aggressively. Based on these findings, Bandura concluded that not all learning was shaped by reward and punishment, as claimed by behaviorists, but rather that learning can also occur through *observation* of others' behavior, as well as through observation of how others' behavior is reinforced, which Bandura called *vicarious reinforcement*.

The findings from the Bobo doll experiments paved the way for Bandura's social learning theory (Bandura, 1977), which holds that most human behavior is learned by observing others. Importantly, social learning theory identified cognitive processes as a key component of learning and behavior change, which was a departure from traditional behaviorist thinking. The theory significantly impacted the course of psychology in the 1980s, sparking wide-ranging interest in modeling and social learning.

In the 1980s, Bandura elaborated on social learning theory and renamed it the social cognitive theory, which stressed that human functioning is the result of reciprocal interactions between the environment, behavior, and a person's psychological processes (e.g., cognition, personality). In contrast to the behaviorist perspective, Bandura proposed that people are not merely shaped by their environment but that they instead have active agency over their lives and the capacity for self-directed change. A central component of the theory is the construct of self-efficacy, which Bandura defined as a person's belief that he or she has the ability to succeed in a given situation or to produce a desired outcome. Bandura proposed that self-efficacy is fundamental to human motivation, emotion, and behavior.

Bandura's work has significantly impacted many areas of psychology, and its applications range from psychological treatments to public health interventions (e.g., televised dramas based on the principles of social cognitive theory have been aired in developing countries to improve social problems). Specific to phobias, his contributions have impacted both theory and practice. In particular, social learning theory explains how individuals without prior negative experience with a phobic stimulus develop a phobia, with observational learning (i.e., seeing another person behaving fearfully around the stimulus) now understood as a pathway to fear acquisition. Further, one of Bandura's earlier books, *Principles of Behavior Modification* (1969), is widely considered to have laid the foundation for what is now known as cognitive behavioral therapy, the first-line treatment for phobias. Relatedly, Bandura also developed an early version of guided mastery therapy, called *participant modeling*, which combined graduated modeling (therapist interacting with the phobic stimulus) with guided participation (client replicating the therapist's actions).

Bandura is acknowledged as the fourth most cited psychologist of all time and the most cited living psychologist (Haggbloom et al., 2002). His contributions are also exemplified through his service on the editorial boards of more than 30 scientific journals in psychology. He has additionally held numerous offices in scientific societies, including president of the American Psychological Association (APA) in 1974—at age 49, he was one of the youngest presidents in the history of the association. Bandura's work has been acknowledged with more than 15 honorary degrees and numerous prestigious awards. He was elected fellow of the American Academy of Arts and Sciences (1980) and is the recipient of the APA awards for Distinguished Scientific Contributions (1980), Distinguished Contributions of Psychology to Education (1999), and Outstanding Lifetime Contribution to Psychology (2004), among many others. Further to his own contributions, Bandura has provided mentorship to numerous students who have themselves made a significant impact in psychology.

Irena Milosevic

See also: Cognitive Behavioral Therapy; Guided Mastery Therapy; Modeling; Self-Efficacy Theory; Social Learning Theory

Further Reading

Bandura, Albert. (1977). *Social learning theory*. Englewood Cliffs, NJ: Prentice Hall.

Bandura, Albert, Blanchard, Edward B., & Ritter, Brunhilde. (1969). Relative efficacy of desensitization and modeling approaches for inducing behavioral, affective, and attitudinal changes. *Journal of Personality and Social Psychology, 13*, 173–199.

Haggbloom, Steven J., Warnick, Renee, Warnick, Jason E., Jones, Vinessa K., Yarbrough, Gary L., Russell, Tenea M., . . . Monte, Emmanuelle. (2002). The 100 most eminent psychologists of the twentieth century. *Review of General Psychology, 6*, 139–152.

Stokes, Donald. (1986). Chance can play key role in life, psychologist says. *Campus Report* (June 4), 1–4.

Barlow, David H. (1942–)

David Barlow (1942–), born David Harrison Barlow, is considered to be one of the most influential pioneers in the field of anxiety disorders and is widely known for his application of scientific principles to improve the understanding and treatment of clinical disorders. Barlow's work in the area of phobias has enhanced our understanding of specific phobia subtypes, including their classification and clinical features. He is also known for his work on the best practices for assessment and treatment of specific phobias. These protocols have been published in books for both professionals and consumers.

David H. Barlow is a leading American researcher in anxiety disorders. Known as a pioneer in the field, he currently focuses his work on the development and evaluation of a transdiagnostic treatment that targets the features that are common to all anxiety disorders rather than the elements that are unique to specific disorders. The major benefit of transdiagnostic treatment is that clinicians will need to learn only one treatment protocol versus one for every disorder, thus greatly advancing dissemination and increasing accessibility to evidence-based treatment. (Dina Rudick/The Boston Globe via Getty Images)

Barlow was born in Needham, Massachusetts, and grew up in the suburbs of Boston, Massachusetts. Just prior to his birth, his father was shot down in World War II while on a mission over Germany, so Barlow and his mother lived with his maternal grandparents as he grew up. Barlow completed his undergraduate degree at the University of Notre Dame where he studied psychoanalytic formulations of literary figures, which sparked his interest in psychology. In 1964, he studied under the mentorship of Joseph R. Cautela at Boston College where he learned the importance of applying scientific principles to the study of clinical applications for human problems. Under Cautela's guidance, Barlow began working with Joseph Wolpe in 1966 to examine behavior therapy applications in the clinic. In 1966, he married and left Boston to begin his doctoral studies at the University of Vermont, where his work focused on an innovative experimental approach to the study of clinical problems known as single-case experimental designs.

After completing his PhD, Barlow took a position in the psychiatry department at the University of Mississippi Medical Center, where he founded a clinical psychology internship program and continued his research program in the study of anxiety and sexual disorders. In 1975, following promotion to professor and the birth of his two children, Barlow returned to the New England region and took a position at Brown University in Providence, Rhode Island, with a joint appointment as professor of both psychiatry and psychology. Here, Barlow founded a clinical psychology internship program and continued his research on anxiety and sexuality. However, he was not able to be as productive as he liked given the administrative demands of his position. Thus in 1979, with the desire to devote more time to research, Barlow took a position at the State University of New York at Albany where he cofounded the Center for Stress and Anxiety Disorders with his long-time colleague and friend, Ed Blanchard.

During the next 17 years, Barlow's clinical research had a major impact on the field, leading to reconceptualizations of panic disorder and generalized anxiety disorder that influenced the definition of these conditions in the *Diagnostic and Statistical Manual of Mental Disorders* (DSM) through Barlow's membership on the American Psychological Association (APA) anxiety disorder work group (DSM-III-R) and task force (DSM-IV). He contributed significant findings to the literature on the nature of anxiety and sexual dysfunction and in the development of evidence-based treatments for anxiety disorders. In 1996, Barlow returned to Boston to join the faculty at Boston University where he is professor of psychology and psychiatry and founder of the Center for Anxiety and Related Disorder (CARD), one of the foremost recognized anxiety treatment, training, and research clinics in North America. CARD offers a one-week intensive treatment program for individuals with specific phobias in addition to standard weekly treatment programs.

A prolific writer, Barlow has published over 500 scientific articles and book chapters and over 60 books for professionals and self-help books for consumers.

His work has had global impact with translations in over 20 languages, including Arabic, Chinese, Hindi, and Russian. In addition to his scholarly work, Barlow has held many key leadership positions in the field of psychology, including president of the Division of Clinical Psychology of the APA and president of the Association for Behavioral and Cognitive Therapies. He has received numerous awards for his lifetime achievements in clinical psychology. In 2000, he was awarded the Distinguished Scientific Award for the Applications of Psychology by the APA.

Barlow has influenced researchers and clinicians alike in their understanding of anxiety and their approach to clinical practice with his seminal texts *Anxiety and Its Disorders*, first published in 1988 and now in its second edition (Barlow, 2004) and the *Clinical Handbook of Psychological Disorders: A Step-by-Step Treatment Manual*, first published in 1985 and now in its fifth edition (Barlow, 2014). The latter broke new ground with the inclusion of detailed therapeutic protocols that greatly facilitated the dissemination of scientific treatment approaches outside the experimental setting. Barlow has also had significant influence on undergraduate students in psychology through his popular course text *Abnormal Psychology: An Integrative Approach*, now in its sixth edition (Barlow & Durand, 2011). Barlow's most recent work continues to be on the forefront of the field with a focus on the development and evaluation of a transdiagnostic approach to treating emotional disorders (Barlow et al., 2011).

Randi E. McCabe

See also: American Psychological Association; Wolpe, Joseph (1915–1997)

Further Reading

American Psychologist. (2000). Award for distinguished scientific applications of psychology: David H. Barlow. *American Psychologist, 55*, 1245–1263.

Barlow, David H. (2004). *Anxiety and its disorders* (2nd ed.). New York, NY: Guilford Press.

Barlow, David H. (Ed.) (2014). *Clinical handbook of psychological disorders: A step-by-step treatment manual* (5th ed.). New York, NY: Guilford Press.

Barlow, David H. & Durand, V. Mark. (2011). *Abnormal psychology: An integrative approach* (6th ed.). Belmont, CA: Wadsworth, Cengage Learning.

Barlow, David H., Farchione, Todd J., Fairholme, Christopher P., Ellard, Kristen K., Boisseau, Christina L., Allen, Laura B., & Ehrenreich-May, Jill. (2011). *The unified protocol for transdiagnostic treatment of emotional disorders: Therapist guide*. New York, NY: Oxford University Press.

Beck, Aaron T. (1921–)

Aaron T. Beck (1921–), psychiatrist and professor emeritus in the Department of Psychiatry at the University of Pennsylvania, is recognized as a revolutionary pioneer who applied the scientific method to testing psychoanalytic theories, which resulted in the development of the cognitive approach to understanding psycho-pathology. At a time when psychoanalysis was the dominant approach to treating mental illness, Beck (known to his friends as Tim) traded in the psychoanalytic couch and Freudian theories of unconscious urges to sit face-to-face with his clients and collaboratively discuss the content of their thoughts. He has come to be known as the father of cognitive therapy and has been described as one of the most influential psychotherapists of all time. Beck's approach has radically shifted the way psychological disorders, including phobias, are conceptualized and treated, and it is considered to be one of the major advances in the treatment of psychiatric disorders in the last half-century.

The youngest of five children, Beck was born in Providence, Rhode Island. After graduating from Brown University in 1942, he completed medical school at Yale University in 1946. Following a rotating internship and subsequent residency in pathology, Beck decided to become a neurologist and went on to complete a residency in neurology in Framingham, Massachusetts, where his exposure to psychiatry sparked his interest in this area. He gained experience in psychoanalytic psychotherapy during a two-year fellowship at Austin Riggs Center at Stockbridge, Massachusetts, a psychiatric hospital internationally recognized for its psychodynamic tradition. He then took a position as chief of neuropsychiatry at the Valley Forge Army Hospital in Phoenixville, Pennsylvania. Beck joined the faculty of the Department of Psychiatry at the University of Pennsylvania in 1954 and graduated from the Philadelphia Psychoanalytic Institute in 1956. At this time, he became interested in empirically validating psychoanalytic theories.

Beck began his research career by examining the dream content of depressed patients to test the psychoanalytic theory that depression is anger turned inward (Beck & Hurvich, 1959). Through a series of studies, he discovered that depressed patients engaged in systematic errors in realistic thinking (Beck, 1963). From this early work, Beck developed the cognitive model of depression and found that teaching depressed individuals to examine and test their negative thought patterns or "schemas" improved their depressive symptoms. He later expanded this model to other disorders, including anxiety and phobic disorders, as well as personality disorders, psychotic disorders, substance use disorders, and marital problems. Beck's cognitive model of anxiety disorders and phobias is outlined in *Anxiety Disorders and Phobias: A Cognitive Perspective* (Beck, Emery, & Greenberg, 2005), now in its 15th edition. In this model, the emotion of anxiety is linked with cognitive themes of threat, danger, and vulnerability. Cognitive techniques focused on promoting more realistic appraisal of threat and vulnerability result in anxiety reduction.

Beck has had a prolific career, publishing over 550 scientific articles and 18 books as well as numerous widely used assessment instruments for measuring depression, anxiety, hopelessness, suicidality, self-concept, and personality. He has developed empirically validated treatment protocols for a broad range of psychological disorders, including anxiety and phobic disorders. Beck has received many prestigious awards and honors, such as the Albert Lasker Clinical Medical Research Award in 2006 for developing cognitive therapy and the Distinguished Scientific Award for the Applications of Psychology in 1989 from the American Psychological Association. Beck is president emeritus of the nonprofit Beck Institute for Cognitive Therapy in Philadelphia, which he founded with his daughter, psychologist Dr. Judith Beck, in 1994. The Beck Institute's mission is to support the growth and dissemination of cognitive behavioral therapy (CBT) globally through leadership, research, and professional training. The Institute also has a therapy clinic specializing in state-of-the-art CBT. In 1998, Beck founded the Aaron T. Beck Psychopathology Research Centre at the University of Pennsylvania, which is dedicated to the study of cognitive therapy and the development of new treatments for psychiatric disorders. The Centre is known for its dissemination of research findings and its training of clinical scientists. Major areas of research have included the development of cognitive therapy for schizophrenia and effective treatment for suicidal behavior.

Beck is known for his signature bow tie, his warm interpersonal style, and his collaborative and generous involvement with students, clinicians, and academics in the pursuit of refining and expanding the applications of the cognitive approach through empirical investigation. He has had a significant influence on the career trajectories of many leaders in the field, as captured in the following anecdote from Dr. Peter Bieling:

In 1995 I was a graduate student who had just spent nearly every dollar I had to get myself to an international conference in Copenhagen, Denmark. On the second day of the conference, feeling a little out of place and out of my depth, I went to the cafeteria and was desperately looking around for the cheapest entrée I could find. The man standing next to me surveying the array of fish dishes said "You seem to be about as confused as I am, maybe we can work together and figure out what's good here." I recognized the voice, and there indeed was Tim Beck, who promptly but needlessly introduced himself to me, now agape. We chose our dishes and he asked me to join him, where we got to talking about my work and my findings, and just things in general. My anxiety melted away as he asked me questions and seemed eager to hear my opinions; he listened far more than he talked. At the end of the lunch he said, "You've done some interesting work, come be a post-doc for me when you're done." Of course I couldn't believe it, thanked him and spent a few more dollars to call home so as to pinch myself and share my chance encounter. Two years later, I started my post-doc with Dr. Beck, an experience which seems to have determined much of my life since. I'll never forget that meeting, his humility, charm, intelligence, listening ear, and the faith he put in me.

Now in his 90s, Beck continues to be involved in training and research and serves as the honorary president of the Academy of Cognitive Therapy, a nonprofit, multidisciplinary organization founded in 1998 to support education and research in cognitive therapy and to maintain standards for certification in CBT. Beck's significant impact on the field of psychotherapy research, practice, and training has been attributed to his collaborative nature, warmth of heart, and ability to have fostered a network of researchers, clinicians, and educators around the world (Padesky, 2004).

Randi E. McCabe

See also: Cognitive Behavioral Therapy; Cognitive Therapy

Further Reading

American Psychologist. (1990). Distinguished scientific award for the applications of psychology: Aaron T. Beck. *American Psychologist, 45*, 458–460.

Beck, Aaron T. (1963). Thinking and depression: I. Idiosyncratic content and cognitive distortions. *Archives of General Psychiatry, 9*, 324–333.

Beck, Aaron T., Emery, Gary, & Greenberg, Ruth. (2005). *Anxiety disorders and phobias: A cognitive perspective*. New York, NY: Basic Books.

Beck, Aaron T., & Hurvich, Marvin S. (1959). Psychological correlates of depression: I. Frequency of "masochistic" dream content in a private practice sample. *Psychosomatic Medicine, 21*, 50–55.

Padesky, Christine A. (2004). Aaron T. Beck: Mind, man and mentor. In Robert L. Leahy (Ed.), *Contemporary cognitive therapy: Theory, research, and practice*. New York, NY: Guilford Publications.

Weishaar, Marjorie E. (1993). *Aaron T. Beck*. Thousand Oaks, CA: Sage.

Websites

www.beckinstitute.org

www.academyofct.org

Behavior Therapy

The historical roots of behavior therapy trace back to the development of behaviorism as a field of study in the early 20th century. In contradistinction to Freud's psychoanalytic theory, which postulated that human thought, emotion, and behavior are a function of latent, unconscious processes, behaviorism turned its focus toward external and observable actions. In 1904, the Russian physiologist Ivan Pavlov (1849–1936) famously observed that behavioral responses are mediated and modulated through pairing of stimuli, in a process called classical conditioning.

Around this same time, Edward Thorndike (1874–1949) put forth the Law of Effect, which states that responses that produce a satisfying effect in a particular situation are likely to occur again in that situation, and conversely responses that elicit an unpleasant effect are less likely to occur. Further developing Pavlov and Thorndike's line of thought, John Watson (1878–1958) argued more broadly that unobservable thoughts and emotions cannot be measured and therefore cannot be objectively understood. He therefore emphasized that behavioral observation should be the sole source of information in studying the human psyche. Further, and more directly relevant to behavior therapy, Watson famously used classical conditioning to create a "fear" in his research subject, Little Albert (1920), by pairing an aversive loud noise together with a fluffy white rabbit. Somewhat later, working together with Watson, B. F. Skinner (1904–1990) developed a series of principles known as operant conditioning, which specified how reward and punishment could be utilized to achieve behavioral changes.

Behavior therapy applies these and other concepts to the clinical realm by employing them in the process of assessing and treating mental disorders. Behavior therapy encompasses a diversity of clinical procedures, including assessment techniques such as functional analysis, self-monitoring, and the behavioral approach test, and treatment techniques such as exposure, response prevention, behavioral activation, habit reversal, social skills training, and relaxation. All of these—and other behavior therapy techniques—are united in several ways. First, they are predicated on the principles of behaviorism, as previously described. Second, and relatedly, behavior therapy is action oriented and facilitates emotional change through behavior change. Third, all methods of behavior therapy focus on objective measurement—treatment techniques aim to provide tangible reductions in symptoms of emotional distress and improvements in psychosocial functioning. And fourth, behavior therapy techniques are well researched and their clinical use tends to be governed by empirical support. Today, behavior therapy is used—either alone or in combination with other treatments (such as cognitive therapy)—for a variety of psychological conditions, including depression, alcohol/substance abuse, attention deficit hyperactivity disorder, and sexual dysfunction. In particular, behavior therapy has been shown to be very effective in the treatment of phobias and other anxiety disorders.

Behavior therapy assessment techniques are methods of conceptualizing and measuring mental disorders using the principles of behaviorism. For example, functional analysis involves identifying links between environmental factors, behavioral responses, and emotional sequela. A functional analysis of a phobic individual's symptoms may assess that persistent fear and aversion (emotional sequela) to a specific object or situation (environmental trigger) is maintained and possibly even exacerbated by avoidance (behavioral response). Another common behavior therapy assessment technique is self-monitoring in which individuals learn to conduct their own functional analyses of their symptoms, employing self-monitoring to learn about how contingencies of reinforcement shape both their behavioral and emotional experiences. The behavioral approach test is another behavior therapy assessment method—commonly used in the context of research, this technique simply involves measuring how close in proximity (e.g., inches) an individual can approach a feared stimulus, and monitoring changes in approach/avoidance over time. In all of these and other behavior therapy assessment techniques, units of measurement are objective, quantitative, and observable—thus, facilitating rigorous scientific study and assessment of human experiences.

Behavior therapy treatment techniques are clinical interventions for mental disorders (i.e., to reduce distress and improve psychosocial functioning) based on the principles of behaviorism. In the context of treatment for anxiety and phobias, the most famous and well-utilized behavior therapy treatment technique is exposure therapy, which involves voluntary confrontation—or exposure—to feared situations. Exposure helps individuals to increase tolerance for high levels of distress, as well as to internalize new information to highlight that fears are irrational and/or overinflated.

In clinical practice, exposure therapy typically commences with the development of a treatment hierarchy—a rank-ordered list of situations, which will reliably elicit an individual's anxiety response. Individuals are then asked to rate the level of distress they anticipate in each feared situation on a scale of 0–100 (known as the Subjective Units of Distress Scale or SUDS). Subsequently, they are encouraged to face their fear at each step of their hierarchy, until they have conquered the entire list. For example, if an individual presents with social anxiety disorder (social phobia) centered on a fear of being embarrassed in front of strangers, the treatment hierarchy may resemble that which is depicted in Table 1. It should be noted that this approach developed from an earlier method known as systematic desensitization, whereby exposure was paired with a relaxation response. Systematic desensitization is typically no longer used because the relaxation response was determined to be unnecessary for clinical gains and, in fact, was hypothesized to potentially interfere with therapeutic gains by teaching people that anxiety needed to be replaced by relaxation rather than just experienced directly until it declined. A similar behavior therapy treatment technique, called behavioral activation, involves purposefully engaging in activities in order to improve one's mood. It is an evidence-based treatment for depression. Specific behavioral activation strategies may include planned engagement in social and pleasure activities throughout one's day; better attending to self-care activities such as sleep, physical exercise, and eating; and devoting adequate time and resources to engage in mastery activities (e.g., tasks that give one a sense of completion) in daily life. However, behavior therapy may also involve identifying and targeting certain behaviors for reduction/elimination, in a process called response prevention. For example, individuals who present with repetitive behaviors aimed at reducing anxiety or distress (e.g., excessive washing, checking, reassurance seeking, or safety behaviors including carrying anxiolytic medications) may be encouraged to reduce and ultimately to cease these and similar behaviors. Similarly, habit reversal—which is commonly used in the treatment of tics—involves replacement of maladaptive and dysfunctional behaviors with other more adaptive responses.

David H. Rosmarin, Aliza Sklar, and Devora Shabtai

See also: Classical Conditioning; Exposure Therapy; Flooding; Obsessive-Compulsive Disorder; Operant Conditioning; Pavlov, Ivan (1849–1936); Phobia, Specific; Rachman, Jack (1934–); Skinner, B. F. (1904–1990); Social Anxiety Disorder (Social Phobia); Subjective Units of Distress Scale; Systematic Desensitization; Thorndike, Edward L. (1874–1949); Watson, John B. (1878–1958); Wolpe, Joseph (1915–1997)

Further Reading

Rachman, Stanley. (1966). Studies in desensitization—II. Flooding. *Behavior Research and Therapy, 4,* 1–6.

Wolpe, Joseph. (1958). *Psychotherapy by reciprocal inhibition.* Stanford, CA: Stanford University Press.

SAMPLE EXPOSURE HIERARCHY FOR SOCIAL ANXIETY DISORDER (SOCIAL PHOBIA)

Feared Situation	Subjective Units of Distress (0–100)
1. Wear an ugly shirt in public	100
2. Forget your wallet at checkout in a store	90
3. Call a "wrong number" on purpose	80
4. Change a food order after placing it	75
5. Give a compliment to a stranger	65
6. Ask a stranger for directions	50
7. Ask a stranger for the time	45
8. Drink coffee and eat a muffin in public	35
9. Order a coffee at a store	30
10. Ride on a crowded train	25

David H. Rosmarin, Aliza Sklar, and Devora Shabtai

Behavioral Approach Test

A behavioral approach test (also known as a behavioral approach task or BAT) is an assessment method for measuring various aspects of a phobia, including factors that influence fear levels, degree of avoidance, anxious thoughts, and safety behavior. The BAT offers several advantages over standard questionnaire assessment measures. Compared to a paper-and-pencil measure where people self-report the aspects of their phobia, a BAT enables the clinician to directly observe the degree of fear and avoidance, as well as to assess various factors that might increase or decrease a client's fear in response to the feared situation or object. BATs are typically used to assess a specific phobia but have also been used for assessment of other anxiety disorders, including social anxiety disorder (social phobia) and agoraphobia. In addition to their use in clinical practice, BATs are commonly used in experimental research on anxiety and phobias to provide an objective assessment of fear before and after treatment. For example, to assess the impact of safety behaviors on therapeutic gains in exposure therapy, Milosevic and Radomsky (2008) used a BAT to measure participants' snake fear comparing levels in those who received exposure treatment with or without incorporation of safety behaviors.

To conduct a BAT with a client who has a specific phobia of spiders, the clinician would ask the client to approach the spider in a series of steps similar to those that might be on an exposure hierarchy. Throughout the BAT, the clinician will ask the client to provide the fear level associated with each step on a 0–100 scale (also called the Subjective Units of Distress Scale or SUDS), with 0 being no fear and 100 being the greatest fear imaginable. In addition to gauging fear levels, the clinician will ask the client about the content of his or her thoughts (e.g., "I am afraid the spider may jump on me," "I want to get out of here"), physical sensations experienced (e.g., "My heart is racing, I feel sweaty, and light-headed"), and note any safety behaviors observed (e.g., looking away from the spider). The clinician will ask additional questions to ascertain other variables that might increase or decrease fear including feared beliefs (e.g., "What are you afraid the spider might do?") and safety behaviors (e.g., "What happens to your fear level when you look away from the spider?"). The clinician will note how close the client can actually come toward the spider in distance (e.g., standing 3 feet away or 1 foot away). Individuals with very severe levels of fear might not be able to take any steps toward the feared stimulus and might not even be able to look at it. Those with more moderate fear levels might be able to look at the feared stimulus and take some steps toward it. Finally, those with more mild fear levels might be able to come right to the feared stimulus and might even be able to touch it despite tolerating a high degree of fear at doing so.

The information gained from the BAT provides an accurate gauge of the severity of the phobia and is used to plan treatment. Specifically, it provides direction for developing the exposure hierarchy, which situations to include on the hierarchy, and where to start in situational exposure. Information from the BAT also helps to identify safety behaviors that should be eliminated through treatment and maladaptive beliefs that should be targeted with cognitive therapy. The BAT can also be used to assess progress in treatment. Depending on the client's fear level, the BAT might include the actual phobic stimulus or a picture or model (e.g., a rubber spider). Studies have tested various formats of the BAT, including live (in person), presentation of steps on a computer, presentation of steps by video, and even a perceived-threat BAT that utilizes a series of opaque jars associated with increasing risk of contact with a spider when in fact none of the jars actually contains a spider at all (Cochrane, Barnes-Holmes, & Barnes-Holmes, 2008). Recent research has examined the role of courage in an individual's ability to approach a feared stimulus despite experiencing significant fear. Researchers studying individuals who were fearful of spiders found that the higher an individual's level of courage, the closer he or she was able to get to a taxidermied tarantula (Norton & Weiss, 2010).

Randi E. McCabe

See also: Cognitive Behavioral Therapy; Cognitive Therapy; DSM-5; Exposure Treatment; Phobia, Specific; Safety Behavior; Subjective Units of Distress Scale

Further Reading

Cochrane, Andy, Barnes-Holmes, Dermot, & Barnes-Holmes, Yvonne. (2008). The perceived-threat behavioral approach test (PT-BAT): Measuring avoidance in high-, mid-, and low-spider-fearful participants. *The Psychological Record, 58*, 585–596.

Milosevic, Irena, & Radomsky, Adam S. (2008). Safety behaviour does not necessarily interfere with exposure therapy. *Behaviour Research and Therapy, 46*, 1111–1118.

Norton, Peter J., & Weiss, Brandon J. (2010). The role of courage on behavioral approach in a fear-eliciting situation: A proof-of-concept pilot study. *Journal of Anxiety Disorders, 23*, 212–217.

GET A LITTLE CLOSER

Michael is a 30-year-old man who has been afraid of heights for as long as he can remember. In childhood, he recalled becoming extremely nervous going to visit his grandparents who lived on the tenth floor of a high-rise building. Although he was able to go to their apartment because he had to, he felt very frightened and avoided looking out the window and stepping out onto their balcony. Now an adult, Michael has noticed that his fear of heights has grown over the years to the point that it is greatly affecting his ability to live his life. He has been managing by avoiding most situations that trigger his fear like using an elevator in high-rise building, standing on a balcony, parking his car on the rooftop garage, standing on a ladder, and driving on bridges. He is specifically afraid of falling and of the physical symptoms of anxiety that he experiences in these situations, including feelings of dizziness, light-headedness, weakness in his legs, shakiness, and rapid heart rate. Michael knew it was time to seek help when he had to decline an exciting job opportunity because the commute to work would have involved driving over a bridge, and there were no alternate routes that did not add an extra two hours to his commute time.

When Michael met with the therapist, he was asked to complete a behavioral approach test (BAT). The therapist asked him to do this so that she could objectively assess his height phobia including the severity of Michael's fear, his reliance on safety behaviors and avoidance, and his cognitions. For the first step, the therapist and Michael went to the roof of the parking garage and stood 20 feet from the edge. The therapist asked Michael to provide a SUDS (Subjective Units of Distress Scale) rating and asked him what thoughts were going through his mind. Michael's SUDS rating was a 70 and he stated that he was focused on his feelings of anxiety, especially feeling dizzy and weak in his legs. The next step of the BAT was to stand 10 feet from the edge. Michael's SUDS rating increased to 85 and he noted his physical symptoms of anxiety were intensified, and he had the thought "I want to get out of here" but he agreed to continue. Next, they stood 5 feet from the edge. Michael reported a SUDS rating of 100 and was unable to look straight out but instead kept his head focused down on the ground. He stated that he could not go any further and that he was unable to think clearly because his physical symptoms of anxiety were so intense. He stated that he thought he would fall down and become overwhelmed by anxiety. The therapist ended the BAT at that point and they went back to the office to review the experience. The therapist used the information she gathered during the BAT to help generate the exposure hierarchy, identify safety behaviors (e.g., looking down at the ground), and potential targets for cognitive therapy (e.g., "Symptoms of anxiety are dangerous" and "I will fall").

Randi E. McCabe

Behavioral Experiment

A behavioral experiment (BE) is a technique used in cognitive therapy. Inspired by the scientific method, the goal of a BE is to help the individual test hypotheses by gathering information about thoughts and beliefs related to his or her fear. Historically, the concept of beliefs as hypotheses to be tested during psychological treatment can be drawn back to Aaron T. Beck, who was one of the first to develop a cognitively based therapy for depression. Although he recognized the importance of examining people's thoughts and beliefs, he also believed that behavioral change, rooted in the concept of learning theory, was one of the most powerful methods of facilitating cognitive change. There is little empirical evidence to date directly examining the effectiveness of BEs in treatment; however, many treatments that incorporate the use of BEs, particularly cognitive therapies for problems such as social anxiety disorder (social phobia) and panic disorder, have been found to be extremely effective forms of treatment (Bennett-Levy et al., 2004).

BEs can be used at any stage of therapy. They can be completed either during the treatment session or between sessions as homework. They can be used to test the validity of the individual's current negative beliefs or to test out new more adaptive beliefs. Devising an effective BE that tests out a given belief in a meaningful way often requires creativity and collaboration on behalf of the client and therapist. Common beliefs related to fear that might be targeted using a BE include beliefs surrounding the meaning of physiological symptoms of anxiety, the necessity of safety behaviors to cope with fearful stimuli, and exaggerated beliefs about the danger of the feared object or situation.

There are two main designs of BEs, those that aim to test hypotheses and those that are primarily discovery oriented. In the first type, which resembles the classical experiment, the individual in treatment generates a hypothesis related to his or her problem and then devises a method to test out that hypothesis, typically by manipulating an aspect of the environment or behavior. After engaging in the new situation or behavior, the individual reviews the outcome in relation to the initial hypothesis, and draws a conclusion about its validity. For example, an individual with social anxiety disorder might hold the belief that if she does something embarrassing people will permanently reject her. In treatment, the therapist assists her to generate an alternative belief that others will not reject her for doing something embarrassing. To test these two competing hypotheses she could devise a BE, whereby she intentionally does something embarrassing in front of others, such as trip up the stairs, and observe people for signs of rejection, such as ignoring or laughing at her. Following the BE, she would review the outcome and draw a conclusion as to which belief was better supported.

In the second type of BE, which resembles observational research, the individual does not generate a specific hypothesis, but rather devises a method to gather more information. For example, an individual with social anxiety disorder, who believes that he is the only person who blushes when giving a speech, might create a survey asking others how likely they are to blush when giving a speech. After gathering the information, the individual would review the responses and generate a conclusion concerning his initial belief that he is the only one who blushes.

It is important to recognize that even though, as with exposure-based treatments, BEs often involve confronting the very thing feared by the individual, BEs are distinct from exposure in a number of ways. Whereas exposure involves repeated confrontation of the feared stimulus with the goal of habituating to the anxiety response, the goal of a BE is primarily to test out a specific belief and facilitate learning. Therefore, reduction of anxiety during the BE is not necessary, nor is repeated exposure to the feared stimulus.

Andrea R. Ashbaugh

See also: Beck, Aaron T. (1925–); Cognitive Restructuring; Cognitive Therapy; Exposure Treatment; Learning Theory; Phobic Beliefs

Further Reading

Bennett-Levy, James, Butler, Gillian, Fennell, Melanie, Hackmann, Ann, Mueller, Martina, & Westbrook, David. (2004). *Oxford guide to behavioural experiments in cognitive therapy*. Oxford, UK: Oxford University Press.

Behavioral Model

The behavioral model is a framework for understanding and treating emotional disorders, including phobias, which was popularized in the early 20th century with the publication of John B. Watson's seminal paper *Psychology as the Behaviorist Views It*, also referred to as the behaviorist manifesto, in 1918. Watson, viewed as the father of behaviorism, was greatly influenced by Pavlov's research on classical conditioning and the idea that behavior could be explained by learned associations. He defined the behaviorist approach as an objective branch of science, whereby behavior is explained through conditioning principles and direct observation and measurement. The goal of behaviorism is to predict and control behavior in both animals and humans. With the founding of the behavioral model, Watson revolutionized psychology by shifting focus away from the mentalist approach of the psychodynamic Freudian model toward an empirical science of psychology in the laboratory.

Throughout the early and mid-20th century, Skinner's work on operant conditioning and Bandura's application of conditioning principles to social learning established the importance of other learning pathways on behavior through reinforcement and modeling. Other important developments that shaped the behavioral model include the work of Dollard and Miller in the area of learning and motivation. They identified four necessary elements for instrumental learning: drive (i.e., motivation), cue (i.e., stimulus), response (i.e., behavior), and reward (i.e., reinforcement). In the 1950s, Wolpe (considered the father of behavior therapy) applied experimental findings to address clinical problems in the beginning of what is now known as the scientist practitioner model. Based on the premise that if behavior is learned it can be unlearned, Wolpe conducted research to extinguish fear reactions in cats through counterconditioning and a process that he called reciprocal inhibition. This work gave rise to a variety of behavioral treatment interventions including systematic desensitization and contemporary exposure therapy. A key assessment methodology in behavior therapy is the functional analysis of behavior, whereby the clinician identifies the variables that influence the occurrence and maintenance of a problem behavior.

According to the behavioral model, fear and anxiety develop and are maintained by a combination of learning processes, including classical and operant conditioning. Therapy aims to gradually expose individuals to the feared stimulus so the physiological fear response habituates and new learned associations are formed. Environmental contingencies are altered to promote functional behavior and reduce maladaptive behaviors such as escape and avoidance.

The behavioral model was the dominant paradigm until the late 1950s when the cognitive model took hold. Since the 1980s, the predominant approach has been the cognitive behavioral model, which acknowledges the important role that both behavior and cognition play in emotional disturbance and well-being. However, some would say that the contemporary behavioral model has been reinvigorated with the development of clinical behavior analysis, which has been defined as the application of modern functional contextual behavior analysis to traditional clinical issues. Therapies developed based on this approach include acceptance and commitment therapy and behavioral activation therapy.

Randi E. McCabe

See also: Behavior Therapy; Exposure Treatment; Pavlov, Ivan (1849–1936); Reciprocal Inhibition; Skinner, B.F. (1904–1990); Systematic Desensitization; Watson, John B. (1878–1958); Wolpe, Joseph (1915–1997)

Further Reading

Dougher, Michael J., & Hayes, Steven C. (2000). Clinical behavior analysis. In Michael J. Dougher (Ed.), *Clinical behavior analysis* (pp. 11–25). Reno, NV: Context Press.

Follette, William C., & Hayes, Steven C. (2000). Contemporary behavior therapy. In C.R. Snyder & Rick E. Ingram (Eds.), *Handbook of psychological change: Psychotherapy processes & practices for the 21st century* (pp. 381–408). Hoboken, NJ: John Wiley & Sons.

Benzodiazepines

Benzodiazepines, also known as "benzos," are among the most widely prescribed class of drugs in the world for treating anxiety symptoms. Chemist Leo Sternbach first created benzodiazepines in the 1950s with the development of chlordiazepoxide, which offered a safer alternative to the then drug of choice for treating anxiety known as barbiturates. Benzodiazepines such as alprazolam, clonazepam, and lorazepam are central nervous system sedating agents and belong to a medication class known as anxiolytics. In addition to treating anxiety, benzodiazepines are also used to treat sleep disturbance, acute agitation, and a variety of other conditions. They are typically prescribed only on a short-term basis (two to four weeks) for individuals suffering from extreme anxiety and panic attacks due to the potential negative consequences associated with their long-term use, including withdrawal and rebound syndrome, as well as tolerance and dependence. The widespread use of benzodiazepines combined with the problems associated with their use led the World Psychiatric Association to create a task force to objectively review the issues associated with benzodiazepines. This resulted in the publication of a clinical guide for their use by the World Health Organization in 1996. In specific phobia, benzodiazepines may sometimes be used to help an individual cope with infrequent situations where he or she must encounter the phobic stimulus. For example, an individual with a phobia of flying who rarely has to travel may be prescribed a benzodiazepine to tolerate a flight. Alternatively, an individual with a phobia of dentists may be given a benzodiazepine to enable him or her to endure a dental procedure.

There is evidence that benzodiazepines may reduce the symptoms of anxiety associated with generalized anxiety disorder, panic disorder, and social anxiety disorder (social phobia). By contrast, there is no evidence to support their use in treating the core symptoms of obsessive compulsive disorder or posttraumatic stress disorder (PTSD). In fact, some evidence suggests that use of benzodiazepines shortly after a trauma may increase the incidence of PTSD. Despite the positive benefits of benzodiazepines in reducing anxiety symptoms of some disorders, the associated negative effects and risk for misuse require clinicians to prescribe these medications judiciously with appropriate precautions to ensure that they are used appropriately. For example, individuals taking benzodiazepines must avoid alcohol due to potentially lethal combination effects. In addition, they should not drive or operate machinery when taking a benzodiazepine due to the sedating effects that could compromise safety.

The negative effects of benzodiazepines include more severe symptoms after the medication is discontinued. Individuals who have taken benzodiazepines over an extended time period (typically a period greater than two months) may have difficulty discontinuing the medication due to uncomfortable withdrawal symptoms. Withdrawal symptoms include agitation, insomnia, seizures, and rebound anxiety, whereby an individual's anxiety level actually increases as the sedating effect of the medication wears off. The onset of withdrawal symptoms depends on the half-life of the medication (i.e., how long it takes for the medication to break down in the body) and may range from one to two days for medications with a shorter half-life and three to seven days for medications with a longer half-life. Thus, the medication needs to be reduced very gradually to minimize negative withdrawal effects and enable the individual to eventually discontinue its use. The longer an individual has taken the medication, the more gradual the recommended taper process. Cognitive behavioral therapy (CBT) has been used to effectively help individuals discontinue benzodiazepines.

Due to the rapid effects of benzodiazepines in reducing anxiety, they are highly addictive and commonly abused, sometimes resulting in unintentional drug overdose resulting in death. When taken over an extended time, the individual may develop tolerance such that the body requires an increasing dose of the medication to achieve the same anxiolytic effects. Benzodiazepines are a particular risk when used in older people where they have been associated with confusion, delirium, and increased risk of hip fractures by as much as 50%. Given the lack of any clear benefits for their use in older adults, it has been recommended that they rarely be used.

Overall, benzodiazepines are not considered a first-line medication treatment of anxiety disorders, including specific phobia. Selective serotonin reuptake inhibitors and other medications have been shown to be far more effective at addressing the core symptoms of anxiety disorders and are considered safe for longer-term use. For specific phobia in particular, cognitive behavioral treatment, including exposure-based strategies, is the optimal choice. Benzodiazepines may actually impede CBT interventions and limit treatment outcome by interfering with the learning of new information, reducing anxiety levels needed for habituation during exposure, limiting motivation to engage in exposure by serving as a safety behavior, and undermining an individual's belief in his or her own personal control over anxiety. Benzodiazepines may be indicated for specific phobia when cognitive behavioral treatment is not available and when there is infrequent, necessary exposure to the phobic stimulus as described in the examples mentioned earlier.

Randi E. McCabe

See also: Cognitive Behavioral Therapy; Exposure Treatment; Habituation; Phobia, Specific; Selective Serotonin Reuptake Inhibitors; World Health Organization

Further Reading

Bostwick, Jolene R., Casher, Michael I., & Yasugi, Shinji. (2012). Benzodiazepines: A versatile clinical tool. *Current Psychiatry, 11*, 55–64.

Otto, Michael W., McHugh, R. Kathryn, Simon, Naomi M., Farach, Frank J., Worthington, John J., & Pollack, Mark H. (2010). Efficacy of CBT for benzodiazepine discontinuation in patients with panic disorder: Further evaluation. *Behaviour Research and Therapy, 48*, 720–727.

World Health Organization. (1996). Program on substance use: Rational use of benzodiazepines.

Beta-Blockers

Beta-blockers such as propranolol, atenolol, and pindolol were first invented by Nobel Prize laureate (medicine, 1988) Sir James Black to treat heart disease by blocking the adrenaline-responsive beta-receptors on the heart, hence the name beta-blockers. The first beta-blocker, created in the early 1960s, was propranolol and its discovery had a revolutionary impact on the medical management of heart disease. Through blockade of the stimulating effects of norepinephrine (also called adrenaline), the physiological effects of the fight-or-flight stress response, such as rapid heart rate (stress-induced tachycardia), increased blood pressure, pounding heart, sweating, and shaky voice and limbs, are inhibited. In the late 1970s, physicians began using beta-blockers to treat the physical symptoms of anxiety in performers such as actors and musicians who experienced extreme performance anxiety and stage fright.

Although not considered a first-line treatment, beta-blockers are currently used in the treatment of social anxiety disorder (social phobia), performance only type, and for individuals with clinically significant anxiety in performance situations such as an individual with severe public speaking anxiety who must give a speech to a large audience, or a professional athlete who experiences extreme competition-related anxiety prior to an event. Beta-blockers are not a long-term anxiety management strategy. They are typically used for short-term relief of the physical symptoms in a specific, time-limited, anxiety-provoking situation. For example, a pianist who experiences severe anxiety about performing in front of an audience may take a beta-blocker 45 to 60 minutes prior to the performance. Although beta-blockers inhibit the physical symptoms of anxiety such as shaky hands, they do not target the psychological and cognitive symptoms of anxiety such as fear and worry. Thus, if cognitive aspects of anxiety are prominent such as fears of making a mistake in the performance or worries about what people think, the beta-blocker will not reduce these symptoms. Limited research on the use of beta-blockers and specific phobia does not support their use. As with other types of phobic anxiety, the treatment of choice for individuals with performance-related fears is cognitive behavioral therapy.

Common side effects of beta-blockers include light-headedness, sleepiness, nausea, and abnormally slow pulse. As with any medication, beta-blockers are not without risk and have been associated with a range of adverse effects. Further, they should not be taken by people with asthma or a history of cocaine use.

An exciting line of research is examining the role of beta-blockers such as propranolol in inhibiting the conditioned fear response in both animal models and humans. For example, a Dutch team of researchers had university students undergo a conditioning paradigm where they learned to associate a picture of a spider with an electric shock. Subsequent exposure to the spider picture triggered a conditioned startle response. Students who were given propranolol no longer exhibited a startle response. Further research is needed to investigate the potential propranolol may have in inhibiting the fear response and weakening or preventing traumatic memories.

Randi E. McCabe

See also: Classical Conditioning; Cognitive Behavioral Therapy; Exposure Treatment; Phobia, Specific; Social Anxiety Disorder (Social Phobia)

Further Reading

Bernadt, M.W., Silverstone, T., & Singleton, W. (1980). Behavioural and subjective effects of beta-adrenergic blockade in phobic subjects. *The British Journal of Psychiatry, 137*, 452–457.

Kindt, Merel, Soeter, Marieke, & Vervliet, Bram. (2009). Beyond extinction: Erasing human fear responses and preventing the return of fear. *Nature Neuroscience, 12*, 256–258.

C

Carbon Dioxide Challenge Test

Carbon dioxide (chemical formula CO_2) is a naturally occurring compound that exists in a gaseous state at standard temperature and pressure and makes up approximately 0.04% of air by volume. The CO_2 challenge test involves the inhalation of CO_2-enriched air and is generally used in laboratory-based studies of fear and anxiety to induce panic attacks or panic attack symptoms. A panic attack involves the sudden onset of intense fear that is accompanied by at least four physical or cognitive panic symptoms. CO_2 challenges are capable of eliciting both physical (e.g., accelerated heart rate, shortness of breath, and dizziness) and cognitive (e.g., feelings of unreality, fear of dying, and fear of losing control) panic symptoms. The CO_2 challenge test is one of a number of procedures that are used to provoke panic and are often referred to as *biological challenges* (e.g., sodium lactate infusion, voluntary hyperventilation, and oral administration of yohimbine). Having the ability to induce panic in the laboratory is useful for helping to elucidate the mechanisms involved in the development, maintenance, and treatment of anxiety disorders.

There are multiple methods for delivering CO_2-enriched air to participants, with one of the most popular being through the use of a respiratory mask. In this method, participants wear a respiratory mask connected by aerosol tubing to one port of a valve system. A second port is open to room air while a third is connected by aerosol tubing to a reservoir containing CO_2-enriched air. Manipulation of the valve allows the experimenter to switch participants' air source from room air to CO_2-enriched air (see Lejuez, Forsyth, & Eifert, 1998, for details).

CO_2 concentration and the duration of delivery can vary greatly and result in somewhat different responses (Zvolensky & Eifert, 2001). For example, low CO_2 concentrations, ranging from approximately 4% to 9% by volume, tend to be delivered continuously over longer periods (e.g., 15–20 minutes) and cause gradual, sustained symptoms. Higher concentrations of CO_2 tend to be delivered for shorter periods (e.g., 20–25 seconds for 20% and possibly only a single vital capacity breath for concentrations greater than 35%) and cause a more rapid, intense reaction.

Inhalation of CO_2-enriched air with time causes hypercapnia, a condition of elevated CO_2 blood levels, and respiratory acidosis, a condition with decreased cell/tissue pH. These conditions lead to increases in respiration, which are accompanied by secondary physiological changes (e.g., increased heart rate). For higher concentrations of CO_2 (e.g., 35%) a rebound effect can occur, temporarily resulting in respiratory alkalosis, a condition with elevated blood pH. While the biological response to breathing CO_2-enriched air is relatively well understood, researchers are still studying the psychological factors that play a role in the extent to which panic symptoms are experienced during CO_2 challenge.

CO_2 challenge procedures have been used in many studies to explore the mechanisms involved in the development, maintenance, and treatment of anxiety disorders. Findings reveal that CO_2 challenge is generally capable of eliciting panic symptoms in those with and without anxiety disorders. Those with panic disorder are more likely to experience a panic attack in response to CO_2 challenge than those without panic disorder (but with another anxiety disorder) as well as those without an anxiety disorder. Interestingly, these groups do not differ much with respect to physiological changes, but do differ with respect to their subjective response to these changes (Barlow 2002). Also, those with panic disorder report that panic attacks experienced during CO_2 challenge are similar to those experienced spontaneously. CO_2 challenge procedures are also used as aversive unconditioned stimuli in Pavlovian fear-conditioning paradigms, to examine theories that posit a role of CO_2 sensitivity as a risk factor for panic disorder, to identify subtypes of panic disorder, and to examine drug and nondrug treatments for preventing panic in response to CO_2-enriched air inhalation. Research has shown that CO_2 challenge procedures are safe and do not contribute to the subsequent development of panic attacks or panic disorder in healthy, nonclinical subjects.

Jason M. Prenoveau

See also: Anxiety and Related Disorders; Fear, Physiology of; Panic Attacks; Panic Disorder

Further Reading

Barlow, David H. (Ed.). (2002). *Anxiety and its disorders: The nature and treatment of anxiety and panic* (2nd ed.). New York, NY: The Guilford Press.

Lejuez, Carl W., Forsyth, John P., & Eifert, Georg H. (1998). Devices and methods for administering carbon dioxide-enriched air in experimental and clinical settings. *Journal of Behavior Therapy and Experimental Psychiatry, 29*, 239–248.

Zvolensky, Michael J., & Eifert, Georg H. (2001). A review of psychological factors/processes affecting anxious responding during voluntary hyperventilation and inhalations of carbon dioxide-enriched air. *Clinical Psychology Review, 21*, 375–400.

Childhood, Phobias in

Fears of different situations and objects commonly wax and wane in childhood. Depending on the child's developmental stage, a fear can be appropriate and expected. For example, preschool-aged children may develop a fear of clowns, reflecting that the child has not yet fully learned to distinguish fantasy from reality. However, a fear of clowns in an adolescent would no longer be considered normative. When fear or anxiety is excessive and unreasonable, is persistent, causes the child significant distress, and interferes with the child's daily life at home, at school, or with peers, the fear may be identified as a "phobia." Phobias in childhood include agoraphobia, social anxiety disorder (social phobia), and specific phobias. The primary difference between these disorders is the focus of the fear.

Specific phobias are the most common phobias in childhood and adolescence with prevalence rates of up to 10% in the community. Specific phobias include animal (e.g., fear of spiders), blood-injection-injury (BII; e.g., fear of needles), natural environment (e.g., fear of the dark), situational (e.g., fear of flying), and "other" (e.g., fear of vomiting) types. Animal, BII, and environmental phobias (i.e., fear of the dark or thunderstorms) tend to occur earliest and are among the most common.

Children and adolescents with social anxiety disorder are excessively fearful of interpersonal situations and negative judgment. Prevalence rate is approximately 7%, and onset typically occurs in late childhood or early adolescence, reflecting the developmental period during which the importance of and reliance on peer relationships begin to increase. Situations that may be avoided or endured with distress include reading out loud, joining conversations, talking to adults, attending

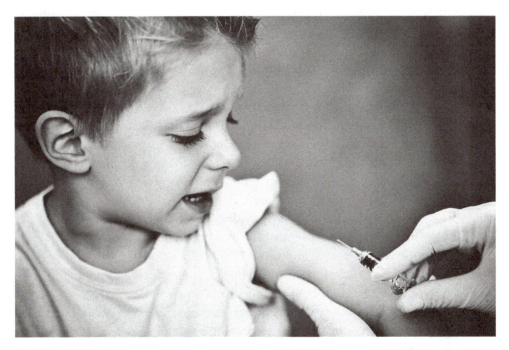

A child winces as he prepares to receive a vaccination. It is very common for young children to fear needles, as they associate them with pain and have limited ability to appreciate their purpose. Most children who are afraid of needles will eventually outgrow their fear, but for a minority the fear persists and may develop into a specific phobia. (Imgorthand/ iStockphoto.com)

social functions like parties or playdates, answering questions in class, and ordering food. School refusal may occur and some adolescents may use substances to alleviate their anxiety in social situations. Adolescents may also experience significant anticipatory anxiety and may ruminate over their perceptions of a social interaction after it occurs.

Children with agoraphobia are afraid that they will not be able to escape a situation easily or without significant embarrassment if they should have panic-like symptoms (dizziness, racing heart, upset stomach, fear of dying, etc.). They may avoid going to school assemblies, going to parks, or sitting in the middle row at movie theatres. Agoraphobia generally begins in the early teens, although it can begin earlier. It is less common than the other phobias among children and youth, and is more common among females than males.

Children who have a phobia may cry, throw tantrums, cling to their parents, or freeze when they are exposed to the feared object or situation. They typically go out of their way to avoid it and refuse to participate in activities that other children their age would typically engage in. Because of this, they may seem to be rigid or defiant. They may develop sleep problems, report somatic complaints (e.g., stomachaches or headaches), and can have difficulties concentrating. Disruption in family relationships can occur as a result of family accommodation, in which family activities and routines are altered to accommodate the demands of the anxious child. There can be significant functional impact, including decrease in academic performance and school refusal, as well as impairment in family and peer relationships.

Genetic and biological causes are among the proposed etiological factors for the development of a phobia during childhood or adolescence. Children are more likely to develop an anxiety disorder when one or both parents have an anxiety disorder. Neuroimaging studies suggest that differences in amygdala and hypothalamic-pituitary-adrenal activity and neural processing may play a role as well. Further, personality and temperament, particularly behavioral inhibition, appear to be associated with social anxiety disorder.

Although it is difficult to disentangle environmental from genetic influence, sometimes phobias develop in children and youth as a result of a particular experience. For example, a child who was bitten by a dog may develop a phobia of dogs. Children and youth also learn by watching others and may develop fears based on parental modeling. If a child sees his or her mother scream every time he or she sees a spider, the child is more likely to develop a fear of spiders as well. Attachment styles, parenting styles, and stressful life events may also render a child more likely to develop an anxiety disorder.

Protective factors help prevent a child or youth from developing an anxiety disorder. These include temperament; supportive home, school, and community environments; cognitive ability; and good general coping. Parents who sensitively encourage and role-model brave behavior can help their child cope better when the child is anxious and can prevent the development of anxiety disorders.

Reliable, structured assessment of childhood phobias is challenged by developmental changes and the fluctuation of anxiety symptoms. Because adults may be less likely to identify a child's anxiety as problematic, child self-report of symptoms is important. However, cognitive and language development often impact younger children's ability to communicate their experiences and to accurately report timelines of symptoms. Discrepancies in informant reports can challenge assessment and determination of treatment outcome, and the frequent comorbidity of phobic disorders increases the complexity.

Although the chronicity of childhood and adolescent phobic disorders is unclear, these disorders may be a precursor to the experience of other mental health problems like depression, or they may be associated with the development of other mental health problems in adulthood. Further, avoidance often results in a dearth of opportunities to develop age-appropriate skills, thereby hindering social, emotional, and behavioral development. It is therefore important that children and youth receive treatment as soon as possible.

Fortunately, treatments have been developed to assist children and youth with phobias. A particularly effective treatment is cognitive behavioral therapy (CBT), which can range from 1 to 12 sessions. CBT helps the child or youth learn to use cognitive coping, replace anxious thoughts with more realistic thoughts, and gradually confront the feared situation. Relaxation strategies may be incorporated as well. Parents, school teachers, and others may be involved in the treatment depending on the age of the child and the nature of the problem. In some cases of social anxiety disorder or agoraphobia, medication may be prescribed together with CBT.

Karen J. Francis

See also: Cognitive Behavioral Therapy; Cognitive Therapy; DSM-5; Exposure, In Vivo; Exposure Treatment; Lifespan, Phobias Across the; One-Session Treatment; Phobia, Animal Type; Phobia, Blood-Injection-Injury Type; Phobia, Natural Environment Type; Phobia, Situational Type; Phobia, Specific; Phobias, Causes of; Phobias, Diagnosis of; Phobias, Family Influences on the Development and Maintenance of; Social Anxiety Disorder (Social Phobia)

Further Reading

Beesdo, Katja, Knappe, Susanne, & Pine, Daniel S. (2009). Anxiety and anxiety disorders in children and adolescents: Developmental issues and implications for DSM-V. *Psychiatric Clinics of North America, 32*, 483–524.

LeBeau, Richard T., Glenn, Daniel, Liao, Betty, Wittchen, Hans-Ulrich, Beesdo-Baum, Katja, Ollendick, Thomas, & Craske, Michelle G. (2010). Specific phobia: A review of DSM-IV specific phobia and preliminary recommendations for DSM-V. *Depression and Anxiety, 27*, 148–167.

Vasa, Roma A., & Roy, Amy K. (2013). Pediatric anxiety disorders: A clinical guide. *Current clinical psychiatry*. New York, NY: Springer.

DEVELOPMENTALLY APPROPRIATE FEARS

Frequent and varied fears are a normal part of childhood. Across cultures, children tend to experience fears of particular stimuli and events at the same age. With experience in the world, and concurrent cognitive development, children tend to "grow out of" fears as they learn that particular stimuli are not dangerous, or in some cases, even real.

Young children (ages 3–5) tend to fear novel stimuli that they have not encountered before such as animals and insects. It is also common for children to fear imaginary creatures like ghosts, witches, and monsters. Fear of the dark is also common at this age, particularly since ghosts, witches, and monsters are thought to lurk in dark rooms, closets, and under beds!

In middle childhood (ages 6–9), worries about animals can continue, as can fears of weather events like thunderstorms, hurricanes, and tornadoes. As children near the teen years (ages 9–12), it becomes common for youth to worry about their physical health. At this age, kids worry about getting shots and blood tests at the doctor and also express concern about vomiting or getting ill. As life becomes more challenging both academically and socially, youth also worry about their school performance and friendships.

In the late teens and early 20s, people begin to worry about driving and other stimuli associated with travel, like bridges, tunnels, and flying. These fears might be associated with the onset of panic attacks. People fear having panic attacks in situations where escape would be difficult or impossible, such as on airplanes or in the middle of long bridges.

Unique to the geriatric population is a fear of falling. Although all older adults should be conscious of falling since a broken bone (most often a hip) can lead to a cascade of other serious health consequences, this fear becomes so intense for some that it leads to significant avoidance of daily activities.

Although fears are very common across the lifespan, clinically significant phobias are far less prevalent. Clinical attention might be warranted if exposure to the feared stimuli causes extreme distress and/or if the fear leads to significant impairment (i.e., avoidance of situations for fear of encountering the feared stimuli). Cognitive behavioral therapy is an effective and efficient means of reducing fears and improving functioning for both children and adults.

Deborah Roth Ledley

Chronicity

Chronicity refers to the enduring and persistent nature of a disorder. Specific phobias tend to have a chronic and unremitting course, comparable to those of other anxiety disorders. On average, individuals with a specific phobia experience symptoms for approximately 20 years (Stinson et al., 2007). Phobias are most likely to develop in childhood, with a mean age of onset being 10 years of age (American Psychiatric Association, 2013). Epidemiological studies suggest that animal, blood-injection-injury, and natural environment phobia types tend to have the earliest onsets. By contrast, situational phobias and agoraphobia tend to have onsets later in life, often in adolescence or adulthood. Although most phobias develop in childhood, they can occur at any age, and later onsets are often the result of a traumatic experience with the phobic stimulus (e.g., the development of a phobia of dogs after being bitten). Phobias can wax and wane over the course of childhood, and many children with a specific phobia show full remission of symptoms. Common childhood phobias that often remit naturally include fears of the dark, strangers, animals, and loud noises. However, phobias that persist into adulthood tend to remain chronic, and remission without psychosocial treatment is unusual.

Individuals with a diagnosis of specific phobia most often have more than one phobia. Similarly, specific phobia is often comorbid with a range of other psychopathologies, such as other anxiety, mood, personality, and substance-related disorders. Due to its early onset, specific phobias tend to precede the development of these comorbid conditions, and individuals with phobic fears are at greater risk of developing additional mental health disorders. Fewer fears and lower fearfulness have both been associated with a less chronic course of specific phobia. Interestingly, severity of the phobia does not appear to be related to chronicity. Various protective factors, including social support and life satisfaction, are associated with higher remission rates of phobic fears. The factors impacting chronicity of phobic symptoms are currently not well understood and require further investigation.

Despite the chronicity of specific phobias and the availability of highly effective treatments, including cognitive behavioral therapy and exposure therapy, most people do not seek help for their phobic fears. In fact, specific phobias are most often diagnosed when individuals present for treatment of another disorder. Some authors have proposed that individuals with specific phobias do not seek treatment because their fears are associated with less distress and impairment due to their circumscribed nature. However, a number of studies have found that impairments associated with specific phobias are substantial and consistent with those observed in other anxiety disorders.

Dubravka L. Gavric

See also: Age of Onset; Agoraphobia; Childhood, Phobias in; Cognitive Behavioral Therapy; Exposure Treatment; Lifespan, Phobias across the; Phobia, Animal Type; Phobia, Blood-Injection-Injury Type; Phobia, Natural Environment Type; Phobia, Situational Type; Phobia Types

Further Reading

American Psychiatric Association. (2013). *Diagnostic and statistical manual of mental disorders* (5th ed.). Arlington, VA: American Psychiatric Publishing.

Stinson, Frederick S., Dawson, Deborah A., Chou, S. Patricia, Smith, Sharon, Goldstein, Rise B. Ruan, W. June, & Grant, Bridget F. (2007). The epidemiology of DSM-IV specific phobia in the USA: Results from the National Epidemiologic Survey on Alcohol and Related Conditions, *Psychological Medicine, 37*, 1047–1059.

Classical Conditioning

Classical conditioning is a type of associative learning in which two stimuli (e.g., tone and shock) are repeatedly paired, and behavioral responses that are first elicited by the second stimulus (shock) are eventually associated with and are produced when the first stimulus (tone) is presented alone. It has been suggested that fears and phobias develop via similar associative processes, thus making classical conditioning models an ideal tool for investigating the development, maintenance, and treatment of phobias.

At the beginning of the 20th century, Russian physiologist Ivan Pavlov (1849–1936) was conducting a series of experiments on the digestive process in dogs when he inadvertently observed one of the most important associative learning processes, now known as classical (Pavlovian) conditioning. He noticed that when the dogs were presented with food they would salivate, a natural, reflexive, behavioral response to food. But more importantly, the dogs eventually began to salivate before they had received the food; specifically, they would salivate at the sight of the lab assistants, who also happened to be the ones who fed them. Pavlov noted that the dogs had learned that the lab assistants were a cue that signaled ensuing food presentation and alone could induce the behavioral responses similar to those induced by food itself (i.e., salivation). Pavlov explored this phenomenon further in a series of follow-up studies in which he rang a tuning fork prior to presenting the dogs with meat powder. At first, only the meat powder elicited salivation, whereas the sound of the tuning fork did not, but after repeated pairings of the sound of the tuning fork followed by the meat powder the dogs began to salivate at the sound of the tuning fork. In fact, the dogs continued to salivate to the sound of the tuning fork even after the meat powder was no longer presented.

From these studies, Pavlov identified four key concepts of classical conditioning. The unconditioned stimulus (US) is a cue that naturally and reflexively elicits a target behavior, also known as the unconditioned response (UR). In his study, the US was the meat powder and the UR was salivation. The conditioned stimulus (CS) is initially a neutral cue, but after being paired with the US comes to elicit the target response. In Pavlov's studies, the CS was the sound of the tuning fork. Importantly, the timing between the presentation of the CS and US is critical. The CS must come before the US, and the closer in time the two occur, the faster and stronger learning will be. In fact, if the stimuli are spaced too far apart in time, associative learning will not occur. The behavioral response produced by the CS after conditioning is called a conditioned response (CR), which may or may not be the same as the UR. The fundamental difference between the UR and the CR is that the UR occurs as a result of the US, and the CR occurs in response to the CS.

In 1920, at Johns Hopkins University, an American psychologist John B. Watson (1878–1958) and his research assistant, Rosalie Rayner (1898–1935), translated Pavlov's studies of classical conditioning in animals to humans. In this seminal, yet highly unethical study by today's standards, Watson and Rayner conducted a classical fear conditioning experiment with a nine-month-old infant known as "Little Albert." At the beginning of the study Little Albert was presented with a white rat (CS), which he initially did not fear. He was also presented with a sudden loud noise (US) made by a hammer hitting a steel bar, which caused him to cry. When Watson and Rayner presented Little Albert with the white rat and seconds later hit the steel bar with the hammer, the boy began to show fear responses to the rat, such as crying and attempts to crawl away (CR). In fact, Little Albert's fear of the white rat generalized to other fuzzy white objects, like a rabbit, a Santa beard, and even Watson's white hair. Not only did Watson and Rayner demonstrate that classical conditioning occurs in humans but they also provided evidence to suggest how phobias may develop through classical conditioning.

This study was important for demonstrating how fears can be learned and become maladaptive, as in the case of phobias, through classical conditioning. Fear learning is an adaptive mechanism that protects an individual from harm. It is a unique form of learning in that it can be acquired in as little as one pairing yet has long-lasting effects. For instance, an individual may consider dogs to be neutral; however, an aversive experience with a dog, like being bitten, could lead to a lasting fear or phobia of all dogs. Classical fear conditioning is the most fruitful behavioral paradigm for exploring how fears are formed and phobias develop. Furthermore, it also has revealed brain mechanisms thought to be important for mediating this type of learning and memory, such as the amygdala.

Christine A. Rabinak

See also: Amygdala; Fear; Fear, Animal Models of; Fear Generalization; Pavlov, Ivan (1849–1936); Phobias, Causes of; Watson, John B. (1878–1958)

Further Reading

Delamater, Andrew R. (2012). On the nature of CS and US representations in Pavlovian learning. *Learning and Behavior, 40*, 1–23.

Classification

Classification refers to the process of categorizing things based on similarities in their qualities or characteristics. Classification is a fundamental aspect of science. In order for experts to be able to communicate with one another, they need a common language. When phenomena are objectively and reliably labeled and organized, experts can build on existing knowledge with new findings. The classification of phobias is part of the broader classification of mental disorders, which is also referred to as *psychiatric nosology* or *taxonomy*.

Classifying behavior and mental phenomena and carving out boundaries between "normal" and "abnormal" present challenges distinct from those involved in classifying things like plants and organic compounds. Accordingly, the classification of mental disorders such as phobias has been associated with numerous controversies, ranging from questions of whether classification is even possible to those relating to boundaries between specific disorder categories. One of the greatest debates is whether the classification of mental disorders should be organized based on distinct categories (e.g., specific phobia, panic disorder, generalized anxiety disorder), along dimensions (e.g., continuum of threat imminence), or some combination of the two. Despite these challenges, current classification systems are based on the best available evidence, and they allow researchers and clinicians to study and understand phobias, as well as to develop effective treatments.

Current classification of phobias is described in published classification systems, most notably the *Diagnostic and Statistical Manual of Mental Disorders*, fifth edition (DSM-5; American Psychiatric Association, 2013) in North America and the *International Classification of Diseases*, 10th revision (ICD-10; World Health Organization, 1992) worldwide. In the United States, a clinical modification of the ICD—the ICD-10-CM—is also used for classification purposes. Whereas the DSM classification is limited to mental disorders, the ICD is a classification system for a broad range of diseases, disorders, injuries, and other health problems. Both classification systems are categorical in nature, whereby a disorder is assumed to be either present or absent based on specific criteria. Further, both systems are used to inform research, policy, and health care. In a clinical context, these classification systems assist clinicians with determining a diagnosis and developing a treatment plan.

The DSM-5 classifies phobias as *anxiety disorders*, which are characterized by excessive fear and anxiety and related behavioral disturbances. This category of disorders includes specific phobias, which are further classified into several types (animal, natural environment, blood-injection-injury, situational, and "other"); social anxiety disorder (social phobia); agoraphobia; and a range of other anxiety disorders such as panic disorder and generalized anxiety disorder. In the DSM-5, anxiety disorders are a stand-alone disorder category that is not subsumed under any other category.

In the ICD-10, phobias are classified as *phobic anxiety disorders*. This group of disorders is characterized by anxiety evoked by circumscribed situations or objects that are not currently dangerous. The situations or objects are avoided or endured with dread. The phobic anxiety disorders include agoraphobia, social phobias, specific (isolated) phobias, other phobic anxiety disorders, and phobic anxiety disorder, unspecified. The ICD-10 does not describe specific phobia subtypes, although it should be noted that the ICD-10-CM includes the same subtypes as the DSM-5. In the ICD-10, phobic anxiety disorders belong to the broader category of *stress-related and somatoform disorders*, which in turn belong to the overarching category of *mental and behavioral disorders*.

Although there is considerable overlap between the two classification systems in the criteria required for a diagnosis of an anxiety disorder, there nevertheless exist differences that might translate to an individual being classified as positive for a diagnosis in one system and negative in the other system. For example, one study reported that the ICD-10 and an earlier version of the DSM (DSM-IV-Text Revision) identify different children as having an anxiety disorder (Adornetto, Suppiger, In-Albon, Neuschwander, & Schneider, 2012). Such differences in classification can hinder communication between experts and impede research progress. In acknowledgment of this concern, there has been increasing effort to "harmonize" the two classification systems, in particular the DSM-5 and the mental and behavioral disorders section of the upcoming version of the ICD, the ICD-11.

Irena Milosevic

See also: Anxiety and Related Disorders; Differential Diagnosis; DSM-5; *International Classification of Diseases*; Phobia Types; Phobias, Diagnosis of; Phobias, History of

Further Reading

Adornetto, Carmen, Suppiger, Andrea, In-Albon, Tina, Neuschwander, Murielle, & Schneider, Silvia. (2012). Concordances and discrepancies between ICD-10 and DSM-IV criteria for anxiety disorders in childhood and adolescence. *Child & Adolescent Psychiatry & Mental Health, 6*, 40.

American Psychiatric Association. (2013). *Diagnostic and statistical manual of mental disorders* (5th ed.). Arlington, VA: American Psychiatric Publishing.

World Health Organization. (1992). *The ICD-10 classification of mental and behavioural disorders: Clinical descriptions and diagnostic guidelines*. Geneva: World Health Organization.

Claustrophobia (Fear of Enclosed Spaces)

Claustrophobia, originating from the Latin *claustrum*, meaning "a shut-in place," and the Greek *phobos*, meaning fear, refers to a fear of enclosed spaces, such as elevators, closets, or crowds. In current diagnostic systems, claustrophobia is classified as a specific phobia of the situational type. About 3.3% of individuals in the population receive a diagnosis of claustrophobia (Depla, ten Have, van Balkom, & de Graaf, 2008). The age of onset is typically 15 years (Depla et al., 2008) and it is more common in women than men (Fredrikson, Annas, Fischer, & Wik, 1996).

Individuals with claustrophobia typically report physiological symptoms of anxiety, such as elevated heart rate, sweating, and shaking when in an enclosed space, such as a crowded room or elevator. They may also report cognitive symptoms of anxiety, such as thoughts that they cannot manage their anxiety, when encountering these situations. As a result of these symptoms, individuals may start to avoid situations where they are likely to encounter enclosed spaces. For example, they may avoid visiting friends who live in a high-rise apartment building in order to avoid being in an elevator. To receive a diagnosis of claustrophobia, these symptoms must cause them clinically significant distress or interference. For example, a person may forgo important medical diagnostic tests in order to avoid being in a magnetic resonance imaging (MRI) scanner.

Symptoms of claustrophobia overlap with symptoms of agoraphobia. Individuals with both disorders may report fear of enclosed spaces. What differentiate individuals with claustrophobia from individuals with agoraphobia are both the range of

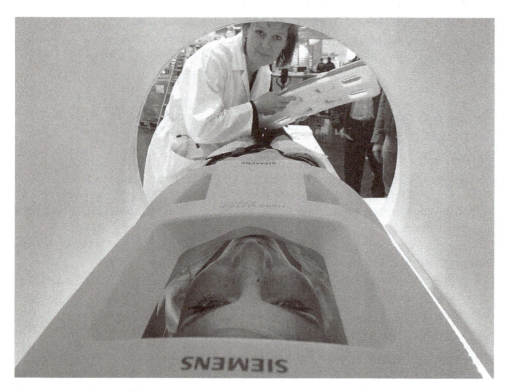

A woman lies in a state-of-the-art magnetic resonance tomograph (MRT) at an international medical fair. This MRT, designed as a short tunnel with a large opening, may be more accessible to people with claustrophobia, who are highly fearful of being in small enclosed spaces. (AP Photo/Martin Meissner)

feared situations and the thoughts associated with these situations. Individuals with claustrophobia will report only fear of enclosed spaces, whereas individuals with agoraphobia will also report fear of other situations, such as wide-open spaces (e.g., parks, parking lots) or public transportation. Individuals with agoraphobia report that they fear these situations because they think that escape might be difficult. By contrast, research suggests that beliefs associated with claustrophobia are related to the fear of suffocation and the fear of restriction (Rachman & Taylor, 1993).

Cognitive behavioral therapy, which involves exposure to feared situations or objects, is currently the recommended treatment for claustrophobia. For example, an individual may be asked to ride a crowded elevator until symptoms of anxiety decline. Virtual reality, in which the individual is exposed to a virtual situation rather than a real situation, has also been used with success in the treatment of claustrophobia (Botella, Villa, Baños, Perpiñá, & García-Palacios, 2000). Treatment may also involve identifying and reevaluating beliefs related to feared situations, such as the belief that one will run out of air or will be unable to manage physiological symptoms of anxiety.

Andrea R. Ashbaugh

See also: Agoraphobia; Anxiety and Related Disorders; Phobia, Situational Type; Phobia, Specific; Phobia Types

Further Reading

Botella, Cristina, Baños, Rosa M., Villa, Helena, Perpiñá, Conxa, & García-Palacios, Azucena. (2000). Virtual reality in the treatment of claustrophobic fear: A controlled, multiple-baseline design. *Behavior Therapy, 31*, 583–595.

Depla, Marja F., ten Have, Margreet L., van Balkom, Anton J., & de Graaf, Ron. (2008). Specific fears and phobias in the general population: Results from the Netherlands Mental Health Survey and Incidence Study (NEMESIS). *Social Psychiatry and Psychiatric Epidemiology, 43*, 200–208.

Fredrikson, Mats, Annas, Peter, Fischer, Håkan, & Wik, Gustav. (1996). Gender and age differences in prevalence of specific fears and phobias. *Behaviour Research and Therapy, 34*, 33–39.

Rachman, Stanley J., & Taylor, Steven. (1993). Analyses of claustrophobia. *Journal of Anxiety Disorders, 7*, 281–291.

Cognitive Behavioral Therapy

Cognitive behavioral therapy (CBT) is a form of psychotherapy that focuses on the relationship between a person's thoughts (i.e., "cognitions"), his or her behaviors, and his or her emotional reactions. The strategies used in CBT help people modify any unhelpful or inaccurate thoughts as well as to change maladaptive behaviors in an attempt to help them manage and/or change difficult symptoms and emotions. CBT has been well researched and is a very effective form of therapy for a number of mental health issues and emotional difficulties, including specific phobias (Dobson, 2010). In fact, exposure therapy (one strategy used in CBT) is the treatment of choice for specific phobias.

CBT has its roots in both behavioral and cognitive therapy traditions. Behavior therapy was a widely used therapeutic style in the mid-1900s and focused explicitly on observable behaviors, with little interest in any unobservable experiences. Behavior therapy was popularized by the work of people like Joseph Wolpe, who paired relaxation strategies with exposure to feared objects in a method called systematic desensitization. Systematic desensitization, used to help people reduce overwhelming fears, is the precursor to modern-day methods of overcoming fears with CBT. In the 1970s and 1980s, there was a renewed interest in understanding people's perceptions and ways of thinking about difficult events, which led to a widespread use of strategies to understand and challenge people's way of thinking. These strategies were known collectively as cognitive therapy and were pioneered by individuals such as Aaron T. Beck and Albert Ellis, who used the strategies to help people suffering from problems like depression and anxiety. Some clinicians paired behavioral and cognitive strategies early on to target stress and emotional difficulties, such as Donald Meichenbaum who called his therapeutic style "cognitive behavior modification." All these efforts provided the groundwork for modern-day CBT.

CBT is a time-limited therapy that aims to teach people strategies for reducing and/or managing difficult emotions such as fear. Depending on the presenting concern and the particular setting, a course of CBT may be as little as one session (in the case of overcoming some specific phobias, such as a mild to moderate fear of spiders; Öst, Salkovskis, & Hellström, 1991) or it may be over 20 sessions (for a more complicated set of symptoms such as severe obsessive-compulsive symptoms). Most research studies suggest that a typical course of CBT for mood, anxiety, or related problems is 12–16 sessions held on a weekly basis, with a decidedly shorter number of sessions for most specific phobias. For the most part, CBT focuses on the present day and on collecting information about the thoughts and behaviors that are contributing to the person's current symptoms and ongoing distress. This does not mean, however, that a therapist conducting CBT should ignore relevant events in a person's childhood or history. For example, if the onset of a height phobia began after a person nearly fell off a high balcony, the therapist needs to know this information and include it in the development of a treatment plan. The emphasis in CBT is simply more on how symptoms are maintained in the present day through the overuse of unhelpful thoughts and behaviors. Consider the case of the fear of heights described earlier; although it is very helpful for the therapist to know that the person almost had a catastrophic experience on a balcony, it is even more important for the therapist to understand how much the client is avoiding almost any high place, even ones that are objectively safe.

CBT has several main components, all of which rely on a good working relationship between therapist and client. Unlike some other forms of therapy where there is a stronger power differential between therapist and client, the relation-ship between client and therapist in CBT aims to be collaborative. In other words, the therapist actively works with the client to help the client develop necessary skills and strategies to meet the client's goals. The client's goals can include both short-term (e.g., "visit my aunt who lives on the 17th floor of an apartment build-ing") and long-term (e.g., "fly to Europe for a vacation at some point in the next two years") goals. Movement toward goals is actively monitored and checked throughout the course of therapy. When providing CBT, therapists also aim to be Socratic in style. *Socratic dialogue* (which stems from the philosopher Socrates's style of questioning) refers to the therapist's efforts to understand the client's experience and to modify the client's understanding of something through the use of strategic questioning rather than by bluntly telling the client what to do or think.

CBT relies on a thorough assessment of a person's presenting concerns, symp-toms, and coping behaviors. Once the assessment is complete, the therapist creates a conceptualization of the presenting problem, which guides him or her in develop-ing a treatment plan. Not all strategies used in CBT will be relevant for each client, so the therapist needs to select the strategies that will most likely help a particular client. For example, the main strategy used in the treatment of phobias is exposure therapy (described later in the entry), and therefore the majority of time spent in ses-sions would be focused on planning, conducting, and reviewing exposure exercises. In some forms of CBT, the most effective strategies identified by research are rec-ommended for all clients with a particular presenting problem, and these strategies may be combined in a manual to be used with all clients. However, even when the strategies are outlined in a manual, it is important for the therapist to have a good understanding of the client's symptoms so that necessary adjustments to tailor the therapy to the particular client can be made.

There are several key strategies used in CBT, including symptom monitoring, cognitive restructuring, exposure therapy, and behavioral activation. Symptom monitoring entails having clients write down examples of their symptoms when they occur along with relevant details. An example of this might be for clients to notice their emotional reaction (e.g., anxiety, sadness, guilt, etc.) in a particular situation, as well as any thoughts, worries, or assumptions that went along with the emotion. For example, a person with a height phobia might notice feelings of anxi-ety and apprehension while anticipating visiting a friend who lives in a high-rise apartment building. This person might also notice having thoughts that the friend will want to sit on the balcony (even if it is a cold winter day) and then predicting that the balcony railing will be faulty. This type of monitoring helps the therapist fully understand the person's concerns.

Cognitive restructuring is a technique in which clients identify their unhelpful or inaccurate thoughts, and work to challenge or rework these thoughts into more adaptive ways of thinking. For example, the height-fearful person described earlier, who worries that the railing on a balcony is not secure, would work with the therapist to search for evidence to support or dispute this prediction. Ultimately, that person would hopefully realize that the risk of the railing collapsing is low.

Exposure therapy is a behavioral technique that involves asking clients to repeatedly and systematically approach feared objects and situations until they are more comfortable. For example, an exposure goal for someone with a fear of heights might be to look out the window of a room on the 10th floor for long enough and repeatedly enough until anxiety levels begin to decline. Another behavioral technique is behavioral activation, which involves planning small and manageable goals in one's day to reverse patterns of avoidance and poor motivation commonly seen when people are depressed.

All of the therapeutic strategies used in CBT have to be practiced on a regular basis, and therefore clients are assigned "homework" after each therapy session of skills to practice between sessions. Regular and consistent homework completion appears to be associated with better outcome from therapy. At the end of a course of CBT, clients are taught skills to help prevent a relapse of their symptoms.

One of the things that sets CBT apart from many other forms of psychotherapy is the extent to which it has been evaluated by research. Researchers have compared the effectiveness of CBT against treatment as usual, waitlists, and other forms of therapy. Researchers have also attempted to figure out the most effective and necessary aspects of CBT in studies known as "dismantling" studies. For some types of problems (e.g., CBT for anxiety disorders), there are so many studies of the effectiveness of CBT that the study results are combined together and evaluated en masse in what is known as a meta-analysis. Less research has tackled the question of exactly how CBT works, but that is a focus of many present-day researchers. The extensive research support of CBT has made this a popular and cost-effective mode of therapy. CBT has been shown to be effective for many types of emotional problems, such as anxiety disorders (including specific phobias), depression, eating disorders, coping with certain health conditions, chronic pain, managing some symptoms of schizophrenia, substance use disorders, and insomnia, among others.

Although traditional CBT is offered in a therapist's office, researchers and therapists have been exploring other ways to offer this treatment, especially to people who live in remote areas or who have physical or psychological barriers to attending an in-person session. For example, studies have examined CBT offered via the Internet, at the client's home, through self-help means (e.g., via a self-help book), and in a group format. It appears that CBT offered in a variety of formats is helpful.

Karen Rowa

See also: Beck, Aaron T. (1921–); Behavior Therapy; Cognitive Restructuring; Cognitive Therapy; Ellis, Albert (1913–2007); Exposure Treatment; Systematic Desensitization; Wolpe, Joseph (1915–1997)

Further Reading

Dobson, Keith S. (2010). *Handbook of cognitive-behavioral therapies* (3rd ed.). New York, NY: Guilford Press.

Öst, Lars-Göran, Salkovskis, Paul M., & Hellström, Kerstin. (1991). One-session therapist-directed exposure vs. self-exposure in the treatment of spider phobia. *Behavior Therapy, 22,* 407–422.

FEAR IN THE LABORATORY: THE ANXIETY AND OBSESSIVE-COMPULSIVE DISORDERS LABORATORY

Founded in 2001, the Anxiety and Obsessive-Compulsive Disorders Laboratory is located at Concordia University in Montreal, Canada. The director of the lab, Dr. Adam Radomsky, is professor of psychology at Concordia University and co-editor in chief of the *Journal of Behavior Therapy and Experimental Psychiatry.* The lab's main focus is experimental psychopathology as it pertains to anxiety and related disorders (such as obsessive-compulsive disorder, or OCD), as well as research on enhancing both the effectiveness and acceptability of cognitive behavior therapy (CBT). Many of the lab's studies are designed to examine key cognitive variables proposed to be at the heart of a range of anxiety disorders and related problems. These include relatively straightforward thoughts/beliefs (e.g., those pertaining to perceived danger), and more novel domains (e.g., beliefs about memory, moral values).

Although many of the studies and experiments taking place in the lab focus on OCD, a large proportion are designed to have transdiagnostic applicability; this is based on the assumption that most anxiety-related problems share similar underlying (cognitive) processes, as do different therapies. Realistic environments and stimuli are created in the laboratory in order to elicit emotional and behavioral responses that are similar to those that anxious individuals would experience when confronting fears in their daily lives. For instance, a spider-phobic individual may be presented with a live tarantula, while a contamination-fearful individual may confront a garbage can. One of the features of the laboratory is a fully functional kitchen designed for the study of obsessions and (mostly checking and washing) compulsions. Assessments of fear are completed using a variety of methods, including Subjective Units of Distress Scale, which require a person to rate his or her fear; standardized questionnaires; behavioral approach tests, which measure how close a person can get to the feared stimulus; and semistructured interviews, which collect detailed information about a person's symptoms and how they impact the person's life.

A current focus of the lab's research is how cognitive-behavioral interventions for anxiety and OCD can be made more acceptable and efficacious, such as by the judicious use of safety behavior. For instance, a study with spider-fearful participants suggested that using safety behavior (e.g., wearing gloves) not only enhanced cognitive change during a behavioral experiment but also enabled fearful participants to approach a live tarantula more closely. This is important because at a closer distance of approach, someone might be able to obtain more (helpful) information about the spider, which would not be available to them at a distance (e.g., patterns of movement, interesting features). At present, research is under way to determine whether these findings can be replicated with samples of contamination-fearful individuals. It is thought that by permitting clients to use safety behavior during therapeutic interventions, such as *in vivo* exposure, they may feel less anxious and more in control, and may therefore be able to obtain more helpful information.

Adam S. Radomsky, Rachael L. Neal, Sarah E. Schell,
and Jessica S. Tutino

Cognitive Bias Modification

Individuals with anxiety disorders have a tendency to automatically and selectively orient their attention to negative or threatening stimuli in the environment (attention bias) and to interpret ambiguous information negatively (interpretation bias). For instance, when giving a speech, individuals with social anxiety disorder (social phobia) are more likely to notice and orient to negative or threatening information (e.g., someone yawning) and to interpret the information as a signal that they are performing poorly. Cognitive bias modification is an innovative approach used to modify the information processing biases that underlie the development and maintenance of anxiety disorders. Cognitive bias modification procedures utilize computer tasks that implicitly teach individuals to orient their attention to neutral/positive stimuli and to adopt neutral or positive interpretations of ambiguous information. Although there is some early evidence for the effectiveness of cognitive bias modification interventions in decreasing anxiety symptoms, this research is still in its early stages and is characterized by several limitations.

The *modified dot-probe task* is most commonly used for attention training. During this task, individuals are first presented a fixation cross in the middle of the computer screen for 500 milliseconds (ms) followed by two stimuli, one neutral and one negative or threatening, that are presented simultaneously. After 500 ms, the stimuli disappear and a neutral probe (an arrow or a dot) appears in the same location as one of the stimuli. Individuals are asked to indicate the location of the probe as quickly as possible by pressing one of two keys. During attention training, the probe consistently replaces the neutral stimuli across repeated trials. Accordingly, individuals learn to orient toward the neutral stimuli since doing so facilitates their ability to identify the probe as quickly as possible. The stimuli that are presented during attention training vary depending on the nature of the anxiety that is being targeted. For instance, for individuals with social anxiety disorder, the stimuli presented include photographs of neutral and negative faces because the main focus of fear is negative evaluation from others. On the other hand, for individuals with specific phobias, the stimuli presented include the feared object (e.g., a dog or a spider) paired with a neutral or pleasant stimulus (e.g., flower).

Although two computerized tasks have been developed for interpretation training, the Mathews and Mackintosh (2000) *scenario paradigm* has been most widely used and studied. During this task, individuals are presented with a brief description of an ambiguous situation that ends with a word fragment that, when solved, disambiguates the scenario in a positive or negative direction. Individuals are required to solve the word fragment as quickly as possible. After solving the word fragment, they are presented with a comprehension question that reinforces the direction in which the scenario was disambiguated. Individuals receive feedback ("You are correct" or "You are incorrect") after answering the comprehension question. In interpretation training, the ambiguous scenarios are consistently disambiguated in a positive direction. The following is an example of a scenario from an interpretation training task targeting social anxiety:

> You arrange to meet a friend in town. Last time you met you had an argument and parted on bad terms. Just before you leave she phones to say that she can't make it. You think that this is because she is feeling unw—l.

The fragment in this example is resolved with the word *unwell*. This disambiguation is in the positive direction because the interpretation of the friend's cancellation is external rather than personal. The Mathews and Mackintosh (2000) scenario paradigm was initially developed for social anxiety disorder but has since been adapted for obsessive-compulsive disorder, anxiety sensitivity (the tendency to respond fearfully to anxiety-related sensations), and worry.

Although early studies suggested much promise for cognitive bias modification as a novel intervention for anxiety disorders, more recent studies have generated mixed findings. There is some evidence that cognitive bias modification procedures decrease self-reported anxiety symptoms and susceptibility to anxiety when encountering a stressor. However, the magnitude of the difference between the training and control conditions ranges from small to medium (Mogoase, David, & Koster, 2014). Moreover, there is a lack of consistent empirical evidence for the generalizability of the effects of attention or interpretation training to naturalistic settings and to measures of information processing biases that are contextually different from the procedures used for training. Studies to date have been limited by small sample sizes, variability in the number of training sessions administered, limited use of clinically anxious participants, and short follow-up periods. There is a need for future research to examine the effects of cognitive bias modification procedures on social functioning and anxiety in real-world situations and to investigate the mechanisms of change underlying cognitive bias modification procedures. Continued research focused on addressing the aforementioned limitations will assist researchers and clinicians in assessing the utility of cognitive bias modification procedures in the treatment of phobias and other anxiety disorders.

Matilda E. Nowakowski

See also: Information Processing Biases

Further Reading

Mathews, Andrew, & Mackintosh, Bundy. (2000). Induced emotional interpretation bias and anxiety. *Journal of Abnormal Psychology, 109*, 602–615.

Mogoase, Cristina, David, Daniel, & Koster, Ernst H. W. (2014). Clinical efficacy of attentional bias modification procedures: An updated meta-analysis. *Journal of Clinical Psychology, 1*, 1–25.

Cognitive Model

The cognitive model is a framework for understanding and treating a range of emotional problems, including phobic disorders. The model is rooted in the work of two pioneers of this approach, Albert Ellis and Aaron T. Beck, who both stressed the role of cognition in emotion and behavior. The cognitive model of phobias centers on the role of maladaptive beliefs in maintaining fear.

In the 1950s, Ellis developed rational emotive behavior therapy. He posited that individuals are well when they hold rational beliefs and that problems develop when they hold irrational beliefs. Subsequently, irrational beliefs lead to dysfunctional behavior. For example, the thought that all animals are unpredictable and dangerous leads to avoidance of them.

In 1963, Beck proposed a cognitive model of depression. This model states that ideas and concepts in our minds, called *schemas*, affect the ways we think. Beck argued that schemas can be dysfunctional and are therefore responsible for causing and maintaining emotional problems. Further, one remembers, notices, and retains information that is consistent with one's distorted views. For example, an individual who fears dogs would more likely remember news about dog attacks than benign experiences with these animals.

In the late 1970s, Albert Bandura proposed another cognitive approach to understanding behavior, the self-efficacy theory. He argued that a person's perceived self-efficacy or ability to carry out specific and effective courses of action, and their expectations for the outcome of such actions, determine subsequent action. For example, an individual who screams upon contact with dogs is more likely to believe that he or she cannot face dogs and will avoid them in the future.

Today, building upon these cognitive approaches, the general cognitive model proposes that human emotion and behavior can be explained by people's thoughts, including other aspects of cognition such as attention and memory. Selective attention and memory for fear-relevant information produce biased automatic thoughts and interpretations of phobic stimuli as dangerous. Therefore, errors in the processing of threatening information are part of the cognitive framework. Specific cognitive models for a variety of emotional problems, including phobias, have been developed based on this proposal. These models are tested experimentally, refined, and used to better understand and treat emotional problems.

The general cognitive model of phobic disorders proposes that an individual's cognitions, promoted by schemas that may in part stem from frightening past experiences, can create a sense of vulnerability to a particular stimulus. These thoughts typically include beliefs that the stimulus is unpredictable, dangerous, disgusting, and/or harmful. Furthermore, thoughts related to a distorted sense of self-efficacy about one's capacity to cope in the presence of a frightening stimulus also contribute to fear. For example, people with a phobia of dogs might believe that a dog can bite them at any time and that they might "die of fright" if they pass a dog in the street. Due to these beliefs, when they see a dog approaching they might cross the road to avoid it. This behavior maintains negative beliefs about the dog (they miss an opportunity to learn that the dog might not, in fact, bite them) and beliefs that they cannot cope with meeting a dog (they miss an opportunity to learn that they can cope with their fear in the dog's presence). Research on the cognitive model of specific phobias confirms that having negative beliefs about phobic stimuli does indeed maintain fear. Further support comes from research demonstrating that instilling a sense of control in phobic individuals and having them learn the predictability of a phobic stimulus reduce their fear/anxiety.

Cognitive therapy for phobias targets dysfunctional beliefs about feared objects or situations and about one's ability to cope with them. Although there are few large-scale trials of cognitive therapy for specific phobia, evidence suggests that this method is most effective for treating claustrophobia (Choy, Fyer, & Lipsitz, 2007). Whereas a cognitive approach is just as good as behavior therapy in reducing fear, it does not enhance treatment for phobias over and above behavioral approaches.

Gillian M. Alcolado, Sasha L. MacNeil, Kelsey Hannon,
and Adam S. Radomsky

See also: Bandura, Albert (1925–); Beck, Aaron T. (1921–); Cognitive Restructuring; Cognitive Therapy; Ellis, Albert (1913–2007); Exposure, Imaginal; Exposure, *In Vivo*; Information Processing Biases; Phobic Beliefs; Rachman, Jack (1934–)

Further Reading

Beck, Aaron T. (1967). *The diagnosis and management of depression*. Pennsylvania, PA: University of Pennsylvania Press.

Choy, Yujuan, Fyer, Abby J., & Lipsitz, Josh D. (2007). Treatment of specific phobia in adults. *Clinical Psychology Review*, 27, 266–286.

Clark, David A., & Beck, Aaron T. (2010). Cognitive theory and therapy of anxiety and depression: Convergence with neurobiological findings. *Trends in Cognitive Sciences, 14*, 418–424.

Cognitive Restructuring

Cognitive restructuring, pioneered by Aaron T. Beck in cognitive therapy and Albert Ellis in rational emotive behavior therapy, is a therapeutic tool used to identify and modify one's maladaptive thoughts and beliefs, to decrease suffering and to improve functioning. With respect to the treatment of specific phobia, cognitive restructuring has been shown to be helpful in the reduction of problematic beliefs related to the danger of feared stimuli such as enclosed spaces, animals, and physical symptoms. Cognitive therapy researchers and practitioners maintain that our thoughts and beliefs about ourselves and the world around us impact our emotions and behavior. Beliefs that lead to negative emotions such as fear or sadness are not necessarily maladaptive; such emotions are normal and at times necessary to maintain safety, relationships, and/or well-being. Maladaptive beliefs impair normal functioning (e.g., social, work/school), or cause undue suffering, typically because they are exaggerated and/or applied to inappropriate situations. For example, the thought "This animal is dangerous" is adaptive when it compels an individual to escape a bear in the woods. When encountering an ant in the bathtub, however, this same belief is maladaptive if the emotional and behavioral consequences (i.e., fear, avoidance) cause needless distress and interfere with daily functioning, as seen in specific phobia.

In therapy, cognitive restructuring typically consists of three main stages. First, the therapist, along with the client, identifies the thoughts and beliefs leading to the dysfunctional behavior and/or emotions. Some thoughts and beliefs may be automatic, firmly held, and not accessible to the client without guided introspection. Second, the therapist and client evaluate the validity and usefulness of these beliefs. The therapist may try to help the client make links between his or her problematic emotions and behavior, and the maladaptive thought pattern that contributes to the disordered function. Finally, when necessary, the therapist and client work together to restructure these cognitions to be more useful and conducive to good mental health.

Although exposure therapy is the treatment of choice for phobias, cognitive restructuring can be applied in conjunction with or in place of exposure therapy.

Maladaptive cognitions are present in all types of phobias (e.g., insect phobia). Cognitive restructuring often begins with *guided discovery*, a series of questions posed to identify the most problematic maladaptive beliefs (e.g., "Insects are dangerous") and automatic, negative assumptions or predictions that arise from them (e.g., "I must escape this insect to stay safe"). *Socratic questioning* promotes evaluation of the evidence that either supports or contradicts the problematic beliefs or biased thinking (e.g., "How many people have been killed by insects?"). Specific tools to generate this evidence include psychoeducation, thought records, informal surveys, or engaging in role-plays. Clients may also test the validity/usefulness of their beliefs in behavioral experiments. Psychological treatments that include cognitive restructuring techniques have received empirical support and are associated with significant reductions in problematic cognitions and symptoms of anxiety.

Kevin C. Barber, Eleanor Donegan, Allison J. Ouimet, and Adam S. Radomsky

See also: Beck, Aaron T. (1921–); Behavioral Experiment; Cognitive Model; Cognitive Therapy; Ellis, Albert (1913–2007); Exposure Treatment

Further Reading

Beck, Judith S. (1995). *Cognitive therapy: Basics and beyond.* New York, NY: Guilford Press.

Hood, Heather K. & Antony, Martin M. (2012). Evidence-based assessment and treatment of specific phobias in adults. In Thompson E. Davis, Thomas H. Ollendick, & Lars-Göran Öst (Eds.), *Intensive one-session treatment of specific phobias* (pp. 19–42). New York, NY: Springer Science + Business Media.

Cognitive Therapy

Cognitive therapy, based on the cognitive model developed by Aaron T. Beck, addresses maladaptive beliefs and cognitive distortions associated with an individual's fear. Cognitive therapy uses specific techniques that aim to change or modify beliefs through the reinterpretation of the content of thoughts, the relationship the individual has with his or her thoughts, and/or the amount of attention/importance these thoughts have received. In fear-based disorders, such as specific phobia, belief change plays a critical role in symptom change. Although behavior therapy techniques, such as exposure, can indirectly achieve belief change, cognitive therapy directly targets the maladaptive beliefs and other thoughts associated with the phobia.

Cognitive therapy begins with psychoeducation about the cognitive model of phobias. The therapist then helps the client identify his or her fear-related beliefs through Socratic questioning (questions aimed at helping the client uncover automatic thoughts, assumptions, or evidence), or the use of thought records (forms used to record fear-related situations and the thoughts that occur during these situations). This process can help identify the maladaptive beliefs a client holds. Two main forms of maladaptive beliefs associated with phobias include *probability overestimation* (believing that feared outcomes are more likely to occur than they actually are; e.g., the spider will definitely bite me) and *catastrophization* (believing that the feared outcome would be much worse than it really would; e.g., a spider bite will kill me instantly). The therapist and client then work together to reevaluate the client's maladaptive beliefs through Socratic questioning, cognitive restructuring, behavioral experiments, and exposure (with a focus on changing thinking and beliefs).

The use of behavioral experiments is a highly promising cognitive therapy technique that was not consistently implemented in earlier forms of cognitive therapy. Behavioral experiments involve choosing a specific maladaptive belief to target, and coming up with an experiment the individual can conduct that will provide him or her with new information about the accuracy of his or her belief. It is suggested that behavioral experiments may lead to more effective belief change than the use of thought records and cognitive restructuring, given their experiential nature (i.e., seeing first-hand that a belief is not necessarily true rather than just discussing this idea).

Cognitive therapy has been shown to be an effective solo or adjunctive treatment for certain specific phobias; however, its effectiveness appears to differ based on the type of phobia. For example, in the treatment of claustrophobia, both cognitive therapy alone and cognitive therapy in combination with *in vivo* exposure have been shown to be successful. Conversely, as an adjunct to *in vivo* exposure, cognitive therapy did not enhance symptom relief in the treatment of spider and flying phobias. Due to its limited utility in the treatment of specific phobias, cognitive therapy is generally not considered a first-line treatment.

Jessica M. Senn, Sarah McIlwaine, and Adam S. Radomsky

See also: Beck, Aaron T. (1921–); Behavioral Experiment; Cognitive Model; Cognitive Restructuring

Further Reading

Choy, Yujuan, Fyer, Abby, J., & Lipsitz, Josh D. (2007). Treatment of specific phobia in adults. *Clinical Psychology Review, 27,* 266–286.

McManus, Freda, Van Doorn, Karlijn, & Yiend, Jenny. (2012). Examining the effects of thought records and behavioral experiments in instigating belief change. *Journal of Behavior Therapy and Experimental Psychiatry, 43,* 540–547.

ODDS OF DEATH FROM COMMON FEARED EVENTS

Individuals with phobias often report that their feared events are highly likely to occur. However, in most cases, these negative predictions are in fact unlikely to be realized. This type of unrealistic prediction is called *probability overestimation*. A common probability overestimation made by individuals with phobias is the prediction of harm, including death, in the feared situation. One way of correcting such predictions is to ask individuals to confront or enter their feared situation so they can learn that it is not dangerous. Another way of helping them to develop a more realistic perspective is to ask them to consider factual information about the likelihood of harm. Such information can be acquired from a variety of places, with reports by the National Safety Council (NSC) being a particularly good resource. The following is a list of the lifetime odds of death in the United States, as reported by the NSC in 2010, for events that are often feared in different types of phobias. When reviewing these, consider whether you have been making any probability overestimations!

Phobia	Feared Situation	Lifetime Odds of Death
Driving phobia	Motor vehicle incidents	1 in 112
Water phobia	Unintentional drowning and submersion	1 in 1,043
Choking phobia	Choking from inhalation and ingestion of food	1 in 3,649
Flying phobia	Air and space transport incidents*	1 in 8,357
Animal phobia (bees, insects)	Contact with hornets, wasps, and bees	1 in 75,852
Storm phobia	Cataclysmic storm	1 in 83,922
Dog phobia	Bitten or struck by dog	1 in 103,798
Storm/thunder & lightening phobia	Lightning	1 in 136,011

*Includes air taxis and private flights

Irena Milosevic

Comorbidity

Comorbidity refers to the coexistence of one or more disorders in addition to the principal or main disorder identified in an individual. The presence of comorbid or co-occurring disorders often has an impact on the course and severity of a person's symptoms, his or her quality of life, the treatment plan, and the anticipated treatment outcome. Phobic disorders have a moderate to high degree of comorbidity with other mental disorders.

The term *comorbidity* was coined by A. R. Feinstein in 1970 in reference to the coexistence of multiple medical conditions within one individual. It was then widely adopted within psychiatry and psychology. There is some controversy about the precise definition of the term within the mental health field, with some arguing that multiple diagnoses within one person reflect independent disorders, whereas others argue that multiple diagnoses can stem from a common underlying issue therefore nullifying the idea that there can be comorbid conditions. Nonetheless, the notion of understanding and recognizing all of the current diagnoses and symptoms that someone presents with at any given time is widely used and valued within the mental health field.

Numerous studies have investigated the most common coexisting mental disorders. A large-scale study by Brown, Campbell, Lehman, Grisham, and Mancill (2001) investigated the most common comorbid diagnoses for a variety of anxiety disorders, including specific phobias. These researchers found that the presence of comorbid diagnoses for people with phobias was lower than the rate found in other types of anxiety disorders, which are highly comorbid. However, over half of people who reported having a phobia as their main problem also reported the presence of at least one other mental disorder at some point in their life. Thus, phobias can but do not often occur in isolation.

This research also pointed out that phobias tend to frequently co-occur with other mood or anxiety disorders as an additional problem of lesser severity than the main problem. For example, 33% of people with a principal anxiety or mood problem also reported the presence of a phobia. Thus, phobias are common comorbid conditions.

The presence of comorbid mental disorders can have an important impact on people's experience of their symptoms and their quality of life. For example, a larger number of comorbid disorders may be related to more severe symptoms and a more challenging course of symptoms. This can have a negative effect on a person's quality of life. This relationship is not completely clear-cut; some people with one disorder may have more severe symptoms from that disorder and poorer quality of life than individuals with multiple comorbid diagnoses. However, greater comorbidity generally tends to be associated with more severe symptoms and difficulties in functioning and enjoyment of life.

The presence of comorbid conditions can also have an impact on a person's treatment plan. For example, someone with a phobia of enclosed spaces who also has depressed mood may benefit from considering using antidepressant medication to help the low mood, even though antidepressants are not typically used to treat a phobia. This would be especially important to consider if the comorbid depression was interfering with treatment for the phobia (i.e., exposure therapy). Exposure therapy for a phobia requires a person to repeatedly be exposed to feared objects or situations, and the low energy and lack of motivation commonly seen in depression could significantly interfere with the person's ability to do the required exposure exercises. Understanding a person's pattern of comorbid diagnoses can also help with decisions about which treatment should come first in a sequence of several potentially beneficial treatments.

Comorbid conditions can also affect treatment outcome. One way that treatment outcome may be affected is through the route of increased symptom severity; the presence of more than one diagnosis may cause the person to have more severe symptoms, which could negatively affect how well he or she does in treatment. Treatment outcome may also be adversely affected simply because comorbidity, in and of itself, may create challenges in treatment (e.g., low mood making it difficult for the person to attend therapy appointments for a phobia).

Although there continues to be some controversy about whether comorbidity means what we think it means for mental disorders, it is a widely used construct with significant helpful clinical implications.

Karen Rowa

See also: Exposure Treatment; Treatment Seeking

Further Reading

Brown, Timothy A., Campbell, Laura A., Lehman, Cassandra L., Grisham, Jessica R., & Mancill, Richard B. (2001). Current and lifetime comorbidity of the DSM-IV anxiety and mood disorders in a large clinical sample. *Journal of Abnormal Psychology, 110*, 585–599.

LIFETIME ASSOCIATIONS BETWEEN SPECIFIC PHOBIA AND OTHER MENTAL DISORDERS

Compared to individuals who have never been diagnosed with a specific phobia, those with a phobia are more likely to also be diagnosed with another mental disorder. The following table provides information on the degree of association between a specific phobia diagnosis and other mental disorders. These data are based on a study of 43,093 participants from a representative sample of the adult population in the United States—the largest epidemiological study to date on specific phobias (Stinson et al., 2007). The adjusted lifetime odds ratios indicate the odds of being diagnosed with another mental disorder across the lifetime for individuals who have been diagnosed with a specific phobia at some point in their life, compared to those who have not. For example, the odds of being diagnosed with another anxiety disorder are 5.6 times greater among individuals with a phobia than those without a phobia. As anxiety disorders are the most common type of comorbidity in specific phobia, detailed information is provided about the odds of having comorbid anxiety disorder diagnoses. The odds ratios take into account (i.e., are adjusted for) sociodemographic factors, such as sex, age, race/ethnicity, and income.

Other Mental Disorder	Adjusted Lifetime Odds Ratio
Any alcohol use disorder	2.2
Any drug use disorder	2.3
Any mood disorder	3.4
Any other anxiety disorder	5.6
Panic disorder with agoraphobia	19.2
Panic disorder without agoraphobia	2.8
Social phobia (social anxiety disorder)	6.6
Generalized anxiety disorder	5.4
Any personality disorder	4.2

Irena Milosevic

Further Reading

Stinson, Frederick S., Dawson, Deborah A., Chou, S. Patricia, Smith, Sharon, Goldstein, Rise B., Ruan, W. June, & Grant, Bridget F. (2007). The epidemiology of DSM-IV specific phobia in the USA: Results from the National Epidemiologic Survey on Alcohol and Related Conditions. *Psychological Medicine, 37*, 1047–1059.

Contingency Management

Contingency management is a process of systematic reinforcement that focuses on the relationship between behaviors and the consequences of behaviors. This technique is based on behavior theory and the principles of operant conditioning. In the treatment of phobias, contingency management aims to modify the frequency and probability of responses to feared stimuli by modifying the consequences of behavior (King, Hamilton, & Ollendick, 1988). A key application of contingency management in the context of phobias is the treatment of childhood phobias (e.g., school phobia; Hersen, 1970).

Animal studies of operant conditioning established important principles upon which contingency management is based. These principles include reinforcement (consequences that increase the probability of a behavior), punishment (consequences that decrease the probability of a behavior), and extinction (removing consequences that reinforce a behavior). Positive consequences involve adding a stimulus, and negative consequences involve removing a stimulus. The study of contingency management as a behavior modification strategy dates to the late 1960s and early 1970s. Its development was influenced by behavior modification methods such as token economies and reinforcement-based substance use interventions (e.g., community reinforcement approach). Contingency management has since become a widely researched method in the treatment of addictions, and it has also been applied to other mental health problems.

The goal of contingency management is to increase the likelihood that functional or adaptive behaviors will occur, and to decrease the probability of maladaptive behaviors. Phobic fear is often maintained by way of negative reinforcement that occurs when a person experiences a decrease in fear after leaving or avoiding a feared situation. Thus, an individual with a height phobia who immediately leaves a balcony when fear increases, or who avoids balconies altogether, will be more likely to escape from or avoid similar situations in the future because doing so provides rapid relief from fear. Another example is when a child with a fear of dogs avoids the presence of a dog and receives comfort from his or her caregiver. The behavior of avoiding the dog is both negatively and positively reinforced, increasing the likelihood that this child will repeat this behavior in the future. The fear of dogs is then maintained because the child's behavior is not allowing new learning to occur (i.e., a positive interaction with a dog).

Before implementing contingencies to change behaviors, a thorough analysis of the factors that are maintaining phobic behaviors is required (King & Ollendick, 1997). In addition, rewards and punishments must be idiographic, as a reward to one person may be a punishment to another. The Premack principle asserts that behaviors that are freely chosen, and more probable to occur, are more reinforcing than behaviors that are less likely to occur. Further, people will often perform a less desirable behavior in order to be rewarded with a more desirable behavior.

It is important to apply the predetermined contingency immediately after the target behavior occurs in order to develop a connection between the behavior and the consequence. Reinforcement and extinction strategies are most commonly used in contingency management for phobias. Desired behaviors (e.g., approaching a feared stimulus) are reinforced, and undesirable behaviors (e.g., avoidance, support seeking) are ignored to establish extinction. For example, a person with a fear of spiders can be rewarded with praise when he or she stands close to a spider, but should not be reinforced with attention for running away from the spider, as this behavior maintains the fear. Alternatively, with someone who has a fear of heights, watching one's favorite television show may be contingent on first standing on a balcony for five minutes. These procedures are often used in combination with other behavioral techniques, such as creating a hierarchy of feared stimuli and exposure treatment. Shaping the behavior by rewarding small successions of the behavior (i.e., reward for thinking about a spider, viewing a picture of a spider, being in close proximity to a spider, holding a spider) is another commonly used behavioral strategy in contingency management.

Criticisms of this approach are based on the lack of research examining contingency management without the use of other behavioral strategies such as exposure, which is a well-supported treatment of phobias on its own. Furthermore, motivation to implement contingencies in response to behavior is necessary, which can be challenging in the context of behavior change related to phobic responses.

Jeanine E. M. Lane

See also: Exposure Treatment; Learning Theory; Operant Conditioning

Further Reading

Hersen, Michel. (1970). Behavior modification approach to a school-phobia case. *Journal of Clinical Psychology, 26,* 128–132.

King, Neville J., Hamilton, David I., & Ollendick, Thomas H. (1988). *Children's phobias: A behavioural perspective.* Chichester, UK: Wiley.

King, Neville J., & Ollendick, Thomas H. (1997). Annotation: Treatment of childhood phobias. *Association for Child Psychology and Psychiatry, 38,* 389–400.

Cortisol

Cortisol, a glucocorticoid produced in the adrenal cortex, is widely considered the primary stress hormone. It is an important marker of hypothalamic-pituitary-adrenal axis activity and is linked to the fight-or-flight response. Cortisol is released spontaneously throughout the day, and its production is increased during times of anxiety to activate the necessary physical and psychological resources. Whereas optimal cortisol levels can have numerous benefits, excess cortisol production—as has been associated with specific phobias—can have harmful effects.

Spontaneous cortisol production is characterized by a strong diurnal rhythm. That is, cortisol levels typically rise rapidly after wakening and reach a peak within 30–45 minutes. They then gradually fall throughout the day until late afternoon, when this decline is interrupted by a brief spike. The morning increase in cortisol is called the cortisol awakening response (CAR). It is considered a marker of individuals' ability to transition from sleep to wakefulness. Basal cortisol levels (measures of naturally occurring cortisol at a given point during the day) are believed to be influenced by baseline physiological and emotional arousal.

In addition to basal cortisol levels, researchers commonly measure cortisol reactivity to specific anxiety-inducing stimuli. In the case of individuals with specific phobias, this constitutes exposure to their source of fear, such as spiders or heights.

Measuring cortisol activity provides insight into whether individuals with a specific phobia differ in their physical response to fear. It also allows researchers to obtain an unbiased and objective measure of anxiety that is not influenced by factors that may alter individuals' self-reports (e.g., influence of the researcher or lack of insight into one's own level of anxiety).

Whereas moderate cortisol levels (and responses to anxiety) are adaptive and necessary, excess cortisol production can disrupt individuals' ability to cope with and regulate their emotions. For example, the hippocampus (a brain region associated with memory) has a higher density of glucocorticoid receptors, and increased cortisol secretion has been shown to damage this area. Excess cortisol production can also disrupt functioning in key emotion-relevant regions of the brain (e.g., the prefrontal cortex and amygdala) and can interfere with the ability to cope effectively with stress. Moreover, increasing evidence demonstrates substantial consequences of cortisol dysregulation on cardiovascular health, immune functioning, and clarity of thinking.

Research findings suggest that individuals with specific phobias exhibit cortisol dysregulation, which may be present even before the onset of phobia. For example, nervous children have been shown to exhibit higher cortisol levels in the morning, which is believed to sensitize them toward exaggerated anxiety symptoms in response to feared stimuli. Although research is mixed, there is evidence that individuals with specific phobias exhibit higher basal cortisol levels compared to those without anxiety. The majority of evidence also indicates that individuals with specific phobias display higher cortisol levels in anticipation and during exposure to their feared stimulus. Individuals with driving phobia, for example, displayed higher cortisol levels beginning one hour prior to a driving exposure compared to those without a specific phobia of driving (Alpers, Abelson, Wilhelm, & Roth, 2003). Cortisol responses to fear may be influenced by individuals' perception of control over their interaction with their feared stimuli. When people with a specific phobia of either spiders or snakes were exposed to their feared stimuli, those who were given less control over the pace of exposure exhibited a greater cortisol response, despite equivalent anxiety ratings. Interestingly, successful treatment with cognitive behavioral therapy (CBT) has been shown to decrease cortisol levels among those with a specific phobia. This was evidenced in a study of Swiss Army recruits suffering from protective mask phobia (Brand, Annen, Holsboer-Trachsler, & Blaser, 2011). Researchers assessed participants' cortisol levels before and after two days of CBT, and they found that cortisol levels decreased from pretreatment to posttreatment.

Joelle LeMoult and K. Lira Yoon

See also: Fight-or-Flight Response; Hypothalamic-Pituitary-Adrenal Axis

Further Reading

Alpers, Georg W., Abelson, James L., Wilhelm, Frank H., & Roth, Walton T. (2003). Salivary cortisol response during exposure treatment in driving phobics. *Psychosomatic Medicine, 65,* 679–687.

Brand, Serge, Annen, Hubert, Holsboer-Trachsler, Edith, & Blaser, Andreas. (2011). Intensive two-day cognitive-behavioral intervention decreases cortisol secretion in soldiers suffering from specific phobia to wear protective mask. *Journal of Psychiatric Research, 45,* 1337–1345.

Khan, Samir, King, Anthony P., Abelson, James L., & Liberzon, Israel. (2008). Neuroendocrinology of anxiety disorders. In M. M. Antony & M. B. Stein (Eds.), *Oxford handbook of anxiety and related disorders* (pp. 111–122). New York, NY: Oxford University Press.

Craske, Michelle G.

Originally from Tasmania, Australia, Michelle G. Craske is recognized as a major figure in the field of anxiety disorders. Her interest in psychology began during her undergraduate work at the University of Tasmania where she conducted research examining the effect of anxiety on performance under stress. After receiving her bachelor's and honors undergraduate degrees, Craske moved to Canada to complete her doctorate in clinical psychology at the University of British Columbia. There, under the supervision of Jack Rachman, she continued her work on performance anxiety and also conducted research on cognitions and escape behavior in panic and agoraphobia. Craske then completed a postdoctoral fellowship under the supervision of David H. Barlow at the State University of New York where her research focused on the phenomenology of panic and on developing and evaluating treatments for anxiety disorders. Craske joined the faculty at the University of California, Los Angeles in 1990 where she is now a professor of psychology and of psychiatry and biobehavioral sciences, as well as director of the Anxiety Disorders Research Centre.

Craske has had a prolific career and continues to maintain a high level of scholarly activity. She has published over 340 scientific papers and written 23 books for both professionals and consumers on such topics as the origins of phobias and anxiety disorders; the translation of basic science findings to clinical applications in fear and learning; cognitive behavioral treatment for phobias, worry, panic, and agoraphobia; gender differences in anxiety; and discontinuation of anxiety medication. As chair of the DSM-5 Anxiety Disorders Subworkgroup, Craske has played a major role in the revision of the anxiety disorders diagnostic criteria from DSM-IV to DSM-5. Craske's research has been awarded funding by the National Institute for Mental Health for over 20 years—a testament to the quality of her work and the innovation of her ideas.

Randi E. McCabe

See also: Barlow, David H. (1942–); Exposure Treatment; Learning Theory; Rachman, Jack (1934–)

Further Reading

Antony, Martin M., Craske, Michelle G., & Barlow, David H. (2006). *Mastering your fears and phobias: Workbook* (2nd ed.). New York, NY: Oxford University Press.

Craske, Michelle G., Liao, Betty, Brown, Lily, & Vervliet, Bram. (2012). Role of inhibition in exposure therapy. *Journal of Experimental Psychopathology, 3*, 322–345.

Cultural Differences

Cultural differences in phobias and anxiety disorders relate to race, ethnicity, and culture. The term *race* refers to physical characteristics that distinguish particular groups of people from other groups, such as White, Black or African American, American Indian or Alaska Native, Asian, and Native Hawaiian or Other Pacific Islander. *Ethnicity* refers to historical behavioral patterns and collective identities shared by groups of individuals from specific geographic regions of the world, such as those pertaining to language, custom, and religion. By contrast, *culture* generally refers to shared sets of social norms, beliefs, and values that particular groups hold and transmit across generations, such as those pertaining to gender and familial roles and relationships, styles of interpersonal communication, and philosophical worldviews. In this entry, however, we use the term *cultural differences* broadly in referring to any differences related to race, ethnicity, or culture that may shape the presentation and treatment of anxiety symptoms.

Phobias and other anxiety disorders often vary greatly across cultural groups. That is, symptom occurrence, severity, presentation, and interpretation of symptoms may vary across cultures. For example, there is general consensus in the literature that cross-cultural variation in anxiety disorders includes differences in catastrophic attribution style, with some groups being more likely than others to attribute symptoms to somatic versus psychological causes. Further, results from epidemiological studies have found key cultural differences in the lifetime prevalence rates of phobias. For example, based on data from the Collaborative Psychiatric Epidemiology Studies, researchers have consistently found that ethnic minority groups have less prevalence for these disorders. In particular, researchers found that Asian Americans are typically less likely to receive social anxiety disorder (social phobia), generalized anxiety disorder, panic disorder, and posttraumatic stress disorder diagnoses than White Americans (Asnaani, Richey, Dimaite, Hinton, & Hofmann, 2010). Similarly, according to the National Comorbidity Survey, Mexican Americans also have lower rates of lifetime phobias and other anxiety disorders compared with rates reported for the U.S. population. Part of these differences may be due to the symptomatology of culture-related forms of anxiety disorders, with variations in content and focus.

There are multiple cultural diversity domains that influence phobias and other anxiety disorders. One of the biggest areas of investigation into cultural differences in phobias is the comparison of collectivistic and individualistic countries, especially with regard to social anxiety disorder. For example, an individual from a country with a collectivistic culture (e.g., Japan, South Korea, and Spain) may report greater levels of social anxiety disorder and more fear of blushing than an individual from an individualistic country (e.g., Australia, Canada, Germany, Netherlands, and the United States). However, other studies have found contradictory results with other collectivistic cultures, such as those of Latin American countries. It has therefore been suggested that although culture-mediated social norms may indeed impact the prevalence and presentation of social anxiety disorder, the dimension of individualism-collectivism may not by itself fully capture the relevant norms. In this regard, other contexts/variables may further shed light on the etiology of social anxiety disorder in a cultural context. For example, social anxiety disorder appears to be more common among groups that have shared styles and behaviors, which may influence fear and shame. Many scholars have proposed that cultures that normalize shame and stress the importance of the opinions of others may influence the occurrence of social anxiety disorder. These types of shared behaviors are common in child rearing practices in Asian families, and may increase the likelihood that some individuals from Asian cultures fear evaluation by others. For example, Dong, Yang, and Ollendick (1994) found that Chinese children and adolescents are more fearful of being evaluated by others than are children and adolescents in Western countries.

It is also important to note that other phobias may be expressed differently and/or appear almost exclusively in different cultural groups. These phobias may not precisely fit the guidelines defined in the *Diagnostic and Statistical Manual of Mental Disorders* (DSM) for the diagnosis of phobias, but they may have some shared characteristics. We will report three specific phobias that may appear almost exclusively in different cultural groups.

Taijin kyofusho (TKS) is a culturally distinctive phobia found in Japan (and much less often among other Asian cultures). This phobia is similar to social anxiety disorder. However, instead of the fear being focused on one's performance in social or performance situations, *taijin kyofusho* focuses on the fear of offending or embarrassing *others*. This fear is consistent with the Japanese cultural emphasis on maintaining interpersonal harmony. Individuals with *taijin kyofusho* may endorse fear related to their own appearance, facial expression, eye contact, body parts, or body odor that may be offensive to others. *Taijin kyofusho* is a recognized disorder in Japan but does not precisely meet the criteria of any particular diagnosis in Western culture.

Ataque de nervios is a culturally distinctive phobia found among Latino individuals (more prevalent among females than males). *Ataque de nervios* shares some symptoms with panic attacks, including heart palpitations, trembling, a sense of fainting, and dissociation, but it also includes uncontrollable screaming, crying, inability to move, loss of memory, and physical/verbal aggression. Further, unlike panic disorder, individuals who experience *ataque de nervios* do not fear the occurrence of further such experiences in the future.

Koro is a culture-specific phobia seen among Asian males, which is characterized by fear that one's genitals are retracting into the body and that this will eventually lead to death. *Koro* is very uncommon in Western countries. Unique to *koro* is that its symptoms involve elements of multiple types of disorders. The fact that *koro* produces extreme fear would typically result in its classification as an anxiety disorder; however, others may view this fear as a strange physical symptom, thereby identifying it as a somatoform disorder. Additionally, others who may not have heard of this condition may consider *koro* as a delusion and thus a symptom of a psychotic disorder.

Oswaldo Moreno, Ariel Kor, and David H. Rosmarin

See also: Fainting Response; Panic Attacks; Phobias, Prevalence of; Risk Factors

Further Reading

Asnaani, Anu, Richey, J. Anthony, Dimaite, Ruta, Hinton, Devon E., & Hofmann, Stefan G. (2010). A cross-ethnic comparison of lifetime prevalence rates of anxiety disorders. *Journal of Nervous and Mental Disease, 198*, 551–555.

Dong, Qi, Yang, Bin, & Ollendick, Thomas H. (1994). Fears in Chinese children and adolescents and their relations to anxiety and depression. *Child Psychology and Psychiatry and Allied Disciplines, 35*, 351–363.

THE SUBTYPES OF TAIJIN KYOFUSHO

Taijin kyofusho (TKS) is a type of social anxiety disorder (social phobia) that is most often identified in Japanese culture. *Taijin kyofusho*, translated literally, means fear (*kyofu*) disorder (*sho*) of interpersonal relations (*taijin*). One of the hallmarks of TKS, which is distinct from the social anxiety disorder diagnosed in Western cultures, is the fear of offending or embarrassing others and thereby bringing shame upon one's social group or family.

In the Japanese classification system, TKS is described by two categories of features, the first of which focuses on specific fears. These fears include (1) *sekimen-kyofu*: fear of blushing, (2) *shubo-kyofu*: fear of a deformed body, (3) *jikoshisen-kyofu*: fear of eye-to-eye contact, and (4) *jikoshu-kyofu*: fear of emitting a foul body odor. When compared to Western classifications of mental disorders, parallels can be drawn between *sekimen-kyofu* and social anxiety disorder and between *shubo-kyofu* and body dysmorphic disorder, although they do not fully map onto one another. *Jikoshisen-kyofu* is understood as being particularly rooted in East Asian cultures where direct eye contact, particularly when speaking to superiors, is considered rude or threatening, as compared to Western cultures where it is strongly encouraged.

In addition to specific fears, TKS varies by disorder severity, which is described on a continuum of four subtypes. These include (1) *transient type*, characterized by short-lived social anxiety typically observed in adolescence; (2) *phobic type*, the most common type, which generally corresponds to Western descriptions of social anxiety disorder (e.g., fear of negative evaluation, avoidance of social situations); (3) *delusional type*, characterized by preoccupation with imagined or exaggerated physical defects or behaviors that might offend others (these perceived inadequacies overlap with the focus of the specific fears described in the first category of features); and (4) *phobic with schizophrenia type*, which reflects a different, more complex disorder category where TKS presents as a symptom of schizophrenia.

The phobic and delusional types of TKS have received the most attention in the literature. They have been described using various terminologies, with the phobic type being termed the *general, sensitive*, or *tension* type and the delusional type being termed the *offensive* or *conviction* type. Importantly, although there is overlap in how these terms are defined within a given TKS type, they are not merely synonyms. For example, individuals with the offensive type of TKS are not always fully deluded or convinced that they are offending others. That is, the degree of conviction likely operates on a continuum within this type.

There is extensive research comparing the Western conceptualization of social anxiety disorder and TKS. Given considerable overlap between the two disorders and similarities in their responsiveness to pharmacologic treatment, some have proposed an expansion of diagnostic criteria for social anxiety disorder to incorporate symptoms of TKS. Specifically, it has been suggested that offensive fears with conviction be added to the spectrum of social fears. Research evaluating the merits and implications of such an expansion is ongoing.

Irena Milosevic

Cynophobia (Fear of Dogs)

Originating from the Greek words *kyno* (dog) and *phobos* (fear), cynophobia is an excessive fear of dogs that is classified as an animal type specific phobia in the *Diagnostic and Statistical Manual of Mental Disorders*, fifth edition. Individuals with cynophobia experience extreme fear and anxiety in the presence of a dog. This anxiety may even escalate into a full-blown panic attack. Efforts are therefore made to avoid encountering dogs. For example, individuals with cynophobia might engage in hypervigilant monitoring for dogs when out for a walk and cross the street if they see a dog approaching. They also might avoid visiting friends or family members who have a dog or request that the dog be placed in a separate room during their visit. Younger children with cynophobia might scream or cry in the presence of a dog. Subsequent efforts by parents to minimize exposure to dogs serve to maintain this phobic behavior. Although many people with cynophobia are able to accommodate their fear to some extent through avoidance and use of safety behaviors, the fear can nevertheless cause significant distress and impairment. For example, it may be difficult for individuals with cynophobia to enjoy outdoor events where dogs may be present. Hearing the word dog or hearing the bark of a dog might also trigger an anxiety response.

Cynophobia most commonly begins in childhood but may develop at any age. As with other specific phobias, there are a number of pathways to the development of the fear (King, Clowes-Hollins, & Ollendick, 1997). Cynophobia might begin following a traumatic experience involving a dog, such as being attacked or bitten or having a panic attack. Alternatively, the fear can develop without any previous direct experience with a dog, through messages received from family members who are fearful of dogs, after seeing or hearing about someone being attacked by

A German Shepherd dog barks from behind a wire fence. Although dogs bark for a variety of reasons, individuals with cynophobia are likely to perceive their barking as a sign of aggression and impending attack. (Sjallen/Dreamstime.com)

a dog, or after observing someone display fearful behaviors when in the proximity of a dog.

Cynophobia is highly treatable with cognitive behavior therapy (CBT) emphasizing situational or *in vivo* exposure strategies. An exposure hierarchy is developed to gradually allow the individual to increase his or her exposure to dogs. It might start with practicing being around a very nice, gentle dog or a puppy where perceived threat is lower. As the individual becomes more comfortable and experiences anxiety reduction, the situations progress (e.g., being in a park near dogs) until the individual is able to comfortably interact with an adult dog (e.g., patting a dog who is on a leash). Other forms of exposure therapy have also been effectively used to treat this fear including a form of imaginal exposure termed *active-imaginal exposure* (Rentz, Powers, Smits, Cougle, & Telch, 2003). Treatment might also include cognitive therapy to challenge feared beliefs and assumptions about dogs (e.g., all dogs are highly dangerous). It can also be conducted in a self-help format using a workbook or with a mental health professional trained in the administration of CBT for anxiety disorders.

Randi E. McCabe

See also: Cognitive Behavioral Therapy; DSM-5; Exposure Treatment; Panic Attacks; Phobia, Animal Type; Phobia, Specific; Three Pathways Theory

Further Reading

King, Neville J., Clowes-Hollins, Viv, & Ollendick, Thomas H. (1997). The etiology of childhood dog phobia. *Behaviour Research and Therapy, 35*, 77.

Rentz, Timothy O., Powers, Mark B., Smits, Jasper A. J., Cougle, Jesse R., & Telch, Michael J. (2003). Active-imaginal exposure: Examination of a new behavioral treatment for cynophobia (dog phobia). *Behaviour Research and Therapy, 41*, 1337–1353.

D

D-Cycloserine

D-cycloserine (DCS) is an established antibiotic treatment for tuberculosis that has been studied for its facilitative effect on the extinction of learned fear. Due to its role in improving certain cognitive processes (memory, learning), DCS has been called a *cognitive enhancer*. It has been shown to be helpful in treating cognitive declines associated with autism, dementia, and schizophrenia and, in the past decade, DCS has also received considerable attention for its potential to improve behavioral treatments for phobias and other anxiety disorders. Its effects as a cognitive enhancer during exposure treatments for anxiety disorders have been supported by research, although not all studies have found it to be beneficial in a treatment context. The mechanisms by which DCS enhances exposure and the specific details regarding how best to administer it during treatment are not fully understood. Additional research is necessary before it can successfully be incorporated into exposure treatment for anxiety disorders. Thus, DCS is considered to be still in the experimental phase and is not part of the standard first-line treatment approach to treating phobias.

The augmentation of exposure treatment for anxiety disorders with DCS is a relatively novel strategy that has emerged from animal studies on the neurological mechanisms of fear extinction—the unlearning of a fear response. Fear extinction depends, in part, on N-methyl-D-aspartate (NMDA) receptors in the basolateral amygdala. Thus, researchers hypothesized that substances that enhance the functioning of these receptors would also enhance extinction. Since DCS is a partial agonist of the glutamatergic NMDA receptor—that is, it facilitates the functioning of this receptor—it became a focus of this line of research. Experiments with animals, typically rats, revealed that DCS enhances extinction of conditioned fear when it is administered prior to or shortly after extinction trials (Vervliet, 2008). DCS was also shown to enhance the generalization of fear extinction. For example, compared to rats treated with a saline solution, DCS-treated rats that were conditioned to fear two different neutral stimuli (light, tone) demonstrated less fear responding to the second conditioned stimulus after they had already achieved fear extinction to the first conditioned stimulus (Ledgerwood, Richardson, & Cranney, 2005).

Findings from animal research on the role of DCS in fear extinction inspired further research that translated this work to clinical applications with humans. An initial study involved virtual reality exposure treatment for individuals with acrophobia (fear of heights). This research demonstrated that participants who received DCS prior to each of two exposure sessions experienced significantly less fear during the second exposure session, as well as one week and three months following the session, compared to participants who received placebo treatment (Ressler et al., 2004). Further research has shown similar positive effects of DCS-augmented exposure treatment for public-speaking phobia and ophidiophobia (fear of snakes); however, other studies have failed to replicate these findings (for a review, see Hofmann, Wu, & Boettcher, 2013). In addition to specific phobias, DCS has been investigated in the context of exposure treatments for other anxiety and related disorders, including panic disorder, obsessive-compulsive disorder, and posttraumatic stress disorder. As with phobias, the findings on its effects as a cognitive enhancer during fear extinction have been somewhat mixed for these other disorders (Hofmann et al., 2013).

One possible reason for discrepancies in the effectiveness of DCS-augmented exposure treatment is the use of nonclinical populations in some studies. In particular, less anxious participants may readily improve with exposure, leaving little room for DCS to facilitate further improvement. Evidence also suggests that the effects of DCS are more nuanced than was previously understood. For example, in a study of exposure treatment for acrophobia, DCS was shown to enhance fear reduction only for successful exposure sessions, where fear is low at the end of the session, and not for unsuccessful sessions, where fear is high at the end of the session (Smits et al., 2013). In other words, it appears that DCS "makes 'good' exposures better and 'bad' exposures worse" (Hofmann et al., 2013, p. 3).

The precise mechanism by which DCS enhances fear extinction is both a topic of debate and a source of considerable research activity. Several hypotheses have been proposed to account for its effects, including the possibilities that it (1) erases fear memories by disrupting their reconsolidation, (2) modifies context-specific fear extinction learning (i.e., it facilitates extinction only if the behavioral procedure first triggers the extinction process), or (3) enhances inhibitory learning that is part of the usual extinction process. To date, no single explanation has been able to account for all of its effects. Further research is necessary not only to improve understanding of the mechanisms of DCS in exposure treatments but also to clarify the optimal dose and the timing of its administration, its interactions with other medications, and its long-term impact on fear and anxiety.

Irena Milosevic

See also: Amygdala; Classical Conditioning; Exposure Treatment; Extinction

Further Reading

Hofmann, Stefan G., Wu, Jade Q., & Boettcher, Hannah. (2013). D-cycloserine as an augmentation strategy for cognitive behavioral therapy of anxiety disorders. *Biology of Mood & Anxiety Disorders, 3*, 1–10.

Ledgerwood, Lana, Richardson, Rick, & Cranney, Jacquelyn. (2005). D-cycloserine facilitates extinction of learned fear: Effects on reacquisition and generalized extinction. *Biological Psychiatry, 57*, 841–847.

Ressler, Kerry J., Rothbaum, Barbara O., Tannenbaum, Libby, Anderson, Page, Graap, Ken, Zimand, Elana, . . . Davis, Michael. (2004). Cognitive enhancers as adjuncts to psychotherapy: Use of D-cycloserine in phobic individuals to facilitate extinction of fear. *Archives of General Psychiatry, 61*, 1136–1144.

Smits, Jasper A. J., Rosenfield, David, Otto, Michael W., Powers, Mark B., Hofmann, Stefan G., Telch, Michael J., . . . Tart, Candyce D. (2013). D-cycloserine enhancement of fear extinction is specific to successful exposure sessions: Evidence from the treatment of height phobia. *Biological Psychiatry, 73*, 1054–1058.

Vervliet, Bram. (2008). Learning and memory in conditioned fear extinction: Effects of D-cycloserine. *Acta Psychologica, 127*, 601–613.

Differential Diagnosis

Differential diagnosis is the process by which multiple possible diagnoses are considered before deciding what diagnosis or diagnoses best fit a person's symptoms. Making an accurate diagnosis and eliminating other competing diagnoses for any disorder, including phobias, is essential in planning an effective course of therapy.

The use of differential diagnosis as applied to mental disorders was pioneered by Emil Kraeplin (1856–1926), a German psychiatrist. Kraeplin argued that mental disorders are best classified by looking at patterns of symptoms that often cluster together instead of grouping similar symptoms together. His ideas about classification were foundational for current classification schemes such as the *Diagnostic and Statistical Manual of Mental Disorders* (fifth edition; DSM-5; American Psychiatric Association, 2013), the most widely used classification scheme in North America. In the DSM-5, guidance is provided not only for what diagnosis the presentation of symptoms might represent but also for what other diagnoses should be ruled out—in essence, the process of differential diagnosis.

The process of differential diagnosis starts with observation or reporting of the symptoms that the person is experiencing. Unfortunately, there are no tests or exams that can definitively rule in or rule out the presence of a particular condition the way a throat swab can confirm strep throat or a blood test can confirm thyroid problems. Clinician judgment and careful questioning are essential. For the phobias, it is important to learn about the symptoms and their development, onset, course, triggers, and frequency. It is also important to understand the focus of the person's fear; in phobias fear is typically focused on a specific object or situation. For example, a phobia of vomiting would center on fears of the act of vomiting or on coming in contact with vomit rather than on things like how embarrassing it would be to vomit in front of others or fearing that vomiting means the person has a serious illness (both of which may suggest diagnoses other than a phobia of vomit).

This information can be gathered in a number of ways, including interviews, observation of the person interacting with his or her feared object, family reports of the person's fears, or self-report questionnaires about fears. Detailed information is important as there is a great deal of overlap in symptoms between the different phobias and other types of disorders. People with phobias may experience panic attacks, an overwhelming rush of physical symptoms, when confronted with their feared object or situation. They may also avoid situations that trigger their fear. The presence of panic attacks and avoidance are common in many other types of anxiety disorders and therefore simply knowing that people experience these symptoms is not enough information to determine an accurate diagnosis. To diagnose a phobia, the anxiety, panic attacks, and avoidance must be triggered by a particular situation or object (e.g., dogs, heights, storms, needles). Once the focus of the fear is clear, alternative diagnoses can be ruled out or more than one diagnosis can be made to account for the person's symptoms. Another example of common overlap of symptoms is avoidance of food. To make an accurate differential diagnosis between eating disorders and phobias, the reason for avoidance must be clear. In eating disorders, avoidance of food is typically linked with fears around gaining weight, whereas in phobias the avoidance of food is often linked with fears about choking. This level of detail about presenting symptoms is necessary for differential diagnosis.

It is also useful to consider a differential diagnosis between the presence of a diagnosable phobia versus a nondiagnosable fear. Fears are common in the general population and should not immediately be considered phobias. Careful questioning about the severity of the fear and the degree to which the fear causes problems in the person's life can help the clinician make a differential diagnosis between fear and phobia.

Another useful piece of information in making a differential diagnosis is the prevalence or frequency of a particular condition in the general population. When deciding between several possible diagnoses, it is important to keep in mind how common each condition is. While this should not be the only piece of information used to decide a diagnosis, it can be useful to carefully consider the most common explanation for the person's symptoms. For example, fear and avoidance of spiders are much more likely to reflect a phobia of spiders (which is very common in the population) than a rare and unusual mental disorder.

An accurate differential diagnosis provides guidance for choosing an appropriate course of treatment. With phobias, ruling out other possible mental disorders also rules out several possible treatments that would have been considered, including a number of medications and therapies. The treatment of choice for a phobia is exposure therapy, and medication therapy is not recommended. Accurate differential diagnosis should lead to appropriate treatment options that have the best chance of successfully helping a person with a phobia.

Karen Rowa

See also: DSM-5; Phobias, Assessment of; Phobias, Diagnosis of

Further Reading

American Psychiatric Association. (2013). *Diagnostic and statistical manual of mental disorders* (5th ed.). Arlington, VA: American Psychiatric Publishing.

DIFFERENTIAL DIAGNOSIS: PHOBIA OR ANOTHER DISORDER?

To distinguish between a specific phobia and a nonclinical fear or another disorder, it is important to clarify the focus of the individual's fear and the context of symptoms such as anxiety and avoidance. The following table highlights the main disorders that may have overlapping symptoms with specific phobia. A thorough assessment will gather the information required (e.g., focus, frequency and severity of fear, context of fear, presence of safety behaviors, degree of distress and impairment) to establish a diagnosis of specific phobia and rule out any possible disorders that may have overlapping features.

Disorder	Features
Specific Phobia	A circumscribed, excessive fear of a specific stimulus or situation (e.g., heights, dogs, vomiting). Panic attacks (if present), anxiety, and avoidance are linked to the specific feared stimulus or situation.
Non-Clinical Fear	The presence of a specific fear that does not lead to any distress or impairment. Unlike in specific phobia, a nonclinical fear is manageable and although it may be a concern, it does not overly bother a person or cause any significant interference in functioning.
Panic Disorder	Unexpected panic attacks that are not cued by an identifiable trigger as in specific phobia. Anticipatory anxiety about experiencing future panic attacks. Avoidance and safety behaviors aimed at minimizing the chance of a panic attack and increasing one's feelings of control are common.
Agoraphobia	Fear and avoidance of situations where an individual may experience symptoms of anxiety or other embarrassing symptoms and where one may not be able to escape or get help if needed. In agoraphobia, avoidance is often generalized across a range of situations, whereas in specific phobia, avoidance is limited specifically to the circumscribed feared object or situation.

(continued)

Disorder	Features
Social Anxiety Disorder (Social Phobia)	Excessive fear about being negatively evaluated by others in a social situation. Often associated with avoidance of anxiety-provoking social situations and use of safety behaviors to manage anxiety symptoms. Although individuals with a specific phobia may be embarrassed by their fear and be concerned that others may judge them negatively, this anxiety is secondary to the central fear of the circumscribed situation/stimulus.
Obsessive-Compulsive Disorder (OCD)	Recurrent and persistent intrusive thoughts (obsessions) that are highly distressing and/or the presence of repetitive behaviors or mental acts (compulsions) intended to reduce the distress associated with the intrusive thoughts. In specific phobia, individuals are preoccupied with thoughts about the particular stimulus or situation they fear, whereas in OCD individuals are focused on the upsetting obsessions. In addition, while individuals with specific phobia may engage in safety and avoidance behaviors, they do not perform these behaviors in a ritualistic and repetitive way as seen with compulsions in OCD.
Anorexia Nervosa	Restriction of food intake in a motivated attempt to lose weight due to negative self-evaluation and overvaluation of being thin. Unlike individuals with a choking phobia who do not eat because they are afraid of choking, individuals with anorexia nervosa do not eat because they are afraid of gaining weight.

Randi E. McCabe

Disease-Avoidance Model

The disease-avoidance model proposes that evolutionary pressures have predisposed humans to experience feelings of disgust when exposed to animals that have the potential to cause harm through disease or contamination. According to this model, an increased proneness to experience disgust in the presence of potentially disease-transmitting animals (e.g., cockroaches) led to avoidance of such situations and provided an adaptive advantage to our ancestors. Earlier accounts, including preparedness theory, posited that phobias are most likely to develop in response to stimuli that posed a threat to ancestral humans and that we therefore readily learn to fear such objects and situations. However, preparedness theory has been criticized for not adequately accounting for the existence of some highly prevalent phobias. For example, it is unlikely that animals such as cockroaches or rats would have posed a substantive threat to early humans. The disease-avoidance model provides a plausible explanation for the development of such phobias by including perceptions of harm caused by contamination or disease into the definition of threat. The disease-avoidance model and the contributing role of disgust sensitivity have received mixed results in the research literature, and some experts have criticized aspects of the model.

Several authors have proposed that animal fears and phobias can be classified into two distinct categories. The first category consists of predatory animals that would pose a clear danger if approached (e.g., shark). The second category consists of nonpredatory animals that are commonly the focus of phobias but would be unlikely to cause serious harm if confronted (e.g., mouse). Results from studies examining these categories suggest that feelings of disgust and the expectation of disgust-related outcomes (e.g., becoming ill) if confronted with the animal are more often found in response to nonpredatory animals, which is consistent with the disease-avoidance model. However, these studies have failed to provide compelling evidence for the causal role of disgust in the development of animal phobias suggesting that additional investigation is required.

Although initially articulated in the context of animal phobias, the disease-avoidance model has since been applied to other anxiety disorders. Notably, research has found that fears of disgust and contamination play a prominent role in blood-injection-injury phobia. Interestingly, evidence suggests that disgust, rather than fear, is the prominent emotional response in this disorder. Similarly, individuals with contamination-related concerns in obsessive-compulsive disorder often describe feeling disgusted when faced with threatening stimuli and identify concerns of disease and infection as feared consequences of contact with perceived contaminants.

A number of criticisms of the disease-avoidance model have been put forth. First, some studies have failed to find the expected relationships between disgust sensitivity and specific animals as predicted by the model (Thorpe & Salkovskis, 1998). As Woody and Teachman (2000) point out, the theory is also unable to explain the high prevalence of some phobias and not others. For example, given the regular occurrence of mosquito-borne illnesses, we might expect phobias of mosquitos to be more common than phobias of snakes (which are not known to transmit diseases to humans). The model's prediction that phobic individuals should experience avoidance of disgust-evoking stimuli more generally has likewise not received support (Mulkens, de Jong, & Merckelbach, 1996). Finally, the validity of the measurement instruments used to assess disgust and disgust sensitivity in previously published studies has also been called into question.

Dubravka L. Gavric

See also: Disgust Sensitivity; Evolution, Role of; Obsessive-Compulsive Disorder; Phobia, Animal Type; Phobia, Blood-Injection-Injury Type; Preparedness Theory

Further Reading

Mulkens, Sandra A. N., de Jong, Peter J., & Merckelbach, Herald. (1996). Disgust and spider phobia. *Journal of Abnormal Psychology, 105*, 464–468.

Thorpe, Susan J., & Salkovskis, Paul M. (1998). Studies on the role of disgust in the acquisition and maintenance of specific phobias. *Behaviour Research and Therapy, 36*, 877–893.

Woody, Sheila R., & Teachman, Bethany A. (2000). Intersection of disgust and fear: normative and pathological views. *Clinical Psychology: Science and Practice, 7*, 291–311.

Disgust Sensitivity

Disgust is considered by many to be a basic emotion that is recognizable across cultures. Disgust, defined literally as *bad taste*, originally evolved to protect humans from ingesting potentially harmful substances, thereby promoting disease avoidance. Over time, disgust has been adapted as a response to a wide range of elicitors, including body products (e.g., feces, urine, vomit), animals (e.g., fleas, cockroaches, rats/mice), body envelope violations (e.g., blood, needles, mutilation), and death. Personality research suggests that individuals vary in how easily they are disgusted by a range of stimuli. Heightened disgust sensitivity, as this personality construct is known, has been linked to the development and maintenance of several anxiety-related disorders, especially specific phobias.

Although the acquisition of disgust sensitivity may have some genetic origins (Rozin & Millman, 1987), recent research suggests that it is acquired primarily through social learning experiences early in childhood. In support of this notion, a recent study found that parents of young children respond with more disgust to their offspring and show greater behavioral avoidance of disgust-relevant stimuli (Stevenson, Oaten, Case, Repacholi, & Wagland, 2010). This transmission of disgust from parent to offspring may be facilitated by the facial expression of disgust, which is especially salient in communicating the threat of contagion. The acquisition of disgust sensitivity in this context may be associated with other personality dimensions, especially neuroticism, that are marked by the tendency to experience negative emotions more broadly.

The observation that a wide range of stimuli elicit disgust has led many researchers to suggest that disgust is not a unitary construct, but rather includes several different domains. A three-domain structure is currently the most widely accepted model of disgust sensitivity. These domains include *Core Disgust* (characterized by a threat of oral incorporation such as urine, feces, or insects), *Contamination Disgust* (elicited by contact with individuals who are thought to be contaminated), and *Animal-Reminder Disgust* (relating to elicitors that somehow remind us of our own mortality including blood or injections), although it is important to note that disgust may also be experienced in the sexual and moral domains (i.e., pedophilia).

A number of self-report measures have been developed to assess how disgust sensitive an individual is. The most commonly used adult measure of disgust sensitivity, the Disgust Scale-Revised (Olatunji et al., 2007), asks individuals to rate how disgusting they find various experiences on a 0 (not disgusting at all) to 4 (extremely disgusting) scale. A sample item from this scale reads "You discover that a friend of yours changes underwear only once a week." Research with similar measures has shown that disgust sensitivity is a stable trait that is present to a lesser or greater extent in all individuals.

In addition to questionnaire measures of disgust sensitivity, many studies employ behavioral tasks. Given that disgust is a relatively easy emotion to elicit, researchers often get creative in their choice of stimuli, which might include artificial vomit, mounted insects, and severed deer legs. Behavioral tasks of disgust sensitivity ask participants how willing they would be to complete steps of increasing difficulty relating to the disgusting stimulus. For example, the steps might range from looking at a mounted cockroach, to touching the space next to the cockroach, and finally touching the actual cockroach.

Several studies have examined the link between disgust sensitivity and specific phobias. Although individuals with specific phobias experience fear when confronted with the feared stimulus, many also report aversion, repugnance, and nausea. Research has also found that measures of disgust sensitivity predict phobic fear and avoidance. Further, individuals with spider phobia, snake phobia, and blood-injection-injury phobia report greater disgust sensitivity and are more avoidant of disgusting stimuli compared to nonphobics. Given that many specific phobias involve fear-provoking yet nonpredatory animals (e.g., spiders, rats) and situations (e.g., blood draws), some researchers have suggested that phobic avoidance may, in part, be due to concerns about contamination. This theory, known as the disease-avoidance model, posits that phobic avoidance is a function of disease-related concerns rather than predatory concerns (Matchett & Davey, 1991). Some researchers have even suggested that the lack of long-term success following the treatment of some phobias may be due to the exclusive focus on fear reduction when reduction of disgust sensitivity is also indicated.

Megan Viar-Paxton and Bunmi O. Olatunji

See also: Disease-Avoidance Model; Phobia, Specific

Further Reading

Matchett, George, & Davey, Graham C. (1991). A test of a disease-avoidance model of animal phobias. *Behaviour Research and Therapy, 29*, 91–94.

Muris, Peter, Mayer, Birgit, Huijding, Jorg, & Konings, Tjeerd. (2008). A dirty animal is a scary animal! Effects of disgust-related information on fear beliefs in children. *Behavior Research and Therapy, 46*, 137–144.

Olatunji, Bunmi O., & McKay, Dean. (2009). *Disgust and its disorders: Theory, assessment, and treatment implications*. American Psychological Association.

Olatunji, Bunmi O., Williams, Nathan L., Tolin, David F., Sawchuk, Craig N., Abramowitz, Jonathan S., Lohr, Jeffrey M., and Elwood, Lisa S. (2007). The Disgust Scale: Item analysis, factor structure, and suggestions for refinement. *Psychological Assessment, 19*, 281–297.

Rozin, Paul, & Millman, Linda. (1987). Family environment, not heredity, accounts for family resemblances in food preferences and attitudes: A twin study. *Appetite, 8*, 124–134.

Stevenson, Richard J., Oaten, Megan J., Case, Trevor I., Repacholi, Betty M., & Wagland, Paul. (2010). Children's response to adult disgust elicitors: Development and acquisition. *Developmental Psychology, 46*, 165–177.

DISGUST SENSITIVITY IN PREGNANCY

The first trimester of pregnancy is a dangerous time for both mother and fetus. Pregnancy suppresses the mother's immune response and the fetus is at its most vulnerable in its early stages. It is for this reason that evolutionary psychologists believe that we see an increase in disgust sensitivity in the first trimester of pregnancy (relative to later pregnancy, and relative to nonpregnant women). Disgust sensitivity serves as protection against disease, thus safeguarding the mother and unborn child.

Disgust sensitivity in pregnancy is most pronounced with respect to food. Pregnant women report more disgust to meat products than to fruit and vegetables. This is likely because meat carries more pathogens and therefore greater risk of disease than do fruits and vegetables. Pregnant women also report heightened aversion to novel foods. Again, this is protective. When women are pregnant, it might not be smart to eat foods that have unknown consequences. Importantly, disgust sensitivity in early pregnancy cannot be explained by morning sickness—the finding holds even after controlling for a woman's level of nausea.

Many women report increased sensitivity to smells in early pregnancy. However, there is no research evidence to support change in sensitivity to smell during pregnancy. In her book, *That's Disgusting: Unraveling the Mysteries of Repulsion*, Rachel Herz (2012) explains that women experience emotional changes during pregnancy and that "emotional sensitivity can feel like physical sensitivity when it comes to odors" (p. 91). In other words, women do not smell meat more acutely when they are pregnant. Rather, they assign emotional meaning to the smell of meat, deciding it is potentially dangerous, labeling it as disgusting, and choosing to not eat it.

Interestingly, there is some evidence that pregnant women also exhibit a heightened "disgust" reaction to unknown people/foreigners (xenophobia) during the first trimester. This finding is harder to explain than disgust reactions to food. Rachel Herz suggests, "it is adaptive to be leery of the unknown," again as a protection of the unborn child.

Deborah Roth Ledley

Further Reading

Herz, Rachel. (2012). *That's disgusting: Unraveling the mysteries of repulsion.* New York, NY: W. W. Norton & Company.

Distraction

Distraction occurs when an individual's attention is directed away from an initial object of focus to the source of distraction. Distraction may be unintentional, as in the case of a sports fan whose attention is taken away from the game by a rowdy person in the crowd, or intentional, such as when individuals purposely shift their focus of attention away from an unpleasant object or situation, including looking away from the screen during a scary movie. In the context of fears and phobias, distraction is a commonly used coping behavior that may, in some instances, contribute to the long-term maintenance of fears, although the relevant research remains somewhat unclear on this issue.

Among individuals with phobias, distraction is often intended to reduce fear and distress in anticipation of a feared situation or event, and/or when confronted with the source of one's fear. It sometimes allows fearful individuals to do something they are afraid of without being fully involved in doing it. Common examples of using distraction as an intentional coping behavior include watching television or surfing the Internet to avoid thinking about a feared situation or event, looking away from a feared object, humming, counting, or listening to music while engaging in a scary task, or purposely focusing on nonthreatening aspects of a feared situation. Within this context, distraction may be classified as a form of avoidance or safety behavior that serves to minimize the individual's distress in the feared situation. Although it is often effective in reducing fear in the short term, cognitive-behavioral theories of fear maintenance suggest that, like other forms of safety behavior, distraction can interfere with the individual's ability to overcome fears in the long run. It is proposed that directing focus of attention away from feared objects or situations via distraction may prevent the individual from fully processing and learning how to handle fear or from noticing "corrective" information (e.g., that the feared object or situation is not actually as dangerous as believed) that might help to disconfirm fear-maintaining beliefs and assumptions. Accordingly, the most widely accepted psychological treatment for phobias, exposure therapy, includes helping individuals face their fears while maintaining their focus of attention on the feared object or situation and eliminating safety behavior such as distraction.

Nevertheless, a debate exists in the scientific literature regarding the hypothesized detrimental effects of distraction during exposure therapy. Some researchers argue that all safety behavior (including distraction) compromises the effectiveness exposure therapy. Thus, they advise that distraction should be targeted for elimination in clinical treatments of phobias, either immediately or in a step-by-step fashion (i.e., facing a feared situation with, and subsequently without, the use of the safety behavior). By contrast, a number of studies have shown that distraction does not necessarily have detrimental effects on exposure therapy and may even help people overcome their fears more quickly and effectively (Podina, Koster, Philippot, Dethier, & David, 2013) by helping them feel a greater sense of control in the feared scenario and/or to remain in the feared situation long enough to process corrective information. This has led some authors (e.g., Rachman, Radomsky, & Shafran, 2008) to suggest that strategic use of distraction and other safety behaviors may be beneficial as a means of making treatment more acceptable and less distressing for individuals with phobias, and helping them disconfirm inaccurate and negative beliefs that previously served to maintain their fears.

Chris L. Parrish

See also: Exposure Treatment; Fear; Safety Behavior

Further Reading

Podina, Ioana R., Koster, Ernst H. W., Philippot, Pierre, Dethier, Vincent, & David, Daniel O. (2013). Optimal attentional focus during exposure in specific phobia: A meta-analysis. *Clinical Psychology Review, 33*, 1172–1183.

Rachman, Stanley, Radomsky, Adam S., & Shafran, Roz. (2008). Safety behaviour: A reconsideration. *Behaviour Research and Therapy, 46*, 163–173.

DSM-5

The DSM-5 is the fifth and most recent edition of the *Diagnostic and Statistical Manual of Mental Disorders* (DSM). The DSM is published by the American Psychiatric Association and describes a classification system for mental illness, including phobias. It identifies a common language and criteria for the diagnosis of mental disorders that are used widely in clinical health settings, research, government policy, the pharmaceutical industry, and the legal system. The DSM is the most widely used nomenclature system for mental disorders in North America. The *International Classification of Diseases* (ICD), produced by the World Health Organization, also classifies mental disorders and is more commonly used in

Europe. In contrast to the DSM, the ICD classifies all types of health disorders rather than focusing solely on mental illness.

The DSM is a categorical classification system that provides diagnostic labels and standardized criteria. The categories provide prototypes with lists of descriptive symptoms. Individuals who are similar to a given prototype (by exhibiting a certain number of the listed symptoms) are determined to have that particular diagnosis. The DSM was designed for the assessment and diagnosis of mental disorders and does not provide information or guidelines related to treatment. It is also said to be atheoretical and generally does not rely on causal theories of mental illness for diagnosis.

The first DSM, which was published in 1952, evolved out of two main sources: (1) census data collection systems and (2) a nomenclature developed for the armed forces during World War II. DSM-I was 130 pages long and described 106 mental disorders. The manual has since gone through several revisions. The DSM-5 was published in May 2013 and now includes over 300 disorders described in 947 pages.

The DSM-5 underwent several significant changes from the previous version. Most notably, the five-axial diagnostic system was removed and replaced with a single axis that combines the former axes I (clinical disorders), II (personality disorders and developmental disorders), and III (relevant physical disorders), while requesting separate notations for psychosocial factors (formerly axis IV) and overall disability (formerly axis V). Additionally, some of the chapters were reorganized and an introduction chapter on the use of dimensional assessment was added. Many of the proposed major revisions for the DSM-5, including a major shift toward a dimensional approach to classifying personality disorders, were ultimately relegated to the section of the manual describing criteria requiring further investigation.

There were several changes made in the anxiety disorders section of the manual. Obsessive-compulsive disorder was moved to a separate chapter titled "Obsessive-Compulsive and Related Disorders," and the new disorders of hoarding disorder and excoriation (skin-picking) disorder were added to this section. Posttraumatic stress disorder was also moved to a separate chapter ("Trauma- and Stressor-Related Disorders") along with acute stress disorder, adjustment disorder, and reactive attachment disorder. Specific phobias remain in the anxiety disorders chapter and the diagnostic criteria have stayed largely the same as those of the DSM-IV; however, there is no longer a requirement that individuals over the age of 18 must recognize that their fear is excessive or unreasonable. Additionally, the duration requirement (lasting for six months or more) is now a requirement for all age groups.

The DSM-5 has been heavily criticized on several fronts. Despite efforts to refine the diagnostic criteria for many disorders, critics state that the DSM-5 remains unscientific and overly subjective, as several of the categories have been shown to have low diagnostic reliability (agreement between professionals when diagnosing). Additionally, as the number of diagnoses has grown with the DSM-5 revision, there have been concerns about a shifting boundary between normalcy and illness. It has been argued that the DSM-5 has moved toward "medicalizing" patterns of behavior and mood that would have been considered normal in the past. The potential for a financial conflict of interest for the DSM authors has also been a source of controversy, as some of the authors have received financial support from the pharmaceutical industry, and this industry generally benefits from increasing the number of diagnoses. Proponents of the DSM-5 state that it is a working document; thus, the current imperfections will be revised over time as the state of the field advances. Despite the debate, the DSM remains widely used and provides a common language for health professionals and patients to communicate about mental illness.

Brenda L. Key

See also: American Psychiatric Association; Cultural Differences; *International Classification of Diseases*; Phobias, Diagnosis of

Further Reading

American Psychiatric Association. (2013). *Diagnostic and statistical manual of mental disorders* (5th ed.). Arlington, VA: American Psychiatric Publishing.

Frances, Allen. (2013). The new crisis in confidence in psychiatric diagnosis. *Annals of Internal Medicine, 159*, 720–721.

Website

www.psychiatry.org/DSM5

Dysmorphophobia (Fear of Deformity)

Dysmorphophobia, a term originating from the Greek *dysmorphia*, meaning ugliness, and currently known as body dysmorphic disorder (BDD), is a chronic psychiatric condition classified in the fifth edition of the *Diagnostic and Statistical Manual of Mental Disorders* (DSM-5; American Psychiatric Association [APA], 2013) under obsessive-compulsive and related disorders. BDD is characterized by marked fear and preoccupation with an imagined deformity, or excessive anxiety and fixation over an existing minor flaw in one's appearance. Concerns typically center on the face or head (e.g., skin, hair, nose) but can also include other areas (e.g., weight; APA, 2013). Due to the time-consuming ritualistic behaviors that distinguish dysmorphophobia, such as frequent mirror checking, excessive grooming, or repeated dermatological or surgical visits, affected individuals experience severe impairments in social and occupational functioning. Additionally, their poor body image may result in self-isolation or avoidance of interpersonal relationships. Dysmorphophobia affects roughly 1% of the general population, is suggested to have a strong genetic component, and often co-occurs with other psychiatric disorders, such as major depressive disorder, obsessive-compulsive disorder, and delusional disorder (APA, 2013). Although successful treatment can be difficult, as individuals with dysmorphophobia tend to seek dermatological or surgical solutions rather than psychiatric interventions, the disorder can be successfully treated with selective serotonin reuptake inhibitors (i.e., antidepressants) and cognitive behavioral therapy (Ipser, Sander, & Stein, 2009).

Michelle Lonergan and Andrea R. Ashbaugh

See also: Cognitive Behavioral Therapy; Selective Serotonin Reuptake Inhibitors

Further Reading

American Psychiatric Association (2013). *Diagnostic and Statistical Manual for Mental Disorders* (5th ed.). Arlington, VA: American Psychiatric Publishing.

Ipser, Jonathan C., Sander, Candice, & Stein, Dan J. (2009). Pharmacotherapy and psychotherapy for body dysmorphic disorder. *Cochrane Database of Systematic Reviews, 1,* CD005332.

Phillips, Katharine A. (2009). *Understanding body dysmorphic disorder: An essential guide*. New York, NY: Oxford University Press.

E

Ellis, Albert (1913–2007)

Albert Ellis was an American psychologist who is considered one of the founders of cognitive therapy. He developed rational emotive behavior therapy (REBT), a pioneering form of cognitive behavior therapy, at the same time that Aaron Beck developed his cognitive therapy approach. Both approaches highlighted the key role of unrealistic expectations and dysfunctional beliefs in creating and maintaining psychological distress, and both use action-based strategies to promote cognitive, behavioral, and emotional change. REBT has been used to effectively treat a range of conditions, including anxiety and phobias, with an emphasis on enhancing, coping, and improving life satisfaction by changing one's philosophy or way of thinking.

Born in 1913 in Pittsburgh, Pennsylvania, Ellis grew up in New York City. He coped with a challenging childhood environment by, in his words, becoming "a stubborn and pronounced problem-solver." Growing up, he had to cope with his own personal health issues (kidney disorder) and his parents' divorce at age 12. He had aspirations of being a writer and planned to make enough money through accounting to retire at age 30 and then be financially free to write. Known to be extremely shy and fearful of public speaking, particularly to young females, Ellis used behavior therapy on himself to overcome his phobias by confronting his fears and approaching and speaking to 100 females at the Bronx Botanical Gardens when he was 19 years old. It is thought that this experience had a significant influence on his development of REBT.

Ellis attended the City University of New York and graduated with a bachelor's degree in business in 1934. He set out in the business field, including a clothing venture with his brother and a position as personnel manager, while devoting his spare time to writing. His fictional manuscripts (he had written over 24 by age 28) were not met with any publishing success. He then began writing nonfiction on the topics of sexuality and family. As he developed his expertise in the area, he was sought out for advice and he discovered that he enjoyed counseling. So in 1942, he enrolled in a doctoral program in clinical psychology at Columbia University. After completing his master's degree in 1943, he began a part-time practice in family and sex counseling. In 1947, Ellis received his doctorate and began training as a psychoanalyst, which he believed at the time to be the most effective therapy approach. He then practiced as a psychoanalyst and taught at Rutgers and New York University. He was a senior clinical psychologist at the Northern New Jersey Mental Hygiene Clinic and later held the position of chief psychologist at the New Jersey Diagnostic Center and then the New Jersey Department of Institutions and Agencies.

Like his contemporary Beck, Ellis began to question the effectiveness of psychoanalysis and developed his own more directive form of psychotherapy, based on his personal experience; his research; and his readings of philosophy, notably Epictetus, Marcus Aurelius, Spinoza, and Bertrand Russell. He observed that his clients improved more quickly with his active and directive approach than with passive psychoanalytic procedures. He coined the term "musterbation" to characterize the unrealistic commands people use on themselves (e.g., "I must do this"), others (e.g., "You must do that"), and the world (e.g., "Things must be this way") that lead to neurotic and maladaptive behavior. According to Ellis, musterbation leads to awfulizing, terribilizing, and catastrophizing, and consequently anxiety, depression, and emotional disturbance. A central REBT technique is known as "disputing," whereby the clinician helps the client dispute dysfunctional beliefs and musts and develop more realistic, helpful beliefs. Ellis was known to emphatically confront clients with their irrational beliefs and persuade them to develop rational beliefs by applying the scientific method to change their personal philosophy and ways of thinking.

His first book on REBT (*How to Live with a Neurotic*) was published in 1957 and in 1959, he founded the Institute for Rational Living, where he gave workshops to train professionals in REBT. Now known as the Albert Ellis Institute (www.alber tellis.org), the organization provides training and certification in REBT, psychotherapy services, and engages in research on REBT.

Ellis was a controversial figure, known for using colorful language and a highly directive, confrontational, often abrasive, approach. He expressed strong opinions on controversial topics such as sex and religion. Ellis's theories were met with much criticism throughout his career, which is likely why his brand of cognitive therapy was less popular than that of Beck.

Throughout his life, Ellis was a prolific writer, publishing over 600 scientific articles and 54 books on a wide range of topics including sex, homosexuality, marriage, relationships, religion, REBT, humanistic psychology, anger, procrastination, optimal aging, happiness, personality, self-esteem, and overcoming the fear of flying. He received numerous awards for his contributions to the field of psychology. In 1985, he was awarded the Distinguished Contribution to Knowledge Award by the American Psychological Association. Ellis worked his entire life, continuing to teach, practice, and conduct research until well into his 90s. He held the position of president emeritus of the Albert Ellis Institute in New York until his death on July 24, 2007. He is recognized as one of the most influential figures in the history of psychology.

Randi E. McCabe

See also: Beck, Aaron T. (1921–); Cognitive Behavioral Therapy; Cognitive Therapy

Further Reading

Ellis, Albert. (1957). *How to live with a neurotic*. Oxford, England: Crown Publishers.

Engels, Gemma A., Garefski, Nadia, & Diekstra, Rene F.W. (1993). Efficacy of rational-emotive therapy: A quantitative analysis. *Journal of Consulting and Clinical Psychology, 61*, 1083–1090.

Website

www.albertellis.org

Emetophobia (Fear of Vomiting)

Emetophobia, the excessive and irrational fear of vomiting, is derived from the Greek word *emetikos*, meaning inducing or causing vomit, and *phobos*, meaning fear. It is classified in the *Diagnostic and Statistical Manual for Mental Disorders*, fifth edition (DSM-5; American Psychiatric Association, 2013) as a specific phobia, other type. Emetophobia has a prevalence of approximately 9%, tends to be more pronounced among women, typically has an early age of onset, and is chronic in course (van Hout & Bouman, 2012).

Symptoms of emetophobia include obsessive thoughts, ritualistic and safety behaviors, and panic attacks (van Hout & Bouman, 2012). Individuals with emetophobia may frequently ask how someone is feeling, or constantly check for signs of illness (e.g., appearing pale or green) in themselves or others. Compulsive, ritualistic behaviors often include excessive cleaning, checking expiration dates, overcooking food, seeking reassurance from others, or taking over-the-counter medication for nausea and stomach upset. Many individuals with emetophobia will avoid eating food that could cause food poisoning or food prepared by others; they may create a list of "safe foods" resulting in a very restrictive diet. Activities or situations that increase the likelihood of vomiting, such as traveling, amusements parks, social occasions involving alcohol, medical procedures, taking prescription medication, or even pregnancy, may be avoided. When confronted with these situations or the possibility of vomiting, individuals with emetophobia experience intense anxiety and panic. The cycle of obsession, compulsion, and avoidance interferes substantially with daily functioning (Veale, 2009).

Individuals with emetophobia are often misdiagnosed with obsessive-compulsive disorder, anorexia nervosa, social anxiety disorder (social phobia), or agoraphobia. Although individuals with emetophobia often display similar symptoms, the underlying cause of the symptoms is usually related directly to the fear of vomiting. For example, some individuals with emetophobia may be severely underweight due to restrictive food intake, an indicator of anorexia nervosa; however, they will fail to exhibit other symptoms of anorexia nervosa such as distorted body image or fear of weight gain. The food restrictions and consequential weight loss are due to the avoidance of foods that are perceived to increase the likelihood of getting sick.

Compared to other specific phobias, emetophobia is more difficult to treat (Veale, 2009). Similar to other phobias and anxiety disorders, emetophobia is often treated with cognitive behavioral therapy (CBT), which can involve psychoeducation, gradual exposure to feared situations, and cognitive restructuring. Exposure may involve looking at pictures of people who are sick, confronting "fake vomit" (mixture of various substances that has the appearance and odor of vomit), and exposure to physiological sensations associated with vomiting, such as feeling dizzy. Although CBT has been successful for some cases, the empirical evidence to date is limited (Veale, 2009).

Michelle Lonergan and Andrea R. Ashbaugh

See also: Cognitive Behavioral Therapy; Phobia, Other Type; Phobia Types

Further Reading

American Psychiatric Association (2013). *Diagnostic and statistical manual for mental disorders* (5th ed.). Arlington, VA: American Psychiatric Publishing.

van Hout, Wiljo J.P.J., & Bouman, Theo K. (2012). Clinical features, prevalence, and psychiatric complaints in subjects with fear of vomiting. *Clinical Psychology & Psychotherapy, 19*, 531–539.

Veale, David. (2009). Cognitive behavior therapy for specific phobia of vomiting. *The Cognitive Behavior Therapist, 2*, 292–288.

Emotional Processing Theory

Emotional processing theory was proposed by Foa and Kozak (1986) to conceptualize pathological fear patterns and was outlined in their seminal article entitled "Emotional Processing of Fear: Exposure to Corrective Information" (Foa & Kozak, 1986). The theory adapts an information processing perspective to conceptualize emotions as information structures (i.e., associative networks) in memory. Fear structures contain a program of information to escape or avoid danger. When the fear structure is activated, anxiety is experienced. The fear structure contains the cognitive representation of the feared situation, the individual's responses in the situation, and the individual's personal meaning/construal of the situation. For example, an individual with a needle phobia would have thoughts such as "Needles are dangerous" and "I can't cope" in the cognitive representation of the needle. The physiological responses would include feeling dizzy, tense, and faint. The behavioral responses would include escape and avoidance. Finally, the associative network for the feared stimulus of needle would be connected to the concepts of blood, nurse, hospital, health, and doctor. Due to escape and avoidance behavior, the individual does not engage the feared stimulus in a manner to allow for habituation and disconfirmation of feared meanings; thus, the phobic fear and anxiety are maintained. Emotional processing occurs when the fear structure is accessed and then modified, which can occur through therapeutic exposure to the feared stimulus. Physiological activation and habituation within and across exposure practices is proposed to reflect successful emotional processing of the feared stimulus. Based on this model of fear development and maintenance, Foa developed the treatment of prolonged exposure for addressing pathological fear. This treatment has been used with great success to treat obsessive-compulsive disorder, posttraumatic stress disorder, and other anxiety disorders and is considered a gold standard evidence-based psychological treatment.

Emotional processing theory extends the work of Lang (1977), who in his bio-informational analysis of fear imagery first described the fear image as a cognitive structure in memory that contained three types of information: (1) information about the feared stimulus or situation; (2) information about the verbal, physiological, and behavioral responses; and (3) information about the personal meaning of the stimulus and response elements. He proposed that the fear structure served as a program to avoid or escape danger and that therapy aims to activate and reorganize the "image unit" to modify the emotion associated with response elements through a process of *emotional processing*.

Foa and Kozak were also strongly influenced by the work of Rachman. In 1980, Rachman published a seminal paper outlining his conceptualization of emotional processing as a "process whereby emotional disturbances are absorbed, and decline to the extent that other experiences and behaviour can proceed without disruption" (Rachman, 1980, p. 51). Successful emotional processing is revealed by an individual's ability to discuss or be reminded of an emotionally upsetting event without experiencing significant distress or disruption. By contrast, unsuccessful emotional processing is reflected in psychological disturbance, which Rachman described as persistent and intrusive signs of emotional activity such as fear, avoidance, nightmares, obsessions, and other inappropriate (e.g., out of context) expressions of emotions. Influenced by the writings of Freud and the work of Lang, Rachman proposed his framework to integrate clinical findings and research evidence and provide an underlying mechanism to explain the success of different behavioral fear reduction methods, such as desensitization, modeling, and flooding.

Emotional processing theory has stimulated much research in the field of anxiety disorders over the past three decades. The theory was elaborated over the years and updated most recently in 2006 by Foa, Huppert, and Cahill, who integrated recent research findings, posed questions for future research, and distinguished between normal fear and pathological fear structures. Normal fear structures represent an accurate depiction of reality, whereas pathological fear structures represent a distorted depiction of reality. The distortion is maintained by behavioral and cognitive avoidance and cognitive biases in information processing, which interfere with acquisition of corrective information (i.e., information that is inconsistent with the fear structure). Emotional processing requires two steps: activation of the fear structure and incorporation of corrective information that disconfirms maladaptive elements. This may occur either through a natural recovery process over time or through cognitive behavioral therapy.

Although it has stimulated much research and helped to integrate the literature on the development and maintenance of anxiety disorders, emotional processing theory has received some criticism. Some have stated that the theory is circular and thus difficult to truly test because the marker of emotional processing is symptom reduction, and symptom reduction is reflected by emotional processing, thus the end point is the same. In addition, the theory proposes that emotional processing works through habituation and extinction; however, some evidence suggests that extinction does not eliminate or replace maladaptive associations in the fear structure but rather enables new associations to develop that compete with prior associations (e.g., Bouton, 2002).

Randi E. McCabe

See also: Exposure Treatment; Extinction; Foa, Edna B. (1937–); Habituation; Lang, Peter J. (1930–); Obsessive-Compulsive Disorder; Posttraumatic Stress Disorder; Rachman, Jack (1934–)

Further Reading

Bouton, Mark E. (2002). Context, ambiguity, and unlearning: Sources of relapse after behavioral extinction. *Biological Psychiatry, 52*, 976–998.

Foa, Edna B., Huppert, Jonathan D., & Cahill, Shawn P. (2006). Emotional processing theory: An update. In Edna B. Foa, Jonathan D. Huppert, Shawn P. Cahill, & Barbara Olasov Rothbaum (Eds.), *Pathological anxiety: Emotional processing in etiology and treatment* (pp. 3–24). New York, NY: Guilford Press.

Foa, Edna B., & Kozak, Michael, J. (1986). Emotional processing of fear: Exposure to corrective information. *Psychological Bulletin, 99*, 20–35.

Lang, Peter J. (1977). Imagery in therapy: An information processing analysis of fear. *Behavior Therapy, 8*, 862–886.

Rachman, Stanley. (1980). Emotional processing. *Behaviour Research and Therapy, 18*, 51–60.

Entomophobia (Fear of Insects)

Originating from the Greek words *entomos* (insect) and *phobos* (fear), entomophobia is an unrealistic or excessive fear of insects such as ants, bedbugs, bees, beetles, butterflies, cockroaches, crickets, dragonflies, fleas, flies, moths, and wasps. In *Diagnostic and Statistical Manual of Mental Disorders*, fifth edition, entomophobia is classified as a specific phobia. Entomophobia typically develops

An *Idea leuconoe* butterfly, also known as the Paper Kite or Rice Paper butterfly, pollinates a flower. Butterflies are considered beautiful by many people, but they can be a source of fear for individuals with entomophobia. (Courtesy of Irena Milosevic)

in early childhood and, as an animal type phobia, it is among the most common of the specific phobias (Becker et al., 2007). In most cases, the individual's fear is focused on a specific type of insect (e.g., fear of bees or fear of butterflies). The individual's fear is out of proportion to the actual danger present and often results in intense distress upon exposure to the feared insect. As a result, the individual will typically engage in efforts to avoid encountering the feared insect. For example, an individual with a fear of moths may avoid being in places where moths are common, such as near porch lights or lampposts at night or near pantries and wardrobes. When near such places, the individual is highly vigilant for signs of moths and may misperceive other flying insects to be moths. Upon seeing a moth, the individual will experience an intense episode of anxiety that may escalate into a panic attack. As a result, the individual will escape the situation as quickly as possible or endure it with a high level of distress. Entomophobia is effectively treated using cognitive behavioral therapy emphasizing situational exposure and may be completed with a therapist trained in this approach or in a self-help format (Antony & McCabe, 2005).

Randi E. McCabe

See also: Cognitive Behavioral Therapy; Exposure Treatment; Phobia, Animal Type; Phobia, Specific

Further Reading

Antony, Martin M., & McCabe, Randi E. (2005). *Overcoming animal and insect phobias*. Oakland, CA: New Harbinger Publications.

Becker, Eni S., Rinck, Mike, Türke, Veneta, Kause, Petra, Goodwin, Renee, Neumer, Simon, & Margraf, Jürgen. (2007). Epidemiology of specific phobia subtypes: Findings from the Dresden Mental Health Study. *European Psychiatry, 22*, 69–74.

Erotophobia (Fear of Sex)

Erotophobia (from the Greek *Eros*, the god of love, and *phobos*, meaning fear) pertains to a fear of sex and to negative attitudes and beliefs about sexuality. The term was coined by Cindy Patton, AIDS activist and health researcher, to describe an irrational fear of the erotic. Patton posited that erotophobia shapes the social organization of sex and sexuality (Patton, 1985). Researchers subsequently began to use the term *erotophobia* in the study of individual differences. In this context, erotophobia-erotophilia is viewed as a personality dimension reflecting variations in emotional and evaluative responses to sex (Fisher, Byrne, White, & Kelley, 1988). The erotophobic side of this dimension is associated with negative responses to sexual situations. From a clinical perspective, erotophobia is somewhat of a misnomer, as it is not classified as a specific phobia in current classification manuals of mental disorders. Rather, it may be present in the context of other disorders, such as sexual dysfunctions, posttraumatic stress disorder (PTSD), and social anxiety disorder (social phobia).

Personality researchers have shown that individuals high in erotophobia endorse negative beliefs, attitudes, expectancies, and emotional reactions related to sex, as well as different sexual behaviors, compared to individuals who are less erotophobic, or erotophillic. Individuals high in erotophobia are more likely to have stigmatizing attitudes toward sexually transmitted infections, to report less sexual knowledge, and to be less likely to pursue sex education and use contraception. Further, they may experience guilt about sex, have difficulty discussing sex, and engage in less sexual activity. Fears surrounding sex may range from fear of intimacy and vulnerability to fear of sexual situations and activities. Specific terms have been coined for different sex-related fears, including *genophobia* (fear of sexual intercourse), *haphephobia* (fear of touching), *philemaphobia* (fear of kissing), *gymnophobia* (fear of nudity), and *paraphobia* (fear of sexual perversion), among others.

As an element of a personality dimension, erotophobia is believed to develop from individuals' early learning experiences and socialization about sex. Exposure to negative perspectives toward sex, in combination with one's direct negative experiences with sexual situations, might increase the tendency to view sex in negative terms. Women are more likely than men to report greater levels of erotophobia, which may, in part, be the result of gender role socialization. Erotophobia may be a vulnerability factor for the development of clinically significant (i.e., highly distressing and disruptive) fear of sex in response to traumatic sexual events and in the context of other conditions (e.g., pain during sexual intercourse, delayed ejaculation, social performance anxiety).

When fear of sex becomes clinically significant, it is important to determine the cause of the fear, as this will have bearing on the treatment choice. For example, if fear of sex is occurring in the context of PTSD following rape, whereby the individual experiences flashbacks to the event during sexual intercourse, the individual would be offered psychological treatment for PTSD. This treatment would help the individual reduce avoidance of feared situations, including sex and intimacy. By contrast, if the individual is fearful of sex due to problems with erectile dysfunction, treatment might involve a combination of medical and psychological interventions, the latter of which would target performance anxiety. Therefore, when it comes to treating fear of sex, treatment might need to address a broader constellation of problems, although one of the more specific treatment goals may involve restoring sexual function and/or pleasure.

Irena Milosevic and Feven Yeshanew

See also: Phobia, Specific; Posttraumatic Stress Disorder; Social Anxiety Disorder (Social Phobia)

Further Reading

Fisher, William A., Byrne, Donn, White, Leonard A., & Kelley, Kathryn. (1988). Erotophobia–erotophilia as a dimension of personality. *Journal of Sex Research, 25*, 123–151.

Patton, Cindy. (1985). *Sex and germs: The politics of AIDS.* Boston, MA: South End Press.

Erythrophobia (Fear of Blushing)

Blushing is commonly defined as the reddening of the face associated with feelings of embarrassment, shyness, or shame. Other parts of the upper body may also redden during a blush, including the neck, ears, and/or upper chest. Everyone blushes, but some people find blushing so distressing that they develop a phobic fear of the response, known as erythrophobia (from the Greek *erythros*, meaning red, and *phobos*, meaning fear). There is limited research on the prevalence of erythrophobia; however, a conservative estimate is that approximately 4% of people will have a fear of blushing at some point in their lives (Dijk & de Jong, 2013).

Individuals with undue fear of blushing believe that blushing damages their image in others' eyes. They view blushing as such an undesirable response that they excessively try to prevent it by avoiding situations where they might blush and, if avoidance is not possible, they will endure these situations with immense fear. The level of fear can vary with context. For example, in a familiar and friendly environment, a fearful-blusher's anxieties may be less problematic than in a less familiar environment. Finally, individuals who fear blushing may go to great lengths to hide blushing by using a scarf or excessive make-up.

Fear of blushing is commonly referred to as a social fear. Typically, fearful blushers are afraid of blushing in interpersonal contexts. They are concerned that others will see them blush and deem them abnormal, weak, or insecure. The fear of blushing has often been described as a marker or subtype of social anxiety disorder (social phobia). Fear of blushing has been found to be the main complaint of about one-third of people who seek clinical help for their social fears (Essau, Conradt, & Petermann, 1999).

Fear of blushing can be a devastating and chronic condition. Fearful-blushers' avoidance of social situations can cause many problems. For example, they may experience difficulties initiating friendships and they may miss important promotions at work, ultimately causing them to earn less money. These resulting difficulties can impair quality of life and give rise to secondary psychological problems, such as alcohol abuse, depression, and/or suicidal ideation.

Fear of blushing can be difficult to treat. One approach to treatment is to surgically eliminate the blushing response through a procedure called endoscopic thoracic sympathectomy (ETS). Although this procedure is effective, there are a number of side effects, including compensatory sweating, which is experienced by most patients (80%), causing approximately one-quarter of patients to regret having undergone ETS (Drummond, 2013). This, however, is not the preferred treatment of choice in reducing the fear in fearful blushers.

Other approaches to treatment focus on helping to reduce the fear around the occurrence of blushing. The focus of these psychological treatments is therefore not on eliminating the symptom of blushing, as blushing is viewed as a symptom that is not under voluntary control. However, if the fear of blushing is reduced, then it is likely that the occurrence of blushing will reduce as well. Treatments used for social anxiety disorder have been typically implemented for fearful blushing. These treatments include social skills training, applied relaxation, exposure therapy, and cognitive therapy. Additionally, more recent treatments have incorporated mindfulness and acceptance-based strategies aimed at cultivating an acceptance of blushing symptoms.

Nancy L. Kocovski, Kayleigh A. Abbott, and Jan E. Fleming

See also: Applied Relaxation; Cognitive Therapy; Exposure Treatment; Social Anxiety Disorder (Social Phobia); Social Skills Training; Treatment, Psychological

Further Reading

Dijk, Corine, & de Jong, Peter J. (2013). Red, hit and scared: Mechanisms underlying fear of blushing. In W. Ray Crozier & Peter J. de Jong (Eds.), *The psychological significance of the blush* (pp. 267–285). Cambridge, UK: Cambridge University Press.

Drummond, Peter D. (2013). Psychophysiology of the blush. In W. Ray Crozier & Peter J. de Jong (Eds.), *The psychological significance of the blush* (pp. 15–38). Cambridge, UK: Cambridge University Press.

Essau, Cecilia A., Conradt, Judith, & Petermann, Franz. (1999). Frequency and comorbidity of social phobia and social fears in adolescents. *Behaviour Research and Therapy, 37,* 831–843.

Evolution, Role of

Pleasant and unpleasant emotions have evolved in humans for the purpose of motivating adaptive behavior. Though pain is unpleasant, it motivates corrective action to avoid injuries or other harmful circumstances. People born with the inability to feel pain provide a natural demonstration of its adaptive value. In one study, over half of them died by the age of 34 (Axelrod & Abularrage, 1982). Fear is another unpleasant motivational state, important for avoiding physical injuries, environmental threats, or even undesirable feelings in social situations such as embarrassment, guilt, or shame. Our ancestors who experienced fear in response to dangerous animals or sick family members, for example, were more likely to survive than those who did not because the experience of fear deterred them from coming into contact with these potential dangers.

Many phobias are considered malfunctions of emotional threat detection mechanisms, to the degree they are characterized by hypersensitivity to stimuli and automatic fear responses, and cause significant impairment in important domains of everyday functioning. Consequently, researchers have attempted to identify malfunctions in the brains of those with phobias. Evolutionary psychologists, however, consider these features as evolved characteristics of the fear response, rather than evidence of malfunction. Thus, many diagnoses of phobia may not be true instances of disorder. An important evolutionary perspective argues that every true instance of disorder involves an adaptation that is malfunctioning (Wakefield, 1992). Once the physiological and psychological characteristics of threat detection mechanisms are completely understood and explained, then instances of disorder can be identified from the deviations from evolved functioning.

From an evolutionary perspective, the diagnostic criteria for phobia can be interpreted as a description of an adaptive stress response, rather than symptoms of malfunction. According to the *Diagnostic and Statistical Manual of Mental Disorders*, fifth edition (DSM-5), the first characteristic of a specific phobia is a persistent fear caused by the presentation or anticipation of the phobic object or situation that is disproportionate to the possible danger. Fear in the presence of safe stimuli, or fear that is caused by simply thinking about the phobic stimulus, is considered "disproportionate." Though sometimes superfluous, this hypercaution is not useless. Humans have evolved fear and threat detection mechanisms that are overly conservative because the cost of not being afraid when the stimulus does present danger greatly outweighs the cost of being afraid in the absence of danger. Although a false positive in danger detection causes unnecessary energy expenditure and subjective feelings of distress, a false negative causes us to be unprepared to deal with a dangerous situation and is more likely to result in injury or death. This hypersensitivity in the fear response can trigger a phobia of generally harmless stimuli or a safe stimulus that resembles a harmful one. For instance, birds are not dangerous to humans but their sharp beaks and talons can, in theory, cause us some harm. Garden hoses are completely harmless, but they resemble snakes, which can be poisonous. In most cases, a fear of birds and garden hoses is unnecessary; however, this fear is beneficial in the off-chance the bird will harm us or the hose is actually a snake. Because the hypervigilance of the fear response is useful to some degree, distinguishing between adaptive fear and a disordered "phobic" state is not clear-cut. Most likely, fear and phobia exist along a continuum, with no fundamental physiological or psychological criteria differentiating between the two. Even when viewing the same stimulus, individuals fulfilling criteria for spider phobia show very similar but elevated response patterns when compared to non-phobic individuals (Gerdes, Uhl, & Alpers, 2009). The increased fear observed in individuals with phobia does not suggest a breakdown in the fear response. Rather, it may reflect adaptive differences in sensitivity to potentially relevant cues, due to developmental or situational factors.

The neurological adaptations that affect threat sensitivity (i.e., the threshold that triggers a fear response) have been partially mapped out (Gray & McNaughton, 2000), and like all adaptations these can malfunction. From a practical standpoint, however, identifying such a malfunction is difficult since the fear response is designed to be hypervigilant. Furthermore, the precise neural mechanisms involved in threat sensitivity have not yet been specified. Diagnoses of phobia are nevertheless established simply by determining how necessary fear seems relative to the environmental trigger. Under this criterion, individuals who exhibit elevated fear responses despite normally functioning threat sensitivity systems are inaccurately diagnosed with a disorder.

Other characteristics contributing to a diagnosis of specific phobia or social anxiety disorder (social phobia) include an immediate fear response when faced with the fear-causing stimulus or situation and subsequent avoidance. Behavioral responses that are automatic are highly preserved over time because they solve crucial adaptive problems. The fear and escape response (also referred to as the *fight-or-flight response*) described in the DSM-5 is a sympathetic nervous system reaction, evolved to assist in the escape of an impending danger or fear-inducing situation. This response is a series of reflexes that include an increased heart rate and blood flow to skeletal muscles, energy liberation, sweating, and pupil dilation. In the context of phobia, feelings of fear are unpleasant, in part because they are involuntary and uncontrollable. However, a fear response that is delayed or activated only under conscious control of an individual is not as adaptive as an automatic one. Each component of the immediate stress response serves a specific purpose in increasing the likelihood of escaping a threatening stimulus, despite any feelings of distress or impairment caused by the inability to suppress it.

The trigger of an automatic response such as anxiety depends on the nature of the stimuli, such that dangerous stimuli are perceived and responded to automatically whereas neutral stimuli are not (Carlsson & Petersson, 2004; Öhman & Soares, 1993). Accordingly, the human body selects which stimuli are potentially dangerous and warrant a reflexive fear response. If phobias, as defined by the DSM-5, are evolved adaptations, the fear response should occur most quickly and reliably in response to stimuli that pose the greatest danger to humans and other mammals (Mineka & Öhman, 2002). Indeed, with some exceptions, phobias typically develop in response to stimuli that were dangerous to humans throughout the evolutionary history. These include fears of poisonous animals such as spiders and snakes, environmental situations such as cliffs and tornadoes, as well as blood, injections, and injuries that can lead to contracting infections from others. Although fears related to social interactions or situations have less overt survival value, they prevent humans from destroying helpful relationships with conspecifics or potential mates. Because the nature of these fears has implications for survival and fitness, the fears were likely selected for (i.e., passed on to subsequent generations more frequently than others) and reflect functional response mechanisms.

According to the diagnostic criteria, phobias also interfere with an individual's normal functioning or daily routine. From an evolutionary perspective, the experience of fear necessarily causes a disruption in expected behavior in order to deter performing actions or staying in situations that evoke fear. Phobias occur most often in response to a particular subset of stimuli that has been consistently dangerous in evolutionary history. Therefore, phobias may have evolved because a strong avoidance in response to these stimuli was particularly beneficial.

The evolved threat detection mechanisms and fear responses in humans are important for promoting behaviors that increase chances of survival. Although these mechanisms and responses can malfunction, subjective distress and impairment are not necessarily evidence of malfunction. From an evolutionary standpoint, the current diagnostic criteria for phobia are written in subjective terms and do not clearly differentiate between functional fear and malfunctioning phobia. This results in inconsistent diagnoses and inaccurate assessments of disorder. This is not to say that treatment of intense fears cannot improve the life of the individuals experiencing them. In modern environments, properly functioning threat detection mechanisms might produce harmful outcomes. Treatment efforts should focus on alleviating distress and minimizing impairment in these situations, regardless if a malfunction is present. Regarding the understanding and assessment of phobias, however, evolutionary perspectives can offer great insight by emphasizing the evolved functions of threat detection and fear response mechanisms.

Marley J. Russell, Marta M. Maslej, and Paul W. Andrews

See also: DSM-5; Fear, Neural Pathways of; Fight-or-Flight Response; Non-Associative Model; Preparedness Theory

Further Reading

Axelrod, Felicia B., & Abularrage, Joseph J. (1982). Familial dysautonomia: A prospective study of survival. *The Journal of Pediatrics, 101*, 234–236.

Carlsson, Katrina, Petersson, Karl M., Lundqvist, Daniel, Karlsson, Andreas, Ingvar, Martin, & Öhman, Arne. (2004). Fear and the amygdala: Manipulation of awareness generates differential cerebral responses to phobic and fear-relevant (but nonfeared) stimuli. *Emotion, 4*, 340–353.

Gerdes, Antje B. M., Uhl, Gabriele, & Alpers, Georg W. (2009). Spiders are special: Fear and disgust evoked by pictures of arthropods. *Evolution and Human Behaviour, 30*, 66–73.

Gray, Jeffrey A., & McNaughton, Neil. (2000). *The neuropsychology of anxiety* (2nd ed.). Oxford, UK: Oxford University Press.

Mineka, Susan, & Öhman, Arne. (2002). Phobias and preparedness: The selective, automatic, and encapsulated nature of fear. *Biological Psychiatry, 52*, 926–937.

Öhman, Arne, & Soares, Joaquim J. F. (1993). On the automatic nature of phobic fear: Conditioned electrodermal responses to masked fear-relevant stimuli. *Journal of Abnormal Psychology, 102*, 121–132.

Wakefield, Jerome C. (1992). The concept of mental disorder: On the boundary between biological facts and social values. *American Psychologist, 47*, 373–388.

IN DARWIN'S WORDS

English naturalist Charles Darwin, often called the "father of evolution," developed the biological theory of evolution. Darwin's theory, which has been extensively supported by scientific evidence, transformed our understanding of the natural world and influenced thinking across a wide range of fields, including psychology. Darwin proposed natural selection as one of the key mechanisms of evolution, whereby organisms that are better adapted to their environment tend to survive and pass on their biological traits to their offspring.

Evolutionary theory has been used to explain how fears and phobias develop. Darwin himself hypothesized that fear has an evolutionary basis. In 1877, when he took his two-year-old son to the zoo, he observed that the boy was frightened of the large animals in cages. Although the boy later expressed a desire to return to the zoo, he stated that he did not want to see the "beasts in houses." This led Darwin to wonder, "May we not suspect that the vague but very real fears of children, which are quite independent of experience, are the inherited effects of real dangers and abject superstitions during ancient savage times?" (Darwin, 1877, p. 288).

Thus, Darwin proposed that childhood fears must be inherited because they arise in the absence of prior experience with the feared situation (e.g., at the first exposure of a large animal). He turned to the process of natural selection to explain the cause of such fears, hypothesizing that they helped our ancestors survive the dangers in their environment and were accordingly passed along to future generations. In other words, Darwin's young son was immediately fearful of large animals because fear of these animals during "savage times" ensured the survival of our distant relatives.

Irena Milosevic

Further Reading

Darwin, Charles. (1877). A biographical sketch of an infant. *Mind, 2*, 285–294.

Exposure, Imaginal

Imaginal exposure is a therapeutic technique used in the treatment of specific phobias, as well as other anxiety disorders. Its main goal is to decrease anxiety and fear by repeatedly having clients engage with (i.e., gain *exposure* to) mental images or scenarios (*imaginal* scenes) involving a feared stimulus, rather than with the feared stimulus itself (i.e., *in vivo* exposure). For example, individuals with a fear of flying (aviophobia) may expose themselves to this fear by repeatedly, vividly imagining an air travel scenario. Imaginal exposure has both theoretical and empirical support in the treatment of fear and anxiety, and it can be tailored for use with specific phobias.

Imaginal exposure has a number of important historical roots, including its use in the original construal of systematic desensitization (Wolpe, 1958). In this type of therapy, clients were taught to use relaxation techniques while repeatedly imagining their feared stimulus in a graded fashion, using increasingly challenging or threatening mental imagery. Although common during Wolpe's systematic desensitization, relaxation techniques are not typically used in contemporary imaginal exposure to facilitate habituation.

Theoretically, imaginal exposure leads to reduced anxiety in two main ways: (1) *habituation/extinction* (see *Habituation* and *Extinction*) and (2) *creating competing cognitive structures. Creating competing cognitive structures* refers to the consequences of gaining new information (e.g., that the object or situation is not as threatening/dangerous as was previously believed), leading to thinking about the feared stimulus in less anxiety-provoking ways. For example, individuals with aviophobia who take several flights would observe that the plane did not crash, perhaps leading to the new belief that airplanes are generally safe.

Imaginal exposure for specific phobia can be used in three main ways: (1) as a stand-alone form of treatment; (2) as a preliminary or preparatory step toward physically engaging with a feared stimulus, with the idea that *in vivo* exposure would follow; or (3) as a way to supplement or extend *in vivo* exposure (Abramowitz, Deacon, & Whiteside, 2011). In each case, imaginal exposure begins by identifying when, where, and how the fear occurs, as well as the expected consequences (e.g., the plane will crash in the case of aviophobia). Next, the therapist and client create a hierarchy of fear, ranking each situation/stimulus by how much anxiety or fear it causes. The least feared stimuli are placed at the bottom of the hierarchy and those that are most fear-provoking are placed at the top. Imaginal exposures begin with the least threatening scenarios on the hierarchy, and gradually increase in difficulty as anxiety declines. The client often creates a written or audio-recorded scenario of an encounter with the feared stimulus using first-person language. The therapist and client refine this scenario together in order to maximize the therapeutic impact of the exercise (e.g., by specifying details, by discussing predictions). The client then imagines the scene while reading or listening to the imaginal exposure scenario repeatedly until the fear decreases. If imaginal exposure is being used to supplement *in vivo* exposure, the client and therapist develop imaginal exposure exercises that best enhance the planned *in vivo* exposure. For example, a person who fears a plane crash may imagine and/or write about a scenario of a plane crash (imaginal exposure) to read repeatedly before and even during plane travel (*in vivo* exposure).

Although *in vivo* exposure is more commonly used in contemporary treatments for specific phobias, imaginal exposure is appropriate when *in vivo* exposure is either impractical or impossible. For example, it would be impractical for most people with aviophobia to take repeated, long plane trips to treat their anxiety. Research findings suggest that imaginal exposure is an effective therapeutic technique for specific phobias. For instance, a review of specific phobia treatments found that imaginal exposure was as effective as *in vivo* exposure several months after completion of treatment, although not immediately following treatment (Wolitzky-Taylor, Horowitz, Powers, & Telch, 2008). This appears to result from individuals continuing to improve following imaginal exposure treatment.

Elizabeth A. Hebert, Rachael L. Neal, and Adam S. Radomsky

See also: Aviophobia (Fear of Flying); Cognitive Restructuring; Exposure, *In Vivo*; Extinction; Habituation; Systematic Desensitization; Wolpe, Joseph (1915–1997)

Further Reading

Abramowitz, Jonathan S., Deacon, Brett J., & Whiteside, Stephen P. H. (2011). *Exposure therapy for anxiety: Principles and practice*. New York, NY: The Guilford Press.

Wolitzky-Taylor, Kate B., Horowitz, Jonathan D., Powers, Mark B., & Telch, Michael J. (2008). Psychological approaches in the treatment of specific phobias: A meta-analysis. *Clinical Psychology Review*, 28, 1021–1037.

Wolpe, Joseph. (1958). *Psychotherapy by reciprocal inhibition*. Palo Alto, CA: Stanford University Press.

Exposure, *In Vivo*

In vivo exposure is a component of cognitive behavioral therapy, a form of treatment used to treat anxiety-related problems, including specific phobias. *In vivo* exposure involves gradually approaching situations and stimuli that are related to one's fear. For example, someone with entomophobia (fear of insects) might be asked to look at and touch insects, while someone with ophidiophobia (fear of snakes) might be asked to approach and touch snakes.

In vivo exposure is based on behavioral theory, which states that remaining in a feared situation or in the presence of something feared and experiencing the associated feelings of anxiety will eventually lead to anxiety reduction (habituation). The theory also states that if this same situation or object is approached again later on, the individual should be less anxious and his or her anxiety should go down even faster. There can often be a return of fear, in which the fear rebounds somewhat between sessions only to decline rapidly upon additional exposure to the relevant stimulus. This process allows individuals to learn that anxiety can go away on its own and that their feared outcomes do not occur, thus weakening associations between feared stimuli and anxiety. With repeated *in vivo* exposures, fear can be extinguished.

The first introduction of *in vivo* exposure, called "systematic desensitization," was described by Joseph Wolpe (1915–1997) in 1958. Systematic desensitization initially involved *imagining* being in a feared situation, and later shifted to being in the presence of feared objects or situations while using relaxation and coping strategies. This evolved to *in vivo* exposure, which does not involve using relaxation strategies, but rather often emphasizes experiencing the feelings of anxiety. Another version of *in vivo* exposure, "flooding," was introduced by Thomas Stampfl (1923–2005) in 1967. Flooding involves confronting one's biggest fear straight away rather than taking steps and slowly progressing to the biggest fear. Thus, someone with a fear of spiders (arachnophobia) might immediately have one or more spiders crawl all over them, whereas an individual doing graded *in vivo* exposure may start by looking at pictures and videos of spiders, then later progress to being in a room with and eventually touching a spider.

Contemporary *in vivo* exposure therapy for specific phobias begins with an in-depth discussion between the therapist and the individual about the individual's specific fears. They also discuss the individual's unhelpful or unrealistic beliefs about the phobic stimulus, and the feared consequences related to those beliefs. For instance, a person with spider phobia may believe that spiders bite aggressively, and that he or she would panic and have a heart attack if bitten. The therapist and individual then collaboratively construct a *fear hierarchy*, which is a graduated series of activities that the individual will engage in (often with the therapist's assistance) to become increasingly close to the feared object or situation. The individual provides ratings for how fear-provoking each step would be, and the steps are then organized from lowest to highest fear level. The therapist then helps the individual proceed through the steps. The individual may be asked to provide ratings of distress at different points during the exposure session(s) in order to monitor changes in anxiety as he or she approaches and becomes accustomed to each step of the exposure. *In vivo* exposure can be conducted during one longer session or over a series of several shorter sessions. The individual may also be asked to do these things on his or her own, between sessions.

Successful *in vivo* exposure results in an extinction of the individual's avoidance of the feared situation or object, such that daily life is no longer negatively impacted by the phobia. Research examining treatments for specific phobia suggests that *in vivo* exposure results in significant decreases in fear and avoidance when symptoms are measured immediately after treatment completion, and that the improvements are typically maintained or enhanced over time (Choy, Fyer, & Lipsitz, 2007).

Rachael L. Neal, Jessica M. Senn, and Adam S. Radomsky

See also: Behavioral Model; Cognitive Behavioral Therapy; Exposure Treatment, Imaginal; One-Session Treatment; Wolpe, Joseph (1915–1997)

Further Reading

Abramowitz, Jonathan S., Deacon, Brett J., & Whiteside, Stephen P. H. (2011). *Exposure therapy for anxiety: Principles and practice.* New York, NY: The Guilford Press.

Choy, Yujuan, Fyer, Abby J., & Lipsitz, Josh D. (2007). Treatment of specific phobia in adults. *Clinical Psychology Review, 27,* 266–286.

Wolitzky-Taylor, Kate B., Horowitz, Jonathan D., Powers, Mark B., & Telch, Michael J. (2008). Psychological approaches in the treatment of specific phobias: A meta-analysis. *Clinical Psychology Review, 28,* 1021–1037.

Exposure, Interoceptive

Therapeutic exposure is a technique used in the treatment of anxiety disorders. This technique involves the planned and predictable confrontation of one's feared object or situation. *Interoceptive exposure* is a specific type of therapeutic exposure that involves intentionally bringing on internal physical sensations (e.g. pounding heart, sweating, shortness of breath, or shaking). This type of exposure treatment is typically applied to individuals with fear of physical sensations of anxiety, also known as anxiety sensitivity. Anxiety sensitivity is a common characteristic of individuals who suffer from panic disorder but also occurs across the anxiety disorder spectrum (Boswell et al., 2013). Interoceptive exposures are often used with individuals who have specific phobias, especially when their fear is related to the physical sensations that are triggered when faced with the feared object or situation.

Claustrophobia (fear of being in enclosed and/or small spaces) is one example of a specific phobia that may involve a fear of physical sensations. Often an individual with claustrophobia will fear hyperventilation, as this sensation can be misperceived as indicating insufficient airflow and suffocation. Fear of internal sensations is also common in height phobias, as feeling weakness in one's legs when standing high above the ground may be misperceived as indicating that one is falling. Fears of physical sensations are also common among individuals with blood-injection-injury type phobias, as light-headedness in response to the sight of blood, for example, can indicate that one will faint. It is always important to assess individuals with any type of phobia to understand whether fear of physical sensations plays a role in their phobia, as interoceptive exposures can be very effective in reducing this fear (Antony, Craske, & Barlow, 2006).

Interoceptive exposures involve using different types of exercises to bring on feared physical sensations. Examples of common interoceptive exposures include shaking one's head from side to side or spinning around in a swivel chair if afraid of feeling dizzy, faint, or light-headed. Individuals can also try shallowly breathing at a rate of 100–120 breaths per minute if afraid of experiencing a racing heart, breathlessness, or smothering sensations, or if afraid of trembling, shaking, numbness, or tingling sensations. Tensing all muscles in the body can also be utilized if an individual is afraid of trembling, shaking, or feeling smothered. Individuals can run on the spot if afraid of experiencing breathlessness, chest tightness, sweating, a racing heart, or blushing. Sitting in a sauna or hot car or wearing warm clothing can be helpful to individuals who are afraid of experiencing breathlessness, smothering sensations, hot flushes, sweating, or blushing, and having a hot drink or hot soup may be used if a person is afraid of sweating, blushing, or having hot flushes.

The first step to deciding which interoceptive exposures may be useful in treatment is to begin with inducing different physical sensations while paying attention to which ones provoke the most fear and which ones are most similar to those that are produced in the phobic situation. In this way, the most appropriate sensations can be targeted. Next, the individual should develop an interoceptive exposure hierarchy, listing the different exposure practices (from least anxiety-provoking to most anxiety-provoking) that he or she will attempt. Finally, the individual should practice the interoceptive exposures, starting with the least anxiety-provoking, and gradually move up the hierarchy. When people progress through their exposure hierarchy systematically and at their own pace, this is called *gradual* interoceptive exposure. Interoceptive exposures can be done more rapidly (i.e., where the individual moves on to more difficult exposure practices before mastering easier ones). However, gradual exposures have been found to be more tolerable for people with specific phobias, and may be useful for individuals who are reluctant to engage in exposures, those who are at risk of dropping out of treatment, and those who report a very high level of fear at the beginning of treatment.

When conducting interoceptive exposures, there are particular guidelines that should be followed to ensure success. The exposures should be planned and predictable (i.e., under the person's control) and repeated frequently (i.e., daily). The person should feel some anxiety during the exposures, stay in the anxiety-provoking situation until his or her anxiety decreases, and try to refrain from using avoidance strategies (e.g., engaging in distraction, using alcohol or other substances). The exposures should be practiced in a number of settings so that the decreased fear can generalize to multiple situations. Finally, exposures should set the person up for success; that is, the person should choose exposures that are anxiety-provoking, but not so anxiety-provoking that it is impossible to complete the exposure.

Interoceptive exposures work by providing individuals with evidence against their belief that the physical sensations they are experiencing are threatening. In turn, these exposures help people gather evidence in support of the belief that they are able to cope with their physical sensations and that the consequences of experiencing these physical sensations are minimal (and often not dangerous). As well, interoceptive exposures promote habituation to the experience of physical sensations. Habituation occurs when there is a diminished response to physical sensations due to repeated exposure to them. Accordingly, through repeated practice, people eventually become accustomed to their sensations.

Brenda L. Key and Caitlin Davey

See also: Anxiety Sensitivity; Claustrophobia (Fear of Enclosed Spaces); Exposure Treatment

Further Reading

Antony, Martin M., Craske, Michelle G., & Barlow, David H. (2006). *Mastering your fears and phobias*. New York, NY: Oxford University Press.

Antony, Martin M., & Swinson, Richard P. (2008). *The shyness and social anxiety workbook*. Oakland, CA: New Harbinger Publications Inc.

Boswell, James F., Farchione, Todd J., Sauer-Zavala, Shannon, Murray, Heather W., Fortune, Meghan H., & Barlow, David H. (2013). Anxiety sensitivity and interoceptive exposures: A transdiagnostic construct and change strategy. *Behavior Therapy, 44*, 417–431.

Exposure Treatment

Exposure treatment ("exposure") is a cognitive behavioral therapeutic approach to treating pathological anxiety. Although exposure may be delivered in a variety of formats, exposure generally involves the systematic and guided confrontation of an anxious individual to feared objects and/or situations. Exposure is thought to reduce anxiety through the modification of underlying maladaptive beliefs about feared stimuli, and by extinguishing conditioned fear responses. Exposure has been shown to be a highly effective treatment for a number of anxiety-related problems compared to medication and other psychological treatments.

The main providers of exposure treatment for anxiety are psychotherapists with a master's or doctorate-level training in psychology. Such exposure therapists include counselors, clinical psychologists, licensed clinical social workers, and psychiatrists. Although exposure has been used to effectively treat a number of psychological problems, recipients of exposure treatments are generally children or adults diagnosed with an anxiety disorder such as specific phobias, obsessive-compulsive disorder (OCD), panic disorder, agoraphobia, posttraumatic stress disorder, or social anxiety disorder (social phobia).

Modern exposure treatments for anxiety disorders derived from earlier approaches such as systematic desensitization, which involved having a client imagine encountering feared stimuli while simultaneously engaging in relaxation techniques. Later research showed that concurrent relaxation was not a necessary treatment component, leading several psychologists (including Isaac Marks, Edna Foa, and David Barlow) to develop a more efficient technique. Modern exposure is usually delivered in weekly, hour-long therapy sessions and is time-limited in nature (e.g., 12–16 weeks). For some anxiety-related problems such as specific phobias, exposure therapy may require fewer sessions. Exposure treatments may be delivered in individual or group format, with or without the assistance of a therapist, or over electronic mediums (such as through video webcams).

The initial stage of exposure treatment is dedicated to functional analysis of a client's presenting problems—a detailed investigation of the client's main concerns, what triggers the client's fears, and what the client does to avoid or reduce the resulting anxiety (i.e., safety behaviors). After collecting this necessary information, the therapist then explains the case conceptualization to the client, provides accurate information regarding the nature of anxiety and the factors that maintain it, and describes a recommended course of exposure-based treatment for the client's approval.

The next step of exposure treatment involves the therapist and client collaboratively devising a fear hierarchy—a rank-ordered list of a client's feared objects and/or situations to be encountered over the course of therapy. The fear hierarchy serves as a sort of road map and task checklist for the therapist and client during treatment. The type and number of items on the fear hierarchy depend on the client's presenting problem(s) and the treatment provider's method. Typically, fear hierarchies are approximately 10 items long per client problem. Exposure tasks can include intentional induction of feared body sensations (interoceptive exposure), repeatedly recalling a traumatic memory or unwanted thought in detail (imaginal exposure), or coming into actual contact with feared objects and/or situations (*in vivo* exposure).

Once a fear hierarchy is constructed, the client begins to systematically encounter the identified stimuli. Clients often complete initial exposure tasks in the presence of the therapist ("therapist-guided exposure"), but they are usually expected to conduct exposures independently outside of therapy sessions as well ("client-directed exposure"). Although clients may choose to start with the least anxiety-provoking task on the fear hierarchy, there is no obligation to do so if a client prefers to start with a more challenging task.

Before beginning an exposure task, the therapist and client briefly discuss the goal of the particular exposure. The therapist also acknowledges that the client is likely to become anxious during the task, but that the anxiety indicates that the task is being conducted correctly. The therapist further emphasizes that the anxiety the client will experience during the exposure is only temporary. It is also valuable to identify what a client is afraid might happen during an exposure task; this way, the client's fearful beliefs can serve as hypotheses to be tested during the exposure "experiment." Therapists also encourage clients to refrain from resisting the anxiety, distracting themselves from the anxiety, or engaging in safety behaviors during exposures in order to maximize the chances of improvement.

During an exposure, the therapist and client usually track predetermined indices of an exposure task's "success." One popular subjective index is the Subjective Units of Distress Scale, which involves clients reporting their level of anxiety, ranging from 0 (no anxiety) to 100 (maximum possible anxiety). Other indices include tracking whether or not the client's feared outcome has happened (e.g., whether or not sitting in an enclosed space has resulted in anticipated suffocation) and the client's perceived ability to tolerate the discomfort evoked by the exposure task. Exposure tasks may be relatively short or long in duration, depending on (1) the nature of the task and (2) how long it takes for the client's fearful beliefs to be disconfirmed and/or the client to experience a significant reduction in anxiety ("habituation"). Following an exposure, the therapist reviews the task with the client, underscoring the client's anxiety toleration during the task and highlighting whether or not the client's feared outcome actually happened. Clients are encouraged to repeat the exposures outside of therapy in varied contexts (such as in different locations) to maximize chances for long-term improvement. Exposure treatments last as long as necessary for the client to experience symptom reduction and improved quality of life. It is also advisable for therapists and clients to continue exposure treatment until the most difficult exposure item on the fear hierarchy has been successfully completed multiple times in multiple contexts.

Throughout the course of treatment, exposure therapists might also provide some form of cognitive therapy—therapy that involves discussing and challenging a client's core beliefs that may be maintaining the psychological problem. Common thought styles that are challenged during exposure treatment include a client (1) overestimating the likelihood and severity of possible negative outcomes associated with feared stimuli (e.g., whether or not a socially anxious client is highly likely to say something embarrassing during a conversation with strangers and, if so, if the embarrassment will truly be unbearable) and (2) being unable to tolerate uncertainty (e.g., needing a 100% guarantee that a feared event will not occur).

Exposure treatments for phobias and other anxiety disorders have been studied in many randomized controlled trials (RCTs). Results from RCTs suggest that exposure-based therapies are the most effective treatment available for anxiety problems. Exposure therapies have demonstrated superiority to no treatment, placebo treatments, and non-exposure-based treatments. Exposure therapy is not generally improved by the addition of medications, and exposure therapy is more effective than medication for some anxiety problems (e.g., OCD and specific phobias). Accordingly, exposure is considered the best first-line treatment for anxiety disorders. Despite the strong research evidence highlighting the effectiveness of exposure treatment for anxiety problems, many therapists are hesitant to provide it. This reluctance often stems from therapist reservations regarding the dangerousness or ethicality of encouraging a client to encounter his or her feared objects and/or situations. For example, some therapists report fears that providing exposure will lead a client to quit therapy, become retraumatized, experience unbearable anxiety, or have a medical emergency in response to experiencing intense distress. Yet research shows that these concerns are unfounded, as these feared outcomes of providing exposure treatment are remarkably infrequent. Therefore, it is beneficial to remind wary therapists as well as anxious clients that a client's long-term improvement will likely outweigh any short-term anxiety associated with conducting exposures.

Shannon M. Blakey and Brett J. Deacon

See also: Barlow, David H. (1942–); Cognitive Restructuring; Exposure, Imaginal; Exposure, *In Vivo*; Exposure, Interoceptive; Foa, Edna B. (1937–); Habituation; Marks, Isaac M. (1937–); Safety Behavior; Subjective Units of Distress Scale; Systematic Desensitization

Further Reading

Abramowitz, Jonathan S., Deacon, Brett J., & Whiteside, Stephen P. H. (2011). *Exposure therapy for anxiety: Principles and practice*. New York, NY: The Guilford Press.

Barlow, David H., Ellard, Kristen K., Fairholme, Christopher P., Farchione, Todd J., Boisseau, Christina L., Allen, Laura B., & Ehrenreich-May, Jill T. (2010). *Unified protocol for transdiagnostic treatment of emotional disorders: Workbook*. New York, NY: Oxford University Press.

Moscovitch, David A., Antony, Martin M., & Swinson, Richard P. (2009). Exposure-based treatments for anxiety disorders: Theory and process. In Martin M. Antony & Murray B. Stein (Eds.), *Oxford handbook of anxiety and related disorders* (pp. 461–475). New York, NY: Oxford Press.

Norton, Peter J. (2012). *Group cognitive-behavioral therapy of anxiety: A transdiagnostic treatment manual*. New York, NY: Guilford Press.

CLIMBING UP THE LADDER

In exposure treatment, individuals gradually confront their fear in a series of steps of increasing difficulty—very much like climbing the steps of a ladder. The bottom steps are least fear-provoking and the top steps evoke the greatest fear levels. This is termed an *exposure hierarchy* and usually consists of about 10–12 steps.

To start, the clinician works with the individual to create a list of feared situations related to the phobia. The list may be generated by asking the individual a series of questions regarding the impact of the phobia on his or her life. For example, "What situations do you avoid because of this phobia?" and "What would you like to be doing but feel you are not able to because you have this fear?" For a person with a spider phobia, this may include such situations as walking in the backyard, going in the basement, entering the garage, and sleeping with the window open. The clinician will also add situations that the individual might not report because including these types of situations in the exposure hierarchy will ensure the greatest fear reduction—for example, the clinician might recommend looking at a spider web, looking at a spider, touching a spider with a pencil, touching a spider with a finger, and holding a spider. The clinician will then ask the individual to rate the amount of fear expected when encountering each situation using a subjective units of distress scale (SUDS). Once all of the situations are rated, they are organized in a hierarchy or ladder from low to high fear.

The clinician uses the hierarchy to guide exposure treatment. Treatment begins with the individual choosing a step on the ladder to start exposure practice with. For some people this may be the bottom step but others may choose to start higher. The step should create some level of anxiety, otherwise a higher step should be chosen. For example, an item with a fear level of 5 will not facilitate fear reduction because it is not associated with any significant fear level. Ideally, the hierarchy ranges from a SUDS of 30 (e.g., walking in the garage) all the way up to 100 (e.g., holding a spider). The individual practices a step repeatedly until he or she achieves significant fear reduction on that step. For example, practicing touching a spider with a pencil may be associated with a SUDS rating of 60 to start, but with prolonged exposure the

SUDS rating will greatly reduce over time (e.g., to 20). The individual will then repeat that practice until the fear associated with the situation is minimal. The individual is then ready to proceed up the next step of the ladder.

Overall, the exposure hierarchy helps break down phobic avoidance into successive steps so that an individual can gradually overcome his or her fear without being overwhelmed. While proceeding up the exposure hierarchy steps, the individual not only experiences significant fear reduction but also has reduced avoidance and increased feelings of mastery and self-confidence.

Randi E. McCabe

Extinction

During extinction the frequency and/or intensity of a behavioral response is reduced. At the beginning of the 20th century, Ivan Pavlov (1849–1936), a Russian physiologist, first noticed that his dogs would salivate at the sound of a bell because the bell predicted the dogs' meal. However, after repeated presentations of the bell without food, the salivary response diminished. This decline in salivary responding to the bell is an example of extinction. Extinction can also occur for operant behaviors. When a behavior no longer produces consequences—either positive or negative—then it will occur less frequently.

Extinction has important clinical applications in the treatment of phobias and other anxiety disorders, as the inability to suppress inappropriate fear responses—that is, to experience extinction of fear—is the hallmark of all phobias. A common, empirically validated approach to treat these disorders is cognitive behavioral therapy (including exposure treatment), which relies on extinction processes. For instance, an individual's fear of spiders can be treated by repeatedly exposing the individual to stimuli associated with spiders without aversive consequences. After repeated presentations, the individual learns that spiders (and/or cues associated with them) no longer predict a negative outcome and anxiety/fear is reduced.

Extinction is not an erasure of the original fear memory. Instead, it is a new learning process that inhibits the original fear memory. There are several situations when fear responding can reemerge even after successful extinction learning. For instance, if fear extinction to a spider occurs in one day, and some time passes before a spider is presented again, the fear response to the spider may return to some extent. This is known as spontaneous recovery of fear, due to the passage of time. Fear extinction is also context-specific, which means that if an individual experiences extinction in a clinician's office he or she will learn not to fear the spider in the clinician's office but might not generalize this safe association to other contexts or places, like the home, office, or stores. Instead, in each new place the individual would experience renewal of fear when presented with the spider and would need to undergo extinction. Lastly, fear may be reinstated if an individual experiences an aversive outcome with the feared cue such as being bitten by a spider (Myers & Davis, 2007).

Enhancing the neural and neurochemical substrates of fear inhibitory learning could solve some of the challenges of extinction and return of fear. Exciting new evidence has shown that pharmacological agents known as "cognitive enhancers" can increase fear extinction in animals and facilitate exposure-based therapy in patients with height phobia and claustrophobia (Kaplan & Moore, 2011).

Shoko Mori and Christine A. Rabinak

See also: Classical Conditioning; Cognitive Behavioral Therapy; D-Cycloserine; Exposure, *In Vivo*; Fear, Return of (Relapse); Habituation; Operant Conditioning; Pavlov, Ivan (1849–1936)

Further Reading

Kaplan, Gary. B., & Moore, Katherine A. (2011). The use of cognitive enhancers in animal models of fear extinction. *Pharmacology, Biochemisty, and Behavior, 99*, 217–228.

Myers, Karyn M., & Davis, Michael. (2007). Mechanisms of fear extinction. *Molecular Psychiatry, 12*(2), 120–150.

Eye Movement Desensitization and Reprocessing

Eye movement desensitization and reprocessing (EMDR) is a psychotherapeutic approach developed by Francine Shapiro to treat posttraumatic stress disorder (PTSD) and the psychological distress associated with trauma memories (Shapiro, 2001). EMDR is recognized as an effective treatment approach for PTSD. Although originally developed for treatment of PTSD, EMDR has been found to be effective in reducing distress associated with other anxiety-related conditions including spider phobia, panic disorder, test anxiety, and public-speaking anxiety. The therapy has also been applied to other types of problems such as depression.

The treatment originated with Shapiro's personal observation that her eye movements reduced the negative feelings she experienced when recalling distressing memories. Hypothesizing that the eye movements had a desensitizing effect, Shapiro began to test her theory with promising effects (Shapiro, 1989). Initially termed *eye movement desensitization*, the treatment was renamed to *eye movement desensitization and reprocessing* in 1991 based on Shapiro's belief that cognitive changes and information processing were critical factors in explaining positive treatment response. She developed the adaptive information processing model to explain the efficacy of the approach.

The EMDR approach is an eight-phase treatment that involves having the individual focus on emotionally upsetting memories while simultaneously focusing on an external stimulus such as therapist-directed lateral eye movements, hand tapping, or audio stimulation. In Phase 1 (history taking, case conceptualization, and treatment planning), treatment targets are identified that may include traumatic memories as well as current situations that evoke distress, and therapy-specific skills are developed. In Phase 2 (client preparation), various coping strategies for managing emotional distress are taught for use between sessions when needed. In Phase 3–6, the EMDR procedures are used to process an identified trauma memory target that encompasses an intense visual image, a negative belief about the self, and any associated emotions and physical sensations. A positive belief is also identified. The individual is instructed to focus on the image, belief, and physical sensations as the therapist encourages processing using sets of bilateral stimulation (e.g., eye movements, taps, or tones that alternate from side to side). For example, the therapist moves his or her index finger side to side in front of the individual, who is instructed to follow the movements in a set of 10–20 movements. The approach is individualized in terms of the length of each set and the type of bilateral stimulation. The sets continue until the target memory is no longer associated with distress and thus desensitization is achieved. The individual then focuses on the positive belief simultaneously with the trauma memory target (installation) and current bodily sensations (body scan) while the procedure is repeated. In Phase 7 (closure), the individual maintains a diary for a week, recording anything that comes up related to the therapy. In Phase 8 (reevaluation), the diary is reviewed and therapeutic progress is discussed.

EMDR has been a source of great controversy in the literature. A lot of media attention was given to the approach in the early days despite limited empirical evidence to support the claims of its proponents and the proposed therapeutic mechanisms of action. Given Shapiro's views in the early days that the treatment was experimental, she controlled training to licensed clinicians through her EMDR Institute. This was a departure from typical modes of psychotherapeutic dissemination, which focus on publishing techniques in academic journals and books accessible to all, and some have considered this controlled training as commercialization of the approach. Critics have also questioned Shapiro's hypothesized mechanism of how the approach is effective, and in particular, the role of eye movements. Studies have found that eye movements were not necessary for a good therapeutic outcome, suggesting that the effective ingredient in EMDR is actually exposure to the trauma memory. Richard J. McNally, a Harvard University psychology professor and leading figure in the field of anxiety disorders, likened EMDR and its meteoric rise to *mesmerism*—a popular therapy that had quickly spread through Europe and America in the 18th century, claiming to cure various conditions by unblocking a fluid termed *animal magnetism*. He has been quoted as saying, "What is effective in EMDR is not new, and what is new is not effective" (McNally, 1999b, p. 619).

Despite the controversy, EMDR has a strong following of clinicians who have been certified through the EMDR Institute. There is an EMDR International Association of practitioners and researchers and a journal specifically devoted to EMDR research.

Randi E. McCabe

See also: Exposure Treatment

Further Reading

Arkowitz, Hal, & Lilienfeld, Scott O. (2007, December). EMDR: Taking a closer look. *Scientific American*. Retrieved from http://www.scientificamerican.com/article/emdr-taking-a-closer-look/

Cahill, Shawn P., Carrigan, Maureen H., & Frueh, Christopher B. (1999). Does EMDR work? And if so, why?: A critical review of controlled outcome and dismantling research. *Journal of Anxiety Disorders, 13*, 5–33.

McNally, Richard J. (1999a). EMDR and mesmerism: A comparative historical analysis. *Journal of Anxiety Disorders, 13*, 225–236.

McNally, Richard J. (1999b). On eye movements and animal magnetism: A reply to Greenwald's defense of EMDR. *Journal of Anxiety Disorders, 13*, 617–620.

Shapiro, Francine. (1989). Eye movement desensitization: A new treatment for post-traumatic stress disorder. *Journal of Behavior Therapy and Experimental Psychiatry, 20*, 211–217.

Shapiro, Francine. (2001). *Eye movement desensitization and reprocessing (EMDR): Basic principles, protocols, and procedures* (2nd ed.). New York, NY: Guilford Press.

Eysenck, Hans J. (1916–1997)

Hans Eysenck (1916–1997), born Hans Jürgen Eysenck, was a highly influential German-born psychologist who established his professional career in Great Britain. Eysenck's most notable contributions spanned several areas of psychology, including personality, intelligence, and psychological treatment, among others. Eysenck was a strong proponent of the application of scientific principles to the study of human nature and was a leader in popularizing psychological science. He is further credited with establishing the profession of clinical psychology in Britain and is considered to be one of the pioneers of behavior therapy. His advocacy of behavior therapy paved the way for the development of current treatments of phobias and other anxiety disorders. A highly prolific thinker and writer, Eysenck was ranked 13th on the list of 100 most eminent psychologists of the 20th century and 3rd on the list of 25 psychologists most frequently cited in the psychological journal literature (Haggbloom et al., 2002). In addition to being recognized for his extensive accomplishments, Eysenck was also a polarizing figure, who espoused controversial views on topics both within and beyond psychology.

Eysenck was born in 1916 in Berlin, Germany, the only child to a silent-film actress and a stage performer. He was raised by his maternal grandmother after his parents divorced when he was two years old. After graduating from high school in 1934, Eysenck hoped to study physics at Berlin University; however, his admission was conditional upon his joining the Nazi Party, which his father had already joined. Eysenck, who openly abhorred Hitler and Nazism, declined the offer and left Germany. Following a brief stay in France, where his mother and her partner had fled, he moved to London. Raised a Lutheran, Eysenck learned that his grandmother was from a Jewish background after her death in a concentration camp during the war.

Eysenck did not initially set out to study psychology. He expected to study physics in London, but when he applied to University College London in 1935, he learned that he did not have the required prerequisites for enrollment. He claimed that he had never heard of psychology at that point but nevertheless enrolled in it because it was the most scientific subject available to him. Following completion of a bachelor of science degree in 1938, he remained at University College for his PhD studies under the supervision of Cyril Burt, a noted educational psychologist, who made controversial contributions to the study of heritability of intelligence.

Eysenck completed his doctorate on the experimental analysis of aesthetic preferences in 1940. As a German national at a time when World War II was escalating, he had few job prospects and worked for a period as a fire watcher, monitoring fires caused by bombs. In 1942, with more relaxed employment restrictions, Eysenck accepted a position as a research psychologist at the Mill Hill Emergency Hospital, which served as the relocated Maudsley Hospital (a psychiatric facility) during the war. With the reopening of the Maudsley Hospital in 1946, the University of London established a new training and research facility there, which was called the Institute of Psychiatry (IOP). Although Eysenck had prestigious job offers from several university departments, he accepted a position at the Maudsley Hospital as the head of the psychology department, where he remained until his retirement in 1983. In 1950, he was appointed reader in psychology (a senior academic appointment) in the department of psychology at the IOP, and in 1955, he was appointed professor of psychology. In the same year, Eysenck also became a British citizen.

In his early career, Eysenck became interested in psychometric (measurement-based) descriptions of personality. He analyzed the questionnaire and experimental data from psychiatric patients and developed a dimensional model of personality, which he published in his seminal book, *Dimensions of Personality*, in 1947. Eysenck proposed two personality factors, neuroticism (N) and introversion-extraversion (I-E). He held that the psychiatric diagnoses of dysthymia and hysteria were, respectively, the introverted and extraverted expressions of a neurotic personality. Eysenck later added a third personality factor, psychoticism (P), which he posited operated along an I-E continuum in psychotic disorders.

He further elaborated his model by examining the relationship between the personality dimensions and neural processes, learning mechanisms, genetics, and behavior. Eysenck also developed several widely used personality measures, including the Maudsley Personality Inventory, the Eysenck Personality Inventory, and the Eysenck Personality Questionnaire.

Further to his influential work on personality, Eysenck was a founder of clinical psychology in Britain, as well as a key figure in the development of behavior therapy. At the IOP, he was involved in promoting graduate training for clinical psychologists. He was also a vocal proponent of the development of clinical psychology as an independent profession and a research-based discipline. Eysenck questioned the reliability of psychiatric diagnosis and the validity of projective tests such as the Rorschach. Such tests evaluate personality features and emotional functioning based on respondents' perceptions of ambiguous pictures or, in the case of the Rorschach, inkblots. Eysenck was also critical of the psychotherapeutic methods practiced at the time and was skeptical of their efficacy. He was fiercely "anti-Freudian" and became widely known for his opposition to psychoanalysis. Accordingly, in the mid-1950s, with Eysenck's leadership, his colleagues at the Maudsley Hospital began applying behavior therapy to individuals with anxiety disorders such as agoraphobia. Their methods were inspired by the work of Joseph Wolpe (1915–1997), who developed a form of behavior therapy called systematic desensitization. Behavior therapy had particular appeal to Eysenck because it was rooted in academic psychology and based on learning and conditioning principles. Although he did not himself practice psychotherapy, Eysenck successfully spearheaded the behavior therapy movement in Britain and internationally in the 1960s. He wrote numerous books on the topic and founded the journal *Behaviour Research and Therapy*, which remains a leading research publication today for behavioral and cognitive behavioral treatments. Eysenck's contribution to behavior therapy was most notable in the area of anxiety disorders as it fostered the development of effective behavioral techniques to reduce fear and anxiety.

Eysenck also contributed influential and, at times, controversial works in the areas of personality and politics, intellectual differences, and personality and physical disease, among others. In the 1950s, he put forth a model of social and political attitudes based on two dimensions, radicalism-conservatism and tough- and tender-mindedness. One of the more controversial implications of the model suggested that Fascism and Communism are underpinned by a similar personality style. From the 1970s to postretirement, Eysenck wrote numerous books on intelligence, promoting the ideas that intelligence is highly heritable, that racial differences in intelligence are partially heritable, and that intelligence is accounted for by a single generalized factor. In the area of personality and physical disease, Eysenck's examination into cancer and personality in the 1960s led him to conclude at the time that the causal role of smoking in cancer had not been conclusively demonstrated.

After his retirement, his interest in personality and health was renewed, and he contributed to research suggesting an important association between different types of personality and physical disease.

In addition to his research publications, Eysenck wrote numerous books on a broad range of topics in psychology, many of which sold millions of copies. Some of this writing helped to popularize psychology among the general public. Other, more provocative, works such as those related to race and IQ, brought about considerable backlash. Eysenck was a brilliant debater and was known for his confrontational style when debating his opponents. As a staunch empiricist, he welcomed skepticism and arguments based on evidence.

Eysenck was highly productive throughout the course of his professional career. He published more than 1,600 journal articles and about 80 books. He continued to write until his death in 1997. At the time of his death, he was the most frequently cited psychologist in the research literature.

Irena Milosevic

See also: Behavior Therapy; Learning Theory; Wolpe, Joseph

Further Reading

Eysenck, Hans J. (1947). *Dimensions of personality*. London, UK: Routledge & Kegan Paul.

Eysenck, Hans J. (1997). *Rebel with a cause: The autobiography of Hans Eysenck* (Rev. and exp. ed.). New Brunswick, NJ: Transaction Publishers.

Haggbloom, Steven J., Warnick, Renee, Warnick, Jason E., Jones, Vinessa K., Yarbrough, Gary L., Russell, Tenea M., . . . Monte, Emmanuelle. (2002). The 100 most eminent psychologists of the twentieth century. *Review of General Psychology, 6*, 139–152.

F

Fainting Response

Approximately 70–75% of individuals with a blood-injection-injury (BII) type specific phobia report a fainting response, also known as syncope, upon exposure to the feared stimulus (e.g., seeing blood, having blood drawn, seeing or receiving an injury). In BII phobia, fainting is triggered by a vasovagal response, which involves two phases. In the first phase, there is sympathetic activation that is commonly seen in fight-or-flight fear responses, whereby heart rate and blood pressure increase as the body responds to the phobic trigger. In the second phase, there is parasympathetic activation that involves a sudden drop of heart rate. The blood vessels in the body expand, which leads to blood pooling in the legs and consequent low blood pressure (hypotension). Blood flow to the brain is reduced, leading to a brief loss of consciousness (i.e., fainting).

A transcranial Doppler is a quick and inexpensive test that may be used to assess the blood flow through the brain and confirm the type of syncope present. Some individuals may experience dizziness or light-headedness without fainting upon exposure to the feared stimulus. This response is known as presyncope. In the context of BII, vasovagal syncope is not dangerous and does not require treatment. The loss of consciousness has a rapid onset, is brief in duration, and is associated with full recovery. Individuals who have a fainting response upon exposure to their feared trigger generally experience signs that they are about to faint, including dizziness, nausea, sweating, "tunnel-like" vision, and loss of skin color in their face. Following fainting, individuals may feel very fatigued.

Evidence suggests that individuals with syncope related to BII have an underlying dysregulation of their autonomic nervous system (bodily system that controls visceral functions, such as heart and respiratory rates), which predisposes them to experience a neurally mediated syncope. Interestingly, this response may also be exhibited when not in the presence of a BII trigger. For example, researchers found that individuals with BII syncope history experienced presyncope or syncope in response to a 45-minute head tilt of 70 degrees (Accurso et al., 2001). They hypothesized that this dysfunction in neural circulatory control could potentially be an etiological factor in the development of the phobia. That is, the phobia may develop in vulnerable individuals after repeated fainting in response to the BII trigger.

The treatment of choice for individuals with BII phobia who faint includes cognitive behavioral therapy, with a focus on exposure combined with applied tension.

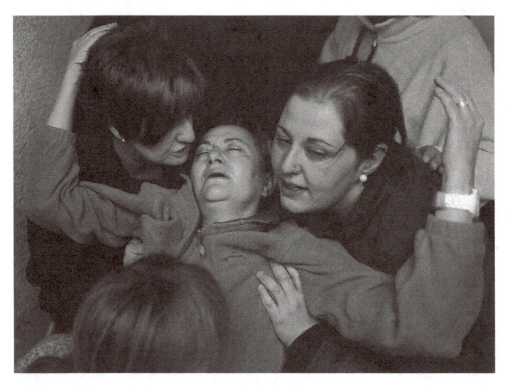

A woman is assisted by her relatives as she faints. Emotional stress can be a trigger for fainting, although the vast majority of individuals with phobias do not faint when they encounter a fear stimulus. BII phobia is unique in that many individuals with this phobia exhibit a fainting response when faced with blood, injection, or injury. (AP Photo/ Andres Kudacki)

Applied tension involves clients simultaneously tensing all the muscles in their body while engaging in exposure to the phobic stimulus. The muscle tension is presumed to counteract the vasovagal response by preventing cardiovascular and autonomic changes, such as the drop in blood pressure and increasing blood flow to the heart and brain. Other tension-related treatment components that have been shown to be helpful include tension only (i.e., muscle tensing in the absence of exposure) and applied relaxation. Applied relaxation involves the use of progressive muscle relaxation (e.g., tensing and relaxing various muscle groups) during exposure to the phobic stimulus. Physical maneuvering, such as combined muscle tensing and leg crossing in the context of exposure to the feared BII stimuli, has also been shown to be helpful in preliminary research.

Randi E. McCabe

See also: Applied Relaxation; Applied Tension; Exposure, *In Vivo*; Exposure Treatment; Phobia, Blood-Injection-Injury Type; Phobia, Specific

Further Reading

Accurso, Valentina, Winnicki, Mikolaj, Shamsuzzaman, Abu S.M., Wenzel, Amy, Johnson, Alan Kim, & Somers, Virend K. (2001). Predisposition to vasovagal syncope in subjects with blood/injury phobia. *Circulation, 104*, 903–907.

Ducasse, Deborah, Capdevielle, Delphine, Attal, Jérome, Larue, Aurore, Macgregor, Alexandra, Brittner, Marie, & Fond, Guillaume. (2013). Blood-injection-injury phobia: Psychophysiological and therapeutic specificities. *Encephale, 39*, 326–331.

Fear

Fear is a fundamental emotion that occurs in response to an imminent actual or perceived threat. It is characterized by a subjective feeling of terror or dread, motivation for behavior (to fight, flee, or freeze), and a distinct physiological reaction. Like all emotions, fear is understood in terms of behavior, physiology, and cognition. It is observed across species and has an evolutionary basis. Although everyone is equipped with the same basic capacity to experience fear in life-threatening situations, the specific objects or situations that elicit fear at other times vary across individuals and are typically acquired through learning experiences. Fear in response to actual danger helps the organism survive; however, when fear is persistently elicited in relatively harmless situations and is associated with distress or impairment in functioning, it is considered a clinically significant anxiety disorder such as a specific phobia.

Although there is variability in how emotion is defined, many theorists understand it as a tendency to engage in a particular behavior, which is driven by an external event and a subjective feeling state and accompanied by a specific pattern of physiological arousal. In the case of fear, the behavioral response most commonly includes the "fight-or-flight" response, whereby the organism confronts a threat (fight) or escapes from it (flight). This response occurs very rapidly and is facilitated by a cascade of reflexive physiological changes (e.g., increased heart and respiration rates) that involve the release of energy to prepare the body for action. These changes are initiated by the sympathetic branch of the autonomic nervous system, which is responsible for involuntary functions such as heart rate, digestion, and perspiration. The physiological fear response is activated during potentially life-threatening situations (even if they are not actually life-threatening but merely perceived as such) to help the organism avert danger.

In actuality, the flight response is much more common than the fight response. Further, in response to some threats, a freezing or tonic immobility response may occur, overriding other action tendencies. This is most likely in situations where escaping or fighting is unlikely to be successful. The freeze response has adaptive significance in increasing the chances of survival and has been well documented in different animal species. For example, if an animal is unable to outrun a predator and movement increases the likelihood of attack, "playing dead" may result in the predator moving on.

Fear also has a well-established neural component, whereby sensory information from the environment is processed in the brain to produce the fear response. The amygdala, in particular, is a brain region critical to fear processing and fear learning. Neuroimaging studies have shown that other areas of the brain are also involved in the perception of and reaction to threat. For example, specific areas of the prefrontal cortex (e.g., anterior cingulate cortex) that are responsible for functions such as physiological changes in the body as well as decision-making and emotional processing are activated during fear-related tasks.

In addition to behavior and physiology, cognition is understood to play a key role in emotion, including fear. Individuals appraise or interpret changes in their environment, and the nature of such interpretations determines which emotion is experienced. Different theories have been proposed to explain the relationship between emotion and cognition, varying in the extent to which they are thought to overlap and in their sequence of activation during an emotional response. When it comes to fear, cognitive processes help the individual detect an external (in the environment) or internal (within the body) change and appraise it as a threat. For example, a pedestrian crossing the street notices a vehicle running a red light and appraises this situation as dangerous. This appraisal activates the fear response, including a rapid effort to get out of harm's way. A further illustration involves a person who detects a slight change in his or her heart rate and appraises this change as a sign of an impending heart attack. He or she might next experience a physiological fear reaction that seems to confirm his or her appraisal that something is terribly wrong in the body. Likely, he or she will call for help or rush to the hospital.

The fear response has a clear benefit when it comes to the survival of a species. Its important protective function is thought to have helped our distant ancestors survive various dangers in their environments, ranging from wild animals to difficult terrain (e.g., cliffs). Accordingly, via the process of evolution, the fear response has been passed on through genes to subsequent generations. By extension, some theorists have proposed that certain fears, such as the fear of water, have a biological basis and do not require a negative experience (e.g., near-drowning) in order to develop. Other theorists hold that prior negative experience is required but that we nevertheless more readily learn to fear objects or situations (e.g., deep water, snakes, heights) that posed a threat to the survival of early humans.

In addition to biological pathways to fear acquisition, learning experiences provide common avenues to developing fear. A person can learn to fear an object or situation based on a direct negative experience with it. For example, a child who is jumped by a dog might subsequently come to fear dogs. Fear can also develop through observation of other individuals behaving fearfully. If the child's parent exhibits apprehension in the presence of dogs, the child might learn that dogs are dangerous. Finally, even hearing about the dangers of a particular object or situation might result in fear. For example, being told that dogs are unpredictable and prone to aggression might make an individual fearful of them.

When fear persists in response to objects or situations that are not dangerous or that are only mildly dangerous and when it causes the individual a great deal of distress or disrupts daily functioning, it is diagnosed as a phobia or another type of anxiety disorder. Phobias are characterized by excessive or unreasonable fear of a particular object or situation. Exposure to the feared stimulus typically triggers the fight-or-flight response, with escape being a common behavioral reaction. Individuals with phobias also typically engage in extensive avoidance to ensure that they do not encounter the target of their fear. To overcome phobic fear, a person must learn that the feared object or situation realistically poses minimal threat. Effective treatments, such as exposure therapy, accomplish this by having the individual gradually and repeatedly confront feared scenarios.

Irena Milosevic

See also: Evolution, Role of; Fear, Neural Pathways of; Fear, Physiology of; Fight-or-Flight Response; Non-Associative Model; Phobia, Specific; Preparedness Theory; Three Pathways Theory

FEAR AND ANXIETY: SAME OR DIFFERENT?

Fear and anxiety are highly overlapping aversive states of emotional arousal. They are universal phenomena that involve a focus on threat. Similarities between these two constructs also include other components, such as increased physiological arousal (e.g., heart rate), bodily sensations (e.g., tingling), a sense of uneasiness, negative affect, and concerns regarding future events. Although the transition between the two may not always be detectable and it may not be possible to distinguish between them in some circumstances at all, important differences exist between fear and anxiety.

Fear is an emotional response to a perceived threat in the environment that is deemed to be imminent. The danger is circumscribed in that fear tends to be evoked by a specific, identifiable threat cue (e.g., a rodent). By contrast, although there is no universally recognized definition of "anxiety," it is commonly understood to be an emotional response to anticipated danger (not imminent), and the threat tends to be intangible (a feeling that something dreadful is about to happen). Whereas there is a clear connection between something a person finds threatening and his or her fear response, the link between the source of a perceived threat and anxiety tends to be less clear, or indefinable.

The onset and culmination of fear are detectable, meaning that there is a definite beginning and endpoint. The fearful individual will experience a tension or mental strain that is restricted to this encounter, and the fear will decline with threat removal. In anxiety, the onset and closing stages are uncertain, and the anxious individual will experience a tension or mental strain that is pervasive and persistent. Fear tends to be episodic, whereas anxiety tends to be prolonged. In particular, fear tends to quickly peak in intensity and then subside as a sense of safety is restored. Anxiety, on the other hand, can persist for longer periods given that an individual might attempt to prepare for all possible negative future outcomes.

Physiological responding associated with fear is akin to an emergency, whereby the fight-or-flight response prepares the body to react rapidly to avert perceived danger. The physiological response associated with anxiety, by contrast, involves a sense of being on guard or vigilant and not in crisis. Fear and anxiety are more easily discernible when they involve severe presentations. For example, an acute episode of fear evoked from seeing a spider would be far removed from a chronic, persistent feeling of anxious uneasiness that arises when dealing with a difficult period at work. Some argue that fear is accompanied by coping skills such as escape and avoidance behavior, whereas coping abilities are hampered in anxiety because the source of the perceived threat is difficult to pinpoint.

Corinna M. Elliott

Fear, Animal Models of

Animal models are vital tools used to identify the basic neural mechanisms underlying normal anxiety as well as psychiatric conditions involving fear and anxiety. These models are based on the assumption that the physiological and neurobiological mechanisms underlying fear and anxiety in animals are comparable to those in humans. Many types of clinical anxiety disorders, such as specific phobias, are mediated through distinct neurobiological systems. Although animal models cannot mimic all features of human psychopathology, fear- and anxiety-related responses in lower-order animals, such as rats and mice, appear to be very similar to human anxiety. Furthermore, there is considerable overlap of neurobiological systems involved in the processing of fear and anxiety in different anxiety disorders; thus, empirical findings from animal models can contribute to theories of the neurobiological basis of these disorders.

Classically, anxiety has been separated into dimensions of state and trait anxiety. *State anxiety* constitutes a discrete and short-lived response to a threatening situation. *Trait anxiety* refers to a relatively stable, innate disposition in which individuals experience anxious symptoms in nonthreatening situations. Unlike state anxiety, the tendency to develop trait anxiety is determined by a combination of genetic and environmental factors. Genetic factors are often examined by identifying genetic differences between mouse strains that vary in their anxiety phenotype or rodent lines selectively bred for high/low anxiety-related behaviors such as avoidance of exposed or brightly lit areas in elevated plus maze, open field, and light/dark box test. The impact of environmental factors has mostly been investigated by examining the influence of exposure to stressors on anxiety-like behavior. Maternal separation paradigms, in which preweaned pups are removed from their mothers, have been used extensively to demonstrate that early-life experiences during critical periods of development may have long-term consequences in brain regions associated with abnormal levels of fear and anxiety later in life. Acute or chronic exposure to unavoidable stressors, such as predator threat, restraint, immobilization, and repeated electric shocks, can induce long-lasting effects on anxiety-like behavior and physiological changes in laboratory animals for days and even weeks. Stress paradigms are also attractive because stress is among the etiological factors mediating subtypes of anxiety disorders.

Like trait anxiety, anxiety disorders are thought to be fairly stable and caused by a combination of genetic and environmental factors. Experiments involving animal models often examine state anxiety, and then relate findings to concepts associated with trait and pathological anxiety. It is still a matter of debate whether trait and pathological anxiety should be conceptualized and assessed in terms of abnormal state reactions. However, it is likely that the enhanced expression and/or impaired ability to inhibit or extinguish state responses may contribute to the etiology and maintenance of persistent fears and pathological anxiety seen in some types of anxiety disorders.

Numerous behavioral testing paradigms have been developed in an attempt to model anxiety in rodents. Different paradigms assess different aspects of anxiety; thus, some tests may be more appropriate for one type of anxiety disorder than for another. Most test models use rodents and involve exposure of animals to external stimuli that induce fear or anxiety, and thus measure state anxiety. Experimental paradigms are often categorized into those that involve conditioned responses or unconditioned responses, but not all tests fit easily into these groups. Tests based on unconditioned responses examine behaviors that occur naturally in response to a given stimulus. Exploration-based paradigms are traditionally used to examine unconditioned anxiety responses in rodents. Trait anxiety is often studied using unconditioned response tests. Models based on conditioned responses rely on anxiety-like behaviors that are learned via an association of a neutral stimulus with an aversive one. Conditioned models can be further divided into procedures that measure classically conditioned responses, punishment-based conflict behaviors, and avoidance behaviors. Many, but not all, test models are sensitive to the administration of classic drugs that reduce anxiety in humans (anxiolytics), such as benzodiazepines and serotonin 5-HT1A agonists. Thus, the following test models are often used to screen and predict the effects in humans:

Exploration-Based Models: The open-field, elevated plus-maze (EPM), and light-dark choice tests are the most commonly used tools to assess anxiety-like behavior in laboratory rodents. These models induce a conflict between the curiosity to explore a new environment and the avoidance induced by the innate aversion in the apparatuses, and they are defined as ethological tests, which focus on animal behavior under natural conditions. The open-field test simultaneously provides measurements of exploration activity and anxiety-like behaviors. This apparatus consists of a square or circular arena with walls to prevent the animals from escaping. When introduced into an open field, the animals tend to stay by the walls of the arena and avoid the more threatening unprotected center area. Rodents with high anxiety display relatively low numbers of entries and time in the center area compared to nonanxious animals. The EPM is composed of two enclosed arms opposed perpendicularly by two open arms, situated above the floor. Anxiety-like behaviors in the EPM are associated with increases in the time and frequency that the animal spends in the aversive open arms. The light-dark apparatus was based on the natural aversion to bright light. It consists of two compartments, one that is dark and covered and another that is unprotected and bright. Anxiety reduction is indicated by an increase in the time spent in the Illuminated light compartment. In rodents, anxiolytic drugs such as diazepam reliably increase the amount of time and number of entries into the threatening/aversive parts of these apparatuses.

Classically Conditioned-Based Models: Fear conditioning tests are based on the principle that animals learn to predict aversive events. In classical conditioning, animals are typically given a training session in which a neutral stimulus (e.g., a tone) and/or neutral context (e.g., training chamber) are paired with an aversive unconditioned stimulus (US) such as the electrical shock. During training (acquisition) and after training (posttraining), the initial neutral stimulus or context serves as a conditional stimulus (CS), which can elicit involuntary conditioned responses (CRs) indicative of the state of fear when presented alone. In rodents, typical fear CR measures include remaining motionless (freezing), potentiation of the auditory startle response, defecation, reduced pain perception (analgesia), changes in heart rate and respiration rate (autonomic responses), and increased release of stress hormones. The administration of anxiolytic compounds often decreases CRs. The repeated presentations of the CS in the absence of the US result in the reduction of fear CRs over time. This reduction, or extinction of fear, can be measured to assess the initial strength of conditioning or how various experimental manipulations influence normal fear reduction.

Punishment-Based Conflict Models: The Geller-Seifter and Vogel paradigms are widely modeled punishment-based procedures in which trained responses for either a food (Geller-Seifter) or a water (Vogel) reward are subsequently suppressed by an electric shock punishment. The subsequent food or water presentation generates a conflict where the animal has to choose between receiving the punishment or reward. Another punishment-based conflict test is the four-plate test. In this test, rodents are exposed to a novel environment with a floor composed of four metal plates connected to a shocker unit. Animals are subjected to an electric shock when crossing from one plate to another and can only escape from this aversive situation by suppressing exploratory behavior. The administration of classical anxiolytics, such as benzodiazepines and 5-HT1A agonists, increases punished responding in these conflict paradigms.

Avoidance-Based Models: Avoidance conditioning involves the learning of a response that serves to prevent the occurrence of an aversive event. Examples of avoidance tests are passive avoidance (PA) and two-way active avoidance (TWAA) behavioral paradigms. Both PA and TWAA paradigms combine fear conditioning with the expression of an operant response. In PA, rodents learn to avoid stepping down to a grid floor or into a dark compartment previously paired with an electrical shock. The TWAA paradigm requires rodents to avoid the foot-shock by actively moving to a different compartment in response to a stimulus cue. Under these conditions, the response prevents the delivery of the aversive event. Avoidance assays exhibit face validity, in that people suffering from anxiety disorders often avoid feared or anxiety-provoking stimuli.

Predator Exposure-Based Models: Measures of anxiety to both conditioned and unconditioned stimuli can be examined using predator exposure tests. An example of this model is the mouse defense test battery (MDTB). This paradigm consists of a test battery which assesses the animal's unconditioned response to the presence of an actual predator (an anesthetized rat) and conditioned stimuli associated with potential threat (the predator context). A major advantage of the MDTB paradigm is the assessment of multiple defensive-related anxiety behaviors, including flight, avoidance, sonic vocalization, risk assessment, threat, and attack.

Eloisa Pavesi and Scott A. Heldt

See also: Anxiety and Related Disorders; Behavioral Experiment; Benzodiazepines; Classical Conditioning; Operant Conditioning

Further Reading

Belzung, Catherine, & Griebel, Guy. (2001). Measuring normal and pathological anxiety-like behaviour in mice: A review. *Behavioural Brain Research, 125*, 141–149.

Campos, Alline C., Fogaca, Manoela V., Aguiar, Daniele C., & Guimaraes, Francisco S. (2013). Animal models of anxiety disorders and stress. *Revista Brasileira de Psiquiatria, 35*(Suppl. 2), S101-S111.

Fuchs, Eberhard, & Flugge, Gabriele. (2006). Experimental animal models for the simulation of depression and anxiety. *Dialogues in Clinical Neuroscience, 8*, 323–333.

Griebel, Guy, & Holmes, Andrew. (2013). 50 years of hurdles and hope in anxiolytic drug discovery. *Nature Review Drug Discovery, 12*, 667–687.

Steimer, Thierry. (2011). Animal models of anxiety disorders in rats and mice: Some conceptual issues. *Dialogues in Clinical Neuroscience, 13*, 495–506.

Fear, Neural Pathways of

The neural pathways of fear are perhaps the most studied emotional circuits in the brain, as work since the early 20th century has been dedicated to identifying these systems. Early work in monkeys and human patients with damage to the temporal lobes of the brain demonstrated that a specific brain region known as the amygdala is essential for learning new fears and producing fear responses. Further anatomical and physiological studies performed by numerous laboratories in the early 1990s established the two main brain pathways of the fear response. In the past decade, animal work and human neuroimaging studies have investigated other brain pathways that feed into these pathways in both healthy people and individuals with anxiety disorders. Although many studies have focused on the pathways of fear in both humans and animal models, much is still unknown regarding the regions and circuits controlling the fear response.

Early experiments established the amygdala as the center of fear processing. The amygdala is a collection of anatomically and functionally distinct nuclei located deep within the temporal lobes of the brain. Work by Kluver and Bucy in 1939 showed that monkeys with damage to the temporal lobes on both sides of the brain did not show the emotional motor and vocal reactions in response to new objects that are typically displayed by normal monkeys without damage in these areas of the brain. Later studies showed that these changes in emotional behavior could be brought about by removal of only the amygdala while keeping the surrounding brain structures. Additionally, studies of human patients with amygdala lesions demonstrated that the amygdala is responsible for processing the social signals of fear. For example, one patient whose amygdalae had hardened due to calcification had no problem identifying most emotions but could not identify the emotion of fear in human faces nor could draw a fearful face.

Additional studies have shown that there are two different pathways through which sensory information of a threat can reach the amygdala and cause a fear

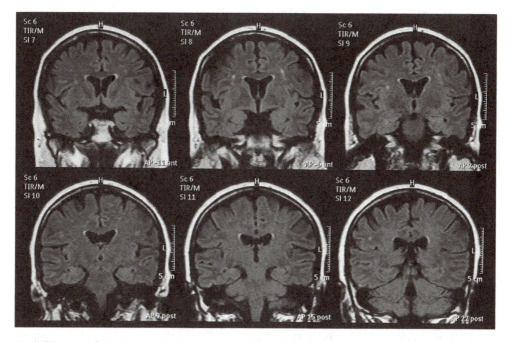

An MRI scan of the human brain. (yumiyum/iStockphoto.com)

response. In both of these pathways, sensory information signaling danger (for instance, a tone preceding an electrical shock) begins in the thalamus. The thalamus is a small brain structure that lies between the cerebral cortex and midbrain, and it can be thought of as the sensory relay between subcortical and cortical regions of the brain. It is from the thalamus that information moves into the two separate pathways. In the first "short" pathway, information is sent directly from the sensory thalamus to the amygdala. This subcortical pathway relays a fast but undetailed picture of the situation. This allows the brain to respond to the threat of danger without wasting the fractions of a second that may mean the difference between life and death.

The second "long" pathway allows for more detailed processing of the threat. Auditory, visual, and other sensory information in the thalamus moves to the cerebral cortex for processing, where then the auditory, visual, and somatosensory unimodal association cortices provide a representation of the object to the amygdala. For instance, in a classical fear-conditioning task, the sound of the tone would move from the thalamus to the primary auditory cortex, where the auditory unimodal association cortex processes this information into a representation of the tone for the amygdala. Further, the polymodal association cortex provides an overall representation of the object, which also includes features about the surrounding environment, to the amygdala and the hippocampus, a region of the limbic system that is responsible for long-term memory formation. In this example, the polymodal association cortex would combine the sound of the tone with the smell, feel, and look of the environment into a representation of the context, and it would then send this information to both the amygdala and the hippocampus. The hippocampus compares this contextual representation with memories of past experiences and provides information about the meaning or significance of the context to the amygdala. In the fear conditioning example, the hippocampus would allow the individual to compare the environment and sound of the tone to past experiences and determine if a shock will or will not be delivered. All of this detailed information sent to the amygdala allows for an appropriate response to be taken to the threat. The immediate response brought about by the short pathway can be called off or intensified, based upon the new information from the long pathway.

Detailed anatomical and physiological studies at the end of the 20th century demonstrated that auditory and other sensory inputs, as well as information about context from the hippocampus, converge in the basolateral nucleus of the amygdala, where associations are formed between the discrete stimuli (e.g., tone, shock) and context. The basolateral nucleus of the amygdala then projects to the central nucleus of the amygdala, where these associations are translated into conditioned fear responses, as well as back to the hippocampus and areas of the cortex. These projections back to the hippocampus help to encode the clear "explicit" memories of fearful events that will establish context for future fearful experiences. For instance, during fear conditioning, the first experiences of fear that are associated with the tone and the environment are sent from the amygdala to the hippocampus, where they are stored for later retrieval. The central nucleus of the amygdala integrates information from the basolateral nucleus of the amygdala as well as contextual information from the hippocampus and projects to regions of the brain that control the physiological and psychological responses to fear (e.g., the brainstem).

The two pathways from the thalamus to the amygdala may explain the basic response to fearful stimuli, but recent work suggests that other brain structures and pathways play a significant role in how humans interpret and react to fear. Numerous human neuroimaging studies have shown increased activation in areas of the prefrontal cortex called the anterior cingulate cortex during fear conditioning and tasks involving emotional images and facial expressions. The anterior cingulate cortex has been shown to be responsible for the regulation of blood pressure and heart rate, as well as cognitive functions such as decision making, reward, and emotional processing. In addition, increased activation in the insula, which is involved in the experience of different emotional states, has also been associated with emotional, fear-related tasks.

The circuitry of fear extinction involves many of the same regions as fear conditioning, with increased contributions from higher brain regions like the prefrontal cortex. Physiological and pharmacological studies have demonstrated that extinction involves neural changes within the amygdala. Anatomical tracing studies and neural recording studies have shown that there are numerous functional connections between the medial prefrontal cortex and the amygdala. Additionally, the hippocampus is activated during extinction learning, suggesting that a prefrontal-hippocampal circuit is at least partially responsible for fear extinction.

In addition to neuroimaging studies of healthy humans, several studies have been published that investigate the neurocircuitry of individuals with social anxiety disorders (social phobia). Individuals with social anxiety disorder clearly demonstrate increased activation of the amygdala while viewing emotional faces or while performing a public-speaking task. This increased amygdala activation has also been observed in individuals with other specific phobias when engaged in tasks or when viewing pictures related to their specific fear. Differences in other areas such as the anterior cingulate cortex and insula have not been consistent in studies of social phobia; however, individuals with other specific phobias show increased activation in areas of the anterior cingulate cortex and insula, which tends to decrease with successful treatment.

To date, evidence from animal and healthy human studies has provided much insight into the underlying brain circuitry responsible for fear learning and memory. Moreover, recent studies with individuals suffering from fear-based disorders have revealed areas in this brain network that are dysfunctional and may be responsible for the development and maintenance of these disorders, as well as potential targets for behavioral and pharmacological treatments.

John A. Greco and Christine A. Rabinak

See also: Amygdala; Classical Conditioning; Extinction; Fear; Fear, Animal Models of; Fear, Physiology of; Limbic System; Neuroimaging

Further Reading

Shin, Lisa M., & Liberzon, Israel. (2010). The neurocircuitry of fear, stress, and anxiety disorders. *Neuropsychopharmacology, 35*, 169–191.

Fear, Physiology of

Organisms experience fear when there is an imminent threat in their environment. In the case of phobias, fear is activated by individuals' perception or anticipation of threat in circumstances that are not currently dangerous. For other individuals, who experience unexpected panic attacks, there is no apparent external threat but rather internal physical sensations (e.g., change in heart rate) are perceived as a signal of danger. Irrespective of the fear trigger, the fear response involves physiological, cognitive, and behavioral changes that function to protect the organism by preparing it for immediate action. The physiological changes involve the nervous, cardiovascular, and respiratory systems, as well as other physical effects.

The physiological effects of the fear response begin in the brain. Sensory information from the environment is transmitted to the thalamus, a brain structure that processes and relays incoming sensory signals. The thalamus sends nerve impulses directly both to the amygdala, a brain structure responsible for emotional processing, and to the sensory cortex, an area of the brain that analyzes these inputs and in turn sends signals to the amygdala. The direct pathway from the thalamus to the amygdala is much faster and therefore permits rapid processing of a potential threat. It does not, however, permit processing of detailed information about the stimulus, which occurs, albeit more slowly, via the sensory cortex. Accordingly, many individuals report "acting before thinking" in the midst of a fear response.

When nerve signals indicating a threat are processed by the amygdala, the amygdala sends signals to the hypothalamus, a brain area that communicates with the rest of the body via the nervous and endocrine systems. In particular, the hypothalamus sends signals to the *autonomic nervous system*, which controls visceral functions that are largely outside of one's awareness (e.g., heart rate, respiratory rate, digestion). In turn, the autonomic nervous system activates one of its subsystems, the *sympathetic nervous system*, which is responsible for releasing energy and preparing the body for action. The hypothalamus simultaneously activates the endocrine system, which results in the secretion of numerous hormones, such as cortisol, by the adrenal cortex in the kidneys. This cascade of actions facilitates the body's stress reactivity.

When the sympathetic nervous system is activated, the stress hormones epinephrine (adrenaline) and norepinephrine (noradrenaline) are released into the bloodstream by the adrenal glands. The rapid flood of these hormones, in addition to those released through the endocrine system, creates numerous changes in the body that help the organism to react quickly. The hormones trigger an increase in blood glucose levels and the release of fats from the body's temporary fat storage to supply needed energy throughout the body.

A major change during the fear response involves *cardiovascular effects*, such as increased heart rate and blood pressure, which prepare the body for action by delivering oxygen to tissues and removing waste products from these tissues. Further, blood vessels are constricted to redirect blood from areas where it is not needed, such as the skin, fingers, and toes, and vessels are expanded in areas requiring more blood, such the heart, vital organs, and large muscles. Accordingly, individuals in a state of heightened fear tend to look pale, and they may report experiencing chills or numbing and tingling in their fingers and toes. Importantly, should an organism be attacked or injured when faced with actual danger, it is less likely to bleed to death because of these changes in blood flow.

The *respiratory system* is also affected by increased sympathetic and endocrine activity during the fear response. In particular, the respiratory rate increases and the lung's small airways are widened to maximize oxygen intake with each breath. Extra oxygen is routed to the brain to enhance alertness. Increased rate of breathing can also produce feelings of breathlessness, chest pain or tightness, and choking or smothering sensations, which individuals experiencing a fear response sometimes find very frightening. Additionally, rapid breathing without increased activity (i.e., when there is no need to fight or flee) can cause *hyperventilation*, whereby the body's level of carbon dioxide is reduced causing the brain's blood vessels to constrict, thus decreasing the blood supply to the brain. Although this is not dangerous, it can lead to sensations of light-headedness, blurred vision, hot flushes, and a sense of confusion.

The physiological effects of the fear response further involve the tensing of the muscles to prepare for action. Perspiration is also increased to cool the organism and, in the case that it is attacked by a predator, to make it more slippery to grip. The pupils additionally dilate to take in as much light as possible, and nonessential bodily systems, such as digestion and immune functioning, slow down to enable more energy for an emergency response. As with the other effects of sympathetic arousal, these changes in physiological functioning can create some unpleasant, though harmless, symptoms. For example, individuals might report trembling and shaking (caused by muscle tension) or abdominal upset (caused by changes in digestion) as a result of experiencing heightened fear.

The intense burst of energy and physiological reactivity triggered by the sympathetic nervous system is short-lived (usually peaking within 10 minutes and then decreasing within 10–30 minutes) and is regulated by another part of the autonomic nervous system, the *parasympathetic nervous system*. The parasympathetic nervous system is responsible for "dampening" the fear response and restoring the body to a normal state. Normal functioning is further restored with the destruction of epinephrine and norepinephrine by other chemicals in the body. In addition, high levels of cortisol are detected by receptors on the pituitary gland and hypothalamus, leading to a decrease in its production. As it takes some time for these hormones to be destroyed or reduced, individuals who have experienced a fear response may report lingering feelings of being "keyed up" after the threat of danger has passed.

Irena Milosevic

See also: Amygdala; Cortisol; Fight-or-Flight Response; Hypothalamic-Pituitary-Adrenal (HPA) Axis

Further Reading

Rapee, Ronald M., Craske, Michelle G., Meadows, Elizabeth A., Moras, Karla, & Barlow, David H. (1991). *The physiology of panic and anxiety*. Center for Stress and Anxiety Disorders, Albany, New York. Unpublished manuscript.

Fear, Return of (Relapse)

There are effective treatments for phobias (e.g., exposure); however, successful fear reductions can often be short-lived and in many instances the previously extinguished fear returns. In fact, approximately 19% to 62% of individuals who have undergone exposure treatment for fear or anxiety will experience a return of fear symptoms (Craske & Mystkowski, 2006).

The most common and effective treatment for phobias involves exposure or extinction techniques, during which the individual is repeatedly exposed to the feared event or object in the hopes of gradually extinguishing the fear. For example, a person who is afraid of spiders would be repeatedly exposed to a spider or spider-related cues (e.g., pictures of a spider), in a hierarchical manner based on level of fear, while in a therapeutic context. In this way, the individual learns, through a gradual exposure process, to approach the fear(s), and doing so gradually leads to reductions in the fear response. This technique has proven successful for individuals with various phobias. Unfortunately, even with techniques targeted at preventing return of fear symptoms, return of fear or relapse is not uncommon following exposure/extinction treatment. Also worth noting is that return of fear symptoms does not always lead to a clinical relapse.

Ways in which fear symptoms can return include spontaneous recovery, reinstatement, and renewal (Vervliet, Craske, & Hermans, 2013). *Spontaneous recovery* refers to the situation where an individual experiences a return of fear symptoms following a period of time in which he or she has not experienced the feared object or event (e.g., seeing a spider after a long period of time). *Reinstatement* is when the previously extinguished fear response returns after an individual has been exposed to an unrelated aversive object or event (e.g., having a panic attack unrelated to spiders causes an increase in fear of spiders). *Renewal* refers to the way in which the fear is presented (i.e., the context) and how this presentation can influence whether the individual has a return of fear symptoms. More specifically, renewal of fear can take place if there are changing external contexts or changing internal states.

Regarding changing external contexts, if an individual encounters the feared object or event and the situation is different from that used during the exposure treatment, this can trigger the previously extinguished fear response (e.g., seeing a spider outside on the lawn posttreatment rather than indoors as was the case during treatment). Further, when presented with a fearful situation or object posttreatment, the lack of treatment cues may inhibit the individual's ability to retrieve the extinction/exposure memories that were formed in treatment. This then causes the initial fear memory to be retrieved, thereby leading to a renewal in the initial fear response. In this instance, the individual is not able to generalize the learning from treatment toward novel contexts. Although the fear symptoms may not be as strong as they were prior to treatment, they can still cause significant distress and/or impairment in day-to-day functioning.

The second factor that may lead to fear renewal relates to the individual's internal state (i.e., the level of physiological arousal). If the individual's internal state is different from that during treatment, this can also trigger the return of fear. For example, individuals who encounter their feared object posttreatment after consuming caffeine may experience a greater return of fear symptoms if they did their treatment exposures caffeine-free (i.e., a different internal state). The memories learned during treatment are not necessarily strong and do not replace the memories developed during the initial fear acquisition. Therefore, when an individual's current state is incongruent to the treatment state, retrieving the in-treatment learned memories can be difficult and, instead, the initially acquired fear response is retrieved leading to a return of fear symptoms. To prevent individuals from experiencing return of fear symptoms, it is important that in-treatment exposures are conducted in varying contexts and with varying internal states to ensure that the skills learned in treatment can be generalized into daily life.

There are also individual difference variables such as anxiety sensitivity that can influence whether an individual will experience a return of fear symptoms. *Anxiety sensitivity* refers to a fear of the physical sensations of anxiety. If an individual who has recovered from having a phobia still fears physical sensations that were once associated with the fear response, it is possible that the individual will misattribute such sensations as being associated with the original fear response instead of just being normal bodily sensations. This misattribution can then trigger a return of the previously extinguished fear.

Nancy L. Kocovski and Amanda J. Desnoyers

See also: Agoraphobia; Anxiety Sensitivity; Exposure Treatment; Phobia, Specific; Social Anxiety Disorder (Social Phobia)

Further Reading

Craske, Michelle G., & Mystkowski, Jayson L. (2006). Exposure therapy and extinction: Clinical studies. In Michelle G. Craske, Dirk Hermans, & Debora Vansteenwegen (Eds.), *Fear and learning: From basic processes to clinical implications* (pp. 214–233). Washington, DC: American Psychological Association.

Vervliet, Bram, Craske, Michelle, & Hermans, Dirk. (2013). Fear extinction and relapse: State of the art. *Annual Review of Clinical Psychology, 9*, 215–248.

Fear Generalization

Fear generalization is the process by which fear of one thing expands to fear of other similar things. One of the first examples of fear generalization was the famous "Little Albert" experiment (Watson & Rayner, 1920). After Albert had acquired fear to a white rat, he generalized his fear to all things white and furry. For example, he demonstrated fear-like behaviors of crying and trying to escape when confronted by an experimenter with a Santa Claus beard that was white and furry. Generalization thus multiplies the number of things that a person may be afraid of after a fearful experience. For this reason, overgeneralization of fear is hypothesized as a contributing factor in anxiety disorders. This process is being studied scientifically, which could lead to identification of the brain regions involved and potential treatments.

Fear generalization can be a useful form of learning. For example, if a person were to be bitten by a black snake, it might be useful to fear and avoid snakes of all colors in case they are also of the biting sort. However, generalization can also be unhealthy if it leads one to fear things that are indeed safe. One example of this is a person who suffers from panic disorder and has a panic attack while grocery shopping. This person may subsequently fear going to grocery stores and additionally generalize the fear to all types of stores such as department stores, gift stores, or convenience stores. The fear may generalize even further to other crowded places like parades and sporting events. Eventually, the person might become fearful of leaving the house, as evident in severe cases of agoraphobia, which often accompanies panic disorder.

Fear generalization can be studied scientifically by measuring the way fear transfers across a variety of events varying in similarity to a dangerous event. Most studies use classical fear conditioning, in which the pairing of an emotionally neutral event with an unpleasant outcome, such as electric shock, leads the features of the neutral event (people, places, and things) to cause anxiety. Studies test for generalization of conditioned fear by measuring fear responses to stimuli, called generalization stimuli, that resemble the danger cue, which was paired with the shock. Studies often use varying degrees of color or size for the danger cue and generalization stimuli. For example, if the danger cue is the color navy blue, generalization cues might be royal blue, teal, and green. Whereas some amount of generalization is normal, overgeneralization can be indicative of abnormal fear processing and is associated with anxiety disorders. Using this example, everybody may generalize fear from navy blue to royal blue but only those with anxiety disorders also fear the teal. Overgeneralization is indicated by increased fear responding to the generalization stimuli. To date, results demonstrate overgeneralization of conditioned fear in people with panic disorder, generalized anxiety disorder, and PTSD when compared to healthy controls (Lissek & Grillon, 2010).

One theory of generalization suggests that a brain area known as the hippocampus categorizes the generalization stimuli as "same" or "different" as the danger stimuli. Individuals with anxiety disorders may have abnormalities in the area of the hippocampus responsible for this categorization, leading to a bias toward categorizing safe stimuli resembling danger cues, as actual danger cues. Essentially, anxious individuals show a bias toward fearing more than is necessary. Further study could help lead to the development of interventions that combine drugs such as D-cycloserine and behavior therapy such as exposure therapy to help anxious individuals learn to overcome those biases and avert overgeneralization of fear.

Brian van Meurs and Shmuel Lissek

See also: Agoraphobia (Fear of Panic-Like Symptoms); Behavior Therapy; Classical Conditioning; D-Cycloserine; Panic Disorder; Watson, John B. (1878–1958)

Further Reading

Lissek, Shmuel, & Grillon, Christian. (2010). Overgeneralization of conditioned fear in the anxiety disorders: Putative memorial mechanisms. *Journal of Psychology, 218*, 146–148.

Watson, John B., & Rayner, Rosalie. (1920). Conditioned emotional reactions. *Journal of Experimental Psychology, 3*, 1–14.

Fear of Driving

Fear of driving pertains to fear of various aspects of driving-related experience, such as operating a motor vehicle or being a passenger under different types of environmental (e.g., during rush hour), social (e.g., with a driving examiner), or psychological (e.g., while experiencing panic symptoms) conditions. Fear of driving can range from mild apprehension during early or novel driving experiences to a severe fear of all driving situations. When the severity of the fear results in significant distress and/or impairment to an individual's functioning, it is diagnosed as one of several anxiety or related disorders, depending on its presentation.

The conceptualization of fear of driving has been a source of some debate in the research literature, as the fear is represented by several diagnostic categories in current classification systems. When driving fear is circumscribed to driving situations (e.g., driving in congested traffic, driving at night, being a passenger), it is generally classified as a situational type of specific phobia. However, when it presents as part of a broader constellation of symptoms, it might instead be diagnosed as part of panic disorder, agoraphobia, posttraumatic stress disorders, or social anxiety disorder (social phobia), depending on the nature of the symptoms. In the context of panic disorder or agoraphobia, individuals might be fearful of experiencing a panic attack or anxiety-related symptoms while driving; indeed, the fear and subsequent avoidance of driving may develop after the occurrence of a panic attack while driving. When fear of driving occurs as a symptom of posttraumatic stress disorder, it typically follows a traumatic motor vehicle accident. In this case, individuals are avoidant of situations that remind them of the accident and might be fearful of the possibility of another collision. Finally, when fear of driving is focused on one's performance as a driver and on other's perceptions of one's driving, it is most likely a symptom of social anxiety disorder. Notably, it is not always easy to distinguish which diagnosis is most appropriate, as individuals with driving fear often report features of several anxiety or related disorders when describing their fear. Researchers continue to investigate features of driving fear that might aid with its classification.

Due to inconsistencies in the conceptualization of driving fear, its prevalence is unclear, although evidence suggests that it may be more common than was once believed (Taylor, Deane, & Podd, 2002). The average age of onset of driving fear ranges from 25 to 29 years, with the onset of significant fear-related distress or impairment occurring approximately 7–10 years after the onset of the fear (Antony, Brown, & Barlow, 1997; Ehlers, Hofmann, Herda, & Roth, 1994). Driving fear might develop following one's involvement in a motor vehicle accident, although it should be noted that many individuals who are fearful of driving have never experienced an accident. Indeed, when comparing driving-fearful and nonfearful individuals, there appear to be no meaningful differences in their histories of accidents. Furthermore, among those who are fearful of driving, the severity of fear is comparable between individuals who had been in a prior accident and those who had not. In addition to direct traumatic experiences, other proposed causes of driving fear include panic attacks, a general predisposition toward anxiety, fear of anxiety-related sensations (anxiety sensitivity), a general fear of high speed, and observation of driving-related traumatic events.

The specific focus of individuals' driving fears is wide-ranging, which is likely explained by the occurrence of the fear across several disorders. Common concerns include being in a car accident, issues of control (e.g., losing control of the vehicle), specific driving situations (e.g., driving in poor weather conditions), being trapped (e.g., in traffic), lack of driving skills, occurrence of anxiety-related symptoms while driving, and being in the company of a critical passenger. Behaviors commonly observed in individuals with driving fear include, among others, various degrees of avoidance (e.g., not driving at all, avoiding driving on freeways or bridges, avoiding driving on unfamiliar roads), driving with a companion, driving very slowly, driving only under certain weather conditions, and driving only in suburban or rural areas. The avoidance associated with driving fear can considerably impair individuals' quality of life by restricting their mobility and independence and by increasing the amount of time spent driving. For example, an individual with a fear of driving on the freeway may take two hours for a trip that would have taken only 30 minutes by freeway.

As with all fears, the most effective treatment for fear of driving is exposure therapy, which involves gradually and repeatedly confronting fear-provoking driving situations until the fear declines. This treatment is typically conducted *in vivo* (i.e., driving in a car), although researchers have also investigated the benefits of virtual reality exposure therapy (VRET). As preliminary findings from this research have shown modest outcomes, VRET might best be applied as a supplement to *in vivo* exposure rather than as a stand-alone treatment for driving fear (Wald, 2004).

Irena Milosevic

See also: Agoraphobia (Fear of Panic-Like Symptoms); Anxiety Sensitivity; Exposure Treatment; Panic Disorder; Phobia, Specific; Posttraumatic Stress Disorder; Social Anxiety Disorder (Social Phobia); Virtual Reality Treatment

Further Reading

Antony, Martin M., Brown, Timothy A., & Barlow, David H. (1997). Heterogeneity among specific phobia types in DSM-IV. *Behaviour Research and Therapy, 35*, 1089–1100.

Ehlers, Anke, Hofmann, Stefan G., Herda, Christoph A., & Roth, Walton T. (1994). *Clinical characteristics of driving phobia. Journal of Anxiety Disorders, 8*, 323–339.

Taylor, Joanne, Deane, Frank P., & Podd, John. (2002). Driving-related fear: A review. *Clinical Psychology Review, 22*, 631–645.

Wald, Jaye. (2004). Efficacy of virtual reality exposure therapy for driving phobia: A multiple baseline across-subjects design. *Behavior Therapy, 35*, 621–635.

Fear of Germs

Fear of germs is an irrational fear of contamination by germs or dirt. This concern is experienced broadly in the general population, and a certain amount of anxiety about germs is normal and adaptive. However, an irrational fear of germs can make a person worry about normal daily exposure to germs, begin to avoid contact with anything that may have germs on it, and use excessive strategies to ensure that no harm comes from possible exposure to germs.

Most people express some concern about exposure to germs (e.g., fears of getting a cold when someone sneezes on them). This concern may be a fear of something bad happening (e.g., getting sick), or it may be more of a disgust reaction (e.g., feeling revolted by the notion of germs on one's body or clothes). In fact, it is useful to be at least a little bit concerned about germs. That helps us remember to wash our hands, to stay home when we are very sick, and to make sensible decisions about what we do or do not touch. On the other hand, the fear of germs can get out of control and become a significant problem. People sometimes refer to themselves as *germophobes* and describe that their fear of germs has become a major problem. These people may feel tremendous anxiety when exposed to possible germs. They may go out of their way to avoid contact with germs, to the point that they are taking excessive measures to do so (e.g., wearing gloves and a mask while grocery shopping). Some people may end up avoiding to such an extent that they can become virtually housebound. For people where the fear of germs is excessive, they may also engage in excessive cleaning, sanitizing, and hand washing.

In some cases, a fear of germs may be part of obsessive-compulsive disorder (OCD). In this case, a person experiences intrusive thoughts and concerns about germs and dirt and may engage in repetitive or ritualized behaviors aimed at reducing his or her distress and ensuring that nothing bad will happen. This is different from a fear of germs because of the presence of obsessive thoughts and/or compulsive behaviors in OCD. For example, people with a fear of germs may feel like they need to use a lot of hand sanitizer, but they would be able to use the sanitizer once or twice when they feel contaminated with no ritual to how they use it. On the other hand, people with contamination concerns in OCD often have particular rituals about how they wash or sanitize, which may include washing in a particular order or a certain number of times.

There are treatments to help people manage their fear of germs, including cognitive behavioral therapy and/or medication treatments.

Karen Rowa

See also: Cognitive Behavioral Therapy; Obsessive-Compulsive Disorder; Treatment, Medication

Fear of Strangers (Stranger Anxiety)

Fear of strangers (or stranger anxiety) refers to anxiety and distress about being with people who are not known to the individual. Whereas stranger anxiety is typically considered in an individual or psychological context, a related term, *xenophobia* (from the Greek *xenos*, meaning foreigner or stranger, and *phobos*, meaning fear) is generally used in a broader social or cultural context, where it pertains to prejudice against outsiders or foreigners. Stranger anxiety, as understood developmentally and clinically, is a normal part of development in infants and is rarely a precursor to a later anxiety problem. However, for a small subset of individuals, stranger anxiety persists well into adulthood and has a negative impact on a person's ability to interact with new people.

Stranger anxiety is developmentally normal. Virtually all infants demonstrate signs of distress about being near, held by, or cared for by someone they do not know. Infants are understandably most comfortable with familiar caregivers. Stranger anxiety often begins between 6 and 12 months, with some infants showing signs of distress as early as 4 months of age. It may persist until 24 months of age (or longer), although it often begins to taper off after 12 months. Signs of stranger anxiety in infants include extreme distress (e.g., crying) when around new people, refusal to go to new or unfamiliar people, or being very quiet and hesitant around new people.

For most infants, stranger anxiety is a developmental phase that tapers off across time. For some infants and children, however, the anxiety persists into childhood and even adulthood. Research suggests that a form of stranger anxiety seen in childhood, called "behavioral inhibition" (i.e., the tendency to "hang back" in new environments and with new people), is associated with higher rates of social anxiety in these children as compared to children who do not show behavioral inhibition (Biederman et al., 2001). Thus, persistent stranger anxiety and inhibition may be related to anxiety difficulties in childhood and beyond.

Stranger anxiety is related to but distinct from separation anxiety. Separation anxiety is anxiety about being away from one's caregiver. Once again, most children

A toddler hides behind her parent, a common behavioral response among young children when they encounter an unfamiliar individual. Stranger anxiety is a normal part of child development, but professional help is recommended if the anxiety begins to interfere with everyday life. (NiDerLander/iStockphoto.com)

will show some signs of separation anxiety during childhood, but only few develop a persistent, problematic form of separation anxiety. In comparison to separation anxiety, stranger anxiety can occur even in the caregiver's presence; thus, it is not simply about being away from a caregiver, but rather about being in the presence of unfamiliar people.

Normal stranger anxiety does not require any intervention. Parents and caregivers can help ease this distress simply by being respectful of their child's distress while slowly and consistently exposing the child to strangers. Problematic stranger anxiety may require professional intervention, such as cognitive behavioral therapy.

Karen Rowa

See also: Behavior Therapy; Cognitive Behavioral Therapy; Temperament

Further Reading

Biederman, Joseph, Hirshfeld-Becker, Dina R., Rosenbaum, Jerrold F., Herot, Christine, Friedman, Deborah, Snidman, Nancy, . . . Faraone, Stephen V. (2001). Further evidence of association between behavioral inhibition and social anxiety in children. *American Journal of Psychiatry, 158,* 1673–1679.

Fear of Success

Fear of success, also known as the *Horner effect*, is a phenomenon where someone poised for or capable of success feels or acts in ways that ultimately discourages success. It is thought of as a psychological barrier to attaining success.

The concept of fear of success was first examined in the late 1960s and early 1970s by psychologist Matina Horner. Dr. Horner noticed that women tended to have high anxiety about achievement. Instead of assuming that women were afraid of failure, she began to question whether they were afraid of success. Her early research focused on the factors that discouraged people from pursuing desired careers. She was especially interested in the factors that discouraged women from pursuing careers in medicine despite the fact that these careers were highly desirable. She gave research participants an incomplete story of a struggling medical student and asked them to finish it—for males, a story about "John" and for women, a story about "Anne." She found that most men finished the story about John with a positive and prosperous outcome, whereas most women finished the story of Anne in a negative way. Her research suggested that many women were worried about the consequences of succeeding, including fears of being seen as unfeminine.

When a fear of success is activated, people may find themselves self-sabotaging on the brink of success. For example, someone might make a careless mistake at work right before an important promotion is finalized. Someone else might procrastinate completing paperwork that would lead to financial reward. Or someone might become stuck in indecision or stick to only "safe" choices. These behavioral indicators of fear of success can be subtle, whereas others are blatant in their negative consequences.

There are numerous current ideas about why some people fear success. One possibility is the fear of change and of the unknown. It is often easier for people to stay in a familiar situation, even if the familiar situation is not ideal. Without the guarantee of success, some people will not even attempt it. Related to the fear of the unknown is the fear of how success will affect someone. Someone might worry about becoming a completely different person with success. Another possible explanation is fear of the responsibility that comes along with success; it may feel overwhelming to take on a sharp increase in responsibility. Some people fear that the success will not last, and they may worry about handling the loss of success so much that they avoid it. For others, a fear of success might be related to feelings of low self-worth. If a person does not feel worthwhile, he or she may not feel deserving of success and may not even pursue avenues of success.

Fear of success can be addressed through cognitive behavioral therapy, including challenging any cognitive distortions a person might hold about the meaning of success.

Karen Rowa

Further Reading

Hoffman, Lois W. (1974). Fear of success in males and females: 1965 and 1971. *Journal of Consulting and Clinical Psychology, 42*, 353–358.

Fear of the Unknown

Fear of the unknown is a common feature among many anxiety disorders. In the current anxiety disorders literature, it is more usually discussed in the context of a related construct, *intolerance of uncertainty* or the tendency to respond negatively to uncertain situations. Intolerance of uncertainty has been identified as a risk factor and maintenance mechanism in anxiety disorders, and it is one of the targets of psychological treatments for these disorders.

An early perspective on the fear of the unknown was presented by an acclaimed writer of horror, H. P. Lovecraft, in 1927. He proposed that "the oldest and strongest emotion of mankind is fear, and the oldest and strongest kind of fear is fear of the unknown" (Lovecraft, 1945, p. 12). Like Lovecraft, many people consider this fear to be among the most fundamental of human fears. Investigations into fear of the unknown originated with Frenkel-Brunswik's (1949) work on the tolerance of ambiguity, which was construed as an individual difference or dispositional variable—that is, people differ in their level of comfort with ambiguous situations. Those who are intolerant of ambiguity will tend to perceive ambiguous situations (e.g., whether or not one is being evaluated; whether or not one has entered a romantic relationship) as threatening. There has been limited clinical research on ambiguity intolerance, and contemporary perspectives have shifted focus to a related construct, intolerance of uncertainty, which also is understood to be a dispositional characteristic (Carleton, 2012). Individuals who have difficulty tolerating uncertainty hold more negative beliefs about uncertainty and perceive situations for which outcomes cannot be known (e.g., whether or not one will pass an examination; whether a romantic relationship will be successful) as threatening.

Intolerance of uncertainty is believed to be a risk factor for the development and maintenance of anxiety disorders, and it is also similarly implicated in depression (Carleton, 2012). Within the anxiety disorders, the concept was originally developed to account for the persistent worry characteristic of generalized anxiety disorder (Freeston, Rhéaume, Letarte, Dugas, & Ladouceur, 1994), but it has since been understood to also have an important role in obsessive-compulsive disorder, social anxiety disorder (social phobia), and panic disorder (Carleton, 2012). Intolerance of uncertainty is associated with another important risk factor for anxiety disorders: anxiety sensitivity or the fear of the physical symptoms of anxiety. Researchers have proposed that low tolerance of the uncertainty surrounding the onset and consequences of physiological arousal (e.g., rapid heart rate) might, in part, account for this relationship (Carleton, Sharpe, & Asmundson, 2007).

Individuals who cannot tolerate the possibility of negative outcomes in uncertain situations, no matter how unlikely they are, suffer a number of undesirable cognitive (e.g., rumination, worry), emotional (e.g., anxiety), and behavioral (e.g., asking people for excessive reassurance) consequences. They are likely to overestimate the probability that negative outcomes will occur in uncertain situations and will therefore try to avoid such situations or to seek further information in an effort to eliminate uncertainty. For example, a person with high intolerance of uncertainty might fail to follow up with results of a medical test for fear of receiving "bad news" or might instead make repeated calls to the doctor's office to see if the results have arrived.

Evidence shows that changes in intolerance of uncertainty predict changes in anxiety symptoms (Carleton, 2012). Cognitive behavioral therapy (CBT) is an effective treatment for anxiety disorders, and one variant of this treatment has been developed specifically for reducing intolerance of uncertainty in generalized anxiety disorder (Dugas & Robichaud, 2007). It involves behavioral exposure to uncertainty (e.g., deciding what movie to see only upon arrival at the theatre), reevaluation of worry beliefs (e.g., challenging the belief that worry ensures that things will get done), modification of a negative problem orientation (e.g., initiating problem solving instead of worrying about the uncertainty of the situation), and imaginal exposure to hypothetical situations that create worry (e.g., imagining testing positively for a serious illness). More broadly, CBT for any anxiety disorder, including phobias, helps individuals reappraise their assumption that uncertainty implies negative outcomes and, more importantly, to learn to cope with uncertainty since it is inherent in all aspects of life.

Irena Milosevic

See also: Anxiety Sensitivity; Cognitive Behavioral Therapy; Exposure, Imaginal

Further Reading

Carleton, R. Nicholas. (2012). The intolerance of uncertainty construct in the context of anxiety disorders: Theoretical and practical perspectives. *Expert Review of Neurotherapeutics, 12*, 937–947.

Carleton, R. Nicholas, Sharpe, Donald, & Asmundson, Gordon J.G. (2007). Anxiety sensitivity and intolerance of uncertainty: Requisites of the fundamental fears? *Behaviour Research and Therapy, 45*, 2307–2316.

Dugas, Michel J., & Robichaud, Melisa. (2007). *Cognitive-behavioral treatment for generalized anxiety disorder: From science to practice.* New York, NY: Routledge

Freeston, Mark H., Rhéaume, Josée, Letarte, Hélène, Dugas, Michel J., & Ladouceur, Robert. (1994). Why do people worry? *Personality and Individual Differences, 17*, 791–802.

Frenkel-Brunswik, Else. (1949). Intolerance of ambiguity as an emotional and perceptual personality variable. *Journal of Personality, 18*, 108–143.

Lovecraft, Howard Phillips. (1945). *Supernatural horror in literature.* New York, NY: Ben Abramson.

Fear Survey Schedule

The Fear Survey Schedule (FSS) is a self-report questionnaire assessing a variety of fears and phobias. Several versions have been developed, each containing a different number of items and different response formats. Two of the most commonly used versions are the FSS-II (Geer, 1965), containing 51 items, and the FSS-III (Wolpe & Lang, 1964), which contains 72 items and was designed for clinical use. These questionnaires assess both common fears, such as spiders and heights, and less common fears, such as strange shapes and ugly people. Child versions are also available that include fears specifically experienced in childhood, such as fear of getting in trouble at school (e.g., Ollendick, 1983). The FSS has been used both in clinical and in research settings to identify people who likely have a phobia, to evaluate the severity of their fear and to assess outcome after treatment. Some experts in the field have recently questioned its use as a diagnostic tool due to the inclusion of uncommon fears and the fact that research suggests that various versions of the FSS do not accurately distinguish individuals with and without a specific phobia.

Andrea R. Ashbaugh

See also: Ollendick, Thomas H. (1945–); Phobias, Assessment of; Wolpe, Joseph (1915–1997)

Further Reading

Geer, James H. (1965). The development of a scale to measure fear. *Behaviour Research and Therapy, 3*, 45–53.

Ollendick, Thomas H. (1983). Reliability and validity of the revised Fear Survey for Children (FSSC-R). *Behaviour Research and Therapy, 21*, 379–399.

Wolpe, Joseph, & Lang, Peter J. (1964). A Fear Survey Schedule for use in behavior therapy. *Behaviour Research and Therapy, 2*, 27–30.

Fear-Potentiated Startle

Fear-potentiated startle (FPS) is the relative increase in the magnitude of the physiological startle reflex that occurs when an organism is in a state of fear. FPS has been extensively studied in the context of conditioned fear in both animals and humans. In humans, it has also been examined with regard to trait fear and psychopathology. FPS is strongly associated with specific phobias and other anxiety disorders, and it has an established neurological basis. FPS can be reduced with medications and psychotherapy.

The naturally occurring startle reflex is an innate defensive response to sudden, unexpected stimuli. It is present in all humans and other mammals. It can be observed, for example, when an individual is surprised with a loud noise. The individual will exhibit rapid involuntary movement of the limbs and jerking of the head, as well as increased heart rate, respiration, and skin conductance. This response serves to protect the individual's body or the eye (through the eyeblink), as well as to facilitate escape from a potentially dangerous situation. When organisms are experiencing fear, there is an increase in their startle reflex; hence the reflex is said to be *potentiated* by fear. In human studies of FPS, the startle reflex is typically assessed through eyeblink rate or heart rate.

FPS is well suited for studies of fear because it provides an objective fear measure and is observed across species. In animal studies, the FPS paradigm involves repeatedly pairing a neutral cue (e.g., light or tone) with an aversive stimulus and then evaluating the magnitude of the startle reflex in the presence of the cue alone. FPS was first described by Brown, Kalish, and Farber (1951) in their work on fear conditioning in rats. They found that after repeated pairings of a light with a foot-shock, the startle response to the light was greater in rats that had been subjected to these pairings than in those that had not. This potentiated startle response to the light is an example of classical conditioning, whereby the previously neutral light had become a conditioned fear stimulus that produces a conditioned fear (i.e., startle) response.

The FPS paradigm in human research is similar to the conditioning procedures in studies with animals. For example, the eyeblink startle response has demonstrated potentiation when participants are presented with a light that was previously paired with a shock. Other research has shown that the startle reflex is potentiated when participants are anticipating the presentation of emotionally arousing (e.g., erotic or fear-provoking) images, suggesting that active anticipation of emotional arousal, whether positive or negative, facilitates motor reflexes. By contrast, evidence suggests that *during* the presentation of emotionally arousing images, the startle response is reduced for pleasant (erotic) pictures and potentiated for unpleasant (danger and threat) pictures (Sabatinelli, Bradley, & Lang, 2001). In general, larger startle reflexes are elicited in response to unpleasant versus pleasant stimuli, and these differences are greatest for highly arousing stimuli. Further, startle potentiation is greater for fear-provoking stimuli as compared to other negative stimuli.

FPS has been associated with trait fear, a dispositional characteristic reflective of one's defensive reactivity to aversive stimuli. It has been proposed that the magnitude of FPS is a physiological indicator of trait fear. That is, individuals high in trait fear tend to exhibit greater FPS in response to threatening versus neutral stimuli than individuals low in trait fear. In terms of psychopathology, there is strong evidence that individuals with phobias exhibit strong startle potentiation when they are exposed to various phobic stimuli. This effect is observed across different types of phobias, such as animal (e.g., snake, spider, dog) and blood-injection-injury phobias. FPS is also evident in posttraumatic stress disorder, a condition that is characterized in part by an exaggerated startle response, and it has also been noted in obsessive-compulsive disorder and generalized anxiety disorder.

The central nucleus of the amygdala has been identified as playing a critical role in FPS. The amygdala is an almond-shaped structure in the temporal lobes of the brain that is involved in fear learning and the activation of fear. Researchers have found that lesioning the central nucleus of animals that have been sensitized to startle blocks their startle response.

FPS can be reduced with medications that reduce anxiety (e.g., diazepam) and with psychological treatment, such as exposure therapy. One study demonstrated significant reduction in startle potentiation in individuals with spider phobia after a one-hour session of *in vivo* exposure therapy (Kashdan, Adams, Read, & Hawk Jr., 2012). Further, evidence suggests that the degree of startle potentiation to a phobic stimulus before treatment predicts the amount of fear reduction at the end of treatment.

Irena Milosevic

See also: Amygdala; Classical Conditioning; Exposure, *In Vivo*

Further Reading

Brown, Judson S., Kalish, Harry I., & Farber, I. E. (1951). Conditioned fear as revealed by magnitude of startle response to an auditory stimulus. *Journal of Experimental Psychology, 41*, 317–328.

Kashdan, Todd B., Adams, Leah, Read, Juliana, & Hawk Jr., Larry. (2012). Can a one-hour session of exposure treatment modulate startle response and reduce spider fears? *Psychiatry Research, 196*, 79–82.

Sabatinelli, Dean, Bradley, Margaret M., & Lang, Peter J. (2001). Affective startle modulation in anticipation and perception. *Psychophysiology, 38*, 719–722.

Fight-or-Flight Response

The fight-or-flight response is the immediate physiological reaction that occurs when danger or a threat to survival is perceived by an organism. This reaction, first described by Cannon in 1929, involves a series of neural and physiological mechanisms that rapidly activate the body to confront the threat (fight) or to escape it (flight). In the case of phobias, the response is activated when an individual is exposed to feared stimuli. A third reaction has recently been described, with researchers and clinicians currently using the term *fight, flight, or freeze response*.

When the potential for danger is perceived or anticipated, the amygdala (an area of the brain involved in the processing of emotional information) activates the autonomic nervous system (the part of the nervous system that controls primarily involuntary bodily functions, such as breathing, digestion, and heart rate) and facilitates the release of stress hormones such as epinephrine (adrenaline) and cortisol. This activation diverts energy from areas of body associated with resting (e.g., the digestive system) to areas of the body that allow the individual to mobilize in an emergency to avoid harm. This change results in the physiological (e.g., increased heart rate and shallow breathing), cognitive (e.g., alertness and worry), and behavioral (e.g., escape) symptoms of anxiety.

From an evolutionary perspective, the fight-or-flight response is an adaptive instinct that developed when predators or environmental stimuli threatened the survival of humans. In some situations, the response still aids in survival (e.g., defending oneself or running from an attacker). However, many of the anxiety-provoking situations today do not threaten people's physical survival and in these situations, the fight-or-flight response can be maladaptive and associated with phobic reactions. As well, frequent or chronic activation of the response may lead to suppression of the immune system and feelings of fatigue. Depression, irritability, and recurrent physiological issues (e.g., headaches and difficulties sleeping) may also develop as a result of chronic activation of the fight-or-flight response.

An example of the fight-or-flight response is the reaction of an individual with arachnophobia (fear of spiders) when exposed to a spider. The individual "fights" by killing the spider or "flees" by running away from it. In fact, people with phobias may experience panic attacks when they are exposed to their feared situations or objects, even though the likelihood of harm is low. Their perception of threat (e.g., "the spider will bite me") automatically activates the biologically programmed fight-or-fight response.

In general, one of the goals of treatment for phobias and other anxiety disorders is to reduce the fight-or-flight response in situations that do not warrant such a reaction. Through exposure treatment, such as *in vivo* exposures (i.e., facing feared stimuli) in the case of phobias and interoceptive exposures (i.e., inducing the physiological symptoms of anxiety) in the case of panic disorder, individuals become accustomed to the experience of the fight-or-flight response being activated. With repeated exposures to feared stimuli, the fight-or-flight response decreases in intensity and duration.

Recently, researchers and clinicians have noted a third reaction—freezing—and thus have begun using the term *fight, flight, or freeze response*. The freeze response involves being rendered immobile when confronted with a potential threat (e.g., the person's muscles may become tense and no visible movements occur). This reaction is particularly associated with posttraumatic stress disorder. However, although this reaction is frequently seen in other mammals, particularly rodents, it has been less studied in humans to date.

Missy L. Teatero and Alexander M. Penney

See also: Amygdala; Arachnophobia (Fear of Spiders); Cortisol; Exposure, Interoceptive; Exposure, *In Vivo*; Exposure Treatment

Further Reading

Cannon, Walter B. (1929). *Bodily changes in pain, hunger, fear, and rage*. Oxford, UK: Appleton.

Flooding

Flooding is a behavioral therapeutic technique based on the learning principles of habituation and extinction, which refer to a progressive decrease in behavioral responses when stimuli are repeatedly presented in the absence of consequence. Flooding is primarily used for treating specific phobias, although the technique has also been applied to treat other anxiety disorders, such as posttraumatic stress disorder and obsessive-compulsive disorder. Flooding entails exposing individuals to their most feared or anxiety-provoking stimuli and preventing escape from the feared object until anxiety symptoms subside. As a result, the person learns to associate the feared object with safety rather than danger. The treatment was initially developed in the late 1950s and early 1960s, although it remains unclear exactly who first developed the procedure. The concept of flooding has variously been associated with A. Tarrence Polin, who used a form of extinction, which he termed *flooding*, in research involving rats; Nicolas Malleson, who used similar extinction procedures in the treatment of test anxiety; and Thomas Stampfl, who is most famously known for the development of implosive therapy.

Flooding is sometimes confused with exposure treatment, a similar therapeutic technique. Although both techniques consist of repeatedly exposing individuals to anxiety-provoking stimuli, they differ in terms of how gradually this exposure is implemented. In exposure treatment, the therapist and client develop a hierarchy of feared and anxiety-provoking stimuli, and with the therapist's assistance, the client confronts each stimulus in a gradual, progressive manner. By contrast, flooding begins by exposing individuals to their most distressing fear and preventing their avoidance or escape until the anxiety recedes. For example, flooding for fear of heights might involve taking the person to the edge of a very tall building as the first and only exercise, whereas exposure would start with less anxiety-provoking situations, such as standing on a second-floor balcony.

In flooding, as with exposure, individuals are confronted with the feared stimulus primarily *in vivo*, meaning in the real world. For example, an individual with snake phobia will be instructed to hold a snake until he or she no longer feels anxiety. However, several adaptations of flooding include an imaginal exposure component in cases where confronting feared stimuli in the real world is impossible or impractical. For instance, it is unrealistic and expensive to treat an individual's flying phobia with repeated plane flights or combat traumas by reexperiencing war. In these cases, imaginal flooding could be used.

Although treating phobias and anxiety disorders with flooding has been successful for some individuals, considerable debate surrounds its appropriateness as a viable treatment option for others (Olatunji, Deacon, & Abramowitz, 2009). Some clinicians express concern that the intensity of the flooding technique may inadvertently lead to retraumatization, and subsequently, a worsening of symptoms;

however, this has not always been supported by the empirical literature (Olatunji et al., 2009). Nevertheless, flooding is still used today for treating various specific phobias (Wolitzky-Taylor, Horowitz, Powers, & Telch, 2008).

Michelle Lonergan and Andrea R. Ashbaugh

See also: Exposure, Imaginal; Exposure, *In Vivo*; Exposure Treatment; Implosive Therapy

Further Reading

Boudewyns, Patrick A., & Shipley, Robert H. (1983). Direct therapeutic exposure. In Patrick A. Boudewyns and Robert H. Shipley (Eds.), *Flooding and implosive therapy* (pp. 1–14). New York, NY: Springer.

Olatunji, Bunmi O., Deacon, Brett J., & Abramowitz, Jonathan S. (2009). The cruelest cure? Ethical issues in the implementation of exposure-based treatments. *Cognitive and Behavioral Practice, 16*, 172–180.

Wolitzky-Taylor, Kate B., Horowitz, Jonathan D., Powers, Mark B., & Telch, Michael J. (2008). Psychological approaches in the treatment of specific phobias: A meta-analysis. *Clinical Psychology Review, 28*, 1021–1037.

Foa, Edna B. (1937–)

Edna B. Foa (1937–) is an internationally renowned psychologist, scientist, master clinician, and expert trainer who is known for her pioneering work in experimental psychopathology of anxiety disorders and the treatments she developed for obsessive-compulsive disorder (OCD) and posttraumatic stress disorder (PTSD) based on her emotional processing model of fear. Foa is professor of clinical psychology in psychiatry at the University of Pennsylvania and director of the Center for the Treatment and Study of Anxiety at the University of Pennsylvania, an internationally recognized clinic dedicated to developing and evaluating psychological treatments for anxiety and traumatic stress disorders, as well as providing specialized training in these treatments to health professionals. In 2010, Foa was named by *Time* magazine as one of the top 100 people to affect our world for the role that she has played in ensuring that individuals experiencing traumatic stress have an evidence-based treatment to help alleviate their suffering.

Foa was born in 1937, in Haifa, Israel, to older parents. Her brother was seven years older than her. Her mother was a housewife, and her father managed an insurance department for a large construction company. Tragedy struck the family when Foa was 10, and her brother was killed in battle during the 1948 war where Israel struggled to establish itself as a state. Her father passed away 4 years later when she was 14 years old. After graduating high school, Foa wanted to enlist in the army and volunteer on a kibbutz. Her mother did not want her to do so and asked her to postpone her army service. She offered to pay for her studies at the Kibbutz Seminary to train as a teacher and Foa agreed. Her training at the Kibbutz Seminary and a job she held directly after at an institution for juvenile criminals shifted Foa's interests to psychology, and she realized she wanted to be a psychologist.

Foa attended Bar-Ilan University in Tel Aviv, Israel, receiving her bachelor of arts degree in psychology and literature in 1962. During that time she met her first husband, Professor Urier Foa, with whom she had three daughters. In 1966, when her husband was invited to be a visiting lecturer at the University of Illinois in Urbana, Foa completed her master of arts there in clinical psychology. She went on to complete her doctor of philosophy degree in clinical psychology and personality from the University of Missouri in Columbia in 1970, where her thesis focused on cognitive structures of aggression and frustration. Foa then moved to Philadelphia where she worked with Joseph Wolpe (1915–1997) at Temple University. Wolpe was a significant influence on Foa's integration of the behaviorist methodology within her cognitive approach. Foa's research interests started with a curiosity about how people process negative information, particularly traumatic information, and what mechanisms are responsible for recovery. This led her to work with Dr. Blackman at the Institute of Psychiatry in London during a sabbatical in 1980 where she conducted her research on rape victims. It was at this time that the diagnosis of PTSD was first included in the *Diagnostic and Statistical Manual of Mental Disorders*, third edition. An important mentor for Foa was Peter Lang who proposed the importance of emotional processing in treating anxiety. Foa followed this idea, working with Michael Kozak, a student of Lang's, to develop the theoretical basis for pathological fear patterns, which they outlined in their seminal article entitled *Emotional Processing of Fear: Exposure to Corrective Information* (Foa & Kozak, 1986).

Based on her theoretical model of fear development and maintenance, Foa developed the treatment of prolonged exposure (PE) for addressing pathological fear. This treatment has been used with great success to treat OCD and PTSD as well as other anxiety disorders and is considered the gold standard evidence-based psychological treatment. The treatment is widely disseminated and is used by psychological treatment services geared to military personnel in many countries, including the United States, Israel, and Canada.

Foa has had an incredibly prolific career with many published books and edited volumes including treatment guides for consumers and clinicians. She has authored over 350 scientific articles and book chapters. Foa developed numerous assessment instruments including the Obsessive-Compulsive Inventory (child and adult versions) and the PTSD Symptom Scale. In addition to her research and writing, Foa is a popular speaker who has been instrumental in disseminating PE around the world through training workshops.

Foa has held many important roles that have had significant impact. She was a major force in the development of the DSM-IV, serving as chair of the subcommittee for OCD and cochair of the subcommittee for PTSD. She was also chair of the treatment guidelines taskforce of the International Society for Traumatic Stress Disorders. Foa has received many awards and honors, including a Lifetime Achievement Award in the Field of Trauma Psychology from the American Psychological Association, an Outstanding Career Achievement Award from the International OCD Foundation, and a Lifetime Achievement Award from the Association of Behavioural and Cognitive Therapies. She has served on the editorial board for many leading journals and has received an honorary doctorate degree of philosophy from the University of Basel.

Today, at age 77, Foa is still as productive as ever. She lives in Philadelphia with her American husband, a professor in ancient philosophy at the University of Pennsylvania. She spends two months each year in Israel where she works with her collaborators, writes, and spends time with family. Her three daughters live in the United States.

Randi E. McCabe

See also: Emotional Processing Theory; Exposure Treatment; Lang, Peter, J. (1930–); Obsessive-Compulsive Disorder; Posttraumatic Stress Disorder; Wolpe, Joseph (1915–1997)

Further Reading

Foa, Edna B., & Kozak, Michael, J. (1986). Emotional processing of fear: Exposure to corrective information. *Psychological Bulletin, 99*, 20–35.

Freud, Sigmund (1856–1939)

Sigmund Freud, born Sigismund Schlomo Freud (1856–1939), was a Viennese physician who developed the theories and methods of psychoanalysis. He was one of the foremost thinkers of the 20th century and his ideas had a profound effect not only in the field of medicine but also on Western culture of the 20th and 21st centuries. Many of his key ideas became incorporated into the everyday understanding of human behavior and psychology. Academically his work has had a major influence on the study of psychology, psychiatry, anthropology, sociology, literature, and the arts.

Freud was born in Freiberg in Moravia. This small town is now known as Pribor and is located in the Czech Republic about 220 miles east of Prague. Freud's family was Jewish. His mother was Amalie Nathanson, the third wife of his father Jacob Freud. Freud had five sisters, two brothers, and two half-brothers. The family moved to Vienna when he was four years old and he lived most of his life there until 1938. In 1896 Freud married Martha Bernays. They had three daughters, Mathilde, Anna, and Sophie, and three sons, Martin, Oliver, and Ernst.

Freud graduated as a doctor of medicine at the age of 25 from the University of Vienna. In his early years, he carried out meticulous research on the brain and

Sigmund Freud in his study. Freud developed the theory and practice of psychoanalysis, a form of psychotherapy that emphasizes the importance of the unconscious. Although Freud's original psychoanalytic methods are no longer widely practiced, he is credited with introducing psychotherapy to psychiatry and psychology. (Library of Congress)

published a number of important papers. He set up in practice as a neurologist, and his office was at No. 19 Bergasse in Vienna. (The Sigmund Freud Museum is now located at this address.)

Freud became interested in the condition known as *hysteria*. Toward the end of 1885, he went to Paris to study hysteria with the renowned neurologist Charcot at the Salpêtrière Hospital. Patients with hysteria presented with neurological symptoms such as paralysis and loss of sensation; however, they did not have any underlying structural neurological disorder. Freud theorized that the underlying basis to the symptoms was psychological in nature and related to unacceptable and unconscious sexual and aggressive thoughts and feelings. In the early years of his practice he used hypnosis to treat these patients and, in 1895, published with his colleague Joseph Breuer, *Studies on Hysteria*.

Freud applied his methods to the treatment of his patients, many of whom suffered from various forms of anxiety, phobias, and obsessions. Freud used the term *neurosis* to categorize these disorders. One of Freud's early cases was that of a five-year-old boy Herbert Graf, referred to in published works as "Little Hans." Hans had developed a phobia of horses. Freud arranged for the boy's father to treat

Hans by following Freud's instructions. Freud derived many important elements of his theory of human psychology from this case.

Freud's original hope was to write a treatise explaining psychology based on the workings of the brain. However, neurological science was not at the level to provide the basis for such a theory. Consequently Freud had to describe mental processes in terms of metaphorical concepts and schemas such as the *id, ego*, and *superego*. He derived his theories by listening with extreme attentiveness to his patients' free associations and accounts of their dreams. His most far-reaching and expansive description of his theory was published in November 1899 in *The Interpretation of Dreams*. Although he continued to modify his theories extensively over the subsequent 30 years, the basic elements are to be found in this volume.

Freud was a prolific writer. His writings pertaining to psychoanalysis have been collected in the 23-volume *Standard Edition of the Complete Psychological Works of Sigmund Freud*. He also produced extensive other writings, including correspondences with many contemporary psychoanalysts and colleagues. Freud's writings consist of detailed case descriptions, as well as general review lectures describing his overall theories and methods. In addition, he wrote a number of philosophical and reflective papers that were more speculative in nature such as "Civilization and Its Discontents," "The Future of an Illusion," "Totem and Taboo," and "Moses and Monotheism." These writings reflected the fact that Freud had witnessed the destructiveness of World War I and had developed a pessimistic view of humanity's inherently aggressive potential. He did not believe in God or an afterlife and felt that religion was an expression of man's need for a protective father figure and provided a delusionary false comfort.

Freud was an avid smoker of cigars and in 1923, at the age of 67, he was diagnosed with mouth cancer. He had to have part of his upper jaw and right side of his palate removed. Over the course of his life, he underwent numerous operations and treatment with radiation. He lived with considerable pain and had to use a prosthesis.

Due to the rise of Nazism, Freud and some of his family members were forced to flee to England in 1938. Four of his sisters, who were unable to leave, were subsequently murdered in Nazi concentration camps. After his escape to London, a reoccurrence of the mouth cancer was identified. Despite further surgery, his condition progressively worsened. He died on September 23, 1939, at the age of 83, after his personal physician, Dr. Max Schur, in accordance with a previous undertaking to Freud, administered high doses of morphine.

Alan B. Eppel

See also: Phobic Neurosis; Psychoanalysis

Further Reading

Clark, Ronald W. (1980). *Freud the man and the cause*. New York, NY. Random House.

THE CASE OF LITTLE HANS: OEDIPUS COMPLEX VERSUS HORSE PHOBIA

Herbert Graf (1904–1973), more commonly known as Little Hans, was the subject of a famous case study published by Sigmund Freud in 1909. Freud analyzed Hans's childhood behavior, primarily focusing on his fear of horses and on how to treat this phobia. Freud used the findings from this case study as support for his concept of the Oedipus complex.

At age three, Hans had developed an active interest in his own genitals. When his mother saw him touching his penis, which he referred to as his *widdler*, she threatened to call the doctor to cut it off if he continued. Hans's fascination with genitals was not limited to his own; he was interested in whether his mother had a *widdler* and was also quite attentive to animal *widdlers*.

When he was about five years old, Hans developed a phobia of horses, causing the outgoing and lively boy to become meek and submissive. Hans even became afraid to go out of his house for fear that a horse would bite him in the streets. His phobia prompted his father to contact Freud, a family acquaintance, for treatment. The father provided Freud with detailed information about Hans's behavior and about his conversations with Hans.

After analyzing the reports from Hans's father, Freud noted that Hans's fear began following the warnings to stop touching his *widdler* and a bad dream he had about losing his mother. He theorized that Hans's phobia was rooted in the *Oedipus complex*, a concept he coined to describe a young child's sexual desires for the parent of the opposite sex and a resultant sense of rivalry and hostility toward the same-sex parent. He arrived at his conclusion based on Hans's claims that he especially feared horses with large *widdlers* and black bits around their eyes and mouth. Freud believed that the horse was a representation of Hans's father with his larger adult *widdler* and moustache and glasses. By extension, he interpreted Hans's phobia as a fear of his father's retaliation for his sexual desire toward his mother; Hans was afraid that his father would castrate him. To cope with the Oedipus complex, Hans was thought to have used a defense mechanism called displacement, whereby he substituted his unacceptable fear of his father with a more permissible fear of horses.

Although Freud met Hans only once during his treatment, he regularly instructed Hans's father on ways to deal with Hans's phobia. In particular, Freud encouraged Hans's father to ask Hans explicit questions concerning subjects like his love for his mother and his fear of his father. Freud believed that Hans's horse phobia had fully resolved following the occurrence of two fantasies in which his unconscious desires were made conscious. In the first fantasy, Hans was married to his mother and had children with her; his father was demoted to the role of grandfather. The second fantasy involved a plumber replacing Hans's small bottom and "widdler" with larger ones. These fantasies allowed Hans to identify with his father, thus resolving his Oedipus complex and horse phobia by about age six.

Lisa Rustom and Irena Milosevic

G

Gamma-Aminobutyric Acid

Gamma-aminobutyric acid (GABA) is one of the inhibitory neurotransmitters in the central nervous system of vertebrates. Its chief physiological role is to activate both ionotropic and metabotropic GABA receptors and to mediate the inhibitory transmissions between neurons. Biochemically, GABA falls in the broad category of amino acid; however, since its amino group is attached to the γ-carbon (and thus a γ-amino acid), it is not involved in the proteinogenic (protein-building) process. In mammalian brains, GABA is synthesized and metabolized in a loop-like process known as GABA shunt. It is synthesized by an enzyme called glutamic acid decarboxylase from glutamate, a key excitatory neurotransmitter, and converted back to glutamate via a multistep process, which involves part of the Krebs cycle (a pivotal metabolic pathway in aerobic organisms). The inhibitory/excitatory balance between GABA and glutamate is particularly important for maintaining proper neuronal signaling, and the loss of such harmony is implicated in anxiety disorders such as specific phobias.

Physiologically, GABA is the common ligand to a family of receptors known as GABA receptors. These receptors can be further categorized into two main groups: (1) ionotropic $GABA_A$ receptors whose activation directly triggers the opening of the chloride channel and results in fast synaptic inhibition; and (2) metabotropic $GABA_B$ receptors whose activation leads to G protein-mediated modulations of certain types of calcium and potassium channels and results in slow inhibitory transmission. GABA receptors are intensively involved in various physiological and psychological processes, such as the expression of anxiety, sleep cycles, and nociception (the perception of pain).

Given the pivotal role of GABAergic system dysregulation in pathological conditions such as anxiety and sleep disorders, many pharmacological agents are designed to positively modulate the $GABA_A$ receptor. Among them are benzodiazepines and non-benzodiazepine drugs (commonly known as Z-drugs). Since different subtypes of $GABA_A$ receptor subunits are known to mediate differential physiological processes, a new generation of subtype-selective drugs is emerging to selectively treat a particular condition (anxiety or insomnia) with minimal unwanted effects.

Yudong Gao and Scott A. Heldt

See also: Benzodiazepines; Fear, Animal Models of

Further Reading

Rudolph, Uwe, & Knoflach, Frederic. (2011). Beyond classical benzodiazepines: Novel therapeutic potential of GABAA receptor subtypes. *Nature Reviews Drug Discovery, 10*, 685–697.

Wiero ska, Joanna M., Stachowicz, K., Nowak, G., & Pilc, A. (2011). The loss of glutamate-GABA harmony in anxiety disorders. In V. Kalinin (Ed.), *Anxiety Disorders*. Rijeka, Croatia: InTech. Retrieved from http://www.intechopen.com/books/anxiety-disorders/the-loss-of-glutamate-gaba-harmony-in-anxiety-disorders

Gender Differences

Phobias are defined as intense fears in the presence or anticipation of a specific object or situation. Gender differences in the prevalence and presentation of phobias are common but tend to vary across types. Women are twice as likely as men to meet the criteria for a diagnosis of any specific phobia (27% vs. 13%) or multiple phobias (5% vs. 2%). Specifically, women are more apt to report animal (12% vs. 3% men), natural environment (5% vs. 3% men), and situational (17% vs. 9% men) phobias. Height and flying phobias tend to be distributed more evenly across gender (60% women), and blood-injection-injury phobia is equally common in both genders (LeBeau et al., 2010).

Gender differences in specific phobias have been linked to biological and environmental factors. The heritability of specific phobias runs between 30% and 60%, with variation across subtypes. Interestingly, there appears to be a genetic factor specifically associated with the development of animal and situational phobias, which might explain why women tend to report more of these phobias than men.

Genetic factors in the development of phobias appear to be most influential during early childhood. As children grow, their genetic vulnerabilities tend to be shaped by social and environmental factors—a process moderated by gender. Socialization processes teach women and men what to fear, how much to fear, and how to respond to fearful stimuli in ways that are consistent with their gender roles. For example, women learn to overestimate the probability that an object or situation is harmful and are more apt to experience these events as unpredictable and uncontrollable. Fear expression and avoidance of fearful stimuli are more consistent with female (vs. male) gender roles and are more apt to be reinforced in women and discouraged in men. Indeed, men are typically encouraged to approach (vs. avoid) fearful stimuli, reducing their risk for phobias through repeated exposure (Craske, 2003). Moreover, women tend to be better at identifying the emotional states of others' through nonverbal cues (e.g., facial expression, body language). This heightened sensitivity to socially transmitted information puts women at greater risk for developing specific phobias through processes of vicarious conditioning, such as observational learning. Research also shows that girls are more susceptible to parental modeling of fear and anxiety than boys.

Most people with specific phobias do not seek treatment either because the symptoms are not debilitating or because they have adapted their lifestyles to avoid contact with the feared stimulus. For example, individuals who fear flying may choose other modes of transportation. Given that women are more apt to seek treatment for mental health issues than men, it is possible (but not confirmed) that women with specific phobias may be more apt to seek treatment than men.

Agoraphobia refers to the fear of situations in which escape might be difficult or help might not be readily accessible if panic-related symptoms occur. Women are more likely to experience agoraphobia than men (3% vs. 2%). Agoraphobia often co-occurs with other mental disorders that vary by gender. For example, women are more likely to report co-occurring anxiety or mood disorders, whereas men are more likely to report co-occurring substance use disorders. Of those affected by agoraphobia, women are significantly more likely to seek treatment than men; men are more reluctant to discuss agoraphobic fears and more apt to exhibit behavioral avoidance.

Agoraphobia, as compared to other phobias, has the highest heritability rate (61%; American Psychiatric Association [APA], 2013). The onset of agoraphobia is later than most other phobias (25–29 years), suggesting that the role of temperamental and environmental factors may be more influential in shaping individuals' genetic vulnerabilities. Such factors may include behavioral inhibition, negative affect, and anxiety sensitivity (i.e., fear of anxiety symptoms), all of which are more prominent in women than men. Moreover, women (vs. men) report greater levels of parental protection during childhood, which is associated with the development of agoraphobic fears.

In the general population, social anxiety disorder (social phobia) is more commonly found in women than men (10% vs. 8%), with greater gender differences observed in adolescence and young adulthood. The prevalence rates are similar or slightly higher for men in clinical samples (APA, 2013). Moreover, the presentation of social anxiety disorder varies across gender. Whereas both women and men share similar levels of fear of informal social situations (e.g., attending a party) and public observation (e.g., eating in public), women tend to report greater fear of professional situations (e.g., performing in front of others, being interviewed). As a result, women with social anxiety disorder may forgo a career working outside of the house and remain unemployed. Men, on the other hand, report greater fear than women of social situations involving the use of public washrooms and dating. Men with social anxiety disorder tend to delay getting married and starting a family.

Women are more predisposed than men to temperamental factors associated with the development of social anxiety disorder, including behavioral inhibition and fear of negative evaluation. Negative affectivity is also implicated in the development and maintenance of social anxiety disorder, and is observed more in women than men across cultures (McLean & Anderson, 2009). Gender differences also emerge when examining disorders that tend to co-occur with social anxiety disorder.

Whereas women display more internalizing disorders (e.g., mood, anxiety), men display more externalizing disorders (e.g., substance use). Women and men appear equally likely to seek treatment, both psychological (62% vs. 64%) and pharmacological (38% vs. 32%; Turk et al., 1998).

Catherine E. Gallagher and Margo C. Watt

See also: Agoraphobia (Fear of Panic-Like Symptoms); Fear; Phobia, Specific; Social Anxiety Disorder (Social Phobia)

Further Reading

American Psychiatric Association. (2013). *Diagnostic and statistical manual of mental disorders* (5th ed.). Arlington, VA: American Psychiatric Publishing.

Craske, Michelle G. (2003). *Origins of phobias and anxiety disorders: Why more women than men*. Oxford, UK: Elsevier Science.

LeBeau, Richard T., Glenn, Daniel, Liao, Betty, Wittchen, Hans-Ulrich, Beesdo-Baum, Katja, Ollendick, Thomas, & Craske, Michelle G. (2010). Specific phobia: A review of DSM-IV specific phobia and preliminary recommendations for DSM-V. *Depression and Anxiety, 27*, 148–167.

McLean, Carmen P., & Anderson, Emily R. (2009). Brave men and timid women? A review of the gender differences in fear and anxiety. *Clinical Psychology Review, 29*, 496–505.

Turk, Cynthia L., Heimberg, Richard G., Orsillo, Susan M., Holt, Craig S., Gitow, Andrea, Street, L. Linda, . . . Liebowitz, Michael R. (1998). An investigation of gender differences in social phobia. *Journal of Anxiety Disorders, 12*(3), 209–223.

Guided Mastery Therapy

Guided mastery therapy (also called therapist-guided therapy, performance-based therapy, or therapist-assisted exposure) is a psychological treatment for phobias and other anxiety disorders. The treatment is based on the self-efficacy model and its clinical extension, participant modeling, put forth by Albert Bandura (1925–). It was subsequently elaborated by Williams and colleagues (e.g., Williams, 1990; Williams, Turner, & Peer, 1985). The approach holds that individuals with phobias experience distress and impairment because they lack self-efficacy, or confidence, that they can capably perform feared tasks. Accordingly, guided mastery therapy helps individuals gain a sense of mastery over their performance during feared activities through active assistance from the therapist. Although there is much overlap between guided mastery and cognitive-behavioral therapy (CBT) techniques, the treatments differ in important ways. Evidence supports the efficacy of guided mastery therapy for the treatment of phobias, although there is mixed support for its theoretical tenets.

The guided mastery model posits that phobias are maintained by individuals' low self-efficacy beliefs about their ability to perform feared tasks. That is, perceptions of danger, feelings of fear, and phobic avoidance are thought to be caused by the belief that one lacks the necessary skills to perform effectively in scary situations. For example, individuals with a dog phobia might believe that they do not have the skills to interact with a dog, and they would therefore perceive dog interactions as dangerous and scary and would likely avoid them. According to the model, people with phobias also typically adopt self-protective behaviors (also called defensive coping rituals) to help them cope with feared situations. A dog-fearful individual might, for instance, cross the street upon noticing a dog approaching. Such behaviors are viewed as a hindrance to self-efficacy because they remind individuals of their limitations (e.g., "I can't walk on the same side of the street as a dog") and provide an inaccurate reason for performance success (e.g., "I managed to walk past the dog but didn't get bitten only because I walked quickly and did not make eye contact with it").

In guided mastery therapy, the therapist works collaboratively with clients and uses several techniques to achieve three main goals: to increase the (1) level, (2) proficiency, and (3) independence of clients' performance. To raise the *level* of performance, the therapist helps clients enter feared situations or to complete tasks that they would typically avoid. The therapist might initially complete the tasks with clients (e.g., walking together through a dog park) or model the tasks to them (e.g., therapist first pets a dog before asking a client to try it). An additional strategy involves identifying a series of progressively more challenging tasks that the client will attempt, which are rated along a 0–100 "confidence" scale to assess self-efficacy. Tasks are deemed ideally challenging when rated in the 20–40 range before they are attempted. To help clients complete the tasks, the therapist might offer physical or mechanical support, such as holding a dog on a leash while the client initially pets it.

Next, to increase the *proficiency* of clients' performance, the therapist helps them complete tasks flexibly and without the use of self-protective coping behaviors. Clients are encouraged to initially reduce their use of such behaviors and then to completely eliminate them. They are also asked to perform tasks in a flexible manner and across a variety of situations (e.g., petting different parts of a dog, petting different types of dogs).

Once the level and proficiency of performance have been sufficiently increased, the therapist fosters *independence* by providing help only as necessary to facilitate progress, and by phasing out assistance as soon as progress is achieved. The therapist also ensures that clients are experiencing independent performance successes by assigning them "homework" between sessions. For example, a client might be asked to walk independently through a dog park or to visit a friend with a dog.

Guided mastery therapy has numerous similarities to CBT, particularly one of its components, exposure treatment. For example, completing progressively more challenging feared tasks is akin to exposure, and the concept of self-protective behaviors is similar to safety behaviors described in CBT models of anxiety disorders. Further, both treatments involve the completion of between-session assignments to facilitate independence and are based upon a collaborative relationship between therapist and client. However, fundamental differences exist between the two. The guided mastery model holds that low self-efficacy is the reason for exaggerated perceptions of danger, feelings of fear, and avoidance behavior, whereas the cognitive behavioral model centers on perceptions of danger as the reason for low self-efficacy in feared situations, feelings of fear, and avoidance behavior. Unlike CBT, guided mastery therapy does not assume that cognitive biases are a barrier to increasing self-efficacy, nor does it require an increase in anxiety during completion of feared activities (i.e., during exposure). Anxiety is viewed as having little value in the context of guided mastery therapy, and anxiety reduction arising from the therapist's assistance during completion of feared tasks is welcomed.

A number of studies have shown that guided mastery therapy is an effective treatment for specific phobias, agoraphobia, and social anxiety disorder (social phobia). For specific phobias, in particular, treatment as short as one or two sessions has been shown to reduce avoidance, phobic beliefs, and fear-related arousal. Some studies have shown that guided mastery treatment is significantly more effective than exposure treatment without therapist assistance. Research that has evaluated the underlying mechanisms for therapeutic change in guided mastery therapy has, however, not consistently demonstrated that the treatment changes self-efficacy or that improvements in self-efficacy lead to reductions in phobic beliefs.

Irena Milosevic

See also: Bandura, Albert (1925–); Cognitive Behavioral Therapy; Exposure Treatment; Self-Efficacy Theory

Further Reading

Williams, S. Lloyd. (1990). Guided mastery treatment of agoraphobia: Beyond stimulus exposure. *Progress in Behavior Modification, 26*, 89–121.

Williams, S. Lloyd, Turner, Samuel M., & Peer, David F. (1985). Guided mastery and performance desensitization treatments for severe acrophobia. *Journal of Consulting and Clinical Psychology, 53*, 237–247.

H

Habituation

Habituation is a type of non-associative learning in which repeated exposure to a stimulus results in a reduction of an innate or biological response. The decrease in responding observed during habituation is not due to motor fatigue (a loss or reduction in the ability to respond) or sensory adaption (a loss or reduction in the ability to detect the stimulus). Rather, habituation is a learned adaptation in which a response to a specific, repeatedly presented stimulus decreases when it is deemed to be irrelevant or harmless. Although it was initially investigated within the context of simple reflex responses, this phenomenon has been observed across a variety of biological processes and species. There is significant consensus regarding the characteristics of habituation, and several theories have been developed to explain this well-studied phenomenon, such as the dual-process theory and memory-based theories. Additionally, the term *habituation* has been used in the context of cognitive-behavioral therapies for the treatment of anxiety disorders, such as phobias, to describe the decrease in anxiety that follows from repeated, prolonged exposure to feared stimuli.

Habituation can easily be confused with *extinction*, which is the elimination of learned behaviors through associative learning (i.e., operant and classical conditioning). By contrast, *habituation* refers to the reduction in responses seen as automatic in nature (e.g., startle response, blinking). An example of habituation can be seen by a turtle's response to having its shell touched. Upon initial contact, sensing potential danger, the turtle may retract its head in an effort to protect itself. With repeated contact, the turtle grows accustomed to the sensation, learns that the contact is not indicative of danger, and stops retracting its head. However, changes in the type, intensity, or frequency of contact will likely result in the return of the turtle's response, demonstrating that it has not lost the ability to respond but rather has stopped responding to a stimulus deemed to be neutral or nonthreatening.

Memory-based theories of habituation (Sokolov, 1963; Wagner, 1979) propose that a model of a response-eliciting stimulus is developed through repeated exposure. Although initial exposures lead to responding, as the memory model is refined to more closely resemble the expected stimulus, the response is inhibited, resulting in habituation. Accordingly, changes in the stimulus (e.g., type, frequency, intensity) result in a mismatch between the stimulus and memory model, resulting in the reemergence of the response. By contrast, the dual-process theory (Groves &

Thompson, 1970) suggests that presentation of a stimulus results in two competing processes, one aimed at reducing responding (habituation) and the other at increasing it (sensitization). It is the net outcome of these competing processes that ultimately determines the observed response. Although they offer different explanations for habituation, both memory-based theories and the dual-process theory have received empirical support.

The construct of habituation has been used clinically, mainly within the context of behavioral treatments for phobias and other anxiety disorders. Individuals are taught that their anxious responses to feared stimuli will eventually subside with more frequent, prolonged, and repeated exposure to them. For example, an individual being treated for a dog phobia may be asked to sit in the same room as a dog. This would result in an initial increase in physiological symptoms and subjective reports of anxiety. However, with the passage of time and absence of a sensitizing response (e.g., the dog acting aggressively), the dog would be recategorized as a neutral stimulus, allowing the symptoms to subside (decreased responding). With repeated, frequent practice in a variety of situations and with different dogs, the habituated response (decrease in anxiety) would be expected to occur more rapidly and to generalize to a number of situations that initially evoked it. Although this has proven useful in clinical settings, some researchers have indicated that the characteristics of habituation described in the literature do not directly coincide with that which has been observed in exposure therapies (see Tryon, 2005, for a review).

Philippe Shnaider and Irena Milosevic

See also: Behavior Therapy; Classical Conditioning; Exposure Treatment; Extinction; Operant Conditioning

Further Reading

Groves, Philip M., & Thompson, Richard F. (1970). Habituation: A dual-process theory. *Psychological Review, 77,* 419–450.

Sokolov, Evgeniĭ N. (1963). *Perception and the conditioned reflex* (S. Waydenfeld, Trans.). Oxford, UK: Pergamon Press.

Tryon, Warren W. (2005). Possible mechanisms for why desensitization and exposure therapy work. *Clinical Psychology Review, 25,* 67–95.

Wagner, Allan R. (1979). Habituation and memory. In Anthony Dickinson & Robert A. Boakes (Eds.), *Mechanisms of learning and motivation: A memorial volume for Jerzy Konorski* (pp. 53–82). Hillsdale, NJ: Lawrence Earlbaum Associates.

Hypnosis

Hypnosis is a state of relaxation and concentration characterized by an increased sense of awareness, imagination, and suggestibility. Although its roots date to the 18th century, it was first applied to the treatment for phobias in the 1970s. Hypnosis is not an effective stand-alone treatment for phobias or other anxiety disorders, but it may be used in conjunction with other approaches, such as cognitive behavioral therapy or exposure treatment, to enhance their effects and facilitate treatment engagement.

Franz Mesmer (1734–1815), a German physician, is credited with the initial development of the hypnotic procedure in the late 1700s. Mesmer believed that there was a natural energetic transference, referred to as *mesmerism*, that occurred between all objects. Sigmund Freud (1856–1939), the founder of psychoanalysis, is noted to have used hypnosis as a technique to access (supposedly) repressed memories. However, Freud later abandoned hypnosis in favor of free association as a technique for interpretation of the unconscious mind. More recently, hypnosis has been used to treat a wide range of medical and psychological difficulties, including addictions, pain, sport performance, obesity, and phobias. The benefits of hypnosis for the treatment of phobias were first investigated in 1974 by Frank Frankel. Since that time, studies on hypnosis as a stand-alone intervention for phobias have achieved mixed results. However, hypnosis is now generally accepted as being useful in phobia treatment when combined with other therapeutic approaches.

Hypnosis physiologically resembles sleep; however, the attention of individuals under hypnosis is more enhanced than in normal conscious states, with a heightened ability to focus intensely and block out distractions. The hypnotic state is typically induced by a hypnotist, but self-hypnosis can also be taught. During hypnosis, people are encouraged to respond to suggestions from the hypnotist for changes in perception, sensation, emotion, thought, or behavior. For example, a person with a phobia of dogs could be induced to envision petting a dog, notice the dog's soft fur and feel calm. Contrary to popular belief, hypnotized individuals have voluntary control over their actions but are more accepting of suggestions. When the subject's responses align with given suggestions, hypnosis is considered to be induced. Individuals vary in how easily they can be hypnotized, and standardized scales can assess the "hypnotizability" of a person.

There are various methods for using hypnosis in the treatment of phobias. In particular, hypnosis is commonly used in combination with cognitive behavioral therapy techniques such as exposure therapy and relaxation training. Hypnosis can be used to enhance imaginal exposure by helping the client focus and remain immersed in the imagined feared scene. During hypnosis, anxiety-provoking scenes are narrated and relevant senses and surroundings are described in expressive detail. Imaginal exposure is particularly valuable in reproducing fear situations that are impractical to re-create, and can also be used as an initial step in building toward real-life (*in vivo*) exposures. Hypnosis is most commonly used for aviophobia (fear of flying), blood-injection-injury phobia, and dental phobia. For example, in aviophobia, imaginal exposure with hypnosis may involve imagining an airplane trip, from buying the tickets through take-off and landing, while the hypnotist suggests better perspectives and ways to cope with the anxiety experienced. Hypnosis can also be used with relaxation training techniques as an aid to deepening relaxation. For example, a hypnotist may take a client through a progressive muscle relaxation exercise and include suggestions that the client is becoming more and more relaxed. In any treatment, therapists make many suggestions to clients. Hypnosis facilitates greater acceptance of these suggestions through enhanced attention, concentration, and relaxation, which can increase the effectiveness of the treatment.

Brenda L. Key and Jennifer M. Yip

See also: Applied Relaxation; Cognitive Behavioral Therapy; Exposure, Imaginal; Exposure, *In Vivo*; Exposure Treatment

Further Reading

Barabasz, Arreed F., Olness, Karen, Boland, Robert, & Kahn, Stephen. (2009). *Medical hypnosis primer: Clinical and research evidence*. New York, NY: Taylor & Francis.

Fredette, Catherine, El-Baalbaki, Ghassan, Neron, Sylvain, & Palardy, Veronique. (2013). Using hypnosis in the treatment of anxiety disorders: Pros and cons. In Federico Durbano (Ed.), *New Insights into anxiety disorders*. Rijeka, Croatia: InTech.

Kohen, Daniel P., & Olness, Karen. (2011). *Hypnosis and hypnotherapy with children* (4th ed.). New York, NY: Routledge.

Hypochondriasis

Hypochondriasis, sometimes called *health anxiety*, is excessive preoccupation with the belief that one has, or will develop, a serious illness. This belief is based on the misinterpretation of mild or benign bodily symptoms, fluctuations, and sensations. An individual with hypochondriasis experiences distress and impairment of daily activities due to preoccupation with health-related concerns. The preoccupation persists despite medical reassurance.

In the fifth edition of the *Diagnostic and Statistical Manual for Mental Disorders* (DSM-5), hypochondriasis has been replaced by somatic symptom disorder (SSD) and illness anxiety disorder (IAD). Individuals with SSD (an estimated 75% of those formerly diagnosed with hypochondriasis) exhibit excessive, persistent thoughts, feelings, and behaviors pertaining to a benign somatic (bodily) symptom (e.g., pain) that is experienced as threatening and harmful. Individuals with IAD (approximately 25% of those formerly diagnosed with hypochondriasis) are distressed by fear of having or getting a serious illness, and interpret normal bodily sensations and fluctuations as indicators of a serious illness (e.g., cancer). Whereas symptom preoccupation is the central feature of SSD, fear and anxiety about the perceived *meaning* of the symptom (i.e., that one has a serious illness) are the central features of IAD.

Illness anxiety is thought to arise from narrow beliefs about health and one's personal vulnerability to illness. For people with illness anxiety, *health* means a total absence of bodily fluctuations and discomfort. Illness anxiety involves somatic hypervigilance (i.e., excessive tendency to scan for and attend to bodily sensations); misinterpretation of normal bodily fluctuations, discomfort, and mild symptoms (e.g. ringing ears, dizziness upon standing, or indigestion) as evidence of a serious illness; and heightened anxiety and worry that one is ill. As the individual becomes anxious, normal bodily sensations and fluctuations increase as part of the autonomic nervous system's normal fight-or-flight anxiety response. These arousal sensations are interpreted as further evidence of serious illness.

In order to escape or reduce anxiety, the individual seeks medical attention, or avoids medical care altogether; he or she also engages in excessive body monitoring and may research symptoms for self-diagnosis. Medical reassurance may provide short-term relief, but individuals with illness anxiety often believe that the doctor missed something or that diagnostic test results are wrong. They will continue to seek medical attention, or come to distrust and avoid medical settings altogether. These *safety behaviors* (body checking, symptom researching, seeking medical care) temporarily relieve anxiety, thereby making it more likely that they will be repeated in the future. Safety behaviors also prevent the individual from experiencing normal bodily discomfort, doing nothing about it, and discovering that nothing catastrophic results. In other words, the individual never has the chance to challenge his or her erroneous beliefs about health.

Estimates suggest that illness anxiety affects between 1% and 5% of the general population over the lifespan. Prevalence rates in men and women are thought to be equal, in contrast with SSD, which is more common in women than in men. Illness anxiety is often comorbid with other somatic disorders, depression, panic disorder, generalized anxiety disorder, and obsessive-compulsive disorder. Illness anxiety generally first occurs in early or middle adulthood, and tends to be chronic—often persisting for years. It usually develops following periods of intense life stress, serious illness, loss of a loved one, or media exposure to illness information (e.g., news stories about an H1N1 flu outbreak). Research suggests that a number of risk factors predict illness anxiety. These include anxiety sensitivity (fear of arousal-related bodily sensations); social isolation, which may increase self- and health-focused attention; direct experience of serious illness as a child or through a family member; and early learning experiences, such as receiving attention for sick-role behavior.

Research suggests that cognitive behavioral therapy (CBT) is at least as effective as medications (i.e., selective-serotonin reuptake inhibitors or SSRIs). CBT may include psychoeducation (broadening the individual's perspective from a biomedical to an alternative biopsychosocial explanation for somatic complaints); cognitive restructuring activities to identify, challenge, and modify erroneous beliefs about health and illness; exposure to feared scenarios (e.g., through imagery or popular media content);

controlled exposure to feared bodily sensations (e.g., spinning in a chair to induce dizziness); and prevention of safety behaviors. These CBT components aim to reduce fear by developing more realistic beliefs about health and the body, and by changing the maladaptive reassurance-seeking or avoidance behaviors that maintain illness anxiety.

Christianne Macaulay and Margo C. Watt

See also: Anxiety Sensitivity; Cognitive Behavioral Therapy; Cognitive Restructuring; Exposure, Interoceptive; Fight-or-Flight Response; Obsessive-Compulsive Disorder; Panic Disorder; Safety Behavior

Further Reading

Allen, Lesley A. & Woolfolk, Robert L. (2010). Cognitive behavioral therapy for somatoform disorders. *Psychiatric Clinics of North America, 33*, 579–593.

American Psychiatric Association. (2013). *Diagnostic and statistical manual of mental disorders* (5th ed.). Arlington, VA: American Psychiatric Publishing.

Hypothalamic-Pituitary-Adrenal (HPA) Axis

Stress—be it physical or emotional—activates the hypothalamic-pituitary-adrenal (HPA) axis. The HPA axis therefore plays a central role in the body's response to fear and phobias. The HPA axis is part of the neuroendocrine system, which controls our body's production of hormones, including hormones that regulate our response to stress. It also influences a variety of other bodily functions, including metabolism, immune function, and the endocrine system more broadly.

When humans encounter a physical or emotional stressor, neurons in the hypothalamus produce arginine-vasopressin (AVP) and corticotrophin-releasing hormone (CRH), two hormones that are transported via blood vessels to the pituitary gland. There, AVP and CRH stimulate the secretion of adrenocorticotrophic hormone (ACTH). ACTH travels via blood vessels to the adrenal gland, where it triggers the production of cortisol, which is typically considered the primary hormone responsible for humans' stress response. An important component of healthy HPA axis functioning is the downregulation of cortisol production, either when enough cortisol has been produced or the stressor has passed. The downregulation of cortisol levels occurs when receptors on the pituitary gland and hypothalamus detect high levels of cortisol in the body and decrease the production of AVP, ACHT, CRH, and ultimately cortisol. This negative feedback loop is necessary to maintain healthy levels of cortisol in the body. Prolonged, heightened, or chronic HPA axis activation can wear down the body over time and may even compromise individuals' physical health.

Although cortisol is the most well-studied hormone in the HPA axis, each hormone is important in its own right. AVP, for example, plays a critical role in the body's ability to maintain homeostasis (a stable or constant level of functioning). One of the main functions of AVP is to regulate the body's retention of water. AVP triggers water conservation when an individual is dehydrated by concentrating the urine and reducing urine volume. AVP also increases peripheral vascular resistance (vasoconstriction), thereby increasing arterial blood pressure. In fact, rapid changes in AVP levels are associated with symptoms of fainting (associated with vasovagal syncope) often associated with blood-injection-injury phobia. Some even believe rapid changes in AVP may be the driving force behind the rapid change in blood pressure that causes some individuals to faint upon exposure to blood. CRH also plays an important role beyond triggering the production of ACHT. In particular, CRH stimulates the sympathetic component of the autonomic nervous system, resulting in increased heart rate, sweating, and respiration, which are some of the more visible signs of encountering a phobic stimulus. Although ACTH is predominantly involved in stimulating cortisol production, ACTH receptors are present in other areas of the body, such as those that affect bone production.

By measuring HPA axis activity, researchers are able to obtain an objective marker of individuals' stress levels when they encounter a feared stimulus. Doing so provides more comprehensive information than could be obtained from self-report alone. For example, some individuals may report heightened anxiety upon exposure to a feared stimulus, but not show excess HPA axis activation. By contrast, some individuals may underreport their experience of anxiety relative to their stress hormone levels. As a result, they may underestimate the effects of stress on their body and long-term physical health.

It is important to test HPA axis functioning as a marker of individuals' ability to adaptively respond to and recover from exposure to a feared stimulus. One of the more direct ways to test HPA axis functioning is the dexamethasone suppression test. Dexamethasone acts on the pituitary gland to suppress the release of ACTH, resulting in the adrenal gland releasing less cortisol. After dexamethasone injection, healthy individuals show lower cortisol. Failure to suppress cortisol secretion after a dexamethasone injection indicates impaired feedback regulation at the pituitary gland, leading to hyperactivity of the HPA axis. Dexamethasone administration can be coupled with an injection of CRH, known as the dex/CRH test, or it can be administered alone via the CRH challenge test. Both examine ACTH production in response to a given level of CRH and allow HPA axis functioning to be tested.

Joelle LeMoult and K. Lira Yoon

See also: Cortisol; Fight-or-Flight Response

Further Reading

Khan, Samir, King, Anthony P., Abelson, James L., & Liberzon, Israel. (2008). Neuroendocrinology of anxiety disorders. In M. M. Antony & M. B. Stein (Eds.), *Oxford handbook of anxiety and related disorders* (pp. 111–122). New York, NY: Oxford University Press.

McEwen, Bruce S., & Stellar, Eliot. (1993). Stress and the individual: Mechanisms leading to disease. *Archives of Internal Medicine, 153*, 2093–2101.

Iatrophobia (Fear of Doctors)

Iatrophobia, (from the Greek *iatros*, meaning physician, and *phobos*, meaning fear) is an excessive and irrational fear of doctors. The fear may encompass being in a doctor's office, interacting with a doctor and other medical staff, and undergoing a physical examination. Iatrophobia is classified as a specific phobia, other type, in the *Diagnostic and Statistical Manual for Mental Disorders*, fifth edition. Notably, although fears of certain medical procedures, such as injections and blood tests, may be associated with iatrophobia, they are classified in a separate category. Iatrophobia can be dangerous for individuals at risk of medical problems or for those who have existing medical conditions because medical appointments are often avoided. The phobia can be effectively treated with cognitive behavioral therapy.

The prevalence rate for iatrophobia has not been reported. Its onset is typically in childhood, although it may develop at any age following a negative experience with a doctor or medical procedure. Importantly, many children experience fear of the pediatrician that, for most, remits naturally over time. In children, iatrophobic fears may relate to being around an unfamiliar person or in an unfamiliar setting, experiencing pain, or being separated from the parent. When the child's fear is reinforced by the parent (e.g., parent exhibits distress or facilitates avoidance behavior when the child is distressed prior to or during the visit), the likelihood that the fear will persist increases. In adults, iatrophobic fear tends to focus on the experience of pain or discomfort, on the mistrust of the physician's skills, on the physician's authority, and on the possibility of receiving "bad news." As a result, avoidance of medical visits is a common feature of iatrophobia. Such avoidance may hinder the detection of medical risks and conditions, as well as access to treatment, which may have dangerous consequences for the individual's health and longevity. Some individuals with iatrophobia are able to attend doctor's appointments but experience considerable anxiety before and during each appointment; they may even experience panic attacks. Iatrophobia may not become significantly distressing or impairing until a person is diagnosed with a condition that requires frequent follow-ups.

A related and more common concern, the *white coat phenomenon*, occurs when individuals experience an increase in blood pressure during doctor's visits, making it difficult to obtain an accurate blood pressure reading and to diagnose certain cardiovascular conditions. This phenomenon is thought to arise due to increased physiological reactivity in response to elevated anxiety during the medical visit.

The effect can be reduced, although not entirely avoided, with automated blood pressure measurements over a longer period of time in a quiet part of the clinic. Unlike individuals with iatrophobia, who experience a broad constellation of anxiety symptoms during medical visits, individuals susceptible to the white coat phenomenon typically only experience blood pressure changes and may nevertheless be willing to regularly see their doctor.

It is important to note that medical fears may be present in several other anxiety disorders. For example, individuals with social anxiety disorder (social phobia) may be anxious about doctor's visits for fear of negative evaluation; individuals with generalized anxiety disorder may avoid doctors because they are worried about being diagnosed with a terrible illness; individuals with obsessive-compulsive disorder may avoid medical settings due to fear of germs and contamination; and, finally, individuals with blood-injection-injury phobia might have a circumscribed fear of needles. A thorough assessment is required to determine whether iatrophobic fear is but one aspect of these conditions or a distinct phobia.

Like other phobias, iatrophobia can be treated effectively with cognitive behavioral therapy, particularly with one of its components, exposure treatment. This method involves educating the individual about the nature of the fear and the factors that maintain it (e.g., postponing medical appointments), developing a hierarchy of avoided situations—from least to most fear-provoking, and proceeding through the hierarchy systematically in order to face one's fears. In the case of iatrophobia, exposure scenarios might involve watching a television show about doctors, walking through a hospital lobby, sitting in a hospital or clinic waiting room, calling to book a doctor's appointment, engaging in discussion with the doctor during the visit, and undergoing a physical exam and any other procedures the individual has been avoiding.

Irena Milosevic and Feven Yeshanew

See also: DSM-5; Obsessive-Compulsive Disorder; Phobia, Other Type; Phobia, Specific; Posttraumatic Stress Disorder; Social Anxiety Disorder (Social Phobia)

Further Reading

Antony, Martin M., & Watling, Mark A. (2006). *Overcoming medical phobias.* Oakland, CA: New Harbinger Publications, Inc.

Implosive Therapy

Implosive therapy (also called implosion therapy) is a psychological treatment for phobias and other mental health concerns. The therapy involves intense and prolonged imaginal exposure to feared scenarios, with the therapist deliberately aiming to induce high levels of anxiety. Although it is considered a behavioral treatment, implosive therapy incorporates psychodynamic elements. Given mixed evidence for its effectiveness, implosive therapy is not considered a treatment of choice for phobias.

Implosive therapy was developed and popularized in the 1960s by psychologists Thomas Stampfl and Donald Lewis. The therapy is rooted in behavioral principles, particularly fear extinction that occurs through repeated exposure to the feared stimulus in the absence of feared consequences and without avoidance or escape. In this way, implosive therapy is considered an early variant of exposure treatment; however, unlike exposure, it incorporates psychodynamic theory and technique (i.e., with a focus on unconscious conflicts). In the context of behavioral treatments, implosive therapy is most closely associated with flooding, in which the individual is rapidly (rather than gradually) exposed to a stimulus that evokes very high levels of fear. Whereas flooding can be conducted either *in vivo* (live) or imaginally (through mental imagery), implosive therapy is exclusively an imaginal treatment. The aim of the therapy is to *implode* or extinguish the fear response through intense, repeated exposure to feared stimuli using imagery.

Implosive therapy differs in several important ways from imaginal flooding. First, whereas flooding requires the individual to describe the feared scenario, implosive therapy additionally involves having the therapist introduce hypothesized feared cues into the scenario. The therapist's hypotheses are based on a psychodynamic formulation of the individual's fear problem (e.g., hostility toward the parents and fear of reprisal). The therapist uses the individual's emotional responses during implosion to determine whether hypothesized cues are relevant. Second, whereas in flooding the individual describes realistic feared scenarios, in implosive therapy the individual is asked to exaggerate the imagined situation to elicit as much fear as possible; indeed, this exaggeration usually has a quality of fantasy. For instance, a person who is afraid of spiders might be asked to imagine hundreds of large spiders crawling around his or her home and eventually crawling up his or her legs and over his or her body and even into his or her mouth and ears. The scenario might be further elaborated by having the individual imagine the spiders invading his or her internal organs and tearing them apart. Finally, whereas flooding involves constructing scenarios before they are presented, the scenarios in implosive therapy are elaborated upon as they are being presented. The therapist asks guiding questions (e.g., "How do you feel about that?") in order to identify additional details that can be incorporated or exaggerated.

Several critiques of implosive therapy are important to note. From a behavioral perspective, the utility of incorporating psychodynamic elements into an exposure-based treatment has been questioned. In fact, research shows that the therapy is just as effective without the psychodynamic component. Further, as with flooding, some individuals might find it difficult to tolerate implosion as compared to a more graduated approach. In terms of its empirical basis, much of the research in support of implosive therapy consists of case studies rather than controlled clinical trials. The evidence for its effectiveness has been mixed, with some studies showing that implosive therapy reduces fear, whereas other studies have not found it to be any more effective than control conditions or other interventions, such as systematic desensitization. Accordingly, implosive therapy is not considered a treatment of choice for phobias, although it is acknowledged as an important precursor to contemporary exposure treatment, the first-line intervention for phobias.

Irena Milosevic

See also: Exposure, Imaginal; Exposure Treatment; Flooding; Psychoanalysis; Systematic Desensitization

Further Reading

Stampfl, Thomas G., & Lewis, Donald J. (1967). The essentials of implosive therapy: A learning theory based on psychodynamic behavioral therapy. *Journal of Abnormal Psychology, 72*, 496–503.

Information-Processing Biases

According to cognitive models of anxiety, biases in the way anxious individuals process information maintain, and potentially cause, anxiety disorders. Specifically, these models theorize that individuals with anxiety disorders, such as specific phobias, tend to selectively pay attention to threatening stimuli, misinterpret ambiguous information as threatening, and display enhanced memory for threatening information. Consequently, threatening information tends to appear and remain salient to anxious individuals. For example, a woman with spider phobia may be more likely to pay attention to cues related to spiders (e.g., spider webs), interpret a spider's movements as dangerous (e.g., "The spider is coming to attack me!"), and remember information related to spiders (e.g., selectively recall the word "web" from a long list of words). As a result, she may be more likely to avoid spiders, and her spider fear will be maintained and potentially exacerbated.

Although cognitive models theorize that anxious individuals have numerous biases in the way they process information, studies evaluating biases among individuals with specific fears and phobias have been mixed. While there is substantial evidence suggesting that individuals with phobias have biases in their judgment (e.g., overestimating the probability of danger) and biased automatic associations (e.g., rapidly and automatically associating phobic stimuli with negative attributes), the evidence is more mixed for whether these individuals have a memory bias or attention bias toward phobic stimuli. Notably, research suggests that information-processing biases predict important clinical outcomes, such as avoidance and distress when in phobia-relevant situations, and that the biases can be reduced following treatment.

Attention Bias

To measure attention bias, researchers often use the modified Stroop task or modified dot-probe task, both of which are completed on the computer. In the modified Stroop task, participants are asked to rapidly say the color in which words are displayed while ignoring the content of the words. For example, one might be asked to say "yellow" in response to the word "web" shown in a yellow text. Response times are compared for words that are threatening, such as the word "tarantula" for an individual with spider phobia, and words that are neutral, such as the word "chair." Many (but not all) studies have found that individuals with spider phobia are slower to name the color of words when the words are related to threat (see Antony & Barlow, 2002), suggesting that their attention is drawn to the threat-related meaning of the words. Notably, this effect also extends to pictures of spiders.

In the modified dot-probe task, participants are shown two stimuli, one threat-related and one not threat-related. For example, the words "ladder" and "carpet" might be presented to a person with height phobia. The stimuli disappear and a probe (such as the letter "E" or "F") appears in the location of one of the stimuli. Participants are asked to determine the probe letter as quickly as possible. Evidence for attention bias using the modified dot-probe task in individuals with specific fears and phobias has been mixed; whereas some studies have suggested spider-fearful and spider-phobic individuals selectively attend to threatening stimuli (i.e., are faster to respond to stimuli when it appears following threat vs. nonthreat stimuli), other studies have not found evidence of attention bias in spider-phobic individuals.

Taken together, studies evaluating attention bias in individuals with specific fears and phobias have been somewhat inconsistent, so it will be important to determine under what conditions the biases emerge (e.g., when stimuli are presented very briefly vs. for a long time). Notably, a number of studies have found that attention bias toward spider stimuli decreases following treatment (see review in Antony & Barlow, 2002).

Judgment and Interpretation Bias

Several studies suggest that individuals with phobias have biases in their judgment, such as a tendency to overestimate danger and probability of harm related to phobic stimuli and situations (for review, see Antony & Barlow, 2002). Additionally, individuals with phobias tend to interpret ambiguous situations related to what they fear in a threatening, or negative way (see Steinman & Teachman, 2011). To evaluate interpretation bias, researchers have developed questionnaires in which individuals are presented with ambiguous scenarios related to the phobic object or situation and then asked to rate the likelihood of several events. For example, after reading about a scenario that involves climbing a ladder, participants are asked to rate the likelihood of falling. Among individuals with specific fears, these question-naires have demonstrated negative interpretation bias, which can predict fear and avoidance of actual phobic stressors. Of note, experimentally manipulating inter-pretation bias using computer paradigms designed to train people to assign benign meanings to ambiguous phobia-related situations has been shown to reduce fear in some cases (e.g., individuals with height fear), suggesting that interpretation bias may maintain, or potentially cause, fear.

The covariation bias, similar to judgment biases, occurs when individuals over-estimate the relationship between what they are afraid of (e.g., spiders) and negative outcomes (e.g., getting shocked). This can be measured by the covariation bias par-adigm, in which participants view fear-relevant or fear-irrelevant stimuli, followed by events that vary by valence (e.g., presence or absence of a shock). Participants are then asked to estimate the co-occurrence of fear-relevant stimuli and negative events. Individuals with high levels of fear tend to overestimate the relationship between fear-relevant stimuli and negative outcomes. The covariation bias has been demonstrated in individuals with various phobias, including blood-injection-injury phobia, flying phobia, and spider phobia (see review in Antony & Barlow, 2002). Moreover, the covariation bias has been proposed to play a role in the maintenance and return of fear; following treatment for spider phobia, individuals who exhibited the bias, compared to those who did not, were more likely to experience return of fear two years later (de Jong, van den Hout, & Merckelbach, 1995).

Memory Bias

Memory bias is often measured by showing participants fear-relevant and fear-irrelevant stimuli, and then evaluating recall or recognition for the stimuli. Studies assessing memory bias in individuals with specific fears and phobias have had inconsistent results (see Antony & Barlow, 2002). Some studies have sug-gested a memory deficit for phobic-relevant stimuli, whereas others have shown enhanced memory for phobic-relevant stimuli, and still others have shown no dif-ference between individuals with and without fears or phobias. One reason for the differences across studies may concern whether or not fear is activated dur-ing exposure to the to-be-recalled information. Of note, at least one study found that treatment reduced a memory deficit for spider cues in individuals with spider phobia (Watts, Trezise, & Sharrock, 1986).

Implicit Associations

Implicit associations are automatic associations in memory that are difficult to con-sciously control. A common measure of implicit associations is the Implicit Asso-ciation Test (IAT), in which participants are asked to rapidly categorize stimuli, such as a picture of a tarantula, into superordinate categories that are paired in a way that they either contradict or match the expected implicit associations (e.g., the category "spider" is paired with the category "safe" vs. with the category "dangerous"). A number of studies have shown that individuals with phobias are faster at categorizing stimuli when category pairings link feared stimuli and negative attributes together, such as when spider is paired with danger. Importantly, among individuals with spider fear and phobia, implicit associations predict distress and avoidance when approaching a spider, and implicit associations decrease following treatment (see Roefs et al., 2011).

Shari A. Steinman and Bethany A. Teachman

See also: Arachnophobia (Fear of Spiders); Attention; Cognitive Bias Modification; Cognitive Model; Memory; Perception, Visual

Further Reading

Antony, Martin M., & Barlow, David H. (2002). Specific phobias. In David H. Barlow (Ed.), *Anxiety and its disorders: The nature and treatment of anxiety and panic* (2nd ed., pp. 380–417). New York, NY: The Guilford Press.

de Jong, Peter J., van den Hout, Marcel A., & Merckelbach, Harald. (1995). Covariation bias and the return of fear. *Behaviour Research and Therapy, 33,* 211–213.

Roefs, Anne, Huijding, Jorg, Smulders, Fren T.Y., MacLeod, Colin M., de Jong, Peter J., Wiers, Reinout W., & Jansen, Anita T.M. (2011). Implicit measures of association in psychopathology research. *Psychological Bulletin, 137,* 149–193.

Steinman, Shari A., & Teachman, Bethany A. (2011). Cognitive processing and acrophobia: Validating the Heights Interpretation Questionnaire. *Journal of Anxiety Disorders, 25,* 896–902. Corrigendum published 2012, *Journal of Anxiety Disorders, 26,* 258–259.

Watts, Fraser N., Trezise, Lorna, & Sharrock, Robert. (1986). Processing of phobic stimuli. *British Journal of Clinical Psychology, 25,* 253–259.

FEAR IN THE LABORATORY: THE PROGRAM FOR ANXIETY, COGNITION AND TREATMENT

The Program for Anxiety, Cognition and Treatment lab (see www.teachman. org), directed by Dr. Bethany Teachman, investigates cognitive processes that contribute to the development and maintenance of anxiety disorders. Dr. Teachman and her team are especially interested in how thoughts that occur outside of people's control or conscious awareness contribute to fear and anxiety. To understand why an intelligent, normally rational person with spider phobia has refused to go down to his or her basement for 10 years because he or she once saw a harmless daddy-long-leg spider down there, or why a person with social anxiety disorder giving a speech sees only the one scowl in an audience full of smiling faces, it is important to consider the role of biased automatic processing of emotional- and disorder-relevant information in these disorders. Each of these seemingly irrational responses is likely fueled by some aspect of biased cognitive processing, whereby anxious individuals attend to and interpret their environment in such a way that these maladaptive reactions make sense to them in the moment. Dr. Teachman's research investigates how these biased cognitive processes contribute to the onset and persistence of anxiety problems, and whether it is important to change these biases to relieve anxiety.

Some of the research in Dr. Teachman's lab involves putting people who are high in anxiety symptoms into situations that may trigger some fear or anxiety and then measuring what they are thinking and how their thinking patterns compare to those of less anxious individuals. For instance, socially anxious individuals will be asked to give a speech in front of a large mirror, after which their thoughts about their performance, or their memory for feedback they received about the speech, will be assessed. Persons with height phobia will be asked to climb a ladder or stand out on a balcony to determine whether they judge the situation as more dangerous than do nonanxious individuals. The lab also investigates people with panic disorder by exposing them to the very bodily sensations they fear, such as inducing shortness of breath by breathing through a very thin straw, and then assessing their tendency to interpret those sensations in catastrophic ways.

One reason that Dr. Teachman and her team measure anxious participants' thinking patterns in these situations is that they want to identify the cognitive biases associated with anxiety disorders so they can then try to change those biases through therapy or other interventions. For example, they found that persons with panic disorder tend to have automatic associations in memory connecting the self with being less calm than nonanxious individuals; these are known as implicit panic associations. They then conducted cognitive behavior therapy for panic disorder and repeatedly measured changes in the participants' implicit panic associations, finding that people did better in therapy the more they reduced these associations. Moreover, Dr. Teachman's lab is now testing computer programs designed to modify these implicit associations and other cognitive biases to directly alter these maladaptive thinking patterns with the goal of reducing vulnerability to, and symptoms of, anxiety pathology.

Bethany A. Teachman

International Classification of Diseases

The *International Classification of Diseases* (ICD) is the most widely used diagnostic tool in the world for the purposes of classifying and studying diseases, disorders, injuries, and other health problems. Phobias are included in this classification system under mental and behavioral disorders.

The earliest version of the classification manual that would eventually become the ICD was developed in 1893 by French physician and statistician, Jacques Bertillon (1851–1922). Many countries subsequently adopted Bertillon's system. In 1948, the World Health Organization assumed responsibility for maintaining the ICD, and its first revision, the ICD-6 in 1949, included for the first time a specific section devoted to the classification of mental disorders. Phobias, termed *phobic reaction*, were classified under psychoneurotic disorders. This early version of the classification of mental disorders was not widely adopted until subsequent revisions to the manual.

The current version of the ICD, the ICD-10 (World Health Organization, 1992), is considered to be the global standard for defining diseases and disorders, as well as monitoring and reporting death and disease rates. As such, it has broad applications, including those related to statistics and epidemiology, management of health care, distribution of resources, research, and clinical care. Examples of the widespread impact of the ICD-10 include its use by more than 100 countries, translation into 43 languages, and citation in more than 20,000 scientific articles. In addition, a clinical modification of the manual, the ICD-10-CM, has been developed by two American federal agencies for classifying diagnoses and reasons for health-care visits in the United States in particular. The ICD-11 is currently in development and expected to be released in 2017.

The ICD-10 classifies phobias under the category of phobic anxiety disorders. These disorders are characterized by an anxiety response in circumscribed situations that are not currently dangerous. Such situations are commonly avoided or endured with dread. Phobic anxiety disorders are classified under neurotic, stress-related, and somatoform disorders, which themselves belong to the broader category of mental and behavioral disorders. The main phobias described in the ICD-10 are agoraphobia, social phobias, and specific (isolated) phobias such as acrophobia and claustrophobia.

Despite the widespread use of the ICD-10, the most widely used classification system for mental disorders in North America is the *Diagnostic and Statistical Manual of Mental Disorders* (DSM). The most recent edition of the manual, the DSM-5 (American Psychiatric Association, 2013), has been revised to align more closely with the ICD-10.

Irena Milosevic

See also: Classification; DSM-5; World Health Organization

Further Reading

American Psychiatric Association. (2013). *Diagnostic and statistical manual of mental disorders* (5th ed.). Arlington, VA: American Psychiatric Publishing.

World Health Organization. (1992). *The ICD-10 classification of mental and behavioural disorders: Clinical descriptions and diagnostic guidelines.* Geneva: World Health Organization.

Website

www.who.int/classifications/icd/en/

J

Jones, Mary Cover (1897–1987)

Mary Cover Jones (1897–1987) was an American psychologist, widely recognized as a pioneer in behavior therapy and life span development. Called the "mother of behavior therapy" by influential behavior therapist Joseph Wolpe (1915–1997), Jones is credited with developing an early form of systematic desensitization. She is best known for successfully curing Peter, a young boy with a rabbit phobia, by associating a pleasant stimulus with the feared animal. Jones also made significant contributions with her longitudinal research on adolescent development. She is noted for the applied implications of her work and for maintaining a balance of scientific and humanistic perspectives in her writing. She was also known to be an engaging teacher, supportive colleague, and community advocate.

Born on September 1, 1897, in Johnstown, Pennsylvania, Jones was the middle of three children. Her mother was a homemaker and her father a businessman who encouraged his children to pursue higher education. Jones was a good student, and in 1915 she successfully enrolled in Vassar College in New York state. She took nearly every psychology course offered in the curriculum before graduating with a bachelor of arts degree in 1919. Jones subsequently attended a weekend lecture by renowned behaviorist John B. Watson (1878–1958). Hearing him describe the *Little Albert experiment* on fear conditioning, Jones wondered whether children's fears could be deconditioned. This interest would eventually lead her to conduct the seminal case study of Peter.

Jones next enrolled in the psychology graduate program at Columbia University in New York and completed her master's degree in 1920, the same year she married fellow graduate student Harold E. Jones. The couple went on to have two daughters. In 1923, Jones was appointed associate in psychological research at the Institute of Educational Research, Teachers' College, Columbia University. In this position, she completed her research with Peter in which she applied conditioning principles to treat the boy's phobia of rabbits. After publishing her results, Jones went on to complete her dissertation on the development of early behavior in infancy. She earned a PhD from Columbia in 1926.

Jones and her family moved to California in 1927, where her husband accepted the position of director of research at the newly founded Institute for Child Welfare at the University of California, Berkeley. Jones became a research associate at the Institute and took on a leading role in the widely influential longitudinal Oakland

Growth Study (OGS), which investigated adolescent development. Beginning in 1932, the study followed about 200 fifth- and sixth-grade students until they graduated from high school. The participants were also assessed in adulthood, at ages 38, 48, and 60. The final set of interviews was conducted in 1980 when Jones was 83 years old. Jones published more than 100 articles on the OGS data. Some of her key findings related to the emotional and behavioral consequences of early and late puberty onset. Other findings focused on the developmental risk factors for adolescent drinking behavior. Jones's approach to this work was noted to be theoretically eclectic and was characterized by a whole-person approach to development. Given the high quality of the OGS research, which was attributed to Jones's commitment to the study and her ability to maintain strong relationships with the participants, data from this project have been used for other important research on development.

In 1952, Jones was appointed assistant professor of education at Berkeley. Due to policies that prevented married women from holding faculty positions, Jones could not become a full professor despite having relevant experience in the department of psychology. She was finally appointed professor in 1959, one year before her retirement. In 1960, she served as president of the American Psychological Association's (APA) Division of Developmental Psychology. She retired together with her husband, who tragically died of a heart attack several months into their retirement.

With increasing recognition of her contributions to developmental psychology, Jones was awarded the prestigious G. Stanley Hall Award from the APA in 1968. She continued to be productive in her academic career and was also known for her commitment to child welfare causes. Reflecting on her early roots in behavior therapy, Jones suggested that after her extensive involvement in longitudinal research, she would be less satisfied with extinguishing fears unless she had an opportunity to follow-up with the individuals and to consider them in a broader context.

Jones died in 1987 shortly before her 90th birthday. Just before passing away, she was noted to have said to her sister, "I am still learning about what is important in life" (Reiss, 1990).

Irena Milosevic

See also: Behavior Therapy; Classical Conditioning; Systematic Desensitization; Watson, John B. (1878–1958); Wolpe, Joseph (1915–1997)

Further Reading

Jones, Mary C. (1924). A laboratory study of fear: The case of Peter. *Pedagogical Seminary, 31*, 308–315.

Jones, Mary C. (1974). Albert, Peter, and John B. Watson. *American Psychologist, 29*, 581–583.

Reiss, Bettyjane K. (1990). *A biography of Mary Cover Jones*. (Unpublished doctoral dissertation). Wright Institute, Berkeley, CA.

THE CASE OF LITTLE PETER

One of the most noted studies by Mary Cover Jones is her investigation into methods to extinguish the fear response of a three-year-old boy named Peter. Reported in 1924, this study followed up on the *Little Albert experiment* by John B. Watson and Rosalie Rayner, who conditioned a baby boy to fear a white rat. Since Albert's fear was acquired through classical conditioning, Jones wondered whether similar methods could also be used to reduce fear. Her study of Peter was conducted under the supervision of Watson. It is considered one of the first case studies of behavior therapy for phobias and an early example of desensitization.

Peter had a fear of furry or fluffy things, particularly of white rabbits, which Jones attempted to treat with several behavioral procedures. On a daily basis, Jones briefly introduced a rabbit into the room where Peter played with three other children, who Jones ensured were not afraid of rabbits. New steps requiring closer contact with the rabbit were gradually introduced within each session (e.g., rabbit in cage 12 feet away; rabbit free in room; helping experimenter return rabbit to cage), and Peter's fear diminished over time. However, at this point, Peter required medical treatment for scarlet fever and was unable to resume the sessions for two months. When he returned to see Jones, his fear had returned to previous levels. Jones hypothesized the return of fear was precipitated in part by Peter being jumped by a dog during the time he was ill; he had found this experience very frightening.

When Peter returned, Jones decided to apply the method of "direct conditioning" to treat his fear. That is, Jones brought the rabbit closer to Peter while simultaneously giving Peter his favorite food—candy! Through the pairing of a pleasant stimulus (candy) with the feared stimulus (rabbit), Peter's fear response to the rabbit was gradually replaced with a positive response, and he was eventually able to pet the animal without fear.

At their final session, Jones tested Peter to see whether his fear reduction generalized to other animals. He was presented with a mouse and some earthworms to which he exhibited mild initial distress followed by subsequent ease. Jones hypothesized that her "unconditioning" procedure with the rabbit increased Peter's tolerance to other strange animals and unfamiliar situations.

Although it did not garner much attention at the time of its publication, Jones's study of Peter was eventually recognized as seminal work that laid the foundation for the development of future behavioral treatments of phobias, particularly Joseph Wolpe's systematic desensitization. This landmark study made Jones a pioneer of behavior therapy.

Irena Milosevic

L

Lang, Peter J. (1930–)

Peter J. Lang (1930–) is a well-known psychologist whose pioneering work in the area of emotion, particularly fear and anxiety, has had a major impact on the field. Lang, who received a PhD from the University of Buffalo in 1958, is director of both the NIMH Center for the Study of Emotion and Attention and the Fear and Anxiety Disorders Clinic at the University of Florida, where he also holds an appointment as professor in the Department of Clinical and Health Psychology. Lang has had a highly productive research career and has received many distinguished awards and honors, including the Distinguished Scientist Award from the Society for a Science of Clinical Psychology (1980), the Award for Distinguished Contributions to Psychophysiology from the Society for Psychophysiological Research (1990), and the Award for Distinguished Scientific Contributions from the American Psychological Association (1993).

Lang's research approach combines psychophysiological experimental methods with cognitive psychology to understand clinical phenomena. One of his most influential contributions is his bioinformational theory of emotional imagery, where he conceptualized emotional imagery as a psychophysiological event that could be understood within an information processing perspective. This bioinformational approach later developed into broader understanding of emotion and emotional memory. Lang (1968) also developed the tripartite model of fear and anxiety that conceptualized these emotions as having three component response systems: physiological responses, subjective distress (cognitive responses), and behavioral responses. This model is central to current cognitive behavioral interventions for anxiety disorders, which target each of these components with specific treatment strategies. Lang also codeveloped the Fear Survey Schedule-III (Wolpe & Lang, 1964), a measure of feared stimuli (e.g., blood and bats) for use in clinical practice with patients.

Randi E. McCabe

See also: Emotional Processing Theory; Tripartite Model of Fear

Further Reading

Lang, Peter J. (1968). Fear reduction and fear behavior. In J. Schlein (Ed.), *Research in psychotherapy* (pp. 85–103). Washington, DC: American Psychological Association.

Lang, Peter J. (1979). A bio-informational theory of emotional imagery. *Psychophysiology, 16*, 495–512.

Wolpe, Joseph, & Lang, Peter J. (1964). A fear survey schedule for use in behavior therapy. *Behavior Research and Therapy, 2*, 27–30.

Learning Theory

Learning theories are theoretical frameworks that describe how information is taken in, integrated, and retained. Learning theories can be loosely categorized into three main theoretical orientations: behavioral learning theories, cognitive learning theories, and social learning theories. Learning theories provide an etiological framework to help us understand the development and maintenance of behaviors, including specific phobias and other anxiety disorders.

Behavioral learning theories are based on the premise that learning occurs through interactions with the environment. Specifically, behavioral theories posit that behaviors are acquired or eliminated through paired conditioning and/or reinforcement and punishment. Two influential behavioral theories include classical and operant conditioning.

Classical conditioning, also referred to as *Pavlovian conditioning* or *respondent conditioning*, states that learning occurs through association, where a previously neutral stimulus (conditioned stimulus; CS) is paired with an unconditioned stimulus (US) that produces a naturally occurring unconditioned response (UR). After repeated pairings of the CS and the US, a conditioned response (CR) will be elicited by the CS, even in the absence of the US. For example, in Ivan Pavlov's famous experiments, dogs naturally salivated (UR) when presented with food (US). Pavlov then presented a tone (CS) prior to providing the dogs with food, and upon repeated pairings of the tone and the food, presenting the tone alone would lead to salivation (CR).

Watson and Rayner's (1920) famous experiment with Little Albert demonstrates how a phobia could form through classical conditioning. In this experiment, Watson conditioned a previously nonfearful child to develop a phobic response to a rat. The rat (CS), which the child was initially not afraid of, was repeatedly paired with a loud noise (US) that distressed the child. After several such pairings, presentation of the rat alone evoked a conditioned fear response. For very aversive experiences, one pairing may be sufficient to condition a fear response. Thus, if an individual gets bitten once by a dog, that could be sufficient to develop a dog phobia.

Operant conditioning, also referred to as *instrumental conditioning*, posits that learning occurs through reward and punishment. Therefore, behaviors are strengthened (more likely to be repeated) or weakened (less likely to be repeated) depending on the subsequent consequence. This theory is based on Edward Thorndike's (1874–1949) *law of effect*, which states that behavior that is followed by reward or pleasure tends to be repeated. B. F. Skinner (1904–1990) further developed this theory, proposing that *reinforcement* refers to any consequence that strengthens a behavior, whereas *punishment* refers to any consequence that weakens a behavior. Reinforcement and punishment can be further broken down into positive or negative categories. In positive reinforcement or punishment, something is added (e.g., giving money for a passing school grade, hitting a dog for peeing on the floor), whereas in negative reinforcement or punishment something is removed (e.g., doing the dishes to avoid a fight, taking a toy away from a child for bad behavior). It is important to note that when it comes to operant conditioning, the terms *positive* and *negative* are entirely unrelated to their common definitions of "good" and "bad," respectively.

Operant conditioning helps to explain how fear is perpetuated and phobias are maintained. Avoidance is considered a form of negative reinforcement because avoidance of a feared stimulus leads to a reduction or removal of anxiety (anxiety being the unpleasant stimulus), which strengthens the behavioral avoidance (makes it more likely to occur). For example, an individual who is phobic of dogs may see a dog on the street and run the other way. Running in the opposite direction reduces the anxiety and makes it more likely that the person will run away in the future.

However, according to social learning theory (also referred to as *observational learning* or *modeling*), directly experiencing the consequences of one's behavior does not fully explain all forms of learning. Accordingly, social learning theory holds that learning can also occur by watching or observing other people. In the famous Bobo doll experiments, Albert Bandura (1925–) demonstrated that children who had watched someone behave violently toward an inflatable Bobo doll were more likely to behave violently as well. This experiment established that children learn and imitate behaviors that they observe. Whereas behavioral learning theories focus on extrinsic reinforcement, social learning theory also considers intrinsic reinforcement (pride and a sense of accomplishment) as important to learning. With regard to phobias, social learning theory hypothesizes that a person could develop a phobia through *vicarious conditioning*, where an individual observes someone else being fearful around a stimulus or having a negative experience with that stimulus. For example, seeing a friend mauled by a dog could contribute to a phobic response during one's subsequent encounters with dogs.

The final category of learning theories focuses principally on cognition (mental experiences, such as thinking and attention). In particular, cognitive learning theory posits that thoughts are central to emotions and behaviors. According to Aaron Beck (1921–), individuals develop expectations based on previous experience or vicarious learning about themselves, other people, and the world. Thus, cognitive theory postulates that irrational responses are driven by learned, automatic, and erroneous beliefs. This theory suggests that phobias are developed and maintained by inaccurate expectations and attributions regarding the safety and danger of the stimulus. Accordingly, individuals with phobias frequently overestimate the probability of negative consequences with regard to feared stimuli. For example, an individual with a flying phobia may overestimate the probability that the plane will crash.

The aforementioned learning theories have an important role in the treatment of specific phobias. The gold-standard, first-line treatment for phobias includes systematic exposure in which the individual is gradually exposed to the feared stimulus. Exposure therapy is based on classical conditioning theory, namely a phenomenon termed *extinction*, whereby the CR is weakened by repeated exposure of the CS without the US. This leads to a gradual reduction in the fear response. Using Little Albert as an example, after fear conditioning has occurred, if the rat (CS) was repeatedly presented without the loud noise (US), the conditioned fear response would subside.

Principles from operant conditioning are also important in the treatment of phobias since it is imperative that treatment address avoidance and escape behaviors. As mentioned previously, both avoidance and escape are highly reinforcing because they eliminate anxiety in the short term; however, these behaviors are problematic because they perpetuate the anxiety cycle. If someone with a phobia always engages in avoidance, extinction of the feared response cannot occur, nor can new learning.

Elements of social learning theory can also be observed in phobia treatment. For example, during exposures the individual will often first observe the clinician modeling an interaction with the feared stimulus prior to the individual interacting with it independently. Thus, by observing a calm interaction with the feared stimulus, the person learns that there is actually nothing to fear.

In addition to exposure, cognitive restructuring, drawn from cognitive learning theory, is often incorporated into treatment for specific phobias. During cognitive restructuring, beliefs, assumptions, and expectations are challenged to help the individual think more flexibly. Cognitive restructuring allows for a more realistic assessment of the danger related to the feared stimulus.

Stephanie Taillefer

See also: Bandura, Albert (1925–); Beck, Aaron T. (1921–); Classical Conditioning; Cognitive Model; Modeling; Operant Conditioning; Pavlov, Ivan; Skinner, B. F. (1904–1990); Social Learning Theory; Thorndike, Edward L. (1874–1949); Watson, John B. (1878–1958)

Further Reading

Beck, Aaron T., & Emery, Gary. (1990). *Anxiety disorders and phobias: A cognitive perspective*. New York, NY: Basic Books.

Skinner, B. F. (1938). *The behavior of organisms: An experimental analysis*. New York, NY: Appleton-Century.

Watson, John B., & Rayner, Rosalie. (1920). Conditioned emotional reactions. *Journal of Experimental Psychology, 3*, 1–14.

Lifespan, Phobias across the

From an evolutionary perspective, fear is necessary and adaptive. Humans have survived over time because of a fear mechanism that caused them to avoid dangerous stimuli. It is interesting to note that children's fears change as they develop and come to understand their own world. It is very normal for children to fear particular stimuli at particular ages—their environments then play a large role in whether they go on to develop a clinically significant phobia.

Between the ages of three and nine, many children fear animals and insects. At this age, children also get a great deal of exposure to animals and insects—in their own environments (bees, dogs), on television, and at the zoo. Developmentally, children must learn what does and does not live in their own environment. Many people fear snakes, but rarely, if ever, encounter them. Part of the process of aging out of fears is coming to an awareness of what we do not typically encounter (and thus, do not need to fear), and what we do encounter and how to figure out if it is safe or dangerous. For example, for the vast majority of people, bees are a nuisance but nothing to be afraid of. People rarely get stung, and if they do, it involves momentary pain. Only children with a life-threatening allergy of bees actually need to be vigilant of bees in their environment.

Children of this age also fear imaginary creatures (ghosts, witches, monsters) and the dark. Again, it is an important part of development for children to learn what is real and what exists only in storybooks and television shows. Parents and teachers play a significant role in educating children about these themes. Some parents perpetuate fear of imaginary creatures due to their own beliefs (i.e., parents who themselves believe in ghosts), in a desire to keep childhood myths alive (i.e., telling their children that witches or monsters on Halloween are indeed real), or inadvertently by trying to help their children. When parents give their children "monster spray" to scare off monsters, it does cause children to wonder why they would need monster spray if monsters are not real!

Between the ages of 9 and 12, as children approach adolescence, fears begin to shift from specific stimuli to more general worries. Children begin to worry about school (doing well on tests), which makes sense as the demands of school increase. This is also the age at which children begin to worry about their personal health. The age of onset for blood-injection-injury phobias is nine and interestingly, this is also the age where vomit phobias emerge. At this age, children are mature enough to have some of the fears commonly seen in vomit phobia, including worrying about losing control and worrying about vomiting in front of others.

Even later (age 13–16), we tend to see the onset of more extreme social fears. Again, this makes sense as the social world becomes more complex. During this time, there is a peak in peer victimization (i.e., bullying, teasing, social exclusion), necessitating skill in navigating social relationships. This is also the time when youth start to explore their sexuality and embark on romantic relationships, which can also lead to intense anxiety for some.

Finally, in the 20s, we begin to see fears that likely have some association with panic attacks. Panic disorder is rarely diagnosed before puberty. It is possible that younger children experience panic attacks but do not have the language skills to describe them. Furthermore, while children experience physical symptoms of anxiety, they might not fear them as is the case in people who have panic disorder. It might be the case that individuals need cognitive maturity to associate particular physical symptoms with feared consequences like having a heart attack or going crazy. Agoraphobia—fear of going into particular situations for fear of having a panic attack—tends to onset in the late 20s, following from repeated panic attacks earlier in the 20s. The 20s is also the age range during which we see fears of driving (and related stimuli like bridges and tunnels), which makes sense because people are driving at this age. Furthermore, these fears might have some association with panic because some people fear driving, bridges, and tunnels because they fear having panic attacks in these situations and not being able to escape.

There is scant research on phobias in older adults, but it is worth noting that fear of falling (ptophobia) is a phobia unique to the geriatric population. Like other phobias seen across the lifespan, fear of falling is associated with significant avoidance.

Deborah Roth Ledley

See also: Age of Onset; Childhood, Phobias in; Evolution, Role of; Panic Attacks; Panic Disorder; Phobias, Causes of; Phobias, Family Influences on the Development and Maintenance of; Ptophobia (Fear of Falling)

Further Reading

Antony, Martin M., & Swinson, Richard P. (2000). *Phobic disorders and panic in adults: A guide to assessment and treatment.* Washington, DC: American Psychological Association.

Beidel, Deborah C., & Turner, Samuel M. (2005). *Childhood anxiety disorders: A guide to research and treatment.* New York, NY: Routledge.

Limbic System

The limbic system is a region in the brain central to emotional processing and drives. It has accordingly been conceptualized as the "feeling and reacting brain." Derived from the Latin word *limbus* meaning "border," the area forms an inner border to the cerebral cortex, also known as the "thinking brain." The limbic system is evolutionarily an older and more primitive brain system than more recent brain systems, and it plays an important role in providing key information for the cerebral cortex to regulate complex behaviors. Other functions associated with the limbic system include various types of memory (spatial, emotional, long-term), sense of smell (through connections with the olfactory system), learning (e.g., fear conditioning), and behavior (reward, conditioning). The limbic system regulates the autonomic nervous system (heart rate, blood pressure) and endocrine system (hormones) in response to emotional triggers. For example, the limbic system controls an individual's level of overall arousal and influences motivation and reinforcing behaviors.

The limbic system consists of a network of interacting brain structures. Cortical structures of the limbic system include the hippocampus and areas of the neocortex (i.e., insular cortex, orbital frontal cortex, subcallosal gyrus, cingulate gyrus, and parahippocampal gyrus). Subcortical structures include the hypothalamus, amygdala, olfactory bulb, and various nuclei (i.e., septal, thalamic, anterior, dorsomedial). The amygdala, in particular, plays a central role in regulating fear, anxiety, and emotionally charged memories.

The origin of the limbic system conceptualization dates back well over a century. The limbic lobe was first described by French surgeon and anatomist Pierre Paul Broca in 1878 and later identified as central in the experience of emotion by American neuroanatomist James Papez in 1937. Paul D. MacLean, an American neuroscientist, first used the term *limbic system* in 1952 to describe the limbic lobe and interconnected subcortical nuclei. MacLean is known for his triune conceptualization of the brain, which proposed the human brain was comprised of three brains: the reptilian complex (R-complex), the limbic system, and the neocortex. The limbic system has been a significant focus of attention by neuroscientists. However, it has also been a subject of controversy over the value of its conceptualization and in terms of varying definitions using a range of criteria (e.g., morphology) that are not empirically proven. There is no consensus in the field on the definitive brain structures comprising the limbic system.

Despite the controversy, the limbic system has proven to be a useful conceptualization that has guided research and teaching of neurosciences and helped to further our understanding in many areas, including the role of brain structures and circuitry in human behavior and various psychological disorders such as phobias and other anxiety disorders. Many advances have been made, especially over the past few decades. For example, cognitive behavior therapy (CBT) has been shown to modify brain circuitry in the limbic system, effectively "rewiring" the brain. In a paper titled *Change the Mind and You Change the Brain: Effects of Cognitive Behavioral Therapy on the Neural Correlates of Spider Phobia*, Paquette et al. (2003) found that individuals with spider phobia who received CBT no longer had significant activation of the parahippocampal gyrus when viewing a film with spiders as measured by functional magnetic resonance imaging and thus their brain activity resembled that of the control participants. Increasingly, neuroscience research on fear and anxiety disorders focuses more specifically on individual structures and circuitry rather than a general "limbic system," finding that specific phobia is particularly associated with hyperactivation in the amygdala and insula.

Randi E. McCabe

See also: Amygdala; Cognitive Behavioral Therapy; Fear, Neural Pathways of; Fear, Physiology of; Neuroimaging

Further Reading

MacLean, Paul D. (1952). Some psychiatric implications of physiological studies on frontotemporal portion of limbic system (visceral brain). *Electroencephalography and Clinical Neurophysiology, 4*, 407–418.

Paquette, Vincent, Levesque, Johanne, Mensour, Boualem, Leroux, Jean-Maxime, Beaudoin, Gilles, Bourgouin, Pierre, & Beauregard, Mario. (2002). "Change the mind and you change the brain": Effects of cognitive-behavioral therapy on the neural correlates of spider phobia. *NeuroImage, 18*, 401–409.

M

Marks, Isaac M. (1937–)

Isaac Marks, born Isaac Meyer Marks (1937–), is a South African psychiatrist known for his seminal work in the area of phobias and anxiety disorders. Marks has been described as an "impassioned behaviour therapist" and "one of the most influential psychopathologists and psychiatric diagnosticians of the outgoing 20th century" in a commentary where he was likened to Sigmund Freud in terms of his keen observations of psychopathology informed by direct clinical practice and his skilled ability to characterize his observations (Katschnig, 2004, pp. 33–34).

Born in Cape Town, South Africa, in 1935, Marks studied medicine there and qualified as a physician in 1956. He then left the country and traveled to London, England, where he completed training in psychiatry at the University of London and Bethlem Maudsley Hospital from 1960 to 1963. Marks was a founding member of the Royal College of Psychiatrists in 1971 and became a fellow in 1976. He spent the majority of his career based at the Institute of Psychiatry, University of London, and the Bethlem-Maudsley Hospital. In 1968, he was appointed honorary consultant psychiatrist and, in 1978, he was appointed professor of experimental psychopathology. Marks has been instrumental in ensuring that clinical approaches to the treatment of anxiety and phobias are rooted in empirically based clinical science. His own clinical practice has greatly informed his research interests, which have focused on a number of areas, including the understanding and treatment of pathological fear, phobias, and other anxiety disorders (panic disorder, obsessive-compulsive disorder), psychodiagnostic classification, and the phenomenology of anxiety and fear.

Marks has had a prolific career, publishing over 150 scientific articles and numerous book chapters and books. His book *Fear and Phobias* (1969) and the follow-up *Fears, Phobias, and Rituals* (1987) were foundational in the rapidly expanding field of anxiety disorders as they furthered our understanding of the nature of fear and panic through a sophisticated integration of scientific findings from biochemistry, physiology, pharmacology, psychology, ethology, and psychiatry. Marks's subclassification of phobias into agoraphobia, social phobia, and specific phobias was incorporated into the third edition of the *Diagnostic and Statistical Manual of Mental Disorders* (1980) and the 10th revision of the *International Classification of Diseases* (1992). Marks also developed the Fear Questionnaire (Marks & Mathews, 1979), a well-validated self-report measure used to assess severity and treatment response in common phobias (including agoraphobia, social phobia, and blood-injection-injury phobia), as well as general anxiety and depression. The Fear Questionnaire has been translated in many languages and has been used around the world.

In addition to his work in anxiety and phobic disorders, Marks has been active in the area of mental health treatment access and implementation. He has advocated for a wider range of care providers to have specialized skills for treating mental health conditions. He is well known for his role in bringing specialized mental health training to nursing in the early 1970s at the Maudsley Hospital. To increase access to mental health treatment, he developed a training program in behavior therapy to provide community mental health nurses with specialized skills. Marks is also a proponent of a stepped care approach to mental health treatment where professional skills are allocated depending on patient needs, with those who need straightforward nonspecific support seen by care providers with limited training and experience and those with more complex needs seen by care providers with more advanced training and experience.

In 2000, Marks became professor emeritus and senior research investigator at Charing Cross Hospital Campus, University of London, where he established a computer-guided self-help clinic and has conducted research on computer-assisted therapy for phobic and other anxiety disorders and on computer aids to psychological treatment.

Marks has been a leader in the development and dissemination of cognitive behavioral therapy. He was a founding member of the British Association for Behavioural Psychotherapy in 1972, which became known as the British Association for Behavioural and Cognitive Psychotherapies in 1992. He served as president-elect (chair-elect) from 1972 to 1974 and president (chair) from 1974 to 1976. Marks's popular self-help book *Living with Fear*, which was first published in 1978, is now in its second edition. Published in several languages, this book is the first self-help book to present evidence-based behavioral techniques. It has helped thousands of people worldwide overcome their fears, including the late Celia Bonham Christie. After overcoming her fear of flying using the book, Christie founded Triumph Over Phobia (TOP UK) in 1987, a registered charity to assist individuals with phobias, obsessive-compulsive disorder, and other anxiety disorders overcome their fears through a network of self-help therapy groups. Marks was the professional advisor for the development of the organization and continues as a clinical advisor to this day.

Randi E. McCabe

See also: Behavior Therapy; Treatment, Evidence-Based

Further Reading

Katschnig, Heinz (2004). Two procrustean or one king-size bed for comorbid agoraphobia and panic? In Mario Maj, Hagop S. Akiskal, Juan J. Lopez-Ibor, &Ahmed Okasha (Eds.), *Phobias* (pp. 33–38). Chichester, England: John Wiley & Sons Ltd.

Marks, Isaac, M. (1969). *Fears and phobias*. London: Heinemann.

Marks, Isaac, M. (1987). *Fears, phobias, and rituals*. Oxford, England: Oxford University Press.

Marks, Isaac, M. (2005*). Living with fear: Understanding and coping with anxiety* (2nd ed.). New York, NY: McGraw-Hill Professional.

Marks, Isaac, M., & Mathews, Andrew. (1979). Brief standard self-rating for phobic patients. *Behaviour Research and Therapy, 17*, 263–167.

Medical Student Syndrome

Medical student syndrome (also known as medical students' disease, hypochondriasis of medical students, and medicalstudentitis) is the tendency for students enrolled in medical school, particularly in their first year, to believe that they are suffering from symptoms of a disease that they are studying as part of their training. Although the individual does not really have the illness, the belief that he or she is ill may cause anxiety and distress. The anxiety and distress may magnify and increase physical sensations that are misinterpreted as further signs of illness. For example, a student learning about the vague and ambiguous symptoms of multiple sclerosis may notice numbness or tingling sensations in his or her arm. He or she may have the thought that perhaps his or her symptoms are a sign that he or she has multiple sclerosis. This thought increases his or her anxiety considerably, including physical symptoms of arousal such as feelings of shakiness and dizziness. In response, the student interprets the additional symptoms as further evidence that he or she may have multiple sclerosis. In an increasing spiral of anxiety, his or her fearful thoughts increase and he or she worries about what his or her life would be like if he or she really did have the disease. He or she finds it increasingly difficult to study as his or her concentration is impaired by his or her heightened anxiety.

Descriptions of this condition date back more than 100 years to Dr. George Lincoln Walton's description of the phenomenon in his book *Why Worry?* (Collier, 2008). The symptoms tend to be transitory and short-lived. As they diminish, so does the accompanying anxiety. In the majority of cases the condition is considered to be a common side effect of the training program rather than a diagnosable condition such as illness anxiety disorder, previously known as hypochondriasis. However, if the anxiety persists and causes significant distress and/or interference in the student's life, a diagnosis of illness anxiety disorder may be warranted. In a very small percentage of cases, the student may be correctly self-diagnosing a condition that requires medical intervention.

In any case, the student may find it helpful to discuss his or her concerns and seek support. Educating students on the nature of this syndrome prior to onset of their training program prepares them to expect that this condition may occur as a normal part of their early medical training and may alleviate anxiety and distress. This syndrome may also be seen in students training in other health professions.

Randi E. McCabe

See also: Hypochondriasis; Nosophobia (Fear of Disease or Illness)

Further Reading

Collier, Roger. (2008). Imagined illnesses can cause real problems for medical students. *Canadian Medical Association Journal, 178*, 820.

Memory

Memory is the cognitive process by which humans and other animals take in, store, and retrieve information. Emotions such as fear can influence the type of information that is processed in memory, leading to preferential or negatively biased recall of the threatening material. In turn, fearful or biased memories can contribute to the development and maintenance of phobias and other anxiety disorders, suggesting that memory biases may be a useful target for intervention in treating these disorders.

The multistore model (Atkinson & Shiffrin, 1968) describes different types of memory, including sensory memory, short-term memory (STM), and long-term memory (LTM). Information taken in from the environment through one of the five senses first enters sensory memory, in which it is held for less than a second. According to information-processing theories of cognition, items that are important are selectively processed and may enter STM. For example, if an individual who is afraid of spiders sees a picture of one in a nature magazine, he or she will pay preferential attention to it and neglect the other words and images on the page. This information will pass from sensory memory into STM, where it can be held for up to 30 seconds without being rehearsed. If the person continues to think about the spider in the picture, this rehearsal will cause the image to enter LTM, a process known as encoding or consolidation. Encoding is associated with long-term changes to the synapses (connections between neurons) in regions of the brain involved in emotional memory. Information can be stored in LTM from minutes to a lifetime. The process of calling this information to mind out of LTM is known as retrieval.

In recent years, researchers have started to examine fear's influence on memory. The amygdala, a structure in the brain's temporal lobe, is now considered more than just the brain's "watchdog" to threat. It interacts with the hippocampus, another brain structure involved in memory, and serves as a filter in encoding and consolidating fear-provoking events or situations into LTM, as well as in the retrieval of these negative events (LaBar, 2007). Research involving spider phobia has demonstrated that people show enhanced recall of spider-relevant information (e.g., words such as *web* and *arachnid*") when in the presence of a large, caged tarantula during encoding (Teachman & Smith-Janik, 2009). Interestingly, having high trait (stable personality characteristic) levels of spider fear was not necessary for the memory bias to be expressed, nor was having the tarantula present during recall. Instead, state (momentary experience) feelings of fear and disgust elicited by the spider seemed to contribute to preferential encoding, and subsequent enhanced recall, of the spider-relevant words for all participants.

Memory biases may play an active role in the development and maintenance of fears, phobias, and anxiety disorders. Information-processing models of anxiety disorders suggest that anxious individuals should be more likely to remember negative or threatening stimuli because these memories have been more deeply encoded and are more accessible to retrieval than other memories. For example, a person afraid of public speaking may remember only the negative feedback that he or she received from the audience after giving a speech, such as a frowning expression or a critical question, instead of positive feedback like smiles or applause. These negative memories may then contribute to increased fear and avoidance in the future. Coles and Heimberg (2002) reviewed memory biases across a range of anxiety disorders and found that panic disorder, posttraumatic stress disorder, and obsessive-compulsive disorder all seem to be associated with biased memory for fear-relevant information. Less evidence was found for memory biases in social anxiety disorder (social phobia) or generalized anxiety disorder, although memory may be biased for personally relevant stimuli in these disorders. For instance, negatively biased memory is typically inferred when study participants with anxiety disorders show enhanced recall of lists of words that are relevant to their feared object or situation (such as in the spider fear study discussed previously), compared to neutral words. However, standardized lists of words do not seem to elicit memory biases in social anxiety disorder or generalized anxiety disorder, whereas realistic social feedback or words that participants select as being relevant to themselves do. Because people who remember more negative information about a particular object or situation are more likely to avoid it and to pay attention to negative information in the future, intervening in memory biases could serve as a way to break the cycle of fear and avoidance that characterizes all of the anxiety disorders.

Meghan W. Cody and Judiann McNiff Jones

See also: Amygdala; Attention; Information Processing Biases

Further Reading

Atkinson, Richard C., & Shiffrin, Richard M. (1968). Human memory: A proposed system and its control processes. In Kenneth W. Spence & Janet T. Spence (Eds.), *The psychology of learning and motivation: II* (pp. 89–195). Oxford, UK: Academic Press.

Coles, Meredith E., & Heimberg, Richard G. (2002). Memory biases in the anxiety disorders: Current status. *Clinical Psychology Review, 22,* 587–627.

LaBar, Kevin S. (2007). Beyond fear: Emotional memory mechanisms in the human brain. *Current Directions in Psychological Science, 16*, 173–177.

Teachman, Bethany A., & Smith-Janik, Shannan B. (2009). Relationship between disgust and memory biases in spider fear. *International Journal of Cognitive Therapy, 2*, 16–36.

Modeling

Broadly speaking, modeling is a prominent component of social learning theory as studied by Albert Bandura. Social learning theory suggests that people can learn not only from the consequences of their own actions but also by observing the consequences of other people's actions. Essentially, individuals learn by watching and then imitating other people. Within the context of psychotherapy, the person doing the learning is typically the client and the person being watched is typically the therapist. Modeling occurs when the therapist is intentionally performing a behavior that the client will then attempt to imitate.

Research to date suggests that specific phobias are very effectively treated using exposure therapy. The process involves education, creating a hierarchy describing graduated levels of interaction with the feared stimulus, and then exposing the client to the graduated levels of interaction. The premise follows operant conditioning models wherein expected consequences dictate behaviors, but the conditioning can be changed with positive reinforcement (e.g., encouragement from the therapist and incremental successes by the client) such that the fear response can eventually be extinguished. The difference for social learning theory, and therein for modeling, involves vicarious reinforcement and extinction; specifically, the learner is, at least initially, *indirectly* exposed to the feared stimulus.

Experimental research has supplemented anecdotal evidence in supporting the effectiveness of modeling. A therapist may model progress entirely through a complete hierarchy of interactions to facilitate the vicarious extinction of a client's fear response. The therapist may then encourage the client to imitate the modeled behaviors and progress through the same hierarchy. Alternatively, a therapist may use a more integrated modeling process and provide modeling for each level of the hierarchy to facilitate the client's subsequent exposure to that level. In either case, the therapist performs each aspect of the interaction very intentionally and demonstrates a calm interaction with a feared stimulus. In doing so, the therapist provides the client with an opportunity to implicitly learn how to interact with the feared stimulus and that the interaction and stimulus are not as dangerous as the client initially believed. The implicit learning facilitates vicarious extinction of the fear response, which facilitates the client's subsequent exposure and direct extinction of the fear response. The modeling and exposures continue until the fear response is no longer elicited.

Modeling itself can be therapeutic, even without the client imitating the therapist and interacting with the feared stimulus. The modeling can be done *in vivo* (directly in the situation) or through a series of images where someone other than the client progresses through the client's fear hierarchy (e.g., for an individual with a cat phobia, this might involve watching a series of video clips that depict an individual first handling toy cats, then entering a room with a live cat, moving closer to the cat, letting the cat brush against his or her leg, petting the cat, and finally picking up the cat). In such cases of vicarious exposure, the process is often called *symbolic modeling*. If the client does imitate the model and engage the feared stimulus, the process is often called *participant modeling*. The available research suggests that participant modeling is more effective for treating a specific phobia than symbolic modeling and more effective than imaginal exposure alone.

As with other exposure processes, modeling does not need to be gradual to be effective. A therapist could readily and successfully model interactions with the feared stimulus following flooding protocols. That said, clients are likely to find that grading the exposures makes the interactions less intimidating and more accessible, which should facilitate participant modeling.

R. Nicholas Carleton and Michelle J. N. Teale Sapach

See also: Applied Relaxation; Bandura, Albert (1925–); Classical Conditioning; Exposure Treatment; Extinction; Flooding; Operant Conditioning; Social Learning Theory; Systematic Desensitization

Further Reading

Bandura, Albert, Blanchard, Edward B., & Ritter, Brunhilde. (1969). Relative efficacy of desensitization and modeling approaches for inducing behavioral, affective, and attitudinal changes. *Journal of Personality and Social Psychology, 13,* 173–199.

Davis III, Thompson E., Ollendick, Thomas H., & st, Lars-Göran. (2012). *Intensive one-session treatment of specific phobias.* doi: 10.1007/978-1-4614-3253-1

Musophobia (Fear of Mice)

Derived from the Greek *muso* (mouse) and *phobos* (fear), musophobia (also called murophobia or suriphobia) is an irrational and excessive fear of mice. Individuals with this phobia also commonly fear other rodents, such as rats and hamsters. Musophobia is classified as an animal type specific phobia in the *Diagnostic and Statistical Manual of Mental Disorders*, fifth edition and is one of the most common animal phobias, alongside snake and spider phobias.

As with other animal phobias, the onset of musophobia is typically in childhood. The phobia can be acquired in a variety of ways, including a direct traumatic experience (e.g., being bitten by a mouse), observation of another person's fear in response to a mouse (e.g., a parent jumping on a chair when startled by a mouse), and/or being exposed to negative information about mice or other rodents (e.g., they spread disease). Musophobia has been reported throughout history, which might be related to the spread of certain diseases by rodents. For example, the very deadly bubonic plague was carried by fleas on rats. Possibly because of this connection between disease and rodents, many individuals with musophobia find mice not only scary but also dirty or disgusting. Accordingly, researchers have proposed that some animal phobias like musophobia are predominantly rooted in disease-avoidance rather than predator-defense concerns (Matchett & Davey, 1991).

Upon encountering a mouse, individuals with musophobia will experience intense fear and/or disgust and will try to quickly escape. They might even experience a panic attack. To prevent such encounters, they will usually avoid places where mice or other rodents might be found, such as attics, subway stations, fields, or even a friend's home if the friend happens to have a pet mouse or rat. In addition to avoiding any exposure to an actual mouse, individuals with musophobia might also avoid looking at photographs or videos that depict mice.

Like that of other phobias, the most effective intervention for musophobia is exposure treatment. This psychological approach involves graduated and repeated exposure to mice-related stimuli.

Irena Milosevic

See also: Disease-Avoidance Model; DSM-5; Exposure Treatment; Phobia, Animal Type; Phobia, Specific

Further Reading

Antony Martin M., & McCabe, Randi E. (2005). *Overcoming animal and insect phobias.* Oakland, CA: New Harbinger Publications.

Matchett, George, & Davey, Graham C.L. (1991). A test of a disease-avoidance model of animal phobias. *Behaviour Research and Therapy, 29*, 91–94.

N

National Institute of Mental Health

The National Institute of Mental Health (NIMH) is the world's largest mental health research organization. It is one of the 27 institutes comprising the National Institutes of Health (NIH), a chief biomedical and health research center of the U.S. government. The mission of the NIMH is "to transform the understanding and treatment of mental illnesses through basic and clinical research, paving the way for prevention, recovery, and cure." The institute supports research programs investigating the causes, diagnosis, prevention, and treatment of anxiety disorders, including phobias.

A precursor to the establishment of the NIMH, the National Mental Health Act was enacted into law in 1946 with the aim of supporting research, prevention, and treatment of mental illness. The NIMH was subsequently formed on April 15, 1949. Over the years, funding for the NIMH increased considerably, and the institute established a significant influence over policy and research into mental illness. It further took on a role in communicating with the public and advocating for the advancement of biomedical science, mental health services, and community-based mental health policies. The current annual budget of the institute is $1.5 billion, which supports, in part, training and research grants. The NIMH also conducts its own internal research.

The NIMH has several wide-spanning research areas, such as neuroscience and basic behavioral science, services and intervention research, and research on disparities and global mental health. Each area has specific research objectives; however, the overarching objectives of the institute are four-fold: (1) promote discovery in the brain and behavioral sciences to fuel research on the causes; (2) chart mental illness trajectories to determine when, where, and how to intervene; (3) develop new and better interventions that incorporate the diverse needs and circumstances of people with mental illness; and (4) strengthen the public health impact of NIMH-supported research.

Notably, shortly before the publication of the *Diagnostic and Statistical Manual of Mental Disorders*, fifth edition (DSM-5) in 2013, the NIMH announced that it will shift away from funding research based on DSM diagnoses in favor of developing its own "brain-based" psychiatric classification system. The rationale for this shift is to facilitate greater objectivity in psychiatric classification and to support research questions that are not constricted by DSM categories. To aid with this effort, the institute's Research Domain Criteria (RDoc) provide a framework for future research that will produce new diagnoses based on basic behavioral neuroscience (i.e., based on genes, cells, neural circuits). Although many mental health researchers and clinicians support this agenda, others consider it controversial. Critiques of the RDoc focus on (1) its assumption that biology is the most fundamental phenomenon in mental illness (with a lesser emphasis on psychology and the social context), (2) the challenge of translating research on neural circuitry to identifiable clinical or treatment targets, and (3) the length of time that will be required for the state of the science to allow the formation of the new classification system.

Many noted mental health researchers receive funding from the NIMH. Aaron Beck, the founder of cognitive therapy, has held numerous NIMH grants and in 2006 was awarded the institute's prestigious Lasker Award for Clinical Medical Research. Beck received the award in recognition of his significant contributions to the understanding and treatment of many psychiatric conditions, including anxiety disorders.

As part of its health and education initiative, the NIMH offers substantial informational resources to the public, which can be accessed through the institute's website and in print format. Information is provided about a broad range of mental disorders and their treatments. For example, a booklet on anxiety disorders details the symptoms of each disorder, the role of research in understanding the causes of the disorders, effective treatments and how to access them, and methods to increase the treatment effectiveness.

Irena Milosevic

See also: Beck, Aaron T. (1921–); DSM-5

Websites

www.nimh.nih.gov

www.nimh.nih.gov/research-priorities/rdoc

Neuroimaging

The term *neuroimaging* broadly refers to a set of scientific methods that are used to investigate the structure and function of the central nervous system. Many different neuroimaging methods are used today. Three popular methods include magnetic resonance imaging (MRI), functional magnetic resonance imaging (fMRI), and diffusion tensor imaging (DTI). These three methods have helped scientists better understand the biological bases of phobias and other anxiety disorders.

Magnetic Resonance Imaging

Magnetic resonance imaging (MRI) is a method used to look at brain structure. In other words, it allows researchers to view a picture of the brain and provides

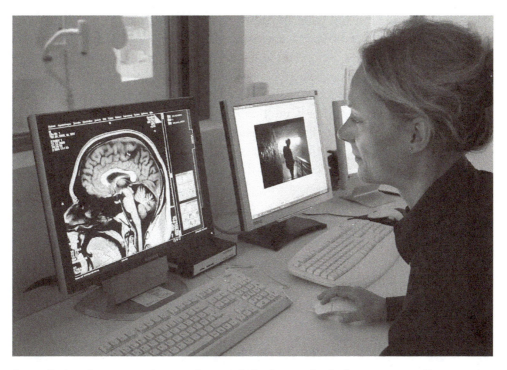

A medical assistant examines an image of the human brain from a magnetic resonance imaging (MRI) scan. MRI has identified abnormalities in the amygdala, a brain structure critical in fear and threat-related processing, across several anxiety disorders. (AP Photo/ Matthias Rietschel)

information about the brain's anatomic properties. The MRI scanner works by producing a strong magnetic field, which temporarily changes the directional spin of some of the hydrogen protons in the brain. Outside of an MRI, hydrogen protons in the human brain spin about on axes that are oriented in many different directions. However, because they have a positive electrical charge, when these hydrogen protons are placed inside of the strong magnetic field of the scanner, they align their axes so that they are parallel with the direction of the magnetic field. The scanner then emits energy in the form of an electromagnetic wave pulse. As the hydrogen protons absorb the energy from this pulse, they are pushed out of alignment with the magnetic field. When the electromagnetic pulse is finished, the hydrogen protons again tilt back into alignment with the magnetic field and emit the energy they have absorbed from the electromagnetic pulse. This energy is emitted in the form of a signal, which is detected by a part of the scanner known as the receiver coil. The receiver coil uses the spatial location and resonance frequency of this signal to generate a detailed picture of the brain.

Researchers use MRI to investigate brain structure in individuals with anxiety disorders. Properties such as the volume and thickness of various brain structures have been examined using MRI. Results of studies employing MRI have been mixed and indicate that different anxiety disorders are correlated with different anatomical abnormalities. For example, by using MRI to measure the thickness of the brain's cerebral cortex, researchers have found altered thickness in the prefrontal and parietal cortices in individuals with social anxiety disorder (social phobia; Brühl et al., 2014). The cortex is the brain's outer layer and, among many other functions, it helps to regulate anxious behaviors. MRI has also been helpful in characterizing specific abnormalities in obsessive-compulsive disorder (OCD), panic disorder (PD), and posttraumatic stress disorder (PTSD). For example, anatomic abnormalities have been found in the basal ganglia and orbitofrontal cortex of individuals with OCD, the temporal lobes of individuals with PD, and the hippocampus of individuals with PTSD. On the other hand, one consistent MRI finding across several anxiety disorders is abnormal volume of a structure known as the amygdala. The amygdala is involved in the regulation of emotions and the production of the fear response. In this way, MRI research has helped to pinpoint brain areas that are both similar and different in people with phobias and other anxiety disorders.

Functional Magnetic Resonance Imaging

Functional magnetic resonance imaging (fMRI) is a method used to investigate brain function. It uses information about alterations in blood flow to identify changes in brain activity by capitalizing on the differences in magnetism between oxygenated and deoxygenated blood. Specifically, when neurons in an area of the brain fire, oxygen-rich blood flows to that region. Once the oxygen is transferred from the blood to the active cells in the region, the blood then becomes deoxygenated. fMRI uses the ratio of oxygenated to deoxygenated blood to examine what is referred to as the *blood oxygen level–dependent* (BOLD) signal. Changes in the BOLD signal during various experimental conditions can be used to identify neuronal activity, telling researchers about how the brain responds to changes in an individual's environment. Changes in the BOLD signal can also provide information about how different areas of the brain work together as part of a functional network. Through the use of fMRI, it is now known that different aspects of behavior such as attention, memory, and motor movement are associated with the activation of specific brain networks.

fMRI has been particularly useful for research into anxiety disorders, and researchers have begun to understand how different parts of the brain function together to produce and maintain anxiety. In particular, several brain regions, which collectively make up the fear network, have been discovered using fMRI. Key players in this network include several regions of the prefrontal cortex, the hippocampus, and the amygdala. The prefrontal cortex is involved in the regulation of the fear response, and the amygdala is involved in the production of the fear response. The hippocampus is involved in memory and learning. Importantly, parts of the fear network have appeared functionally abnormal in several anxiety disorders, indicating a common neural circuitry across the anxiety disorders, including phobias. fMRI has also examined pediatric populations, and studies have shown that the fear network may develop abnormally in children and adolescents at risk for developing an anxiety disorder. Finally, fMRI has been useful for tracking changes in brain activity that occur before and after the treatment of anxiety with cognitive behavioral therapies (CBTs) and medications. For example, it has been shown that the treatment of arachnophobia with CBT can significantly reduce the activation of the amygdala during exposure to pictures of spiders. Additionally, treatment of social anxiety disorder with CBT significantly reduces activation of the amygdala and hippocampus during public-speaking tasks.

Diffusion Tensor Imaging

Diffusion tensor imaging (DTI) is another imaging method used by researchers to examine the biological bases of anxiety and phobias. DTI measures the structural properties of the white matter tracts in the brain. White matter is composed of myelinated axons (long pathways by which messages are transported from one cell to another) and helps to speed up the transmission of information between different regions of the brain, making it an important aspect of the brain to study.

By measuring how freely water molecules are able to move about (diffusion) in white matter, DTI provides information about the structure of the white matter fibers. When water molecules are restricted in their movement by the long myelinated axons, the direction of their movement defines a tract or white matter pathway. By looking at the structural integrity of white matter fibers through DTI, researchers can better understand the structure of brain networks in people with anxiety disorders. DTI is a relatively new area of research used to study anxiety, and some anxiety disorders have not been thoroughly examined using this method. However, DTI studies have identified important white matter tracts that may be altered in people with PTSD and OCD. DTI studies have found that PTSD may be characterized by abnormalities in the white matter of the prefrontal cortex. In OCD, several abnormalities in white matter connecting different parts of the brain's cortex (outer layer) have also been found. These findings are important for two reasons. First, they have allowed for a white matter characterization of certain anxiety disorders. Second, these findings support MRI and fMRI studies that have found abnormalities in neighboring gray matter regions (regions of dark brain tissue that contain cell bodies). In addition, other DTI studies have begun to examine anxiety disorders such as generalized anxiety disorder, and findings have revealed abnormalities in the white matter connecting the fear network. For example, reduced integrity of the uncinate fasciculus, a white matter tract connecting the prefrontal cortex and the amygdala, has been found in adults with generalized anxiety disorder (Hettema et al., 2012), and reduced integrity of this amygdala-prefrontal pathway has also been correlated with higher trait anxiety (Kim & Whalen, 2009). Thus, DTI appears as a promising and informative neuroimaging technique in the study of phobias and other anxiety disorders.

Jenna M. Traynor and Geoffrey B. C. Hall

See also: Amygdala; Arachnophobia (Fear of Spiders); Cognitive Behavioral Therapy; Limbic System; Neuroimaging; Obsessive-Compulsive Disorder; Posttraumatic Stress Disorder; Social Anxiety Disorder (Social Phobia)

Further Reading

Brühl, Annette Beatrix, Hänggi, Jürgen, Baur, Volker, Rufer, Michael, Delsignore, Aba, Weidt, Steffi, . . . Herwig, Uwe. (2014). Increased cortical thickness in a frontoparietal network in social anxiety disorder. *Human Brain Mapping, 35*, 2966–2977.

Hettema, John M., Kettenmann, Brigit, Ahluwalia, Vishwadeep, McCarthy, Christopher, Kates, Wendy R., Schmitt, James E., . . . Fatouros, Panos. (2012). Pilot multimodal twin imaging study of generalized anxiety disorder. *Depression and Anxiety, 3*, 202–209.

Kim, M. Justin, & Whalen, Paul J. (2009). The structural integrity of an amygdala-prefrontal pathway predicts trait anxiety. *The Journal of Neuroscience, 29*, 11614–11618.

PHOBIC VERSUS NONPHOBIC BRAINS

The way in which our brains function to process information greatly influences our behavior. Neuroimaging research examining anxiety disorders, including phobias, has revealed that these conditions are associated with abnormal structure and function of the human brain. Compared to healthy individuals, there are marked differences in the brains of people with anxiety disorders. Although specific causes of abnormal brain function in anxious individuals are still unknown, researchers now know that a combination of genetic and environmental factors may disrupt brain development and function.

Two areas of the brain that are important in the study of anxiety disorders are the amygdala and the prefrontal cortex. These two areas are a part of a larger network in the brain known as the fear network. In healthy individuals, these two structures function together as a balanced team. However, in people with anxiety disorders they function in a dysregulated manner.

The amygdala is an almond-shaped brain structure located deep inside the brain. It is a part of the emotion regulation system and helps us assess the meaning and relevance of our environment. The amygdala is active during conditions that elicit strong emotional responses. It is important in assessing threat and in the production of fear. Activation of the amygdala is also highly correlated with autonomic nervous system function and is implicated in the fight-or-flight response. Accordingly, amygdala activity is adaptive and is thought to fulfill a protective function during healthy development. Also important in the study of anxiety is the prefrontal cortex (PFC), which is located near the bottom of the frontal lobe. The PFC is implicated in complex, higher-order thinking such as the planning and execution of behavior, and it helps to modulate the amygdala's fear response to perceived threat. It is particularly important for the suppression and extinction of fear and the regulation of emotions.

In healthy individuals, the amygdala and prefrontal cortex work together to produce and inhibit appropriate fear responses. However, in people with phobias and other anxiety disorders, these structures function atypically. That is, the amygdala tends to overactivate in situations that pose no real threat. In addition, the prefrontal cortex is often underactive and unable to regulate the production of the fear response. This underactivation may be due to abnormalities in development at an early age. Studies have made analogies to the amygdala as the "gas" and the prefrontal cortex as the "breaks," with anxious individuals having "too much gas, and not enough breaks." This functional imbalance results in individuals displaying anxious behaviors at higher levels.

Thus, there are clear neural influences on anxiety that have great effects on our behavior. These neural differences can help us better understand why some individuals develop phobias and other anxiety disorders. In addition, these differences have helped researchers monitor the effects of treatment on the brain. For example, successful treatment of anxiety with cognitive behavioral therapy has been shown to increase activation in fear-regulating regions of the prefrontal cortex.

Jenna M. Traynor and Geoffrey B. C. Hall

Non-Associative Model

The non-associative model was proposed by Menzies and colleagues (Menzies & Clarke, 1995; Poulton & Menzies, 2002a, 2002b) as a theory of the origin of fears and phobias. The researchers noted that fear can be evoked by stimuli without prior direct or indirect learning. That is, not all individuals who develop a phobia have previously had an aversive experience with the phobic stimulus. For example, some parents of individuals with water phobia recall that their child's fear was apparent at the very first exposure to water. The non-associative model therefore proposes that certain fears have a biological basis. Further, it holds that these fears naturally extinguish for most individuals through normal developmental processes. However, for some individuals the fears persist or are reactivated during times of stress. According to the model, these individuals are at greater risk for developing a clinical phobia.

Like the preparedness theory of phobias, the non-associative model views certain fears as being biologically relevant because, from an evolutionary perspective, they ensured the survival of our distant ancestors. These fears include, for example, fears of heights and water. However, the non-associative model differs from the preparedness account as the latter requires at least one negative associative learning experience for a phobia to develop, whereas the non-associative model does not. Importantly, the non-associative model does not preclude that associative learning underlies the development of some "evolutionarily neutral" fears and phobias. Rather, it proposes that associative learning is *not necessarily required* for fear development. Accordingly, a non-associative pathway was proposed as a fourth pathway to fear acquisition, in addition to the three pathways that account for learning experiences (direct conditioning, vicarious learning, and negative information transmission). Subsequent to the initial formulation of the non-associative model (Menzies & Clarke, 1995), its proponents presented the argument that the model is superior to conditioning theory in accounting for fear phenomena (Poulton & Menzies, 2002b).

The non-associative model has received some empirical support—for example, its proponents point to genetic findings as being consistent with the model (Poulton & Menzies, 2002a). However, the model has also been subject to critique. It has been argued that its claims are difficult to test. In particular, to establish support for the theory, one must look for the absence of prior associative learning; however, the absence of a learning history does not necessarily confirm a biological fear vulnerability. Further, as with all theories that incorporate evolutionary perspectives, it is difficult to determine the exact survival pressures of our distant ancestors (e.g., we cannot know for certain whether avoidance of water allowed our ancestors to survive). Finally, critics have pointed to the importance of possible interoceptive conditioning. That is, rather than an obvious external cue (e.g., a barking dog) being associated with a fear response, it is possible for a more subtle internal cue (e.g., changes in one's heart rate) to become associated with fear. In this case, individuals might report no history of associative learning, whereas in fact associative learning had actually taken place. Further critique of the non-associative model has been detailed by Mineka and Öhman (2002), whereas rebuttals to these critiques are presented by Poulton and Menzies (2002a).

Irena Milosevic

See also: Classical Conditioning; Phobias, Causes of; Preparedness Theory; Three Pathways Theory

Further Reading

Menzies, Ross G., & Clarke, J. Christopher. (1995). The etiology of phobias: A nonassociative account. *Clinical Psychology Review, 15*, 23–48.

Mineka, Susan, & Öhman, Arne. (2002). Born to fear: Non-associative vs associative factors in the etiology of phobias. *Behaviour Research and Therapy, 40*, 173–184.

Poulton, Richie, & Menzies, Ross G. (2002a) Fears born and bred: Toward a more inclusive theory of fear acquisition. *Behaviour Research and Therapy, 40*, 197–208.

Poulton, Richie, & Menzies, Ross G. (2002b). Non-associative fear acquisition: A review of the evidence from retrospective and longitudinal research. *Behaviour Research and Therapy, 40*, 127–149.

Nosophobia (Fear of Disease or Illness)

Nosophobia (also known as nosemaphobia) derives from the Greek *nosos*, meaning disease, and *phobos*, meaning fear. More specifically, it is an irrational fear of contracting a disease. Nosophobia does not appear in the *Diagnostic and Statistical Manual of Mental Disorders*, fifth edition (DSM-5) but fits with one of the two new DSM-5 diagnoses that replace hypochondriasis, namely illness anxiety disorder (IAD). Whereas 75% of individuals formerly diagnosed with hypochondriasis would now meet the criteria for somatic symptom disorder (SSD), the other 25% would meet the diagnostic criteria for IAD. Whereas people with SSD fear that physical symptoms (e.g., pain) signify illness, people with IAD fear having or acquiring a specific illness, such as cancer. The prevalence of IAD in community samples is estimated to range from 1.3 to 10%, with higher rates (3–8%) in ambulatory medical samples.

In the past, nosophobia was believed to be more common in people engaged in the study of illness, such as medical students. Indeed, nosophobia was sometimes referred to as *medical student's disease*. More recent studies, however, have found no evidence that medical students are more health anxious than others. Nosophobia is presumed to arise from a combination of diathesis (e.g., a genetic predisposition to be anxious) and stress (e.g., trauma, poor general health, chronic pain). It may arise in the aftermath of a friend or family member contracting, or dying from, the feared illness. In one case, a man whose father had died young of heart disease became convinced that he too suffered from heart disease, despite medical reassurances to the contrary. Nosophobia may arise in the context of a major depressive episode (if patient ruminates about health) and remit with treatment for depression. People with nosophobia reveal symptoms characteristic of anxiety (e.g., feelings of terror, dread, panic) and often take extreme measures to avoid the feared illness (e.g., avoiding contact with others who may be "contaminated" by the illness). Other symptoms can include ruminating about the disease or death (thanatophobia); obsessively collecting or avoiding information on the disease; repeated bodily monitoring and self-examinations; and constant need for reassurance from others (medical practitioners, family, friends) that the disease is not present.

Cognitive behavioral therapy (CBT) is considered to be the most effective treatment for phobias. CBT typically includes three components: (1) providing information about the disorder, (2) helping individuals identify and challenge the thoughts that maintain the disorder (e.g., overestimating the probability of illness), and (3) exposure. Exposure involves helping individuals face their fear through a personalized program of desensitization. An exposure program involves the client moving through a series of steps in his or her hierarchy of fears, and staying in the fear while practicing anxiety reduction techniques (e.g., breathing, relaxation, cognitive challenging). With nosophobia, exposure could include reading about the feared illness (e.g., cancer), looking at pictures of cancerous cells, and visiting a cancer ward. Reducing reassurance behavior usually involves a concerted effort by medical and mental health practitioners, family, and friends to remind the individual of his or her need to refuse reassurance.

Margo C. Watt

See also: Anxiety and Related Disorders; Anxiety Sensitivity; Cognitive Behavioral Therapy; Cognitive Restructuring; Exposure, Interoceptive; Hypochondriasis; Medical Student Syndrome; Thanatophobia (Fear of Death)

Nyctophobia (Fear of the Dark)

Fear of the dark, or nyctophobia (from the Greek *nyktos*, meaning night, and *phobos*, meaning fear), is a natural environment type specific phobia. Natural environment type phobias generally onset in childhood. Many children, at one time or another, are frightened of the dark. A fear of the dark is considered to be clinically significant if exposure to the dark causes an extreme distress reaction and/or if the fear leads to significant impairment. For example, if a child really wants to go to sleepovers and overnight camp but cannot due to his or her fear of the dark, a diagnosis of specific phobia would be made. Furthermore, to differentiate the typical transient fears of childhood, fear of the dark must last for six months or more to be considered a clinically significant phobia.

Fear of the dark is extremely common in childhood, but the prevalence rate for clinically significant phobias in the general population is only around 3.5%. Although phobia of the dark is one of the most common phobias in childhood (endorsed by 29% of children in one clinical sample), it is rarely the sole reason for families to seek treatment. Rather, children who have a fear of the dark often have several other specific phobias. Fear of the dark is also frequently seen with separation anxiety disorder. When children sleep independently, they tend to feel more frightened of the dark than if they sleep with their parents. Similarly, children with generalized anxiety disorder focused on the safety of self and others often have fear of the dark. They are particularly worried about bad things happening (e.g., robberies, burglaries, fires) when they are alone in a dark room.

Fear of the dark causes sleep impairment. Some children want their lights so bright that it interferes with sleep. In families where parents insist on turning out the lights, intense anxiety also interferes with sleep. Because children who fear the dark also tend to have other sleep issues (fear of separation from parents; and other nighttime worries), bedtime can be associated with behavioral issues, somatic complaints, and bedtime rituals. Interestingly, one study has also shown that poor sleep in adulthood might be related to fear of the dark. Although scant research has been done on fear of the dark in adults, this study by Carney, Moss, Atwood, Crowe, and Andrews (2014) suggests that it is worth further exploration.

Treatment varies from child to child depending on the issues that go along with fear of the dark. In general, children should do gradual exposure to darkness. It is often helpful to begin by doing exposure to a dark room during the daytime, gradually moving exposures closer and closer to bedtime. In addition, exposures can first be done with a parent present, gradually moving them further from the child's room. Although it is important to do some exposures to a completely dark room, it is usually acceptable to allow children to sleep with a night-light on an ongoing basis.

Concurrent with exposures, children must learn how to challenge the anxious thoughts that they experience in the dark. For example, if they fear that a robber will come in the house, they can remind themselves, "not happening here." Similarly, if they fear ghosts or other "made-up" creatures, they can say, "not real," or "you're telling me lies, brain." Children should also be taught coping statements like, "It is dark in here, but I am safe."

Many children who fear the dark also lack good strategies for falling and staying asleep independently. Teaching these strategies is another integral part of treatment. For example, children can be taught relaxation strategies like positive imagery, progressive muscle relaxation, and breathing exercises as a means of soothing themselves to sleep.

Deborah Roth Ledley

See also: Behavior Therapy; Childhood, Phobias in; Cognitive Therapy; Exposure Treatment; Phobia, Natural Environment Type

Further Reading

Carney, Colleen E., Moss, Taryn G., Atwood, Molly E., Crowe, Brian M., & Andrews, Alex J. (2014). Are poor sleepers afraid of the dark? A preliminary investigation. *Journal of Experimental Psychopathology, 5*, 2–13.

Chansky, Tamar E. (2004). *Freeing your child from anxiety: Powerful practical solutions to overcome your child's fears, worries, and phobias.* New York, NY: Broadway Books.

O

Obsessive-Compulsive Disorder

Obsessive-compulsive disorder (OCD) is a mental disorder characterized by obsessions and/or compulsions. In order to receive a diagnosis of OCD, one's obsessions and/or compulsions must be time consuming (occupy more than one hour per day), cause significant distress, or interfere with daily functioning. OCD is classified under obsessive-compulsive and related disorders in the *Diagnostic and Statistical Manual of Mental Disorders*, fifth edition.

Obsessions are thoughts, images, or impulses that repeatedly intrude into a person's mind and cause anxiety or distress. The obsessions are unwanted and often very inconsistent with the person's normal thoughts and how they view themselves. Some common obsessions include doubting thoughts (e.g., Did I lock the door?), thoughts about contamination (e.g., I have contacted germs), aggressive impulses (e.g., impulse to punch someone), obscene or horrific images (e.g., image of mutilated bodies), disturbing religious thoughts (e.g., blasphemous thoughts), and thoughts about causing accidental harm (e.g., Maybe I hit someone with my car). Other thoughts, images, or impulses can also be obsessions if they are repetitive and unwanted. Importantly, obsessions must be more than just excessive worries about problems.

Compulsions are repetitive behaviors, mental actions, or rituals that a person feels driven to do. The goal of the compulsions is to prevent or reduce the distress caused by obsessions. The majority of people with OCD recognize that their compulsions are excessive but nevertheless feel compelled to do them. Common compulsions include hand washing, checking (e.g., locks, appliances), counting, internal repetition of phrases (e.g., a prayer), adhering to certain rules or sequences (e.g., lining up books on a shelf), and repeating rituals (e.g., rereading or rewriting). A person with OCD may spend many hours per day performing compulsions, often needing to repeat a compulsion until it feels "just right." Often people with OCD will attempt to avoid experiencing obsessions or compulsions by avoiding things that have triggered their OCD symptoms in the past. For example, people with fears of contamination may avoid touching door knobs or wear gloves when they go out in public.

OCD affects 2–3% of people in the general population at some point in their life, and occurs approximately equally across gender and cultures. There are generally two age ranges when OCD first appears: between ages 8 and 12 or between ages 18 and 24. An earlier age of onset is more common in males. Without treatment,

OCD tends to be a chronic disorder that may fluctuate in severity depending on one's general life stress, but it does not go away on its own.

There is no known single cause of OCD. It is likely caused by a combination of biological, psychological, and social factors. Evidence suggests that individuals may inherit a biological predisposition toward anxiety disorders generally. It has also been shown that certain brain structures and neurochemicals are involved. OCD may also be more likely to develop in people who hold certain rigid beliefs that they learned through their upbringing, culture, or personal experiences. These problematic beliefs can come in various forms. Many people with OCD have difficulty with ambiguous situations and are likely to hold beliefs that overestimate the potential threat and underestimate their ability to cope with challenges. They might also put too much importance on their intrusive thoughts, believing that the thoughts mean something about them as a person or that merely having a thought is just like doing an action. Overresponsibility and perfectionism beliefs are also quite common, where the individual believes that failing to prevent something bad from happening is the same as causing it or that even minor mistakes are unacceptable.

Treatment of OCD over the past few decades has greatly improved. There are currently two main approaches to treatment that have been shown to be effective for decreasing symptoms of the disorder: medication and cognitive behavioral therapy (CBT). The most commonly used medications are serotonin reuptake inhibitors. Significant symptom improvement is seen in about 50–60% of people who take medication; however, complete elimination of symptoms is rare, and about 90% of people will relapse if the medication is discontinued (Dougherty, Rauch, & Jenike, 2004). CBT is a psychological treatment that typically involves 12–20 weekly one-hour meetings with a trained therapist and includes exposure to obsession-related fears without engaging in compulsive behaviors (exposure with response prevention). This treatment also involves examining thinking patterns and challenging beliefs that are contributing to the OCD. CBT with exposure and response prevention is effective in reducing symptoms for 60–80% of people who complete the treatment, and it has lower relapse rates compared to medication treatment (Fisher & Wells, 2005). Evidence indicates that adding CBT to medication has superior results to medication alone.

Brenda L. Key

See also: Cognitive Behavioral Therapy; DSM-5; Exposure Treatment; Fear of Germs; Selective Serotonin Reuptake Inhibitors

Further Reading

Dougherty, Darin D., Rauch, Scott L., & Jenike, Michael A. (2004). Pharmacotherapy for obsessive-compulsive disorder. *Journal of Clinical Psychology, 60,* 1195–1202.

Fisher, Peter L., & Wells, Adrian. (2005). How effective are cognitive and behavioral treatments for obsessive-compulsive disorder? A clinical significance analysis. *Behaviour Research and Therapy, 43,* 1543–1558.

Hyman, Bruce M., & Pedrick, Cherlene. (2010). *The OCD workbook: Your guide to breaking free from obsessive-compulsive disorder* (3rd ed.). Oakland, CA: New Harbinger Publications.

Website
Obsessive Compulsive Foundation: www.ocfoundation.org

Ollendick, Thomas H. (1945–)

Thomas H. Ollendick (1945–) is a leading American psychologist in the field of child and adolescent clinical psychology, where his work has focused on evidence-based assessment and treatment of anxiety disorders and phobias. The fourth of seven children, Ollendick was born and raised on his family farm in rural Nebraska. He received his bachelor's degree from Loras College in Dubuque, Iowa, and then attended Purdue University in Indiana, where he received a doctorate in philosophy in clinical psychology in 1971. After completing a postdoctoral fellowship at the Devereux Foundation in Devon, Pennsylvania, Ollendick joined the faculty of Indiana State University. In 1980, he left Indiana and moved to Blacksburg, Virginia, to join the faculty of Virginia Tech, where he is currently appointed a university distinguished professor in clinical psychology and the director of the Child Study Centre.

Known for both his research findings and his ability to skillfully translate science to practice, Ollendick is a prolific writer who has had a major impact on training clinicians around the world. He has published over 300 scientific papers, 75 book chapters, and 25 books. Ollendick is a powerhouse in the field, authoring and editing the seminal readings on anxiety disorders and phobias in children and adolescents.

Randi E. McCabe

Further Reading
Ollendick, Thomas H., & Davis III, Thompson E. (2012). Evidence-based assessment and treatment of specific phobias in children and adolescents. In Thompson E. Davis III, Thomas H. Ollendick, and Lars-Göran Öst (Eds.), *Intensive one-session treatment of specific phobias* (pp. 43–58). New York, NY: Springer Science.

One-Session Treatment

One-session treatment (OST) is an intensive exposure-based psychological therapy for the treatment of specific phobias. Originally developed by Öst (1987, 1989), this single-session intervention incorporates exposure to the feared stimulus, psychoeducation, therapist modeling (also called participant modeling), positive reinforcement, and challenging of catastrophic cognitions. Treatment sessions last a maximum of three hours, during which the therapist guides the client to face feared situations using a graduated approach. A substantial body of research has demonstrated that OST is comparable to longer evidence-based treatment approaches and can be applied to a wide range of specific phobias.

Prior to beginning OST, the therapist meets with the individual to conduct an initial assessment that ideally includes a clinical interview, self-report measures, and a behavioral assessment. The goals of such an assessment are threefold. First, it allows the therapist to confirm that the person meets diagnostic criteria for a specific phobia. Second, it provides an opportunity to develop a case conceptualization of the person's idiosyncratic fears, anxious beliefs, maladaptive coping strategies, and avoidance behaviors. Such a conceptualization is necessary so that treatment can target the specific factors maintaining the individual's phobia, and this information is used in the development of an exposure hierarchy. Finally, the assessment provides an opportunity to collaboratively develop therapy goals, assess motivation, and provide a treatment rationale.

Following the assessment, the therapy session itself consists of a series of massed *in vivo* exposure exercises in which the individual confronts the feared stimulus. In OST, exposures are framed as behavioral experiments designed to evaluate the validity of a person's catastrophic predictions. For example, individuals with spider phobia often fear that if given the chance, spiders will readily crawl onto them and underneath their clothes. An exposure to test this prediction can therefore be carried out by observing how a spider actually behaves and by challenging the person's anxious cognitions. The goal for each exposure is for the person to remain in the situation, without using any behavioral or cognitive avoidance strategies (e.g., distraction), until there is a marked reduction in subjective anxiety. Once significant anxiety reductions have occurred and the individual recognizes that feared outcomes are unlikely to happen, he or she progresses to a more challenging exposure task. Öst (1989) recommends that therapists encourage individuals to engage in exposures that go above and beyond those that would be expected to occur naturally in their everyday lives (a process known as "overlearning"). For example, an individual with a snake phobia may intentionally wrap a snake around his or her neck as a final exposure. Overlearning allows individuals to interact with the phobic stimulus in a more extreme manner than would typically be experienced, thus helping to inoculate them against future encounters that are more probable. Throughout the session, the therapist also models appropriate behavior (when relevant), monitors the individual's subjective feelings of distress, challenges irrational anxious thoughts, and provides positive reinforcement when the individual exhibits approach behaviors.

OST consists of a single therapy session, and most individuals experience substantial anxiety reductions to feared stimuli during this time; however, it is not expected that fear is completely eradicated following this session. Rather, individuals are encouraged to view OST as the *beginning* of therapy. In order to maintain and further treatment gains, individuals must continue to engage in exposure to feared objects and situations in their daily lives and resist engaging in escape or avoidance behaviors. Individuals are encouraged to be their own therapists and to view contact with phobic stimuli as an opportunity to practice the skills acquired during OST. At the end of OST, specific exposure tasks to be completed following the session may be developed collaboratively with the therapist to promote the generalizability of new learning and maintenance of gains. Some therapists may also choose to schedule a booster session for additional consolidation of new learning.

Although the treatment techniques and interventions utilized in OST are similar to those applied in exposure therapy and cognitive behavioral therapy, the structured, massed, and single session of exposure is unique to this approach. The treatment is similar to flooding (which involves facing one's worst fears from the outset), but OST takes a more graduated approach and places greater emphasis on the single-session protocol and on testing of negative predictions.

Current empirical evidence appears to suggest that longer exposure sessions or those spaced closer together in time are superior, findings that OST capitalizes on, although research on this topic has produced inconsistent results (Zlomke & Davis III, 2008). Studies that have compared treatment outcomes consistently demonstrate that OST is comparable or superior to other evidence-based approaches (e.g., manualized exposure therapy) across a wide range of specific phobias, including animal, blood-injection-injury, and situational phobias. There is evidence for its application with children, adolescents, and adults, as well as in individual and group therapy formats. OST is generally well tolerated, although it is most appropriate for individuals with at least moderate levels of motivation to overcome their phobia.

Dubravka L. Gavric

See also: Behavioral Experiment; Cognitive Behavioral Therapy; Exposure, *In Vivo*; Exposure Treatment; Flooding; Modeling; Öst, Lars-Göran; Phobia, Specific; Phobias, Assessment of; Treatment, Evidence-Based

Further Reading

Öst, Lars-Göran. (1987). One-session treatments for a case of multiple simple phobias. *Scandinavian Journal of Behavior Therapy, 16*, 175–184.

Öst, Lars-Göran. (1989). One-session treatment for specific phobias. *Behaviour Research and Therapy, 27*, 1–7.

Zlomke, Kimberly, & Davis III, Thompson E. (2008). One-session treatment of specific phobias: A detailed description and review of treatment efficacy. *Behavior Therapy, 39*, 207–223.

Operant Conditioning

Operant conditioning is a type of associative learning between the action of an organism and the consequences of the organism's behavior in a given situation. This learning can serve to increase or decrease the behavior depending on whether the consequence is rewarding or punishing. The initial account of operant learning was Edward Thorndike's *law of effect*, which was further refined by B. F. Skinner who coined the term *operant conditioning*. Operant conditioning is one of the main ways through which humans learn how to interact with their environment, and impairments in operant learning can contribute to phobic behaviors such as avoidance. However, the principles of operant conditioning are also at the core of the treatments used to counter these behaviors in phobic individuals.

Thorndike proposed that stimulus-response (S-R) associations were responsible for the learning of operant behavior through the law of effect (Thorndike, 1933). Specifically, the law of effect states that given a preexisting situation or stimulus, a response that is accompanied or closely followed by pleasure will reinforce the association between the situation or stimulus (S) and that response (R). When pleasure follows a response (i.e., behavior) the likelihood of the response being chosen again more quickly and/or more frequently increases when the organism is confronted with that situation again, as the organism has learned that the consequence of the response is pleasure. Consider, for example, a hungry mouse that comes across a jar of honey in the garbage (S). The mouse decides to approach the jar and lick it (R). The sweetness is perceived as pleasurable, and the mouse is therefore likely to approach and lick jars filled with honey-like substances in the garbage in the future. Operant conditioning theories are subsequently built on this theory of reinforcement to include the inverse of reinforcement, punishment, which involves the weakening of the relationship between the stimulus and response, or, in other words, a decrease in the behavior when the response is followed by displeasure. Consider another hungry mouse that comes across a honeycomb (S), decides to approach and lick it (R), and is then stung by a bee. The mouse is displeased by the sting and is less likely to try and lick honeycombs in the future.

While Thorndike relied on internal states such as pleasure and displeasure to explain the increase and decrease in behavior, B. F. Skinner rejected the notion of unobservable mental states and relied only on observable behavior and observable consequences for his theories. Skinner developed the operant conditioning chamber or "Skinner Box," which could deliver either reinforcing consequences such as food or punishing consequences such as electric shock after behaviors such as pressing a lever. While one is tempted to say positive consequences for food or negative consequences for shock, both of these are actually considered positive in operant terms, which highlights the confusing terminology of operant conditioning. While we are often prone to think about events as good or bad, pleasurable or unpleasant, given Skinner's stance on unobservable states, these terms have no place in the field. Rather everything is defined by observable characteristics. In operant conditioning, whenever a behavior results in something with motivational value being added to the environment, it is considered positive, regardless of whether it is "good" or "bad" or the behavior increases or decreases. Adding shock often decreases the behavior, making it a positive punishment, whereas adding food increases the behavior, making it a positive reinforcement. Alternatively, if something with motivational value is removed from the environment, it is termed negative. Removing a toy from a child for bad behavior, which hopefully decreases the behavior, is thus negative punishment. Of particular interest to the study of phobias is negative reinforcement, which involves escape and avoidance behaviors. As either escape or avoidance behaviors serve to remove feared stimuli from an individual's environment, it is considered negative; since this behavior results in outcomes that the individual prefers, it is reinforcing and the behavior is strengthened.

To understand the contribution of operant conditioning to the development and maintenance of phobias, consider the example of an individual who sees a spider and becomes frightened. The individual's response may be to escape the situation. Doing so both removes the spider from the environment and reduces fear, which could make the individual more likely to repeat that behavior in the future. The effectiveness of this escape behavior could lead the individual to avoid any interaction with spiders in the future and this avoidance is characteristic of phobias.

Exposure therapy for phobias also relies on operant conditioning principles for changing behavior and reducing phobic avoidance. Importantly, avoidance behavior limits future learning experiences because it prevents the learning of new consequences in the given situation because that situation is avoided. Exposure therapy has the individual learn that the fear response will eventually go away even if the avoidance response is not performed. Given the situation of encountering a spider, a new behavior of continuing to expose oneself to the feared stimulus is encouraged, and the consequence that the fear response eventually subsides is learned. This reinforces the approach behavior and, through repetition, the fear response can subside more quickly until it is manageable and the spider is no longer avoided.

Brian van Meurs and Shmuel Lissek

See also: Arachnophobia (Fear of Spiders); Behavior Therapy; Safety Behavior; Skinner, B. F. (1904–1990); Thorndike, Edward L. (1874–1949); Two-Factor Theory of Avoidance Learning

Further Reading

Thorndike, Edward L. (1933). A proof of the law of effect. *Science, 77*(1989), 173–175.

Ophidiophobia (Fear of Snakes)

Ophidiophobia, originating from the Greek *ophis*, meaning serpent or snake, and *phobos*, meaning fear, is a persistent and irrational fear of snakes. This phobia belongs to the broader category of herpetophobia (fear of reptiles) and is classified as an animal type specific phobia in the *Diagnostic and Statistical Manual of Mental Disorders*, fifth edition. It is a common animal phobia, and its development is believed to be influenced by both environmental and biological factors. Ophidiophobia can be treated effectively with exposure treatment, a type of cognitive behavioral therapy.

Point prevalence rates based on questionnaire surveys in the general population suggest that ophidiophobia is among the most common animal phobias, with estimates ranging from 1.2% (Oosterink, de Jongh, & Hoogstraten, 2009) to 5.5% (Fredrikson, Annas, Fischer, & Wik, 1996). Similar to other animal phobias, ophidiophobia is much more likely to be reported by women than men (it is up to 3.5 times more prevalent among women; Fredrikson et al., 1996). The onset of animal phobias, including ophidiophobia, is typically between ages five and nine (LeBeau et al., 2010). There is evidence of familial aggregation of ophidiophobia,

A green coiled snake flicks out its tongue. Individuals who are fearful of snakes, and in fact most people, assume that a flicker of a snake's tongue is a sign of threat. However, snakes use their tongues to "smell" their environment, as their nostrils are used exclusively for breathing. (Courtesy of Irena Milosevic)

whereby having a mother with ophidiophobia increases one's risk of having the phobia versus having a mother with a spider phobia; this aggregation may be due to both environmental and genetic influences.

Ophidiophobia can develop through several pathways that comprise different types of learning experiences. These include direct traumatic conditioning (e.g., being bitten by a snake), vicarious observation (e.g., seeing one's parent run away from a garter snake in the yard), and informational transmission (e.g., being told to stay away from snakes because they are all dangerous and venomous). Additionally, some researchers believe that because snakes posed a significant danger in the environment of early humans, evolutionary mechanisms have facilitated our *biological preparedness* to readily learn to fear snakes. Findings in support of this theory show that humans and other primates learn to fear snakes more readily than other stimuli through direct or vicarious conditioning. It has also been shown that people tend to perceive associations between snakes and aversive stimuli when these associations do not actually exist (illusory correlation). Further, when presented with complex visual displays, people more readily detect snakes in the display than stimuli such as flowers and frogs (Öhman & Mineka, 2003). Not all individuals, however, develop snake phobia through conditioning experiences. An alternative account holds that fear is mediated by the disgust-eliciting properties of snakes. Disgust is believed to be important in preventing people from coming into contact with things that might spread disease (e.g., blood, feces). Snakes possess features of primary disgust-elicitors, such as mucous and feces, because they appear to be slimy. Accordingly, researchers posit that phobic avoidance of snakes can be explained, in part, by concerns about contamination.

In considering models of the development of ophidiophobia, it is worth noting that snakes hold an important symbolic value in the psychoanalytic school of thought, where they are viewed as a phallic or sexual symbol. In psychoanalysis, phobias are considered a displacement of unconscious fears to a neutral object. Accordingly, a fear of snakes is interpreted as a symptom of unconscious castration anxiety and fears of sexual activity. This perspective has not been empirically supported, with no evidence to suggest that individuals with ophidiophobia disproportionately suffer from sexual difficulties. Interestingly, snakes and serpents have long held various symbolic meanings across history, cultures, and religions. Although they have been associated with many positive elements (e.g., fertility, immortality, healing, guardianship, wisdom), they have also been linked with evil, deception, and vindictiveness. For example, in the Christian tradition, serpents are associated with Satan. It is therefore unsurprising that some individuals with ophidiophobia endorse beliefs that snakes are evil.

Individuals with ophidiophobia typically fear coming into contact with a snake. They may believe that if they encounter a snake, the snake will come toward them and attack or bite them. They may also believe that all snakes are venomous and dangerous to humans. They might interpret the snake's behavior (e.g., snake flicking out its tongue) as a sign of imminent danger. Realistically, however, snakes use their tongues to gather information about their environment; it is not a sign of aggression. Upon encountering a snake or snake-related stimuli (e.g., photograph, video, rubber snake), individuals with ophidiophobia experience intense fear and may even have a panic attack. Some individuals might also experience a disgust response and report feeling "grossed out" by a "slimy and slithering" snake. Interestingly, by contrast to the popular belief that snakes are slimy, the skin of reptiles, including snakes, is dry and scaly.

A common behavioral response among individuals with ophidiophobia is rapid escape from the situation in which a snake or related stimulus is encountered. To prevent such encounters, individuals with ophidiophobia typically engage in pervasive avoidance of places where snakes might be present, such as yards, parks, gardens, zoos, and pet shops. They might also avoid looking at pictures or photos of snakes, watching nature shows, and vacationing in destinations where snakes are prevalent. If avoidance is not always possible, they might wear protective clothing (e.g., long pants and boots) and remain on guard in the environment, checking that no snakes are nearby.

To receive a diagnosis of a specific phobia of snakes, an individual's fear must cause significant distress and/or disruption to daily life and must be out of proportion to the realistic threat of snakes. For example, for individuals who live in environments where there is minimal to no possibility of encountering a *dangerous* snake, it would be considered excessive to avoid parks and backyards for fear of snakes, whereas for individuals who live in environments populated by venomous or otherwise harmful snakes, avoiding areas where such snakes have been encountered might be an appropriate response. Notably, most individuals who report symptoms that meet the criteria for a diagnosis of ophoidiophobia have not had a prior encounter with a dangerous snake, nor have they been attacked by a snake.

The treatment of choice for ophidiophobia, like other specific phobias, is exposure treatment. This intervention includes psychoeducation about fear and the factors that maintain it (e.g., avoiding places where there might be snakes) and gradual exposure to feared or avoided situations. For example, an individual might initially work on saying the word "snake," then move on to looking at photos and videos of snakes, holding a rubber snake, and walking through grassy areas. Eventually, the individual would advance to situations that provoke the greatest amount of fear, such as looking at snakes in a pet store, watching someone handle a snake, and ultimately holding a snake. Exposure treatment for ophidiophobia can be conducted over a series of sessions or in a single session (approximately three hours in length).

Irena Milosevic and Feven Yeshanew

See also: Disease-Avoidance Model; DSM-5; Exposure Treatment; Phobia, Animal Type; Phobia, Specific; Preparedness Theory

Further Reading

Fredrikson, Mats, Annas, Peter, Fischer, Hakan, & Wik, Gustav. (1996). Gender and age differences in the prevalence of specific fears and phobias. *Behaviour Research and Therapy, 34*, 33–39.

LeBeau, Richard T., Glenn, Daniel, Liao, Bette, Wittchen, H. U., Beesdo-Baum, K., Ollendick, T., & Craske, M. G. (2010). Specific phobia: A review of DSM-IV specific phobia and preliminary recommendations for DSM-V. *Depression and Anxiety, 27*, 148–167.

Öhman, Arne, & Mineka, Susan. (2003). The malicious serpent: Snakes as a prototypical stimulus for an evolved module of fear. *Current Directions in Psychological Science, 12*, 5–9.

Oosterink, Floor, de Jongh, Ad, & Hoogstraten, Johan. (2009). Prevalence of dental fear and phobia relative to other fear and phobia types. *European Journal of Oral Sciences, 117*, 135–143.

Ornithophobia (Fear of Birds)

Ornithophobia (from the Greek *ornithos* meaning bird and *phobos* meaning fear) is an excessive and persistent fear of birds. In the *Diagnostic and Statistical Manual of Mental Disorders*, fifth edition, ornithophobia is classified as an animal type specific phobia. Animal phobias are among the most prevalent phobias, although the specific prevalence of ornithophobia is not known.

Individuals with ornithophobia are typically fearful of being attacked or swarmed by birds. They might also be concerned about the spread of disease by birds. Ornithophobia can be acquired directly through a prior negative experience with birds (e.g., being bitten by a friend's pet parrot), through observing another person responding fearfully to birds (e.g., sister running away in tears when seagulls swarm around a family picnic), or through hearing negative information about birds (e.g., a warning from parents that an owl near the home had attacked a small child). More broadly, an evolutionary account suggests that humans might be predisposed to develop this fear because our early ancestors faced the threat of attack from predatory birds; thus, learning to fear birds may have been important to our survival.

Because birds are nearly impossible to avoid in everyday life, ornithophobia can be very debilitating. Individuals with this phobia may partially or completely avoid being outdoors. To avoid exposure to birds, they might get around almost exclusively by car. When this is not possible, they might avoid walking in areas with an abundance of trees or foliage. Further, they might require their windows at home or in their vehicle to be closed at all times. Individuals with ornithophobia might also have difficulty seeing videos or pictures of birds. When exposed to a bird, they respond with intense distress and may even experience a panic attack.

Ornithophobia, similarly to other phobias, can be successfully treated with exposure therapy. This form of psychological treatment involves gradual and repeated exposure to fear-provoking stimuli. For example, an individual might begin by looking at pictures and videos of birds and then move on to visiting a museum to look at bird specimens, watching birds through a closed window, being near a caged bird, walking through a park, sitting near a duck pond, feeding birds at the park, and ultimately to touching and handling a bird.

Irena Milosevic

See also: DSM-5; Exposure Treatment; Phobia, Animal Type; Phobia, Specific

Further Reading

Antony, Martin M., & McCabe, Randi E. (2005). *Overcoming animal and insect phobias.* Oakland, CA: New Harbinger Publications.

Lassen, Maureen K., & McConnell, Stephen C. (1977). Treatment of a severe bird phobia by participant modeling. *Journal of Behavior Therapy and Experimental Psychiatry, 8*, 165–168.

Öst, Lars-Göran

Lars-Göran Öst, PhD, is a prominent clinical researcher in cognitive behavioral therapy (CBT) for anxiety disorders. Öst is the founder of CBT in Sweden and a leading figure in the dissemination of CBT worldwide. He has pioneered innovative treatment methods for phobias, including one-session treatment and applied tension. He also developed applied relaxation, a widely used treatment method in anxiety disorders and other conditions.

Öst first became involved in research at Uppsala University in Sweden and completed his thesis in educational psychology at Stockholm University in Sweden in 1976. He continued his work at Uppsala University in the Department of Psychiatry, where he completed a thesis in psychiatry in 1985. He went on to collaborate with prominent CBT and anxiety disorders researchers at Oxford University in England, and in 1992 he returned to Stockholm University where he was appointed professor of clinical psychology. Öst subsequently also became chair of clinical psychology at Stockholm University and further developed affiliations with other institutions, such as Bergen University in Norway and a prestigious medical university, the Karolinska Institute, in Stockholm. In 2012, Öst retired from his position at Stockholm University, and a conference featuring international researchers and his former students was held to honor his career accomplishments (Andersson, Holmes, & Carlbring, 2013).

Öst is recognized as a prolific researcher and innovator in the evidence-based treatment of anxiety disorders. He has evaluated the efficacy of CBT for various anxiety disorders through numerous controlled clinical trials. His work has also focused on other elements of anxious psychopathology, such as perfectionism and cognitive biases. Among his most notable contributions is his development of treatments for specific phobias. In particular, Öst established an effective one-session treatment (OST) for phobias, which is an exposure-based intervention that can be applied in a single two- to three-hour session. OST has been applied to a broad range of phobias, including phobias of snakes, spiders, blood-injection-injury (BII), dentists, flying, and enclosed places (Öst, 2012). Öst also developed applied tension, a technique used in the treatment of BII phobias, particularly in cases where individuals with the phobia are susceptible to fainting upon exposure to feared stimuli (Hellström, Fellenius, & Öst, 1996).

In addition, Öst is credited with developing applied relaxation (AR), which is comprised of various relaxation techniques and methods for detecting early signs of anxiety or tension. AR has been used both in the treatment of anxiety disorders, particularly generalized anxiety disorder, and medical conditions such as headaches and chronic pain.

As a clinical researcher, Öst's productivity is exemplified by his publication of approximately 200 scientific articles, book chapters, and books. He is a former editor of the *Scandinavian Journal of Behaviour Therapy* and *Behavioural Psychotherapy* and has served on the editorial boards of numerous other scientific journals geared toward CBT and psychopathology. He has also presented extensively at major professional conferences and universities worldwide. His efforts in the dissemination of CBT are further illustrated with his career-long supervision and training of students and clinicians in CBT methods.

Irena Milosevic

See also: Applied Relaxation; Applied Tension; Cognitive Behavioral Therapy; Exposure Treatment; One-Session Treatment; Phobia, Specific

Further Reading

Andersson, Gerhard, Holmes, Emily A., & Carlbring, Per (2013). Lars-Göran Öst. *Cognitive Behaviour Therapy, 42*, 260–264.

Hellström, Kerstin, Fellenius, Jan, & Öst, Lars-Göran. (1996). One versus five sessions of applied tension in the treatment of blood phobia. *Behaviour Research and Therapy, 34*, 101–112.

Öst, Lars-Göran. (2012). One-session treatment: Principles and procedures with adults. In Thompson E. Davis III, Thomas H. Ollendick, & Lars-Göran Öst (Eds.), *Intensive one-session treatment of specific phobias* (pp. 59–95). New York, NY: Springer.

P

Panic Attacks

The *Diagnostic and Statistical Manual of Mental Disorders*, fifth edition (DSM-5; American Psychiatric Association, 2013) describes a panic attack as the sudden onset of intense fear with at least four symptoms. Physical symptoms include heart palpitations, sweating, trembling, chest pain, shortness of breath or smothering, choking feeling, dizziness, nausea, numbness or tingling, chills or hot flushes, and feeling disconnected from the body or from reality. Cognitive symptoms include fear of losing control of the body (e.g., fainting or vomiting) or of going crazy, and fear of dying. Panic attacks peak rapidly and usually subside in 30 minutes.

Panic attacks are part of the fear response in anxiety disorders and can also occur in the context of any other DSM disorder (e.g., depression). In the DSM-5, panic attacks are a "specifier," informing what is understood about the origins, severity, and prognosis of any associated disorder. *Unexpected* attacks occur in threat-free situations (e.g., at home), whereas *expected* attacks may occur where a person previously had an attack (e.g., a mall) or in response to other feared objects or situations (e.g., flying). Panic attacks are the basis of panic disorder (recurrent panic attacks) and are frequently associated with agoraphobia, specific phobia, and social anxiety disorder (social phobia).

Fear is the body's automatic alarm reaction to danger. Fear triggers normal, adaptive preparations to fight or flee (e.g., heart rate increases to pump extra blood to muscles). Panic attacks, however, are a "false alarm" in the brain's fear network, possibly triggered by abnormal neurotransmitter activity, a biological vulnerability to anxiety, or heightened vigilance for and misinterpretation of bodily sensations. Misinterpretation of fight-or-flight sensations, such as believing that a rapid heartbeat signals a heart attack, creates anxiety, which subsequently intensifies the physiological response, further worsening symptoms and leading to a panic attack.

Over the lifespan, 12–20% of adults (more women than men) experience at least one panic attack. Onset is typically in early adulthood, during periods of stress. People may avoid places associated with the initial attack and activities that arouse similar sensations (e.g., aerobic exercise). In 3–5% of people, this anxiety and avoidance leads to the development of panic disorder. Approximately 50% of people with specific phobia or social anxiety disorder also experience panic attacks; the phobia usually develops first. Risk factors for panic attacks include life stress, a hypersensitive biological fear response, smoking, fear of fight-or-flight sensations ("anxiety sensitivity"), and learned beliefs that the world is scary and uncontrollable.

A young man is comforted as he experiences a panic attack. People with phobias and other anxiety disorders commonly experience panic attacks when they encounter feared objects or situations. Panic attacks are not dangerous and help to prepare the body for a fight-or-flight response in the face of actual or perceived danger. (AP Photo/ Rachelle Blidner)

Culture-specific symptoms of panic attacks include localized heat, ringing in the ears, neck pain, screaming, and crying. Some groups tend to report certain symptoms, such as numbness (African Americans), cardiac-respiratory distress (Caucasians), and dizziness (Asians), possibly because of different illness incidence rates, concepts of illness and the body, or cultural metaphors for distress.

Most people having their first panic attack unnecessarily seek emergency medical help. An acute panic attack can be treated with fast-acting (highly addictive) benzodiazepines. Early psychological intervention is important. The treatment of choice, cognitive behavioral therapy, involves education, examination, and modification of beliefs about panic, and controlled exposure to panic-like sensations (e.g., breathing through a straw to trigger hyperventilation). Treatment reduces anxiety about future panic attacks, helping to prevent the development of panic disorder.

Christianne Macaulay and Margo C. Watt

See also: Agoraphobia; Anxiety Sensitivity; Cognitive Behavioral Therapy; DSM-5; Exposure Treatment; Panic Disorder; Phobia, Specific; Social Anxiety Disorder (Social Phobia)

Further Reading

American Psychiatric Association. (2013). *Diagnostic and statistical manual of mental disorders* (5th ed.). Arlington, VA: American Psychiatric Publishing.

Barlow, David H. (2002). *Anxiety and its disorders* (2nd ed.). New York, NY: The Guilford Press.

Panic Disorder

Panic disorder (PD) is an anxiety disorder characterized by recurrent and unexpected panic attacks. Panic attacks are sudden onset episodes of intense fear characterized by increased respiration, perspiration, heart rate, and other physiological sensations such as nausea and dizziness. A diagnosis of PD requires that a person has experienced one or more panic attacks, accompanied by persistent worry about future panic attacks and the potential consequences of those attacks (e.g., losing control, dying, "going crazy"). Following the initial attack, people may avoid places where they fear a panic attack may occur or activities that may trigger panic-like symptoms (e.g., physical exercise). Typically, PD begins in early adulthood. If not treated, it tends to follow a chronic, waxing, and waning course. PD affects approximately 2–3% of the population and is more common in women than men. Lower prevalence rates are found in Asian, African, and Latin American countries. PD commonly co-occurs with other anxiety disorders, especially agoraphobia (i.e., intense fear and/or avoidance of situations where help might not be available or where it may be difficult to leave in the event of panic symptoms or other incapacitating or embarrassing symptoms), but also mood (depression) and substance use disorders, which can complicate its course and treatment (American Psychiatric Association, 2013).

Although the exact cause of PD is unknown, several risk factors have been identified (Taylor, Asmundson, & Wald, 2007). Genetics are implicated in its development, with first-degree relatives (e.g., children, siblings) of people with PD having a 10–20% increased risk for the disorder. Environmental factors, such as childhood physical and sexual abuse, are more common in PD than in some other anxiety disorders. High sensitivity to arousal-related sensations (i.e., anxiety sensitivity or "fear of fear") is also a known risk factor for PD. In addition, learning experiences (e.g., witnessing a parent's panic, being reinforced for sick-role behavior related to anxiety) have been found to increase a person's risk for PD.

Anxiety surrounding future panic attacks is a key maintenance factor in PD. Effective treatments for PD include medication (e.g., antidepressants) and cognitive behavioral therapy (CBT) (Taylor et al., 2007). CBT involves education about anxiety, such as the nature of the body's fight-or-flight response and how panic attacks are "false alarms." Affected individuals are taught to examine and modify faulty beliefs, such as catastrophizing about anxiety-related sensations. For example, individuals may misinterpret a rapid heartbeat, fearing that it signifies a heart attack, and begin to panic. CBT for PD also includes exposure to feared situations (*in vivo* exposure) and feared physical sensations (interoceptive exposure) allowing for practice of new skills and reduction of fear (Watt & Stewart, 2008).

Catherine E. Gallagher and Margo C. Watt

See also: Agoraphobia; Anxiety Sensitivity; Cognitive Behavioral Therapy; Exposure, Interoceptive; Exposure, *In Vivo*; Panic Attacks

Further Reading

American Psychiatric Association. (2013). *Diagnostic and statistical manual of mental disorders* (5th ed.). Arlington, VA: American Psychiatric Publishing.

Taylor, Steven, Asmundson, Gordon J.G., & Wald, Jaye. (2007). Psychopathology of panic disorder. *Psychiatry, 6,* 188–192.

Watt, Margo C., & Stewart, Sherry H. (2008). *Overcoming the fear of fear: How to reduce anxiety sensitivity*. Oakland, CA: New Harbinger Publications.

Pavlov, Ivan (1849–1936)

Ivan Pavlov (1849–1936), born Ivan Petrovich Pavlov, was a Russian physiologist most renowned for his work on classical conditioning (also called Pavlovian conditioning or learning). His famous findings on the conditioned response have been highly influential to the field of behavioral psychology. Pavlov's conditioning principles not only made a significant contribution to theories on how phobias are acquired but they also served as the foundation for the development of behavior therapy for phobias and other anxiety disorders.

Pavlov was born in Ryazan, Russia, to a village priest and his wife. Intending to follow in the footsteps of his father, he attended a church school and subsequently a seminary. However, at age 21, Pavlov abandoned his religious studies to pursue the study of science. This change was inspired by progressive thinkers and academics of his time, including the prominent Russian physiologist, Ivan Sechenov (1829–1905). While completing a major in animal physiology and a minor in chemistry at the University of St. Petersburg, Pavlov developed a passion for physiology and conducted his first research project on the physiology of pancreatic nerves.

After graduating from the University of St. Petersburg in 1875 with an exceptional academic record and a degree in natural sciences, Pavlov continued his studies at the Academy of Medical Surgery where he earned a doctor of medicine degree in 1883. In 1890, he was appointed director of the Physiology Department at the Institute of Experimental Medicine in St. Petersburg. He held this position for 45 years and conducted some of his most important work on the physiology of digestion during this period. Until this point, the mechanisms responsible for digestion were not well understood, so Pavlov established a new surgical method, using dogs as models,

Russian physiologist Ivan Pavlov. Pavlov's work on classical conditioning critically contributed to theories of fear learning and to the development of effective phobia treatments. (Library of Congress)

that allowed him to study digestive processes without disrupting normal functioning of the organs. This groundbreaking method paved the way for advances in physiology and resulted in many important discoveries, including the significance of neural control on the regulation of the digestive process, the observation that different food types affect the quantity of gastric juices released, and the fact that the sight of food can itself lead to gastric secretions and salivation. In recognition of this work, Pavlov was awarded the Nobel Prize in physiology or medicine in 1904. Notably, instead of discussing the findings from his digestion research during his acceptance speech, he instead spoke about what was eventually to become his most significant contribution to the understanding of phobias: his discovery of the conditioned reflex or response.

During his investigations into digestion, Pavlov began noting that the dogs in his experiments experienced gastric secretions and salivation not only at the sight of food but also at the sight of the research assistants, in the total absence of food. This observation resulted in Pavlov's shift in focus from the study of digestion to the study of what is now known as classical conditioning. Pavlov hypothesized that the dogs had begun salivating in response to the white coats of the research assistants because they had learned to associate the assistants with food presentation.

Following this discovery, Pavlov began attempting to generate responses of salivation to previously neutral stimuli.

One of Pavlov's most distinguished experiments involved conditioning a salivation response to the ringing of a bell by training dogs to associate the sound of the bell with the presentation of food. Whereas the typical salivary response to the presentation of food was considered to be natural and unlearned or *unconditioned*, the salivary response to the bell had been acquired through association or *conditioned*. In essence, Pavlov demonstrated that inborn reflexes, such as salivation, can be conditioned by environmental stimuli, such as the sound of a bell, that had no initial relation to the salivation reflex. This discovery has also been applied to fear learning, whereby a previously neutral stimulus (e.g., a tone) can be conditioned to elicit a fear response after being paired with an aversive stimulus (e.g., an electric shock).

Pavlov continued to study classical conditioning in both animals and humans until his death from pneumonia at age 86. He left a remarkable legacy across several scientific areas, including physiology, medicine, psychology, and neurological science. Within psychology, he influenced many prominent figures such as Carl Jung (1875–1961) and John B. Watson (1878–1958). Watson's work, in particular, translated Pavlov's findings into the field of behaviorism.

Pavlov's concept of classical conditioning has been extensively applied to the study of phobias. In particular, it laid the groundwork for understanding the mechanisms of how fears are acquired. His findings have also influenced the development of phobia treatments such as exposure therapy, which is based, in part, on the extinction of the conditioned fear response and is widely considered to be one of the most effective treatments for phobias and other anxiety disorders.

Lisa Rustom and Irena Milosevic

See also: Behavior Therapy; Classical Conditioning; Exposure Treatment; Extinction; Learning Theory; Systematic Desensitization; Watson, John B. (1878–1958)

Further Reading

Delgado, Mauricio R., Olsson, Andreas, & Phelps, Elizabeth A. (2006). Extending animal models of fear conditioning to humans. *Biological Psychology, 73*, 39–48.

Field, Andy P. (2006). Is conditioning a useful framework for understanding the development and treatment of phobias? *Clinical Psychology Review, 26*, 857–875.

Wolpe, Joseph, & Plaud, Joseph J. (1997). Pavlov's contributions to behavior therapy. *American Psychologist, 52*, 966–972.

Perceived Control

Perceived control is the belief that one can effectively influence the experience or consequences of an event. This feeling of control is most relevant in situations where there is a perceived threat and associated fear. The extent to which perceived control aligns with one's actual control can vary. Research suggests that individuals with phobias tend to have lower perceived control than those without psychological disorders. Low perceived control tends to worsen fears and increase avoidance, thereby contributing to the development and maintenance of anxiety disorders, including phobias. Although low perceived control is associated with anxiety, the benefits of actually giving an individual control over a feared object during exposure treatment is unclear. Some studies have shown that having more control (e.g., the individual gets to control the distance from a feared animal) actually increases fear, whereas others have found no differences when individuals had control over the duration of an exposure session versus when they did not.

There are three main theories related to perceived control: locus of control, learned helplessness, and self-efficacy. In *locus of control theory*, it is proposed that anxiety becomes problematic for individuals who rigidly believe that threats occur due to external factors that are outside their control. For example, people with arachnophobia may believe that spiders are unpredictable and that they will not be able to protect themselves if a spider approaches. *Learned helplessness theory* focuses on the problems associated with the belief that circumstances will remain negative regardless of any actions taken. For example, an individual who developed hydrophobia due to a past near-drowning incident may believe water will be dangerous no matter how well he or she learns to swim. In *self-efficacy theory*, beliefs about one's capability to manage a situation are seen as central to whether a person will be willing to face the situation and also how anxious they will feel. For example, people with claustrophobia (fear of enclosed spaces) typically expect that they will panic if they become caught in an enclosed space and that they will be unable to cope. In all three theories, low perceived control is believed to be problematic and to contribute to anxiety.

The two main elements of perceived control are perceived control over one's own physiological response and perceived control over the feared object or event itself. Perceived physiological control is related to fear of anxiety-related symptoms (e.g., increased heart rate, respiration, and perspiration) and emotional experiences (e.g., anticipation of intense anxiety). Perceived control of the object or event is related to the people's beliefs about their ability to exercise control over the object/event and prevent undesirable outcomes.

Understanding an individual's unique beliefs about perceived control helps to determine the best intervention. Some patients may benefit more from learning to cope with physiological responses, whereas others benefit more from adjusting their expectations about event outcomes. For example, people with blood-injection-injury phobia who believe that they will faint when they get a needle can be taught applied tension, which decreases the chances of fainting and which might increase their perceived physiological control. Although events are not always controllable, individuals should learn to match perceived control to actual potential dangers in the environment. For example, individuals with arachnophobia (fear of spiders) who believe that all spiders will attack might benefit from greater perceived control and less anxiety after learning that most spiders in fact tend to avoid humans.

Brenda L. Key and Jennifer M. Yip

See also: Arachnophobia (Fear of Spiders); Exposure Treatment; Fear, Physiology of; Perception, Visual; Phobia, Blood-Injection-Injury Type; Phobia, Specific

Further Reading

Antony, Martin M., & McCabe, Randi E. (2005). *Overcoming animal & insect phobias: How to conquer fear of dogs, snakes, rodents, bees, spiders & more.* Oakland, CA: New Harbinger Publications.

Eifert, Georg H., Coburn, Kendall E., & Seville, Janette L. (1991). Putting the client in control: Perception of control in the behavioral treatment of anxiety. *Anxiety, Stress & Coping, 5,* 165–176.

Perception, Visual

Visual perception refers to the visual representation of a sensory stimulus—what one literally sees. Empirical studies and clinical case reports indicate that people with phobias may have distorted perceptions of feared stimuli. For example, fearful (relatively to nonfearful) individuals may report that spiders or snakes are very large, or moving very rapidly toward them. One limitation with research in this area, however, is that it is challenging to determine whether fearful persons *visually* perceive things differently, or if differences are due to cognitive, judgment, self-report, or recall biases. Thus, it is critical for researchers to develop tools to try to capture what participants truly see (distinct from their self-report or other cognitive phenomena).

In recent years, researchers have applied the theory of embodied perception to the area of visual perception and fear in an effort to evaluate what fearful individuals truly *see*. According to the theory of embodied perception, "visual perception promotes survival by making people aware of both the opportunities and the costs associated with action" (Proffitt, 2006, p. 111). For example, hills may appear steeper when one is wearing a heavy backpack or when standing on a skateboard.

Research on height-fearful individuals lends some support to the theory of embodied perception, or the idea that one's goals, physiological state, and emotions may influence what one sees. Applying this theory, researchers speculate that for individuals who are afraid of heights, the costs of interacting on a high place like a balcony or mountain (e.g., the costs of falling) might actually cause high places to be seen as taller. For instance, one study asked individuals high and low in height fear to estimate the vertical height of a two-story balcony using several different measures designed to capture what participants truly saw when they looked over the balcony (Teachman, Stefanucci, Clerkin, Cody, & Proffitt, 2008). Results indicated that individuals high in height fear made greater estimations of the balcony's height, even when taking into account measures of cognitive bias. This finding suggests that emotional factors, such as fear, may influence what one sees at a visual level. A follow-up study asked participants to estimate the height of two different balconies (Clerkin, Cody, Stefanucci, Proffitt, & Teachman, 2009). This time, however, on one of the balconies participants engaged in an imagery exercise where they imagined themselves falling off the balcony. Results indicated that all individuals overestimated the height of the balcony after they imagined themselves falling, and this overestimation was greater for individuals high in height fear. This finding led researchers to hypothesize that a more persistent fear of heights may function as an underlying vulnerability that leads to differences in visual perception when accompanied by a stressor (in this case, imagining oneself falling off the balcony).

Other research outside the area of height fear lends support to the idea that fear and other emotions may influence visual perception. For instance, one study found that participants evaluated a bed of nails as larger when they were instructed to imagine themselves falling onto it (Stefanucci, Gagnon, Tompkins, & Bullock, 2012). In another study, participants with social phobia, depression, and no mental illness (control) saw faces that had been morphed, or altered, to display 0% to 100% of a given emotion (e.g., a given face might consist of a morph of 70% anger and 30% neutral; Joormann & Gotlib, 2006). Results indicated that participants with social phobia (vs. depressed and control participants) needed less emotional intensity to correctly identify an angry face, whereas participants with depression (vs. social phobic and control participants) needed greater emotional intensity to correctly identify a happy face.

Despite evidence that fears and phobias may influence visual perception, the theory of embodied perception remains controversial, with some visual scientists claiming that vision is an encapsulated process that cannot be influenced by outside factors, including fear. Indeed, some studies have not found the anticipated differences in visual perception among fearful individuals. One thing seems clear: compared to nonfearful individuals, fearful individuals frequently *report* differences in what they see, and there are hints that they may actually be *visually seeing* things differently. However, further research needs to be conducted to understand whether fear and anxiety can actually influence visual perception, and if so, the conditions under which these influences emerge.

Elise M. Clerkin and E. Marie Parsons

See also: Acrophobia (Fear of Heights); Arachnophobia (Fear of Spiders); Fear; Information Processing Biases; Ophidiophobia (Fear of Snakes); Phobia, Specific

Further Reading

Clerkin, Elise M., Cody, Meghan W., Stefanucci, Jeanine K., Proffitt, Dennis R., & Teachman, Bethany A. (2009). Imagery and fear influence height perception. *Journal of Anxiety Disorders, 23*, 381–386.

Joormann, Jutta, & Gotlib, Ian H. (2006). Is this happiness I see? Biases in the identification of emotional facial expressions in depression and social phobia. *Journal of Abnormal Psychology, 115*, 705–714.

Proffitt, Dennis R. (2006). Embodied perception and the economy of action. *Perspectives on Psychological Science, 1*, 110–122.

Stefanucci, Jeanine K., Gagnon, Kyle T., Tompkins, Christopher L., & Bullock, Kendall E. (2012). Plunging into the pool of death: Imagining a dangerous outcome influences distance perception. *Perception, 41*, 1–11.

Teachman, Bethany A., Stefanucci, Jeanine K., Clerkin, Elise M., Cody, Meghan W., & Proffitt, Dennis R. (2008). A new mode of fear expression: Perceptual bias in height fear. *Emotion, 8*, 296–301.

IT WAS THIS BIG: BIASED PERCEPTION OF SPIDER SIZE

Individuals with phobias exhibit various biases in how they process phobic stimuli. For example, a person who is fearful of rodents might report seeing a "giant rat" after encountering a small field mouse. In this particular example, the exaggerated report suggests distortions in the way that the person is taking in (encoding) and processing visual information about the threatening stimulus. Given that few studies have specifically investigated the association between fear and visual perception, researchers in the Department of Psychology at the Ohio State University decided to do just that.

Vasey and colleagues (2012) recruited 57 individuals with a phobia of spiders. The research participants were asked to interact with different varieties of live tarantulas, ranging in size from about 1 to 6 inches long, over the course of two test sessions. During each session, participants completed several behavioral approach tasks in which they approached a tarantula in an uncovered glass tank. A total of five approach tasks were completed across two sessions.

Each encounter with a spider began 12 feet from the tank, and participants were then asked to approach the spider. Once they were standing by the tank, the researchers asked them to use an 8-inch probe to touch the spider for two minutes. They then asked them to repeat this task with a 5.5-inch probe. Throughout each spider encounter, participants rated their fear on a 0–100 scale. At the end of a test session, participants also completed a questionnaire assessing more generally their tendency to be afraid of spiders.

Following the spider encounters, the tank was covered with a white sheet so that the spider could no longer be viewed. Participants were then asked to estimate the spider's size by drawing a line on an index card to indicate its length from the tips of its front legs to the tips of its back legs.

Analyses showed that fear was significantly associated with a magnified perception of spiders. That is, the higher the participants' peak fear during the spider encounters the greater their spider size overestimates. The results also indicated that fear experienced during a phobic encounter was a stronger predictor of size overestimates than a more general tendency to fear spiders.

The researchers concluded that fear appears to alter visual perception of feared stimuli. Their study was the first to demonstrate an association between fear experienced *during* a phobic encounter and a perceptual bias. When in a fearful state, people seem to magnify the object of their fears. Understanding how fear influences visual perception may help us better understand how phobias are maintained and how to more effectively treat them.

Irena Milosevic

Further Reading

Vasey, Michael W., Vilensky, Michael R., Heath, Jacqueline H., Harbaugh, Casaundra N., Buffington, Adam G., & Fazio, Russell H. (2012). It was as big as my head, I swear! Biased spider size estimation in spider phobia. *Journal of Anxiety Disorders, 26*, 20–24.

Personality

Personality refers to relatively stable patterns in a person's thinking, behavior, and emotions. It is often conceptualized in terms of personality traits, which are enduring qualities that affect a person's behavior across most situations, whereby the behavior is consistent from one situation to another. The majority of personality traits are considered to be dimensional; that is, they occur on a continuum ranging from a low to a high level of a particular trait. Several personality traits have been associated with anxiety disorders, although there has been scant research into personality and phobias in particular, with existing evidence suggesting weak associations between specific personality factors and phobias.

Personality is linked to temperament, which is a genetically influenced predisposition to emotional reactivity that manifests very early in childhood. A child's temperament interacts with the environment and thereby serves as the foundation for the development of personality. Although there is overlap in how temperament and personality are conceptualized, temperament is typically discussed in the context of infant and child development, whereas personality is associated with adolescence and adulthood and is generally thought to comprise more complex patterns of evaluations, beliefs, goals, values, and behaviors (Taylor, Abramowitz, McKay, & Asmundson, 2010). Factors important in the development of personality broadly include both genetic and environmental influences (e.g., social learning).

Several personality traits are thought to influence the development and maintenance of anxiety disorders. These include narrow traits such as *trait anxiety* (the tendency to respond with tension, apprehension, and increased physiological reactivity), *anxiety sensitivity* (the tendency to respond fearfully to arousal-related physical sensations), and *intolerance of uncertainty* (the tendency to respond negatively to uncertain outcomes), as well as broader traits such as *neuroticism* or *negative affectivity* (the tendency to experience negative emotions). The narrow personality traits are understood as vulnerability factors for developing particular anxiety problems (e.g., high anxiety sensitivity is a vulnerability factor for panic disorder), whereas the broader traits have been identified as vulnerability factors for developing emotional problems more generally (e.g., various mood and anxiety disorders). An individual's unique vulnerability for developing a given anxiety disorder is thought to be comprised of a combination of these traits, which interact with environmental stressors and biological risk factors (e.g., genes).

Numerous models have been proposed with the aim of delineating the most fundamental personality traits and their subcomponents and describing the relationships between them. The leading general model of personality is the five-factor model (e.g., McCrae & Costa, 1987), which provides a hierarchical organization of personality, comprised of five broad higher-order traits (neuroticism, extraversion, agreeableness, conscientiousness, and openness) and six narrow lower-order traits within each broad trait. Of the broad traits, neuroticism has been most closely linked to anxiety disorders. In addition to general models of personality, several specific models of personality vulnerability to anxiety disorders have also been proposed. A prominent model is Clark and Watson's (1991) tripartite model of anxiety and depression. The authors specify three broad personality traits, including negative affectivity, positive affectivity (the tendency to experience positive emotions), and physiological arousal (the tendency to become physiologically aroused). The risk for developing anxiety disorders is thought to be greater when negative affectivity and physiological arousal are high. Narrow personality traits (e.g., anxiety sensitivity) that increase anxiety disorder vulnerability are also included in the model and subsumed under negative affectivity. The tripartite model has been extensively evaluated, with findings generally supporting the tenets that negative affectivity and physiological arousal are associated with anxiety symptoms (for a review, see Taylor et al., 2010). Contrary to the model's assumption that low positive affectivity is uniquely associated with depression, low levels of this trait have also been linked with social anxiety disorder (social phobia).

In an effort to understand patterns of comorbidity across mental disorders, Krueger (1999) proposed a two-factor model, comprised of externalizing (e.g., substance use disorders) and internalizing (e.g., anxiety and depressive disorders) factors. The internalizing factor is similar to the broad personality trait of negative affectivity and is further divided into two narrower factors—anxious-misery and fear proneness. Fear proneness, in particular, is thought to be associated with symptoms of specific phobias, social anxiety disorder, and agoraphobia. However, research into the application of the two-factor model to specific anxiety disorders is yet in the early stages.

In consideration of more narrow personality traits, trait anxiety has been shown to be robustly associated with anxiety disorders. Cognitive explanations of this association have garnered substantial empirical evidence. Specifically, studies have shown that individuals with high trait anxiety tend to be hypervigilant to threat and are prone to making threat-based interpretations of ambiguous stimuli. Anxiety sensitivity has also been associated with various anxiety disorders and predicts the risk for panic attacks, although there is little research on the association between anxiety sensitivity and specific phobias. In fact, with the exception of a study reporting an association between fear of somatic symptoms and specific phobias after neuroticism was accounted for (McWilliams et al., 2007), findings generally do not support an association between anxiety sensitivity and phobias. In terms of the intolerance of uncertainty trait, much of the research to date has evaluated its association with generalized anxiety disorder and obsessive-compulsive disorder, although recent studies suggest associations with a broader range of anxious psychopathology, including social anxiety disorder and panic disorder. The association between intolerance of uncertainty and specific phobias has yet to be investigated.

Clearly, despite voluminous literature on personality and various anxiety disorders, there is very little research into personality and specific phobias in particular. The existing literature in this area is mixed, with some studies suggesting no association between personality traits (e.g., neuroticism) and the diagnosis of a specific phobia, whereas others have shown weak associations and yet others reported strong associations. Generally, it appears that individuals with specific phobias are higher in neuroticism than individuals in the general population but lower than individuals diagnosed with other anxiety disorders. However, an important limitation of studies reporting associations between personality traits and phobias is that they did not control for other mental disorder diagnoses, which may account for some or all of the reported associations. Although neuroticism or negative affectivity is characteristic, to varying degrees, of all of the anxiety disorders, it is most weakly related to disorders characterized by behavioral avoidance (i.e., specific phobias). Overall, it appears that personality factors relevant to anxiety disorders do not have as significant of a role in specific phobias (Pagura, Cox, & Enns, 2008).

Irena Milosevic

See also: Anxiety Sensitivity; Fear of the Unknown; Temperament

Further Reading

Clark, Lee Anna, & Watson, David. (1991). Tripartite model of anxiety and depression: Psychometric evidence and taxonomic implications. *Journal of Abnormal Psychology, 100*, 316–336.

Krueger, Robert F. (1999). The structure of common mental disorders. *Archives of General Psychiatry, 56*, 921–926.

McCrae, Robert R., & Costa, Paul T. (1987). Validation of the five-factor model of personality across instruments and observers. *Journal of Personality and Social Psychology, 52*, 81–90.

McWilliams, Lachlan A., Becker, Eni S., Margraf, Jürgen, Clara, Ian P., & Vriends, Noortje. (2007). Anxiety disorder specificity of anxiety sensitivity in a community sample of young women. *Personality and Individual Differences, 42*, 345–354.

Pagura, Jina, Cox, Brian J., & Enns, Murray W. (2008). Personality factors in the anxiety disorders. In Martin M. Antony and Murray B. Stein (Eds.), *Oxford handbook of anxiety and related disorders* (pp. 190–206). New York, NY: Oxford University Press.

Taylor, Steven, Abramowitz, Jonathan S., McKay, Dean, & Asmundson, Gordon J. G. (2010). Anxious traits and temperaments. In Dan J. Stein, Eric Hollander, & Barbara O. Rothbaum (Eds.), *Textbook of anxiety disorders* (2nd ed., pp. 73–86). Washington, DC: American Psychiatric Publishing.

Phobia, Animal Type

Animal type specific phobia is among the most common of the phobia subtypes with a prevalence rate ranging from 3.3% to 7% that is similar across child, adolescent, and adult samples. Individuals with this phobia display excessive fear of a specific animal or insect such as snakes, spiders, dogs, and fish. To be diagnosed as a specific phobia according to the *Diagnostic and Statistical Manual of Mental Disorders*, fifth edition, the fear must be associated with significant distress and/or impairment. For example, a person with a phobia of spiders may experience an extreme anxiety response when confronted with a real spider or even just the word "spider." This response may escalate into a full-blown panic attack. In response to the fear of spiders, the person may avoid going anywhere there may be spiders present, such as the basement, garage, or backyard. Animal type phobia has been associated with a number of indicators of impairment, including the seeking of professional help and reported interference in daily activities and social interactions.

Onset of animal type phobia is typically in early childhood between the age of six and nine years. The focus of fear may include fear of danger or harm (such as being bitten by a dog or shark) and/or internal feelings of disgust and revulsion (common with phobias of spiders and snakes, for example). Recent research comparing animal phobia to blood-injection-injury phobia suggests that the phobia subtypes may be associated with distinct neural response patterns in the brain activated by the presence of the feared stimulus. Specifically, animal phobia is associated with activation of the dorsal anterior cingulate cortex (i.e., area of the brain involved with appraisal and expression of negative emotion) and the anterior insula (i.e., area of the brain involved in consciousness and emotional awareness). As with other phobia subtypes (natural environment and situation type), animal type specific phobia is more than twice as common in females than males, with prevalence rates ranging from 4.3% to 12.1% in women compared to 2.7 to 3.3% in men. Interestingly, compared to other phobia subtypes, individuals with animal phobias report fewer symptoms of anxiety and little focus on internal sensations of arousal.

Risk factors for the development of animal type phobia include direct experience (e.g., being bitten by a dog) and other learning pathways (e.g., observation and informational transmission), as well as genetic transmission. For example, children with parents who have an animal type phobia are at greater risk to also develop an animal type phobia with the heritability of the phobia estimated at 47%. In addition, this genetic transmission may even be specific to the type of feared animal. For example, one study found that a snake phobia in a mother increased the likelihood of a snake phobia in the child specifically versus other animal phobias such as spider phobia. Although the research clearly shows that genetic factors play an etiological role in the development of animal type phobia, the specific mechanisms have yet to be elucidated.

Animal type phobias are effectively treated using cognitive behavioral treatment emphasizing *in vivo* exposure to the feared animal or insect. Compared to other phobia types, animal type phobias are particularly amenable to intensive one-session treatment.

Randi E. McCabe

See also: Cognitive Behavioral Therapy; Cognitive Therapy; DSM-5; Exposure, *In Vivo*; Exposure Treatment; One-Session Treatment; Phobia, Blood-Injection-Injury Type; Phobia, Natural Environment Type; Phobia, Situational Type; Phobia, Specific; Phobia Types; Phobias, Causes of

Further Reading

LeBeau, Richard T., Glenn, Daniel, Liao, Betty, Wittchen, Hans-Ulrich, Beesdo-Baum, Katja, Ollendick, Thomas, & Craske, Michelle G. (2010). Specific phobia: A review of DSM-IV Specific Phobia and preliminary recommendations for DSM-V. *Depression and Anxiety, 27*, 148–167.

Phobia, Blood-Injection-Injury Type

Individuals with blood-injection-injury (BII) type specific phobia have a marked fear or anxiety that is triggered by seeing blood, receiving an injection or transfusion, undergoing an invasive medical procedure, receiving medical care, or sustaining an injury. The focus of an individual's fear is typically on the physical symptoms of anxiety (e.g., feeling dizzy and light-headed) and fainting, as well as on feelings of disgust or revulsion, rather than on the possibility of harm. An individual with a fear of blood may faint at the sight of blood. An individual with a fear of injuries may be unable to attend to a cut and might have to look away. Someone with a fear of medical procedures may avoid seeking medical care despite needing to do so (e.g., refusing a biopsy for a lump). Someone with a fear of injections may refuse to receive an injection or have blood drawn even though it is medically necessary. BII phobia may shape education and job choices (e.g., a student who wants to be a doctor may drop out of medical school because he or she is unable to see blood), as well as major life decisions (e.g., a woman may avoid future pregnancy for fear of medical procedures). Impairment from BII phobia may be severe and may have serious health implications, particularly for those with a major medical illness requiring treatment.

BII phobia most commonly begins in childhood, with an average age of onset between five and nine years old. Lifetime prevalence rates range from 3.2% to 4.5% and tend to be more frequent in younger versus older age groups (LeBeau et al., 2010). There is no clear evidence of gender differences in BII phobia. Some research has shown slightly higher prevalence in females compared to males, whereas other studies have found no gender differences. Common comorbid conditions include another specific phobia, another anxiety disorder (i.e., panic disorder, social anxiety disorder [social phobia], agoraphobia), obsessive-compulsive disorder, depression, and marijuana abuse. Having a parent with a BII phobia increases the likelihood of developing BII phobia through both environmental and genetic factors. The genetic heritability of BII phobia has been estimated at 59%.

Research on BII phobia shows that it is associated with a distinct physiological profile compared to other specific phobia types. Upon exposure to the feared stimulus, individuals with BII phobia experience a vasovagal response involving an initial increase in heart rate and blood pressure, followed by a sharp decrease that contributes to the likelihood of fainting. By contrast, individuals with other specific phobia types typically experience heart rate acceleration and blood pressure elevation when exposed to their feared objects or situations. Up to 75% of individuals with BII phobias have a history of fainting in response to the feared stimulus. Recent research comparing BII phobia to animal phobia suggests that the phobia types may be associated with distinct neural response patterns in the brain activated by the presence of the feared stimulus. Specifically, BII phobia is associated with activation in the thalamus (the area of the brain involved in sensory perception and regulation of motor functions) and the bilateral occipito-temporo-parietal cortex (the area of the brain involved in visual attention and spatial processing).

BII phobia is treated with cognitive behavioral therapy emphasizing *in vivo* exposure. For individuals who experience fainting, *in vivo* exposure is modified to counteract the vasovagal response by incorporating muscle tension to increase blood pressure during exposure to the feared stimulus. This variation on exposure is known as applied tension.

Randi E. McCabe

See also: Applied Tension; Exposure, *In Vivo*; Exposure Treatment; Fainting Response; Phobia, Animal Type; Phobia, Natural Environment Type; Phobia, Other Type; Phobia, Situational Type; Phobia, Specific

Further Reading

LeBeau, Richard T., Glenn, Daniel, Liao, Betty, Wittchen, Hans-Ulrich, Beesdo-Baum, Katja, Ollendick, Thomas, & Craske, Michelle G. (2010). Specific phobia: A review of DSM-IV specific phobia and preliminary recommendations for DSM-V. *Depression and Anxiety, 27*, 148–167.

Phobia, Choking

Choking phobia is the excessive fear that one may develop difficulty breathing and die due to a blockage of the airway (i.e., choking) caused by ingestion of food, liquid, or pills. Fear of choking may be associated with *pseudodysphagia*, which is the sensation of feeling a lump in the throat that leads to difficulty in swallowing, and with *globus*, which is the sensation that the throat is constricting. Choking phobia often has a sudden onset after a traumatic choking experience and may occur at any age. At the mild end of the severity continuum, individuals with this phobia fear and/or avoid certain foods that may increase the likelihood of choking, such as sticky items (e.g., peanut butter) and items that are difficult to chew (e.g., meat). At the extreme end of the continuum, an individual with choking phobia avoids all food and thick fluids, and sustains a diet limited to clear fluids. It is no surprise then that this phobia may be associated with significant medical complications due to restriction of nutrition and consequent extreme weight loss. The effects of the phobia may be greatly debilitating, including limited function in day-to-day activities due to fatigue and loss of energy as well as ability to engage in social activities that often revolve around social eating. It may be associated with social withdrawal and depression.

Individuals with choking phobia often engage in a range of safety behaviors aimed at reducing the likelihood of choking. Examples of such behaviors include eating very slowly, chewing excessively until food is liquefied, pureeing solid food, taking very small bites, and swallowing food with liquid. The anxiety and increased focus on swallowing accompanying eating may paradoxically increase difficulty swallowing and reinforce the fear of choking. For example, try for yourself to swallow three times in succession. You will find this increasingly difficult, and one can see how this would increase choking fears.

In the *Diagnostic and Statistical Manual of Mental Disorders*, fifth edition, choking phobia is diagnosed as a specific phobia, other type. This is due to the fact that there is very limited research on this fear to establish it as a distinct subtype. The information we do have on choking phobia comes primarily from published uncontrolled case study reports. From this limited data, choking phobia appears to be somewhat more common in females than males and often co-occurs with panic disorder and depression. Upon presentation for treatment, individuals with choking phobia may at first be mistaken as having an eating disorder, particularly anorexia nervosa, which is also characterized by restricted food intake and weight loss. However, careful assessment can distinguish the two disorders by focusing on the nature of the fear. In choking phobia, an individual fears/avoids eating due to the fear of choking, and weight loss is a consequence of the fear. By contrast, in anorexia nervosa, an individual fears gaining weight and intentionally restricts food intake to achieve the goal of weight loss.

There are currently no randomized controlled treatment trials on choking phobia. However, case study reports demonstrate that choking phobia may be effectively treated using cognitive behavioral treatment, which may include psychoeducation, cognitive restructuring, interoceptive exposure, and *in vivo* exposure. Cognitive restructuring strategies aim to reduce maladaptive thoughts that contribute to the phobia such as overestimation of choking risk. Behavioral experiments may also be used to correct maladaptive thoughts. *In vivo* exposure for choking phobia consists of gradual exposure to eating a variety of liquids and foods, and reducing safety behaviors by increasing bite size and rate of eating. Finally, interoceptive exposure exercises are aimed to trigger the gag reflex and may involve using a tongue depressor or toothbrush to reduce fear associated with the gag response.

Randi E. McCabe

See also: Behavioral Experiment; Cognitive Behavioral Therapy; Cognitive Therapy; DSM-5; Exposure, Interoceptive; Exposure, *In Vivo*; Exposure Treatment; Phobia, Other Type; Phobia, Specific; Phobia Types; Phobias, Causes of; Safety Behavior

Further Reading

McNally, Richard J. (1994). Choking phobia: A review of the literature. *Comprehensive Psychiatry, 35*, 83–89.

Phobia, Dental

Fear of the dentist is one of the most common fears, with an estimated 24.3% of individuals reporting the fear in a Dutch study, right behind fear of snakes (34.8%), heights (30.8%), and physical injury (27.2%; Oosterink, de Jongh, & Hoogstraten, 2009). The majority of people with dental fear are able to manage the fear and continue to attend the dentist and receive necessary oral hygiene care without significant emotional and other negative consequences. For a smaller proportion of individuals, approximately 2.4–3.7%, the dental fear causes significant distress and impairment in functioning and warrants diagnosis as a specific phobia (LeBeau et al., 2010).

Individuals with dental phobia report a range of fears, including fear of dental procedures involving injury or injections (e.g., extractions), witnessing surgical operations, receiving anesthetic injections, and seeing blood. Individuals with this phobia often avoid attending the dentist for treatment and therefore have worse dental health than those without dental phobia. They may also avoid any reminders of the dentist including brushing their teeth. Without treatment, dental phobia tends to have a chronic course and has been associated with intrusive reexperiencing of fear, disrupted sleep, impaired social relationships, avoidance of certain foods, and negative effects on physical health, as well as secondary social anxiety related to poor dental health.

In the *Diagnostic and Statistical Manual of Mental Disorders*, fifth edition, dental phobia is classified as a specific phobia, blood-injection-injury (BII) type due to the focus of fear on invasive medical procedures. Some have advocated for dental phobia to be classified as a distinct type of specific phobia. However, a thorough review comparing dental phobia to BII phobia and other phobia types found that it

A child who fears the dentist is comforted by his mother. Odontophobia, fear of the dentist, can begin at a young age and carry on through adulthood. (slobo/iStockphoto.com)

shared many features with BII phobia and that there was insufficient evidence to support a separate classification (LeBeau et al., 2010).

There are a number of assessment tools used to measure dental fear. Common measures include the Dental Anxiety Scale, the Dental Cognitions Questionnaire, and the Dental Fear Survey. These measures are useful for screening for the presence of dental fear and anxiety, quantifying the level of dental fear, and identifying targets for treatment such as feared situations and catastrophic cognitions.

A review of treatment approaches for dental phobia found that cognitive behavioral treatment (CBT) targeting catastrophic cognitions and emphasizing exposure to feared situations was the treatment of choice with the most evidence supporting its efficacy (Gordon, Heimberg, Tellez, & Ismail, 2013). Studies included in the review used a variety of formats of CBT, including one-session treatment. Cognitive therapy, relaxation, and strategies aimed to increase the person's perceived control over dental care were also found to be helpful but were most effective when combined with exposure to avoided situations (e.g., calling to make an appointment, visiting the clinic, sitting in the waiting area, meeting with the dentist). CBT has been associated with reduced dental anxiety, increased acceptance of dental treatment, and improvements in quality of life and oral health.

Dental anxiety is a factor that dental practitioners must manage on a regular basis to ensure that they are able to provide the best care while minimizing distress to patients. Dentists are trained in approaches to help in identifying and caring for individuals with dental anxiety. A good dentist-patient relationship is essential to optimizing care, and dentists may use a variety of techniques to foster this relationship, including open and clear communication and increasing a patient's perceived control. In some cases, medication is used to treat a patient with dental phobia. This is more of a short-term strategy to ensure that the patient receives a necessary procedure and may range from having the patient take a benzodiazepine or other sedative drug to undergo a checkup to the use of general anesthesia to complete more invasive work (such as a root canal or tooth extraction). Generally, medication does not treat the anxiety directly and may in fact maintain or increase anxiety in the long term. Therefore, it is used more as a supplement to CBT provided by a qualified practitioner.

Randi E. McCabe

See also: Cognitive Behavioral Therapy; Cognitive Therapy; DSM-5; Exposure Treatment; Exposure, *In Vivo*; Phobia, Blood-Injection-Injury Type

Further Reading

Gordon, Dina, Heimberg, Richard G., Tellez, Marisol, & Ismail, Amid I. (2013). A critical review of approaches to the treatment of dental anxiety in adults. *Journal of Anxiety Disorders, 27*, 365–378.

LeBeau, Richard T., Glenn, Daniel, Liao, Betty, Wittchen, Hans-Ulrich, Beesdo-Baum, Katja, Ollendick, Thomas, & Craske, Michelle G. (2010). Specific phobia: A review of DSM-IV specific phobia and preliminary recommendations for DSM-V. *Depression and Anxiety, 27*, 148–167.

Oosterink, Floor M., de Jongh, Ad, & Hoogstraten, Johan. (2009). Prevalence of dental fear and phobia relative to other fear and phobia subtypes. *European Journal of Oral Sciences, 117*, 135–143.

Phobia, Natural Environment Type

A phobia is an excessive fear of a specific situation or stimulus that causes significant distress and impairment and is diagnosed as a specific phobia according to the *Diagnostic and Statistical Manual of Mental Disorders*, fifth edition. There are five types of specific phobia: animal, situational, blood-injection-injury, other, and natural environment. The phobia subtypes vary with regard to a number of features, including age of onset and gender differences in prevalence. Individuals with natural environment type phobia fear specific situations in nature such as heights, storms (e.g., wind, lightning), water, and the dark. The focus of an individual's fear in the particular situation may vary, although an overwhelming majority report a fear of danger or harm. For example, an individual with a fear of water may fear drowning. Someone with a fear of heights may be afraid of falling as well as the physical symptoms they may experience as they get close to the edge of a high place, such as stepping out onto a balcony or even looking out the window from a high floor of an apartment building. Individuals with natural environment type phobia typically avoid the situation that they fear or endure it with extreme anxiety and distress. For someone with height phobia, for example, the situations avoided may range from stepping on a chair or a low step on a ladder to visiting a friend who lives on a high floor of a building. Natural environment type phobias have been associated with significant interference in life activities as well as reduced quality of life. For example, one study that examined a sample of children and adolescents found that those with natural environment type phobia had significantly lower levels of life satisfaction than did those with an animal phobia. Studies that look at symptom clusters across the different phobia types have generally found that natural environment type phobias and situational type phobias cluster together. The two phobia types share a number of core features, including fear that is focused broadly on an environment or situation versus more discretely on a specific trigger, such as a needle in blood-injection-injury type phobia or a dog in animal type phobia.

Altogether, the prevalence of natural environment type phobia ranges from 8.9% to 11.6% (LeBeau et al., 2010) and is similar to that seen in situational type phobia. The most common natural environment type phobia is fear of heights. Water and storm phobias are less common but are higher in children and adolescents. Onset of natural environment phobia ranges from childhood to early adolescence (6–13 years old); however, it can occur at any age. Females are more likely to have a natural environment type phobia than males. However, among males who report a specific phobia, height phobia is the most common. Individuals with natural environment type phobia often have other psychological disorders as well. The most common co-occurring conditions include other phobias, other anxiety disorders, and depression.

As with other phobias, the treatment of choice for natural environment type specific phobia is cognitive behavioral therapy emphasizing *in vivo* exposure. The exact combination of treatment strategies utilized will depend on the individual characteristics of the phobia. It may be difficult to create exposures for an individual who has a storm phobia, as storms are relatively infrequent and unpredictable. Thus virtual reality may be incorporated as well as exposure to video and audio clips of storms. Height phobia is treated most typically with a combination of *in vivo* exposure and cognitive therapy. If an individual's fear is focused on anxiety symptoms in the phobic situation, then incorporation of interoceptive exposure strategies may be beneficial.

Randi E. McCabe

See also: Cognitive Behavioral Therapy; Cognitive Therapy; DSM-5; Exposure, Interoceptive; Exposure, *In Vivo*; Exposure Treatment; Phobia, Animal Type; Phobia, Blood-Injection-Injury Type; Phobia, Other Type; Phobia, Situational Type; Phobia, Specific; Virtual Reality Treatment

Further Reading

LeBeau, Richard T., Glenn, Daniel, Liao, Betty, Wittchen, Hans-Ulrich, Beesdo-Baum, Katja, Ollendick, Thomas, & Craske, Michelle G. (2010). Specific phobia: A review of DSM-IV specific phobia and preliminary recommendations for DSM-V. *Depression and Anxiety, 27*, 148–167.

Phobia, Other Type

Like all specific phobias, "other type" phobias are diagnostically classified by a marked and persistent fear of a clearly discernable stimulus for at least six months. Usually, this fear is out of proportion to the actual threat of danger or harm. Importantly, intense fear of a particular object or situation is diagnosed as a phobia only if the fear causes marked distress or impairment. Phobias that fall under the other type category are not easily classified by the four other phobia categories (animal type, natural environmental type, blood-injection-injury type, and situational type). Technically, one can develop a phobia for any stimulus, and there are many online lists that document unusual phobias (e.g., "porphyrophobia," the fear of the color purple). More common other type phobias include the fear of choking or vomiting and, in children, fears of costumed characters and loud noises. Some other less common phobias of this type include heliophobia (fear of sunlight) or pyrophobia (fear of fire). Usually, the excessive fear associated with the phobia leads to avoidance of the feared object or situation or else enduring it with intense distress. In some cases, this avoidance may contribute to actual functional impairment. For example, someone who has a phobia of contracting an illness may avoid any contact with other people, leading to social isolation and/or impairment in vocational functioning.

In general, it is estimated by the National Institute of Mental Health that phobias have a lifetime prevalence of 8.7%—18.1% of the population. Because of the wide variety of other type specific phobias, no prevalence data for this subtype are available. Onset of phobias can occur at any age, but more typically occurs during childhood or adolescence. Theories about the etiology of specific other type phobias include both biological and learning perspectives. Studies investigating the genetic contribution of specific phobias have shown that an individual who has a family member with a specific phobia is at increased risk of developing the disorder, and the pattern of phobia types is similar within families. There is also support for learning history involving various pathways (e.g., a traumatic incident with the feared object or situation or through observational learning) in the development of phobias. For example, a child may develop a fear of dolls if his or her parent demonstrates irrational fear around dolls. Alternatively, a traumatic experience with a seemingly benign object or stimulus (e.g., a popping balloon) may lead to a future phobic response when faced with the object.

Treatment for other type specific phobias is highly effective. In cognitive behavioral therapy, *in vivo* exposure of the feared stimulus is used to gradually introduce the stimulus and allow natural learning to occur (i.e., one learns that the perceived threat of the feared object or situation does not exist or is not as great as one thought). In time, with repeated exposures and learning, fear decreases and the individual is no longer motivated to avoid the feared object or situation. Pharmacotherapy is not considered to be a treatment of choice for specific phobias of any type.

Sheryl M. Green and Angela M. Lachowski

See also: Phobia, Specific; Phobia Types

Further Reading

Antony, Martin, M., & Swinson, Richard P. (2000). *Phobic disorders and panic in adults: A guide to assessment and treatment.* Washington, DC: American Psychological Association.

Phobia, School

School phobia, also known as school refusal, is seen across the anxiety disorders. Significant school refusal occurs in approximately 5% of youth, with prevalence higher in adolescents than in younger children. Youth with school refusal either avoid school completely or attend school but with subtle avoidance and distress. Children who refuse school typically exhibit tearfulness and/or oppositional behavior on school mornings, numerous somatic complaints (e.g., stomach aches and headaches), and difficulty falling asleep at night. If they go to school, they frequently visit the school nurse or counselor and often ask to go home early. School performance and social relationships are impacted by school refusal.

It is essential for clinicians to understand why youth fear or avoid school because there is much variability from child to child. In clinical practice, the majority of children who cannot attend school have *separation anxiety disorder*. These children have a very difficult time separating from their parents and are distressed to be away from them during the school day. They worry that something will happen to their parents (e.g., a car accident) or to themselves (e.g., a kidnapping) when they are apart. A child with separation anxiety typically asks his or her parents numerous questions about where they will be during the day, what the pick-up arrangements are at the end of the day (even if they are the same every day), and seeks a great deal of reassurance that everyone will be "okay" when they are apart. Children with separation anxiety also worry about being unable to cope with their anxiety independently if they are not with their parents.

Other children fear and avoid school due to *specific phobias*. It is very common to see children with vomit phobia refuse school. These children worry about contracting illnesses from other kids at school, the social implications of vomiting at school, and whether anyone will help them if they were to get sick. Although less common, other specific phobias can also interfere with school (e.g., fear of mascots, fear of loud noises).

Other anxiety disorders can also lead to school refusal, including obsessive-compulsive disorder, social anxiety disorder, and generalized anxiety disorder. For children with these diagnoses, school refusal is often brought on by a particular trigger like a class presentation (in the case of a child with social anxiety disorder) or a challenging test (in the case of a child with generalized anxiety).

Treatment for school refusal involves working collaboratively with the family, the therapist, and school personnel, with the goal being a complete return to school. Children are taught cognitive techniques, particularly with respect to having confidence in their own ability to cope when apart from their parents. Safety behaviors, such as visiting the school nurse, frequent calling and texting with parents, and reassurance seeking, are gradually eliminated. Behavioral strategies are used to rework the morning routine so that children begin their day calmly instead of riddled by anxiety. Children are also taught cognitive and behavioral skills to help them reduce their anxiety during the school day without needing to rely on parents or other adults.

Deborah Roth Ledley

See also: Behavior Therapy; Childhood, Phobias in; Cognitive Therapy; Emetophobia (Fear of Vomiting); Test Anxiety

Further Reading

Kearney, Christopher A., & Albano, Anne Marie. (2007). *When children refuse school: A cognitive-behavioral therapy approach. Therapist Guide.* New York: Oxford University Press.

Phobia, Situational Type

A *phobia* refers to a circumscribed fear of a specific situation or stimulus, which is diagnosed as a specific phobia according to the *Diagnostic and Statistical Manual of Mental Disorders*, fifth edition. There are five different types of specific phobia: animal, natural environment, blood-injection-injury, other, and situational. These types vary in terms of their age of onset, gender differences in prevalence, and other features. Individuals with situational type phobia fear specific situations such as flying in an airplane, driving or riding as a passenger in a car, taking public transportation, going over bridges or through tunnels, and being in enclosed places. The focus of an individual's fear in a particular situation may vary, although the majority report a fear of danger or harm. For example, a phobia of flying may be associated with fears of crashing, having anxiety symptoms, or feeling trapped. Individuals with a situational type phobia typically avoid the situation that they fear, or endure it with extreme anxiety and distress. They may also engage in various safety behaviors to cope with their anxiety. For example, a person who has a phobia of flying but must take a flight for work may manage anxiety by drinking heavily. Studies that look at symptom clusters across the different phobia types have generally found that situational type phobias and natural environment type phobias cluster together. The two phobia types share a number of core features, including fear that is focused broadly on a situation or environment versus more discretely on a specific trigger, such as a needle in blood-injection-injury type phobia or a dog in animal type phobia.

The prevalence of situational type phobia ranges from 5.2% to 8.4% and is similar to that seen in natural environment type phobia. With a later onset than the other specific phobia types, situational type phobia typically begins in the teenage years to early adulthood (13–21 years). However, onset may occur at any age. Females are more likely to have a situational type phobia than males. The presence of a situational type phobia is associated with significant impairment and may interfere with daily activities, social and leisure activities, as well as role obligations (e.g., work or school). Individuals with situational type phobia often have other psychological disorders as well. The most common co-occurring conditions include other phobias, mood disorders, substance use disorders, and panic attacks.

The treatment of choice for situational type specific phobia is cognitive behavioral therapy emphasizing *in vivo* exposure. The exact combination of treatment strategies utilized will depend on the phobic situation. For example, *in vivo* exposure combined with cognitive therapy is used for the treatment of driving phobia. For flying phobia, virtual reality may be incorporated. For fear of enclosed places (i.e., claustrophobia), the addition of cognitive strategies and interoceptive exposure is beneficial. Medications are not considered a first-line treatment for situational type phobias. However, in some instances they may be beneficial. For example, an individual with claustrophobia who needs to receive an MRI (a brain scan procedure that involves being confined in a small space) but is unable to do so because of extreme anxiety may benefit from taking an anxiolytic medication just prior to the procedure. Although this will help the individual undergo the diagnostic test, it is not a long-term treatment strategy.

Randi E. McCabe

See also: Cognitive Behavioral Therapy; Cognitive Therapy; DSM-5; Exposure, Interoceptive; Exposure, *In Vivo;* Exposure Treatment; Phobia, Animal Type; Phobia, Blood-Injection-Injury Type; Phobia, Natural Environment Type; Phobia, Other Type; Phobia, Specific; Virtual Reality Exposure

Further Reading

LeBeau, Richard T., Glenn, Daniel, Liao, Betty, Wittch, Hans-Ulrich, Beesdo-Baum, Katja, Ollendick, Thomas, & Craske, Michelle G. (2010). Specific phobia: A review of DSM-IV specific phobia and preliminary recommendations for DSM-V. *Depression and Anxiety, 27*, 148–167.

Phobia, Specific

Specific phobia is an anxiety disorder that is characterized by marked fear or anxiety about a specific object or situation, such as flying, driving, heights, enclosed spaces, animals, injections, or blood. Although some fear and discomfort to novel or frightening stimuli is normal, intense fear that is distressing and interferes with an individual's day-to-day functioning may meet criteria for a diagnosis of specific phobia. Specific phobias cluster into five subtypes, and are associated with a range of physiological, cognitive, and behavioral features.

Although fear and anxiety have been noted in literature since the time of the ancient Greek philosophers, the diagnosis of simple phobia (a precursor to specific phobia) did not appear in the American Psychiatric Association's *Diagnostic and Statistical Manual of Mental Disorders* until the publication of the third edition (DSM-III) in 1980 (before that, the terms *phobic reaction* and *phobic neurosis* were used in DSM-I and DSM-II, respectively). In the DSM-III and the DSM-III-R, the term *simple phobia* referred to an excessive fear of an object or situation that was not better accounted for by another phobic disorder (e.g., agoraphobia, social phobia). The term *specific phobia* first appeared in the diagnostic nomenclature with the publication of the DSM-IV in 1994, with the name change intended to better describe the circumscribed nature of the fear. Included in the DSM-IV for the first time were the five phobia subtypes associated with distinct demographic and physiological characteristics. There have been few changes to the diagnostic criteria since that time.

Etiology

The etiology of specific phobia is thought to involve an interaction of biological, psychological, and environmental factors. Specific phobia tends to run in families; however, the subtype of phobia is often of a different category than that of the first-degree biological relative. In addition, there is preliminary evidence suggesting specific chromosomal regions and personality factors (e.g., neuroticism) are associated with specific phobia. However, the majority of evidence points to a stronger contribution of environmental influences in the etiology of specific phobia, such as a traumatic experience with the phobic stimulus or observational or instructional learning from others.

Diagnostic Features

According to the fifth edition of the *Diagnostic and Statistical Manual of Mental Disorders* (DSM-5; American Psychiatric Association, 2013), a specific phobia is characterized by intense fear or anxiety in anticipation of or immediately upon encountering a specific feared object or situation. In children who may not be able to articulate their fears as clearly as adults, the phobia may be expressed by crying, tantrums, freezing, or clinging. As a result, the feared object or situation is actively avoided or, when the stimulus cannot be avoided, it is endured with intense distress. This leads to significant impairment in everyday functioning or considerable distress about having the fear.

In addition, the fear must be out of proportion to the actual threat posed by the object or situation. Although some people, including young children, may not readily acknowledge that their fear is unreasonable, most people admit that their fear is excessive compared to that of others. Despite this awareness, people with a specific phobia have difficulty inhibiting their fear response. Finally, the fears must be persistent. To distinguish specific phobia from normal, occasional, or transient fears, the anxiety or avoidance must persist for at least six months.

There are five subtypes of specific phobia: animal type (e.g., dogs, spiders, snakes), natural environment type (e.g., storms, heights), situational type (e.g., flying, enclosed spaces), blood-injection-injury (BII) type (e.g., injections, surgery, blood), and a residual category, other type, for fears that do not fit into one of the other categories, such as fears of choking or vomiting. These subtypes tend to differ in a variety of ways, including age of onset, gender differences, focus of the fear, and type of phobic reaction. For example, animal and BII phobia subtypes have an earlier age of onset compared to phobias of the situational type, which tend to begin later, around 13 years of age (Becker et al., 2007). Some subtypes, including animal and situational phobias, are more common among women than men, whereas BII phobias are equally common across genders.

Specific phobia is also described in other classification systems, such as the *International Statistical Classification of Diseases and Related Health Problems*, 10th Revision (ICD-10). Although the conceptualization of specific phobia in the ICD-10 is largely consistent with the DSM-5, the diagnostic criteria are not as clearly defined. The most notable difference is the inclusion of the term *isolated* in parentheses within the disorder title in ICD-10 to indicate that the phobic trigger is restricted to specific stimuli.

Associated Features

Specific phobias tend to be associated with unique physiological, cognitive, and behavioral features. While the predominant presentation of specific phobias involves focus on the danger posed by a phobic object or situation, individuals with specific phobias also tend to report more fear of internal physical sensations (e.g., racing heart, dizziness, hot flashes, or chills) compared to nonanxious individuals (Wheaton et al., 2012). Further, some subtypes are characterized by greater fear of physical sensations. For example, people with situational phobias report more fear of hyperventilation than other phobia subtypes, and individuals with BII phobias are more likely to focus on internal sensations, such as light-headedness, faintness, and disgust. It is not uncommon for individuals to have a panic attack in the phobic situation; however, BII phobia is the only subtype associated with a fainting response (Antony, Brown, & Barlow, 1997), occurring in up to 75% of cases. The fainting response is caused by a vasovagal reaction, in which there is an initial increase in blood pressure followed by a rapid decrease in heart rate and blood pressure and, consequently, an increased likelihood of fainting.

Individuals with specific phobias also tend to demonstrate characteristic biases in information processing. For example, people with a specific phobia show enhanced attention for fear-relevant information compared to nonanxious individuals. That is, they are hypervigilant for signs of threat. They also tend to misinterpret uncertain cues as threatening and have difficulty disengaging from signs of threat. For example, an individual with a spider phobia may scan a room upon entering, quickly detect a dark spot, which he or she may perceive to be a spider, and have difficulty diverting his or her attention from that spot. Consequently, these cognitive biases are thought to enhance and maintain specific phobias.

One of the diagnostic features of specific phobias is active avoidance of the feared stimuli. Avoidance can be overt, such as preventing or minimizing contact with the feared object or situation (e.g., avoiding important medical tests for fear of injections, taking the stairs instead of elevators for fear of enclosed spaces). Individuals may escape from a fearful situation, such as leave the room as soon as they spot a spider, which reduces anxiety and, therefore, reinforces avoidance behavior. Avoidance can also be subtle and might entail the use of safety behaviors, distraction, or family accommodation. Safety behaviors are unhelpful coping strategies that are intended to reduce one's anxiety and prevent some feared outcome from occurring. Common safety behaviors include alcohol and drug use to decrease anxiety in the feared situation; wearing protective clothing to prevent contact with feared animals, insects, or objects; or driving overly slowly to avoid a car accident. Individuals with specific phobias may attempt to divert their attention to distract themselves from the feared stimulus, or use some other form of mental distraction, such as thinking about pleasant or neutral thoughts, to reduce their anxiety in the feared situation. Family accommodation refers to having a family member, friend, or caregiver perform tasks that the individual fears, allowing the individual to effectively avoid the feared situation. In many cases, the avoidance behaviors are pervasive and long-standing, severely limiting the activities and lifestyles of those with specific phobias. Consequently, they may not experience anxiety in their day-to-day lives; however, they may experience significant limitations in their physical, social, and occupational functioning, and quality of life.

Treatment

Psychological interventions are considered the treatments of choice for specific phobia. In particular, the majority of individuals who receive exposure-based therapy for their phobia experience significant improvements in their symptoms, often in as little as a single session. Exposure therapy involves having the client confront the feared object or situation in a systematic and controlled manner for long enough to learn that the feared consequences do not occur, and that they can tolerate the fear and anxiety. Variations of exposure therapy have also been found to be effective, including virtual reality exposure therapy for flying and height phobias, and applied tension for BII phobias. Despite the frequency with which anxiolytic medications are prescribed for specific phobias, there is no evidence that medications are effective in the treatment of specific phobias and they may lead to relapse upon discontinuation.

Heather K. Hood and Martin M. Antony

See also: Anxiety and Related Disorders; Classification; Differential Diagnosis; Etiology; Fear; Information Processing Biases; Lifespan, Phobias across the; Phobia Types; Phobias, Diagnosis of

Further Reading

American Psychiatric Association (2013). *Diagnostic and statistical manual of mental disorders* (5th ed.). Arlington, VA: American Psychiatric Publishing.

Antony, Martin M., Brown, Timothy A., & Barlow, David H. (1997). Heterogeneity among specific phobia types in DSM-IV. *Behaviour Research and Therapy, 35,* 1089–1100.

Becker, Eni S., Rinck, Mike, Türke, Veneta, Kause, Petra, Goodwin, Renee, Neumer, Simon, & Margraf, Jürgen. (2007). Epidemiology of specific phobia subtypes: Findings from the Dresden Mental Health Study. *European Psychiatry, 22,* 69–74.

Davis, Thompson E., Ollendick, Thomas H., & Öst, Lars-Göran. (Eds.) (2012). *Intensive one-session treatment of specific phobias*. New York, NY: Springer.

Wheaton, Michael G., Deacon, Brett J., McGrath, Patrick B., Berman, Noah C., & Abramowitz, Jonathan S. (2012). Dimensions of anxiety sensitivity in the anxiety disorders: Evaluation of the ASI-3. *Journal of Anxiety Disorders, 26,* 401–408.

CLINICAL PHOBIA: A CASE EXAMPLE

Jennifer, a 23-year-old college student, had been afraid of birds for as long as she could remember. When she was very young, her parents would take her to feed ducks at a pond near their house. During one of these occasions, Jennifer was holding a bag of bread, not realizing that it would attract the ducks. The ducks began following her and acting aggressively. They surrounded her and honked at her loudly. Jennifer was extremely frightened during this experience and began screaming for her parents. Eventually, she dropped the bag of bread and the ducks flocked around it, leaving her alone. Although she was not physically injured, she was terribly upset by the ordeal.

Since experiencing that event, Jennifer made every effort to avoid birds. She refused to go to the pond with her family and would hide behind her parents whenever she saw pigeons while walking on the street. Jennifer believed that if a bird got too close, other birds would begin to flock toward her and peck at her body. She was also concerned that this would make her so anxious that she would faint, leaving her unable to protect herself. As she grew older and began going places on her own, she would worry about encountering birds en route to her destinations. For example, Jennifer refused to go to places in the city where pigeons tended to gather. This fear of birds increasingly limited the places that she would go to and led her to continuously decline invitations to go downtown with her friends.

Although she had been afraid of birds for most of her childhood and adolescence, Jennifer only realized how problematic her fear had become when she and her friends went on a trip to Florida. When she arrived at the beachfront hotel where they were staying, she instantly noticed the seagulls that were walking around on the sand. She became upset and refused to go down to the beach. With her friends' persistent encouragement, she was able to go down the next day. However, she constantly scanned her surroundings, checking to see how close the birds were. Jennifer refused to sit down, explaining that she needed to make sure that the birds did not approach. Whenever a bird came within 20 feet of her, she panicked and ran toward the hotel. Her friends laughed at her and were embarrassed by her dramatic reactions. Jennifer returned to the hotel exhausted and upset. She felt humiliated and guilty about spending money on a trip that she could not enjoy.

When Jennifer returned home, she began noticing that her fear of birds had spiraled out of control. She found herself constantly scanning for pigeons in the downtown area where she went to school. Eventually, she began skipping certain classes because she noticed that birds would congregate outside of specific buildings. At the end of the semester, having failed two classes due to her fear of encountering birds, Jennifer decided to seek out therapy for her bird phobia.

Philippe Shnaider and Irena Milosevic

Phobia Types

The *Diagnostic and Statistical Manual of Mental Disorders*, fifth edition (DSM-5) categorizes specific phobias into five distinct types. These types include *animal* (e.g., spiders, snakes, fish), *natural environment* (e.g., heights, water, darkness), *blood-injection-injury* (e.g., needles, seeing blood, invasive medical procedures), and *situational* (e.g., flying, elevators, driving). Additionally, an *other* type is included for fears of objects or situations not captured by the predefined categories (e.g., choking, vomiting, clowns). In order to meet diagnostic criteria for any of these phobias, it is necessary that the individual experience excessive anxiety in response to the feared object/situation as well as distress or impairment in important areas of functioning. Typically, individuals with this disorder fear more than one specific object or situation, with approximately 75% meeting diagnostic criteria for multiple specific phobias (American Psychiatric Association, 2013). Phobias in a given subtype are more likely to co-occur within the same individual. That is, someone with one animal phobia is more likely to have a second phobia of an animal, as opposed to one of the other phobic categories.

Despite the relatively small number of phobia categories described by the DSM-5, various authors and sources have identified hundreds of names for phobias of specific objects and situations, such as astraphobia (fear of thunder and lightning), aviophobia (fear of flying), and ptophobia (fear of falling). Although the identification of such a vast number of phobias has been a source of public intrigue, it has been argued that such descriptions serve little utility in clinical or research settings given that the number of commonly observed fears is relatively small. Various studies have demonstrated that phobias of animals, heights, elevators, closed spaces, driving, and blood-injection-injury (BII) have the highest prevalence rates.

The DSM-5 phobia types were developed based on evidence suggesting that meaningful differences exist between categories. Research has shown that specific phobia types can be differentiated based on prevalence, age of onset, male-to-female ratio, socioeconomic status, comorbidity patterns, distress in daily living, focus of apprehension, and physiological and neurological response patterns (Antony & Barlow, 2002). For example, although specific phobias are generally more common among women, certain types tend not to show this gender bias (e.g., flying). Similarly, relative to other phobia types and anxiety disorders more generally, BII phobias are characterized by a distinct physiological response. Many individuals with BII phobia experience vasovagal syncope (a rapid drop in heart rate and blood pressure), which results in fainting when exposed to the phobic stimulus. Such a physiological response is unique to this phobia, and fainting is not observed in the other phobia types. Situational specific phobias have also been differentiated based on their similarities to agoraphobia as there is substantial overlap in the types of situations that are feared across these disorders (e.g., driving, elevators, enclosed spaces).

The existing classification of phobias has been criticized by a number of authors. Although markers differentiating the categories have been identified, a relatively small number of studies have specifically focused on phobia subtypes and the identified distinctions have not emerged across all published studies. Furthermore, much of the existing research has suffered from methodological problems (e.g., inconsistencies in which phobias are included). Certain phobias are also challenging to classify as they do not clearly fit into any of the defined categories. For example, one could argue that fears of enclosed spaces could be considered a situational or a natural environment phobia. Similarly, fears of going to the dentist could be subsumed under BII phobia or may better fit into the "other" type. Finally, from a clinical perspective, identifying the precise focus of fear is more informative than providing a general subtype category. Knowing that someone has a fear of tunnels or a fear of flying is more useful in terms of case conceptualization and treatment planning than is knowing that someone has a specific phobia, situational type.

Cognitive behavioral therapy, with a focus on *in vivo* exposure to feared objects and situations, is considered the empirically supported treatment of choice for all phobias. Regardless of phobia type, most individuals who engage in this form of treatment demonstrate substantial reductions in fear responding.

Dubravka L. Gavric

See also: Age of Onset; Agoraphobia (Fear of Panic-Like Symptoms); Astraphobia (Fear of Thunder and Lightning); Aviophobia (Fear of Flying); Cognitive Behavioral Therapy; DSM-5; Exposure, *In Vivo*; Exposure Treatment; Fainting Response; Fear of Driving; Phobia, Animal Type; Phobia, Blood-Injection-Injury Type; Phobia, Natural Environment Type; Phobia, Other Type; Phobia, Specific; Phobias, Causes of; Phobias, Diagnosis of; Ptophobia (Fear of Falling)

Further Reading

American Psychiatric Association. (2013). *Diagnostic and statistical manual of mental disorders* (5th ed.). Arlington, VA: American Psychiatric Publishing.

Antony, Martin M., & Barlow, David H. (2002). Specific phobia. In D. H. Barlow (Ed.), *Anxiety and its disorders: The nature and treatment of anxiety and panic* (2nd ed., pp. 380–417). New York, NY: Guilford.

Phobias, Assessment of

Psychological assessment has a number of important functions, including providing a diagnosis, measuring severity and clinical features, case conceptualization (understanding the factors involved in the development and maintenance of the disorder), treatment planning, and monitoring of treatment progress and outcome. Consequently, assessment typically involves a number of components, including semistructured interviews, self-report questionnaires, behavioral assessment (e.g., behavioral approach tests, diaries, behavioral observation), and other strategies (e.g., skills assessment, psychophysiological assessment), when relevant.

One goal of assessment is to establish a diagnosis for the individual's presenting problem. A diagnosis facilitates communication about the individual's symptoms and enables the selection of treatments that are most likely to be helpful. Semistructured interviews are often used for the diagnosis of psychological disorders, including specific phobias. Semistructured interviews provide clinicians with a standard list of questions to assess the diagnostic criteria for psychological disorders while also providing clinicians the flexibility to ask their own follow-up questions based on their clinical judgment and to clarify answers provided by patients. Two widely used semistructured interviews for the diagnosis of phobias (and other psychological disorders) are the Structured Clinical Interview for DSM-5 Disorders (First, Williams, Karg, & Spitzer, 2014) and the Anxiety and Related Disorders Interview Schedule for DSM-5 (Brown & Barlow, 2014).

The assessment process also provides a basis for case conceptualization and treatment planning. In order to better understand the nature of the individual's difficulties, clinicians identify the cognitive (e.g., "The dog will attack me," "I will faint if I get a needle"), physiological (e.g., sweating, heart racing, rapid breathing), and behavioral (e.g., avoidance) symptoms that individuals experience when exposed to the feared object or situation. In addition to assessing the presence of overt avoidance, clinicians also assess the use of "safety behaviors," defined as subtle avoidance strategies that individuals may use to prevent harm or manage fear. For instance, individuals with a phobia of spiders may avoid wearing shorts to prevent spiders from touching their skin. Clinicians also inquire about factors that increase or decrease the individual's fear of the object or situation (e.g., small vs. large dogs, driving alone vs. accompanied). Given that the treatment of specific phobias involves gradual exposure to feared objects or situations, this information is helpful in identifying potential situations for exposure practice.

In addition to semistructured interviews, self-report questionnaires also provide information about the severity of the fear, avoidance behaviors, and associated cognitions. A number of different questionnaires have been developed that focus on various specific phobias, including snakes, spiders, dogs, heights, and dentists. The questionnaires typically consist of statements that describe various cognitions, behaviors, and fears related to a specific object or situation and ask patients to rate the degree to which each statement is consistent with their experiences.

In some cases, especially following years of avoidance, individuals may have difficulty describing their responses to a feared object or situation. In these cases, behavioral assessment methods (e.g., behavioral observation, diaries) may be useful. One such method is the behavioral approach test or BAT. BATs involve facing a feared object or situation (e.g., moving as close as possible to a spider, in the case of spider phobia) and measuring a number of relevant responses (e.g., self-reported fear level, ability to approach the feared object, anxiety-provoking predictions). In some cases, an individual's psychophysiological response (e.g., heart rate) may also be measured. Specific phobias may also be associated with skills deficits, especially if the patient has been avoiding the situation for an extended period of time. Therefore, clinicians also assess for any skills deficits that may be associated with the specific phobia. For instance, a person with a driving phobia may undergo an assessment with a professional driving instructor to determine if there are any skills deficits. Any identified skills deficits are addressed either prior to initiating treatment or concurrently with treatment.

The assessment may also involve asking about an individual's treatment history, including the types of treatments received, outcome following treatment, and any barriers or challenges that were experienced. This information provides the clinician with insight regarding both helpful and unhelpful strategies that had been tried previously, as well as potential challenges that might arise during treatment. For instance, if during a previous course of treatment the patient struggled with completing homework between therapy sessions then the clinician might place a greater emphasis on planning between-session homework exercises.

A final purpose of the assessment process is to monitor treatment progress and outcome. This can be done in a number of ways. First, the individual and clinician can identify changes in the individual's fear and symptoms by examining changes in self-report questionnaires completed throughout treatment. As well, a BAT can be completed at different points throughout treatment, and any changes in self-reported fear as well as the individual's ability to approach the feared object or situation can be noted. It is important to monitor treatment progress and outcome as a lack of progress may suggest the need to modify the current treatment approach. Moreover, highlighting progress can motivate individuals to continue facing fear-provoking situations.

Matilda E. Nowakowski and Martin M. Antony

See also: Anxiety Disorders Interview Schedule; Behavioral Approach Test; Phobia, Specific; Safety Behavior; Structured Clinical Interview for DSM Disorders

Further Reading

Brown, Timothy A., & Barlow, David H. (2014). *Anxiety and Related Disorders Interview Schedule for DSM-5 (ADIS-5)—Adult version.* New York, NY: Oxford University Press.

First, Michael B., Williams, Janet B. W., Karg, Rhonda S., & Spitzer, Robert L. (2014). *Structured Clinical Interview for DSM-5 Disorders—Patient Edition (SCID-5).* New York, NY: Biometrics Research Department, New York State Psychiatric Institute.

Hood, Heather K., & Antony, Martin M. (2012). Evidence-based assessment and treatment of specific phobias in adults. In Thompson E. Davis, Thomas H. Ollendick, & Lars-Göran Öst (Eds.), *Intensive one-session treatment of specific phobias* (pp. 19–42). New York, NY: Springer.

McCabe, Randi E., Ashbaugh, Andrea R., & Antony, Martin M. (2010). Specific and social phobias. In Martin M. Antony & David H. Barlow (Eds.), *Handbook of assessment and treatment planning psychological disorders* (2nd ed., pp. 186–223). New York, NY: Guilford Press.

Phobias, Causes of

Over the years, progress has been made regarding the underlying etiology of phobias and more specifically, theories have been proposed to explain how individuals, regardless of the phobia, acquire such fears. Prominent among these explanations is the behavioral viewpoint that regardless of the type of phobia the individual has acquired (e.g., social, specific, or agoraphobia), phobias are predominately caused by learning. However, other researchers suggest that a combination of multiple factors, such as behavioral, environmental, and genetic influences, most accurately describe the development of anxiety and phobic disorders.

Behavioral theories have suggested that phobias are acquired through one of four ways: conditioning, vicarious learning, through the transmission of fear-inducing information and through no prior association (Rachman, 1990). Conditioning suggests that when a previously neutral stimulus is continually paired with a pain-producing or a fear-producing event, both become closely associated in the individual's mind. This association then causes the once-neutral stimulus to evoke the same pain or fearful response in the individual as initially caused by the fear or pain-inducing event, in turn causing it to become a conditioned fear response. Conditioning of fears has been demonstrated in a well-known study completed by John B. Watson and Rosalie Rayner (1920) in which they conditioned a young child to fear a white rat (a previously neutral stimulus). They did so by continually exposing the child to a loud noise (fear-producing event) while the child was in the presence of the rat. The continual pairing of the noise and the rat conditioned the child in such a way that eventually just presenting the child with the rat evoked the same fear response that the loud noise had initially produced.

The strength of the conditioned fear response is determined by the number of times the neutral stimulus has been paired with the fear or pain-producing event and the intensity of the fear or pain experienced by the individual. Therefore, with more pairings and more intense responses being generated, stronger fear responses are acquired. Conditioning, as a cause of phobias, has been attributed to the development and acquisition of many fears, including those associated with specific phobia, social anxiety disorder (social phobia) as well as agoraphobia.

Another way in which individuals may acquire phobias is through vicarious learning or modeling. In this way, individuals who observe other people enduring an intense fearful situation or observe others fearing certain objects or situations may develop similar fears. These fears are developed through observational experiences that have provided the individual with negative information about the object or event. For example, a young boy whose mother is afraid of doctors and is frequently expressing those fears may develop a fear of doctors himself just by observing his mother's fearful behavior. Further, related to social fears, a child whose parents continually display fear of being negatively evaluated at parties or while asking others for help may develop similar social fears. Vicarious learning or modeling has been found to play an influential role in the acquisition of specific phobias as well as social anxiety disorder but appears to be less relevant for the acquisition of agoraphobia.

The third way in which fears may be behaviorally acquired is through the transmission of fear-inducing information. An individual who is given information that may contain a possible threat or is given information that could be misinterpreted as being threatening may develop a phobia as a result. For example, a child who is told that aggressive dogs may bite or otherwise attack may develop a fear of all dogs just through the transmission of such negative information. In comparison to those fears acquired through conditioning and vicarious learning, fears acquired through the transmission of fear-inducing information often tend to be less severe and tend to be more prevalent among specific phobias (e.g., animal phobias) rather than agoraphobia or social anxiety disorder.

One final point with respect to these aforementioned behavioral models concerns avoidance. Once an individual has acquired a fear response in relation to a certain object or situation, a secondary fear response typically emerges. The individual begins to adopt specific behavioral strategies (i.e., avoidance) in order to successfully reduce the fear and the anxiety associated with the fear. These behavioral strategies increase in prevalence as the fear increases in strength. For example, if a child has been bitten or scared by a dog, that child may now fear dogs and the secondary fear response will likely be to avoid all dogs or places where dogs may be present (e.g., parks, neighbors' houses who have dogs) and to escape from any situations where there are unexpected encounters with dogs (e.g., going back in the house once neighbors approach with their dog). This avoidance of dogs then serves to perpetuate the fear of dogs. Choosing to avoid rather than approach the feared object or event is a common reaction, resulting in missed opportunities to learn skills to handle such fears.

Finally, some individuals may develop a fear response without any prior learned association with the object or event. Further, some phobias (e.g., fear of animals, heights, and darkness) are much more prevalent than other phobias, and the reason for such increased prevalence and lack of associative learning may speak more to evolutionary factors rather than behavioral explanations. In support of this, some individuals report no recollection as to when or how their fear may have developed. It has then been suggested that individuals may have a biological predisposition to develop certain fears, an idea that has been referred to as *preparedness*. Such a predisposition stems from the fact that individuals may be innately susceptible to acquire certain fears (e.g., fear of snakes or fear of the dark), which in an evolutionary stance may threaten the individual's survival.

Preparedness can be seen in not only the development of specific phobias but also in the development of social anxiety disorder. Social anxiety has been argued to have evolved as a mechanism to help individuals deal with socially threatening situations (see Gilbert & Trower, 1990). From an evolutionary standpoint, situations that would have evoked social anxiety would have been deemed threatening to the ongoing survival of the individual. For instance, if individuals are biologically predisposed to fear angry faces, which from an evolutionary stance would favor increased survival, then certain individuals may be innately inclined to do so even in the absence of a learned association. Additionally, this type of predisposition would allow individuals to gauge which interactions are more likely to elicit approval and interest, thereby fulfilling a fundamental need to belong to social groups. However, taken to an extreme, this type of predisposition could result in excessive levels of social anxiety and therefore play a role in the acquisition of social anxiety disorder.

Phobic disorders tend to be prevalent within first-degree family members, suggesting that individuals may also be genetically predisposed to develop or acquire a phobia. Inherent in this supposition is that individuals may inherit a cognitive style that biases the way in which they perceive their surroundings. Specifically, individuals may inherit a tendency toward fearfulness or may have an innate tendency to see the world as being more threatening, which when combined with a fearful situation may result in the development of a phobia. Such cognitive biases may be more of a factor in the development of agoraphobia and social anxiety disorder than in the development of specific phobias. Further, genes responsible for the regulation of neurotransmitters (chemical messengers in the brain) may be, in part, responsible for the development of anxiety and phobic disorders. However, there has not been consensus as to which genes may be involved. It is important to note that rather than inheriting a specific anxiety or phobic disorder, individuals may be predisposed to some fundamental trait or temperament that contributes to the development of a spectrum of mental health problems. This perspective on heritability may, in part, account for why individuals who develop phobias also tend to suffer from other mental health problems. It is possible that some underlying trait may be partially responsible for the development of several related mental disorders.

Other biological factors that may influence the acquisition of anxiety and phobic disorders include dysfunctions within the nervous system. People with anxiety and phobic disorders tend to have an overactive autonomic nervous system (the part of the nervous system responsible for the activation and regulation of fear responses), reflected by physiological symptoms such as increased heart rate, blushing, and sweating. Through conditioning (i.e., continual pairing of the heightened fear response with a stimulus), individuals can erroneously learn to excessively fear previously neutral or mildly fearful stimuli (e.g., dentist, heights). An area of the brain that is particularly prominent in the fear response is the amygdala. The amygdala plays a key role in the perception of threatening stimuli and response to fear. By sending messages to other parts of the brain in response to threatening stimuli, the amygdala controls automatic responses to fear, such as increased heart rate and respiration. Through the use of neuroimaging studies, researchers have found that the amygdala appears to be overactive in a variety of anxiety disorders, including social anxiety disorder, agoraphobia, and specific phobias. For example, in one neuroimaging study, Irle and colleagues (2010) found that those with the generalized type of social anxiety disorder (i.e., the form of social phobia where most social situations are feared) had an amygdala that was, on average, 13% smaller than those of healthy controls. However, it is not clear whether hyperactivity and reduced size of the amygdala contribute to the development of anxiety and phobic disorders or if anxious symptoms lead to hyperactivity and reduced amygdala size.

One final important point to keep in mind with respect to the overall etiology of phobias is that not just one, but multiple influences (biological, cognitive, genetic, learning, etc.) appear to be at play, especially in more complex phobic disorders, such as agoraphobia and social anxiety disorder. Further, how phobic disorders develop may vary across individuals. Whereas one individual may develop a certain phobia primarily due to conditioning or vicarious learning, another individual may develop the same phobia due to a combination of environmental and genetic factors.

Nancy L. Kocovski, Rebecca A. Blackie, and Amanda J. Desnoyers

See also: Agoraphobia (Fear of Panic-Like Symptoms); Amygdala; Classical Conditioning; Evolution, Role of; Operant Conditioning; Phobia, Specific; Phobias, Genetics of; Preparedness Theory; Social Anxiety Disorder (Social Phobia); Temperament; Twin Studies; Watson, John B. (1878–1958)

Further Reading

Gilbert, Paul, & Trower, Peter. (1990). The evolution and manifestation of social anxiety. In W. Ray Crozier (Ed.), *Shyness and embarrassment: Perspectives from social psychology* (pp. 144–177). New York: NY: Cambridge University Press.

Irle, Eva, Ruhleder, Mirjana, Lange, Claudia, Seidler-Brandler, Ulrich, Salzer, Simone, Dechent, Peter, . . . Leichsenring, Falk. (2010). Reduced amygdalar and hippocampal size in adults with generalized social phobia. *Journal of Psychiatry and Neuroscience, 35,* 126–131.

Rachman, Stanley. (1990). The determinants and treatment of simple phobias. *Advanced Behavioural Research, 12,* 1–30.

Watson, John B., & Rayner, Rosalie. (1920). Conditioned emotional reaction. *Journal of Experimental Psychology, 3,* 1–14.

Phobias, Diagnosis of

Accurate diagnosis is a first step in effective treatment planning. To receive a diagnosis of specific phobia based on the *Diagnostic and Statistical Manual of Mental Disorders*, fifth edition (DSM-5; American Psychiatric Association, 2013), seven diagnostic criteria must be met: (1) the individual must experience intense fear or anxiety in response to a circumscribed object (e.g., snakes, needles) or situation (e.g., heights, driving); (2) the feared object or situation almost always triggers an immediate fear or anxiety reaction; (3) the feared object or situation is typically avoided or endured with intense fear or anxiety; (4) the fear or anxiety is out of proportion to the actual danger and is greater than what is typically experienced in the individual's sociocultural group; (5) the fear, anxiety, or avoidance are chronic, typically lasting at least six months; (6) the fear, anxiety, or avoidance are distressing to the individual or interfere with important life domains (e.g., work, social functioning); and (7) the fear, anxiety, and avoidance are not better explained by another disorder (e.g., avoidance of driving for fear of experiencing panic-like symptoms, as in agoraphobia).

The DSM-5 requires that the clinician specify the type of specific phobia, from among five options: (1) animal (e.g., spiders, mice, snakes), (2) natural environment (e.g., being near water, high places, storms), (3) blood-injection-injury (e.g., needles, blood, surgery), (4) situational (e.g., elevators, enclosed spaces, flying), or (5) other (e.g., vomiting, choking, clowns). Individuals may fear objects or situations from more than one type, in which case each relevant type would be specified as distinct phobias.

Although the DSM-5 diagnostic system is the most frequently used in North America, the World Health Organization's *International Classification of Diseases* (ICD-10; World Health Organization, 1993) is also used around the world. The ICD-10 diagnostic criteria for specific phobias (also called isolated phobias) are similar to those in the DSM-5, requiring fear or avoidance of a specific object or situation that is not included among those in the definition of agoraphobia or social phobia. As in the DSM-5, the ICD-10 includes five types of specific phobias, although the "natural environment" type from the DSM-5 is referred to as *nature-forces type* in the ICD-10.

Differentiating specific phobias from other mental disorders, a process known as differential diagnosis, can be challenging as phobias often share features with one another and with other disorders. In addition to identifying the specific feared objects or situations, a diagnosis requires an understanding of the underlying motivation for the fear or avoidance. For example, an individual may avoid air travel because of a specific phobia of flying (e.g., fear of an airplane crashing), another specific phobia such as heights or enclosed places, agoraphobia (e.g., fear of being unable to escape in the event of a panic attack), obsessive-compulsive disorder (OCD; e.g., fear of contamination), or generalized anxiety disorder (e.g., worry about travel-related risks such as lost luggage), to name a few.

Individuals sometimes experience panic attacks when faced with a feared object or situation. If panic attacks are recurrent and unexpected, a diagnosis of panic disorder may be warranted (if all of the required diagnostic criteria are met). However, if the panic attacks occur only when the individual is exposed to a specific object or situation, they may be a symptom of specific phobia. Agoraphobia may also be mistaken for a specific phobia of enclosed places for example, because both disorders can be associated with the same fear. However, in agoraphobia, fear occurs in a variety of situations in which escape might be difficult or in which the individual might experience panic-like, incapacitating, or embarrassing symptoms (i.e., not just enclosed places), whereas a specific phobia of enclosed places (i.e., claustrophobia) is limited to these situations only, although the focus of the fear is often on similar themes (e.g., suffocation, being unable to escape).

Specific phobia is not to be confused with social anxiety disorder (social phobia). In social anxiety disorder, the anxiety is focused on the possibility of being judged, embarrassed, or humiliated in social or evaluative situations. For example, an individual might avoid visiting the dentist either due to fear of negative evaluation by the dentist (e.g., social anxiety disorder) or due to fear of painful dental procedures (e.g., specific phobia of dentists). Generalized anxiety disorder (GAD) can sometimes be mistaken for multiple specific phobias. In GAD, individuals experience persistent and pervasive worry about a variety of events or situations, whereas individuals with specific phobias typically experience anxiety or fear only upon exposure (or anticipation of exposure) to the feared object. It can be similarly difficult to differentiate between a somatic symptom and related disorder (e.g., illness anxiety disorder) and a specific phobia of blood-injection-injury. If the focus of the anxiety is on having or acquiring a serious illness rather than fears concerning specific medical procedures, a diagnosis of illness anxiety disorder is likely more appropriate. OCD can appear to share features with specific phobias since both disorders are associated with fear and avoidance of situations and objects. Fears that are based on OCD-related themes (e.g., avoiding seeing or touching spiders for fear of contamination) would generally be seen as part of the individual's OCD, whereas fears related to non-OCD themes (e.g., general danger or disgust associated with spiders) would more likely receive a specific phobia diagnosis. Similarly, avoidance of food must be carefully assessed to distinguish between phobias of choking and vomiting versus other disorders (e.g., eating disorders).

It is also important to assess the individual's level of insight regarding the fear. Fear-related beliefs that are of delusional intensity (i.e., a firmly held unusual belief that persists despite obvious evidence to the contrary, such as a fear-related belief that dogs communicate with one another and are plotting to attack the individual) may be symptomatic of a schizophrenia spectrum or other psychotic disorder.

Understanding the course of the fear can also be important. For example, for an extreme fear of driving that begins after an auto accident, it is important to distinguish between specific phobia and posttraumatic stress disorder (PTSD). Both conditions are associated with fear and avoidance of potential threat cues, but PTSD is also associated with a variety of other symptoms (e.g., intrusion symptoms, mood disturbances, changes in reactivity and arousal) that are generally not seen in specific phobia.

When considering specific phobias in children, fear and anxiety may be expressed in different ways, including crying, tantrums, freezing, or clinging. In addition, special considerations should be taken when diagnosing specific phobias in older adults and in those with medical concerns that contribute to fear. For example, if an older adult avoids going out on icy days due to fear of falling, it is important to determine whether the fear is out of proportion to the actual risk of falling and the harm that could be caused by falling. If the risk is high, a diagnosis of specific phobia may not be warranted. Similarly, an individual with small veins might appropriately fear needles due to the pain and bruising experienced when having blood drawn. In these cases, it is important to identify whether the fear is out of proportion to the actual danger in the situation.

Reliability and validity of specific phobia diagnosis can be increased by using established semistructured interviews such as the Anxiety and Related Disorders Interview Schedule for DSM-5 (Brown & Barlow, 2014) and the Structured Clinical Interview for DSM-5 Disorders (First, Williams, Karg, & Spitzer, 2014).

Hanna McCabe-Bennett and Martin M. Antony

See also: Anxiety Disorders; Classification; Differential Diagnosis; Fear; Phobia, Specific; Phobia Types; Phobias, Assessment of

Further Reading

American Psychiatric Association (2013). *Diagnostic and statistical manual of mental disorders* (5th ed.). Arlington, VA: American Psychiatric Publishing.

Brown, Timothy A., & Barlow, David H. (2014). *Anxiety and related disorders interview schedule for DSM-5 (ADIS-5)—Adult version*. New York, NY: Oxford University Press.

First, Michael B., Williams, Janet B. W., Karg, Rhonda S., & Spitzer, Robert L. (2014). *Structured clinical interview for DSM-5 disorders (SCID-5)—Patient edition*. New York, NY: Biometrics Research Department, New York State Psychiatric Institute.

World Health Organization. (1993). *The ICD-10 classification of mental and behavioural disorders*. Geneva, Switzerland: World Health Organization.

PHOBIAS VERSUS NONCLINICAL FEARS

Fear is a universal, normal, and adaptive human emotion that has been essential for our survival as a species because it helps us mobilize our resources to deal with threats in our environment. We all have fears. So when do fears become a phobia? This is an important question that really focuses on when a fear is "normal" or realistic (what we would term *nonclinical*), and when does a fear cross into the realm of being clinically significant and potentially warranting of treatment? To answer this question, one must consider a range of factors including the nature of the fear, the environmental context, and the impact on the individual.

In terms of the nature of the fear, one must assess the degree to which the fear is *excessive* or beyond what most people would experience in a given situation. For example, it is normal for most people to fear being stung by a bee and to experience discomfort or even some distress at a bee flying around their head. However, if a bee flying around triggers an extreme level of fear to the point that a person becomes highly distressed and perhaps even experiences a full-blown panic attack, this is suggestive of a clinical fear or phobia. One must also consider how *persistent* the fear is. If one feels fearful of encountering bees on a daily basis and feels little control over the ability to manage the fear, this is suggestive of a clinically significant fear.

Further, it is also important to consider the *environmental context* of when the fear occurs. Although most people may fear a bee if they encounter one, they are likely not too concerned about bees when they are not around. By contrast, if a person continues to fear encountering a bee anywhere outdoors and is vigilant for detecting a bee even when there is no sign of one, then the fear is more likely to be clinically significant.

In the *Diagnostic and Statistical Manual of Mental Disorders*, fifth edition, the clinical significance of a fear is determined by consideration of the *impact* of the fear on the individual. A fear is deemed clinically significant if it causes the individual marked distress and/or interferes significantly with the ability to function on a daily basis. For example, an individual who is greatly upset by having the fear such that he or she spends a substantial amount of time thinking about the fear, about when it might be triggered, as well as about his or her ability to manage the fear, is experiencing clinically significant distress. An individual who is so fearful of bees that he or she is not able to comfortably remain outdoors in nice weather is being significantly impacted in the ability to enjoy social and leisure activities.

The consideration of all of these factors assists a clinician in determining whether a person has a nonclinical fear versus a clinical fear or phobia. This important distinction typically determines whether treatment is warranted.

Randi E. McCabe

Phobias, Family Influences on the Development and Maintenance of

There are two major family factors that lead to the development of phobias: genetics and social learning. Both the distinct effects of each of these factors and their interaction influence the onset and maintenance of phobias.

Family studies have shown that anxiety disorders run in families. However, the specific fear seen in one family member is typically not the same as the specific fear seen in another family member. This suggests that the tendency to develop anxiety is heritable, but that specific anxiety disorders are not directly heritable from one family member to another. Some data suggest that children might inherit a tendency toward physiological hyperarousal from their parents, and it is this tendency that puts them at risk for the development of anxiety. In other words, when confronted with potentially fear-inducing stimuli, some people feel fear very intensely and experience a slow habituation to that fear. This style of physiological reactivity might predispose individuals to develop anxiety disorders.

An interesting finding in the genetics of anxiety disorders concerns blood-injection-injury (BII) phobias. In contrast to the findings that most anxiety disorders are not directly heritable between family members, this specific phobia does tend to be inherited from one family member to another. Almost 70% of individuals with BII have a relative with BII (Beidel & Turner, 2005). In general, when confronted with feared stimuli, individuals tend to experience an increase in heart rate and blood pressure. However, in the case of BII, this initial increase is rapidly followed by a sharp decrease in heart rate and blood pressure, leading to feelings of faintness and actual fainting in some individuals. This unique physiology might be passed from one family member to another.

In addition to genetic factors, social learning within the family most definitely plays a role in the development of phobias. In 1977, Jack Rachman described three pathways to the development of fears: direct conditioning (i.e., when a traumatic event results in the development of a fear); observational learning (i.e., when a fear develops after watching someone else experience a traumatic event or after exhibiting fear toward particular stimuli); and verbal information transfer (i.e., receiving information that certain stimuli should be feared because they pose a threat). The last two pathways are particularly relevant within the context of families.

It is completely normal for young children to experience transient fears as they are learning about their worlds. Because of this, the *Diagnostic and Statistical Manual of Mental Disorders*, fifth edition (American Psychiatric Association, 2013) requires a particular fear to last for at least six months for a phobia to be diagnosed. Clinically, there are features that are often present in families where normal childhood fears develop into full-blown phobias. Notably, parents of these children tend to facilitate avoidance of feared stimuli. As an example, many young children are fearful of dogs. Parents who cross the street with their children to avoid dogs, leave the playground when a dog arrives, or ask friends to put dogs in a separate room during social visits are more likely to have a child who ends up developing a full-blown phobia of dogs than parents who facilitate gradual and calm interactions with dogs.

With respect to observational learning, parents might also transmit a fear of dogs to their children if they themselves are fearful of dogs. Similarly, children might come to fear flying if their parents always choose to drive places where it would really make more sense to fly. This transmission of fear comes about in two ways. First, children acquire the message that particular stimuli are dangerous—even if their parents never directly say so. And second, children are denied the opportunity to be exposed to these stimuli and see that, in fact, they are not that frightening. For example, flying can be a fun and adventurous experience for children if framed that way by their parents.

Verbal information transfer can be circumscribed to particular feared objects or situations, and it can occur on a broader scale. This, in addition to teaching children to fear specific stimuli, some parents communicate to their children that the world, more generally, is a dangerous place. These parents tend to be overprotective, constantly warning their children to be careful, to watch out, and to avoid anything that involves even the tiniest potential for harm. Children of these parents, particularly when biologically predisposed, tend to internalize these messages and approach the world in a very cautious way. This leads to less exposure to objectively safe stimuli (e.g., playing with insects in the backyard, swimming, going on rides at amusement parks), perpetuating the belief that such stimuli are scary and likely to lead to bad outcomes.

It is important to recognize that genetics and social learning can interact to lead to the development of phobias. Some children are biologically predisposed to have very extreme reactions to certain stimuli, particularly those that are novel. These same children might have sensitive parents who have a difficult time tolerating distress in their children. Therefore, parents might choose to avoid these stimuli in the future rather than deal with the extreme emotional reaction to them, thus maintaining the fear over time.

Deborah Roth Ledley

See also: Childhood, Phobias in; Phobia, Blood-Injection-Injury Type; Phobia, Specific; Phobias, Causes of; Phobias, Genetics of; Rachman, Jack (1934–); Three Pathways Theory

Further Reading

American Psychiatric Association. (2013). *Diagnostic and statistical manual of mental disorders* (5th ed.). Arlington, VA: American Psychiatric Publishing.

Antony, Martin M., Craske, Michelle G., & Barlow, David H. (2006). *Mastering your fears and phobias: Workbook (treatments that work)*. New York, NY: Oxford University Press.

Beidel, Deborah C., & Turner, Samuel M. (2005). *Childhood anxiety disorders: A guide to research and treatment*. New York, NY: Routledge.

Chansky, Tamar. (2004). *Freeing your child from anxiety: Powerful practical solutions to overcome your child's fears, worries, and phobias*. New York, NY: Broadway Books.

THE DOS AND DON'TS OF SUPPORTING LOVED ONES WITH PHOBIAS

Providing support to friends or family members struggling with a phobia can be very helpful to them. Indeed, many people would not be able to overcome their fears without the support or assistance of their loved ones. Unfortunately, sometimes very well-intentioned support can turn out to be unhelpful or hurtful to the individual. The following are some tips to help you provide effective support and to avoid common pitfalls.

Dos	Don'ts
☑ Do listen to the person's concerns, and ask questions to learn more about his or her fear. Even if the fear seems irrational or unusual to you, focus on how hard it must be for the person.	☒ Don't joke about the person's phobia or respond with comments such as "You're afraid of *that*?" This can trivialize the person's distress and may contribute to feelings of shame or embarrassment.
☑ Do ask the person how you can be of help.	☒ Don't assume you know what is helpful for the person.
☑ Do learn about effective treatments for phobias and encourage the person to do the same.	☒ Don't attempt to "treat" the person by pushing him or her into feared situations or through other means.
☑ Do understand that surprising someone with a feared object or situation (e.g., dangling a spider near someone with a spider phobia) can reinforce the phobia.	☒ Don't attempt to surprise the person with the feared object or situation. The person will likely find this very distressing and not humorous despite your light-hearted intentions.
☑ Do convey acceptance and understanding when you see the person experiencing fear or panic. Ask how you can be of help.	☒ Don't laugh when you see the person experiencing a fear response. This can add to distress and make the person feel very embarrassed.
☑ Do remember that the person with the phobia is in charge. It is important that he or she feels in control. Be patient and supportive.	☒ Don't force the person to do something that he or she is not ready for. This will only increase fear and create a sense of low control over the situation.
☑ Do model nonfearful coping behavior. Try to demonstrate that you feel safe and comfortable in the situation of which the person is afraid.	☒ Don't display fear or avoidance in the person's feared situation. This will only reinforce his or her fear. If you are indeed uncomfortable, help the person to focus on other people's nonfearful responses, or identify another nonfearful support person who could be of help.
☑ Do encourage the person to explore his or her fearful thoughts and to consider the evidence in the situation (e.g., "How likely is that to happen?").	☒ Don't tell the person that his or her thoughts or predictions are irrational. The person likely knows this already, so this feedback is not constructive.

☑ If the person is currently receiving treatment for the phobia, ask how you can be of help. Encourage the person to reflect on gains made so far when he or she feels discouraged.

☒ Don't suggest to the person that getting help means that he or she must be "really crazy." Disparaging attitudes toward treatment can contribute to stigma surrounding mental illness and discourage people from seeking help.

Irena Milosevic

Phobias, Genetics of

Phobias cluster within families to a moderate degree, with genetics contributing 24% to 40% to their development. Studies have identified several areas in the genetic material of some families that may be related to phobias, but these areas still need further replication in more families. A few specific genes (*COMT, MAO-A, DAT, BDNF, 5HTT, CNTNAP2*) involved in neurotransmission and neuronal function have also been found to be associated with various types of phobias. Although there have not been very large-scale genetic investigations of the whole human genome for phobias, two studies have examined a personality trait closely linked to phobias (neuroticism) and one has found a gene (*MDBA2*) of potential interest.

Several types of study methodologies have been used to investigate the genetics of phobias. They include (1) family studies, (2) twin studies, (3) linkage studies, (4) candidate gene studies, and (5) genome-wide association studies (GWAS).

The family study approach examines the presence of phobias in biologically related family members of individuals with and without phobias. The family study compares the rates of phobias between the two sets of family members and calculates the degree to which the phobia "runs" or clusters within the families. Numerous family studies have been conducted investigating different types of phobias, specifically agoraphobia, social anxiety disorder (social phobia), and specific phobia. These studies show that individuals with a first-degree relative with agoraphobia have a nine-fold higher chance of developing agoraphobia compared to someone who has no relatives with agoraphobia. For social anxiety disorder and specific phobia, individuals with an affected first-degree relative have a six-fold increased chance of developing social anxiety disorder or specific phobia compared to someone who has no relatives with these conditions. Therefore, phobias have a moderate degree of familial clustering.

Twin studies use identical twins (monozygotic twins who share 100% of their DNA) and fraternal twins (dizygotic twins who share 50% of their DNA) to estimate the contribution of genes to the development of phobias. If identical twins have higher rates of phobias than fraternal twins, then it is assumed that the greater amount of shared DNA in the identical twins is the reason why their rate is higher. From the twin studies that have been conducted, genetics or DNA contributes 25% to 40% to the development of phobias.

Linkage studies are another way to investigate the genetics of phobias. Traditionally, linkage studies have been the next step after family studies to establish that a disease clusters within families. Their main purpose is to locate the chromosomal segments (large portions of the DNA) in the human genome that are "linked" or co-inherited with the disease of interest. They require the collection of many families with the disease. Families in which multiple family members have the disease are more informative. All members of the family are examined to see if they have the disease, and their blood is taken for a DNA sample. The DNA of all family members contributes to locating the chromosomal segments related to the disease. Family members with the disease give information about the possible locations where the disease gene is, and family members without the disease help eliminate areas where the disease gene is not. Linkage studies report a score for each chromosomal segment in the genome tested in relation to the disease, known as the logarithm of odds or LOD score. The higher the LOD score, the more likely that location is related to the disease. If the LOD score is 3, for example, this means that the location is 10^3 times more likely to be related to the disease, compared to that location being related to the disease by random chance. An LOD score of 10 indicates a very high likelihood (that is, 10^{10} times greater likelihood compared to chance alone) that a particular location is related to the disease.

Several linkage studies of phobias have been conducted. The number of families examined ranges from 14 to 20 and has implicated several chromosomal segments. The chromosomes that have been implicated in phobias are chromosome 3 for agoraphobia, chromosome 14 for specific phobia, chromosome 16 for social anxiety disorder, and chromosomes 4 and 7 for all types of phobias. However, the LOD scores for several segments have been fairly low (less than 3) and, to date, no specific gene has been located, nor have the locations been subsequently confirmed or replicated in other families. Therefore, the evidence from linkage studies for phobias has been inconsistent because studies do not report the same findings. A common explanation for the limited findings is that multiple genes may contribute, but each only modestly, to the development phobias. If this were the case, the number of families needed to find the chromosomal segments is much greater than what has been investigated thus far.

Candidate gene studies use yet another approach to examine the genetics of a disease. Based on the known biology of the diseases, specific "candidate" genes are proposed to be tested in individuals with and without the disease. The frequency of the genes in those with and without the disease is compared and if the gene is more common in those with the disease, it is presumed the gene is involved in the disease. In phobias, as in many other mental disorders, the genes related to brain neurotransmitters have been examined in candidate gene studies. *COMT* (catechol-O-methyltransferase), *MAO-A* (monoamine oxidase A), *DAT* (dopamine transporter), *5HTT* (serotonin transporter), *BDNF* (brain-derived neurotrophic factor), and *CNTNAP2* (contactin-associated protein-like 2) are genes that have been found to be related to phobias. The *COMT* and *MAO-A* genes are involved in the breakdown of catecholamines, a group of neurotransmitters that include dopamine, epinephrine, and norepinephrine. These neurotransmitters are involved in emotion (pleasure, excitement), cognition (memory, concentration), and motor function. The *DAT* gene is involved in the transmission of dopamine at the cellular level. Dopamine is a neurotransmitter involved in reward, pleasure, and excitement. Serotonin is another neurotransmitter involved in sociability, sleep, and anxiety, and the *5HTT* gene regulates its transmission. Finally, the *BDNF* gene encodes for a nerve growth factor in the brain, and the *CNTNAP2* gene is related to the supporting structures of the nervous system.

Lastly, GWAS are the most recent approach to study the genetics of disease. In contrast to candidate gene studies where candidate genes are proposed based on the known biology of the disease, GWAS have no a priori (predefined) candidate genes. Instead they examine the whole genome for locations with variations in the genetic code. These locations are called single nucleotide polymorphisms or SNPs. The variations in these locations are being tested to see if they occur more frequently in many individuals with and without the disease. Because so many SNPs are being tested at one time, statistical correction needs to be made before an accurate result can be reported. In addition, GWAS require very large numbers of individuals with and without the disease under investigation; typically, the number of individuals needed is in the thousands or tens of thousands.

To date, no GWAS have been published in social anxiety disorder, agoraphobia, or specific phobia populations. However, two GWAS have been conducted on the anxious personality trait of "neuroticism," which is often present in individuals with phobias. Neuroticism is the tendency to experience negative feelings, such as being sad or blue, and it is also characterized by being unable to relax, being tense all the time, worrying a lot, and getting nervous easily. The first GWAS had no significant findings on any of the 450,000 SNPs that were examined. The second GWAS yielded one SNP in the *MDBA2* gene, which codes for a protein found in the central nervous system.

Nancy C. P. Low and Matthew E. Sloan

See also: Agoraphobia (Fear of Panic-Like Symptoms); Anxiety and Related Disorders; Phobia, Specific; Phobias, Family Influences on the Development and Maintenance of; Social Anxiety Disorder (Social Phobia)

Further Reading

Hettema, John M., Webb, Bradley T., Guo, An-Yuan, Zhao, Zhongming, Maher, Brion S., Chen, Xianging, . . . van den Oord, Edwin J. (2011). Prioritization and association analysis of murine-derived candidate genes in anxiety-spectrum disorders. *Biological Psychiatry, 70,* 888–896.

Kendler, Kenneth S., Neale, Michael C., Kessler, Ronald C., Heath, Andrew C., & Eaves, Lindon J. (1992). The genetic epidemiology of phobias in women. The interrelationship of agoraphobia, social phobia, situational phobia, and simple phobia. *Archives of General Psychiatry, 49,* 273–281.

Villafuerte, Sandra, & Burmeister, Margit. (2003). Untangling genetic networks of panic, phobia, fear and anxiety. *Genome Biology, 4,* 224.

Phobias, History of

Phobias have likely been a part of our nature since the dawn of humankind. The famous Greek physician Hippocrates (470–410 BC) wrote the earliest account of someone having what we might today call a phobia. In *The Seventh Book of Epidemics*, he wrote of a patient who became terrified at the sound of flute music but only when he heard it played at night. However, a Roman writer named Aulus Cornelius Celsus (25 BC–AD 50) was the first to use the term *phobia*. Specifically, Celsus coined the term *hydrophobia* as a way to describe the aversion to water documented in people with advanced rabies. *Phobia* was derived from the name of the Greek god *Phobos*, the son of *Aries*. Phobos was believed to be so terrifying that warriors would paint a picture of his face on their shields in order to terrify their enemies. The modern use of the term emerged in the late 1800s, with phobia generally defined as an exaggerated and usually illogical fear of a particular object, class of objects, or situation.

As recognition of phobias grew in the late 1800s and early 1900s, physicians and psychiatrists began to document and study them. Of the early writers and thinkers, one of the most influential was Sigmund Freud (1856–1939), a Viennese neurologist. Freud described two types of phobias: (1) common phobias, which consisted of things that many people feared (e.g., spiders, death, or snakes); and (2) contingent phobias, which consisted of things that people rarely feared (e.g., leaving home or socializing). Freud argued that phobias were rooted in traumatic childhood memories of sexual feelings, and were means for these hidden emotions to be expressed. Of particular importance was Freud's report on the case of "Hans" (now commonly called "Little Hans"). When Hans was four years old he saw a horse that was pulling a large cart collapse in the street, and he subsequently became fearful of horses and large carts. Freud argued that Hans's phobic fears were due to his desire to replace his father and be with his mother, as well as due to unconscious conflicts related to masturbation, and a fear of a loss of attention after the birth of his younger sister. This case study, along with the rise of psychoanalysis (psychological therapy based on Freud's theories of mental illness), had significant influence on the understanding of phobias for many years.

World War II led to the need for an improved system of classifying mental illness. Accordingly, the U.S. Armed Forces developed a new classification system of mental disorders known as the *Medical 203*. Psychiatrists, returning to work in hospitals and clinics from military duty, adopted the Medical 203. From this document, the Américan Psychiatric Association (APA) would create the *Diagnostic and Statistical Manual of Mental Disorders*, first edition (DSM-I; 1952). The DSM-I and the second edition, the DSM-II (1968), were heavily influenced by psychoanalytic thought. Phobias were defined as one of six types of *psychoneuroses* and were termed *phobic reactions*. In the DSM-II, phobias were assumed to be due to unconscious conflicts, with afflicted individuals believed to be displacing their underlying fears and anxieties onto the phobic object or situation.

While Freud's theories were gaining popularity among psychiatrists and the APA, researchers working in universities started to use a more scientific approach to explore behavior. American psychologist John B. Watson (1878–1958) established the early tenets of behaviorism in the 1910s and 1920s, which dictated that psychology should focus on observable behavior, and that the mind and cognition have little role in human behavior. As the work of Russian physiologist Ivan Pavlov (1849–1936), whose research led to the development of classical conditioning principles, became widespread, Watson sought to test classical conditioning in humans. This led to the study of "Albert B" (now commonly known as "Little Albert"). By exposing Albert to a loud sound while he was near a white laboratory rat (which Albert did not initially fear), Albert developed a fear of white rats that subsequently generalized to include fear of many furry objects. This study led researchers and clinicians to see phobias as the result of behavioral principles, which challenged the psychoanalytic view of phobias. With the continued rise of behaviorism through the work of B.F. Skinner (1904–1990) and Joseph Wolpe (1915–1997) between the 1940s and 1960s, new treatments for phobias emerged. These early treatments included systematic desensitization and flooding, both of which emphasized that phobias could be treated through behavioral principles such as exposure. It was also at this time that the first medications for phobias, barbiturates and benzodiazepines, began to be formally studied.

As behaviorism reached its peak in the 1950s and 1960s, a new line of thought began to emerge in both psychology and psychiatry. With pioneers Aaron T. Beck, a psychiatrist who established cognitive therapy, and Albert Ellis, a psychologist who established rational emotive therapy, the cognitive revolution began. Researchers and therapists began to consider the role that thoughts and beliefs play in human behavior. Beginning with the development of new treatments for depression and other anxiety disorders, cognitive techniques began to be incorporated into the treatment of phobias in the 1970s, creating early forms of cognitive behavioral therapy (CBT) for phobias. CBT combined exposure elements of behavioral therapy with cognitive restructuring elements (i.e., challenging dysfunctional beliefs about a phobic stimulus) of cognitive therapy.

With the publication of the DSM-III in 1980, the definition of phobias was radically changed, due in part to behaviorism and the cognitive revolution. However, the DSM-III focused on symptoms for classification purposes and did not align with any particular theoretical perspective. For phobias, this meant that the psychoanalytic view of phobias as a form of displacement from some unconscious desire was no longer included. Instead, the DSM-III defined a *phobic disorder* (or *phobic neurosis*) as a persistent and irrational fear of a specific object, activity, or situation that leads to a desire to avoid the object, activity, or situation. Phobic disorders were placed in a newly created *anxiety disorders* category. The DSM-III also established subcategories of phobic disorders of *social phobia, agoraphobia without or without panic attacks*, and *simple phobias*. When a revision of the third edition, the DSM-III-R, was published in 1987, the phobic subtypes were moved to separate diagnostic categories of anxiety disorders, with the higher-order category of phobic disorders removed. Agoraphobia was linked with panic disorder, and social phobia was given its own category, as was simple phobia.

Changes to the treatment of phobias coincided with the revised classification. The 1970s and 1980s saw CBT gain substantive empirical support, and it has since become the dominant form of therapy for phobias. New medications were also being tested at this time with initial research into selective serotonin reuptake inhibitors (primarily considered antidepressant medications) and the second generation of benzodiazepines.

The diagnosis of simple phobias was further refined in the DSM system in the 1990s. With the introduction of DSM-IV in 1994, the diagnosis of *specific phobia* (formerly termed *simple phobia*) now included five major subtypes: (1) animal type; (2) natural environment type (e.g., lightning or water); (3) blood-injection-injury type; (4) situational type (e.g., planes or elevators); and (5) other type (e.g., vomiting or choking). At the same time, increased understanding of the pervasive nature of social phobia led to calls for it to be renamed *social anxiety disorder*. Although agoraphobia was largely unchanged from DSM-III-R to DSM-IV, it was revised with the publication of the fifth edition of the DSM, the DSM-5 (2013). With new research indicating that agoraphobia was no more strongly related to panic disorder than it is with other anxiety disorders, agoraphobia was moved into its own distinct category with updated diagnostic criteria. Criteria for specific phobia and social phobia were largely unchanged with the DSM-5, although social phobia was renamed *social anxiety disorder*.

With the dawn of the Information Age of the 1990s, advances in technology brought new methods for researching and treating phobias. For example, researchers and therapists are investigating how to combine CBT with virtual-reality systems to enhance the effectiveness of treatment. The development of cognitive science research has also increased our understanding of phobias, with new studies examining the role of information processing, perception, and attention in phobias and other anxiety disorders. Neuroscience, genetic studies, and new technologies propel our understanding of phobias forward at a rate never before possible.

Alexander M. Penney and Missy L. Teatero

See also: American Psychiatric Association; Beck, Aaron T. (1921–); Behavior Therapy; Classical Conditioning; Cognitive Behavioral Therapy; Freud, Sigmund (1856–1939); Skinner, B. F. (1904–1990); Watson, John B. (1878–1958); Wolpe, Joseph (1915–1997)

Further Reading

Compton, Allan. (1992). The psychoanalytic views of phobias: Part 1: Freud's theories of phobias and anxiety. *Psychoanalytic Quarterly, 61*, 206–229.

Watson, John B., & Rayner, Rosalie. (1920). Conditioned emotional reactions. *Journal of Experimental Psychology, 3*, 1–14.

WHAT'S IN A NAME? HOW ARE PHOBIAS NAMED?

Do you have *ichthyophobia*, or perhaps *tachophobia*? Would it help to first know what these phobias refer to? You might be able to decode them if you happen to speak Greek!

As you might have noted already, all phobia names end with the suffix *-phobia*, which is derived from the Greek word *phobos*, meaning fear, and the suffix *-ia*, indicating a condition or disease. In ancient Greek mythology, Phobos, son of Aphrodite (goddess of love) and Ares (god of war), is described as the personification of fear. His twin brother, Deimos, was the god of panic and terror.

The word preceding the suffix *-phobia*, or the prefix, is typically also Greek and pertains to the feared object or situation. Thus, to decode *ichthyophobia* and *tachophobia*, it is useful to know that *ichtus* is Greek for fish and *tachys* is Greek for rapid or accelerated. *Ichtus + phobos = ichthyophobia* or fear of fish, and *tachys + phobos = tachophobia* or fear of speed. Sometimes this naming rule is broken and a Latin word is used instead to describe the feared object or situation. For example, *ranidaphobia* is a fear of frogs and is based in part on the Latin word for frog, *rana*.

Interestingly, not all words containing the suffix *-phobia* refer to a clinical condition. For example, words like *homophobia* are used to describe negative attitudes, hostility, and fear in relation to a particular group of people (in this case, toward individuals who are lesbian, gay, bisexual, or transgender). Another example is *hydrophobia*, which means fear of water and refers to illness-related difficulty with drinking water or a chemical compound that repels water.

Many websites, magazines, and books offer lists or examples of interesting phobia names (see www.phobialist.com). However, it is important to note that clinicians and researchers typically do not use this naming system and prefer instead to rely on English terms to describe the feared object or situation. For example, instead of saying *zoophobia*, they simply say animal phobia, and instead of *arachnophobia*, they say spider phobia. *Agoraphobia* (from the Greek *agora*, meaning marketplace or open space) and *claustrophobia* (from the Latin *claustrum*, meaning closed or "shut in" place) are exceptions in that these terms are listed in contemporary classification systems for mental disorders and are accordingly also used clinically and in the scientific literature.

Although reviewing phobia name lists is fun (it might even boost your knowledge of Greek!), it is important to be aware of the possible consequences resulting from the discrepancy between popular culture and clinical practice and research when it comes to phobia terminology. First, creating phobia names for just about any imaginable fear might erroneously suggest to people that they have a clinical disorder when in fact they have a normal or manageable fear or aversion. Conversely, simply because a fear is included in a fun list of phobia names does not mean that it is not clinically important.

Irena Milosevic

Phobias, Impairment Related to

Impairment is the state of being unable to perform daily activities due to the effects of substance use, physical injury, a physical condition and/or a mental health condition, rather than an absence of skill. Depending on the severity of impairment, the quality of life in impaired individuals might be greatly reduced. Specific phobias are generally considered to cause relatively low impairment compared to other anxiety disorders since the feared object or event is typically limited to particular settings, such as avoidance of flowers or gardens in a bee phobia. However, it is more accurate to state that impairment in phobias ranges from mild to severe, depending on the individual, the type of phobia, the number of phobias, and whether there is more than one psychological disorder involved. For example, a needle phobia could result in severe impairment for a person with diabetes who is required to receive daily insulin injections to stay healthy.

Definitions of impairment vary widely across professions, and there is considerable overlap between impairment and the symptoms of a physical or mental problem, as well as impairment and disability. From a clinical standpoint, it is essential to distinguish between these terms as the definitions contribute to the accuracy of diagnoses and therefore also influence treatment decisions. Impairment is highly individualized and cannot be judged solely on the basis of diagnosis or symptoms.

The requirement for impairment is built into the diagnostic criteria for phobias. Specifically, for an individual to be diagnosed with a phobia, the avoidance, anxious anticipation, or distress in feared situations must significantly impair normal functioning (American Psychiatric Association, 2013). Because impairment is based on disruption of normal functioning, it depends on the extent to which an individual has to face a feared object or situation on a regular basis. If encounters are limited and easily avoided, individuals might lead relatively unaffected lives. For example, many individuals with aviophobia (fear of flying) can choose to avoid flights without significant disruption to their daily life, but this phobia might cause greater impairment if a person is frequently required to travel by plane for business.

Different domains of an individual's life may be impaired as a result of a specific phobia. Daily routine tasks in particular are frequently impacted. For example, individuals with spider phobia might avoid doing laundry if the laundry is in the basement and if they believe that they are likely to encounter a spider there. Furthermore, people with phobias might be less productive in their work and bypass advancement in their occupation due to the disruptive nature of their fear. For instance, a person with social anxiety disorder (social phobia) might refuse an attractive job offer if it involves public speaking. Individuals with medical phobias might avoid seeking professional help and medication to the point that their physical health is negatively impacted. For example, those with dental phobias commonly avoid going to the dentist even when experiencing serious problems with their teeth. Phobias can also influence social interactions and disrupt romantic relationships and friendships. For instance, individuals with dog phobia might avoid going for walks or hikes with their spouse even if this is an important leisure activity for their partner.

Since interference with daily living is a primary reason that individuals seek treatment, specific impairments in various areas must be identified, evaluated, and targeted during treatment. Additionally, successful treatment should be measured based on both the reduction of impairment and symptom change rather than symptom change alone.

Brenda L. Key and Jennifer M. Yip

See also: Phobia, Specific; Phobias, Social and Economic Impact of

Further Reading

American Psychiatric Association. (2013). *Diagnostic and statistical manual of mental disorders* (5th ed.). Arlington, VA: American Psychiatric Association.

Goldstein, Sam, & Naglieri, Jack A. (Eds.) (2009). *Assessment of impairment: From theory to practice.* New York, NY: Springer.

Phobias, Life-Threatening

Typically, individuals who have a phobia of a particular object or situation go out of their way to avoid the feared stimulus. In rare cases, this avoidance can be so severe that it becomes life-threatening.

Blood-injection-injury (BII) phobias are one example of possible life-threatening phobias. Individuals with a BII phobia are irrationally and pervasively afraid of seeing blood, being injected by a needle, or being injured. Although the fear response itself is not likely to lead to death, this phobia can become dangerous in the instance that avoidance of injections or blood leads to serious medical consequences. For example, anaphylactic shock (a severe allergic reaction) can be lethal if not treated immediately with an injection of adrenaline. A BII phobia of injections may prevent a person from carrying around the necessary dose of adrenaline or refusing the injection, possibly resulting in death. Further, individuals who are fearful of needles might avoid medical tests that include blood draws or treatments that involve injections (e.g., insulin injections for diabetes), which could result in adverse health outcomes.

Phagophobia is the fear of choking and represents another example of a life-threatening phobia. Individuals with phagophobia may fear the act of eating foods, especially those that are anything other than liquid, and they can have an extreme sensitivity to the "gag reflex." The consequences of this phobia can be severe, including malnutrition or starvation. It is often diagnostically confused with anorexia, which is a refusal to maintain a healthy weight with the focus being on body image. Phagophobia might also involve a fear of choking on a medication (e.g., pills). It can become life-threatening when individuals with a serious disease or injury avoid taking a needed medicine because they fear that they will choke on the medication.

For phobias that have possibly life-threatening consequences, it is especially important that individuals seek and receive treatment in a timely manner. Cognitive behavioral therapy is a very effective psychological treatment for phobias. It helps individuals change their beliefs and behaviors surrounding feared objects or situations. For instance, in the case of phagophobia, individuals would learn to examine their beliefs about what might happen if they consumed a feared food or medication. Their therapist would help them develop a more accurate prediction, and this would be accompanied by a slow progression of tasting and ultimately eating the feared food (or swallowing the feared medication) to recognize that their catastrophic predictions do not come true.

Sheryl M. Green and Angela M. Lachowski

See also: Phobia, Blood-Injection-Injury Type

Phobias, Prevalence of

Specific phobia is one of the most common psychiatric disorders and it is the most prevalent of the anxiety disorders. Estimates indicate that between 9% and 13% of the population experience a specific phobia at some time in their life. Within any given year, approximately 7% of people will report symptoms consistent with a diagnosis of specific phobia. However, there is wide variability in the prevalence of phobias across phobia subtypes, age groups, genders, and cultural groups.

The rates of specific phobias vary across subtype of phobia. For example, one study found that among the DSM-5 (*Diagnostic and Statistical Manual of Mental Disorders*, fifth edition) specific phobia subtypes, situational (e.g., flying, enclosed spaces) and natural environment phobias (e.g., heights, storms, water) are the most common at 5.2% and 5.9%, respectively, followed by animal (4.7%) and blood-injection-injury (BII; 4.0%) phobias (Stinson et al., 2007), although there are some inconsistencies across studies. The majority of individuals with a specific phobia report having multiple phobias; in fact, one study of over 4,000 individuals with a specific phobia found that the average number of phobias reported among individuals was 3.1 (Stinson et al., 2007). In this study, 16% of the sample reported a lifetime history of six or more specific phobias. Further, fewer than 10% of individuals with a specific phobia reported having only a single subtype, suggesting that most people with a phobia will report several fears across a range of objects or situations.

The prevalence of specific phobias also tends to vary by age. The average age of onset for specific phobias is around eight years of age. The age of onset distribution for specific phobia subtypes appears to parallel experiences consistent with one's developmental stage. That is, the onset of phobias varies throughout the lifespan as one encounters different stimuli and situations. For example, phobias of animals, blood, storms, and water (which are typically first encountered early in life) tend to begin in early childhood, whereas phobias of flying and driving (which are often not encountered until later) tend to begin in adolescence, on average. Despite the variability in age of onset, the overall prevalence of phobias levels off with age and remains relatively stable throughout adulthood. However, there is some evidence that the prevalence of phobias decreases among older adults. There are several possible explanations for this decline in prevalence rates among older adults. Older adults may minimize their symptoms, phobias may cause less interference or distress because of changes in lifestyle, or older adults may experience anxiety differently and thus the diagnostic criteria are less sensitive in detecting clinical phobias.

Specific phobias are significantly more common among women than men, and women tend to report greater fear associated with their phobias. In particular, women are more likely than men to report animal and situational phobias, although height and BII phobias are equally prevalent among men and women (Stinson et al., 2007). It is unclear what accounts for this sex difference. Although it may reflect actual differences in the vulnerability to develop phobias, it may also reflect response bias (men may underreport their fears) or differences in gender role socialization (women may be more likely to seek treatment for phobias; it may be more socially acceptable for women to fear and avoid frightening stimuli). This sex difference appears to level off after the age of 65 years, with men and women reporting similar rates of specific phobia.

Although there are limited data available on the prevalence of specific phobias across racial and cultural groups, most studies indicate that there is wide variability in the prevalence of specific phobias across cultural groups. The highest prevalence estimates of specific phobia have been reported in samples from North America (8.7%) and the lowest are typically seen in Asian countries, such as China (1.9%; Lewis-Fernández et al., 2010). Limited cross-cultural validity of diagnostic criteria and measurement instruments likely contribute to the variability in rates of specific phobias among Western countries compared to Asian countries; however, to date, no clear explanation has been found to account for these differences. Within the United States, there appears to be less variability across cultural groups. Studies indicate that specific phobias are slightly less common among Asian and Hispanic adults compared to non-Hispanic White adults. Comparisons of the prevalence of specific phobias among African American and White adults have produced mixed results, with some studies showing a small increase in prevalence among African Americans, and other studies showing no differences compared to Whites.

Heather K. Hood and Martin M. Antony

See also: Anxiety and Related Disorders; Cultural Differences; Fear; Gender Differences; Lifespan, Phobias across the; Phobia, Specific; Phobia Types

Further Reading

Lewis-Fernández, Roberto, Hinton, Devon E., Laria, Amaro J., Patterson, Elissa H., Hofmann, Stefan G., Craske, Michelle G., . . . Liao, Betty. (2010). Culture and the anxiety disorders: Recommendations for DSM-V. *Depression and Anxiety, 27,* 212–229.

Stinson, Frederick S., Dawson, Deborah A., Chou, S. Patricia, Smith, Sharon, Goldstein, Rise B., Ruan, W. June, & Grant, Bridget F. (2007). The epidemiology of DSM-IV specific phobia in the USA: Result from the National Epidemiologic Survey on Alcohol and Related Conditions. *Psychological Medicine, 37,* 1047–1059.

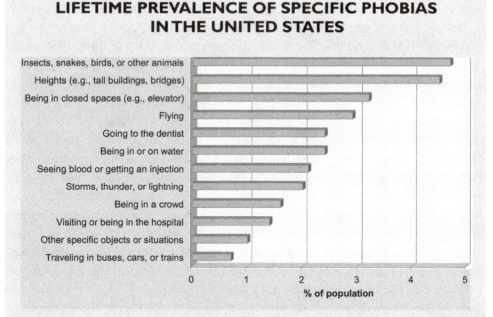

LIFETIME PREVALENCE OF SPECIFIC PHOBIAS IN THE UNITED STATES

Source: Stinson, Frederick S., Dawson, Deborah A., Chou, S. Patricia, Smith, Sharon, Goldstein, Rise B., Ruan, W. June, & Grant, Bridget F. (2007). The epidemiology of DSM-IV specific phobia in the USA: Result from the National Epidemiologic Survey on Alcohol and Related Conditions. *Psychological Medicine, 37*, 1047–1059. Used by permission.

Phobias, Social and Economic Impact of

People with phobias can suffer significant impairment in their functioning, which is associated with broader social and economic consequences. The high level of fear experienced in phobic situations often leads sufferers down a path of avoidance. The degree of avoidance can range from a very specific situation, such as avoiding the dentist in the case of dental phobia, to a wide range of situations in the case of agoraphobia or social anxiety disorder (social phobia). Depending on the nature of the phobia, the anxiety and related avoidance can lead not only to significant social and occupational impairment for the individual but also to more extensive societal costs associated with unemployment and other factors.

The estimated annual cost of anxiety disorders, including phobias, in the United States is $40 billion (Greenberg et al., 1999). This figure includes both direct costs related to treatment and indirect costs such as those related to employment. Of note, unlike most anxiety disorders, specific phobias are not always associated with workplace impairment due to the circumscribed nature of specific fears (e.g., fear of animals, fear of heights). Therefore, the type and severity of the phobia play a significant role in the degree of social and economic burden. Comparatively more is known about the social and economic costs associated with some phobias (e.g., social anxiety disorder) than others (e.g., specific phobias).

The economic costs related to phobias are especially pronounced in social anxiety disorder. Less than one-third of individuals with this diagnosis reported working full-time compared to more than half of the psychiatrically well population (Patel, Knapp, Henderson, & Baldwin, 2002). High unemployment rates have negative implications for the phobic individual as well as society at large. In these cases where the phobia is severe enough to interfere with employment, government organizations or insurance companies may be required to provide disability support. In fact, most of the costs associated with social anxiety disorder are not directly associated with treatment but rather are indirect costs related to lost wages and disability support. In addition to unemployment, there may be other occupational impairments such as decreased work productivity and lower occupational attainment. For example, an individual with social anxiety disorder may choose a career as a data entry clerk to avoid interacting with other people, despite being otherwise capable of a higher occupational status. Similarly, a person with a fear of flying may turn down a promotion that involves frequent travel, thereby leading to a lower level of occupational attainment and a lower salary than would otherwise be the case. Further to occupational impairments, those with social anxiety disorder also have lower levels of educational attainment.

Given the significant impairment that can result from a variety of phobias, early diagnosis and intervention are necessary to mitigate the associated economic cost. Despite some variability in treatment-seeking rates across the various phobias (e.g., people with agoraphobia tend to seek treatment more often than those with specific phobias), treatment seeking remains low for all phobias. Further, when treatment is sought, it is commonly years after the onset of the phobia despite available and effective treatments for phobic disorders. Rather than pursuing treatment, many individuals attempt to manage the phobia themselves by avoiding the feared object or situation, which has long-term social and economic ramifications. The delay in treatment is especially problematic given that people with phobias are at greater risk of developing other disorders, especially depression, later on, which leads to even greater impairment and associated economic cost.

Despite being unlikely to seek treatment, people with phobias tend to be significant users of primary health-care and outpatient services. Rather than obtaining help for the phobia, the individual often seeks treatment for related symptoms from general rather than specialized healthcare professionals. Therefore, the phobic disorder often remains undiagnosed and untreated. This practice of treating related symptoms, but not the phobia itself, is associated with increased primary care visits, overuse of health-care services, and reduced cost-effectiveness for the phobia treatment. Although the most cost-effective therapies for treating phobias are still unknown, treating phobias with any effective, evidence-based treatment may increase work productivity, reduce financial dependency and, by extension, reduce the economic burden of the phobic disorder.

Nancy L. Kocovski and Rebecca A. Blackie

See also: Agoraphobia (Fear of Panic-Like Symptoms); Phobia, Specific; Phobias, Impairment Related to; Social Anxiety Disorder (Social Phobia)

Further Reading

Greenberg, Paul E., Sisitsky, Tamar, Kessler, Ronald C., Finkelstein, Stan N., Berndt, Ernst R., Davidson, Jonathan R. T., . . . Fyer, Abby J. (1999). The economic burden of anxiety disorders in the 1990s. *Journal of Clinical Psychiatry, 60,* 427–435.

Patel, Anita, Knapp, Martin, Henderson, Juliet, & Baldwin, David. (2002). The economic consequences of social phobia. *Journal of Affective Disorders, 68,* 221–233.

Phobias in Popular Culture

There is a long-standing history of phobias being depicted in popular culture. Poets, novelists, playwrights, and the like, have long capitalized from the horrific and at times humorous portrayals of phobia-inducing situations and objects, as well as individuals' corresponding responses. The widespread presence of phobias in popular culture is likely due to their bidirectional relationship. Specifically, the situations and objects feared by a given society will influence popular culture, and popular culture itself can at times drive that which is feared in a particular society. This mutually informed connection, with the respective elements evolving together over time, can be advantageous for the dissemination of information to the public about phobic disorders and their treatments. However, it can also be problematic by providing misinformation, reinforcing maladaptive behaviors such as avoidance, preventing individuals from seeking treatment, and being exploitive in the context of some mass media.

Popular culture may be defined as a collection of widespread beliefs that prevail during a specific period of time in a given society. These beliefs can be transmitted via mass media (newspaper articles, books, television, movies, radio broadcasts, and Internet websites) and can change over time. This means that there are differences in current popular beliefs between cultures, as well as within a culture over time. For example, phobias portrayed in popular Western culture have shifted from depictions of fictional characters to everyday people featured on reality television programs.

A poster for Alfred Hitchcock's classic thriller *Vertigo*. In this movie, a detective goes into early retirement because an experience in the line of duty causes him to develop a severe fear of heights (acrophobia) and vertigo. (Library of Congress)

At the dawn of civilization, oral tradition, art, music, and literature stood out as the primary means by which popular cultural beliefs regarding fears were communicated. One early example of this appears in Homer's *Iliad*, an ancient Greek epic poem (800 BCE). With the aim of inducing fear in their opponents during battle, Greek warriors had the image of Phobos, the god of terror, crafted on their shields.

The rise of the Judeo-Christian tradition brought with it new religious beliefs that permeated many aspects of Western society. Dante Alighieri's *Divine Comedy* (1321), a poem that chronicles the author's fictional journey through hell and the tortures that condemned souls were forced to endure, illustrates how phobias can influence the development of popular culture. Dante's tormenting descriptions reflect situations and objects commonly associated with phobias, including vipers, insects (hornets and worms), blood, water, and diseases. These were possibly chosen because of fears that they produced in Dante himself or in others.

Playwrights have also disseminated information about phobias through works that became part of popular culture. *The Merchant of Venice* (Shakespeare, 1623/1992, p. 143) noted the fear and behavioral reactions that some individuals display in the presence of a phobic stimulus:

Some that are mad if they behold a cat,
And others, when the bagpipe sings I'th'nose
Cannot contain their urine

However, Shakespeare did not attempt to explain the origin of these phobias or how those afflicted might rid themselves of these fears.

Until the end of the 19th century, literature, art, music, and oral tradition were the dominant means by which popular culture transmitted information about phobias. Although these mediums still play a role in communicating this knowledge, the advent of technology by way of film, radio, television, and the Internet has both widened and quickened the distribution of these cultural beliefs to the masses. One of the first such examples came to us on October 30, 1938. At the time, Orson Welles, an American actor and filmmaker, performed a radio drama adopted from the H. G. Wells novel, *The War of the Worlds* (1898), a science fiction story about the invasion of earth by aliens. Although announcements were made throughout the program indicating that it was merely a fictional account of an extraterrestrial attack, it went on to cause mass panic as many took it to be an actual event. After the airing, reports appeared of people seeking treatment for issues related to this panic. Although no evidence emerged of specific phobias developing from this incident, it serves as an example of the power that media have on the emotional reactions of people on a large scale.

Similarly, films have played a pivotal role, and continue to do so today, in the spreading of cultural knowledge to the masses. Countless films from different genres broach the topic of phobias. Suspense and horror films tend to utilize particular situations or objects known for their phobic responses with the aim of inducing fear in their audience. For instance, director Alfred Hitchcock featured a protagonist with a fear of heights in his film *Vertigo* (1958). The storyline explores the development of the fear (witnessing someone fall to their death), the disabling effect that the phobia has on the character (quitting his job and failing to prevent a suicide), and his eventual success at conquering this anxiety by facing his fear. Another example of the depiction of phobias in movies includes *Arachnophobia* (1990). In this film, a poisonous South American spider finds its way to America and mates with a local spider, resulting in the proliferation of offspring that begin to kill off residents of a small town. The main character must face his arachnophobia (fear of spiders) to save the townspeople. Both of these films appear to suggest that phobias can be conquered only through exposure. Other notable movies that depict phobias include *Jaws* (1975; fear of water and sharks), *Raiders of the Lost Ark* (1981; fear of snakes), *What about Bob?* (1991; claustrophobia, agoraphobia, acrophobia, fears of illness, toothbrushes, water, darkness, and thunderstorms), *The Truman Show* (1998; fear of water), and *Batman Begins* (2005; fear of bats).

Several television programs have also featured phobias. One example comes from *The Maury Povich Show*, an American tabloid talk show. This program has featured individuals suffering from a variety of unusual specific phobias, including those of olives, flowers, peanut foam, human hair, chalk, pickles, mustard, peaches, and cotton balls. The typical show follows the format in which guests are brought on stage to tell their stories, and then the elements of the feared object are presented either by audio clips or visually on a television screen. This is followed by live presentation of the phobic object, which is brought on stage toward the guest. In one particular episode (aired June 14, 2007), a woman with a cotton phobia is followed around the studio by a man dressed up as a bunny made of cotton balls. While being pursued, the woman screams and cries while the host and many people in the audience laugh at her reaction. Episodes commonly end by treating the affected individuals with techniques that are not empirically supported treatments of phobias, such as time with a "motivational hypnotist" or "success coach."

Although reality-based television shows first made their appearance in the 1940s, this genre gained significant attention and momentum in the 1990s. Competitive reality shows emerged out of this increased popularity and were unique in that they offered a monetary reward to the winners of challenging situations. Three shows in this genre stand out with regard to their portrayal of phobias: *Survivor, The Amazing Race*, and *Fear Factor. The Amazing Race* aired one episode in which a contestant exhibited a phobic reaction to heights and water that involved screaming, protests, and tears. In the end, she could not bring herself to travel down a steep slide into a pool of water and lost her team the million dollar prize. Another reality show called *My Extreme Animal Phobia* featured individuals with a range of specific animal phobias, such as phobias of bats, rats, and insects. The show portrays the story of each afflicted person and examines the impact of the phobia on his or her life. It then brings together three of these people by having them reside in a home for five days, where they are treated with intensive exposure and response prevention therapy by a psychologist. During the five-day stay, the psychologist has them carry out exposure-based strategies such as picking up rats off a bathroom floor and placing them into a terrarium.

Popular culture may influence phobias in many ways, including acquisition of fear, prevalence rates, the types of common phobias, and treatment-seeking behavior. It is possible for a phobia to be acquired through an indirect pathway. For example, negative information transmission through the media about West Nile virus may influence the development of a phobia of insects. Subsequent avoidance of insects will reinforce the fear of insects because the acquisition of new, disconfirming information is stymied. Prevalence rates may be influenced by popular culture as new movies and reality television shows are developed. In addition, a specific phobia such as aviophobia (fear of flying) may become more prevalent when a plane crash is reported in the news or shown in films, even though flying in an airplane is statistically less dangerous than driving in a car.

Diagnostic manuals, such as the *Diagnostic and Statistical Manual of Mental Disorders*, fifth edition and *International Classification of Diseases*, 10th revision, characterize a specific phobia as involving excessive fear that is unreasonable given the small degree of possible harm, whereas phobias are often portrayed in popular culture as involving either a humorous or rational response. A comical depiction may involve an exaggerated fear response to a seemingly innocuous object. For example, a large, muscular man appearing to be extremely afraid of a small creature, such as a mouse, would be outside of the stereotypical definition of masculine. However, this type of portrayal may be harmful to those suffering from phobias because it minimizes their distress and likely discourages them from disclosing their excessive fear and seeking treatment.

A seemingly rational depiction may involve portraying a degree of fear that is not excessive enough and therefore appears to justify escape and avoidance behavior. For instance, many common specific phobias have an evolutionary basis akin to other anxiety disorders. Being afraid of poisonous snakes and carnivorous predators likely served a purpose at one point in time in many geographical contexts. The problem is that these types of fear are unnecessary for many city dwellers. For example, a family living near a swamp in Northern Australia would benefit from a certain degree of fear of crocodiles, whereas people living in Manhattan would be considered to possess an excessive fear if they reported a fear of crocodiles living in the sewers. Horror movies depict certain fears as adaptive and thereby reinforce avoidance and escape behavior. For example, it is unwise to go into the dark outside alone when you are staying in a cabin in the woods. Depictions of phobias in this manner reinforce beliefs regarding overestimations of degree of harm. Additionally, prevailing phobias in popular culture may involve situations and objects that would be difficult to access in everyday life. Exposure to an unlikely phobia through popular culture may paradoxically inflate individuals' sense of probability about encountering their feared situation or object, and their erroneous beliefs about probability might maintain their irrational fears.

Popular culture can influence the development of a phobia, and then interfere with treatment by reinforcing avoidance and escape behavior. If psychological treatments depicted on television are portrayed as too challenging and too unpredictable, such as exposure and response prevention gone wrong, individuals will be less likely to seek treatment. In turn, these portrayals may lead individuals to underestimate their ability to cope when confronted with a feared situation and object.

Radek Budin and Corinna M. Elliott

See also: Cultural Differences; Phobia, Specific; Phobias, History of; Phobias, Prevalence of

Further Reading

Mowat, B. A., & Werstine, P., (Eds.). (1992). *The Merchant of Venice* (pp. 1–235). Toronto, Canada: Washington Square Press. (Original work by William Shakespeare, published in 1600). Retrieved from http://www.worldcat.org/title/merchant-of-venice/oclc/26381794.

Phobic Beliefs

Phobic beliefs are ideas that people strongly believe to be true of a particular object, situation, or place that serves to initiate and maintain excessive fear and avoidance related to the phobic stimulus. These ideas are often unlikely, flawed, or make situations more frightening than they would be for other people. In addition, phobic beliefs include personal attitudes that underestimate an individual's ability to manage the feared situation by emphasizing personal vulnerability and lack of control. For example, someone afraid of elevators might believe that elevators cannot hold his or her weight, that they frequently have cables break, or that the doors will get stuck and trap people. Fear and avoidance of real danger ensures survival (e.g., fear of poisonous snakes and spiders); however, phobic beliefs often focus on exaggerated or inaccurate threat and danger (e.g., fear of insects such as dragonflies and ladybugs that do not pose harm to humans). Many beliefs that are inaccurate disappear as people age and learn from experience that these dangers are unlikely to cause real harm (e.g., fear of the dark). However, phobic beliefs remain a problem into adolescence and adulthood for some people. These errors fall into three main areas. First, individuals with phobias tend to overestimate how often bad things occur, a belief that is referred to as *probability overestimation* (e.g., thinking there is a high chance that their plane will crash). Second, they tend to assume the worst possible outcome if the bad thing does occur, which is referred to as *catastrophizing* (e.g., any sound on the plane means the plane will crash and all will die). Third, they also worry about how they will react to the related situations by assuming they will panic, feel out of control, or make a fool of themselves.

Many psychological theories have been developed to explain these beliefs. One explanation is that when individuals experience a threatening situation, (*direct conditioning*) they develop inaccurate beliefs about the situation (e.g., a person bitten by a dog may develop a belief that all dogs want to bite people). Alternatively, phobic beliefs may develop just by watching someone act fearfully (*observational learning*; e.g., a child whose parents pull him or her away from all dogs may develop a belief that dogs are dangerous). Phobic beliefs may also develop from the things children hear (*information transfer*; e.g., a teenager who wants to try ice skating may be more anxious after hearing his or her parents say, "You could seriously hurt yourself on the ice," leading the teenager to overestimate negative outcomes on the ice).

Usually, the factors that influence the development and maintenance of phobic beliefs are more complex than this. Often several direct and indirect experiences lead a person to develop and keep a strong phobic belief. For example, a person may come to believe that highway driving is dangerous after being in a car accident, seeing someone badly injured while driving (direct learning), seeing others avoid the highway (observational learning), or seeing a news program about the dangers of young people in motor vehicle accidents (information transfer). On the other hand, potentially threatening situations are not necessarily required for the development of phobic beliefs and not all dangerous situations leave a person with inaccurate beliefs. For instance, not everyone who has been stung by a bee develops a bee phobia. Although exposure to negative experiences may impact who develops an inaccurate belief, positive experiences may also prevent someone from subsequently developing a strong phobic belief. For example, one person who travels by plane often may not be fearful about flying, even after a particularly turbulent flight, whereas another person who is flying for the first time might come to believe that airplanes are unsafe and likely to crash due to the same turbulence.

The development and maintenance of phobic beliefs are important to study because the way that people think about situations affects their feelings and behaviors. Some people may develop significant problems due to the errors in their thinking. For example, due to their phobic beliefs, some people go to great lengths to avoid feared situations. However, this avoidance guarantees that they will not have experiences that disprove the phobic beliefs. This situation results in a way of thinking that grows stronger and eventually becomes difficult to reevaluate and change. For people with phobias, this way of thinking becomes such a problem that it prevents them from taking care of normal daily activities, like time with friends and family or school or work activities. Research suggests that the stronger the belief that something is dangerous, the more the person fears that situation. Similarly, the stronger the belief that one cannot control or protect oneself from the fear, the more the phobia will interfere with one's life. Fortunately, psychological interventions such as cognitive behavioral therapy may be useful in changing phobic beliefs, and by doing so, reduce people's avoidance and improve their lives. In fact, some scientists believe people's recovery from a phobia is partly due to changes in the accuracy of their phobic beliefs.

Nina Wong Sarver, Antonina S. Farmer, Kirstin Stauffacher Gros,
and Daniel F. Gros

See also: Anxiety and Related Disorders; Cognitive Model; Information Processing Biases; Learning Theory; Phobia, Specific; Risk Factors

Further Reading

Field, Andy P. (2006). Is conditioning a useful framework for understanding the development and treatment of phobias? *Clinical Psychology Review, 26,* 857–875.

Fisak Jr., Brian, & Grills-Taquechel, Amie E. (2007). Parental modeling, reinforcement, and information transfer: Risk factors in the development of child anxiety? *Clinical Child and Family Psychology Review, 10,* 213–231.

Thorpe, Susan J., & Salkovskis, Paul M. (1995). Phobic beliefs: Do cognitive factors play a role in specific phobias? *Behaviour Research and Therapy, 33,* 805–816.

COMMON PHOBIC BELIEFS

Individuals with phobias often report negative and unrealistic beliefs about the focus of their fear. Such beliefs typically increase their fear and make it more likely that they will engage in unhelpful coping behaviors, such as avoidance or escape.

Two of the most common beliefs reported by individuals with phobias are *probability overestimations* and *catastrophizing*. Probability overestimations are predictions that exaggerate the likelihood of something bad happening. Individuals with phobias often expect that negative outcomes are highly likely to occur in feared situations when, in fact, the likelihood of their occurrence is usually very low. Catastrophizing, on the other hand, is the tendency to assume that it would be absolutely terrible and unmanageable if something negative did indeed happen in a feared situation.

Here are some examples of these two types of beliefs in phobias:

Probability Overestimations

- The plane will crash
- The dog will bite me if I get too close
- The spider will jump on me
- The elevator will break while I'm in it
- I will be hit by lightning
- The boat will capsize
- People will point and laugh at me if they see I'm afraid
- I will be so scared that I will go crazy
- My heart will beat so quickly that I will have a heart attack

Catastrophizing

- It would be unbearable to experience turbulence on a flight
- It would be absolutely terrible to sit in a room with a dog

- If a spider crawled on me, I couldn't cope
- Getting in a crowded elevator is one of the worst things I can imagine
- I couldn't manage being outdoors during a storm
- Having to take a ferry on my vacation would be devastating
- If people saw that I was afraid, it would be a complete disaster
- Entering this scary situation would ruin my entire week
- Feeling afraid is the most awful thing ever

Effective strategies are available for changing phobic beliefs. These typically include cognitive and behavioral methods, such as examining the evidence for the phobic belief and entering feared situations to determine whether one's negative assumptions are true.

Irena Milosevic

Phobic Neurosis

Phobic neurosis is a term rooted in psychoanalysis and pertains to an irrational fear of a particular object or situation. According to famed psychoanalyst Sigmund Freud (1856–1939), neuroses arise from unresolved unconscious conflicts. To manage such conflicts, the individual employs unconscious defense mechanisms. In phobic neurosis, in particular, displacement and avoidance are commonly observed pathological defenses. For example, in Freud's case study of Little Hans, a young boy's phobia of horses was understood to represent the boy's fear that he would be castrated by his father for desiring his mother. Accordingly, the boy's fear was thought to be displaced onto a symbolic object: horses.

The *Diagnostic and Statistical Manual of Mental Disorders*, second edition (DSM-II), which was influenced by psychoanalytic theory, described several types of neuroses, all of which were understood to have anxiety as a main characteristic. Phobic neurosis was described as an intense fear in response to an object or situation that an individual recognizes is not actually dangerous. Symptoms may include faintness, fatigue, heart palpitations, perspiration, nausea, tremor, and panic. Consistent with Freud's theory, the DSM-II posited that the fear observed in phobic neurosis is a displacement onto the phobic object or situation from another object of which the individual is unaware.

With a shift away from the psychoanalytic influence in classification and toward a more standardized descriptive approach, the term *phobic neurosis* did not appear in subsequent versions of the DSM.

Irena Milosevic

See also: Freud, Sigmund (1856–1939); Phobias, History of; Psychoanalysis

Further Reading

American Psychiatric Association. (1968). *Diagnostic and statistical manual of mental disorders* (2nd ed). Washington, DC: American Psychiatric Association.

Posttraumatic Stress Disorder

Posttraumatic stress disorder (PTSD) is a mental disorder that can arise after a person has been exposed to a traumatic event. PTSD was previously classified as an anxiety disorder but in the *Diagnostic and Statistical Manual of Mental Disorders*, fifth edition (DSM-5) it has been moved to the newly created section on trauma and stressor-related disorders. In order to receive a diagnosis of PTSD, the person must experience a trauma followed by the occurrence of symptoms from four cluster areas that cause significant distress or impairment for more than one month.

U.S. Army soldiers during a combat operation in Iraq in 2004. The prevalence rate of PTSD among military service members who were deployed in Iraq and Afghanistan has been estimated at 14%. (Department of Defense)

According to the DSM-5, a traumatic event is defined as an event where the person is exposed to "actual or threatened death, serious injury, or sexual violence." Examples of traumatic events include physical or sexual assault; natural disasters (e.g., earthquakes, hurricanes); experiences of war; and severe motor vehicle accidents. The person may have directly experienced the event, witnessed the event as it occurred to others (in person, not through media), learned that a traumatic event occurred to a close friend or family member, or experienced repeated exposure to aversive details of traumatic events (e.g., first responders collecting human remains).

The majority of individuals who experience a traumatic event will experience some PTSD-like symptoms immediately following the trauma; however, these will typically resolve within a few weeks. Some individuals will experience persistent symptoms that interfere with their lives. These symptoms can be divided into four clusters: (1) intrusions, (2) avoidance, (3) alterations in cognitions and mood, and (4) alterations in arousal and reactivity. Intrusions are so named because they intrude into the mind without warning. These intrusions may come in the form of nightmares related to the traumatic event, flashbacks (feeling like you are back in the situation), or unwanted memories of the event. Avoidance symptoms reflect attempts to gain psychological distance from the trauma and to prevent the intrusions from happening. The individual may attempt to avoid internal reminders of the trauma such as thoughts and feelings, as well as external reminders of the trauma such as situations, people, or objects. In addition to intrusions and avoidance, individuals with PTSD also experience changes in their thinking patterns and emotions. Alterations in cognition may include exaggerated negative beliefs about the self, world, or others (e.g., I'm a horrible person; the world is very dangerous; others can never be trusted). Alterations in mood are typically characterized by persistent negative emotions such as fear, guilt, and anger, as well as feelings of detachment from others and difficulties experiencing positive emotions such as happiness. The trauma survivor may also experience increased physiological arousal (e.g., being easily startled by noises, difficulties sleeping) and increased emotional reactivity (e.g., angry outbursts, reckless behavior). In order to be diagnosed with PTSD an individual needs to experience difficulties in all four of the symptom clusters.

The symptoms of PTSD usually begin within three months of the trauma, although this is not always the case. When symptoms surface more than six months after the trauma, the PTSD is said to have a delayed onset. Although the majority of adults (60%) will experience a traumatic event sometime in their life, only a minority of these people will develop PTSD (7% lifetime prevalence rate). There are several risk factors that have been linked to increased chances of developing PTSD, including gender, age, and type of trauma. Women are more than twice as likely to experience PTSD compared to men (10% vs. 4%) at some point in their lifetime, and children under the age of 10 are less likely to be diagnosed with the disorder. Rape has been identified as the trauma most likely to lead to PTSD. Combat exposure, childhood abuse, and physical assault have moderate risk levels for the development of PTSD, whereas accidents and natural disasters are less likely to precipitate PTSD. Individuals with PTSD often develop additional mental health difficulties, such as alcohol abuse or dependence (52% of men and 28% of women with PTSD) and depression (48% of men and 49% of women with PTSD), which further interfere with functioning and can complicate treatment.

The causes of sensitivity to traumatic events are complex and involve a combination of biological and psychological factors. Humans are equipped with a stress response system that interprets events, decides whether they are threatening, and responds with anxiety and physical activation when threat is detected. Individuals with PTSD are said to have a hypersensitive stress response system, which leads the person to be on high alert even when there is no real threat anymore. Science suggests that some people inherit a strong disposition to develop a hypersensitive stress response and PTSD. The experience of past traumas earlier in life can also sensitize the individual to the development of PTSD. Attempts to prevent the development of PTSD by providing critical incident stress debriefing or psychological debriefing shortly after the occurrence of a trauma have been largely unsuccessful. This intervention involves a single session, usually conducted in a group format, designed to promote emotional processing through recollection and discussion of the traumatic event. Several meta-analyses have concluded that psychological debriefing is unhelpful and potentially even harmful.

Even though psychological debriefing has been unsuccessful, the good news is that there are a number of scientifically supported treatments for PTSD. There are currently two main approaches to treatment that have been shown to be effective for decreasing symptoms of PTSD: medication and cognitive behavioral therapy (CBT). The medications that are most commonly used in treatment are a class of antidepressant medications called selective serotonin reuptake inhibitors. CBT involves a number of treatment sessions with a therapist, either individually or in a group. Several different forms of CBT for PTSD have been developed (e.g., cognitive processing therapy, prolonged exposure therapy) but all contain the core components of education about PTSD, exposure (facing feared thoughts, feelings, or situations), and cognitive restructuring (exploring how the event has changed beliefs and shifting unhelpful thinking patterns). Medications and CBT can also be used in combination for the treatment of PTSD.

Brenda L. Key

See also: Cognitive Behavioral Therapy; DSM-5; Exposure Treatment; Selective Serotonin Reuptake Inhibitors

Further Reading

Kessler, Ronald C., Sonnega, Amanda, Bromet, Evelyn, Hughes, Michael, & Nelson, Christopher B. (1995). Posttraumatic stress disorder in the National Comorbidity Survey. *Archives of General Psychiatry, 52,* 1048–1060.

Roberts, Neil P., Kitchiner, Neil J., Kenardy, Justin, & Bisson, Jonathan. (2009). Multiple session early psychological interventions for the prevention of post-traumatic stress disorder. *Cochrane Database of Systematic Reviews, 3.*

Rose, Suzanna, Bisson, Jonathan, Churchill, Rachel, & Wessely, Simon. (2002). Psychological debriefing for preventing post traumatic stress disorder (PTSD). *Cochrane Database Systematic Reviews, 2*(2).

Website

National Center for PTSD: http://www.ptsd.va.gov/

Preparedness Theory

Preparedness theory (also known as the selective association model) holds that organisms are biologically predisposed or "prepared" to easily learn to fear objects or situations that were once dangerous to the survival of their species. Proposed by Seligman (1971) and expanded by Öhman and colleagues (e.g., Öhman, Dimberg, & Öst, 1985), this evolutionary account of fear learning explains why phobias are not randomly distributed but instead involve a limited number of fears focused on life-threatening objects or situations. Preparedness theory has provided a widely influential account of the origins of fears and phobias, although the validity of several of its tenets has been a source of dispute.

Preparedness theory represents an early effort by researchers to describe fears within an evolutionary framework. They hypothesized that the ability to easily learn to fear environmental dangers was advantageous to a species' survival and that such prepared fears thus evolved into adaptive traits through the process of natural selection. Indeed, research has shown that the content of most clinical phobias was likely more relevant to the survival of our early ancestors than it is to that of modern-day humans. For example, early humans likely had frequent encounters with dangerous animals, such as venomous snakes and spiders, and were at greater risk of falling from heights in their environment, which promoted the evolution of certain animal phobias and acrophobia (fear of heights), respectively.

Several specific observations about phobic fears influenced the development of preparedness theory. These include their nonrandom distribution (i.e., some stimuli are more likely to be feared than others), ease of acquisition, irrational nature, and high resistance to being extinguished. Within this framework, cognition is viewed as having little influence on fear.

Preparedness theory is considered to be a modification of the classical conditioning model of fear learning. By contrast to this model, which posits that any neutral stimulus can develop phobic properties by being associated with an aversive stimulus, preparedness theory instead predicts that fear conditioning occurs through *selective associations* (also called belongingness) between certain classes of stimuli. For example, according to the theory, it is expected that people would more quickly learn to associate a snake (a prepared or fear-relevant stimulus) with a shock (an aversive stimulus) than they would a flower (an unprepared or fear-irrelevant stimulus) with a shock. However, experimental studies of this particular hypothesis have yielded mixed results. Instead, the most consistent finding in support of the theory has shown that conditioned fear is significantly more resistant to extinction with a fear-relevant conditioned stimulus than a fear-irrelevant one (e.g., Öhman, Erixon, & Lofberg, 1975). Thus, once the fear is acquired through a classical conditioning paradigm, it is more difficult to stop fearing a stimulus such as a snake than it is to stop fearing one such as a flower.

Preparedness theory has been applied to understand not only fear learning but also taste aversion learning. This type of learning, also called the Garcia effect (Garcia & Koelling, 1966), occurs when an organism rapidly learns to avoid a substance that has resulted in sickness during prior consumption. Taste aversion learning is remarkable for its occurrence often after just one trial of association between a specific sensory cue (e.g., taste, smell) and a negative outcome such as feeling sick. According to the preparedness model, it is highly adaptive for organisms to be able to quickly learn to avoid substances that have resulted in illness, as this may have significant bearing on their survival.

The validity of various tenants of preparedness theory has been called into question. Criticism of the theory includes evidence of relatively equivalent fear conditioning of fear-relevant and fear-irrelevant stimuli and lack of consistent evidence to support the notion of selective associations or belongingness in fear acquisition. The theory is also unable to explain the high prevalence of some phobias (e.g., cockroaches were probably not life-threatening to our ancestors) and low prevalence of others (e.g., bears likely did pose a significant threat to our ancestors). Furthermore, contrary to what the theory would predict, phobias, including those hypothesized to be prepared, have a very high rate of positive response to treatment.

Another critique of the preparedness model is its minimization of the role of cognitive factors in fear acquisition. Current knowledge suggests that cognition does in fact play a role in fear learning. For example, researchers have demonstrated that the ease with which a stimulus becomes associated with an aversive outcome is rooted, in part, in information-processing biases about the threatening stimulus (Davey, 1995). In particular, increased expectation that there will be an aversive or traumatic outcome following a fear-relevant stimulus produces and maintains a strong learned association between them. Such an expectancy bias would be evident if one were to expect to be bitten by a snake upon seeing it. Cultural and developmental factors are considered to be important in determining expectancy bias. It is also possible that preparedness has an influence on expectancy bias; thus, the two models are not mutually exclusive.

Irena Milosevic

See also: Aversions; Classical Conditioning; Evolution, Role of; Information Processing Biases; Learning Theory

Further Reading

Davey, Graham C. L. (1995). Preparedness and phobias: Specific evolved associations or a generalized expectancy bias? *Behavioral and Brain Sciences, 18,* 289–297.

Garcia, John, & Koelling, Robert A. (1966). Relation of cue to consequence in avoidance learning. *Psychonomic Science, 4,* 123–124.

Öhman, Arne, Dimberg, Ulf, & Öst, Lars-Göran. (1985). Animal and social phobias: Biological constraints on learned fear responses. In Steven Reiss & Richard R. Bootzin (Eds.), *Theoretical issues in behavior therapy* (pp. 123–178). New York, NY: Academic Press.

Öhman, Arne, Erixon, Gosta, & Löfberg, Ingrid. (1975). Phobias and preparedness: Phobic versus neutral pictures as conditioned stimuli for human autonomic responses. *Journal of Abnormal Psychology, 84,* 41–45.

Seligman, Martin E. P. (1971). Phobias and preparedness. *Behavior Therapy, 2,* 307–320.

Psychiatry

Psychiatry is the branch of medicine that comprises the diagnosis and treatment of psychological disorders. This includes illnesses affecting mood, emotions, thoughts, perceptions, memories, and intellectual functioning. Disturbances in these areas are often manifested by abnormalities of behavior. The treatment of phobias and other anxiety disorders falls within the scope of psychiatry.

At one time it was felt that psychological disorders were disorders of the "mind." It is now generally accepted that psychological functions and symptoms of psychiatric disorder are the result of abnormal brain function.

There is an overlap in the practice of psychology and psychiatry. The principal differentiation is that in order to become a psychiatrist one must first qualify as a medical practitioner, whereas in order to become a psychologist one must complete graduate studies instead of medical school. Both psychology and psychiatry involve the treatment of psychological or psychiatric disorders.

There is also an overlap between the specialty of neurology and psychiatry. Neurology is primarily focused on structural disorders of the brain and spinal cord. This includes strokes, tumors, seizure disorders, and degenerative diseases. Dementias, such as Alzheimer's disease, may be treated by either neurologists or psychiatrists.

Within psychiatry, treatment is principally with medications and with psychotherapy. Medication treatment of phobias and other anxiety disorders is principally with serotonin reuptake inhibitors. Other medications, such as benzodiazepines, beta-blockers, gabapentin, and pregabalin, may have a secondary role. Psychotherapeutic treatments used in psychiatry principally include cognitive behavioral therapy and psychodynamic therapies.

Advances in neuroscience, particularly the use of magnetic resonance imaging and positron emission scanning, are adding to our understanding of the underlying causes of psychiatric disorders. These tools have helped to identify the specific neurocircuits and neurotransmitters that appear to be involved in phobic disorders.

Alan B. Eppel

See also: Benzodiazepines; Beta-Blockers; Fear, Neural Pathways of; Neuroimaging; Selective Serotonin Reuptake Inhibitors; Treatment, Medication

Psychoanalysis

Psychoanalysis is the name given to the theories and methods developed by Sigmund Freud (1856–1939). It encompasses a theory about how the mind works, as well as a method of treatment of psychological disorders. Freud wanted to develop a neurological theory of mental functioning but this was not possible due to the limited knowledge of the workings of the brain during his lifetime. The term *psychoanalysis* was first used in March 1896 in a paper published by Freud in French. Practitioners of this method are referred to as *psychoanalysts* or *analysts* and the patients are referred to as *analysands*.

Over the past 120 years or so since its beginnings, psychoanalysis has evolved and developed into many different strands. The term *psychoanalysis* is now restricted to the practice of the classical method, which involves the patient lying on a couch and free-associating (reporting anything that comes to mind). Psychoanalytic therapy generally lasts a number of years and the patient is required to attend up to four or five times per week. Because of the length of time commitment required for this form of therapy, the theory and methods have been considerably modified and adapted. Forms of therapy and schools of thought that have been derived from Freud's original psychoanalysis are referred to as *psychodynamic psychotherapies*. These therapies are practiced face-to-face and involve no more than one or two visits per week. They may be short-term, lasting as little as a dozen sessions, or they may extend over one or more years.

Although many of Freud's original concepts are no longer accepted by the majority of psychodynamic therapists, he is recognized as having introduced to the fields of psychiatry and psychology the basic elements of the psychotherapeutic approach. Fundamentally, Freud revolutionized the practice of psychiatry and psychology by introducing "the talking cure." Freud demonstrated the importance of the expression of unconscious or unspoken thoughts and feelings as essential for the alleviation of psychological suffering. He, more than any of his predecessors, stressed the importance of the unconscious. Freud theorized that many thoughts, feelings, and memories were kept out of our awareness. He gave the name *repression* to the psychological mechanism that keeps unacceptable thoughts and feelings out of our consciousness. He theorized, however, that these repressed thoughts and feelings remain a source of psychological conflict and symptoms.

Freud viewed symptoms as being symbolic and imbued with meaning. Symptoms are the result of internal unconscious conflict between unacceptable aggressive and sexual drives and the opposing forces of morality and probity dictated by society. He expressed these ideas in the forms of metaphorical categories: the *id* represents unconscious aggressive and sexual instinctual drives; the *superego* describes the standards and morality imposed by society and corresponds to our conscience; and the *ego* represents the rational thinking part of our psychological functioning.

Anxiety, or irrational fear, had a central place in Freud's theories of psychoanalysis. His ideas about this changed over the years, but eventually Freud came to believe that anxiety had an essentially warning function and indicated the presence of threat and danger. External threats result in an inborn physiological response to mobilize a defense against the danger. Internal threats arise from conflict between the id and the ego or superego. Psychological defense mechanisms evolve to reduce the anxiety. When defenses fail, symptoms result.

Principal concepts that have derived from psychoanalysis and that are still critical components to all forms of psychodynamic therapy include the idea of the unconscious, the importance of childhood relationships, transference, countertransference and defense mechanisms. *Transference* refers to the universal tendency to repeat the patterns of our childhood relationships in our new relationships. *Counter-transference* is used to describe the therapist's transference reactions to the patient.

Psychoanalysis was originally described as an intrapsychic theory in that it described conflict that was internal to an individual. As psychodynamic therapies have evolved, the focus has been more on the relationship aspects of human development and psychological functioning. *Object relations theory*, developed in the United Kingdom after World War II, provided the basis for this. Its major proponents were Melanie Klein, Ronald Fairbairn, and Donald Winnicott. The major shift was from a focus on internal conflicts to a focus on interpersonal relationships. This was a precursor to attachment theory, which emphasizes the mother-infant bond as the central determinant of future relationships.

A second major branching within psychoanalysis is the school of *self-psychology* established by Heinz Kohut in the United States in the 1970s and 1980s. Self-psychology stresses the importance of self-esteem and the problems of narcissism.

An intensive short-term form of psychodynamic therapy was developed by Habib Davanloo in Montreal in the 1980s and this in turn has led to further modifications of the technique. The practice of psychodynamic therapy has shifted from interpretations based on intrapsychic conflict and moved to a focus on the dyad, the relationship between the therapist and the patient. The newest wave in psychoanalytic theory is known as *relational psychoanalysis*. The emphasis in treatment is on the interactions between the patient and the therapist and how these affect the patient's sense of self and impact on the patient's relationships with others.

In the treatment of phobias and other anxiety disorders, this means that the therapist looks beyond the specific symptoms to a wider context. What is the meaning of the symptoms in terms of the patient's early relationships and his or her interactions with other people in the present? What are the triggers to panic attacks and their origins in past relationships or separations? The phobia is not seen as the primary source of the disorder but an expression of a disturbance in the relationship templates based on early childhood relationships, separations, and losses.

In face-to-face psychodynamic therapy of phobias and other anxiety disorders, the patient is asked to begin each session by stating whatever is on his or her mind. The therapist will probe and explore particularly looking for areas that are emotionally charged. Whereas in classical psychoanalysis, dreams were felt to be the "Royal Road" to the unconscious, a contemporary practitioner is more likely to explore the expression of feelings in order to uncover significant themes and memories that impact on the patient's symptoms and behavior.

There has been a resurgence of interest in psychoanalytic concepts as a result of advances in neuroscience. Many neuroscientific research findings have provided support to some of Freud's general ideas and constructs. A new discipline of *neuropsychoanalysis* has been established to explore the interface between neuroscience and psychoanalysis.

Alan B. Eppel

See also: Freud, Sigmund (1856–1939)

Further Reading

Della Selva, Patricia C., & Malan, David. (2007). *Lives transformed: A revolutionary method of dynamic psychotherapy*. London, UK: Karnac Books.

Gabbard, Glen G. (1994). *Psychodynamic psychiatry in clinical practice* (2nd ed). Washington, DC: American Psychiatric Press.

Psychoeducation

Psychoeducation is the process of providing individuals with information to help them better understand characteristics of their phobia, its progression, causes, symptoms, typical treatment course, and expected treatment results. It is generally considered to be a part of good clinical care and is incorporated into most phobia treatments.

Psychoeducation can be delivered through various methods such as verbal communication, pamphlets, books, videos, or websites. It can be a stand-alone intervention but is often combined with other treatments such as cognitive behavioral therapy. This lower intensity intervention may be sufficient for certain individuals as it can help them understand and manage their symptoms. After receiving psychoeducation, individuals often become more receptive and cooperative toward additional treatment and are less likely to drop out, effectively decreasing health-care costs.

During psychoeducation for phobias, individuals learn about the thoughts, behaviors, and physiology involved in the phobic disorder, and how these factors interact to influence the development and maintenance of fear. They learn that although excessive fear or anxiety is maladaptive, fear is a normal response that helps to prepare a person to respond rapidly in a situation involving actual danger. Therefore, it is the fear response to perceived rather than actual threat that is the target of treatment. Education about the feared situation or object may also be provided, as individuals with phobias often hold unrealistic beliefs about the dangers of the things they fear. For example, in aviophobia (fear of flying), statistics about how often planes crash would be discussed as patients with aviophobia usually overestimate the risk of a crash.

Brenda L. Key and Jennifer M. Yip

See also: Anxiety and Related Disorders; Aviophobia (Fear of Flying); Cognitive Behavioral Therapy; Exposure Treatment

Further Reading

Kase, Larina, & Ledley, Deborah R. (2007). *Wiley concise guides to mental health: Anxiety disorders*. Hoboken, NJ: John Wiley & Sons.

Psychology

Psychology is both an applied and academic field that involves the scientific study of mind and behavior. The first psychology lab was founded in 1879 by Wilhelm Wundt, a German physician also known as the "father of experimental psychology." The goal of psychology is to try to understand individuals and groups by examining social, cognitive, developmental, and biological influences. In this field, a professional practitioner, teacher, or researcher is called a psychologist. Psychologists receive their training in graduate school and typically hold a master's or a doctoral degree. They engage in research, applied practice, and teaching across a wide range of topics having to do with how people think, feel, and behave. Whereas a large part of psychological knowledge is often applied to the assessment, diagnosis, and treatment of mental health problems, it is also directed toward understanding and solving problems in many different domains of human activity. Applied psychological services are provided in schools, private practices, businesses, health clinics, hospitals, jails, courts, social welfare agencies, and rehabilitation centers, to name a few. These services are offered by governments or the private sector. Each regional government (e.g., state, province) is responsible for public psychological services and the regulation of psychology. Research psychologists can focus their research on animals or people on a wide range of topics related to mental processes and behavior. Psychological researchers typically work in university psychology departments or other academic settings such as medical schools or hospitals and industrial and organizational settings, among others.

Sheryl M. Green

Ptophobia (Fear of Falling)

Ptophobia (from the Greek *ptosis*, meaning fall, and *phobos*, meaning fear) is an intense fear of falling from a standing or walking position. The term was coined in 1982 by researchers Bhala, O'Donnell, and Thoppil, who noted that fear of falling was a common concern among elderly and disabled individuals. Prevalence estimates of ptophobia vary widely, from 3% to 85% among community-dwelling older adults, with most studies reporting prevalence rates between 21% and 85% (Scheffer, Schuurmans, van Dijk, van der Hooft, & de Rooij, 2008). This broad range might be accounted for by methodological differences across studies. Risk factors for the development of the phobia include a prior fall, older age, and female gender.

Although ptophobia is not specifically described in current classification systems of mental disorders, if the fear of falling is excessive, persistent, and very distressing or impairing, it would be classified as a specific phobia. Ptophobia is understood to develop as a conditioned response to prior falling incidents, which are typically associated with physical and/or medical problems (e.g., hip fractures, dizzy spells, visual impairments). However, it can also develop in the absence of a falling history if an individual believes that he or she is vulnerable to falling. In either case, the fear of falling is considered to be excessive relative to actual risk of falling. Research has shown that ptophobia is itself a predictor of future falls, although a number of additional variables, such as restricted participation in activity and low balance confidence, likely contribute to this association.

Physical assessments of individuals with ptophobia often indicate adequate physical coordination, balance, and strength. Nevertheless, individuals with ptophobia exhibit low confidence in their balance ability and in their ability to avoid falls. Accordingly, they avoid standing or walking without assistance and experience significant distress when required to walk independently, even for short distances. To prevent falls, they might rely excessively on ambulatory aids, such as canes, walkers, and crutches, as well as on the assistance of family members and healthcare providers. Due to reduced mobility and activity, individuals with ptophobia suffer considerable physical and social impairment. They are also at higher risk for depression.

Ptophobia can be assessed with clinical interviews, self-report instruments, and behavioral observation. One of the most common self-report measures is the *Falls Efficacy Scale* (Tinetti, Richman, & Powell, 1990), which assesses respondents' confidence in accomplishing basic activities of daily living without falling.

Observation of individuals who report fear of falling typically reveals a distinct gait, which is characterized by very slow, cautious shuffling or walking, short steps, and a broad-based stance.

Treatment of ptophobia involves a combination of behavioral and physical therapy and is typically facilitated by a physiotherapist in collaboration with other health-care personnel and the individual's family members. The treatment specifically focuses on graduated exposure to walking situations and habituation to the fear response. Exposure begins with assisted walks for short durations (e.g., walking from bed to dresser using a walker and with assistance from physiotherapist) and progresses toward increasingly autonomous walks for longer durations (e.g., walking down a hallway unassisted). Treatment might also involve strength and balance training.

Irena Milosevic

See also: Exposure Treatment; Phobia, Specific

Further Reading

Bhala, Ram P., O'Donnell, John, & Thoppil, Ephrem. (1982). Ptophobia: Phobic fear of falling and its clinical management. *Physical Therapy, 62,* 187–190.

Scheffer, Alice C., Schuurmans, Marieke J., van Dijk, Nynke, van der Hooft, Truus, & de Rooij, Sophia E. (2008). Fear of falling: Measurement strategy, prevalence, risk factors and consequences among older persons. *Age and Ageing, 37,* 19–24.

Tinetti, Mary E., Richman, Donna, & Powell, Lynda. (1990). Falls efficacy as a measure of fear of falling. *Journal of Gerontology, 45,* 239–243.

R

Rachman, Jack (1934–)

Jack Rachman (1934–), born Stanley Rachman, is professor emeritus of psychology at the University of British Columbia in Vancouver, Canada. He received his PhD from the University of London in 1961, which he completed under the supervision of Hans Eysenck. During this time, he also worked with Joseph Wolpe, a key figure in the development of treatments for a range of anxiety disorders, including phobias. Professor Rachman has published in excess of 200 peer-reviewed articles as well as over a dozen books on fear, the anxiety disorders and related topics (e.g., obsessions, compulsions, courage), behavior therapy, cognitive therapy, and behavioral medicine. For many years, he was the editor in chief of *Behaviour Research and Therapy*, one of the top-ranked journals in clinical psychology. His work is known for its clarity and ability to get to the heart of understanding a particular problem or process. He is renowned for inspiring students, researchers, and therapists to explore new ideas in their laboratories and clinics. Indeed, the clinical relevance of his research is one of its many strengths.

Professor Rachman's early research was devoted to a number of important topics, but arguably his most important early contributions attempted to address issues related not only to the effectiveness of exposure and other behavioral techniques used to treat fear- and anxiety-related problems (including phobias) but also to understand *how* they work. Some of this research (e.g., Rachman, 1965) examined the relative contributions of applied relaxation and systematic imaginal exposure to behavior therapy for anxiety disorders, while others explored the positive and negative implications of various ways to apply systematic desensitization, including the more typical graded, hierarchical approach, and approaches more closely associated with flooding or implosive therapy. Much of this work explored how symptoms change over time during exposure, and how various strategies employed by the research participants (e.g., avoidance and compulsions) could interfere with habituation. This work has important implications for understanding psychological treatments for fear and phobias because it provided a first account of the essential ingredients in behavior therapy for phobic and other anxiety disorders, most notably exposure in the absence of neutralizing behavior.

Moving beyond these basic processes associated with fear change, Professor Rachman conducted a number of studies of courage—especially in British bomb disposal workers during the Irish Republican Army bombing campaign, and also coined the term "emotional processing" (see Rachman, 1980) when trying to account for how it is that people might come to experience the resolution of very unpleasant emotions following especially difficult, sometimes even traumatic, experiences.

Later in his career, Professor Rachman's theoretical orientation underwent a major shift from behaviorist to cognitivist. That is, rather than seeing people's problems grounded in behavioral theory, he conceptualized psychopathology and its treatment as based in the significance or meaning that individuals ascribe to their surroundings, their actions, and even to their thoughts. This shift led to dramatic reconceptualizations of the nature and treatment of a wide range of anxiety disorders—especially on obsessive-compulsive disorder (OCD; Rachman, 1997). Indeed his more recent work focused more specifically on arriving at a cognitively based understanding of and treatments for obsessions, compulsive checking, and contamination-related symptoms in OCD.

Beyond his research, Professor Rachman was responsible for implementing Britain's first national clinical psychology training program. In addition, he has supervised an impressive number of students, many of whom are now internationally known for their research and clinical work in the anxiety disorders and publically acknowledge the influence of Professor Rachman's mentorship.

Those who have spent time with him (colleagues, patients, students, etc.) describe Professor Rachman as warm, brilliant, funny (even silly), and generous with his ideas. He is not only respected for his research but is also much cherished as a therapist, supervisor, mentor, colleague, and friend.

Professor Rachman continues to see patients with a range of anxiety disorders, and to engage in research and writing, and most importantly thinking about cognitive behavioral therapy (CBT) for anxiety disorders and related problems. His current interests revolve around OCD; the intersection of psychology and medicine; and ways to improve the understanding, delivery, and effectiveness of CBT.

Adam S. Radomsky and Roz Shafran

See also: Cognitive Model; Cognitive Restructuring; Exposure, Imaginal; Eysenck, Hans J. (1916–1997); Flooding; Habituation; Obsessive-Compulsive Disorder; Panic Disorder; Systematic Desensitization; Wolpe, Joseph (1915–1997)

Further Reading

Rachman, Stanley. (1965). Studies in desensitization: I. The separate effects of relaxation and desensitization. *Behaviour Research and Therapy, 3*, 245–252.

Rachman, Stanley. (1980). Emotional processing. *Behaviour Research and Therapy, 18*, 51–60.

Rachman, Stanley. (1997). A cognitive theory of obsessions. *Behaviour Research and Therapy, 25*, 793–802.

Reciprocal Inhibition

Reciprocal inhibition, from a physiological perspective, refers to the automatic spinal reflex process by which an antagonist muscle is inhibited from contracting when the opposing agonist muscle is contracted, such that both muscles cannot be contracted simultaneously. For example, if you contract your quadriceps muscle (agonist) and extend your leg at the knee, the hamstring muscle (antagonist) stretches. This is reversed as you pull your knee back in by contracting your hamstring muscle and stretching your quadriceps muscle. In the 1950s, a South African psychiatrist named Joseph Wolpe (1915–1997) applied this process to fear extinction. He noted that the autonomic nervous system has two systems that oppose each other in a similar agonist/antagonist process: the sympathetic nervous system and the parasymapathetic nervous system. From this perspective, anxiety resulting from activation of the sympathetic nervous system could be inhibited by activation of a competing response from the parasympathetic nervous system such as digestion.

Wolpe, who is also known as the father of behavior therapy, used this idea to guide his research on counterconditioning in cats and later in humans. Wolpe's work was based on the research of Jules Masserman, who exposed cats to electric shocks in a box so that they experienced a conditioned anxiety response when placed in the box where they were previously shocked. Later, when Masserman fed the cats while they were in the box, they became less anxious. Masserman interpreted this behavior from a psychodynamic perspective. He concluded that cats made to be neurotic could lose their neurosis by addressing their motivational conflict. Wolpe extended this research and observed that as he fed the anxious cats gradually closer and closer to the box where they were shocked, the cats became less anxious. Wolpe proposed that the anxiety response was incompatible with eating and thus the anxiety reduction occurred due to the process of reciprocal inhibition. This was the first development of the gradual and stepwise process of exposure therapy, which is now the treatment of choice for treating phobias.

Wolpe found that a new learned association could inhibit or prevent a previously conditioned response through counterconditioning or deconditioning. He identified three types of responses that are antagonistic or incompatible with the experience of anxiety: assertive responses, sexual responses, and relaxation responses. A number of effective behavioral techniques for anxiety reduction and treatment of fears and phobias have been based on this process, including avoidance conditioning, assertiveness training, and systematic desensitization. For example, an individual who is fearful of snakes may be trained in a relaxation response. The relaxation response is then repeatedly paired with the feared stimulus (the snake) until the snake no longer evokes fear. The relaxation response is considered to be mutually incompatible with the fear response (i.e., it is impossible to feel relaxed and fearful at the same time). In 1958, Wolpe published his approach in a book called *Psychotherapy by Reciprocal Inhibition.* This seminal work stimulated many researchers in the field who contributed significantly to the development of the science and practice of behavior therapy over the following decades.

Randi E. McCabe

See also: Behavior Therapy; Systematic Desensitization; Wolpe, Joseph (1915–1997)

Further Reading

Wolpe, Joseph (1954). Reciprocal inhibition as the main basis of psychotherapeutic effects. *Archives of Neurology and Psychiatry, 72,* 205–226.

Wolpe, Joseph (1958). *Psychotherapy by reciprocal inhibition.* Redwood City, CA: Stanford University Press.

Risk Factors

Fear of things that cause harm is common, healthy, and normal. In fact, upward of 90% of children in preschool age and middle childhood have significant fears. However, as children cognitively and emotionally develop, most learn to use coping strategies to reason and calm themselves when they are afraid. However, this part of development can go awry and result in a person developing a phobia. Phobias are fears that are intense, long-lasting (i.e., *persistent*), automatic (i.e., *involuntary*), and problematic (i.e., *maladaptive*). Factors that *increase* the likelihood that a person develops problems are called *risk factors.* For example, younger ages are more likely to have intense fears, so they evidence higher risk. Similarly, factors that *decrease* the likelihood of awry development are called *protective factors.* Studies suggest both kinds of factors affect the chances or probability someone will develop a phobia. It is important to understand that no one risk factor guarantees that someone will develop a phobia, no one protective factor guarantees that one will not develop one, and factors do not usually simply cancel each other out. For example, most studies have found that phobic fears are similar across culture, socioeconomic status (i.e., income, career, education), and race once other risk factors are accounted for. This is why risk and protective factors are said to be *multiplicative* in how they affect the development of problems.

Risk and protective factors are often broken down into specific psychological vulnerabilities (e.g., learning what is dangerous), generalized psychological vulnerabilities (e.g., diminished sense of control), and generalized biological vulnerabilities (e.g., genetic contributions). Common psychological vulnerabilities include experiences that either teach the person to fear something or teach him or her how to cope well with fears (e.g., parents' behavior and how adults and friends respond to fear). Humans learn through observing others and by experiencing the consequences (positive and negative) of doing something. Experiences that are frightening or traumatic can be a risk factor for developing a phobia, especially in children older than seven years. People find fear uncomfortable but fear goes away temporarily when someone avoids the feared thing; this teaches the lesson that avoiding feels better immediately. However, as time goes on, the person avoids more and more types of things to escape the fear. This is why people may generalize a fear to include more things or situations over time. Humans also learn from observing others who have fears. Children are more likely to develop fears if they see their caregiver avoiding and fearing certain objects or situations. This risk is greater if the child has other rewards for his or her avoidance, such as when others help the person avoid or praise the person for avoiding. In fact, children whose caregivers are insensitive or nonresponsive to their fears and needs (e.g., an insecure attachment) are more likely to develop anxiety later. The opposite is also true; children who are encouraged and supported for safely confronting fears are less likely to develop phobias and thus these children overcome fears faster.

Biological or heritable factors linked to phobia development include genes, temperament, and gender. The research on gender is mixed in that some studies found males were more likely to develop phobias, others found equal rates in males and females, and some have found higher rates in females. It is likely that the rate for each gender is highly dependent on the type of fear and other risk factors that may be present. For example, there is some evidence that the genes inherited from parents play an important role in children's risk for developing a phobia, but the data have been inconsistent. Studies of children with identical genes (monozygotic twins) and those with very similar genes (dizygotic twins) have suggested that the risk for developing a phobia is partly related to inherited genes, with excessive fears of animals and blood/needles as the phobias demonstrating the greatest heritability.

However, these genetics studies have also shown that genes do not explain who develops a phobia. Research suggests that genes interact, or work uniquely, with certain life experiences. In these cases, the genetic "risk" becomes active only when the person is also exposed to certain frightening experiences. Frightening, uncontrollable, or unpredictable events over time (especially at a young age) can help increase a person's generalized psychological risk for developing a phobia by changing how he or she thinks or how his or her brain interprets new information. For example, temperament can be thought of as a stable way that a person approaches or interprets the world. High fear sensitivity, emotion dysregulation (poor ability to soothe self), high amounts of behavioral inhibition (sensitivity to punishment), and behavioral disinhibition (approach-withdrawal) are all temperament dimensions that appear to be heritable or biological risk factors for phobia development. However, the impact they have depends on the context of fearful experiences. For example, the behavioral inhibition system (BIS) has been linked to an increase of the activity of certain brain (neural) pathways. These pathways being used more often increases the person's risk for responding fearfully in the future and possibly developing a phobia. People with phobias also tend to have increased focus and memory for dangerous things around them and often to believe things are more dangerous than they really are. Since life experiences cannot always be controlled, knowing how risk and protective factors work together can help researchers develop ways to prevent the development of phobias for those most at risk and help treat those who already have phobias.

Kirstin Stauffacher Gros, Antonina S. Farmer,
Nina Wong Sarver, and Daniel F. Gros

See also: Evolution, Role of; Phobias, Family Influences on the Development and Maintenance of; Phobias, Genetics of

Further Reading

Gerulle, Friederike C., & Rapee, Ronald M. (2001). Mother knows best: The effects of maternal modeling on the acquisition of fear and avoidance behaviour in toddlers. *Behaviour Research and Therapy, 40,* 279–287.

Lichtenstein, Paul, & Annas, Peter. (2000). Heritability and prevalence of specific fears and phobias in childhood. *Journal of Child Psychology and Psychiatry, 41,* 927–937.

Vasey, Micahel W., & Dadds, Mark R. (Eds.) (2001). *The developmental psychopathology of anxiety.* New York, NY: Oxford University Press.

Rothbaum, Barbara O.

Barbara Olasov Rothbaum, PhD, is a professor and psychologist who specializes in research on the treatment of anxiety disorders. She has pioneered the application of virtual reality exposure therapy for psychological disorders such as phobias, and she is a leading figure in the development of cognitive behavioral therapy (CBT) for posttraumatic stress disorder (PTSD).

Rothbaum holds a doctoral degree in clinical psychology and a diplomate in behavioral psychology from the American Board of Professional Psychology. At Emory University's School of Medicine in Atlanta, Rothbaum is professor in psychiatry, director of the Trauma and Anxiety Recovery Program, and the associate vice chair of clinical research. Rothbaum additionally serves as a member of the Blue Ribbon Panel for Pentagon officials. This panel is comprised of notable experts who are appointed to investigate specific topics. Further, she serves as a committee member on the Institute of Medicine's Study on Assessment of Ongoing Efforts in the Treatment of PTSD.

Having published more than 200 scientific articles, book chapters, and books, Rothbaum is a highly productive researcher. Her work has been recognized with both state and national awards. In terms of her research on phobias, her most notable contribution is the development of virtual reality exposure therapy (VRET), which involves exposing individuals to feared situations in an immersive, computer-simulated environment. In 1995, Rothbaum and her colleagues published the first study evaluating this intervention and demonstrated that it was effective in treating acrophobia (fear of heights). In further studies, VRET has been successfully applied to aviophobia (fear of flying), social anxiety disorder (social phobia; particularly public speaking), and PTSD. In 1996, Rothbaum founded Virtually Better, Inc., a company that creates virtual reality environments. The company has been extensively involved in the development, research, and dissemination of virtual reality applications for various health conditions.

In addition to her work on phobias, Rothbaum is an internationally recognized expert on trauma and CBT, particularly exposure treatment, for PTSD. She has published extensively in this area, including numerous research articles and several therapist manuals and client workbooks. She is a past president of the International Society for Traumatic Stress Studies and has also served as associate editor of the *Journal of Traumatic Stress*. Combining her interests in virtual reality treatment and trauma, Rothbaum's recent work has focused on evaluating VRET for military-related PTSD.

Irena Milosevic

See also: Acrophobia (Fear of Heights); Aviophobia (Fear of Flying); Cognitive Behavioral Therapy; Exposure Treatment; Foa, Edna B. (1937–); Posttraumatic Stress Disorder; Virtual Reality Treatment

Further Reading

Rothbaum, Barbara Olasov, Foa, Edna B., & Hembree, Elizabeth A. (2007). *Reclaiming your life from a traumatic experience: Workbook*. New York, NY: Oxford University Press Inc.

Rothbaum, Barbara Olasov, Hodges, Larry F., Kooper, Rob, Opdyke, Dan, Williford, James, & North, Max M. (1995). Effectiveness of computer-generated (virtual reality) graded exposure in the treatment of acrophobia. *American Journal of Psychiatry, 152*, 626–628.

S

Safety Behavior

Safety behavior is any strategy used to protect oneself from actual or perceived threat. Safety behaviors can be overt (observable) or covert (mental) actions. In the general population, individuals use safety behavior adaptively to cope with and decrease anxiety in various situations. For instance, carrying an umbrella on a cloudy day and mentally rehearsing a speech prior to delivering it are common examples of overt and covert safety behavior, respectively. Like the general public, individuals with anxiety disorders also use safety behavior. However, for these individuals, safety behavior tends to be employed in unnecessary contexts, at a higher frequency and to a greater degree (Thwaites & Freeston, 2005). For example, a person suffering from achluophobia (fear of darkness) may never leave home without a flashlight or may drink excessive amounts of alcohol prior to bedtime in order to induce sleepiness. Thus, by using safety behavior, anxious individuals are (sometimes) able to manage or entirely avoid their distress in feared situations. Nevertheless, employing these strategies may be problematic. According to Salkovskis (1991), a fear persists because continuous use of safety behavior prevents an individual from confronting his or her fears and/or from discovering important, sometimes therapeutic, information about feared situations. Therefore, as described in cognitive models of various anxiety disorders, safety behavior may be a maintenance factor for anxiety-related problems.

Some researchers argue that safety behavior interferes with psychological treatments for anxiety disorders because it prevents patients from disconfirming their fears. For example, if an individual with trypanophobia (fear of needles) consistently applies numbing cream to his or her arm prior to receiving a vaccination, he or she will never have the chance to learn that the needle does not cause unbearable pain. Consistent with this view, several research studies have shown that individuals who refrain from using safety behavior during treatment fare better than those who use it. In one study, Sloan and Telch (2002) compared exposure therapy with and without safety behavior for claustrophobia (fears of restriction and/or suffocation) and found that those who did not use safety behavior during exposure experienced the largest reductions in claustrophobic fear. By contrast, other research comparing exposure therapy with and without safety behavior has failed to find such differences. For instance, Milosevic and Radomsky (2008) compared exposure therapy with and without safety gear (e.g., gloves, masks) for ophidiophobia (fear of snakes) and found no differences in fear reduction between the two treatment conditions. Based on these mixed findings, it is unclear whether safety behavior indeed interferes with exposure therapy for anxiety disorders. In fact, some researchers have proposed that safety behavior may actually enhance the efficacy and acceptability of exposure-based treatments (Rachman, Radomsky, & Shafran, 2008).

Given the controversial results, a greater understanding of whether safety behavior interferes with treatment for anxiety disorders is warranted. By clarifying how these behaviors affect treatment outcome, clinicians may be able to more effectively administer psychotherapy and better assist their clients. Because the majority of research on safety behavior has been conducted on nonclinical (e.g., undergraduate students) samples, future research should aim to replicate and extend these findings in clinical (e.g., individuals with anxiety disorders) samples. Testing on clinical samples may inform us about the specific characteristics (e.g., for which disorders and with which types of safety behavior) necessary for the enhancement of and/or interference with psychological treatments. Investigating these characteristics may therefore help to resolve the aforementioned controversy related to the use of safety behavior in the treatment of anxiety disorders.

Joelle N. Soucy, Hannah C. Levy,
and Adam S. Radomsky

See also: Anxiety and Related Disorders; Cognitive Behavioral Therapy; Cognitive Model; Distraction; Exposure Treatment

Further Reading

Milosevic, Irena, & Radomsky, Aadam S. (2008). Safety behaviour does not necessarily interfere with exposure therapy. *Behaviour Research and Therapy, 46,* 1111–1118.

Rachman, Stanley, Radomsky, Adam S., & Shafran, Roz. (2008). Safety behaviour: A reconsideration. *Behaviour Research and Therapy, 46,* 163–173.

Salkovskis, Paul M. (1991). The importance of behaviour in the maintenance of anxiety and panic: A cognitive account. *Behavioural Psychotherapy, 19,* 6–19.

Sloan, Tracy, & Telch, Michael J. (2002). The effects of safety-seeking behavior and guided threat reappraisal on fear reduction during exposure: An experimental investigation. *Behaviour Research and Therapy, 40,* 235–251.

Thwaites, Richard, & Freeston, Mark. (2005). Safety-seeking behaviours: Fact or function? How can we clinically differentiate between safety behaviours and adaptive coping strategies across anxiety disorders? *Behavioural and Cognitive Psychotherapy, 33,* 177–188.

Selective Serotonin Reuptake Inhibitors

Selective serotonin reuptake inhibitors (SSRIs) are a class of psychiatric medications used in the treatment of anxiety disorders. SSRIs are believed to have their effects by increasing the amount of serotonin available in certain brain regions. Because of this, it has been assumed that low levels of serotonin are responsible for causing depression and anxiety disorders.

The first medication in this class was fluoxetine, known by the brand name Prozac. Prozac was first released for the treatment of depression in 1987 by the Eli Lilly pharmaceutical company. Prior to that time, the main antidepressant drugs belonged to the tricyclic and monamine oxidase (MAO) inhibitor families. Prozac was found to be effective without the common troublesome side effects of the tricyclics and the MAO inhibitors. Subsequently, many other SSRIs were developed: sertaline, paroxetine, citalopram, fluvoxamine, and escitalopram.

SSRIs are often effective in the treatment of panic disorder. They can block the panic symptoms. However, cognitive behavioral therapy is still required to overcome agoraphobic symptoms. SSRIs are also used in the treatment of general anxiety disorder, social anxiety disorder (social phobia), obsessive-compulsive disorder, and posttraumatic stress disorder. SSRIs have been used in the treatment of specific phobias, but the evidence for their effectiveness is limited.

SSRIs are generally well tolerated. The most common side effects in up to 30% of individuals include nausea, stomach upset, vomiting, reduced sexual drive, feelings of emotional blunting, restlessness, and tremor. Occasionally, SSRIs can cause an increase in suicidal thoughts or behavior. This is more likely in teenagers and those with bipolar mood disorders.

SSRIs are believed to have their therapeutic effects by increasing the amount of serotonin in the synaptic gaps between nerve cells in specific neurocircuits. Serotonin is a neurotransmitter, a chemical that is responsible for transmitting nerve impulses from one neuron to another. Nerve cells, or neurons, are separated from each other by a microscopic gap known as a synapse. When an electrical impulse travels along the branches of a neuron, it causes the release of a neurotransmitter at the synaptic junction. The neurotransmitter floats across the gap and combines with receptor molecules in the cell wall of the next neuron. Neurons are connected to each other by millions of synapses. Groups of neurons are connected along millions of neurocircuits.

Although the theory of low serotonin has some explanatory power, many researchers believe that it is an oversimplification. The true basis of phobic disorders may be more complex, involving gene expression in neurons and the action of multiple chemical cascades inside the cell. Other neurotransmitters may also be implicated: epinephrine, norepinephrine, gamma-aminobutyric acid, and glutamate.

SSRIs are widely used because of their relative safety and tolerability. Serious side effects are rare. They are not addictive or habit-forming. However, there can be withdrawal symptoms if the medication is stopped suddenly after extended periods of treatment. This is referred to as the *SSRI discontinuation syndrome*. The major symptoms of this syndrome are dizziness or light-headedness, general malaise, and strange electric shock–like sensations in the head. These symptoms are not at all dangerous but can be very uncomfortable.

In a minority of individuals, the beneficial effects of SSRIs may wear off after a period of a year or longer. This is known as *SSRI poop out* or more properly as *tachyphylaxis*. Often a switch to an alternate SSRI is effective in regaining symptom control.

Alan B. Eppel

See also: Treatment, Medication

Self-Efficacy Theory

Self-efficacy is defined as "the belief in one's capabilities to organize and execute the courses of action required to produce given attainments" (Bandura, 1997, p. 3). In other words, self-efficacy reflects a person's confidence in being able to effectively achieve a goal. Self-efficacy theory, developed by Albert Bandura in the 1970s, holds that self-efficacy beliefs determine cognitive processing, motivation, emotional arousal, and behavior. The theory is a central component of Bandura's broader social cognitive theory of learning and development. It has been applied to numerous domains, including phobias and their treatment.

Self-efficacy theory delineates two types of expectations for success: *outcome expectations* and *efficacy expectations*. *Outcome expectations* refer to one's beliefs that certain behaviors will produce certain outcomes, whereas *efficacy expectations* pertain to beliefs about one's capabilities to perform the behavior required to produce an outcome. It is possible to have high outcome expectations (i.e., that a behavior will lead to an outcome) but low efficacy expectations (i.e., low confidence in one's ability to perform the required behavior). Bandura proposed that it is the efficacy expectations that are the critical determinant of the goals people set and the choices they make, as well as their expenditure of effort and perseverance.

Self-efficacy is understood to be a multidimensional construct, varying in magnitude (degree of difficulty of adopting a specific behavior), strength (certainty in being able to perform a task), and generality (degree to which self-efficacy beliefs are related within or across behavioral domains or across time). In social cognitive theory, self-efficacy is considered significant because of its direct impact on behavior and influence on other important psychological variables. For example, people with greater self-efficacy believe that they are more capable of coping with obstacles and tend to therefore embrace challenges to fulfill their goals. By contrast, people with low self-efficacy believe that there is little they can do to change their circumstances and accordingly feel helpless. When faced with challenges or set-backs, they tend to lower their ambitions and give up quickly or suffer a decrease in the quality of their performance.

Bandura proposed that self-efficacy has a powerful impact on cognitive, motivational, emotional, and choice processes. People with high self-efficacy tend to be more cognitively resourceful and future-focused. They envision achieving successful outcomes and engage in effective problem solving. Further, self-efficacy helps to maintain consistency in levels of motivation. It determines the goals that people set, the effort they place in achieving those goals, and their perseverance in the face of challenges. Given sufficient ability and motivation, high self-efficacy can enhance task initiation and persistence. However, if a person does not believe that his or her actions can produce desired outcomes, motivation to act will be low. Self-efficacy additionally has a role in regulating emotional states. High self-efficacy makes it more likely that demands will be interpreted as manageable challenges, thereby reducing a person's worry and anxiety. It further facilitates problem-focused coping geared toward changing stressful circumstances, and it enables individuals to seek social support and engage in self-soothing to reduce emotional arousal. Low self-efficacy, on the other hand, is associated with stress and can directly produce depression. Finally, self-efficacy influences the choices people make, such as the kinds of activities and environments they choose throughout their life.

Bandura detailed four factors that determine a person's self-efficacy, including one's prior performance experiences of success or failure (*mastery experience*), observation of others' success or failure (*vicarious experience*), others' verbal encouragement or negative messages about accomplishing a task (*verbal persuasion*), and one's subjective physiological and emotional arousal (*physiological state*). All four factors can have a role in either increasing or decreasing a person's self-efficacy. Mastery experiences are believed to be the most influential and reliable determinant of self-efficacy, as they provide the most direct information about one's capability to perform a task.

Since Bandura conceptualized self-efficacy theory, the construct of self-efficacy has become prominent in psychological theory and research. Self-efficacy theory has further been applied to a broad range of domains, including education, health, and occupational choice. In terms of its application to phobias, the early work of Bandura and colleagues identified self-efficacy as an important mechanism of change in phobia treatment (e.g., Bandura & Adams, 1977). Based on a series of studies of behavioral treatment of snake phobia, Bandura concluded that the relationship between fear and phobic avoidance is explained by self-efficacy. He found that treatment is effective in reducing avoidance because it teaches individuals that they can successfully cope with the phobic stimulus. Guided mastery therapy, a type of phobia treatment, was subsequently developed based on this premise. The therapy aims to change individuals' self-efficacy in feared situations. More generally, according to self-efficacy theory, if people can learn that they are capable of tackling challenges, they are expected to experience less anxiety when faced with stressors and to engage actions that will help them overcome the challenges.

Self-efficacy theory has been supported by extensive correlational and experimental studies showing that self-efficacy beliefs contribute to people's development, adjustment, and achievement (Bandura, 1997). Critiques of the theory suggest that the focus on a single variable as a major determinant of performance and choice is limiting. Additionally, debate surrounds one of the theory's key tenets, which holds that self-efficacy causes expected outcomes for behavior but not vice versa. Contrary to this position, research has shown that expected outcomes can also causally influence self-efficacy (for a review, see Williams, 2010).

Irena Milosevic

See also: Bandura, Albert (1925–); Guided Mastery Therapy; Social Learning Theory

Further Reading

Bandura, Albert. (1977). Self-efficacy: Toward a unifying theory of behavioral change. *Psychological Review, 54*, 191–215.

Bandura, Albert. (1986). Fearful expectations and avoidant actions as coeffects of perceived self-inefficacy. *American Psychologist, 41*, 389–391.

Bandura, Albert. (1997). *Self-efficacy: The exercise of control*. New York, NY: Freeman.

Bandura, Albert, & Adams, Nancy E. (1977). Analysis of self-efficacy theory of behavioral change. *Cognitive Therapy and Research, 4*, 287–310.

Williams, David M. (2010). Outcome expectancy and self-efficacy: Theoretical implications of an unresolved contradiction. *Personality and Social Psychology Review, 14*, 417–425.

Skinner, B.F. (1904–1990)

B.F. Skinner, born Burrhus Frederic Skinner (1904–1990), was an influential American psychologist, author, and inventor. Skinner established his own brand of the scientific study of behavior, and he made critical contributions to learning theory by developing the principles of operant conditioning. Skinner's work has had wide-reaching influence in psychology and other fields such as education. His ideas have shaped the understanding and treatment of phobias. He is recognized as the most eminent psychologist of the 20th century (Haggbloom et al., 2002).

Skinner was born on March 20, 1904, in the small town of Susquehanna, Pennsylvania. He was the eldest of two sons of a lawyer and a homemaker. Skinner described his upbringing as "warm and stable." A naturally curious boy, he spent

Renowned behaviorist psychologist B.F. Skinner. Skinner is credited with developing operant conditioning principles, which explain that certain responses, such as escape from a feared situation, are reinforced because they eliminate an unpleasant stimulus. (AP Photo)

his childhood building things, including a shack in the woods, a flotation system that separated ripe berries, and a cart with backward steering. Skinner's construction abilities would come in handy in his future research in psychology.

After graduating from a small high school with a group of only eight students, Skinner went on to attend Hamilton College in upstate New York with the goal of becoming a writer. At Hamilton, Skinner felt at odds with the students and faculty. He complained of the students' low intellectual interest and, as an atheist, he was critical of the school's religious teaching and policy. He graduated in 1926 with a BA in English literature and moved back home to further his writing. This proved a struggle, however, and Skinner was not productive. He eventually moved to Greenwich Village in New York City hoping to advance his career there. Although he did not achieve success writing fiction, a brief stint working as a bookstore clerk exposed him to the work of Ivan Pavlov (1849–1936) and John B. Watson (1878–1958), which piqued his interest in psychology.

At age 24, Skinner enrolled as a graduate student in psychology at Harvard University, where he was mentored by a physiologist with an interest in animal behavior. He earned a master's degree in 1930 and a PhD in 1931. Skinner was subsequently awarded a fellowship that allowed him to remain at Harvard for another five years and extend his research.

Skinner built numerous apparatuses that allowed him to study animal behavior. The two most important devices included the "Skinner box" (also called the operant conditioning chamber) and the cumulative recorder. The Skinner box facilitated the training of animals, typically rats or pigeons, to perform specific behaviors (e.g., pressing a bar) in response to a cue (e.g., a light or sound). Once a desired behavior was performed, the mechanisms in the box delivered a food pellet or another reward. The cumulative recorder allowed Skinner to record the rats' behavior graphically. Critically, Skinner discovered that the rats' rate of bar pressing did not depend on the stimulus that preceded this behavior (as proposed by Pavlov and Watson) but rather on what followed it.

Skinner was influenced by the work of notable behaviorist Edward L. Thorndike (1874–1949), particularly Thorndike's *law of effect*, which holds that the specific consequences of behavior will make that behavior either more or less likely to be repeated. Skinner elaborated on Thorndike's ideas by developing the principles of *operant conditioning*, a type of learning in which behavior is influenced by the consequences that follow it. These consequences can be *reinforcements*, which make a behavior more likely to occur again, or *punishments*, which make a behavior less likely to occur again. Skinner used the term *operant* because organisms operate on their environment to produce consequences.

Sharing Watson's view that all behavior must be understood through observable events, Skinner rejected a mentalist, introspective approach to psychology. As he continued to develop his ideas, he articulated his own version of behaviorism, *radical behaviorism*, which held that all behavior is environmentally determined and that personal freedom is thus an illusion. Skinner proposed that all behavior is to some extent governed by reinforcement. A rat's bar pressing, for example, is reinforced by the delivery of food after the bar is pressed. Parents are reinforced if their baby stops crying when they pick it up.

Skinner also discovered how to *shape* behavior; that is, he successively reinforced smaller elements of a desirable behavior until the full behavior was achieved. In this way, Skinner taught pigeons to play Ping-Pong and to play a tune on a toy piano. Like Thorndike, Skinner believed that using *punishment* to change behavior was not effective in the long term and held that the best way to develop new behavior is to positively reinforce desired behavior. Skinner detailed his principles of operant conditioning in his first book and seminal work, *The Behavior of Organisms* (1938). He went on to publish numerous additional books and articles on operant conditioning and behavior.

In 1936, Skinner married Yvonne Blue, with whom he had two daughters. In the same year, the couple moved to Minnesota, where Skinner took up a teaching position at the University of Minnesota. In 1945, the family moved to Bloomington, Indiana, where Skinner was appointed chair of the Psychology Department at Indiana University. His appointment, however, was short-lived as he was invited to return to the Psychology Department at Harvard in 1948. Skinner remained at Harvard as professor until his retirement in 1974. During his tenure, he trained many graduate students who themselves made notable contributions to psychology (e.g., Ogden R. Lindsley, Herbert Terrace, William K. Estes).

Although Skinner was renowned for his laboratory research with animals, his work extended well beyond the laboratory. He wrote extensively on the applications of behaviorism and operant conditioning to various problems in society. His most notable projects and inventions included attempts to train pigeons to guide missiles during World War II (Project Pigeon); the "baby tender" or Air-Crib, an enclosed, heated crib designed to make early childcare easier, which garnered Skinner unintended infamy when it was likened to the Skinner box; and the "teaching box," a mechanical device that provided reinforcement to students when they produced a correct response. In 1948, Skinner published a well-known novel, *Walden Two*, in which he provided a fictional account of a society where positive reinforcement was used to control human behavior. About two decades later, he published another widely read work, *Beyond Freedom and Dignity* (1971), in which he denied the idea of free will, emphasizing instead the role of operant conditioning in determining human behavior and proposing solutions to societal problems based on operant conditioning principles.

Skinner received many awards for his work, including the prestigious Gold Medal Award for Distinguished Scientific Contribution from the American Psychological Association (APA; 1958) and the National Medal of Science (1968). He maintained a high degree of productivity across his lifetime, publishing more than 20 books and 180 articles. In 1990, he received a Special Presidential Citation for Lifetime Contributions to Psychology, the first award of its kind, at the APA's 98th Annual Convention. During his keynote address, Skinner expressed a critical view of the rise of cognitive psychology. He wrote his final paper, *Can Psychology Be a Science of Mind?*, based on this talk. He completed the paper within a week of the keynote and the night before his death. Diagnosed with leukemia the year prior, Skinner died on August 18, 1990, at age 86.

Skinner's principles of operant conditioning continue to influence our views of learning. Further, his ideas have laid the groundwork for behavior modification therapies, such as contingency management, which involve reinforcement of desirable behaviors and extinction (elimination of reinforcement) or punishment of undesirable behaviors. Operant conditioning principles have also contributed to our understanding of phobias and their treatment. In particular, escape from or avoidance of feared situations is understood to maintain the fear problem through a mechanism of reinforcement.

Irena Milosevic

See also: Contingency Management; Operant Conditioning; Pavlov, Ivan (1849–1936); Thorndike, Edward L. (1874–1949); Two-Factor Theory of Avoidance Learning; Watson, John B. (1878–1958)

Further Reading

Haggbloom, Steven J., Warnick, Renee, Warnick, Jason E., Jones, Vinessa K., Yarbrough, Gary L., Russell, Tenea M., . . . Monte, Emmanuelle. (2002). The 100 most eminent psychologists of the twentieth century. *Review of General Psychology, 6*, 139–152.

Rutherford, Alexandra. (2009). *Beyond the box: B. F. Skinner's technology of behavior from laboratory to life, 1950s–1970s*. Toronto: University of Toronto Press.

Skinner, B. F. (1938). *The behavior of organisms: An experimental analysis*. New York, NY: Appleton-Century.

Social Anxiety Disorder (Social Phobia)

The hallmark characteristic of social anxiety disorder (SAD), also referred to as *social phobia*, is a fear of situations that could involve evaluation. The fear of being evaluated in one or more social or performance situations is sufficiently intense that the anticipation of evaluation causes anxiety, which can escalate into a panic attack. Therefore, a person with SAD avoids such situations or endures them with great distress. The anxiety or avoidance significantly impairs quality of life.

Most people report experiencing occasional social anxiety, such as before a critical presentation or while interacting with someone important; however, this type of social anxiety tends to be short-lived and does not stop someone from giving presentations or meeting new people. By contrast, there is a significant portion of the population (12-month prevalence is approximately 7%; American Psychiatric Association [APA], 2013) for whom the social anxiety is more intense, enduring, and disruptive to life functioning. The distinction between "common" social anxiety and pathological social anxiety was formalized over several versions of the *Diagnostic and Statistical Manual of Mental Disorders* (DSM). Pathological social anxiety was initially narrowly defined within the context of a *specific phobia* in the DSM-II. In the DSM-III, social anxiety was designated as a distinct diagnostic category termed *social phobia*. In the DSM-IV, the category was relabeled as *social anxiety disorder* (SAD) and included specifiers distinguishing between a specific phobia (e.g., public speaking) and an anxiety disorder generalized across several situations. In the fifth and most recent version of the DSM (APA, 2013), SAD refers to persons who fear several social situations, with a specifier now used to indicate persons who fear only performance situations (Kerns, Comer, Pincus, & Hofmann,

2013). The SAD diagnosis requires that the symptoms are consistent and persistent, and cause clinically significant distress or impairment in social, occupational, or other important areas of functioning, which represents something very different from common character traits (e.g., shyness, introversion).

The DSM is only one set of criteria for assessing SAD. Perhaps equally common is the World Health Organization's *International Classification of Diseases* criteria, currently in version 10 (ICD-10). The ICD-10 diagnostic criteria share a great deal with the DSM-5 diagnostic criteria, referring to fears of being the focus of attention, being embarrassed, or being humiliated, as well as avoidance of social situations where such fears might be realized.

People with SAD typically report a desire to be social with others, but also report significant anxiety about doing something embarrassing or humiliating (e.g., visibly shaking, stumbling over one's words). To cope, people with SAD often withdraw in social settings (e.g., be quiet or avoidant). They might also experience increased levels of physiological arousal (e.g., sweating, blushing, trembling) in response to social situations, either during the situation or for weeks to months in anticipation of the situation. Attempts to hide or minimize the symptoms of physiological arousal (e.g., not shaking hands because of sweaty palms) can cause someone with SAD to appear rude or conceited, therein eliciting negative responses from others. Despite such outward appearances, people with SAD are often overly self-critical, have low self-esteem, and can be excessively submissive.

SAD is associated with school dropouts, lower workplace productivity, and overall decreased quality of life. People with SAD may seek out jobs that have limited social contact, live at home longer, experience a delay in marrying or having children, or may avoid such experiences altogether. People with SAD also tend to self-medicate, using drugs or alcohol to help them endure social situations. Accordingly, SAD often co-occurs with other anxiety, depressive, and substance use disorders, as well as with avoidant personality disorder.

The onset of SAD is typically during childhood or early adolescence and remains distinct from shyness. Many children who report extreme shyness will outgrow their shyness, and many people who have SAD do not report a childhood history of shyness. Having a first-degree relative with SAD increases the chance of developing the disorder (two to six times more likely; APA, 2013); however, the manifestation of SAD is at least partly dependent on environmental influences such as stressful social events and parental modeling. SAD is typically chronic in nature because people are often reluctant to seek treatment; nevertheless, there are several empirically supported treatments for SAD, including cognitive, cognitive behavioral, and pharmacological therapies.

In the general population, women are more likely than men to report SAD (1.5–2.2 times more likely; APA, 2013). In treatment-seeking samples, the gender difference in prevalence disappears, or is even slightly higher in men. Social pressures to conform to gender roles may prompt more men than women to seek help (e.g., it is less socially acceptable for a man to be shy than for a woman to be shy). Gender may also contribute to differential presentations of SAD between men and women; specifically, men are more likely to fear dating and use substances to cope with social anxiety symptoms. By contrast, women are more likely to report comorbid bipolar, depressive, and anxiety disorders. The manifestation of SAD may also differ slightly in Eastern cultures than in Western cultures. In Western cultures the fear often focuses on embarrassing oneself, whereas for people from Eastern cultures the central concern can focus on offending others or making others feel uncomfortable (e.g., *taijin kyofusho* syndrome in Japan and Korea).

Life stage may also influence the type and intensity of social anxiety symptoms. Older adults may experience a lower level of social anxiety in several situations, which may be related to declining function (e.g., hearing or vision) or concerns about appearance (e.g., aging, visible symptoms of other medical conditions). Younger adults and adolescents seem to experience higher levels of anxiety in fewer but more specific situations (e.g., dating). Finally, levels of social anxiety may rise and fall naturally with changes in life circumstances (e.g., engaging and leaving relationships, vocation changes).

Historically, research and theory have focused on fearing negative evaluation (e.g., being humiliated) as the key concern for persons with SAD; however, more recent research has suggested that for some people fearing positive evaluation (e.g., being honored) may be just as problematic (Weeks, Jakatdar, & Heimberg, 2010). Researchers have also found that fears of arousal (e.g., blushing) and intolerance of uncertainty (e.g., fear of the unknown) are related to higher social anxiety symptoms (Carleton, Collimore, & Asmundson, 2010).

R. Nicholas Carleton and Michelle J. N. Teale Sapach

See also: Anxiety and Related Disorders; Cognitive Behavioral Therapy; Panic Attacks; Safety Behavior; Social Skills Training

Further Reading

American Psychiatric Association (APA). (2013). *Diagnostic and statistical manual of mental disorders* (5th ed.). Arlington, VA: American Psychiatric Publishing.

B gels, Susan M., Alden, Lynn, Beidel, Deborah C., Clark, Lee Anna, Pine, Daniel S., Stein, Murray B., & Voncken, Marisol. (2010). Social anxiety disorder: Questions and answers for the DSM-V. *Depression and Anxiety, 27,* 168–189.

Carleton, R. Nicholas, Collimore, Kelsey C., & Asmundson, Gordon J. G. (2010). "It's not just the judgements—it's that I don't know": Intolerance of uncertainty as a predictor of social anxiety. *Journal of Anxiety Disorders, 24,* 189–195.

Kerns, Caroline E., Comer, Jonathan S., Pincus, Donna B., & Hofmann, Stefan G. (2013). Evaluation of the proposed social anxiety disorder specifier change for DSM-5 in a treatment-seeking sample of anxious youth. *Depression and Anxiety, 30,* 709–715.

Weeks, Justin W., Jakatdar, Tejal A., & Heimberg, Richard G. (2010). Comparing and contrasting fears of positive and negative evaluation as facets of social anxiety. *Journal of Social and Clinical Psychology, 29*, 68–94.

Social Learning Theory

Social learning theory, developed by Albert Bandura in the 1960s, is a theory of learning that incorporates both behavioral and cognitive learning components and emphasizes observational learning. Bandura developed social learning theory in response to traditional theories of learning, particularly operant conditioning, which theorized that learning a new behavior requires a person to engage in this behavior and to directly experience its consequences. The social learning theory was one of the first learning models to implicate the role of cognitive factors, in addition to behavioral factors, in the learning of new behavior. Social learning theory has had important implications for our understanding of how fears and phobias develop as it suggests that these fears could arise without direct contact with the threatening object.

According to the operant conditioning theory, complex behaviors are learned via trial and error and selective reinforcement of progressively more complex behaviors. Both Bandura and renowned language acquisition theorist, Noam Chomsky, argued that purely behavioral theories could not account for the range and complexity of human behavior. For example, Chomsky argued that it is virtually impossible for language to be acquired via trial and error, as predicted by models of operant conditioning, since individuals are able to correctly use words with which they have had no prior experience. In response to the limitations of purely behavioral learning theories, Bandura proposed the social learning model, which holds that individuals can learn not only via direct experiences with the new behavior but also by observing other people and imitating their behaviors and responses.

According to the social learning theory, individuals can learn how to respond to stimuli in their environment by observing how other people respond to the same stimuli. One of the best demonstrations of this principle can be found in a series of Bandura's seminal experiments, commonly known as the *Bobo doll experiments* (Bandura, Ross, & Ross, 1961). In these experiments, preschool children observed an adult interacting with a Bobo doll, a child-sized inflatable doll. Some children observed the adult behaving aggressively toward the doll (e.g., hitting, kicking the doll) and other children observed the adult behaving nonaggressively toward the doll. Later in the experiment, the children were given the opportunity to interact with the doll and their behavior was observed. Critically, it was demonstrated that children who observed the adult acting aggressively toward the doll themselves acted more aggressively toward the doll compared to children who observed the adult acting nonaggressively toward the doll. These experiments clearly demonstrated that individuals do not require direct interaction with stimuli in order to acquire new learning, but rather that they can learn simply by observing another individual engage in certain behaviors and by observing the consequences of that behavior.

Bandura proposed several different pathways through which an individual can acquire new learning without directly engaging in the learned behavior or experiencing the consequences of a new behavior. An individual may learn a new behavior by observing a live model engage in the behavior. Bandura referred to this type of observational learning as *modeling*. A new behavior can also be learned by verbal instruction of how to engage in that behavior. Finally, a new behavior can be learned via media, such as film, literature, and the Internet. Observed behavior that results in positive consequences and therefore increases the likelihood that the observee will also engage in that behavior is called *vicarious reinforcement*.

According to Bandura's social learning theory there are four factors that influence the learning of information via observation. First, the individual must direct attention toward the behavior that is to be modeled (*attention*). Factors that influence whether a given behavior is attended to include the perceived importance or relevance of the behavior and the individual engaging in the behavior, as well as characteristics of the individual observing, such as his or her cognitive and perceptual abilities. Second, the individual observing must store that information in long-term memory (*retention*). According to Bandura, retention involves two types of memorial representations: an imaginal and verbal representation of the modeled sequence and its consequences. These retention processes are particularly important when the imitation of the behavior is delayed. Factors influencing this stage of social learning include individual characteristics, such as cognitive and memorial abilities, as well as characteristics of the observed behavior, such as its complexity. Third, the individual must be able to reproduce the observed behavior (*reproduction*). Characteristics that influence the ability to reproduce the observed behavior once again include the complexity of the behavior, as well as the motoric capabilities of the person learning the behavior. The execution of the new behavior is typically refined via self-correction based upon performance feedback. Finally, the individual must have a reason to reproduce the new behavior (*motivation*). An individual will not engage in a new behavior unless there is some reason to do so. Motivation to engage in a new behavior can be influenced by factors such as the personal standards of the individual, past experiences, and perceived consequences of the behavior. Another important component of social learning theory is the concept of reciprocal determination, the idea that individuals are not only influenced by their environment but also influence the environment around them.

Social learning theory has greatly expanded our understanding of how fears develop. Prior to the development of social learning theory it was believed that an individual must have had direct experience with the feared object in order to develop fear of that object. For example, an individual could develop a fear of dogs only if he or she had had a negative interaction with a dog, such as being attacked. A major limitation of this theory was that many individuals with significant fears reported no prior direct experience, or at least an overtly negative experience, with the object of their fears. Accordingly, social learning theory posited an alternative avenue through which fears could develop: an individual could develop a fear not only through direct experience but also by observing another person interact fearfully with the object or even by being told that the feared object was dangerous. Rather than being directly attacked by a dog, an individual could develop a fear of dogs by observing someone else being attacked or simply by being told that dogs are dangerous. Support for the social learning theory of fear comes from studies of rhesus monkeys, which found that monkeys that were not initially fearful of snakes developed a fear of snakes after observing another monkey interacting fearfully with either a real or toy snake (Cook & Mineka, 1990). Vicarious reinforcement and modeling may also play important roles in the reduction of fear. For example, children who are fearful of dogs are more willing to approach and interact with dogs if they had observed models interacting with a variety of dogs (Bandura, & Menlove, 1968).

Social learning theory also has important implications for the treatment of phobias and fears. Whereas purely behavioral theories suggest that fear can be reduced only via extinction (e.g., presentation of the fearful stimulus, such as a snake in the case of snake phobia, in the absence of negative consequences, such as being bitten by a snake), social learning theory also suggests that fears can be treated via modeling and observation. Treatments incorporating concepts from social learning theory may involve having the therapist first model interacting with the fearful object, such as how to handle a snake in the case of snake phobia. Social learning theory can also be used to help the individual acquire new skills. For example, in treating an individual who is fearful of social situations, the therapist may model various social skills pertinent to having a conversation and ask the patient to practice these new skills.

It is important to note that although social learning theory provided a more complete explanation on how fears can develop as compared to earlier purely behavioral theories, it does not offer a complete explanation for the development of fears and phobias. For example, only a proportion of individuals who observe an individual behaving fearfully in the presence of a snake will go on to develop a fear of snakes. Other factors, such as individual differences in personality or genetics, are also important.

Andrea R. Ashbaugh

See also: Bandura, Albert (1925–); Classical Conditioning; Cognitive Model; Learning Theory; Modeling; Operant Conditioning; Phobias, Causes of; Social Skills Training

Further Reading

Bandura, Albert. (1977). *Social Learning Theory*. Upper Saddle River, NJ: Prentice Hall.

Bandura, Albert, & Menlove, Frances L. (1968). Factors determining vicarious extinction of avoidance behavior through symbolic modeling. *Journal of Personality and Social Psychology, 8*, 99–108.

Bandura, A., Ross, Dorothea, & Ross, Sheila A. (1961). Transmission of aggression through the imitation of aggressive models. *Journal of Abnormal and Social Psychology, 63*, 575–582.

Cook, Michael, & Mineka, Susan. (1990). Selective associations in the observational conditioning of fear in monkeys. *Journal of Experimental Psychology: Animal Behavior Processes, 16*, 448–459.

Social Skills Training

Cognitive behavioral models of social anxiety disorder (social phobia) implicate thoughts of personal inadequacy and fears of behaving in a way that is socially unacceptable as central to the development and maintenance of symptoms; however, some researchers believe that a deficit in social skills, rather than cognitive distortions, may contribute to social anxiety. Accordingly, social skills training has been applied as an independent treatment and has been integrated into other empirically supported therapies (e.g., cognitive behavioral therapy [CBT]) for treating social anxiety disorder. The results of integrating social skills training remain mixed and, as such, research is ongoing.

Social skills training begins with identifying deficient social behaviors that would benefit from improvement. Several skills may be addressed, but training typically focuses on nonverbal communication (e.g., frequency of eye contact), speech patterns (e.g., speaking with more confidence), conversation skills (e.g., generating ideas for small talk), and presentation skills (e.g., using adequate volume and appropriate tone). The therapist providing training typically begins didactically and then moves to modeling the skills for the client. The therapist and client then engage in role-played scenarios where the client can practice the skills and receive feedback in a safe and constructive environment. In some cases, the role-played scenarios are videotaped so the client can watch and more objectively assess his or her behaviors. The therapist and client can collaboratively identify areas for additional practice. As the process improves the client's confidence, the therapist encourages the client to progressively implement the new skills in real-life scenarios.

The research results are mixed as to whether people with social anxiety disorder actually have deficits in social skills. Some evidence suggests that people with social anxiety disorder demonstrate social skill deficits when compared to people without social anxiety disorder; however, in other research, no such differences have been found. There is also evidence that although people with social anxiety disorder may not demonstrate large social skills deficits relative to other groups, they are more likely to have social skills deficits. In any case, research has not supported a consistent difference in the skills deficits between people with social anxiety disorder (generalized) and people with performance-specific social anxiety disorder. The results are complicated by evidence that for some people with social anxiety disorder, the skills deficits do not appear while they know they are being watched (e.g., during recorded role-playing), but do appear when they do not know they are being watched (i.e., naturalistic observation). Furthermore, a lack of consensus among researchers regarding the definition and measurement of social skills hinders the interpretation and application of these research findings. The lack of consensus may be inevitable in this line of research since social skills are not always generalizable (e.g., what is acceptable at a party may not be acceptable in a classroom); as such, teaching and producing socially desirable behaviors for all interactions can be challenging. The research does suggest that a social skills deficit makes the person appear more anxious, compliment others less, talk infrequently, and convey less warmth. All of these behavioral differences result in the individual being rated as less likable than nonsocially anxious people.

Assessing skills deficits in specific phobia may provide useful clinical insights. For example, some individuals who fear deep water may be afraid because they cannot swim; accordingly, swimming lessons may help to alleviate the client's fear. A parallel process for social anxiety disorder provides theoretical support for social skills training, but the diagnostic criteria and available research reviewed earlier do not require deficits for the disorder. Indeed, people without social anxiety disorder can display social skills deficits and people without social skills deficits can have social anxiety disorder.

In general, social skills training as a stand-alone treatment for social anxiety disorder has not been as effective as other empirically supported treatments (e.g., CBT). People with social anxiety disorder who display social skills deficits appear to respond less favorably to treatment overall and do not display additional gains from social skills training. In other words, matching individuals who display social skills deficits to treatment including social skills training does not yield greater improvement.

Integration of social skills training into other therapies, such as CBT, exposure therapy, or interpersonal therapy, demonstrates equivalent treatment gains and maintenance when compared to other treatment groups without social skills training; however, social skills training appears to improve performance in role-plays and may serve to facilitate participation in real-life behavioral exposures.

R. Nicholas Carleton and Michelle J. N. Teale Sapach

See also: Cognitive Behavioral Therapy; Exposure Treatment; Modeling; Phobia, Specific; Social Anxiety Disorder (Social Phobia); Video Feedback

Further Reading

Antony, Martin M., & Rowa, Karen. (2008). *Social anxiety disorder (Advances in psychotherapy—evidence-based practice)*. Cambridge, MA: Hogrefe & Huber Publishers.

Hood, Heather K., & Antony, Martin M. (2012). Evidence-based assessment and treatment of specific phobias in adults. In Thompson E. Davis III, Thomas H. Ollendick, & Lars-Goran st (Eds.), *Intensive one-session treatment of specific phobias* (pp. 19–42). doi: 10.1007/978-1-4614-3253-1_2

Stravynski, Ariel, Kyparissis, Angela, & Amado, Danielle. (2010). Social phobia as a deficit in social skills. In Stefan G. Hofmann, & Patricia M. DiBartolo (Eds.), *Social anxiety: Clinical, developmental, and social perspectives* (pp. 147–181). San Diego, CA: Elsevier.

Structured Clinical Interview for DSM Disorders

The Structured Clinical Interview for DSM Disorders (SCID) is a semistructured interview designed to assess the major disorders listed in the *Diagnostic and Statistical Manual of Mental Disorders* (DSM). Along with the Anxiety Disorders Interview Schedule (ADIS), the SCID is considered one of the gold standard assessment tools for diagnosing anxiety disorders, although it is less detailed than the ADIS for assessing the range of specific phobias.

The current version of the SCID is the SCID-IV, developed to assess the mental disorders characterized in the DSM-IV. The SCID-5 is currently in development and is expected to be released in late 2014 based on the recent publication of the DSM-5. There are different versions of the SCID for varying purposes. The Research Version (SCID-RV) is for use in clinical and research settings and consists of one booklet containing interview questions, diagnostic criteria, and ratings. There is a patient edition of the SCID-RV for use when assessing individuals presenting with psychiatric disorders. There is also a nonpatient edition of the SCID-RV for studies using participants with no previously identified psychiatric illness, such as a community survey. The Clinician Version (SCID-CV) is a shortened version of the SCID covering the main categories of diagnoses seen in clinical settings and can also be used for research settings. It consists of a reusable test booklet and separate scoring sheets. The Clinical Trials Version of the SCID (SCID-CT) is a modified form of the Research Version that has been adapted to include typical inclusion and exclusion criteria for use in studies investigating the effectiveness of drugs for treating major depressive disorder, bipolar disorder, schizophrenia, and generalized anxiety disorder.

The SCID is designed to be administered by trained mental health professionals or clinicians such as psychologists or physicians experienced in psychodiagnostic assessment. The length of time to complete the SCID can range from 15 minutes in the case of an individual with no major mental disorders to 4 hours in the case of an individual with multiple diagnoses. The reliability of the SCID-IV diagnoses has been found to be moderate to excellent (Lobbestael & Leurgans, 2010), although reliability is greatly influenced by the context and training of the person administering the interview.

Randi E. McCabe

See also: Anxiety Disorders Interview Schedule; DSM-5; Phobias, Diagnosis of

Further Reading

First, Michael B., Spitzer, Robert L., Gibbon, Miriam, & Williams, Janet B. W. (1996). *Structured clinical interview for DSM-IV Axis I Disorders. Patient edition (SCID-I/P)*. New York, NY: Biometrics.

Lobbestael, Jill, & Leurgans, Maartje. (2010). Inter-rater reliability of the Structured Clinical Interview for DSM-IV Axis I Disorders (SCID I) and Axis II Disorders (SCID II). *Clinical Psychology and Psychotherapy, 18*, 75–79.

Subjective Units of Distress Scale

The Subjective Units of Distress Scale (SUDS) is a quick and simple way for a therapist or researcher to measure how much fear people are experiencing in a given moment. Wolpe (1958) proposed that by having people relax while they were in situations that provoked fear, subsequent exposures to the situations would become less distressing, and in order to measure how much fear a situation produced, Wolpe and Lazarus (1966) developed the SUDS. The SUDS requires respondents to estimate the severity of their fear in a particular situation by giving a numerical value ranging from 0 (no fear) to 100 (most severe fear or distress ever experienced). Alternatively, a 0–10 scale may be used.

The SUDS is still commonly used in the development of fear hierarchies in the context of exposure treatment. For example, prior to starting treatment, individuals are asked to create a list of about 10–12 fear-provoking situations and to attribute a SUDS rating to each as if they were in that situation. These ratings are then arranged by order of severity and used to plan subsequent exposure sessions.

SUDS ratings are also used while individuals are being exposed to feared situations during exposure sessions. When a person is about to begin an exposure, a therapist will ask for a SUDS rating to establish an initial measure of the person's fear level. As the person remains in the situation, the therapist will ask for SUDS ratings at regular intervals to monitor change in fear. The ratings are expected to decrease as the individual begins to habituate to the situation. People may also be asked to use SUDS ratings to monitor changes in fear during between-session exposure exercises and to report these back to the therapist.

The SUDS is frequently used in exposure treatment because it is easy to understand, is very brief, and is useful for showing individuals how they habituate to different fear-provoking situations. SUDS ratings are also frequently used in research on phobias and other anxiety disorders, particularly PTSD and panic disorder.

Measures that correlate highly with the SUDS include measures of state anxiety, state affect, depressive symptoms, and, to a lesser extent, trait affect.

Alexander M. Penney and Missy L. Teatero

See also: Behavioral Approach Test; Exposure Treatment; Habituation; Systematic Desensitization; Wolpe, Joseph (1915–1997)

Further Reading

Barlow, David H. (2002). *Anxiety and its disorders: The nature and treatment of anxiety and panic* (2nd ed.). New York, NY: The Guildford Press.

Wolpe, Joseph. (1958). *Psychotherapy by reciprocal inhibition*. Stanford, CA: Stanford University Press.

Wolpe, Joseph, & Lazarus, Arnold A. (1966). *Behavior therapy techniques: A guide to the treatment of neuroses*. Elmsford, NY: Pergamon Press, Inc.

Substance Use

People with phobias are at least 1.5 times more likely to have a substance use disorder compared to the general population (Bolton, Cox, Clara, & Sareen, 2006). Moreover, having a phobia is associated with greater alcohol and drug use, regardless of the type of phobia. However, there are differences in substance use rates across phobias; individuals with agoraphobia and social anxiety disorder (social phobia) may be more likely than those with specific phobia to have a substance use disorder. It also appears that individuals with phobias who have a substance use disorder experience greater impairments in their day-to-day life compared to those who do not abuse substances.

Theories as to why there is an increased prevalence of substance use and substance use disorders among individuals with phobias have been developed and, in part, are based on the fact that the phobia is typically present prior to the onset of the substance use. For example, the *self-medication hypothesis* suggests that the individual with a phobia may in fact turn to alcohol or drug use as a coping mechanism to help reduce the anxiety and tension that he or she is experiencing (Khantzian, 1985). Inherent in this model is the subjective individual belief that using the substance may actually be successful in helping to reduce the anxiety. Such a thought process is believed to help perpetuate the continued cycle of substance use and misuse and, in general, may actually serve to exacerbate the phobic symptoms. Evidence in support of the self-medication hypothesis is not only greatest for agoraphobia and social anxiety disorder but is also present for specific phobias. A possible reason as to why there may be a lower prevalence of self-medication among individuals with specific phobias compared to other types of phobias is that they simply choose to avoid the object or thing that they fear (e.g., flying, animals) eliminating the need to use alcohol or drugs to reduce anxiety.

More recently, the self-medication hypothesis has been broadened and is now conceptualized as being part of a larger *motivational model*. Motivational models posit that an individual may turn to substance use to achieve an internal (i.e., mood change) or external (i.e., social approval) reward and to obtain a positive outcome or to avoid a negative outcome (Cooper, 1994). Individual motives for substance use can include coping (as seen in the self-medication hypothesis), conformity, enhancement, and social factors, and each is associated with different patterns of substance use among individuals with phobias.

Despite the belief that alcohol reduces stress, using alcohol as a motive for coping is actually associated with greater distress among individuals with phobias when compared to those who choose not to self-medicate. Further, individuals with social anxiety disorder, a disorder characterized by a fear of social scrutiny and negative evaluation, may perceive drinking to be a socially acceptable strategy to help reduce their anxiety. This perception may then lead the individual to use alcohol to help manage and reduce the distress they may be feeling, thereby increasing their vulnerability to substance-related problems. Using a strategy such as this may also limit the use of more adaptive coping strategies causing the individual to then rely on the alcohol as his or her primary means of coping with his or her internal distress. This overreliance on alcohol as opposed to more adaptive coping strategies is prominent with not only social anxiety disorder but also with all phobias where substances are used to help reduce distress.

Nancy L. Kocovski and Amanda J. Desnoyers

See also: Agoraphobia (Fear of Panic-Like Symptoms); Comorbidity; Phobia, Specific; Social Anxiety Disorder (Social Phobia)

Further Reading

Bolton, James., Cox, Brian, Clara, Ian, & Sareen, Jitender. (2006). Use of alcohol and drugs to self-medicate anxiety disorders in a nationally representative sample. *The Journal of Nervous and Mental Disease, 194*, 818–825.

Cooper, M. Lynne. (1994). Motivations for alcohol use among adolescents: Development and validation of a four-factor model. *Psychological Assessment, 6*, 117–128.

Khantzian, Edward J. (1985). The self-medication hypothesis of addictive disorders: Focus on heroin and cocaine dependence. *American Journal of Psychiatry, 142*, 1259–1264.

Suicide

Suicide is the act of intentionally causing one's own death. It is often but not always associated with mental illness such as depression, bipolar disorder, schizophrenia, borderline personality disorder, and substance abuse. Suicide results from a complex interplay of factors, including mental illness, financial difficulties, physical health problems, major life stressors, and lack of social support. Specific phobias can have a negative impact on a broad range of life domains, and individuals with a specific phobia have an increased risk of suicide attempt compared to those without anxiety disorders.

Rates of suicide vary considerably across age groups, race, and gender. About 11 out of every 100,000 people in the United States and Canada die by their own hands. Although men are approximately three times more likely than women to complete suicide, women are about four times more likely than men to attempt it. This difference in suicide rates may be due to the fact that women tend to use less lethal methods. Males are most likely to complete suicide by hanging and are much more likely to use a firearm than females. Women are most likely to complete suicide by poisoning (including medication overdose). Regardless of gender, suicide rates tend to gradually increase with age, with elderly Caucasians having the highest suicide rate.

Research indicates that many people who are considering suicide often change their minds if they are helped. Therefore, identifying individuals at high risk of suicide and providing them with treatment is very important. Depression is the most common mental illness associated with suicide, thus early recognition and treatment of depression are key to preventing suicide. Although suicide is less strongly associated with anxiety disorders, it is important to routinely screen individuals with phobias for suicidal thoughts because anxiety and depression often co-occur. In fact, research indicates that the combination of a mood and anxiety disorder is associated with a higher risk for a suicide attempt compared with a mood disorder alone. Additionally, data reveal that individuals with anxiety disorders, such as generalized anxiety disorder, panic disorder with agoraphobia, and posttraumatic stress disorder, have increased rates of suicide, suicidal thoughts, and suicide attempts compared to those without an anxiety disorder. Research shows that phobias are associated with an increased risk of suicidal thoughts and suicide attempts; however, once the co-occurrence of phobias with other disorders is accounted for, this relationship largely disappears.

Suicide attempts are treated as psychiatric emergencies and typically lead to hospitalization. Individuals can be hospitalized against their will if they appear to be at imminent risk of harming themselves or others. Decisions about hospitalization are based on a suicide risk assessment that takes into consideration a broad range of factors that influence the level of risk, including the severity of an individual's mental illness, the availability of social support, history of previous suicide attempts, substance abuse, and psychosis (loss of contact with reality), as well as protective factors.

Brenda L. Key

See also: Panic Disorder; Posttraumatic Stress Disorder; Substance Use

Further Reading

Kanwar, Amrit, Malik, Shaista, Prokop, Larry J., Sim, Leslie A., Feldstein, David, Wang, Zhen, & Murad, Mohammad H. (2013). The association between anxiety disorders and suicidal behaviors: A systematic review and meta-analysis. *Depression and Anxiety, 30,* 917–929.

Sareen, Jitender, Cox, Brian J., Afifi, Tracie O., de Graaf, Ron, Asmundson, Gordon J., ten Have, Margreet, & Stein, Murray B. (2005). Anxiety disorders and risk for suicidal ideation and suicide attempts: A population-based longitudinal study of adults. *Archives of General Psychiatry, 62*, 1249–1257.

Other Resources

American Association of Suicidology. Suite 408, 4201 Connecticut Avenue, NW, Washington, DC 20008. (202) 237–2280. Fax: (202) 237-2282. *http://www.suicidology.org*

United States National Suicide Hotline: (800) 273-TALK (1–800–273–8255)

Systematic Desensitization

Systematic desensitization is a behavioral treatment for phobias and anxiety-related disorders. It was pioneered by South African psychiatrist Joseph Wolpe (1915–1997), also known as the father of behavior therapy, through his research on counterconditioning in cats and later humans in the 1950s. Systematic desensitization involves having an individual imagine feared scenarios of increasing difficulty while simultaneously engaging in relaxation. The approach is based on Wolpe's application of reciprocal inhibition to fear extinction—whereby it is impossible to experience anxiety and relaxation at the same time. Thus, repeated pairing of the feared stimulus with relaxation leads to weakening and ultimately extinction of the anxiety response. Wolpe described this approach in his 1961 paper titled, *The Systematic Desensitization Treatment of Neurosis.*

The procedure of systematic desensitization involves three phases as described by Wolpe (1958). In the first phase, the individual is trained in relaxation using the method of progressive relaxation developed by Edmund Jacobson in the 1930s. In progressive relaxation, the state of deep muscle relaxation is clearly delineated by having an individual engage in muscle tightening and then releasing through various muscle groups while focusing on the contrast between initial tension when a muscle is contracted and the feeling of relaxation when the muscle is released. The individual works from practicing in individual muscle areas to larger groups of muscles until the feeling of relaxation can be brought on without the tensing of muscles. The individual can then intentionally induce the relaxed state at will. This phase takes place over a number of sessions. In the second phase, the individual works with the therapist to develop a fear hierarchy consisting of various scenarios related to the feared stimulus. The scenarios are arranged in order of the amount of fear that they provoke, ranging from low fear-inducing scenarios, such as standing on the first step of a stepladder in the case of an individual with a fear of heights, to extreme fear-inducing scenarios, such as standing on the balcony of a 10th floor apartment while looking over the edge. In the third phase, the therapist uses the fear hierarchy to guide sessions such that the individual starts at the bottom of the list and works toward the top. With each step, the individual imagines the feared scenario while engaging in relaxation, and the therapist provides encouragement, support, and direction. Once a feared scenario can be imagined while total relaxation is achieved, the individual is ready to move up the fear hierarchy to the next step. Through this process of gradual desensitization, the association between the feared stimulus and the fear response (conditioned response) is weakened and then extinguished as it is replaced with the new conditioned response of relaxation.

Wolpe's research showed that systematic desensitization was an effective intervention for fear reduction for a variety of phobias, including phobias of flying, public speaking, driving, and animals. The approach was a major area of research throughout the 1960s and 1970s but experienced a sharp decline in the late 1970s. Clinical practice in systematic desensitization was widespread until the early 1980s and thereafter was typically practiced only by those clinicians who were trained before the mid-1980s. It was largely left behind as the field moved on and later-trained clinicians practiced alternative treatments that were equally effective or that led to enhanced outcome such as exposure treatment and cognitive behavioral therapy (McGlynn, Smitherman, Gothard, 2004).

In systematic desensitization, the feared stimulus is confronted imaginally and not *in vivo* (live). Thus, systematic desensitization was the forerunner to imaginal exposure, which also has people confront their feared stimulus through mental imagery. Unlike systematic desensitization, however, individuals do not engage in relaxation during imaginal exposure. Rather, they are encouraged to process aspects of the imagined scenario with the therapist, including their thoughts, sensory perceptions, feelings, and the personal meaning of the experience. Although systematic desensitization and imaginal exposure have shown to be helpful in the clinical management of phobias, the most effective treatment option is *in vivo* exposure where individuals gradually confront their fear directly in real-life situations.

Randi E. McCabe

See also: Applied Relaxation; Behavior Therapy; Exposure, Imaginal; Exposure Treatment; Reciprocal Inhibition; Wolpe, Joseph (1915–1997)

Further Reading

McGlynn, F. Dudley, Smitherman, Todd, A., & Gothard, Kelly, D. (2004). Comment on the status of systematic desensitization. *Behavior Modification, 28*, 194.

Wolpe, Joseph. (1958). *Psychotherapy by reciprocal inhibition*. Redwood City, CA: Stanford University Press.

Wolpe, Joseph. (1961). The systematic desensitization treatment of neuroses. *The Journal of Nervous and Mental Disease, 132*, 189–203.

T

Temperament

Temperament refers to emotional reactivity that appears early in life. Temperamental traits are influenced by genetic factors and typically develop before 18 months of age. They tend to be at least moderately stable throughout the lifespan. Temperament is related to personality. Indeed, there is disagreement in the literature as to the distinction between them. Some argue that temperament is an enduring and distinct component of personality, whereas others view it as a foundation for later development of more complex personality traits. In general, research has shown that temperamental traits in early childhood predict personality traits in adulthood, although these findings do not speak to the distinction between the two constructs. Certain temperamental traits have been associated with the development of anxiety disorders.

Numerous models of temperament have been proposed. In most models, temperament is conceptualized as consisting of several dimensional temperamental traits, with more narrow traits clustering together to form broader higher-order traits (Rettew & McKee, 2005). There are three commonly discussed broad traits, the first of which describes the tendency to experience negative emotions and the degree of sensitivity to punishment. This trait has been termed *harm avoidance, behavioral inhibition, negative affectivity*, or *neuroticism*. Behavioral inhibition, in particular, pertains to a child's tendency to display a high degree of fear and reticence in unfamiliar situations. It is one of the most stable temperamental traits in childhood, although it can abate somewhat over time with the influence of other traits. The second broad temperamental trait pertains to the tendency to seek out novelty and to experience positive emotions. It has also been conceptualized as extraversion and associated with the tendency toward impulsivity. The terms used to describe this trait include *novelty* or *sensation seeking, surgency, extraversion*, and *behavioral activation*. Finally, the third trait describes a person's ability to regulate emotions and encompasses abilities such as voluntary management of one's attention, delayed gratification, planning, and modulation of emotional responses. These abilities have been termed *effortful control* or *persistence*. Effortful control can influence the emotional reactivity encompassed by the other two traits. For example, a child with high levels of effortful control and behavioral inhibition may become less inhibited over time.

Research suggests a higher risk of developing an anxiety or mood disorder among children with certain temperamental traits, such as high levels of negative affectivity and behavioral inhibition and low levels of extraversion and effortful control (Taylor, Abramowitz, McKay, & Asmundson, 2010). A key model in explaining the association between temperament and psychopathology is the diathesis-stress model, which holds that a child's temperament and stressors in his or her environment interact to give rise to an emotional disorder (Taylor et al., 2010). This model allows for the possibility that some children might have a temperamental predisposition to develop a disorder but might not necessarily develop it if there are appropriate supports in their environment that buffer against stressors and promote adjustment. On the other hand, when temperamental vulnerabilities are present (e.g., high behavioral inhibition) and there are few supports and/or the presence of significant stressors (e.g., persistent bullying), there is a greater likelihood of the development of psychopathology (e.g., social anxiety disorder [social phobia]).

Temperamental traits can additionally indirectly influence a child's psychological adjustment by informing the child's choice of activities, situations, and people (Taylor et al., 2010). A highly behaviorally inhibited child will tend to avoid novel situations and may therefore miss out on important learning experiences, which may in turn influence the development of emotional problems. For example, a child who refuses to attend summer camp may not have other opportunities to be exposed to swimming or water sports, which may increase the child's vulnerability toward fearing water and swimming.

In addition to the role of temperament in the subsequent development of anxiety disorders, it is important to note that once a disorder develops, temperament may influence its severity and course. Further, it is also possible for psychopathology to influence temperament, a relationship that has been termed the *scar effect* (Rettew & McKee, 2005). For example, a person who is highly phobic of dogs and always on the lookout for them may become avoidant of novel situations (i.e., behaviorally inhibited) for fear of an unexpected encounter with a dog. However, there are few empirical studies of this model.

An additional model of the relationship between temperament and anxiety disorders proposes that both are caused by another variable, such as factors in the individual's environment (e.g., parents' mental health problems), as well as genes. Research shows, for example, that genes that play a role in negative emotionality or neuroticism also influence certain anxiety symptoms (Goldsmith & Lemery, 2000).

Research to elucidate the complex relationship between temperament and anxiety disorders is ongoing. It should be noted that current models are not mutually exclusive and that there are numerous pathways to developing an anxiety disorder, some of which are not shaped by temperament. Nevertheless, the understanding that certain temperamental traits serve as a risk for future development of pathological fear suggests a promising avenue for early intervention. Indeed, work in this area suggests that early interventions for children with high behavioral inhibition decrease subsequent anxiety disorders (e.g., Kennedy, Rapee, & Edwards, 2009).

Irena Milosevic

See also: Personality; Phobias, Genetics of

Further Reading

Goldsmith, H. Hill, & Lemery, Kathryn S. (2000). Linking temperamental fearfulness and anxiety symptoms: A behavior-genetic perspective. *Biological Psychiatry, 48*, 1199–1209.

Kennedy, Susan J., Rapee, Ronald M., & Edwards, Susan E. (2009). A selective intervention program for inhibited preschool-aged children of parents with an anxiety disorder: Effects on current anxiety disorders and temperament. *Journal of the American Academy of Child and Adolescent Psychiatry*, 48, 602–609.

Rettew, David C., & McKee, Laura. (2005). Temperament and its role in developmental psychopathology. *Harvard Review of Psychiatry, 13*, 14–27.

Taylor, Steven, Abramowitz, Jonathan S., McKay, Dean, & Asmundson, Gordon J. G. (2010). Anxious traits and temperaments. In Dan J. Stein, Eric Hollander, & Barbara O. Rothbaum (Eds.), *Textbook of anxiety disorders* (2nd ed., pp. 73–86). Washington, DC: American Psychiatric Publishing.

Test Anxiety

Test anxiety is excessive anxiety, worry, and arousal either leading up to a test situation or during a test situation. High levels of test anxiety are associated with poorer performance. Unfortunately, poor outcomes on a test only fuel anxiety about future tests. Test anxiety is not a diagnosis. Researchers have found that test anxiety does not fit particularly well within one type of anxiety disorder. Instead, it appears to share features with several anxiety disorders, including specific phobia, generalized anxiety disorder, and social anxiety disorder (social phobia). Fortunately, there are a number of ways to manage and treat test anxiety.

Most people are nervous about test situations, which could involve writing an exam for school or completing a performance test such as a driving test. Some anxiety is helpful leading up to a test; it encourages us to prepare for tests and to take them seriously. However, some people experience significant levels of anxiety before or during a test. This type of anxiety can manifest itself in several ways. Physical signs of significant test anxiety include nausea, heart palpitations, sweating, or dizziness. Cognitive signs of test anxiety include negative predictions about how things will go (e.g., I will fail this exam!), unhelpful comparisons to other people (e.g., Everyone else seems to find this stuff easy), difficulty focusing, racing thoughts, or finding that one's mind "goes blank." Having one's mind go blank may occur even when one has adequately prepared for the exam. Behaviors associated with test anxiety include procrastination instead of preparing, skipping exams,

A student experiences anxiety during an exam. High levels of anxiety in a test situation can interfere with students' performance even when they have adequately prepared for the exam. (4774344sean/iStockphoto.com)

overpreparing for an exam, or being very restless during the exam. Test anxiety is associated with a number of negative emotions, including depression, anger, frustration, and low self-esteem.

The exact cause of test anxiety is unknown. One suggestion is that test anxiety arises from high expectations from important others, such as parents. If a parent reacts to poor performance on a test with criticism and disappointment, the child may develop a fear of poor performance on future tests. Or if a parent routinely emphasizes the importance of top performance, the child might fear the prospect of failure, even if failure has never occurred. These high expectations and pressure do not necessarily arise only from parents; high standards may be held by teachers or coaches, or even by the person taking the test. Perfectionistic tendencies are linked with test anxiety.

Previous poor performance can also have an impact on test anxiety. Individuals who have not done well on an important test may put undue pressure on their future performance (e.g., If I don't pass this next test, my life is over). They may also engage in unhelpful behaviors that exacerbate test anxiety (e.g., procrastinating instead of studying). Other suggestions of what contributes to test anxiety include the ability of the test-taker to focus on the task at hand (i.e., the exam) versus focusing on other, irrelevant information (e.g., internal sensations of anxiety or the ticking of a clock in the room).

Test anxiety is treated using medications to help manage the arousal and/or with cognitive behavioral therapy (CBT) techniques. The most commonly used medications are selective serotonin reuptake inhibitors, benzodiazepines, and beta-blockers (which block some of the physical symptoms of anxiety). CBT techniques include developing realistic thinking about the test, using breathing and relaxation techniques, and engaging in practice test situations.

Karen Rowa

See also: Benzodiazepines; Beta-Blockers; Cognitive Behavioral Therapy; Cognitive Restructuring; Phobia, Specific; Selective Serotonin Reuptake Inhibitors; Social Anxiety Disorder (Social Phobia)

Thanatophobia (Fear of Death)

Thanatophobia (from *Thanatos*, the Greek god or daemon of nonviolent death, and *phobos* meaning fear) is an excessive and persistent fear of one's own death. It is more commonly referred to as *death anxiety* in the research and clinical literature. Death anxiety has been conceptualized from a variety of theoretical perspectives, including the psychological, philosophical, cultural, and religious, among others. Clinically, death anxiety is not classified as a distinct mental disorder; rather, it may present as a feature of other disorders, particularly anxiety disorders and illness anxiety disorder (previously classified as hypochondriasis). Interventions for death anxiety have not been extensively investigated, although, as with other anxiety problems, cognitive behavioral therapy (CBT) is the recommended treatment.

One of the earliest theories regarding death anxiety was put forth by Sigmund Freud (1856–1939). Freud held that fear of death represented unresolved childhood conflicts, and he theorized that humans were not able to truly accept their mortality. A number of other theories about death-related fears have since been proposed, with *terror management theory* (TMT) being among the most extensively researched. According to TMT, people have a fundamental desire to live but are simultaneously aware that death is inevitable; this conflict is believed to create "terror" that requires constant management. When people are reminded of their mortality, they tend to seek greater structure and meaning, which they derive from increased emphasis on personally and culturally valued goals. TMT also holds that people with lower self-esteem have less tolerance of death-related situations and thus experience greater death anxiety. The main tenets of TMT have received substantial empirical support and have been used to explain a broad range of human behavior.

Although death is a prospect faced by all organisms and fear of death is a common concern, intense and persistent fear of death is less prevalent. In a community study, about 4% of individuals reported that they are much more nervous than others about death or dying, and about 10% of individuals reported that they are somewhat more nervous than others (Noyes et al., 2000). Individuals who have mild levels of death anxiety may experience significant increases during periods of illness or when a loved one dies. Importantly, however, not all individuals faced with a serious illness will experience intense fear of death.

Women generally report greater death anxiety than men. In both men and women, death anxiety appears to peak in the 20s and declines thereafter; however, women experience a second spike in death anxiety in their 50s (Russac, Gatliff, Reece, & Spottswood, 2007). Hypotheses about the peak in young adulthood relate to reproductive status and concerns about the impact of one's death on one's children. Speculation about the second peak in women relates to the possibility that menopause serves as a reminder that one is growing older. Notably, death anxiety stabilizes at a low level in the sixth decade of life. Some researchers have hypothesized that death anxiety declines with age because death threatens fewer values in older age, and because coming to terms with one's mortality is a developmental process that resolves with age (Kastenbaum, 2000).

Evidence also suggests that there is a modest association between higher socio-economic status and lower levels of death anxiety. Further, stable family background is associated with lower levels of death anxiety (Kastenbaum, 2000). A greater degree of religious belief and participation in religious practice does not appear to be associated with less death anxiety. The relationship between religiosity and fear of death is complex, as the nature of religious belief can either attenuate (e.g., protective beliefs) or facilitate the fear (Kastenbaum, 2000).

When death anxiety becomes persistently distressing and disruptive to one's daily life, assessment and treatment are warranted. It is important to conduct a thorough assessment to clarify the nature of the concerns and to rule out competing diagnoses. Although death anxiety can be present in a range of mental disorders (e.g., obsessive-compulsive disorder, generalized anxiety disorder, panic disorder), it is most strongly associated with illness anxiety disorder in which the individual is principally fearful of the possibility of having a serious illness and/or of death. Individuals may persistently worry about dying and be unable to enjoy their life unless they can be sure that they are not facing imminent death. They may therefore seek frequent reassurance that they are not dying. They may also often engage in checking behavior (e.g., self-examinations, looking up symptoms online) and rely on maladaptive safety behavior (e.g., rigid reliance on health foods and supplements) to prevent death. Common beliefs endorsed by individuals with death anxiety include expectations that one will not be able to cope with a terminal diagnosis, that the path to death will be very painful and characterized by suffering and loss of control, and that one's family (particularly children) will be catastrophically affected if the person were to die.

The recommended treatment for death anxiety is CBT, which may be applied to death anxiety in particular (see Furer & Walker, 2008) or to a broader problem of which death anxiety is a symptom. Specific treatment strategies include (1) psychoeducation (e.g., about adaptive and maladaptive avoidance of death-related issues); (2) reduction of excessive reassurance seeking, checking, and safety behavior; (3) exposure to avoided situations (e.g., reading obituaries), distressing physical symptoms, and death-related thoughts and memories; (4) cognitive restructuring of unhelpful or irrational thoughts about death; (5) increasing enjoyable activities; (6) establishing a healthy lifestyle (for individuals who have neglected this part of their life); and (7) relapse prevention to ensure maintenance of treatment gains (Furer & Walker, 2008). Preliminary evidence suggests that CBT for death anxiety in the context of hypochondriasis produces significant declines in the anxiety.

Irena Milosevic

See also: DSM-5; Fear of the Unknown; Hypochondriasis; Nosophobia (Fear of Disease or Illness); Obsessive-Compulsive Disorder

Further Reading

Furer, Patricia, & Walker, John R. (2008). Death anxiety: A cognitive-behavioral approach. *Journal of Cognitive Psychotherapy, 22*, 167–182.

Kastenbaum, Robert. (2000). *The psychology of death* (3rd ed.). New York, NY: Springer Publishing Company.

Noyes, Russell, Hartz, Arthur J., Doebbeling, Caroline C., Malis, Richard W., Happel, Rachel L., Werner, Elizabeth A., & Yagla, Steven J. (2000). Illness fears in the general population. *Psychosomatic Medicine, 62*, 318–325.

Russac, R.J., Gatliff, Colleen, Reece, Mimi, & Spottswood, Diahann. (2007). Death anxiety across the adult years: An examination of age and gender effects. *Death Studies, 31*, 549–561.

Thorndike, Edward L. (1874–1949)

Edward L. Thorndike, born Edward Lee Thorndike (1874–1949), was an American psychologist and a pioneer in behaviorism and the study of learning. He revolutionized the experimental analysis of animal behavior, and his laws of learning were critical for subsequent learning theory that contributed to our understanding of phobias. Further to his contributions on the learning process in both animals and humans, Thorndike was also an influential figure in educational research and is considered by many to be the "father of educational psychology."

Thorndike was born on August 31, 1874, in Williamsburg, Massachusetts, to a homemaker and a Methodist minister. He was the second of four children, all of whom would go on to have successful academic careers. Due to the demands of his father's position, the family moved frequently. Thorndike lived in eight different New England towns before leaving home to attend university in 1891. Thorndike fulfilled his family's expectations of academic excellence; however, on matters of religion, he rejected his father's views in favor of secularism.

Thorndike completed a BA at Wesleyan University in Connecticut in 1895. He earned a second BA at Harvard University in Cambridge the following year and an MA from Harvard in 1897. His early research was conducted under the influential philosopher and psychologist William James. Thorndike had hoped to study children in graduate school, in particular their responsiveness to facial expressions in a series of "mind-reading" experiments. However, after failing to obtain approval from the university for this work, he shifted his focus to research with animals and took up the study of behavior in chickens. Thorndike initially conducted this research in his bedroom but was forced to stop once his landlady discovered he was keeping chickens. When he could not secure research space for the animals at Harvard, James invited him to continue the work in his cellar.

With two of his "most educated chickens" in tow, Thorndike subsequently transferred to Columbia University in New York City to study the inheritance of acquired traits under James McKeen Cattell, who is noted for his work on intelligence theory and testing. When this topic proved fruitless, Thorndike began to study animal intelligence. He completed his PhD at Columbia in 1898 at age 23. In the same year, he published his dissertation, *Animal Intelligence: An Experimental Study of the Associative Processes in Animals.* Notably, Thorndike's dissertation was the first in psychology to investigate nonhuman subjects, earning him recognition as a pioneer in comparative psychology (the study of mental processes and behavior in nonhuman animals). The dissertation, considered one of the most influential publications in psychology during the first half of the 20th century, is renowned for its conceptualization of learning as a function of an animal's ability to make new associations. It also details Thorndike's innovative research methods for studying learning. Thorndike went on to publish additional research articles and monographs on animal learning, and in 1911, he compiled his earlier studies in a seminal volume titled, *Animal Intelligence: Experimental Studies.*

Thorndike's research critically marked a shift from speculative and anecdotal study of animal behavior to controlled, objective observation using highly technical experiments. In particular, his investigations using cats as subjects in home-made puzzle boxes helped him establish that learning is incremental (occurring in small steps over time rather than all at once), automatic (not influenced by thinking), and the same across all mammals, including humans. His learning theory, referred to as *connectionism*, focuses on the formation of associations between sensory stimuli and responses. Thorndike was principally concerned with the way that experience changes the strength of these associations. He proposed several specific laws and principles to explain how the associations are strengthened and notably did not refer to any internal, unobservable mechanisms. With new insights from his research, Thorndike would go on to revise his theory, eliminating certain laws and modifying others.

After earning his doctoral degree, Thorndike worked as an instructor at Case Western Reserve University in Cleveland but left this position after a year to return to the Teachers College at Columbia, where he remained until his retirement in 1940. He held positions of instructor in genetic psychology and adjunct professor of educational psychology before being appointed professor in 1904. With greater demand in psychology for applied research than for studies of animal intelligence, Thorndike shifted his focus to applied psychology and focused much of the remainder of his career on educational psychology.

Thorndike made many contributions to educational psychology, particularly on topics relating to human learning, intelligence, and mental testing. For example, during World War I, he developed the Alpha and Beta versions that led to the development of the contemporary Armed Services Vocational Aptitude Battery (administered to determine qualification for enlistment). When soldiers completed the written Alpha test, it became apparent that not all of them could read well enough to complete it. Accordingly, the Beta test, which consisted of pictures, would then be administered. Thorndike is also known for developing word books, such as *A Teacher's Word Book of the Twenty Thousand Words Found Most Frequently and Widely in General Reading for Children and Young People*, to help teachers with reading instruction.

A prolific researcher and writer, Thorndike published more than 500 articles and books. His accomplishments were acknowledged with many awards, and he was elected to numerous scientific honors. He served as president of several professional societies, including the American Psychological Association (1912), the New York Academy of Sciences (1919–1920), the American Association for the Advancement of Science (1934), the American Society for Adult Education (1934–1935), and the Psychometric Society (1936–1937).

Thorndike died in 1949, shortly before his 75th birthday. His work has far-reaching influence and has contributed to our understanding of phobias. In particular, Thorndike's *law of effect* laid the conceptual foundation for B. F. Skinner's studies of operant conditioning, which involved manipulating the consequences of behavior to change the frequency of a response. These learning principles were eventually applied to the study of phobias and elucidated how certain coping strategies (e.g., escape, avoidance) maintain a phobia. In turn, this understanding informed effective treatments for phobias.

Irena Milosevic

See also: Operant Conditioning; Skinner, B. F. (1904–1990); Two-Factor Theory of Avoidance Learning

Further Reading

Chance, Paul (1999). Thorndike's puzzle boxes and the origins of the experimental analysis of behavior. *Journal of the Experimental Analysis of Behavior, 72*, 433–440.

Dewsbury, Donald A. (1998). Celebrating E. L. Thorndike a century after animal intelligence. *American Psychologist, 53*, 1121–1124.

Thorndike, Edward L. (1898). Animal intelligence: An experimental study of the associative processes in animals. *Psychological Review: Monograph Supplements, 2*, i-109.

THORNDIKE'S PUZZLE BOX PARADIGM AND THE LAW OF EFFECT

Thorndike's method for examining animal learning was to present the animal with a problem that it needed to solve. His most famous experiments involved placing a hungry cat in a *puzzle box* from which it needed to escape to access food that was in plain sight but out of reach. The puzzle box was a small wooden enclosure that the animal could open if it performed a simple action to unlock the door. Typically, this action involved pressing a lever or pulling a wire loop. Once the cat found a way to exit the box, it was rewarded with access to the food. It would subsequently be placed back in the box and the procedure would be repeated numerous times until the cat mastered the task.

In early trials of the puzzle box paradigm, the cat would exhibit various behaviors in an effort to get to the food (e.g., clawing, meowing) and would eventually, by chance, perform the correct behavior that opened the door. With repeated trials of such *trial-and-error learning*, the cat gradually became faster at opening the door, and it ultimately learned to immediately press the lever or pull the loop.

Thorndike plotted the time taken to escape from the box (response latency) during each trial, generating what is known as a learning curve. He observed a gradual decline in response latency characterized by many fluctuations. This discovery led him to conclude that the cats were not solving the problem through an intellectual process leading to insight (in which case the curve would reveal a sudden drop in response latency). Instead, he proposed that the cats' tendency to produce their original responses in the box, which he believed were based on prior learning or innate predisposition, became weaker because they failed to open the door with these responses. By contrast, the new behavior (e.g., pressing the lever) was strengthened over trials because it provided access to a reward.

Thorndike proposed the *law of effect* to explain his observations of cats in a puzzle box. According to this law, responses that are followed by a reward or pleasure will be strengthened (more likely to be repeated) and those that are not rewarded or that are followed by discomfort will be weakened (less likely to be repeated). Thorndike posited that the strength of a response is determined by the "effect" that follows it. In other words, he believed that behaviors are controlled by their consequences. Thorndike embedded his theory in evolutionary terms, stating that, "He who learns and runs away, will live to learn another day" (Thorndike, 1899. p. 91). He later went on to revise the law of effect by removing its second tenet; that is, with further research, Thorndike concluded that punishment is ineffective in modifying behavior.

Irena Milosevic

Further Reading

Thorndike, Edward L. (1899). *The associative process in animals. Biological lectures from the Marine Biological Laboratory at Woods Hole.* Boston, MA: Athenaeum.

Three Pathways Theory

The three pathways theory, proposed by Rachman (1977), is an expansion of the classical conditioning theory of fear acquisition. It posits that fears and phobias are learned through one or more common processes or "pathways," including classical conditioning, vicarious learning, and negative information transmission. These pathways to fear may operate alone or in combination with one another. The three pathways theory focuses only on associative learning and does not account for genetic and biological influences on fear development, although, more recently, a fourth non-associative pathway involving evolutionary preparedness has been proposed. The theory has been well supported by research and continues to influence fear-related research and clinical practice.

Early behavioral theorists used classical conditioning theory to explain the acquisition of fears and phobias. Classical conditioning occurs when a previously neutral stimulus becomes capable of eliciting fear by being paired or associated with an aversive stimulus. Thus, the acquired fear is the result of direct negative experiences with an object or situation. For example, roughly 41% of children who develop a spider phobia recall directly experiencing a prior aversive event related to spiders (Merckelbach, Muris, & Shouten, 1996). Importantly, the majority of individuals who experience a traumatic event do not go on to develop a phobia. One of the reasons for this is the phenomenon referred to as *latent inhibition*, whereby previous relatively positive exposure to a stimulus serves as a buffer against acquiring a fear during subsequent aversive experiences with this stimulus.

Rachman (1977) noted that contrary to the classical conditioning model of fear development some individuals develop phobias without ever having encountered the object of their fears. Accordingly, he suggested two additional *indirect* pathways by which fear responses can be learned. One of these pathways is vicarious learning (also called vicarious conditioning or modeling). Vicarious learning occurs when an individual develops a fear response after witnessing another individual acting fearfully in a given situation, despite a lack of direct negative experience. One example of vicarious learning is the phenomenon of *social referencing* in infants. Social referencing occurs when infants interpret ambiguous situations based on cues (e.g., facial expressions, vocalizations) provided by their caregivers and then behave in ways (e.g., approach, escape) consistent with the interpretation. For example, infants who observe their parents make a fearful expression in response to a potentially dangerous object (e.g., a snake) will be less likely to approach this object.

The third pathway to fear acquisition is negative information transmission. Information may be transmitted through several means, such as family members and the media. Negative information can contribute to the development of fears and phobias when an individual is specifically warned by others that a given situation or object is dangerous and is instructed to be cautious or to avoid it altogether. This is thought to alter the individual's beliefs regarding the danger posed by a given situation, such that he or she is more likely to experience fear during subsequent exposure to the situation and/or to avoid it. Mowrer's (1960) two-factor theory of fear development suggests that avoidance of feared situations, in turn, serves to maintain fears by preventing the disconfirmation of negative/catastrophic predictions.

Both empirical and anecdotal evidence seems to support the validity of three pathways theory. However, given the theory's roots in behaviorism, it is a purely learning-based model, which does not account for other potential contributors to fear acquisition. Indeed, one of the primary critiques of the theory is that the role of genetics or biology in the origins of fear is ignored. Interestingly, Rachman (1978) posited that some fears are innate and that individuals who demonstrate clinical levels of such predisposed fears may have failed to learn not to respond fearfully. More recently, Poulton and Menzies (2002) proposed the addition of a fourth, non-associative pathway involving evolutionary preparedness to the three associative pathways of fear acquisition highlighted by Rachman (1977). Incorporating this fourth pathway would aid our understanding of how some individuals are unable to identify an event precipitating the onset of their fear and recall instead that they have always been afraid of a certain stimulus or situation.

Corinna M. Elliott and Chris L. Parrish

See also: Classical Conditioning; Fear; Fear Generalization; Non-Associative Model; Preparedness Theory; Two-Factor Theory of Avoidance Learning

Further Reading

Merckelbach, Harald, Muris, Peter, & Shouten, Eerik. (1996). Pathways to fear in spider phobic children. *Behaviour Research and Therapy, 34*, 935–938.

Mowrer, Orval H. (1960). *Learning theory and the symbolic processes*. New York, NY: Wiley.

Poulton, Richie, & Menzies, Ross G. (2002). Non-associative fear acquisition: A review of the evidence from retrospective and longitudinal research. *Behaviour Research and Therapy, 40*, 127–149.

Rachman, Stanley. (1977). The conditioning theory of fear-acquisition: A critical examination. *Behaviour Research and Therapy, 15*, 375–387.

Rachman, Stanley. (1978). *Fear and courage*. San Francisco, CA: Freeman.

THREE PATHWAYS TO FEAR

The cases of Malcolm, Zara, and Alvaro each illustrate one of Rachman's three pathways to fear development.

Classical conditioning: Malcolm and his parents have planned a camping trip during his summer vacation, as he has always enjoyed spending time outdoors, swimming, hiking in the woods, and building campfires. One day during their vacation, Malcolm experiences an unfamiliar and very unpleasant, sharp pain after being stung by a bee while hiking. He cries, runs back to the camp site, and immediately wants to go home, even though there are still a couple of days left of the family trip. He also tells his parents that he no longer likes hiking and that he does not want to go on his Scouts retreat later in the summer. In this example, Malcolm is exhibiting a conditioned fear of camping/hiking (the conditioned stimulus) due to his direct experience of pain (the unconditioned stimulus) caused by the bee sting.

Vicarious learning: Zara, who has just entered grade school, is an inquisitive and playful little girl whose parents would describe as an "animal lover." However, to her parents' surprise, one day Zara begins to scream and insists on crossing the street when they encounter a dog on their walk to the park. After talking to Zara about this change in her behaviour, her parents learn that Zara's schoolmate, Tanya, has repeatedly shrieked and run away every time she sees a dog near the school playground. Thus, in this example, Tanya has "modeled" a fear of dogs, which Zara has acquired vicariously.

Negative information transmission: Alvaro is invited to spend a weekend at his friend's lakeside cottage. The weather is very hot, but Alvaro refuses to join his friends when they go swimming. Although he has trouble explaining why he does not wish to swim, he realizes that his fear might stem from his parents' overprotectiveness, and their repeated warnings about the dangers of drowning while swimming. Because he has always heeded his parents' advice and avoided the water, Alvaro has never learned that he is able to enjoy the water safely, and so, his fear of the water has persisted.

Chris L. Parrish

Treatment, Evidence-Based

There are many types of treatments and some treatments work better than others. Fortunately, researchers have been able to use science to develop and test treatments to find the ones that work well. These treatments are considered *evidence-based* (or *empirically supported*). Researchers use established methods and guidelines to build the scientific evidence for a treatment. Furthermore, evidence-based treatments may be labeled and categorized according to how much evidence is in favor of that particular treatment. Although clinical research is an ongoing process, cognitive behavioral therapy (CBT) has the strongest evidence for effectively reducing anxiety and phobias at this time.

Researchers gather evidence for treatments that work by using a careful scientific approach. One way to test if treatments work is by comparing how individuals feel before and after receiving treatment. The best treatments demonstrate that most individuals feel better or less afraid (phobia-related fears decrease considerably or go away) after treatment. Another scientific way to test if treatments work is with a *randomized controlled trial* (RCT). For this scientific method, researchers assign individuals randomly into two (or more) groups. They have one group get one treatment, while the second group gets no treatment (often called a *wait-list* condition) or a different treatment. Researchers monitor each group's symptoms before and after treatment and determine which group improved the most. Since participants are randomly assigned to a treatment, and each individual has the same chance of being in a particular group, the results of this sort of study are less likely to be influenced by other factors (e.g., differences in age, gender, or other group characteristics due to chance) so these findings are considered stronger evidence. However, researchers do not believe that it is enough for a treatment to be effective in one study. Rather, researchers have to build strong evidence by showing that the treatment works well for many different groups of people and that the findings can be repeated by different research teams.

Researchers established guidelines to help people understand how much scientific evidence each treatment has. A treatment may be called "possibly efficacious" if there has been one well-designed study demonstrating that the treatment works, but the findings have not been repeated in a different setting or with different people. A treatment may be called "efficacious" if multiple studies show that the treatment is better than no treatment. A treatment may be called "efficacious and specific" when multiple well-designed RCT studies support that it works better than another common treatment. On the other hand, a treatment may be labeled "controversial" if only some of the research studies are in support of its effectiveness while others are not. There is also a category of "potentially harmful" treatments—ones that make individuals worse, rather than better, after treatment.

Scientists have been using RCTs and other methods to compare different medical and psychological treatments for phobias for decades. These studies suggest that a specific form of psychotherapy, called CBT, is supported by the most scientific evidence. Briefly, CBT is a form of treatment that focuses on examining the relationships between emotions, thoughts (or cognitions), and actions (or behaviors). Several versions of CBT have been found to successfully treat phobias. One option is situational or *in vivo* exposure therapy, which involves gradually and directly confronting feared objects or situations in a controlled safe manner until the fear decreases over time. For example, a therapist treating an individual with dog phobia may have the individual sit across from a dog, approach the dog, pet the dog, and perhaps even hug the dog as the individual's fear reduces for each stage. A second option is *in virtuo* exposure, which involves the individual confronting feared objects or situations in a computer-generated virtual environment. For example, a therapist may instruct an individual with dog phobia to look at a computer that shows vivid images and sounds of dogs barking until the individual's anxiety decreases over time. A third option is cognitive therapy, which involves questioning and changing inaccurate beliefs until the fear decreases. For example, a therapist may help an individual with dog phobia evaluate the real danger of dogs until the individual is less afraid of dogs. Cognitive therapy is often combined with exposure therapy.

As an alternative to CBT, medication treatments have also been used to treat phobias. Development of these has received less attention due to the considerable success of CBT. With the exception of very short-term benefits, medications are generally not recommended for treatment of phobias because they do not change fears or phobic beliefs; rather, they just reduce the physical sensations of anxiety. For example, an individual with dog phobia may take an anxiolytic medication to reduce discomfort in the moment just before visiting a friend who has dogs, but he or she will still be afraid of dogs after the effects of medications wear off. Some medications may also have dangerous risks, like the potential for addiction.

As CBT is currently the most evidence-based treatment for phobias, it should be attempted before receiving alternative, non-evidence-based treatments (e.g., medications, supportive psychotherapy, relaxation therapy, or hypnosis).

Nina Wong Sarver, Antonina S. Farmer, Kirstin Stauffacher Gros,
and Daniel F. Gros

See also: Applied Relaxation; Behavior Therapy; Benzodiazepines; Cognitive Behavioral Therapy; Cognitive Restructuring; Cognitive Therapy; Exposure, *In Vivo*; Exposure Treatment; Hypnosis; Selective Serotonin Reuptake Inhibitors; Treatment, Psychological; Virtual Reality Treatment

Further Reading

Barlow David H. (2002). *Anxiety and its disorders: The nature and treatment of anxiety and panic* (2nd ed.). New York, NY: Guilford Press.

Chambless, Dianne L., & Hollon, Steven D. (1998). Defining empirically supported therapies. *Journal of Consulting and Clinical Psychology, 66*, 7–18.

Choy, Yujuan , Fyer, Abby J., & Lipsitz, Josh D. (2007). Treatment of specific phobia in adults. *Clinical Psychology Review, 27*, 266–286.

Kazdin, Alan E. (2008). Evidence-based treatment and practice: New opportunities to bridge clinical research and practice, enhance the knowledge base, and improve patient care. *American Psychologist, 63*, 146–159.

Silverman, Wendy K., Pina, Armando A., & Viswesvaran, Chockalingam. (2008). Evidence-based psychosocial treatments for phobic and anxiety disorders in children and adolescents: A review and meta-analyses. *Journal of Clinical Child & Adolescent Psychology, 37*, 105–130.

Treatment, Medication

The use of medications in the treatment of phobias tends to be limited to a few specific situations. When a medication is prescribed for a phobia, it is usually taken during or just prior to an encounter with the feared object or situation, and is usually taken for a very brief period of time rather than on an ongoing basis. In these cases, the medication prescribed is usually a benzodiazepine. Additional classes of medications used in the treatment of phobias include beta blockers and antidepressant medication, although these are prescribed more rarely and in very circumscribed cases. Another medication, d-cycloserine, is being investigated as an augmentation strategy for psychological treatment of phobias.

Benzodiazepines cause a reduced emotional sense of anxiety, reduced physical symptoms of anxiety, decreased muscle tension, and increased drowsiness. The effects are observed soon after taking the medication, and are short-lived (onset and duration of action differ between the various benzodiazepines). Long term, regular use of benzodiazepines can result in dependence and abuse, so the use of these medications must be closely monitored. For these reasons, it is normally suggested that benzodiazepines should not be taken for long periods of time.

Benzodiazepine medications such as lorazepam (Ativan), clonazepam (Rivotril, Klonapin), diazepam (Valium), or alprazolam (Xanax) can be prescribed for people who infrequently encounter feared situations and require a rapid and reliable method of reducing anxiety in such situations. Examples of situations in which such short term use of a benzodiazepine is appropriate include during infrequent air travel (for those with a fear of flying), during medical/surgical/dental procedures (for those with blood-injection-injury phobias), or during MRI or CT scans (for those with fear of enclosed spaces). Benzodiazepines may also be taken by people who are unable or unwilling to engage in cognitive behavioral therapy (CBT), the treatment of choice for phobias.

Benzodiazepines may also be prescribed during the initial stages of exposure therapy (a component of CBT). If a person with a phobia is too frightened of participating in gradual exposure, even at its simplest step, a benzodiazepine may be used to lower the anxiety response enough to allow engagement in therapy. This would be done with the eventual plan of discontinuing the medication and proceeding with exposure therapy medication-free, once a certain level of comfort is realized.

Beta-blocker medications (e.g., propranolol), originally designed for the treatment of high blood pressure, are another class of short-term antianxiety medications used even less frequently than benzodiazepines in the treatment of phobias. Because of their ability to inhibit many physical symptoms of anxiety (e.g., rapid heartbeat, shaking), beta-blockers are used to combat anxiety in performance situations (e.g., public speaking, performing on stage, playing a musical instrument), usually diagnosed in the context of social anxiety disorder (social phobia) rather than specific phobia. They are usually taken just prior to the performance itself and are not used on an ongoing basis. They also carry a risk of side effects and must be prescribed cautiously.

Because there is little evidence for the usefulness of the antidepressant class of antianxiety medications (e.g., selective serotonin reuptake inhibitors [SSRIs], serotonin-norepinephrine reuptake inhibitors [SNRIs]) in the treatment of phobias, they are rarely prescribed for people who suffer from specific phobias alone. As an aside, they are commonly prescribed for other anxiety disorders, including social anxiety disorder, panic disorder, and agoraphobia. That being said, there are a few small-scale reports that describe one or two individuals with flying phobias and thunderstorm phobias responding to SSRI medication.

D-cycloserine is another medication that deserves special mention. In recent years, this medication has been found to aid in CBT/exposure therapy. In controlled experiments, taking d-cycloserine prior to an exposure exercise has been shown to enhance learning/fear extinction versus exposure therapy without d-cycloserine, thereby significantly reducing the duration of therapy. Studies of this medication and its usefulness in treating phobias (and other anxiety-related disorders) are ongoing.

Mark A. Watling

See also: Beta-Blockers; Benzodiazepines; D-Cycloserine; Selective Serotonin Reuptake Inhibitors

Further Reading

Stahl, Stephen M., & Moore, Bret A. (Eds.) (2013). *Anxiety disorders: A guide for integrating psychopharmacology and psychotherapy*. New York, NY: Routledge.

Swinson, Richard P., Antony, Martin M., Bleau, Pierre, Pratap, Chokka, Craven, Marilyn, Fallu, Angelo, . . . Walker, John R. (2006). Clinical practice guidelines. Management of anxiety disorders. *Canadian Journal of Psychiatry, 51*(Suppl. 2), 1S–92S.

Treatment, Psychological

When people feel distressed by excessive fears or find themselves avoiding meaningful activities due to their fears, they may seek professional psychological help to lessen the intensity, frequency, or interference of those fears. *Psychological treatments* are interventions that help individuals learn to think, behave, and feel differently so that a situation becomes no longer feared, or at least causes less distress and is not avoided. There are various psychotherapy options available to individuals with phobias. They all typically involve an individual interacting with a trained mental health professional to discuss the individual's thoughts, feelings, behaviors, and relationships with the aim of improving his or her well-being. For phobias, exposure treatments based on behavior therapy tend to be the most effective, although variations of this approach can be useful for specific types of problems. There are also options for nontraditional therapy approaches including group therapy and computer-based interventions.

Psychological treatments begin with assessment, a process by which the psychotherapist attempts to understand the nature of the problem, the extent of its impact on the individual's life, and possible reasons for the problem originating and enduring. For example, a person may come in for treatment because of feeling stressed at work, but during the assessment interview, the therapist may learn that the person stopped using his or her primary coping strategy of gardening due to a preexisting snake phobia and a (harmless) chance encounter with a snake in the garden the previous month. Once the therapist identifies that the individual has a phobia, he or she works together with the individual in developing a treatment plan to address the concerning fears. The approach a psychotherapist uses will differ based on his or her theoretical orientation and training, as well as the individual's presentation and preferences.

Modern psychological treatment for phobias began with *psychoanalysis*, based on the theories of Sigmund Freud (1856–1939). This school of thought viewed phobias as originating from unconscious psychological conflicts in which repressed impulses (typically of a sexual or aggressive nature) were displaced onto a specific object or situation. The treatment aimed to help people develop insight about the underlying source of their fears with the hope that resolving the displacement would eliminate the phobia. Psychodynamic therapists progressed this view by taking into account that conscious past experiences and relationships could contribute to fears and avoidance, and they helped people make this connection. Although there is some support for psychodynamic approaches being useful for social fears, psychodynamic therapies have *not* been rigorously studied for the treatment of specific phobias (Choy, Fyer, & Lipsitz, 2007). Thus, their use is generally not recommended as a first-line intervention.

In the 1920s, behaviorists came to view phobias as learned fearful reactions and later developed some of the most effective techniques for treating phobias. *Behavior therapy* assumes that a phobic fear occurs when a normal fear response, usually reserved for dangerous stimuli (e.g., being in front of a poisonous snake), is generalized to nonthreatening stimuli (e.g., all snakes or things that resemble snakes, such as a garden hose). If a person were to face the nonthreatening stimuli many times without any dangerous consequences, the fear should lessen over time. However, people with phobias attempt to completely avoid such situations, so their fear continues and intensifies over time. *Exposure treatments* involve having the individual repeatedly and purposefully confront their feared object or situation while preventing them from escaping the situation behaviorally (e.g., not looking at the feared object) or internally (e.g., thinking about something else).

Psychotherapists can control the format, pace, and dose of treatment. For example, they may gradually expose individuals to more and more fear-provoking stimuli or immerse them in the feared situation straightaway. Psychotherapists may use different kinds of exposures, such as encountering the feared object or situation in real life through *situational* or *in vivo* exposure (e.g., handling a live snake), imagining being in the feared situation through *imaginal* exposure (e.g., imagining/describing oneself handling snakes), or even interacting with the feared stimulus using technology through *virtual reality* exposure (e.g., handling a virtual snake through a computer interface). The main goal of each exposure is for the individual to stay in the situation long enough to learn that he or she can tolerate the experience of fear and anxiety and to observe that the feared consequences do not occur (e.g., snake does not kill them).

Although exposure treatments usually take several weeks or even months to reduce fears and avoidance, individuals can show significant improvements in their symptoms in as little as a single prolonged session of two to three hours (Zlomke & Davis, 2008). Most often, people will meet with a therapist on multiple occasions (often weekly) and complete assigned exposures between sessions. Exposures outside of the therapist's office are particularly helpful for fears or situations that may not be easily replicated in sessions. Regular attendance and practice of skills outside of sessions are important components of effective exposure treatments. Thus, it is important for people to be highly motivated for treatment.

In addition to standard exposure treatments, several variations of behavior therapy have been used for treating phobias. For example, eye movement desensitization and reprocessing (EMDR) is one such technique that involves the individual imagining the feared object or situation while quickly moving his or her eyes back and forth, guided by the therapist. It is unclear whether the eye movements offer any benefit over and above the exposure alone. Thus, EMDR is not recommended as an alternative to exposure treatments. Another example involves methods to counteract the fainting response present in some individuals with blood-injection-injury (BII) phobias. Therapists have developed two specific techniques to help individuals reduce this unpleasant and possibly dangerous response (e.g., if injured while fainting). First, applied tension involves the individual tensing up the muscles of the body during exposure to increase blood pressure and thus reduce the likelihood of fainting. Alternatively, applied relaxation teaches individuals to relax their body during exposure. Comparison studies suggest exposure alone to be more effective than applied relaxation, but applied tension appears to be at least as effective as exposure for BII phobias, even when people do not have a history of fainting (Ayala, Meuret, & Ritz, 2009).

By the 1960s, another psychological treatment emerged that also addressed problematic thoughts, beliefs, and expectations that contribute to fear and avoidance. *Cognitive behavioral therapy* for phobias incorporates cognitive techniques for challenging people's assumptions about the likelihood or consequences of a feared situation to reduce their distress, and challenging beliefs about their (in)ability to tolerate a feared situation to reduce avoidance. For example, by helping an individual who fears snakes recognize the rarity of poisonous snakes and the even lower likelihood of encountering a poisonous snake in the wild, the individual may experience less anxiety when taking a walk through a grassy park. This approach can be useful as an adjunctive treatment to behavioral approaches, particularly for individuals with claustrophobia. However, recent summaries of all available research to date suggest that cognitive strategies offer little benefit over exposure alone, which produces significant improvement in 80–90% of individuals who complete treatment (Wolitzky-Taylor, Horowitz, Powers, & Telch, 2008).

Psychological treatments need not always occur one-on-one. Parents and families are often involved in therapy with young children and adolescents. Additionally, group therapy tends to be an effective approach to helping reduce some fears. Cognitive behavioral group therapy, which combines exposure and cognitive techniques in a group setting, has been effective for certain types of phobias. For example, a group setting facilitates devising exposures specific to social fears (e.g., mimicking a classroom presentation with an audience).

Although psychological treatments typically occur with the help of a psychotherapist, they do not necessarily require face-to-face therapist contact. Some therapists offer treatment over the Internet using time-delayed communication (e.g., e-mail), real-time chat, or video conferencing, or they might provide treatment over the telephone. Additionally, computer programs are available for providing self-directed treatment based on evidence-based approaches. Self-help treatments and self-administered therapies can be similarly effective, as long as the individual is motivated and performs exposure exercises regularly. In the long run, though, people who work with a therapist tend to have longer-lasting symptom reduction than those who engage in self-directed exposure. Thus, computer-based self-administered treatments will often include periodic communication with a therapist to answer questions and to provide feedback and motivation.

An alternative to psychological treatments is *pharmacological treatment*, which involves using medications to directly change how a person responds to the world on a biological level (e.g., how the neurons communicate in the brain, how the body responds to threatening situations). Sometimes people will receive both medication and psychological treatment. For example, some providers will pair anxiety-reducing medications with psychological treatments to help individuals get through exposures with less discomfort. However, this practice tends to make the exposures less effective in the long term (Choy, Fyer, & Lipsitz, 2007). This may be because individuals attribute their successes to the medication and do not actually learn to fear the object or situation less. In sum, psychological treatments—namely, exposure therapies—appear to be the most effective option for long-lasting reductions in fear and anxiety symptoms and improvements in daily function in people with phobias.

Antonina S. Farmer, Kirstin Stauffacher Gros,
Nina Wong Sarver, and Daniel F. Gros

See also: Cognitive Behavioral Therapy; Cognitive Therapy; Exposure Treatment; Psychoanalysis; Treatment, Medication; Treatment, Self-Help; Treatment Outcome, Predictors of

Further Reading

Ayala, Erica S., Meuret, Alicia E., & Ritz, Thomas. (2009). Treatments for blood-injection-injury phobia: A critical review of current evidence. *Journal of Psychiatric Research, 43,* 1235–1242.

Choy, Yujuan, Fyer, Abby J., & Lipsitz, Josh D. (2007). Treatment of specific phobia in adults. *Clinical Psychology Review, 27,* 266–286.

Wolitzky-Taylor, Kate B., Horowitz, Jonathan D., Powers, Mark B., & Telch, Michael J. (2008). Psychological approaches in the treatment of specific phobias: A meta-analysis. *Clinical Psychology Review, 28,* 1021–1037.

Zlomke, Kimberly, & Davis III, Thompson E. (2008). One-session treatment of specific phobias: A detailed description and review of treatment efficacy. *Behavior Therapy, 39*, 207–223.

HOW DOES PHOBIA TREATMENT HELP PEOPLE LEARN NEW WAYS OF THINKING ABOUT FEARED OBJECTS OR SITUATIONS?

Beliefs that maintain a person's phobia can be challenged in two ways using cognitive behavioral therapy (CBT), the preferred method of treatment for phobias: directly through a process called cognitive therapy and indirectly through a process called exposure (behavior) therapy.

Cognitive therapy directly examines the unrealistic beliefs a person has about a feared object/situation. It helps the person examine the logical evidence that supports or refutes these beliefs, and it allows less accurate, anxiety-inducing beliefs to be replaced with more accurate, anxiety-reducing beliefs. For example, a person with claustrophobia might think that being stuck in an elevator would be impossible to handle. In cognitive therapy, this individual might be asked to consider whether he or she has experienced any prior scary situations that seemed impossible to handle but that ultimately turned out to be more manageable than expected. The individual might also be asked to gather information about what happens when an elevator gets stuck (e.g., relating to safety features, emergency response, air flow) and about the frequency of elevators getting stuck.

Exposure therapy is another way of gaining perspective regarding phobias. When a person fears something, the usual coping strategy is avoidance. But, avoidance strengthens the phobia through maintenance of the initial faulty beliefs about that object or situation. For example, individuals who believe that high places are dangerous and that they can't handle feeling scared in high places will continue to hold these beliefs as long as they avoid such places because they are not getting any new information to contradict their beliefs. To overcome a phobia, a person must enter a feared situation rather than avoid it. Exposures allow a person to gradually confront the feared stimulus in a controlled, predictable, and repeated manner. By doing this, the person is able to gain new information about the feared object or situation, specifically information that contradicts the fearful beliefs held prior to exposure. For example, a person who is fearful of taking elevators for fear of getting stuck in one would learn by repeatedly riding elevators that getting stuck is a very rare event. Further, if indeed an elevator were to get stuck while the person was in it, the person would have the opportunity to learn that this situation is not "impossible" to handle.

Mark A. Watling

Treatment, Self-Help

In a given year, approximately 19.2 million American adults have some type of specific phobia (Kessler, Chiu, Demler, Merikangas, & Walters, 2005). However, the majority of these individuals never receive professional treatment. Further, when patients with phobias present for treatment, it is most often to seek treatment for another mental health problem (e.g., depression). Nevertheless, when offered help for their phobia, most will accept treatment, suggesting that a lack of awareness of effective treatments for phobias may be a barrier. Other possible barriers to treatment include costs, embarrassment associated with help seeking, and a lack of availability of treatment, especially outside of major cities. One way to increase the availability and affordability of treatment is to use methods based on self-help. *Self-help* refers to self-guided management of mental health difficulties through the use of literature and techniques with minimal or no direction from relevant professionals. Self-help treatments are typically offered through written manuals or books, and recently through a number of Internet and computer-based self-help treatment programs, as well as phone "apps" (mobile phone applications).

There are a number of self-help books available for the treatment of phobias. Many of these are empirically based, meaning that they were written based on strategies that have been found to be effective in traditional in-person treatments. These self-help books are largely based on traditional cognitive behavior therapy (CBT) techniques including exposure to the feared situations and strategies focused on challenging anxious thoughts. For example, *Overcoming Animal and Insect Phobias: How to Conquer Fear of Dogs, Snakes, Rodents, Bees, Spiders, and More* by Antony and McCabe (2005) aims to teach readers how to use CBT to treat their animal and insect phobias, and *The Shyness and Social Anxiety Workbook: Proven, Step-by-Step Techniques for Overcoming Your Fear* by Antony and Swinson (2008) teaches socially anxious individuals how to use traditional CBT. Some recent self-help books have also included mindfulness and acceptance-based strategies. For example, *The Mindfulness and Acceptance Workbook for Social Anxiety and Shyness* by Fleming and Kocovski (2013) guides readers to use mindfulness meditation (using audio files downloaded via the Internet) in addition to exposure and other strategies.

Most self-help books start with psychoeducation (informing the reader about the phobia) before getting into how to treat it. Psychoeducation typically involves information about common symptoms, prevalence, and theories on etiology, and other information that helps to describe the nature of phobias to the reader. Self-help books also commonly contain case examples (brief descriptions of people with phobias). Case examples typically include information about a person's symptoms, how these symptoms have affected the person's life, and strategies that have been helpful. The aim for including case examples is to allow readers the opportunity to connect with others with similar problems. Self-help books also typically include various written exercises to be completed as each chapter is read as a way of engaging the reader and ensuring the reader is applying the information to himself or herself. In many books, full worksheets are also included and homework practices are suggested.

Studies have examined the effectiveness of self-help as a treatment for various phobias. Some of this research has investigated self-help as an adjunct to traditional therapy sessions (i.e., patients attend several traditional therapy sessions, as well as complete several online self-help sessions), whereas other studies have evaluated self-help as a stand-alone treatment. In either case, there has been support for self-help as a viable treatment option for various specific phobias, social anxiety disorder (social phobia), and agoraphobia. In some cases, results for self-help treatments have rivaled traditional in-person treatments. Further, self-help treatments can represent an easily accessible and quick treatment option. For example, one study evaluated the effectiveness of a one-session self-induced computer-based exposure treatment in people with arachnophobia (fear of spiders). Individuals who completed this 27-minute exposure treatment, where nine spider pictures were shown, showed significant fear reduction that day and one month later compared to people who were exposed to neutral pictures (Müller, Kull, Wilhelm, & Michael, 2011). These findings lend support for the effectiveness of computer-based self-help for the alleviation of fear in people with arachnophobia.

In addition to being easily accessible, and in some cases efficient, self-help treatments are associated with reduced costs and a lower level of anxiety about seeking help. Self-help treatments for those with more severe phobias have also been found to assist individuals with seeking in-person therapy by getting them "ready" for treatment and reducing anxiety about treatment (Rickwood & Bradford, 2012). These additional features are significant advantages when one considers the high prevalence and low treatment-seeking rates for phobias. However, one significant disadvantage associated with self-help is that it is difficult for some people to stay motivated and to continue reading and working through the exercises (perhaps in particular the exposure exercises) without the help and encouragement of a therapist. Some researchers have also expressed skepticism about the validity and usefulness of these self-help treatments. Rosen (1987) reviewed the research on self-help materials and found three potential problems with self-help treatments: (1) self-help techniques are not always easy to administer and can be administered incorrectly, (2) self-help treatments have higher drop-out rates, (3) the effectiveness of self-help treatments has not all been empirically tested.

A general approach to selecting a good self-help book includes choosing one that focuses on one main problem (or a small subset of problems) and is written by doctoral-level professionals with expertise in the topic area of the book. The book should also be based on research showing that the strategies are helpful, should avoid claims that appear too good to be true, and provide detailed guidance regarding how to implement the treatment strategies (ideally including when and where the strategies should be implemented).

Treatment services around the world are limited in their reach and scope. In addition, a large proportion of people with phobias do not seek help from traditional services, with many of these people reporting that they prefer to deal with their difficulties themselves. For these people, self-help treatments may provide an acceptable alternative to traditional treatments. Overall, self-help treatments have been found to provide a more easily accessible and less stigmatizing alternative for individuals who are unwilling or unable to access more traditional treatments.

Nancy L. Kocovski, Jan E. Fleming,
and Kayleigh A. Abbott

See also: Agoraphobia (Fear of Panic-Like Symptoms); One-Session Treatment; Phobia, Specific; Social Anxiety Disorder (Social Phobia); Treatment Seeking

Further Reading

Antony, Martin M., & McCabe, Randi E. (2005). *Overcoming animal and insect phobias: How to conquer fear of dogs, snakes, rodents, bees, spiders, and more.* Oakland, CA: New Harbinger Publications.

Antony, Martin M., & Swinson, Richard P. (2008). *Shyness and social anxiety workbook: Proven, step-by-step techniques for overcoming your fear* (2nd ed.). Oakland, CA: New Harbinger Publications.

Fleming, Jan E., & Kocovski, Nancy L. (2013). *The mindfulness and acceptance workbook for social anxiety and shyness.* Oakland, CA: New Harbinger Publications, Inc.

Kessler, Ronald C., Chiu, Wai T., Demler, Olga, Merikangas, Kathleen R., & Walters, Ellen E. (2005). Prevalence, severity, and comorbidity of 12-month DSM-IV disorders in the National Comorbidity Survey Replication. *Archives of General Psychiatry, 62,* 617–627.

Müller, Birgit H., Kull, Sandra, Wilhelm, Frank H., & Michael, Tanja. (2011). One-session computer-based exposure treatment for spider-fearful individuals—Efficacy of a minimal self-help intervention in a randomised controlled trial. *Journal of Behavior Therapy and Experimental Psychiatry, 42,* 179–184.

Rickwood, Debra, & Bradford, Sally. (2012). The role of self-help in the treatment of mild anxiety disorders in young people: An evidence-based review. *Psychology Research and Behavioral Management, 2,* 25–36.

Rosen, Gerald M. (1987). Self-help treatment books and the commercialization of psychotherapy. *American Psychologist, 42,* 46–51.

HELP IN YOUR HANDS: SELF-HELP THROUGH MOBILE APPS

With the increasingly widespread use of mobile devices such as smartphones and tablet computers, there has been a proliferation of health-focused applications or "apps" for these devices. Apps are software programs designed for mobile devices. They range widely in their purpose—for example, some are designed for entertainment, whereas others provide information about the weather and news, assist with navigation, facilitate social networking, and promote health and fitness. Health apps, in particular, are geared toward helping individuals monitor their health behavior and implement change. In this way, many of these apps are designed to provide self-help treatment. A distinct feature of apps in the context of self-help treatment is that their technology allows for multimedia (e.g., audio, video, photos, location sensing) and interactive experiences. Numerous apps that specifically target phobias and other anxiety concerns are currently available.

Self-help apps for phobias vary widely, but many include elements of cognitive behavioral treatment, such as education about the target problem, self-monitoring (which can be accomplished through voice or video recording, photos, and text logs), and guided exposure to feared stimuli. One app for spider phobia, for example, provides an interactive interface through which the individual can observe and manipulate virtual spiders of varying degrees of threat (e.g., cartoon spider, small spider, tarantula). Further, the technology of *augmented reality* can place these virtual spiders in the individual's actual environment. That is, the camera in the mobile device superimposes the spider on the screen so that it appears as though it is in the individual's real-time environment (e.g., in the person's hand, crawling across a desk). Other elements of this app require the individual to go out and take photos of real spiders with the mobile device.

Self-help apps for phobias have several advantages. As with other self-help tools, they tend to be cost-effective and can be used as a stand-alone intervention or as an adjunct to therapist-facilitated treatment. They have also been shown to be acceptable to a broad range of clients, including low-income and ethnically diverse groups. They can be particularly useful to individuals living in remote communities where access to treatment is sparse. Specific to their format, apps on mobile devices can be taken anywhere and used discretely, and they use powerful technologies to provide an immersive treatment experience.

Although mobile technology offers a promising avenue for self-help treatment for phobias, several cautions must be noted. Few mobile apps have been subjected to empirical evaluation, and the evidence base for their effectiveness is still in the early stages. Anyone can create and market an app; the content of self-help apps is not regulated by experts or health organizations. Further, some individuals may be reluctant to use this technology due to concerns about privacy. Given both the drawbacks and the great potential of apps for phobias and other mental health problems, mental health organizations are starting to develop guidelines to help clinicians and consumers identify safe and effective apps.

Irena Milosevic

Treatment Outcome, Predictors of

Specific phobia is the third most common anxiety disorder in adults with a 12-month prevalence rate of 8.7% (Kessler, Berglund, Demler, Jin, & Walters, 2005), but is also one of the most treatable anxiety disorders. Psychosocial treatments are empirically supported and demonstrate high success rates, making them the treatment of choice for specific phobia. Graded *in vivo* exposure therapy preceded by a rationale for the therapy and some tailored didactic education appear to be the most effective and well-tolerated intervention. The predictors of treatment outcome for specific phobia relate to the (1) treatment protocol, (2) therapist, (3) client, and (4) the combination of all three; however, research suggests there is no singularly correct protocol, therapist, client, or combination.

Available research supports exposure therapy as more efficacious than control conditions and more efficacious than alternative therapies for the treatment of anxiety disorders, including phobias. Among types of exposure therapy, *in vivo* exposure appears to be the most effective. Individuals who receive *in vivo* exposure therapy report and demonstrate larger fear reductions following therapy than individuals who receive imaginal exposure or virtual exposure; nevertheless, the differences in gains between exposure therapy types are not sustained at follow-up. In other words, *in vivo* exposure may produce more rapid gains, but it is not actually more effective than other types of exposure. That said, there are several treatment-related factors that may influence the efficacy of any exposure therapy, including the degree of therapist involvement, exposure pacing, exposure intensity, exposure context, distraction tasks, and applied muscle tension. In all cases, exposure therapy should be preceded by a rationale and some didactic education before exposing the individual to the feared object or situation, and the therapeutic factors should be tailored to the individual.

The degree of therapist involvement in exposure therapy ranges from none at all to very high levels of structured involvement in exposure sessions. There are many self-help and self-directed exposure therapies for specific phobia that have been empirically supported, and for many individuals a lack of therapist involvement may be sufficient. Despite the success with self-help, research supports therapist-guided exposure therapy as more effective. The additional effectiveness may come from having the added structure, diligence, and support that comes from attending therapy sessions with prescribed exposures.

The frequency and duration of exposures (i.e., pacing) can vary substantially depending on the specific protocol. Individuals often demonstrate clinically significant improvement after one session of exposure therapy; however, multiple exposure sessions appear to produce greater improvement than a single session of exposure, particularly when the exposure sessions are staggered over several days. Multiple exposure sessions also lead to further posttherapy improvements and sustained improvements. Longer sessions (e.g., two-hour sessions vs. multiple one-hour sessions) and shorter intersession periods (e.g., seeing individuals multiple times a week compared to seeing them once a week) also increase the effectiveness of exposure therapy.

The intensity of exposure to the feared object or situation also varies substantially within exposure sessions depending on the specific protocol. Some protocols are graded, moving along a hierarchy with exposures starting relatively small (e.g., looking at a photograph of the feared object or situation), and increasing as rapidly as possible (e.g., having the feared object or situation in the room but away from the individual) to some agreed-upon goal (e.g., directly interacting with the feared object or situation). Other protocols, referred to as *flooding*, are very intense and begin with exposure to the most intensely feared activity (e.g., starting with direct interaction with the feared object or situation). Research has supported the effectiveness of graded and flooding approaches; however, people may be better able to tolerate graded exposure, which decreases the risk a person will quit, and therein may increase the overall effectiveness.

Exposure therapy is most beneficial when the new learning associated with the feared object or situation is generalized to as many contexts and variants as possible. Accordingly, most therapists will vary the context and type of stimuli over the course of exposure therapy to maximize treatment gains. For example, exposing the individual to the feared object or situation in different settings as well as having different forms of the feared object or situation (e.g., exposure to different types of spiders in different rooms).

Some clinicians suggest that success with exposure therapy may increase with a distraction task (e.g., performing simple math tasks while approaching the feared object or situation). Including a distraction task may make exposure therapy less frightening for individuals, making them more willing to participate; however, distraction tasks may also interfere with the efficacy of exposure therapy. The possible reduction in efficacy is large enough that most clinicians advise against using distraction during exposure therapy.

In cases where encounters with the feared objects or situations involve a tendency to faint—most commonly for blood and needle phobias—successful exposure therapy may require additional education about how fainting occurs coupled with a technique called applied muscle tension. Applied muscle tension is not intended as a distraction task. The patient flexes various muscle groups throughout the body while breathing as normally as possible. The technique temporarily increases blood pressure, which reduces the probability of fainting, and in doing so facilitates exposure therapy.

All therapies can be influenced by several factors specific to the therapist or the client. A strong therapeutic alliance (i.e., a positive working relationship between client and therapist) is thought to be critical for successful treatment outcomes. The therapist's expression of empathy through verbal (i.e., choice of what and how things are said, voice intonation) and nonverbal communication (i.e., body language, eye contact, facial expression, listening skills) is also important in developing a strong therapeutic alliance and, therein, critical for successful treatment outcomes. Therapists with more training are more likely to have positive therapeutic outcomes. There is also evidence that therapists with more experience also have better outcomes, but the associated research is relatively limited and having experience does not guarantee successful outcomes. Treatment success can also be impacted by client characteristics, such as self-efficacy, belief in the efficacy of treatment, and meta-cognitive abilities (i.e., the capacity to reflect on one's own thoughts in the moment). Clients who participate voluntarily, have strong self-motivation, or have personality traits that facilitate forming stable relationships with others are all more likely to have success with therapy. Clients who present with more severe symptoms or a comorbid psychological disorder tend to have less successful treatment outcomes; that said, up to a point, symptom severity can increase client motivation to change and participate in psychotherapy. Finally, most types of psychotherapy require the client to engage in activities between treatment sessions (i.e., homework); accordingly, personal traits, lifestyle choices, and socioeconomic statuses that facilitate such activities will also support positive therapeutic outcomes.

R. Nicholas Carleton and Michelle J. N. Teale Sapach

See also: Applied Relaxation; Applied Tension; Exposure, Imaginal; Exposure, *In Vivo*; Exposure Treatment; Flooding; One-Session Treatment; Systematic Desensitization; Treatment, Self-Help; Virtual Reality Treatment

Further Reading

Kessler, Ronald C., Berglund, Patricia, Demler, Olga, Jin, R., & Walters, Ellen E. (2005). Lifetime prevalence and age-of-onset distributions of DSM-IV disorders in the national comorbidity survey replication. *Archives of General Psychiatry, 62*, 593–602.

Wolitzky-Taylor, Kate B., Horowitz, Jonathan D., Powers, Mark B., & Telch, Michael J. (2008). Psychological approaches in the treatment of specific phobias: A meta-analysis. *Clinical Psychology Review, 28*, 1021–1037.

Treatment Seeking

Despite effective treatments, people with phobias generally delay seeking treatment for the disorder. Compared to other psychiatric disorders, treatment seeking is typically lowest in phobic and anxiety disorders. Further, individuals are most likely to seek treatment as time progresses, rather than at the onset of the disorder. The likelihood of seeking professional help for anxiety and phobic disorders ranges from 9 to 23 years after the initial onset of the disorder (Wang et al., 2005). Several factors may contribute to why people with phobias delay seeking treatment, such as type of phobia, severity of condition, and comorbidity of other mental health disorders.

Treatment seeking varies depending on the type of phobia or anxiety disorder and is generally lowest among specific phobias. Because individuals with specific phobias are often able to avoid the feared object or situation, few individuals generally express interest in seeking treatment for the phobic disorder. However, the percentage of individuals who seek treatment for other anxiety disorders is somewhat higher. Approximately 35% of those with lifetime social anxiety disorder (social phobia) report seeking treatment primarily for the disorder (Ruscio et al., 2008). Generally, those who seek treatment for social anxiety disorder also tend to have the greatest number of social fears, suggesting that treatment seeking increases as a function of severity. The likelihood of treatment seeking is generally the highest in agoraphobia. This may be, in part, due to the panic attacks (sudden episodes of extreme fear) that often accompany the disorder.

Another factor influencing treatment seeking includes the extent of comorbidity (co-occurrence) of other mental disorders. Specifically, among those with anxiety disorders, the likelihood of seeking treatment increases as the number of comorbid mental disorders also increases (Johnson & Coles, 2013). However, oftentimes these individuals seek treatment primarily for a comorbid disorder rather than the phobic condition. It appears that those with phobic disorders believe the disorder is not severe enough to require professional help and that the disorder will improve without treatment. They might also underestimate the efficacy of professional treatment for the phobia and/or simply lack knowledge regarding treatment options.

Nancy L. Kocovski and Rebecca A. Blackie

See also: Agoraphobia (Fear of Panic-Like Symptoms); Cognitive Behavioral Therapy; Exposure Treatment; Phobia, Specific; Phobias, Impairment Related to; Social Anxiety Disorder (Social Phobia); Treatment, Evidence-Based

Further Reading

Johnson, Emily M., & Coles, Meredith E. (2013). Failure and delay in treatment-seeking across anxiety disorders. *Community Mental Health Journal, 49*, 668–674.

Ruscio, Ayelet M., Brown, Timothy A., Chiu, Wai T., Sareen, Jitender, Stein, Murray B., & Kessler, Ronald C. (2008). Social fears and social phobias in the United States: Results from the National Comorbidity Survey Replication. *Psychological Medicine, 38*, 15–28.

Wang, Philip S., Berglund, Patricia, Olfson, Mark, Pincus, Harold A., Wells, Kenneth B., & Kessler, Ronald C. (2005). Failure and delay in initial treatment contact after first onset of mental disorders in the National Comorbidity Survey Replication. *Archives of General Psychiatry, 62*, 603–613.

CONSEQUENCES OF UNTREATED PHOBIAS

Untreated phobias may significantly impact a person's life, affecting quality of life and daily functioning across many domains. Research shows that the disease burden associated with phobias is such that phobias should be considered a public health priority. This view is based on the high prevalence of phobias and the reality that phobias are associated with a chronic course if left untreated. The consequences of untreated phobias are unique to each individual in terms of their impact. Some people may be affected in just one area of functioning, whereas others may be severely impaired across numerous domains as described in the following examples:

Work functioning: A phobia can interfere with a person's ability to fulfill his or her duties at work or to travel to work in the first place. For example, Jim has a phobia of elevators. His fear did not initially have a substantial impact on his life, as he was able to take the stairs when needed. However, when his office relocated from the ground floor to the 25th floor, Jim found it increasingly difficult to get to work. Due to increased anxiety, he eventually took a leave of absence.

School functioning: A phobia can interfere with a person's ability to attend school or participate in class and complete assignments. For example, Traci is a teenage girl who developed a phobia of vomiting. Over the course of the school year, she experienced increasing difficulty with concentrating in class due to her preoccupation with the thought that she might vomit. She spent her time focusing on her internal physical state to monitor for feelings of nausea and stomach upset. Her fear became so great that she started to avoid attending school.

Social: Social functioning reflects a person's ability to engage in social activities and interactions. Traci (from the previous example) was unable to engage in activities with friends that she had previously enjoyed because of her fear of vomiting. She refused invitations to visit friends because she never knew how she might feel. Her social life became increasingly restricted due to her phobia. The impact on her family was also significant as she no longer wanted to go out with them to eat or to family gatherings because she was afraid of vomiting.

Health: Untreated phobias may have a significant impact on a person's physical health and ability to receive necessary medical tests and care. For example, Phil has a phobia of needles and avoids any situations that would require getting a needle. For example, he refuses to get necessary blood work during routine medical check-ups. He was recently diagnosed with diabetes and requires insulin injections. His doctor warned him of the major medical complications he will experience if he does not manage his blood sugars using insulin injections. Phil is now considering having an insulin pump inserted permanently to avoid receiving needles.

Personal well-being/self-care: The consequences of an untreated phobia often have effects on personal enjoyment, freedom, and ability to engage in small yet important activities that we all may take for granted. For example, Dawn has a phobia of spiders and is constantly on the lookout for them. She scans for spiders in every room she enters and is unable to sleep with the window open in the summertime for fear of a spider entering her room. She avoids going into her basement, garage, or backyard because she may encounter a spider. Dawn feels that her fear of spiders consumes much of her personal energy so that she can never really relax and enjoy herself.

These examples illustrate the many areas of a person's life that a phobia can impact. Thus, it is not surprising that phobias are associated with a significant disease burden that is comparable if not greater to many chronic medical conditions. The good news is that we have effective treatments that can lead to complete remission of a phobia and improve quality of life and overall functioning in a relatively short time duration. However, lack of awareness of available treatments and limited treatment accessibility may contribute to phobias remaining untreated.

Randi E. McCabe

Tripartite Model of Fear

The tripartite model of fear, developed by Lang (1967, 1979), is a theory regarding the components of a fear response. Lang's tripartite model states that the fear response is characterized by three components of a neural network: physiological arousal, a cognitive (subjective) component, and a behavioral response.

Physiological arousal refers to the physical/bodily sensations of anxiety, including a racing heart, sweating, nausea, and breathing change. The *cognitive component* refers to the thoughts or cognitions that an individual has about safety—for example, the thought that exposing oneself to the feared stimulus (e.g., approaching a dog) is dangerous and will result in harm. The *behavioral response* refers to the fearful individual's behaviors and might include avoiding the feared object or situation or escaping when confronted by the feared stimulus. The behavioral component may also include hypervigilance (being on guard) or safety behaviors, the latter which are used to reduce anxiety and/or to prevent anticipated catastrophe. Examples of safety behaviors include requiring a companion in fear-provoking situations or engaging in a mental routine (e.g., counting to 10 or praying) to reduce discomfort.

These three components of the fear response could be activated either individually or simultaneously. Thus, it is possible for one of the components to be activated, while the other components remain dormant. This could account for individual differences in the fear response. That is, the differential activation of the components may explain why some individuals experience a lot of physiological arousal and cognitive distress but do not engage in behavioral avoidance when confronted with a feared stimulus, whereas other individuals may engage in substantial behavioral avoidance. The number of components activated in the model is dependent on the strength of the fear response.

Concordance refers to the simultaneous activation of the physiological, cognitive, and behavioral components of the fear response, whereas *discordance* refers to individual activation of the components. The degree to which the components are concordant is thought to be a function of the strength of the fear reaction. Since the fear response is heightened in specific phobias, in comparison to other anxiety disorders, it is thought that the concordance between the three components is likely to occur more frequently in specific phobias (Lang & Cuthbert, 1984).

The tripartite model of fear conceptualizes a typical fear response in specific phobias. A phobia of flying in airplanes (aviophobia) will be used to examine the component parts of this theory. Physiological arousal may occur in anticipation of the flight and/or during the flight itself (e.g., racing heart, sweating, shortness of breath, nausea, and shaking). The cognitive component might include thoughts such as "Flying is not safe," "The plane is going to crash," and "I am going to be injured or killed." The behavioral component might take the form of avoiding flying altogether and instead driving long distances, even though flying is the faster or more cost-effective alternative. For those who attempt to fly, behavioral avoidance might include trying to escape from the plane before takeoff. Safety behaviors might include flying only with a companion, holding a companion's hand, or mentally rehearsing a prayer during takeoff.

The tripartite model of fear has also been utilized in the clinical treatment of phobias, particularly cognitive behavioral therapy. All three components of the fear response are addressed in treatment. Individuals are first taught to identify the three components of their fear response. The physiological component is then targeted by introducing relaxation and breathing techniques. The cognitive component is targeted by examining and challenging dysfunctional beliefs and expectations. For example, in the case of the flying phobia described earlier, the thought "The plane is going to crash" could be challenged and altered by examining the probability of the plane crashing. The behavioral component is targeted by gradually exposing the individual to the feared situation while eliminating safety behaviors.

Stephanie Taillefer

See also: Cognitive Behavioral Therapy; Fear; Fear, Physiology of

Further Reading

Lang, Peter J. (1967). Fear reduction and fear behavior: Problems in treating a construct. In John M. Shlien (Ed.), *Research in psychotherapy* (pp. 332–368). Washington, DC: American Psychological Association.

Lang, Peter J. (1979). A bio-informational theory of emotional imagery. *Psychophysiology, 16*, 495–512.

Lang, Peter J., & Cuthbert, Bruce N. (1984). Affective information processing and the assessment of anxiety. *Journal of Behavioral Assessment, 6*, 369–395.

Triskaidekaphobia (Fear of the Number 13)

Triskaidekaphobia (from the Greek *tris* meaning three, *kai* meaning and, *deka* meaning ten, and *phobos* meaning fear) is an irrational fear of the number 13. Another common and related superstitious fear is the fear of Friday the 13th or paraskevidekatriaphobia (from *paraskevi*, meaning Friday in Greek) or friggatriskaidekaphobia (from Frigg, the Norse God of Friday). Both of these fears are based on superstitious or magical thinking. Notably, although the number 13 is perceived as unlucky and is feared in Anglo-Saxon culture, in other cultures (e.g., Italian) 13 is believed to be a lucky number.

The exact origin of triskaidekaphobia and paraskevidekatriaphobia is unknown. At least three different sources have been implicated in the development and prevalence of these fears, particularly in Anglo-Saxon cultures. In Christian tradition, Judas, the disciple who is said to have betrayed Jesus, was the 13th disciple at the last supper, making the number 13 an inherently unlucky number. Similarly, in Nordic mythology, Loki, the 13th god of the pantheon, was responsible for the murder of Balder, another Norse god, and was said to be the last guest to arrive at his funeral, making the number 13 an evil or undesirable number. Finally, it is believed that paraskevidekatriaphobia may have its roots in the fact that the Knights Templar, a medieval military order created to protect pilgrims traveling to the Holy Land, were executed on Friday, October 13, 1307, after losing favor with Philip IV of France.

Superstitiousness and fear of the number 13 have resulted in a number of interesting phenomena within Western culture. For example, many high-rise buildings do not have a 13th floor, and the 13th row on airplanes is often eliminated. Confirming the popularity of this superstitious fear, a Gallup poll in 2007 found that 13% of respondents would feel uncomfortable if assigned to a hotel room on 13th floor (Carroll, 2007).

Neither triskaidekaphobia nor paraskevidekatriaphobia are represented in current classification systems for mental disorders. Additionally, very little research has been conducted examining these types of superstitious fears from a clinical or treatment perspective, suggesting that for most individuals who subscribe to these superstitious beliefs there is little impact on their daily functioning and that such beliefs cause little distress. Symptoms of obsessive compulsive disorder (OCD) may be associated with superstitious beliefs, such as triskaidekaphobia. These beliefs may function in a similar manner as other magical or idiosyncratic beliefs in OCD. For example, the individual may take extreme steps to avoid the number 13, such as checking a light switch 12 or 14 times, but never 13 times, or having to perform a certain ritual if the number 13 is encountered to "undo" any potential harm that may arise.

As to whether the number 13 and Friday the 13th are actually unlucky, the jury appears to be out. For example, at least one research study found an increase in the number of traffic accidents on Friday the 13th (Scanlon, Luben, Scanlon, & Singleton, 1993), although others have found no relation between Friday the 13th and injuries (Radun & Summala, 2004). Whether accident proneness on Friday the 13th is related to being unlucky or to simply being more anxious remains to be determined.

Andrea R. Ashbaugh

See also: Obsessive-Compulsive Disorder

Further Reading

Carroll, Joseph. (2007). Thirteen percent of Americans bothered to stay on Hotels' 13th floor. Retrieved from http://www.gallup.com/poll/26887/Thirteen-Percent-Americans-Bothered-Stay-Hotels-13th-Floor.aspx

Radun, Igor, & Summala, Heikki. (2004). Females do not have more injury road accidents on Friday the 13th. *BMC Public Health, 4*, 54.

Scanlon, T. J., Luben, Robert N., Scanlon, F. L., & Singleton, Nicola. (1993). Is Friday the 13th bad for your health? *British Medical Journal, 307*, 1584–1586.

Trypophobia (Fear of Holes)

Trypophobia (from the Greek *trypo*, meaning boring or drilling holes, and *phobos*, meaning fear) is an intense fear of a repetitive pattern of holes. In particular, individuals with trypophobia are fearful of clusters of holes that are found in a variety of objects and matter such as skin, coral, honeycombs, seed pods, and even aerated chocolate. This unusual phobia has only recently been described in the scientific literature (Cole & Wilkins, 2013) and is understood to have possible evolutionary origins.

The prevalence of trypophobia in the general population is not known. However, preliminary research suggests that the tendency to experience aversion in response to trypophobic stimuli is relatively common. For instance, 16% of a sample of 286 participants reported discomfort or repulsion when presented with an image of a lotus seed pod (Cole & Wilkins, 2013). Individuals with trypophobia describe feeling fearful, disgusted, itchy, or physically ill when confronted with a trypophobic stimulus, and they endorse beliefs about the possibility that something might be living in the holes or that they might fall into them.

When researchers analyzed images of trypophobic objects, they found a common visual feature among them: a high spatial frequency with a greater energy at midrange. Importantly, images of many poisonous animals (e.g., certain types of aquatic animals, frogs, snakes, insects, and spiders) possess the same visual characteristics. This led the investigators to hypothesize that trypophobia has an evolutionary basis and serves to alert humans of dangerous organisms. Indeed, they found that even nontrypophobic individuals reported higher discomfort ratings when viewing images with this spectral pattern compared to when viewing neutral images (Cole & Wilkins, 2013).

Trypophobia is not specifically described in current classification systems of mental disorders but would fall under the broad category of specific phobia provided the fear was excessive, persistent, and associated with significant distress and/or impairment. Although there are no reported studies of treatments for this particular fear, existing evidence-based treatments for phobias, such as exposure treatment, would likely be effective interventions for trypophobia.

Irena Milosevic

See also: Evolution, Role of; Exposure Treatment; Phobia, Specific; Phobias, Diagnosis of; Preparedness Theory

Further Reading

Cole, Geoff G., & Wilkins, Aarnold J. (2013). Fear of holes. *Psychological Science, 24,* 1980–1985.

Twin Studies

Twin studies are studies that use monozygotic (identical) and dizygotic (fraternal) twins to attempt to quantify the degree to which genetic and environmental factors lead to the development of complex traits. Twin studies rely on the fact that monozygotic twins share nearly all of their genetic material since they develop from a single fertilized egg, whereas dizygotic twins share on average 50% of their genetic material since they develop from two fertilized eggs. In classical twin studies, one compares the degree to which monozygotic twins share a complex trait to the degree to which dizygotic twins share this trait. Through this comparison, it is possible to estimate the extent to which a trait is due to genetic factors. Thus, twin studies can be used to estimate the heritability of both phobias and personality traits that predispose to the development of phobias.

Twin studies report a heritability estimate (H^2), which represents the proportion of variation in the complex trait due to variation in genes. The H^2 estimate ranges from 0% to 100%. Classical twin studies also report other factors that contribute to the development of the complex trait. They assume that each trait is accounted for by three main factors. The first factor is *additive genetic effects* (A), which refer to the genes inherited by each twin. The second factor is *common environmental effects* (C), which consist of elements of the environment shared by both twins such as the socioeconomic status of the family. The third factor is *unique environmental effects* (E), which consist of individual experiences that do not occur in both twins such as accidental injury. For example, if a study shows that a trait is 16% due to additive genetic effects, 34% due to common environmental effects, and 50% due to unique environmental effects, the study will report this as A = 0.16, C = 0.34, and E = 0.50. Since it is assumed that these three factors fully account for the trait, A + C + E is always equal to 1.

More sophisticated twin-based methodologies are also employed. For example, in twin adoption studies, twins are adopted and hence raised in different environments. If adoptees and adoptive parents or siblings do not develop a trait at similar rates, it suggests that genetic factors are more important than environmental factors for the development of this trait. If, on the other hand, adoptees and adoptive parents or siblings develop the trait at similar rates, it suggests a shared environmental influence on the trait given that adoptees and adoptive families are genetically dissimilar.

The development of twin studies is often incorrectly attributed to a paper published by Sir Francis Galton (1822–1911) in 1875 (see Rende, Plomin, & Vandenberg, 1990). Galton, a Victorian scientist who published on a dizzying array of topics ranging from forensics to meteorology, was a cousin of Charles Darwin and is perhaps most famous for coining the term *eugenics*. Although he stressed the need to study twins over time to determine how different environments can lead twins to become dissimilar, he never proposed comparing monozygotic and dizygotic twins. The first two publications describing twin study methodology appeared in 1924 (Rende et al., 1990). One was an article by Curtis Merriman, then a doctoral student at Stanford, examining mental abilities in twin pairs, and the other was a book chapter by Hermann Siemens, a German dermatologist, looking at skin disorders in twin pairs. Merriman described the methodology but did not actually compare monozygotic to dizygotic twins in his study. Siemens, however, used the twin study methodology to study skin moles and found that monozygotic twins have more closely correlated mole count than dizygotic twins, thus highlighting the importance of hereditary factors in determining mole count. Some of the earliest twin studies in psychiatry were performed by Franz Kallman, who used twin study methodology to investigate the heritability of schizophrenia in the 1940s. These early studies were methodologically flawed but the methodology has greatly improved over time and has now been applied to a wide variety of psychiatric conditions.

Numerous twin studies have been conducted looking at the heritability of the diagnosis of specific phobias, although none have been adoption studies. A recent comprehensive review that integrated the findings of these studies found that the average heritability was 33% for blood-injury-injection (BII) type phobias, 32% for animal type phobias, and 25% for situational phobia (van Houtem et al., 2013). Agoraphobia is estimated to be 48% heritable whereas estimates for social anxiety disorder (social phobia) range from 37% to 39%. These results are comparable to heritability estimates for other anxiety disorders, such as generalized anxiety disorder and panic disorder, and indicate that phobias are moderately heritable. It is likely that there is a shared vulnerability to these disorders, meaning that certain genes predispose people to multiple anxiety disorders and phobias rather than a single specific disorder. These studies also indicate that environmental factors play a large role in the development of phobias. Relevant environmental factors likely include stressful life events, observational learning, and classical conditioning (the repeated pairing of a neutral stimulus with a stimulus that provokes a fear response).

Other twin studies have looked at the heritability of personality traits that predispose to phobic disorders. The most studied of these traits is neuroticism. Neuroticism is a risk factor for both depression and anxiety, including phobias. A large twin study estimated that neuroticism is 56% heritable in women and 49% heritable in men. Other twin studies have found high genetic correlations between neuroticism, specific phobia, social anxiety disorder, and agoraphobia. There are likely shared genetic factors that predispose to both neuroticism and phobic disorders.

Another type of twin study of phobias looks at the heritability of scores of different types of fear scales. For example, one twin study investigated the heritability of scores on the brief version of the Fear of Negative Evaluation Scale, a scale that measures sensitivity to disapproval or criticism. High scores on this scale tend to occur in both individuals and family members of individuals with social anxiety disorder. The study examining this particular scale estimated that the scores were 48% heritable. A similar study evaluated the heritability of subscales of the Fear Questionnaire. These subscales measure BII fear, social fear, and agoraphobic fear. This study estimated that the heritability for these three fear subscales ranged from 36% to 51%.

Nancy C. P. Low and Matthew E. Sloan

See also: Personality; Phobias, Genetics of

Further Reading

Boomsma, Dorret, Busjahn, Andreas , & Peltonen, Leena. (2002). Classical twin studies and beyond. *Nature Reviews Genetics, 3*, 872–882.

Rende, Richard D., Plomin, Robert, & Vandenberg; Steven G. (1990). Who discovered the twin method? *Behavior Genetics, 20*, 277–285.

van Houtem, C. M. H. H., Laine, M. L., Boomsma, D. I., Ligthart, L., van Wijk, A. J., & De Jongh, A. (2013). A review and meta-analysis of the heritability of specific phobia sub-types and corresponding fears. *Journal of Anxiety Disorders, 27*, 379–388.

Two-Factor Theory of Avoidance Learning

The two-factor theory of avoidance learning, proposed by Mowrer (1947), posits that it is the combination of classical conditioning and operant conditioning that leads to the development and maintenance of anxiety disorders, including phobias.

Pavlov (1927) proposed that in classical conditioning, an unconditioned stimulus automatically triggers an unconditioned response. When a neutral stimulus is repeatedly paired with an unconditioned stimulus, the neutral stimulus can become a conditioned stimulus, which provokes a conditioned response that is similar to that of the unconditioned response triggered by the unconditioned stimulus. For example, a dog might be a neutral, nonthreatening stimulus to an individual. However, if a dog bites this individual, he or she will experience pain. Pain from the dog bite is an unconditioned response because it is an automatic reaction to the dog bite. Through pairing of the painful bite with the presence of the dog (originally a neutral stimulus), the dog can become a conditioned stimulus that evokes a conditioned response, such as fear, that is similar to that of the unconditioned response. The individual may develop a phobia of dogs (cynophobia) because he or she now associates the pain experienced from the dog bite with dogs in general. Thus, from a classical conditioning learning perspective, anxiety disorders can develop when a neutral stimulus is paired with an unconditioned stimulus. However, classical conditioning alone does not explain avoidance behaviors associated with anxiety disorders.

Thorndike (1898) thought that organisms have drives, such as hunger and thirst, and that a response to a drive in a given situation may not achieve the desired result. Thorndike believed organisms learn through trial-and-error by replacing responses to drives that have unsatisfactory results with responses that lead to satisfactory results. For example, Thorndike placed a cat in a locked puzzle box with food outside of the box. Only a particular behavior, such as pressing a bar, would enable the cat to escape the box. The cat would perform many behaviors (e.g., meowing, pacing) that would not get it out of the box or satisfy its hunger drive. However, when it chanced upon performing the correct behavior, it could escape the box and eat the food, thus satisfying its hunger. In future trials, the cat would be able to escape the box more quickly because it learned the behavior that enabled it to satisfy its hunger. Thus, the cat replaced ineffective responses with a response that achieved the desired result. Based on such drive theory, if individuals experience the drive of fear, they will behave in ways intended to reduce their fear. The earliest version of the two-factor theory combined classical conditioning and drive theory to explain the development of avoidance behaviors associated with anxiety disorders (Mowrer, 1947). Mowrer later refined and elaborated upon his two-factor theory to include operant conditioning.

Operant conditioning is learned behavior that is contingent upon the consequences following the behavior. Skinner (1938) proposed that if a response is reinforced, this will increase the probability of that response occurring again in the future. Negative reinforcement occurs when a behavior is followed by the removal of an aversive stimulus (e.g., electric shock), which increases the probability of that behavior. For example, individuals with social phobia may consider social interactions at a party to be aversive stimuli and experience fear during such interactions. By leaving the party, they remove the aversive stimuli and decrease their fear, thus increasing the likelihood that they will escape social interactions in the future. Avoidance behaviors occur when organisms learn responses that allow them to circumvent aversive stimuli (such as the experience of anxiety symptoms). Thus, these avoidance behaviors are increased through negative reinforcement.

Mowrer (1960) believed that classical conditioning and operant conditioning could be synthesized to explain avoidance behaviors associated with anxiety disorders. He proposed that avoidance learning develops through classical conditioning and operant conditioning by the following: (1) through classical conditioning, fear becomes associated with a conditioned stimulus through paired association of the conditioned stimulus with an aversive unconditioned stimulus; and (2) through operant conditioning, an organism avoids the conditioned stimulus (a feared stimulus), reducing fear, thus negatively reinforcing the organism's response to continue avoiding the conditioned stimulus. In sum, Mowrer posited that organisms learn to fear conditioned stimuli preceding aversive unconditioned stimuli, and that avoidance of the conditioned stimuli is then maintained through negative reinforcement.

Mowrer (1960) viewed avoidance responses as learned behaviors that temporarily reduce fear. For example, an individual who had a negative experience (e.g., being trampled) in a crowded space may associate his or her unconditioned emotional and physiological arousal response, which may include fear, to crowded spaces. Through the process of classical conditioning, crowded spaces can come to evoke a conditioned fear response for the individual in the absence of being trampled. The individual may experience fear at the thought of running an errand that involves entering a crowded space. If the individual decides to avoid running the errand, he or she will experience a reduction in fear. Thus, the avoidance behavior reduces fear, or allows the individual to avoid experiencing fear associated with the crowded space, which results in negative reinforcement of the avoidance behavior. The individual is likely to avoid crowded spaces in the future to avoid the fear associated with crowded spaces. If the individual repeatedly exposed himself or herself to crowded spaces without escaping when experiencing fear, this would lead to a reduction of fear to the crowded spaces. However, when feared stimuli are avoided, fears of conditioned stimuli are maintained and can even be amplified through negative reinforcement. For a more thorough treatment of the two-factor theory of avoidance learning and the various versions of the theory, see Mowrer (1960).

There are criticisms of Mowrer's (1960) two-factor theory of avoidance learning. Behaviorists criticize this two-factor theory because the internal experience of fear is used to explain avoidance conditioning. By contrast to this view, behaviorists believe that only directly observable behaviors should be measured to ensure that the scientific study of behavior is as objective as possible. Cognitive researchers have criticized the two-factory theory of avoidance, because fear or anxiety were not measured but rather assumed to be involved in the avoidance process (Seligman & Johnston, 1973). Further, Rachman (1984) proposed that people with phobias (e.g., agoraphobia) are not motivated by avoidance of their fear but rather by positive feelings that they experience in safe places; that is, they are motivated to search for safety signals that make them feel comfortable as opposed to avoiding fear-producing stimuli. Another critique of the two-factor theory is based on the work of Herrnstein and Hineline (1966), who showed that animals maintain avoidance behavior simply by the reduction of an aversive unconditioned stimulus (i.e., rate of electrical shocks); further, these researchers imply that avoidance conditioning can occur without classical conditioned stimulus and that the reduction of the unconditioned stimulus is sufficient to develop and maintain avoidance behavior.

Mark E. Pierson and Jason M. Prenoveau

See also: Anxiety and Related Disorders; Classical Conditioning; Fear; Learning Theory; Operant Conditioning; Pavlov, Ivan (1849–1936); Skinner, B. F. (1904–1990); Thorndike, Edward L. (1874–1949)

Further Reading

Herrnstein, Richard J., & Hineline Phillip N. (1966). Negative reinforcement as shock-frequency reduction. *Journal of the Experimental Analysis of Behavior, 9*, 421–430.

Mowrer, Orval H. (1947). On the dual nature of learning—A re-interpretation of "conditioning" and "problem-solving." *Harvard Educational Review, 17*, 102–148.

Mowrer, Orval H. (1960). *Learning theory and behavior.* New York, NY: Wiley.

Pavlov, Ivan. (1927). *Conditioned reflexes.* New York, NY: Oxford University Press.

Rachman, Stanley. (1984). Agoraphobia: A safety-signal perspective. *Behaviour Research and Therapy, 22*, 59–70.

Seligman, Martin E., & Johnston, James C. (1973). A cognitive theory of avoidance learning. In Frank J. McGuigan & D. Barry Lumsden (Eds.), *Contemporary approaches to conditioning and learning* (pp. 69–110). Washington, DC: Winston.

Skinner, Burrhus F. (1938). *The behavior of organisms: An experimental analysis*. New York, NY: Appleton Century Company.

Thorndike, Edward L. (1898). *Animal intelligence: An experimental study of the associative processes in animals*. New York, NY: Columbia University Press.

V

Video Feedback

Individuals with social anxiety disorder (social phobia) tend to report negative self-worth and consistently underestimate their social skills; accordingly, they often rate their social performance more negatively than objective observers. Models of social anxiety disorder posit that this biased negative self-perception may contribute to the development and maintenance of anxiety-related psychopathology. Empirically based therapies, including cognitive behavioral therapy, are designed to modify negative self-perceptions and thereby to reduce anxiety. Many protocols also use video feedback to help correct the biased self-perceptions. The visual aid provides individuals with compelling evidence for the discrepancy between perceived performance and actual performance.

Video feedback consists of having individuals watch video recordings of themselves performing a task on which they perceive their performance to be poor. The most common task is giving a speech. Research has demonstrated that having individuals high in social anxiety view a video of themselves giving a speech helps them to rate their performance more accurately. The increased accuracy leads to ratings that are closer to ratings of objective observers. The improvements have been most dramatic for individuals whose initial self-ratings were highly discrepant from objective ratings; as such, video feedback appears most effective for individuals who incorrectly believe they have skill deficits.

Video feedback begins with an overview of the process, followed by the recording itself; thereafter, prior to viewing the video, individuals are provided with cognitive preparation in three steps. In step one, individuals are instructed to predict in great detail what they will see in the video. The predictions are facilitated through a semi-structured interview using self-ratings of specific behaviors. In step two, individuals are given time to create a mental image or representation of themselves giving the videotaped performance. Doing so is believed to help individuals identify the discrepancies between their perceived performance and their actual performance. In step three, individuals are instructed to watch the video as an objective observer or as if they are watching a stranger. The intent is to avoid the video prompting recollections of the performance that would interfere with paying attention to the video, such as recollections of how their presentation felt (e.g., recalling feeling flush). Although the video feedback could be presented without cognitive preparation, research suggests the preparation increases the gains made by the participant. The video feedback process then concludes with a subsequent interactive review of discrepancies. This review appears to help individuals internalize more accurate and less negative representations of themselves, which is thought to further reduce symptoms of anxiety.

Video feedback has demonstrated clinical utility in altering distorted self-perceptions of performance tasks and has anecdotally helped individuals with their social anxiety symptoms; however, there was relatively little empirical support that correcting the distorted perceptions causally reduced symptoms of social anxiety until recently. Current research suggests that video feedback, combined with cognitive preparation and the subsequent interactive review, does indeed causally reduce anticipatory anxiety associated with future performance situations.

Most video feedback research to date has focused on the utility for social anxiety disorder; however, the process may also have benefits for other phobias. For example, video feedback could be used to augment exposure therapy more generally or to serve as modeling for specific phobias. Such use remains speculative but certainly warrants future exploration.

R. Nicholas Carleton and
Michelle J. N. Teale Sapach

See also: Behavior Therapy; Cognitive Behavioral Therapy; Cognitive Restructuring; Cognitive Therapy; Social Anxiety Disorder (Social Phobia)

Further Reading

Orr, Elizabeth M. J., & Moscovitch, David A. (2010). Learning to re-appraise the self during video feedback for social anxiety: Does depth of processing matter? *Behaviour Research and Therapy, 48*, 728–737.

Rodebaugh, Thomas L., Heimberg, Richard G., Schultz, Luke T., & Blackmore, Michelle. (2010). The moderated effects of video feedback for social anxiety disorder. *Journal of Anxiety Disorders, 24*, 663–671.

Virtual Reality Treatment

In the context of phobias and anxiety disorders, people often refer to virtual reality as a technology used to immerse a patient in a three-dimensional (3D) context where exposure sessions can be conducted. Pratt, Zyda, and Kelleher (1995, p. 17) offered a simple and practical definition of what virtual reality is: an application that allows a patient to navigate and interact in real time with a 3D and computer-generated environment. Many technologies are available to immerse phobic and anxious patients in virtual reality, from the high-end very expensive immersive rooms where images are projected on large walls and objects are perceived as floating in front of the patient, to more affordable goggles where small computer displays are combined with tiny motion trackers and mounted on a kit that patients can put on their head. This technology is now used with success to conduct exposure with people suffering from anxiety and related disorders.

Conducting exposure in virtual reality allows a therapist to expose a person to fear-provoking stimuli, just as with traditional means, in order to develop new internal representations and associations between the feared stimuli and the lack of threat (Richard & Lauterbach, 2007). It is important to remember that conducting exposure in virtual reality is not a "virtual exposure" or a "virtual therapy" because, although the stimuli are virtuals, the exposure and the therapy are quite real for the patient. More precise expressions such as "exposure conducted in virtual reality" or "*in virtuo*" exposure, a term coined by Tisseau (2008), are instead favored. *In virtuo* exposure offers several advantages as it allows the therapist to have much greater control of the stimuli used for exposure (e.g., controlling the behavior of the audience during exposure for social anxiety), to easily vary contexts (e.g., such as the size of spiders and where the patient can encounter them), and to access locations that would otherwise require traveling outside the office (e.g., for phobia of heights or flying in a plane). It is also perceived as more enticing by patients, who

A monitor displays images that are viewed by an individual in 3D through a virtual reality headset. This technology allows the individual to become immersed in a virtual environment that simulates feared situations. (AP Photo/Bebeto Matthews)

A screenshot of a virtual environment for generalized anxiety disorder (GAD), a disorder in which individuals worry excessively about a variety of everyday matters. This virtual environment depicts a hospital waiting area, where a woman wearing a mask sits in front of the user, a man and a little girl are coughing, a crying mother can be observed through the door to another area, and a receptionist calls the next number in line. (Courtesy of Stephane Bouchard)

expect that exposure will be easier and less frightening in virtual reality than *in vivo*. However, with children it seems important to explain in advance the virtual stimuli to reduce their apprehension, which is not a problem with adults.

To conduct *in virtuo* exposure, therapists must become familiar with two concepts, including presence and virtual reality–induced negative side effects. *Presence* refers to two ideas: (1) the impression that the stimuli are real, as opposed to being created and displayed through some form of computer media, and (2) the feeling of "being there" inside the virtual environment instead of being in the therapist's office (Sadowski & Stanney, 2002). Clinical experience and preliminary empirical data suggest that the relationship between anxiety and presence felt during the immersion in virtual reality is probably not linear (Bouchard, Robillard, Larouche, & Loranger, 2012). Indeed, when facing anxiety-provoking stimuli during immersion, it is difficult for patients to be frightened when they do not feel present at all. However, even when presence is only minimal, anxiety can rise to a full panic. Also, nonphobic patients can feel highly present in the virtual environment yet feel no anxiety at all. Finally, presence can remain high during an exposure session while anxiety is actually decreasing. It is also clear that virtual stimuli do not have to be a perfect replica of the objective reality to achieve successful *in virtuo* exposure. Research has shown that people suffering from an anxiety disorder will react strongly to virtual stimuli that are relevant to their fear, even with low-end affordable technologies (e.g., a less expensive system with goggles), with imperfect stimuli (e.g., with spiders that do not behave exactly like spiders do), or when some human senses are not activated (e.g., during a virtual flight that has no hydraulic motion system to replicate the movements of the airplane).

Being immersed in virtual reality can sometimes induce unwanted negative side effects, often called "cybersickness" (Lawson, Graeber, & Mead, 2002). Some of the side effects include general discomfort, nausea, dizziness, headaches, or eyestrain. These side effects are not dangerous and are influenced by several factors, including an individual's strong susceptibility to motion sickness and the use of older, less powerful technologies. Between 5% and 10% of the general population may experience side effects during an immersion in virtual reality. These symptoms are easily managed by an experienced therapist (e.g., by asking the patient to move and rotate his head more slowly), who will know how to differentiate them from anxiety and when to stop the immersion if necessary. These side effects are not a significant cause of attrition in outcome trials and clinical practice.

The scientific literature shows that cognitive behavior therapy (CBT), which includes exposure treatment, is an effective treatment for phobias and other anxiety disorders, and *in virtuo* exposure is simply a different way to conduct exposure. It is not surprising that randomized controlled trials (David, Matu, & David, 2013) support the efficacy of *in virtuo* exposure when used alone (in the case of specific phobias) or in conjunction with other CBT techniques (in the case of anxiety disorders that are more complex than phobias). A treatment program using virtual reality usually follows the same structure as traditional CBT treatments, with the exception of paying attention to having at least a minimal sense of presence and keeping an eye on unwanted negative side effects (Bouchard et al., 2012).

Several virtual environments have been developed and tested to treat phobias (e.g., flying, height, dog, cat, spider, and snake phobias), as well as nonphobic fears (e.g., test anxiety, needles, and venipuncture). Virtual environments also exist for more complex anxiety disorders like panic disorder with agoraphobia; social anxiety disorder (both for fear of public speaking and interpersonal situations); obsessive-compulsive disorder (for subtypes related to contamination, doubt, aggression, sexuality, religion, checking and hoarding); posttraumatic stress disorder (both military- and nonmilitary-related sources of trauma); and even generalized anxiety disorder.

Stéphane Bouchard

See also: Acrophobia (Fear of Heights); Agoraphobia (Fear of Panic-Like Symptoms); Arachnophobia (Fear of Spiders); Aviophobia (Fear of Flying); Claustrophobia (Fear of Enclosed Spaces); Cynophobia (Fear of Dogs); Exposure, *In Vivo*; Exposure Treatment; Obsessive-Compulsive Disorder; Ophidiophobia (Fear of Snakes); Posttraumatic Stress Disorder; Social Anxiety Disorder (Social Phobia)

Further Reading

Bouchard, Stéphane, Robillard, Geneviève, Larouche, Serge, & Loranger, Claudie. (2012). Description of a treatment manual for in virtuo exposure with specific phobia. In Christiane Eichenberg (Ed.), *Virtual reality in psychological, medical and pedagogical applications* (pp. 82–108). Rijeka, Croatia: InTech.

David, Daniel, Matu, Silviu-Andrei, & David, Oana A. (2013). New directions in virtual reality-based therapy for anxiety disorders. *International Journal of Cognitive Therapy*, 6, 114–137.

Lawson, Ben D., Graeber, David A., & Mead, Andrew M. (2002). Signs and symptoms of human syndromes associated with synthetic experience. In Kay M. Stanney (Ed.), *Handbook of virtual environments: Design, implementation, and applications* (pp. 589–618). Mahwah, NJ: Lawrence Erlbaum Associates.

Pratt, David R., Zyda, Michael, & Kelleher, Kristen. (1995). Virtual reality: In the mind of the beholder. *IEEE Computer, 28*, 17–19.

Richard, David C. S., & Lauterbach, Dean. (2007). *Handbook of exposure treatment*. Burlington, MA: Elsevier Inc.

Sadowski, Wallace, & Stanney, Kay M. (2002). Presence in virtual environments. In Kay M. Stanney (Ed.), *Handbook of virtual environments: Design, implementation and applications* (pp. 791–806). Mahwah, NJ: Lawrence Erlbaum Associates.

Tisseau, Jacques. (July, 2008). *In vivo, in vitro, in silico, in virtuo*. 1st Workshop on SMA in Biology at Meso or Macroscopic Scales, Paris, France.

W

Watson, John B. (1878–1958)

John B. Watson, born John Broadus Watson (1878–1958), was an influential American psychologist and the founder of behaviorism, a psychological school of thought concerned with studying observable behavior. Watson is credited with revolutionizing psychology by shifting its focus away from a mentalistic approach, which emphasized internal states and mental processes, to an objective experimental method concerned with classical conditioning principles and the prediction and control of behavior. Watson popularized psychology as an empirical science and sparked the dominance of behaviorism in the field for more than 50 years. His work stimulated a large body of research, and its applications resulted in innovations in behavior modification that were applied broadly across psychology, education, medicine, and advertising. Watson had a significant influence on behavioral techniques for treating phobias.

Watson was born on January 9, 1878, in Travelers Rest, a rural community in South Carolina. His mother was a devout Baptist who subjected Watson to religious teachings that would ultimately lead Watson to reject religion. His father, who abused alcohol and had problems with the law, left the family when Watson was 13 years old. Watson subsequently rebelled; his grades were poor and he was twice arrested for violent behavior. Nevertheless, with a move to the larger nearby community of Greenville and his mother's social connections, Watson succeeded in enrolling in Furman University in Greenville at age 16. There, one of his teachers helped him focus on academics. Watson graduated from Furman with a master's degree at age 21 and enrolled in doctoral studies at the University of Chicago, where he majored in experimental psychology and minored in neurology and philosophy. He arrived in Chicago with only $50 to his name. To support himself, he worked as waiter, janitor, and caretaker of laboratory rats.

As a doctoral student, Watson studied under several influential psychologists and philosophers. He was influenced by prominent functionalist thinkers at the University of Chicago, who held that mental events and behavior are adaptive adjustments to an organism's environment. It was at the University of Chicago where Watson developed an interest in comparative psychology, the study of mental processes and behavior in animals. His dissertation examined the neurological correlates of learning ability in rats. Watson completed his doctoral degree in 1903 at age 25 and

American psychologist John B. Watson, founder of behaviorism, about 1935. (Hulton Archive/Getty Images)

was said to be the youngest person at the university to earn a PhD. Watson stayed on at the university as a researcher and instructor. In 1904, he married one of his students, Mary Amelia Ickes, with whom he had two children.

By 1907, Watson had developed a reputation for his work in animal psychology and took the position of associate professor at Johns Hopkins University in Baltimore, Maryland. Soon after, he was promoted to chair. Watson also took up editorship of the *Psychological Review*, a prominent academic journal, which afforded him the opportunity to disseminate his views on behaviorism.

Strongly influenced by Ivan Pavlov's (1849–1936) work on classical conditioning, Watson was highly critical of the state of psychology in the early 20th century, particularly its introspective approach. He rejected the concept of consciousness and the study of mental states, instead pushing for psychology to embrace a scientific approach that was as objective as the study of physiology. In 1913, Watson gave a series of public lectures at Columbia University in New York, which launched the behaviorist movement. He detailed his position on psychology in the most famous of these lectures, titled *Psychology as the Behaviorist Views It* (also widely known as the *Behaviorist Manifesto*). In this lecture, which Watson later published in the *Psychological Review*, he called for a paradigm shift in psychological research:

> Psychology as the behaviorist views it is a purely objective experimental branch of natural science. Its theoretical goal is the prediction and control of behavior. Introspection forms no essential part of its methods, nor is the scientific value of its data dependent upon the readiness with which they lend themselves to interpretation in terms of consciousness. The behaviorist, in his efforts to get a unitary scheme of animal response, recognizes no dividing line between man and brute. (Watson, 1913, p. 158)

After delivering the Columbia lectures, Watson became a public advocate of behaviorism. In his next notable publication, *Behavior: An Introduction to Comparative Psychology* (1914), Watson argued for the importance of using animals to study reflexes and proposed that the most optimal experimental tool was the study of conditioned responses. Although Watson initially focused on animal subjects in his studies, he eventually took interest in human behavior. Radically, Watson pushed for the application of behaviorism to understand all human behavior. He believed that all behavior is acquired through conditioning and similarly held that any individual differences among humans are the result of learning. Although it took several years for his ideas to gain popularity after the introduction of the *Behaviorist Manifesto*, Watson was nevertheless elected president of the American Psychological Association (APA) in 1915 when he was only 36 years old. His APA presidential address proposed the conditioned reflex in place of introspection in psychology.

In 1920, Watson and his research assistant, Rosalie Rayner, conducted what is now known as one of the most famous and controversial experiments in psychology. To determine whether classical conditioning could be used to condition fear in humans, Watson conditioned a young boy, "Little Albert," to fear a white rat. The boy's fear subsequently generalized to other white fluffy objects. One of the most objectionable elements of this research was Watson's failure to decondition the boy's fear.

Watson's career at Hopkins ended abruptly in 1920 when he was forced to resign his chair because of a scandalous affair with Rayner. Watson divorced his wife in 1921 and married Rayner with whom he went on to have two children. He did not work again in full-time academia but continued to do research and write, particularly for the popular press, after moving to New York with Rayner. He often used his two sons with Rayner in his investigations on behaviorism. In 1928, Watson published a best-selling parenting manual, *Psychological Care of the Infant and Child*, in which he criticized affectionate and permissive child-rearing practices, endorsing instead relative emotional detachment and methods based on behavioral principles. This publication is said to have transformed American child-rearing practices at the time, although it also garnered much criticism.

In New York, Watson also began a second highly successful career as an applied psychologist in the advertising field. In 1924, he was appointed vice president of the J. Walter Thompson Company, an advertising agency, and in 1935 he moved on to become vice president of William Esty Advertising, where he remained until his retirement at age 67. Watson's success in advertising was built upon his strategy to influence sales by manipulating images associated with brand names.

After Rayner died unexpectedly at age 36 in 1935, Watson was said to become reclusive. He lived on the couple's estate, Whippoorwill Farm, in Connecticut, until moving to a small farm in the 1950s, where he remained for the rest of his life. In 1957, he was honored with the prestigious gold medal from the APA for his lifetime contributions to psychology. He died the following year at age 80. Shortly before his death, Watson burned a large collection of his unpublished papers and letters.

Watson's work left a long-standing legacy in psychology and related fields. His ideas influenced prominent figures, including the noted behaviorist B. F. Skinner (1904–1990) and the "father of behavior therapy" Joseph Wolpe (1915–1997). Conditioning principles and behavior modification are still widely applied in various therapies, including those aimed at reducing phobic fear.

Irena Milosevic and Feven Yeshanew

See also: Classical Conditioning; Jones, Mary Cover (1897–1987); Pavlov, Ivan (1849–1936); Skinner, B. F. (1904–1990); Wolpe, Joseph (1915–1997)

Further Reading

Watson, John B. (1913). Psychology as the behaviorist views it. *Psychological Review, 20*, 158–177.

Watson, John B., & Rayner, Rosalie. (1920). Conditioned emotional reaction. *Journal of Experimental Psychology, 3*, 1–14.

THE CASE OF LITTLE ALBERT

As the "father of behaviorism," John Watson has made many notable contributions to the field of psychology. Although Watson was not principally concerned with psychopathology, one of the most famous examples of his work is his experiment on fear acquisition with a baby boy named Albert, now famously called the *Little Albert experiment*. This experiment marks one of the first successful attempts to classically condition fear in the laboratory.

In 1919, Watson's interest in fear acquisition was piqued by his observation of a child who demonstrated an irrational fear of dogs. This inspired Watson to investigate whether an emotionally stable child could be conditioned to have a phobia. Along with his research assistant at Johns Hopkins University, Rosalie Rayner, Watson conducted an experiment with nine-month-old Albert. Two months after an initial assessment that established that Albert was not afraid of a series of live animals and objects, the boy was presented with a fluffy white rat. He was not afraid of the animal and enjoyed playing with it. The experimenters then introduced a jarring noise (produced behind Albert by striking a steel bar with a hammer) every time he reached for the rat. Albert responded to the noise with distress. He was subsequently presented with the rat in the absence of the noise and became similarly distressed in the rat's presence. It took only seven trials of the rat-noise pairings for Albert to become fearful and avoidant of the rat.

Albert was tested five days later to determine whether his fear response had generalized to other objects. Indeed, he responded with fear to a white rabbit, a dog, and a sealskin coat, and he even had a negative response to the beard of a Santa Clause mask. After one month without any conditioning trials, Albert was tested again and demonstrated fear when confronted with the rat, rabbit, dog, sealskin coat, and mask.

Watson and Rayner's experiment demonstrated that fear can be classically conditioned. That is, through pairings of the fluffy white rat (a neutral stimulus) with the aversive noise (an unconditioned stimulus, in response to which Albert produced an unconditioned fear response), Albert was conditioned to respond to the rat (conditioned stimulus) with fear (conditioned response). Watson used this experiment to support his views on the importance of the environment or *nurture* in human behavior as compared to innate biological factors or *nature*.

Notably, Watson and Rayner failed to "recondition" or remove Albert's fear upon completion of their study. Accordingly, their experiment by today's standards would be considered unethical and would not be approved to be conducted. A further ethical controversy relates to researchers' later discovery that Albert had not been healthy but instead suffered from congenital hydrocephalus (excessive fluid buildup in the brain), of which he died at age 6. Researchers now speculate that Watson had controversially misrepresented Albert's health. Conducting research on a neurologically impaired child limits the generalizability of the findings to healthy humans.

Irena Milosevic

Wolpe, Joseph (1915–1997)

Joe Wolpe, born Joseph Wolpe (1915–1997), is often described as the father of behavior therapy. A native of Johannesburg, South Africa, he obtained his medical degree in psychiatry at the University of Witwatersrand. For his doctoral dissertation in medicine (1948), Wolpe investigated fearful behaviors in animals, which he used to develop what would become the first successful treatment of phobias. He was a determined and dedicated scientist, who worked with many influential psychologists and psychiatrists of his time, such as Hans J. Eysenck and Stanley J. Rachman. He completed a fellowship at the University of Stanford at the Centre for Advanced Study in the Behavioral Sciences (1956–1957), worked in the Psychiatry Departments at the University of Virginia (1960–1965) and Temple University (1965–1982), and then settled at Pepperdine University in Malibu, California (1989–1997). He was a prolific researcher and writer, best known for his influential book *Psychotherapy by Reciprocal Inhibition* (Wolpe, 1958). In addition to therapeutic advancements, he developed the Fear Survey Schedule and the Subjective Units of Distress Scale (SUDS). He has been recognized widely for his contribution to the field and in 1995 received a Lifetime Achievement Award from the Association for the Advancement of Behavior Therapy. He has been described as gentle and modest, yet highly inspirational to those who knew him. He was very active and dedicated to his work to the end of his life.

During World War II, Wolpe worked as a medical officer in the South African military. He became dissatisfied with his lack of success with standard treatments for posttraumatic stress disorder, which included psychoanalytic and drug therapies. This led him to seek a more effective treatment. As a firm believer that psychological treatments should be empirically based, he devised a series of experiments with animals to examine a novel method of treating anxiety. Wolpe proposed that if much of behavior was learned, then it could also be unlearned. Based on this notion, he sought to extinguish learned fearful reactions in cats. He started by repeatedly pairing a neutral stimulus (a sound) with a feared stimulus (shocks) so that the cats would learn to fear the sounds. Once the sounds alone elicited a fearful response, Wolpe began the process of extinguishing the response. To do so, he repeatedly paired the sounds with a pleasant, calming stimulus (food). As predicted, every time food was paired with the sound, the fearful response diminished, and eventually, the once-feared sounds, when presented alone, ceased to elicit any fearful response. Wolpe theorized that the feared response was extinguished because the fear caused by the sounds was not compatible with the new pleasurable response to the food. This notion—that fear responses could be extinguished by repeatedly eliciting an incompatible response—became the foundation for the theory of reciprocal inhibition.

Building on the theory of reciprocal inhibition, Wolpe devised a method called systematic desensitization for treating phobias and anxiety in humans. Similar to the technique he used with cats, systematic desensitization involved diminishing a fear response to a phobic stimulus such as a spider by repeatedly pairing that stimulus with an incompatible response: relaxation. Unlike his experiments with cats, however, relaxation was not paired with the actual feared stimulus, but instead with imaginal exposure (imagining the spider). With repeated pairings, this technique proved to be highly successful in the treatment of phobias and other anxiety-related problems. Systematic desensitization subsequently evolved into modern-day exposure therapy.

Wolpe helped to lay the groundwork for many of the hallmark features in the field of clinical psychology today. He was a true pioneer of the model "scientist practitioner." His SUDS is still used in clinic and research settings to measure fear and change in fear over the course of therapeutic and experimental inductions. His early work as a student ultimately led him to develop the first successful evidence-based treatment of phobia. The basic tenet of his treatment—exposure—has become the most widely and successfully implemented technique in the treatment of all anxiety disorders.

Sarah E. Schell, Gillian M. Alcolado, Kristin G. Anderson,
and Adam S. Radomsky

See also: Association for Behavioral and Cognitive Therapies; Behavior Therapy; Behavioral Model; Exposure, Imaginal; Exposure, *In Vivo*; Exposure Treatment; Eysenck, Hans J. (1916–1997); Fear Survey Schedule; Rachman, Jack (1934–); Reciprocal Inhibition; Subjective Units of Distress Scale; Systematic Desensitization

Further Reading

Poppen, Roger. (1995). *Joseph Wolpe*. London, UK: Sage Publications.

Rachman, Stanley. (2000). Joseph Wolpe (1915–1997): Obituary. *American Psychologist, 55*, 431–432.

Wolpe, Joseph. (1958). *Psychotherapy by reciprocal inhibition*. Palo Alto, CA: Stanford University Press.

World Health Organization

The World Health Organization (WHO) is an agency of the United Nations that specializes in international public health. It is a leader in global health matters, including areas such as research, standards for health care, policy, and monitoring of health trends. The WHO is also responsible for the *International Classification of Diseases*, a classification system for a broad range of diseases and disorders, including mental health problems such as phobias and anxiety disorders.

The WHO was formed on April 7, 1948, with the aim of improving global health. This date has since been established as World Health Day. Since its inception, the WHO has grown in membership from 55 to 194 nations, encompassing nearly all of the countries in the world. Representatives of these countries meet annually at the World Health Assembly in Geneva, Switzerland, to set policy for the organization. Its agenda has varied over the years and has focused on issues such as fighting diseases, improving health-care and health inequalities in developing countries, and improving health-care funding. The WHO is credited with eradicating smallpox by leading a global vaccination program, and it is leading efforts toward eradicating other serious diseases.

The Department of Mental Health and Substance Abuse is a division of the WHO that focuses specifically on mental, neurological, and substance use disorders. Its goals are to reduce the burden associated with these disorders and to promote mental health globally. One of the initiatives of the department is the Mental Health Gap Action Programme (mhGAP), which was launched in 2008 with the aim of increasing mental health services in low- and middle-income countries.

Irena Milosevic

See also: International Classification of Diseases

Website

www.who.int

LIST OF EDITORS AND CONTRIBUTORS

Volume Editors

Irena Milosevic, PhD
St. Joseph's Healthcare Hamilton
McMaster University

Randi E. McCabe, PhD
St. Joseph's Healthcare Hamilton
McMaster University

Contributors

Kayleigh A. Abbott, BSc
Wilfrid Laurier University

Gillian M. Alcolado, MA
Concordia University

Kristin G. Anderson, MA
Concordia University

Paul W. Andrews, PhD
McMaster University

Martin M. Antony, PhD
Ryerson University

Andrea R. Ashbaugh, PhD
University of Ottawa

Kevin C. Barber, BA
Concordia University

Jessica R. Beadel, MA
University of Virginia

Rebecca A. Blackie, MA
Wilfrid Laurier University

Shannon M. Blakey, MS
University of North Carolina

Stéphane Bouchard, PhD
Université du Québec en Outaouais

Radek Budin, MA
Concordia University

R. Nicholas Carleton, PhD
University of Regina

Elise M. Clerkin, PhD
Miami University

Meghan W. Cody, PhD
Mercer University School of Medicine

Caitlin Davey, MA
Ryerson University

Brett J. Deacon, PhD
University of Wollongong

Amanda J. Desnoyers, MA
Wilfrid Laurier University

Eleanor Donegan, MA
Concordia University

Corinna M. Elliott, PhD
Massachusetts General Hospital/
Harvard Medical School

Alan B. Eppel, MB, FRCPC
McMaster University

Antonina S. Farmer, PhD
Randolph-Macon College

Jan E. Fleming, MD
The Mindfulness Clinic

Karen J. Francis, PhD
McMaster University

Catherine E. Gallagher, BSc
St. Francis Xavier University

Yudong Gao, BEng
The University of Tennessee Health
Science Center

Dubravka L. Gavric, PhD
St. Joseph's Healthcare Hamilton

John A. Greco, BS
University of Michigan

Sheryl M. Green, PhD
St. Joseph's Healthcare Hamilton

Daniel F. Gros, PhD
Ralph H. Johnson VAMC

Geoffrey B. C. Hall, PhD
McMaster University

Kelsey Hannon, BA
Concordia University

Elizabeth A. Hebert, MA
Concordia University

Scott A. Heldt, PhD
The University of Tennessee Health
Science Center

Heather K. Hood, PhD
Ryerson University

Judiann McNiff Jones, MS
University of Alabama at Birmingham

Brenda L. Key, PhD
McMaster University
St. Joseph's Healthcare Hamilton

Nancy L. Kocovski, PhD
Wilfrid Laurier University

Ariel Kor, MA
Teachers College, Columbia
University

Angela M. Lachowski, MA
Ryerson University

Jeanine E. M. Lane, MA
Ryerson University

Deborah Roth Ledley, PhD
Private Practice

Joelle LeMoult, PhD
Stanford University

Hannah C. Levy, MA
Concordia University

Shmuel Lissek, PhD
University of Minnesota

Michelle Lonergan, MSc
McGill University

Nancy C. P. Low, MD
McGill University

Christianne Macaulay, MA
York University

Sasha L. MacNeil
Concordia University

Marta M. Maslej, BA
McMaster University

Hanna McCabe-Bennett, MA
Ryerson University

Sarah McIlwaine
Concordia University

Oswaldo Moreno, MA
Clark University

Shoko Mori, BS
University of Michigan

Rachael L. Neal, MA
Concordia University

Matilda E. Nowakowski, PhD
St. Joseph's Healthcare
   Hamilton

Bunmi O. Olatunji, PhD
Vanderbilt University

Allison J. Ouimet, PhD
University of Ottawa

Chris L. Parrish, PhD
The Mindful Living Centre

E. Marie Parsons, BA, BS
Miami University

Eloisa Pavesi, PhD
Universidade Federal de Santa
   Catarina

Alexander M. Penney, PhD
MacEwan University

Mark E. Pierson, MS
Johns Hopkins University

Jason M. Prenoveau, PhD
Loyola University Maryland

Christine A. Rabinak, PhD
Wayne State University

Adam S. Radomsky, PhD
Concordia University

David H. Rosmarin, PhD
McLean Hospital/Harvard Medical School

Karen Rowa, PhD
St. Joseph's Healthcare Hamilton
McMaster University

Marley J. Russell, BSc
McMaster University

Lisa Rustom, BSc
McMaster University

Nina Wong Sarver, PhD
University of Mississippi Medical Center

Sarah E. Schell, BSc
Concordia University

Jessica M. Senn, MA
Concordia University

Devora Shabtai, BA
Center for Anxiety

Roz Shafran, PhD
UCL Institute of Child Health

Philippe Shnaider, MA
Ryerson University

Aliza Sklar, BA
Center for Anxiety

Matthew E. Sloan, MD
McGill University

Joelle N. Soucy, BA
Concordia University

Kirstin Stauffacher Gros, PhD
Ralph H. Johnson VAMC

Shari A. Steinman, PhD
New York State Psychiatric Institute

Stephanie Taillefer, MA
Ryerson University

Bethany A. Teachman, PhD
University of Virginia

Michelle J.N. Teale Sapach, BA Hons
University of Regina

Missy L. Teatero, MA
Lakehead University

Jenna M. Traynor, BA
McMaster University

Jessica S. Tutino
Concordia University

Brian van Meurs, MA
University of Minnesota

Megan Viar-Paxton, MA
Vanderbilt University

Mark A. Watling, MD
Western University

Margo C. Watt, PhD
St. Francis Xavier University

Feven Yeshanew
McMaster University

Jennifer M. Yip, BSc
University of British Columbia

K. Lira Yoon, PhD
University of Notre Dame

ABOUT THE EDITORS

Irena Milosevic, PhD, is a clinical psychologist at the Anxiety Treatment and Research Clinic at St. Joseph's Healthcare Hamilton and an assistant professor in the Department of Psychiatry and Behavioural Neurosciences at McMaster University, both in Ontario, Canada. Her research interests focus on factors related to the development and maintenance of anxiety disorders, and on the development and evaluation of cognitive behavioral interventions for anxiety disorders. She has authored a number of peer-reviewed articles and book chapters on these topics and has presented her work at numerous national and international conferences.

Randi E. McCabe, PhD, is director of the Anxiety Treatment and Research Clinic and chief psychologist at St. Joseph's Healthcare Hamilton and professor in the Department of Psychiatry and Behavioural Neurosciences at McMaster University, both in Ontario, Canada. Dr. McCabe is on the editorial board of *Cognitive and Behavioral Practice* and is President-Elect of the Canadian Association of Cognitive and Behavioural Therapies. She has published over 80 articles and book chapters in the areas of anxiety, eating disorders, and cognitive behavior therapy. She has coauthored six books including *10 simple solutions to panic* and *Overcoming animal and insect phobias: How to conquer fear of dogs, snakes, rodents, bees, spiders and more.* Her work has reached a global audience, with editions published in many languages including Chinese, Japanese, Polish, Spanish, French, Italian, Dutch, and Hebrew.

INDEX

Note: Page numbers in **boldface** reflect main entries in the book.